W9-AXZ-050

TOP EXPERIENCES MAP | NEXT PAGE

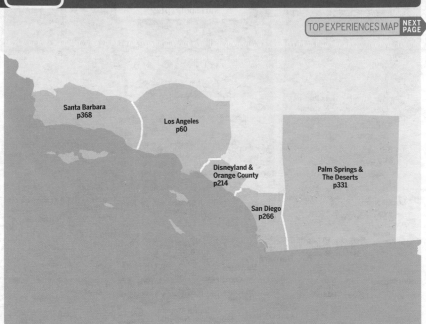

Santa Barbara
p368

Los Angeles
p60

Disneyland &
Orange County
p214

Palm Springs &
The Deserts
p331

San Diego
p266

THIS EDITION WRITTEN AND RESEARCHED BY

Sara Benson,
Andrew Bender, Adam Skolnick

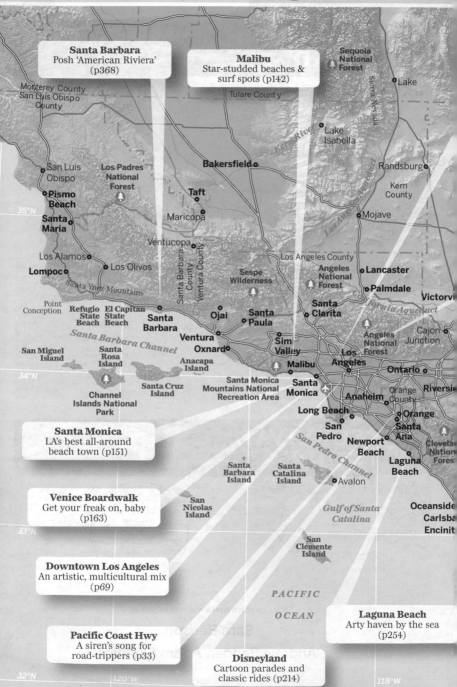

Santa Barbara
Posh 'American Riviera'
(p368)

Malibu
Star-studded beaches &
surf spots (p142)

Santa Monica
LA's best all-around
beach town (p151)

Venice Boardwalk
Get your freak on, baby
(p163)

Downtown Los Angeles
An artistic, multicultural mix
(p69)

Pacific Coast Hwy
A siren's song for
road-trippers (p33)

Disneyland
Cartoon parades and
classic rides (p214)

Laguna Beach
Arty haven by the sea
(p254)

California

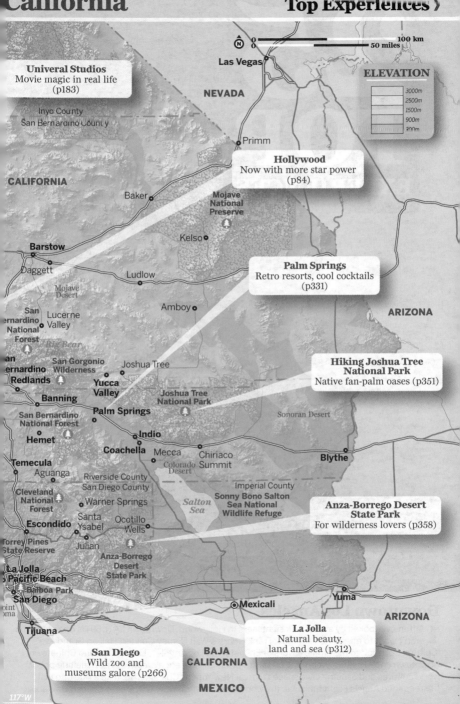

ELEVATION

	3000m
	2500m
	1500m
	900m
	300m

Univeral Studios
Movie magic in real life
(p183)

Hollywood
Now with more star power
(p84)

Palm Springs
Retro resorts, cool cocktails
(p331)

**Hiking Joshua Tree
National Park**
Native fan-palm oases (p351)

**Anza-Borrego Desert
State Park**
For wilderness lovers (p358)

La Jolla
Natural beauty,
land and sea (p312)

San Diego
Wild zoo and
museums galore (p266)

NEVADA

CALIFORNIA

ARIZONA

ARIZONA

BAJA
CALIFORNIA

MEXICO

Las Vegas

Primm

Inyo County
San Bernardino County

Baker

Mojave
National
Preserve

Kelso

Barstow

Daggett

Ludlow

Mojave
Desert

Amboy

San
Bernardino
National
Forest

Lucerne
Valley

Big Bear

San
Bernardino

San Gorgonio
Wilderness

Joshua Tree

Redlands

Yucca
Valley

Banning

Joshua Tree
National Park

San Bernardino
National Forest

Palm Springs

Hemet

Indio

Coachella

Mecca

Chiriaco
Summit

Blythe

Temecula

Aguanga

Riverside County
San Diego County

Colorado
Desert

Cleveland
National
Forest

Warner Springs

Imperial County
Sonny Bono Salton
Sea National
Wildlife Refuge

Escondido

Santa
Ysabel

Ocotillo
Wells

Salton
Sea

Torrey Pines
State Reserve

Julian

La Jolla
Pacific Beach

Balboa Park

San Diego

Anza-Borrego
Desert
State Park

Yuma

Point
Loma

Mexicali

Tijuana

Sonoran Desert

25 TOP EXPERIENCES

Downtown Los Angeles

1 Often overlooked by star-struck sightseers in Hollywood, Downtown LA (p69) is one place you won't want to miss. From architect Frank Gehry's Walt Disney Concert Hall on Grand Ave's 'Cultural Corridor' to the ethnic flavors of El Pueblo de Los Angeles, Little Tokyo and Chinatown, Downtown encapsulates everything LA has to offer: cutting-edge creative arts, a melting pot of world cultures and aspiring civic spaces to rival New York or Chicago. Tip: take a ride into history on the reopened Angels Flight funicular, the world's shortest railway. Walt Disney Concert Hall, above

Disneyland

2 Where orange groves and walnut trees once grew, there Walt Disney built his dream, throwing open the doors of his Magic Kingdom in 1955. Today, Disneyland (p217) is SoCal's most-visited tourist attraction. Inside Anaheim's most popular theme park, beloved cartoon characters waltz arm-in-arm down Main Street USA and fireworks explode over Sleeping Beauty's castle on summer nights. If you're a kid, or just hopelessly young at heart, who are we to say that Disneyland can't really be 'the happiest place on earth'?

Pacific Coast Highway

3 This legendary highway (p33) snakes past dizzying sea cliffs and dozens of beach towns, each with its own idiosyncratic personality, from offbeat bohemian to glamorously rich. PCH also connects the dots between SoCal's coastal cities, from surfin' San Diego to rockin' LA. Make your escape from tangled, traffic-jammed freeways and cruise in the slow lane. You'll uncover hidden beaches and locals' fave surf breaks, rustic seafood shacks dishing up the day's freshest catch and old-fashioned piers where you can walk out and catch the sun setting over boundless Pacific horizons.

Santa Monica

4 With more than 250 miles of Pacific coastline, SoCal has an overwhelming number of beaches to choose from. If you only have time for one, Santa Monica (p151) can grant instant happiness. Learn to surf, ride a solar-powered Ferris wheel, dance under the stars on an old-fashioned pier, let the kiddos explore the aquarium's tidal touch pools, pump iron at Muscle Beach, or just dip your toes in the water and let your troubles float away. Did we mention jaw-dropping sunsets?

DAVID PEEVERS

San Diego Zoo & Balboa Park

5 An enormous urban green space – an increasingly rare sight in SoCal – Balboa Park (p267) is where San Diegans come to play (when they're not at the beach). Take the family and spend the day immersed in more than a dozen art, cultural and science museums, or just marveling at the Spanish Revival architecture while sunning yourself along El Prado promenade. Meet the local wildlife at the world-famous zoo or see a show at the Old Globe theater, a faithful reconstruction of the Shakespearean original. Giant Panda, left

KEVIN LEVESQUE

Getty Center

6 Who says LA has no culture? (Other than pop culture of the American Idol variety, that is.) You can prove those SoCal critics and LA naysayers wrong by getting to the Getty (p129). An island in the sky in the City of Angels, this architecturally postmodern museum's hilltop campus can only be reached by tram, elevating you above the city's smog and grime. Then wander billion-dollar art galleries, botanical gardens, fountain courtyards and outdoor cafes. Incredibly, it's all free (except for parking – this is still LA, you know).

RICHARD CUMMINS

LEU / IMAGEBROKER

Venice Boardwalk

7 New-agey bohemians, muscled bodybuilders à la Arnold Schwarzenegger, goth punks, hippie tribal drummers and genuine freaks all gravitate toward Venice Beach's Ocean Front Walk (p163). It's the place where the crazy side of SoCal really lets it all hang out. Imagine an experimental human zoo, or an outdoor carnival in which audience participation is practically required. Strap on those Rollerblades, hop on a pastel-pink beach cruiser or just strut in your bikini and shake what yo' mama gave you.

Malibu

8 What, you didn't see any stars in Hollywood? We're so not surprised. Big-wig producers and A-list stars hide out in beachy Malibu (p142), a quick drive up the Pacific Coast Hwy. Whoever said Malibu is a state of mind more than a place was right: there's no real center here (apart from shopping malls). Just miles of white-sand beaches and rolling Pacific waves backed by million-dollar oceanfront mansions. Luckily, those beautiful beaches are public-access up to the high tide line – any paparazzi photographer can tell you that.

Shopping Robertson Boulevard

9 Yes, Beverly Hills may have glitzy, over-the-top Rodeo Dr, where desperate housewives carrying pocket pooches and wearing movie-star sunglasses walk clickety-clack along sidewalks that may as well be paved with gold. Meanwhile, young rockers and 'celebutantes' desperate to keep up with the Kardashians haunt the edgier shops of Melrose Ave. But chic Robertson Blvd (p141), discreetly lined with boutiques both label-savvy and sexy, is where you'll realize that LA really is a fashion capital. Stay ahead of the supermodel and *Project Runway* curve here.

Universal Studios

10 Some days, it seems like everyone in LA is trying to break into the TV and movie biz (aka 'the Industry'). Your waiter is usually an out-of-work actor, and that person yapping on their cell phone seems to be a producer cutting a deal. Turn all that serious business into funny business at Burbank's Universal Studios (p183), a family-friendly theme park. Take a behind-the-scenes tram tour past working soundstages, then pick up free tickets to join a live TV studio audience later in the Valley.

HERMES IMAGES / PHOTOLIBRARY

Hollywood

11 The movie and TV studios have all moved away, but Hollywood (p84) and its pink-starred Walk of Fame still attracts millions of wide-eyed visitors every year. Snap a souvenir photo outside Grauman's Chinese Theatre or with the Hollywood sign as a backdrop inside the Babylon Court at Hollywood & Highland – go ahead, we know you can't resist. Like an aging starlet making a comeback, this once-gritty urban neighborhood in LA is undergoing a rebirth of cool, with hip hotels and glitzy velvet-roped bars and nightclubs. Preparing for the Oscars, below

Griffith Observatory

12 Even some locals don't know that LA's Griffith Park is the second-biggest urban park in the country, bigger even than NYC's Central Park. Its sparkling white art-deco centerpiece is Griffith Observatory (p99), on the slopes of Mt Hollywood. From the same terrace where James Dean got into a knife fight in *Rebel Without a Cause*, the city views are unmatched (as long as it's not smoggy). Show up early to score tickets for a planetarium show, or wander the cutting-edge science exhibition halls and peer inside the solar telescope for free.

La Jolla

13 On what some argue is the most beautiful stretch of San Diego's coastline, La Jolla (p312) is definitely not just another SoCal beach town. Atop rocky bluffs just a whisper's breath from the sea, its richly adorned downtown is crowded with boutiques and cafes. But what's right on the shoreline is even more of a treasure, especially the all-natural fish bowl of La Jolla Cove or windswept Torrey Pines State Reserve, further north along the coast, where migratory whales swim by.

EDDIE BRADY

BILL LACHMANN

Santa Barbara

14 Proudly calling itself the 'American Riviera,' and that's honestly not such a stretch: Santa Barbara (p370) is so beautiful, you just have to sigh. Waving palm trees, powdery beaches, fishing boats clanking about in the harbor – it'd be a travel cliché if it wasn't the plain truth. California's 'Queen of the Missions' is a beauty, especially with its signature red-roofed, whitewashed adobe buildings. In fact, all of downtown was rebuilt in harmonious historical style after a devastating earthquake in 1925. Come escape LA just for the day, or maybe a whole wine-drenched weekend.

Gaslamp Quarter

15 If you can tear yourself away from San Diego's bodacious beaches after dark, then go bar-hopping, clubbing and restaurant-tasting in this revitalized downtown district (p291). Cobblestone streets and gas lamps evoke 19th-century nostalgia, but this rollickin' neighborhood's true historical legacy lies in long-gone gambling dens, saloons and bordellos. These days the party scene still spills out onto the sidewalk nightly, while bands, DJs and serious cocktails mix it up indoors. The Gaslamp Quarter takes all comers: don't worry, you won't have to fight velvet-rope bouncers here.

Channel Islands

16 Tossed like so many lost pearls off the coast, the Channel Islands are SoCal's last outpost of civilization. They've been that way for thousands of years, ever since seafaring Chumash tribespeople established villages on these remote rocks. The islands also support an abundance of marine life, from coral-reef creatures to giant elephant seals. Get back to nature in rustic Channel Islands National Park (p405), a wildlife haven with fantastic sea kayaking and snorkeling opportunities, or make a posh getaway to Mediterranean-esque Catalina Island (p210), with its harborfront hotels.

Ojai

17 The scenery is so surreal that Frank Capra set the 1937 movie *Lost Horizon* about a mythical Shangri-La right here in this mountain valley, flush with orange orchards. Ojai (p401) has delighted generations of artists, bohemians and new-age mystics. Doing nothing much is the goal for most visitors, especially on retreat at one of Ojai's spas. Spend an afternoon ambling around downtown's quaint shops or drop by the bountiful Sunday farmers market. Come around sunset to catch a legendary 'pink moment,' when the mountains emanate a rosy glow.

Anza-Borrego Desert State Park

18 When you start feeling crushed by SoCal's 22 million residents, head inland from San Diego until you can breathe easy again in the wide-open desert. California's largest state park (p358) is an incredible place to get lost. Follow 4WD roads or hiking trails to find hidden canyons, wind caves, cactus gardens or even herds of endangered bighorn sheep. Outside the park, the Old West gold-rush mining town of Julian and Temecula's wine country feel far away from the urban rat race.

ANGUS OBORN

19 In Orange County, Huntington Beach draws the hang-loose trust-fund surfer crowd, while teens and yachties play in the soap-opera fantasyland of Newport Beach. But Laguna Beach (p254) is a more sophisticated blend of money and SoCal culture. Oh, and natural beauty, too: the startlingly beautiful seascapes here led to an artists' colony taking root in the early 20th century. Today, Laguna Beach's bohemian past still shows through in downtown's art galleries, adorable arts-and-crafts bungalows tucked amongst multimillion-dollar mansions and the annual Festival of Arts and Pageant of the Masters.

LEFT LANE MUST TURN LEFT

Palm Springs

20 A star-studded oasis in the Mojave ever since the retro days of Frank Sinatra's Rat Pack, 'PS' (p332) is a chic getaway for LA denizens. Do like A-list stars and hipsters do: lounge by your midcentury modern hotel's swimming pool, go art-gallery hopping and vintage shopping, then drink cocktails from sunset till dawn. Feeling less loungey? Break a sweat on hiking trails that wind through desert canyons across Native American tribal lands, or scramble to a summit in the San Jacinto Mountains, reached via a head-spinning aerial tramway. City National Bank, above

Hiking Joshua Tree National Park

21 With their crooked arms reaching up toward heaven like a biblical prophet (at least, so early Mormon migrants thought), Joshua trees are SoCal desert icons. Leave the windshield scenery behind for this national park's network of hiking trails (p352), which will take you to gawk at even more natural wonders, from native fan-palm oases that almost look airlifted out of Africa to vistas of the strange Salton Sea and snow-dusted San Bernardino Mountains. Kids love boulder-hopping among the park's Wonderland of Rocks, an outdoor playground for rock jocks.

BRENT WINEBRENNER

Foxen Wine Trail

22 Forget Northern California's Napa and Sonoma. SoCal enfolds the fog-kissed Santa Ynez and Santa Maria Valleys (p389), aka *Sideways* wine country. Less than an hour's drive from Santa Barbara, you can wander through golden fields of grapes, tipple pinot noir and other prized varietals, and live the good life. Start in the dandified village of Los Olivos, overflowing with wine-tasting rooms and cafes. Then wind north along the Foxen Wine Trail, a winding back road where big-name wineries rub shoulders with more risk-taking boutique producers.

Mission San Juan Capistrano

23 When you visit SoCal, you can't help but follow in at least a few of the footsteps of early Spanish conquistadors and Catholic priests. Mission San Juan Capistrano (p261), nicknamed the 'Jewel of the Missions,' was founded by peripatetic Padre Junípero Serra in 1776. Authentically restored, the mission today deserves its nickname, with gorgeous gardens, stone arcades and fountains, and a chapel adorned with spiritual frescoes. In mid-March the whole town celebrates the swallows' famous return from South America to nest in the mission's walls.

Taquerías

24 *Taquerías* are a staple of the SoCal lifestyle, whether you're a beach-bum surfer or an actor rushing between auditions, or both. Taco shops are ubiquitous, particularly in San Diego where the Baja-style fish taco (a corn tortilla wrapped around fried or grilled fish on a bed of cabbage slathered with *pico de gallo* salsa, sour cream or citrusy mayonnaise) reigns supreme. In SoCal you'll see taco trucks parked by the side of the road almost wherever you go – go ahead and try 'em. We bet you'll like 'em.

JERRY ALEXANDER

Surfing

25 Even if you never set foot on a board – and we, like, totally recommend that you do, dude – there's no denying the influence of surfing on all aspects of SoCal life, from fashion to environmentalism to the way everyday people talk. Experience the adrenaline rush for yourself by riding the world-class waves off Malibu (p143), Santa Barbara's Rincon Point (p401), San Diego's Windansea Beach (p316) or Orange County's Huntington Beach (aka 'Surf City USA'; p238). You can also get schooled at 'surfari' camps up and down the coast.

welcome to Southern California

In all of your California daydreaming, palm trees, golden sands and Pacific sunsets beckon, right? The good news: SoCal is where those cinematic fantasies really can come true.

Pop Culture

Surf, sand and sex will always sell SoCal. Even though you won't find many real-life stars in Hollywood these days, you might spot celebs shopping at LA's boutiques or walking along the beach in Malibu. Or just take a sneak peek behind the scenes on a movie studio tour (p184) or join a live TV audience (p90). Then round up the whole family to see where Hollywood's high-tech magic really happens – at SoCal's theme parks. Universal Studios Hollywood and Orange County's Disneyland and Disney's California Adventure, with their cartoon characters and adventure rides, are all classic choices. Or take a walk on the wild side at the San Diego Zoo and Wild Animal Park, where giraffes and zebras roam. Loosen up, and live a little.

Beaches & Natural Beauty

SoCal may be best known for its artificial beauty (whoa, botox and silicone!), but its beaches (p39) are really an ace in the hole. Whether you're a punk surfer, aspiring pro volleyball nut or new-agey bohemian, SoCal's beach towns, each with its own idiosyncratic personality, give you a perfect excuse to take a vacation. Then hop a boat out to the Channel Islands, a jewel-like archipelago encompassing civilized Catalina and a truly wild national park. If you can tear yourself away from the ocean, more adventures await on land. Escape to the cooler alpine climes of Big Bear Lake or turn up the heat in SoCal's deserts with a getaway to retro-modern Palm Springs. Then gear up to dig deeper into the desert: Death Valley, Joshua Tree or Anza-Borrego, where dusty 4WD roads and hiking trails lead to hidden canyons and native fan-palm oases.

California Cuisine & Wine

Or maybe your SoCal sojourn will be an epicurean quest (p442). Finding the most killer fish tacos in San Diego alone could take days. Meanwhile, LA is an all-around foodie winner, where denizens passionately argue about where the best sushi bar, gourmet food truck or underground supper club is. LA is also a melting pot of ethnic cooking, from Little Tokyo and Thai Town to the tamale shops of East LA. Jam up the Pacific Coast Hwy to Malibu, stopping at seafood shacks, then follow back roads through the fog-kissed vineyards of Santa Barbara's wine country.

need to know

When to Go

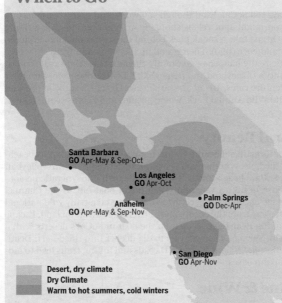

Santa Barbara
GO Apr-May & Sep-Oct

Los Angeles
GO Apr-Oct

Palm Springs
GO Dec-Apr

Anaheim
GO Apr-May & Sep-Nov

San Diego
GO Apr-Nov

- Desert, dry climate
- Dry Climate
- Warm to hot summers, cold winters

High Season (Jun–Aug)
» Accommodation prices up 50–100%

» Major holidays are even busier and more expensive

» Thick clouds may blanket the coast during 'June gloom'

» Coincides with low season in the desert

Shoulder (Apr–May & Sep–Nov)
» Crowds and prices drop off, especially along the coast

» Temperatures remain mild, with sunny cloudless days in September and October

» Weather typically wetter in spring, drier in autumn

Low Season (Dec–Mar)
» Accommodation rates drop near the coast, but not always in cities

» Chillier temperatures, more frequent rainstorms and mountain snow

» Coincides with peak season in the desert regions

Your Daily Budget

Budget less than
$75
» Dorm beds $25-40

» Find farmers markets and taquerías for cheap eats

» Skip theme parks, hit the beaches and plan around 'free admission' days at museums

Midrange
$75-$200
» Two-star inland motel or hotel double room $75-150

» Rental car from $30 per day, excluding insurance and gas

Top end over
$200
» Three-star coastal lodging from $150 per night in summer high season

» Three-course meal in top restaurant: $75 plus wine

Money

» ATMs are widely available. Credit cards are usually required for hotel reservations. Out-of-state checks are rarely accepted. Tipping is customary, not optional.

Visas

» Generally not required for citizens of Visa Waiver Program (VWP) countries, but only with ESTA approval (apply online at least 72 hours in advance).

Cell Phones

» Cell-phone coverage is spotty in the deserts. The only foreign phones that will work in the USA are GSM multiband models.

Driving

» Traffic in cities and coastal areas can be nightmarish. Avoid weekday rush hours (roughly 7am to 10am and 3pm and 7pm).

Websites

» **CalTrans** (www.dot.ca.gov) Current highway conditions and construction updates.

» **California Tourism** (www.visitcalifornia.com) Multilingual trip-planning guides.

» **LA Times Travel** (www.latimes.com.travel) Daily news, SoCal travel deals and theme-park blogs.

» **Lonely Planet** (www.lonelyplanet.com/california) Destination info, hotel bookings, travelers' forums and more.

» **Theme Park Insider** (www.themeparkinsider.com) Reviews and discussion boards.

Exchange Rates

Australia	A$1	$0.95
Canada	C$1	$0.97
Euro zone	€1	$1.31
China	Y10	$1.49
Japan	¥100	$1.06
Mexico	MXN10	$0.78
New Zealand	NZ$1	$0.73
UK	£1	$1.56

For current exchange rates see www.xe.com.

Important Numbers

All phone numbers have a three-digit area code followed by a seven-digit local number. For long-distance and toll-free calls, dial 1 plus all 10 digits.

Country code	☎1
International dialing code	☎011
Operator	☎0
Emergency (ambulance, fire & police)	☎911
Directory assistance (local)	☎411

Arriving in Southern California

» **Los Angeles International Airport** (LAX; see p206)
Taxis – $30-50, 30 minutes to one hour
Door-to-door shuttles – $15-26, operate 24 hours
Bus & Metro – FlyAway bus ($7) to downtown LA or free Shuttle C to LAX Transit Center

» **San Diego International Airport** (SAN; see p300)
Taxis – $10-25, 15 to 30 minutes
Door-to-door shuttles – $8-20, operate 24 hours
Bus – No 992 'the Flyer' ($2.25) to downtown San Diego every 15 minutes from 5am to 11pm

Earthquakes

Earthquakes occur almost daily in SoCal, but most are so tiny you won't feel them. If you're caught in a serious shaker, stay indoors, get under a desk or table or stand in a doorway, and protect your head. If outdoors, get away from buildings, trees and power lines. If you're driving, pull over to the side of the road away from bridges, overpasses and power lines. Turn on the radio and listen for bulletins. For more earthquake safety tips, see p459.

what's new

For this new edition of Los Angeles, San Diego & Southern California, our authors have hunted down the fresh, the transformed, the hot and the happening. These are some of our favorites. For up-to-the-minute recommendations, see lonelyplanet.com/usa/california.

Food Trucks

1 Sure, there have always been taco trucks in SoCal. But recently, a gourmands' street-food revolution has taken over, especially in LA. Whatever you're craving, from Korean BBQ to Indian dosa, haute grilled cheese to good ol' fried chicken, there's a restaurant-on-four-wheels serving it. Find 'em all on Twitter; the Southern California Mobile Food Vendors Association website (www.socalmfva.com) has links and a real-time map. (p169)

LA Live

2 Reason number one to visit downtown LA's new entertainment complex is the Grammy Museum, a glittering musical homage to everyone from Yo-Yo Ma to MJ. (p73)

Hollywood & Vine

3 Newly glam Hollywood keeps pushing the boundaries of its urban renaissance further east. Now the W Hollywood hotel towers near the iconic Capitol Records building. (p92)

Disneyland

4 It's a Small World got dolled up, animatronic Mr Lincoln and Captain EO returned, Toy Story Mania opened and the Pixar Play Parade and World of Color spectacular debuted. (p215)

LACMA's 'Transformation'

5 On a 20-acre museum campus installed with new public art, an ambitious multiyear construction project has already opened the Broad Contemporary Art Museum. (p109)

Echo Park

6 So long, Silverlake, once LA's uncontested alternative cultural capital. These days, the cutting edge of hipsterdom is in this traditionally Latino neighborhood. (p104)

LA County's Lifeguard Towers

7 Brightly splashed with new murals and artwork, these repainted sentinels of the sand, called 'Portraits of Hope,' are visible from Malibu to the South Bay. (p154)

Shorebreak Hotel

8 Party animals still rule in Huntington Beach, but this hip downtown boutique property is upping the ante with a 'surf concierge,' yoga studio and dog-friendly lodgings. (p240)

East Village

9 Popping up around San Diego's Petco Park you'll find gastropubs, epicurean pizzerias, bistros and bars that are making stiff competition for the Gaslamp Quarter. (p291)

New Children's Museum

10 Ingeniously disguised as a playground, San Diego's reborn space for tots and tykes to learn about art and science is mega-fun for young families. (p277)

if you like...

Theme Parks

Southern California's theme parks are the best hands-down, ranking high among family favorites nationwide (who needs Orlando?). If visiting Disney's 'happiest place on earth,' getting a thrill from Hollywood's movie magic or just feeling a powerful need for speed on a rad roller coaster is on your itinerary, you've definitely come to the right place.

Disneyland Topping almost every family's must-do fun list is Walt Disney's 'imagineered' theme park, along with next-door Disney's California Adventure (p215)

Universal Studios Hollywood Cinematic theme park with a studio backlot tram tour, tame rides and live-action, special-effects shows (p183)

Six Flags Magic Mountain Hair-raising roller coasters will scare the bejeezus out of speed-crazed teens (p212)

San Diego Zoo Safari Park Take a safari-style tram tour through an 'open-range' zoo (p326)

Legoland California Low-key theme park made of beloved building blocks for tots (p325)

Beaches

Think SoCal, and you're already dreaming about golden and white-sand beaches with frothy surf, bronzed bods hanging out in the lifeguard huts and palm trees lazily waving in the wind. The SoCal lifestyle is all about the beach, it's true. With over 250 miles of Pacific coastline, you'll be spoiled for choice, whether you're a surfer, volleyball player, whale-watcher or beach bum.

Santa Monica Learn to surf, ride a solar-powered Ferris wheel or dance under the stars (p151)

Huntington Beach Orange County's 'Surf City USA' lives up to its moniker (p238)

Leo Carrillo State Park Malibu's most family-friendly beach, with tide pools, hiking trails, swimming and surfing galore (p154)

Mission & Pacific Beaches For that quintessential SoCal day at the beach in sunny San Diego (p303)

Butterfly Beach Chic hidden strand in Santa Barbara where you may even spot celebs (p375)

Wine

Northern California's Napa and Sonoma Valleys may be more famous, but SoCal's wine countries hold their own. Just crack open a bottle of pinot noir from the sun-kissed Santa Ynez and Santa Maria Valleys and you'll become a believer. Despite the antics of Miles and Jack in the indie movie *Sideways,* Santa Barbara's wine country is actually among California's most civilized. Temecula, near San Diego, has younger, brasher wineries catering to a weekend party crowd.

Foxen Canyon Wine Trail Pastoral country roads wind past some of Santa Barbara's most famous vintners (p392)

Los Olivos The posh hub of Santa Barbara's wine country, where quaint streets are lined by wine-tasting rooms (p395)

Santa Rita Hills Where independent innovators artfully crush grapes in the Santa Maria Valley (p393)

Temecula Stroll past Old West–style storefronts downtown, where olive oil, wine, cheese and candy shops await (p329)

> Shopping, Abbot Kinney Blvd (p170)

Ethnic Food

California cuisine may have reached *Iron Chef* peaks of hauteness, especially around LA, where celebrity restaurateurs have invaded most neighborhoods. But dollar for dollar, SoCal's flavorful cornucopia of mom-and-pop ethnic eateries is what will really satisfy your belly and soul.

Little Tokyo Settle your entourage into an *izakaya* (gastropub) and just go nuts (p75)

Koreatown Juicy aromas of do-it-yourself barbecue grills will pull you in off the street (p197)

Thai Town East of Hollywood's walk of fame, with tastes as authentic as a Bangkok night market (p94)

San Gabriel Valley Let the Chinese seafood feasts commence (p194)

Little Saigon Orange County's mecca for Vietnamese cooking – *pho* (noodle soup) is just the beginning (p234)

San Diego Just north of the border, Mexican taco shops are serious business here (p444)

Freebies

Who says you need to throw around a lot of money just to have a good time in SoCal? Many of the most beautiful beaches are free, just for starters. Look for weekly free admission or pay-what-you-will days at museums too.

El Pueblo de Los Angeles Get a feel for LA's earliest days along lively, adobe building–lined Olvera St (p69)

Getty Center Arrive by public transportation, and you're free to stroll a multimillion-dollar art collection gratis (p129)

Griffith Observatory Be amazed by family-friendly science demonstrations in Griffith Park (p99)

Hollywood Forever Cemetery Free outdoor movies and DIY tours of the gobsmacking graves of bygone stars (p89)

Getty Villa Malibu's trove of ancient Greco-Roman art is another can't-miss freebie (p143)

Old Town San Diego's historic 19th-century Mexican *pueblo* (p281)

Anza-Borrego Desert State Park Hike to hidden canyons, drive to jaw-dropping viewpoints and even pitch your tent for free (p358)

Scenic Drives

In SoCal the open road always beckons. So drop the convertible top, cue up the Red Hot Chili Peppers and step on it. The Pacific Coast Hwy delivers surreally beautiful ocean vistas and serpentine cliffside stretches. Inland you'll find SoCal has even more detours for adventure-seeking road trippers.

Pacific coastin' SoCal's most famous scenic drive hopscotches between beach towns from San Diego to Malibu and beyond (p33)

Mountain highs The Angeles Crest Hwy (p192), the Rim of the World Dr to Big Bear Lake (p212) and Palms to Pines Scenic Byway (p344), carved into the San Jacinto Mountains above Palm Springs, are all classics

Seeing stars So famous David Lynch named a movie after it, LA's Mulholland Drive (p91) winds past movie-star mansions and glittering vista points

If you like... hot-air balloonimg
Del Mar (p321), in San Diego's North County, is a capital spot to take flight
If you like... hot springs
detour to Glen Ivy Hot Springs (p233), aka 'Club Mud,' and soak in natural-springs pools

Shopping

From vintage clothing shops and deeply discounted outlet malls to high-end boutiques where celebrities drop thousands of dollars, SoCal is a shoppers' paradise. It doesn't matter where you go there's a rack of haute couture or bargain finds just begging to be stashed in your suitcase.

Robertson Blvd Forget Rodeo Dr: this short stretch has LA's highest density of star-worthy boutiques per block (p141)

It's a Wrap! Castoffs from real TV shows and movies hang on the racks of this unique resale shop in LA (p187)

Abbot Kinney Blvd Browse an eclectic, arty mix of shops in Venice Beach (p170)

Costa Mesa Skip power shopping at South Coast Plaza for the Camp and the Lab, offbeat anti-malls for indie tribes (p253)

Palm Springs Heaven for vintage and thrift-store shoppers looking for 20th-century gems from decades past, and outlet malls too (p349)

Nightlife

You've seen the red carpet rolled out for movie-star premieres. Now it's your turn to step out in style at ultra-chic nightclubs. Oh, you're not a fan of velvet ropes and attitudinous bouncers? No problem. You'll find casual watering holes all over SoCal, from hipster bars around LA to Orange County's true-blue dives and oceanfront tiki bars. LGBT travelers will find plenty of hangouts too.

Hollywood Hip-hop to world beats, techno to trance, DJs spin for SoCal's most elevated club scene (p95)

West Hollywood WeHo's Santa Monica Blvd is ground zero for LA's thriving gay and lesbian scene (p115)

Gaslamp Quarter Go on a pub crawl in the city's historic red-light district (p295)

Palm Springs Groove with Rat Pack–era martinis, or check out the desert's alternative LGBT bars and clubs (p348)

Las Vegas The Strip's high-powered nightclubs measure up to any clubber's fantasy (p366)

Celebrity Spotting

Celebrity spotting is a favorite SoCal pastime. While we can't guarantee you'll run into Halle Berry or Matthew McConaughey walking around incognito wearing big ol' dark sunglasses while being followed by photographers with giant zoom-lens cameras, it's more likely to happen here than anywhere else. Check out our A-list hot spots below.

Malibu Millionaire movie stars love their privacy, but you can catch a glimpse of them grabbing a latte, doing their grocery shopping and otherwise trying to be normal everyday people in Malibu's shopping plazas (p142)

Los Angeles From Beverly Hills west to the beaches, keep your eyes open for who's next to you at the coffee shop, movie theater or celeb-happy restaurants like the Ivy (p138)

Join a live TV studio audience Watch your fave sitcom or late-night talk-show taping, and you never know who the special guest star will be (p90)

If you like... historic hotels
nothing tops the Hotel del Coronado (p301), an oceanfront dazzler

If you like... parades
Pasadena's Rose Parade (p67) is a New Year's cavalcade of flower-festooned floats

Outdoor Action

On land, in the water and in the sky you'll find plenty of opportunities to get your heart pumping in SoCal – and no, we're not talking about spotting Pamela Anderson or Leonardo DiCaprio in the flesh. Everyone goes swimming or surfing. Water babies can also don a mask, strap on a tank or grab a paddle for close-ups with marine creatures. Back on dry land, hikers have a huge variety of trails and terrain. And that's just a taste of what awaits outdoors (see p39).

Snorkeling & diving La Jolla Underwater Park Ecological Reserve is full of subaquatic creatures (p316)

Kayaking Find adventure in the Channel Islands (p405) or tamer trips along Santa Barbara's coast (p376)

Hiking SoCal's deserts have incredible scenery, from Palm Springs' aerial tramway (p335) and Native American canyons (p339) to three iconic parks – Joshua Tree (p351), Death Valley (p363) and Anza-Borrego (p358)

Weird Kitsch

SoCal truly is a capital of quirk, and you'll encounter unique characters, odd places and bizarre experiences wherever you go. SoCal's deserts especially rope in kooks and offbeat bohemian souls, but even metro areas like loopy LA are jam-packed with just plain weird stuff you won't want to miss.

Venice Boardwalk If aliens landed here, they'd probably blend right in with the human zoo of chainsaw-jugglers, Speedo-clad snake-charmers and a roller-skating Sikh minstrel (p163)

Integratron With the help of aliens, this giant rejuvenation and time machine still stands in the middle of the Mojave (p357)

Salvation Mountain Monumental folk-art piece is a testament to one man's mystical beliefs (p358)

World's Biggest Dinosaurs Vintage roadside attraction ironically now houses a museum of creationism (p340)

Palm Springs Follies Where octogenarian showgirls do the can-can (p348)

Solvang Danish-flavored tourist trap spirited out of a Hans Christian Andersen fairy tale (p396)

Museums

Who says SoCal has no culture? Not us. You could easily spend most of your trip inside mighty fine museums, forgetting about all those theme parks, and still have a great time. Get immersed in multimillion-dollar art galleries or family-friendly interactive science spots (we've got out-of-this-world planetariums, aquariums and more to show you).

Balboa Park Go all-day museum hopping, with top-notch art, history and science exhibitions, near the San Diego Zoo (p272)

Getty Center & Villa Art museums that are as beautiful as their hilltop settings and ocean views in West LA (p129) and Malibu (p143)

LA County Museum of Art More than 150,000 works of art spanning the ages and crossing all borders (p109)

Aquarium of the Pacific Meet SoCal's denizens of the deep in Long Beach (p177)

Museum of the American West Learn the true stories behind cowboys and Native Americans at Griffith Park's storied museum (p101)

> World's Biggest Dinosaurs (p340)

Architecture

SoCal has been on the leading edge of American architecture since the early 20th century. Whether you're admiring the intricate handiwork of arts-and-crafts bungalows, the stark angular lines of mid-century modernism or the groovy sculptural forms and sheer unpredictable whimsy of postmodernism, SoCal has plenty to see.

Gamble House Where brothers Charles and Henry Greene birthed the 'ultimate' California bungalow (p190)

Schindler House Rule-breaking modernist Rudolph Schindler's home and studio, now a living architectural center (p112)

Hollyhock House Not Frank Lloyd Wright's finest work, but still a singular experience (p100)

Palm Springs Mid-century modern playground in the desert; show up in February for Modernism Week (p338)

Getty Center Pritzker Prize–winner Richard Meier's cutting-edge design perches above LA's smog (p129)

Walt Disney Concert Hall Globe-trotting maverick Frank Gehry defies gravity in downtown LA – love it or loathe it, you won't be unmoved (p69)

History

Gold is usually the reason given for the madcap course of California's history, and it's true that mining ghost towns fill SoCal's deserts. But Native American people, Spanish colonial *presidios* (forts), Catholic missions and Mexican pueblos (towns) have all left traces for you to delve into.

Julian Pan for real gold in this historic mining town in the hills east of San Diego (p361)

Chumash Painted Cave State Historic Park See 400-year-old pictographs painted by Native Americans (p389)

San Diego's Old Town Time travel on the site of California's first civilian Spanish colonial *pueblo* (p281)

Mission Santa Barbara The 'queen of the missions' was the only survivor of Mexican secularization (p370)

La Brea Tar Pits Discover where prehistoric mammoths, sloths and saber-toothed cats once roamed around LA (p110)

Spiritual Life

Judging by the tabloids, you might think SoCal is Sodom and Gomorrah reincarnate, but it actually ranks among the USA's most religiously diverse areas (see p426). California's recorded history begins with a string of Spanish missions. Jump two centuries ahead and you have some of the world's finest architects building grand houses of worship. SoCal is famous for spawning new religious movements, as well as importing spiritual philosophies from around the world.

Mission San Juan Capistrano A painstakingly restored jewel along 'El Camino Real,' California's mission trail (p261)

Heavenly architecture José Rafael Moneo's Cathedral of Our Lady of the Angels (p76), Lloyd Wright's Wayfarers Chapel (p175) and Philip Johnson's Crystal Cathedral (p234)

New-age retreats Yogi Paramahansa Yogananda's Self-Realization Fellowship retreats in LA (p144) and San Diego (p323), Deepak Chopra's center in Encinitas (p326) and bliss-out Ojai (p401)

month by month

Top Events

1 **Rose Bowl & Parade,** January

2 **Beach season,** July & August

3 **Cinco de Mayo,** May

4 **Miramar Air Show & Fleet Week,** September

5 **Coachella Music & Arts Festival,** April

January

Typically the wettest month in SoCal, January is a slow time for coastal travel. Mountain ski resorts are busy, as are desert destinations, particularly Palm Springs.

 Rose Bowl & Parade

Held before the Tournament of Roses college football game, this famous New Year's Day parade of flower-festooned floats, marching bands and prancing equestrians draws more than 100,000 spectators to the LA suburb of Pasadena. (p67)

 Chinese New Year

Firecrackers, parades, lion dances and street food celebrate the lunar new year, falling in late January or early February. SoCal's biggest celebrations happen in LA. (p67)

February

Another rainy month for coastal California, but things stay busy at mountain ski resorts. The low desert sees more visitors as wildflowers start blooming. Valentine's Day is booked solid at restaurants and resorts.

 Modernism Week

Can't get enough of Palm Springs' retro vibe? Join other mid-century modern aficionados in mid-February for more than a week of architectural tours, art shows, film screenings, lectures and swingin' parties. (p341)

★ Academy Awards

The red carpet gets rolled out for Hollywood's A-list stars on Oscar night at the Kodak Theatre in late February or early March, while mere mortals scream from the bleachers nearby when stretch limos arrive. (p67)

March

Less rainy, so travelers head back to the coast, especially for spring break (varies, depending on school vacation schedules and Easter holidays). Peak season in the deserts. Ski season ends.

 LA Marathon

On the first Sunday in March, more than 25,000 athletes race along a 26.2-mile course from Dodger Stadium to Santa Monica Pier. Even if you're not a runner, come cheer 'em on and enjoy the live entertainment on stages through the city. (p67)

◉ Wildflowers bloom

Little splotches of color pop up on newly green hillsides from February through May (sometimes even later in the mountains), but March is the peak month for wildflower viewing, with especially dramatic desert displays.

Festival of the Swallows

After wintering in South America, the swallows famously return to Mission San Juan Capistrano in Orange County around March 19. The historic mission town celebrates its Spanish and Mexican heritage with events all month. (p262)

April

Peak wildflower bloom in the high desert. Shoulder season in the mountains and on the coast means lower prices, except during spring break (varies, depending on when the Easter holiday falls).

Dinah Shore Weekend & White Party

Palm Springs' lesbian social event of the year sees pool parties, dances and mixers coinciding with the LPGA golf tournament. For men, the four-day White Party gets crazy over Easter weekend. (p341)

Coachella Music & Arts Festival

Indie no-name bands, cult DJs and superstar rock bands and rappers all converge in Indio, outside Palm Springs, for a three-day musical extravaganza. Bring lots of sunscreen and drink tons of water. (p342)

May

The weather starts to heat up, although some coastal areas remain blanketed by fog ('May grey'). The Memorial Day holiday weekend is the official start of summer, and one of the year's busiest travel times.

Cinco de Mayo

Viva Mexico: margaritas, music and merriment commemorate the victory of Mexican forces over the French army at the Battle of Puebla on May 5. LA and San Diego really do it up in style. (p67)

June

Once school lets out for the summer, nearly everywhere in SoCal gets busy, from beaches to inland theme parks and mountain resorts. In the deserts, it's just too darn hot. Some coastal fog lingers ('June gloom').

LA Pride

Out and proud since 1970, SoCal's biggest, boldest LGBT pride celebration takes place over a long weekend of partying in mid-June, with a parade, live music and more. (p67)

Summer Solstice Celebration

Kick off the official start of summer as Santa Barbara lets its hair down with this wacky parade up State St, filled with characters straight out of a Burning Man festival, in late June. (p377)

July

Beach season gets into full swing everywhere in SoCal. Theme parks are mobbed by vacationing families, as are cooler mountain resorts, but the deserts are deserted. July 4th holiday is the summer's peak travel weekend.

Beach Season

Southern California's mostly Mediterranean climate means that you'll see locals hitting the beach year-round (even with wetsuits in winter to surf giant waves). But the Pacific Ocean's waters only warm up later in summer, meaning the best time for beachgoers is July and August.

Opening Day at Del Mar Racetrack

Horse racing returns in late July to Del Mar's elegant Spanish Mission–style racetrack, built by Hollywood stars in the 1930s. Tickets are tough to get, but worth it just to see the ladies' hats. (p321)

Festival of Arts & Pageant of the Masters

Exhibits by hundreds of artists and a pageant of masterpiece paintings 're-created' using actors makes Orange County's Laguna Beach a hot spot during July and August. (p257)

Comic-Con International

Affectionately known as 'Nerd Prom,' the alt-nation's biggest annual convention of comic book geeks, sci-fi and animation lovers, and pop-culture memorabilia collectors brings out-of-this-world costumed madness to San Diego in late July. (p286)

Orange County Fair

A million people come to ride the giant Ferris wheel, cheer on pie-eating contestants and rodeo cowboys, browse the blue-ribbon agricultural and arts-and-crafts exhibits, and listen to live bands in late July and early August.

August

Warm weather and water temperatures keep SoCal beaches busy. School summer vacations start ending, but everywhere (except for the hot, hot deserts) stays packed. Travel slows just slightly before the Labor Day holiday weekend.

Old Spanish Days Fiesta

Santa Barbara celebrates its early Spanish, Mexican and American *rancho* culture with parades, rodeo events, crafts exhibits and performances all happening in early August. (p377)

Sunset Junction Street Fair

For two days in late August, Silverlake's big-deal block party brings the hipsters out into the streets for food vendors, crafty wares and a killer line-up of bands. (p68)

September

Summer's last hurrah is the Labor Day holiday weekend, which is super-busy almost everywhere (except in the deserts). After kids go back to school, the beaches and cities start to see fewer visitors.

Miramar Air Show & Fleet Week

San Diego's military pride is on display during this week (or actually, more like a month) of land, air and sea events, including parades, concerts, ship-board tours and the USA's largest air show in late September or early October.

October

Shoulder season means things quiet down just about everywhere in SoCal, even though the weather is sunny and balmy. Travel deals abound along the coast, in cities and in the desert, where temperatures are finally cooling off.

West Hollywood Halloween Carnival

More than 350,000 revelers come out to LA's most established gay-and-lesbian neighborhood for all-day partying, dancing and an infamous street fair. The over-the-top, often X-rated costumes must be seen to be believed. (p68)

November

Temperatures drop everywhere, with scattered winter rainstorms just beginning. Coastal beach areas, cities, theme parks and even the deserts are less busy for travelers, except around the Thanksgiving holiday. Ski season just barely begins.

Día de los Muertos

Mexican communities honor their deceased relatives on November 2, with costumed parades, sugar skulls, graveyard picnics, candlelight processions and fabulous altars, including in LA and San Diego. (p68)

December

Winter rains usually begin in coastal areas, while travel to typically sunny, drier desert regions picks up. Christmas and New Year's Eve are extremely crowded travel times, though there's usually a short-lived lull between them.

Christmas Boat Parade

Ho, ho, ho! For more than a century this parade of brightly illuminated and decorated boats, including multimillion-dollar yachts, has floated through the harbor at Orange County's Newport Beach the week before Christmas. (p248)

itineraries

Whether you've got three days or 30, these itineraries provide a starting point for the trip of a lifetime. Want more inspiration? Head online to lonelyplanet. com/thorntree to chat with other travelers.

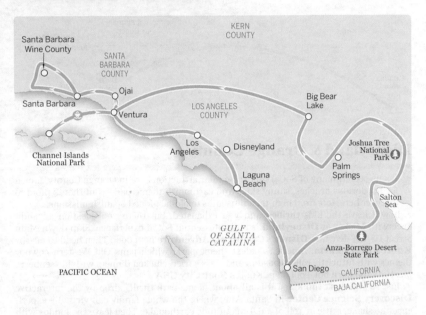

Two Weeks
SoCal Classics

Kick things off in **Los Angeles**, where top-notch sights, bodacious beaches and tasty food form an irresistible trifecta. Follow up with a date with Mickey at **Disneyland** or a day of sybaritic downtime in **Laguna Beach** before heading south to **San Diego** for arts and culture in Balboa Park and a wild night out in the Gaslamp Quarter. Leaving civilization behind, head out to starkly beautiful **Anza-Borrego Desert State Park**. Cruise around the eerie **Salton Sea** and into iconic **Joshua Tree National Park**, beckoning with its 'Wonderland of Rocks.' Squeeze in a day of margarita-sipping and lazing poolside in **Palm Springs** before heading to **Big Bear Lake** for hiking, biking, fishing and skiing. Wind west via the scenic Rim of the World Drive to **Ventura** for a boat trip to **Channel Islands National Park**, then inland to arty, alternative **Ojai** to catch a 'pink moment' at sunset. Take a breather in seaside **Santa Barbara**, whose gorgeous Spanish-Mediterranean downtown offers boutique shopping and dining. Before heading south to LA via star-studded **Malibu**, stock up on fine pinots in the **Santa Barbara Wine Country**.

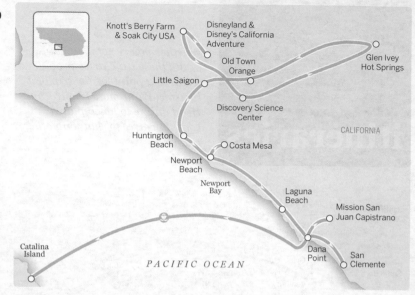

One Week
Disneyland & Orange County

It's no secret: many of SoCal's most popular attractions are in Orange County, famed for its glorious beaches, sunny skies and cartoonish theme parks. But there's more to discover here, too, from high-tech museums to old-fashioned Spanish missions.

It will leave the kids thrilled and you exhausted, but there's no question an audience with Mickey at **Disneyland** is a quintessential SoCal experience. Skip down Main Street USA or dive into **Disney's California Adventure** next door. Then head to nearby **Knott's Berry Farm**, America's oldest theme park, which pairs Old Western cowboy themes with futuristic roller-coasters and classic fried-chicken dinners with boysenberry pie. If it's too darn hot, cool off at Knott's **Soak City USA**.

Just so you don't think SoCal is all about theme-park thrills, drop by the interactive **Discovery Science Center** in Santa Ana, where the whole family can virtually experience the shake, rattle 'n' roll of a 6.9-magnitude earthquake. Then leave the kiddos with a sitter and make a detour inland to adults-only **Glen Ivey Hot Springs,** aka 'Club Mud,' for a long, therapeutic soak. Back closer to Anaheim, **Old Town Orange** is another break from Disneyfied magic, with its antique and vintage shops and eclectic restaurants. **Little Saigon** is not far away, where you can trade those theme-park hot dogs and funnel cakes for a steaming bowl of *pho* (noodle soup).

Cruise toward the OC's unbeatable beaches. Take a day off in **Huntington Beach**, aka 'Surf City USA.' Rent a board, play beach volleyball, build a bonfire at day's end – whatever, just kick back and chill, dude. The next day, roll south to **Newport Beach**, for soap opera–worthy people-watching by the piers. Make a quick stop for power shopping and eclectic eats in **Costa Mesa**, then keep going to **Laguna Beach**, a former artists' colony with more than two dozen public beaches to spoil you, plus an art museum and a chic downtown shopping and eating scene.

From **Dana Point** you could catch a ferry to **Catalina Island**. Otherwise slingshot back toward the I-5, stopping off at **Mission San Juan Capistrano** for a taste of Spanish colonial and Mexican rancho history. Or keep the beach-bum attitude by slacking south to retro **San Clemente**, near Trestles, a year-round surf break.

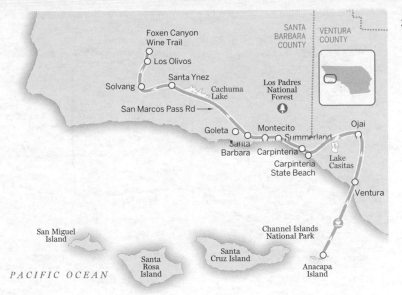

One Week
Santa Barbara & Wine Country

❯ Leave behind star-struck LA and uncover the pacific charms of Santa Barbara and its vineyards. If you crave a little solitude first, hop a ferry over to **Channel Islands National Park** and spend a day or two exploring 'California's Galapagos.' Back on dry land, oceanfront **Ventura** has a walkable downtown, plum full of vintage shops and cafes. Mountainous **Ojai** is an inland Shangri-la with an artsy pedigree, stunning scenery, a spiritual vibe and unbeatable spa experiences.

It's less than an hour's drive from Ojai to Santa Barbara, but why rush? Once you hit the coast, drop by **Carpinteria** for a lazy day at the beach and a plate of Mexican tacos or fresh seafood downtown, where the retro main street is lined with surf shacks and unusual shops. Just up Hwy 101, **Summerland** and **Montecito** are more affluent suburbs, beloved by antiques, art and boutique shoppers.

Ah, **Santa Barbara**. Strut down State St, with its quaint sea of red-tile roofs, then climb to the top of the courthouse for bird's-eye vistas. Down at Stearns Wharf, dig into a bowl of chowder on the pier. Meet local hotties in a pickup game of volleyball on East Beach, or take your sweetheart to romantic Butterfly Beach. If fog hides the ocean views, Santa Barbara's 'Queen of the Missions' awaits inland, as do jewel-like museums, from art and rare manuscripts to maritime and Spanish colonial history. After dark, university students light up downtown's bars and live-music clubs.

Santa Barbara lies at the edge of the **Los Padres National Forest**, an outdoor wonderland of rocks, creeks and waterfalls great for overnight camping. Or take a scenic drive on **San Marcos Pass Rd** (Hwy 154) past Cachuma Lake up to the farming and ranch town of **Santa Ynez**, a back door to Santa Barbara's wine country. Drive west to kitschy Danish **Solvang**, with its pancake houses, faux windmills and tiny mission, then north to the hoity-toity village of **Los Olivos**. From there, follow the **Foxen Canyon Wine Trail**, which lazily winds on back roads past big-shouldered wineries and small artisan producers, where you can tipple to your heart's content.

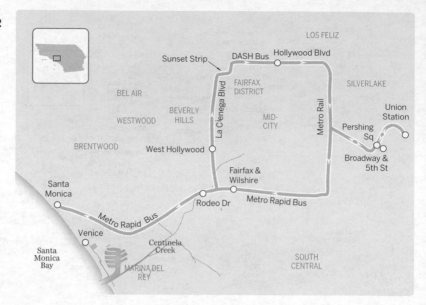

Three Days
Los Angeles: No Car Required

> Hollywood Walk of Fame. Walt Disney Concert Hall. Melrose Ave. Beverly Hills. The beaches. Yup, it can all be done in LA without a car, we promise. You'll need patience, an open mind, a good sense of direction and a couple of Metro day passes. Get an early start and plan on being back at your hotel by dinnertime. Double-check bus and subway route maps and timetables with the **Metro's online trip planner** (www.metro.net) before heading out.

Without further ado, may we present: the logistics for three fun-filled carless days in LA, the city infamous for its traffic. **West Hollywood** makes a handy base of operation and puts you within walking distance – or a short DASH bus ride – of the Original Farmers Market and Grove shopping mall, Mid-City's Museum Row, fashion-forward shopping on Melrose Ave and hip restaurants and bars.

Explore your immediate surroundings on day one, then the following morning catch the DASH bus north on La Cienega Blvd, then east along the legendary **Sunset Strip** to **Hollywood Boulevard**. Explore the famous star-studded walk, then board the **Metro Rail** Red Line subway at Hollywood & Highland and head to **Union Station** in downtown LA. Spend the afternoon exploring downtown's neighborhoods on foot, making sure to return to Union Station before 5pm to catch the Red Line to Pershing Sq, then take Metro Rapid Bus 720 from Broadway & 5th St west to Fairfax & Wilshire, catching the last DASH bus at 6pm.

On day three, pack a swimsuit because you're headed to the beach. But first, Beverly Hills. Board the DASH bus on La Cienega, transferring to the Metro Rapid 720 west bus at Fairfax & Wilshire. Get off at **Rodeo Drive** for a whiff of the lifestyles of the rich and famous and perhaps breakfast at Nate 'n Al delicatessen. Then it's back on the bus and on to **Santa Monica**. Spend a couple of hours on the sands, check out the pier or squeeze in some shopping along the Third St Promenade or Montana Ave. Catch the Metro Rapid 720 east no later than 5pm, again transferring to the last 6pm DASH at Wilshire & Fairfax.

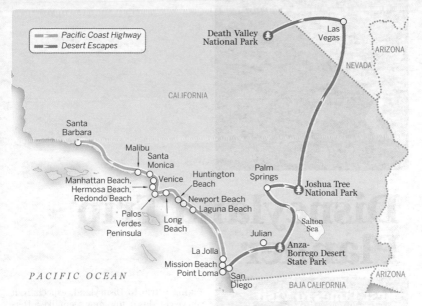

One Week
Pacific Coast Highway

❭ Drop the convertible top, cue up 'California Girls' and step on it! This famous route hugs the Pacific throughout most of coastal Southern California.

Before you steer northward, admire the 360-degree views from **Point Loma**, the buff surfers in **Mission Beach** and the underwater treasures of **La Jolla** in San Diego. Our vote for prettiest Orange County town is artsy **Laguna Beach**, whose secluded coves, craggy cliffs and azure waves enchant. Want ritzy? Plow on to **Newport Beach**, where bobbing yachts are tell-tale signs of the rich and famous. Officially 'Surf City USA,' **Huntington Beach** is just up the road.

Head across the LA County line to **Long Beach**, where families find plenty of fun. Continue around the surreally beautiful **Palos Verdes Peninsula** before plunging headlong into LA's South Bay towns: **Redondo Beach**, **Hermosa Beach** and **Manhattan Beach**. North of boho-chic **Venice**, **Santa Monica** beckons with a carnival pier, superb restaurants and shopping.

The busy coast highway delivers surreal ocean vistas en route to **Malibu**, a celebrity hideaway. Wrap up your tour in **Santa Barbara**, a symphony of red-tile roofs, wine-country restaurants and idyllic beaches.

One Week
Desert Escapes

❭ Start your trip in surfside **San Diego,** then head for the hills and **Julian,** an Old West mining town where you can pan for gold and gorge on apple pie. Drop into ginormous **Anza-Borrego Desert State Park**, where dirt roads and trails lead to hidden canyon oases, Native American petroglyphs and 19th-century stagecoach stops.

Gaze into the mirage-like **Salton Sea**, then head north to retro-chic **Palm Springs**, the once-again hip resort hangout of Elvis and the Rat Pack. Then it's goodbye to poolside cocktails and off to mystical **Joshua Tree National Park**, whose twisted namesake trees have inspired artists and poets, while its desert-baked boulders invite world-class rock climbers.

By now, you're ready for a big-city fix: **Vegas**, baby. It's seductive, cheesy and absolutely outrageous. Where else can you climb the Eiffel Tower, make out in a gondola and witness pirate battles with exploding pyrotechnics, all in the same day? Before you gamble away your life savings, drive west to sere **Death Valley National Park**, a jigsaw puzzle of sand dunes, sun-baked salt flats, volcanic cinder cones and mining ghost towns.

Disneyland Trip Planner

Best Times to Visit

Mid-April–mid-May Miss both spring-break and summer-vacation crowds but still have a good chance of sunny weather.

Mid- to late September Summer vacationers depart after Labor Day and temperatures cool down, but it's still sunny.

Late November–early December As visitation dips between Thanksgiving and Christmas, holiday decorations spruce up the parks.

Weekdays Year-round, they're less busy than weekends.

Top Rides & Attractions

Disneyland Pirates of the Caribbean, Indiana Jones Adventure, Haunted Mansion, Space Mountain, Finding Nemo Submarine Voyage, It's a Small World, Fantasmic! show

Disney's California Adventures Soarin' Over California, Twilight Zone Tower of Terror, California Screamin', Grizzly River Run, Pixar Play Parade, World of Color show

For More Information

Disneyland Resort (☎ recorded info 714-781-4565, live assistance 714-781-7290; www.disneyland.com)

Taking a trip to Disneyland, especially if you've got kids in tow, may seem like a Herculean task. But really, it couldn't be easier. We've got advance-planning tips and strategies to help you out, including the best times to go (and when *not* to go), and we'll show you how to save money on tickets, hotels, restaurants and more.

For in-depth coverage of both of the resort's theme parks, Disneyland and Disney's California Adventure (DCA), including reviews of rides and attractions, lodgings, dining and shopping, see p215.

Timing Your Visit

» Both theme parks, Disneyland and DCA, are open 365 days a year. Check the **current schedule** (☎714-781-4565; www.disneyland.com) in advance.

» Park hours vary, depending on forecast attendance, and are subject to change at any time.

» During peak summer season (roughly mid-June to early September), Disneyland's hours are usually 8am to midnight; the rest of the year, 10am to 8pm or 10pm. DCA closes at 10pm or 11pm in summer, earlier in the off-season.

» Opening hours may be extended during spring break (March/April) and the winter holidays, from a week before Christmas through New Year's Day.

DISNEYLAND DOS & DON'TS

Dos

☐ Designate a meeting place if someone in your group gets lost.

☐ Drink plenty of fluids and eat salty snacks to avoid dehydration (see p456).

☐ Arrive early at the parks, then take a midday break back at your hotel.

☐ Use the Fastpass system to skip long lines at select rides and attractions.

☐ Buy tickets in advance so you don't have to wait even longer to get in. (And keep your ticket if you leave and want to return later.)

☐ Leave your pets at home, or board them for the day at Disneyland's kennels (p228).

Don'ts

X Don't try to cram both theme parks into one day – it takes two days minimum.

X Don't arrive at 11am, almost always the busiest time to buy tickets and enter the parks.

X Don't bring soft-sided coolers bigger than a six-pack or any kind of wheels (eg rolling luggage, bikes, skateboards, in-line skates, even shoes with wheels!) into the parks.

X Don't show up without restaurant reservations if you want to sit down and eat in the parks.

X Don't walk up *and* down Downtown Disney – use the monorail (p230) as a one-way shortcut to/from Disneyland.

X Don't light up in the parks, except at specially designated smoking areas.

» If you visit off-season, some attractions and shows may not be running, like Disneyland's evening fireworks, so check the website in advance to avoid disappointment.

» Concerned about getting stuck waiting for a ride or attraction at closing time? Don't worry! The parks stay open until the last guest in line has had their fun.

Busiest Times to Go

» **March/April** Unless you love crowds and a chance of rain showers, don't visit when schools take their 'spring break' vacation, especially the weeks before and after Easter.

» **July & August** The hottest dog days of summer are the busiest time in the parks, with families taking summer vacations.

» **October** Although the weather is balmy and summer crowds have vanished, Halloween celebrations make this a busy time, too.

» **Mid- to late November** The week leading up to the Thanksgiving long weekend is another crowded period. Plus, there's a chance of rainfall, and not all of the holiday decorations are up yet.

» **Special events** High schoolers take over the parks on 'Grad Nites' in late May and June. Although unofficial, queer-friendly 'Gay Days' in early October are also popular.

» **Weekends** Year-round, the parks are busiest on Saturdays and Sundays.

Beating the Crowds

» Disneyland Resort parking lots and ticket booths open an hour before the theme parks' official opening times, so if you want to get in right away, show up early.

» The busiest time of day in the parks is between 11am and 4pm, making that a great time to go back to your hotel for a mid-day swim (and a nap!), then return after dinner.

» Downtown Disney's restaurants and shops get crowded after 5pm, so try to visit around lunchtime for less crowded shops and cheaper lunch menus, too.

» Fo find out about Disneyland and DCA's Fastpass system, which can cut your wait time significantly for some rides and attractions, see p228.

» A shorter, single-rider line may be an option on some rides (see p222).

» For smartphone apps that may also help you avoid long queues in the parks, see p229.

Buying Tickets

» Tickets never sell out, but buying them in advance will save you time waiting in line at the park and probably some money too.

» Remember that ticket prices increase annually; check www.disneyland.com for the latest information and to buy tickets directly, including convenient print-at-home e-tickets.

» One-day admission to *either* Disneyland or Disney's California Adventure (DCA) theme park costs $76 for adults and $68 for children aged three to nine.

» To visit *both* parks in one day, buy a one-day 'Park Hopper' ticket ($101/91 per adult/child).

» Multi-day 'Park Hopper' tickets cost from $161/146 for two days up to $256/230 for six days of admission within a two-week period.

» Some 'Park Hopper' bonus tickets include one 'Magic Morning' early-bird admission to select attractions on certain days, based on availability (show up 75 minutes before the theme park opens to the general public).

» An annual passport for unlimited theme-park entry on 315 pre-selected days of the year costs $329 per person, regardless of age; a premium annual passport with no blackout dates costs $459, including parking (which otherwise costs $15 per day).

Discounts & Deals

» Disneyland sometimes makes promotional ticket offers available, like five-day 'Park Hopper' tickets for the regular three-day price; check for specials online.

» If you're a resident of Southern California (defined by zip code, extending as far north as San Luis Obispo County), you're eligible for discounted theme-park admission tickets and seasonal and annual passports (subject to blackouts and valid only on pre-selected off-peak days).

» Anyone can buy a **Southern California CityPass** (www.citypass.com), allowing three-day 'Park Hopper' admission to Disneyland and DCA, as well as one-day admission to three other major SoCal attractions (see p455). Purchase online in advance to save time and money.

» You might save substantially by booking your trip through the **Walt Disney Travel Company** (☎714-520-5060, 800-225-2024; www.disneytravel.com), which sells vacation packages that include air, hotel and theme-park tickets, plus extra perks like early-morning park admission and dining plans.

Bringing the Kids

You're never too young or too old for Disneyland. You'll see huge, multi-generational families all enjoying the park's rides and attractions together, from mothers with newborn babes in arms to young honeymooners to elderly great-grandparents.

Infants & Toddlers

» Stroller rentals are available (see p229), but rental strollers can only be used in the theme parks, not Downtown Disney.

» Bringing your own stroller will save time, money and a headache if the parks' rentals are all taken, especially during peak season or later in the day.

» Strollers are not allowed on escalators or the parking lot tram. You need to fold up strollers before bringing them on the monorail.

» Stroller parking areas are available outside most park rides and attractions.

» Baby centers, including diaper-changing and nursing facilities with comfy rocking chairs, are available at Disneyland (Main Street USA) and DCA (Pacific Wharf).

» If you're toting a lot of stuff, day lockers are available (see p228).

» The 'rider swap' system lets two parents with babies or small children each ride without standing in line twice. Ask a staff member at any ride for a pass (both adults must be present). The first adult waits in line and rides, while the other stays with the kids, then they swap.

Kids & Tweens

» Tell your kids that if they get lost, they should contact the nearest Disney staff, who will escort them to a 'lost children' center (on Disneyland's Main Street USA or at DCA's Pacific Wharf).

» Study the online minimum-height charts for rides and attractions in advance, to avoid whining and disappointment when you get to the park.

» If you've booked a Disneyland Resort vacation package, don't forget to schedule a complimentary pre-trip phone call for your kids from Mickey, Minnie or Goofy.

» Every restaurant has a kids' menu. If you're here for a birthday, call and ask about decorate-your-own-cake parties and personal-size cakes (order at least 48 hours in advance).

» Stop by Disneyland's City Hall to pick up a special free 'It's My Birthday!' badge.

» Kids aged 9 years and under may wear costumes inside the park (but no masks, toy weapons or other sharp objects). During Halloween time, preteens may also wear costumes.

» Note for sensitive children: many kids' rides – including Roger Rabbit's Car Toon Spin and Mr Toad's Wild Ride – can be surprisingly scary.

Teens

» Tell your teens that if their cell phones don't work, they can leave a message for 'Lost Parents' at City Hall, just inside Disneyland's entrance.

» If you'd rather send your teens off by themselves, buy tickets in advance for special 'Grad Nites,' when high-school seniors and prom-goers flood the parks in late May and June.

» Clothing or tattoos with any language, graphics or designs deemed offensive are prohibited, as is displaying what Disneyland deems an 'excessive' amount of bare skin (eg bikini tops).

Visitors with Special Needs

Surprisingly, the Disneyland Resort may be the most accessible place in all of Southern California for anyone with mobility issues or other disabilities. If you need something, just ask.

Mobility Support

» Rental wheelchairs and motorized scooters are available (see p229), but it's best to bring your own because rentals are only for use in the parks (not Downtown Disney). They may also sell out, especially later in the day.

» Most rides are either fully accessible to those in wheelchairs or scooters or allow guests to board via a 'transfer access vehicle.' Only a few rides have ambulatory requirements.

» Companion restrooms are available at Disneyland and DCA; consult park maps.

Other Services

» Service animals (eg guide dogs) are welcome to accompany guests into the parks, but they must remain on a leash or harness at all times and are not allowed on some rides and attractions.

» If you have sight or hearing impairments, then Braille guides, digital audio tours, supplemental audio descriptions, assisted listening systems, captioning and sign-language interpretation services are all available.

» Visual and audio support services are complimentary, but may require a same-day refundable deposit (eg for portable audio systems) or advance notice (for live interpretation).

Where to Sleep
At Disneyland Resort

» For the full-on Disneyland experience, stay in one of the resort's three **hotels** (☑reservations 714-956-6425, 800-225-2024; www.disneyland. com). For hotel reviews, see p221).

» Resort hotel guests usually get bonus perks, from early admission to the parks' attractions to preferred seating for live shows and parades.

DISNEYLAND TO-DO LIST

A Month or More in Advance

☐ Make area hotel reservations or book a Disneyland vacation package

☐ Sign up online for Disney Fans Insider e-newsletters and resort updates

A Week or Two Ahead

☐ Check the parks' opening hours and live show and entertainment schedules online

☐ Make dining reservations for sit-down restaurants or special meals with Disney characters

☐ If you haven't already, buy print-at-home tickets and passes online

The Day or Night Before

☐ Recheck the next day's park opening hours and Anaheim or hotel shuttle schedules

☐ Pack a small day pack with sunscreen, hat, sunglasses, swimwear, an extra change of clothes, a jacket or hoodie, a lightweight plastic rain poncho, and extra batteries and memory cards for digital and video cameras

☐ Make sure your electronic devices (including cameras and phones) are fully charged

☐ If you have a smartphone, consider downloading a Disneyland app (p229)

» One-night stays at Disneyland Resort's hotels are comparatively expensive, but rates fluctuate almost daily, so shop around if your schedule is flexible.

» You might save money by booking multinight stays or vacation packages, including theme-park admission tickets and optional dining plans, with the **Walt Disney Travel Company** (☎714-520-5060, 800-225-2024; www. disneytravel.com).

» Booking your Disneyland Resort hotel online usually gets you the cheapest rates.

Outside the Parks

» Many Anaheim area motels and hotels offer packages combining lodging with theme-park tickets; most have family rooms or suites that sleep four to six people.

» Some local accommodations operate complimentary guest shuttles to Disneyland.

» Otherwise, consider staying within walking distance of the parks or along Anaheim's public shuttle route (see p230).

» It's possible to stay anywhere in Orange County, or even LA or San Diego, and commute to Disneyland for the day, but then you'll probably have to drive (see p229) and miss out on the least busy times in the park (early morning and late night).

Dining & Drinking

» Technically, you can't bring any food or drinks into the parks, but security-inspection staff usually look the other way if you're just carrying small water bottles and a few snacks.

» Store soft-sided coolers and other food in the all-day lockers (see p228) by the not-so-appealing picnic area outside the main entrance.

» If you haven't made restaurant reservations (see the next section), plan on eating at off-peak times (eg outside the noon to 3pm lunch rush, and before 6pm or after 9pm for dinner).

» Convenient, if overpriced, fast food and carnival-style snacks are sold everywhere in the parks.

» Park maps indicate restaurants and cafés where you can find healthy-food options – look for the apple icon.

» For good-value eats and fresher menu options, exit the parks and walk to Downtown Disney (or ride the monorail; see p230).

» You can't buy any alcohol in Disneyland, but you can at DCA, in Downtown Disney and at the resort's hotel restaurants, bars and lounges.

» Drinking fountains are everywhere, so bring a refillable water bottle.

Reservations & Special Meals

» If you want to do any sit-down dining in the parks or at resort hotels, reservations are essential, especially during peak season. For restaurant reviews, see p224.

» For both parks, call **Disney Dining** (☎714-781-3463) if you have dietary restrictions, need to make dining reservations or want to inquire about character dining (meals during which Disney characters work the dining room and greet the kids) or dinner-and-a-show picnics.

» Disneyland Dining Plans (DDPs) may save you money if you are eating at least two meals a day in the parks. DDPs include at last one character meal, but vouchers are only valid at selected restaurants, they can't be used for alcohol or tips, and no change is given. DDPs are only available with a Disneyland vacation package (see p37).

The Beaches & Outdoors

SoCal's Best Beaches

Los Angeles Santa Monica, Venice, Malibu, South Bay
Orange County Huntington Beach, Newport Beach, Crystal Cove State Park
San Diego La Jolla, Coronado, Mission Beach, Pacific Beach
Santa Barbara Leadbetter Beach, East Beach, El Capitán & Refugio State Beaches

Best Times to Go

Swimming & beach volleyball Jul–Sep
Surfing & windsurfing Sep–Nov
Kayaking, snorkeling & diving Jun–Oct
Whale-watching Jan–Mar
Hiking Apr–Jun

Top Outdoor Experiences

Surfing Malibu, Huntington Beach, Trestles or Rincon Point
Sea kayaking and **whale-watching** in the Channel Islands
Snorkeling or **scuba diving** at La Jolla
Beach volleyball at LA's Manhattan Beach
Cycling in LA's South Bay or Santa Barbara
Rock climbing or **hiking** in Joshua Tree National Park

Weather forecasters in Southern California probably have the easiest job in the world. 'Today it's…sunny and mild. Tomorrow will be…sunny and mild. And our extended forecast is…' You get the picture. With its Mediterranean climate, SoCal is an ace place to find yourself outdoors at any time of year. There are indeed changes with the seasons and in different regions, but they are milder than elsewhere in California. Here we'll let you in on the prime times and locations to get out and about, pump those legs and lungs and enjoy one of the USA's greatest natural playgrounds.

Beaches & Swimming

With miles and miles of wide, sandy beaches, you won't find it hard to get wet and wild in Southern California. Ocean temperatures become tolerable by about May, peaking in July and August. For safety tips about riptides, see p459.

Another way to keep kids' temperatures cool is by taking them to a water park, such as **Hurricane Harbor** north of LA, **Legoland** north of San Diego or Knott's **Soak City USA** in Anaheim and Palm Springs.

SMOOTH SAILING

Choppy seas can be nauseating for some landlubbers. To avoid seasickness, sit outside on the boat's second level – not too close to the diesel fumes in back. Over-the-counter motion-sickness pills (eg Dramamine) are effective but will make you drowsy. Staring at the horizon works for some people, as does chewing ginger or wearing acupressure wristbands.

Top Swimming Beaches

» **Santa Monica**, Los Angeles
» **Main Beach**, Laguna Beach
» **Leadbetter Beach**, Santa Barbara
» **Torrey Pines State Beach**, San Diego
» **San Buenaventura State Beach**, Ventura

Best Family-Friendly Beaches

» **Leo Carrillo State Beach**, Malibu
» **Arroyo Burro Beach**, Santa Barbara
» **Silver Strand State Beach**, San Diego
» **Newport Beach**, Orange County
» **Carpinteria State Beach**, near Santa Barbara

Best for Beach Volleyball

» **Manhattan Beach**, LA's South Bay
» **Hermosa Beach**, LA's South Bay
» **Huntington Beach**, Orange County
» **Ocean Beach**, San Diego
» **East Beach**, Santa Barbara

Safety Tips

» Most beaches have flags to distinguish between surfer-only sections and sections for swimmers. Flags also alert beachgoers to dangerous water conditions.

» Stay out of the ocean for at least three days after a major rainstorm because of dangerously high levels of pollutants flushed out through storm drains.

» Check the weekly Beach Report Cards issued by the nonprofit organization **Heal the Bay** (www.healthebay.org) for current water conditions and beach closures.

Books & Maps

» The outstanding *California Coastal Access Guide* (University of California Press; www.ucpress.edu) has comprehensive maps and breakdowns of every public beach, reef, harbor, cover, overlook and coastal campground. It's especially helpful for finding secret pockets of uncrowded sand.

Surfing

Surf's up! Are you down? Even if you never set foot on a board, there's no denying the influence of surfing on every aspect of So-Cal beach life, from clothing to lingo; it's an obsession up and down the coast, particularly in San Diego and Orange County. For more on surf culture, see p427.

The most powerful swells arrive in late fall and winter, while May and June are generally the flattest months, although they do bring warmer water. Speaking of temperature, don't believe all those images of hot blonds surfing in skimpy swimsuits; without a wet suit, you'll likely freeze your butt off except at the height of summer.

Top Surf Spots for Pros

See the map on p42 for more places to catch killer waves.

» Santa Barbara's **Rincon Point** is a legendary right point-break that peels forever.

» Near San Clemente in Orange County, **Trestles** is a premier summer spot with big but forgiving waves, a fast ride and both right and left breaks.

» Malibu's **Surfrider Beach** is a clean right break that just gets better with bigger waves.

» San Diego's **Windansea Beach** is a powerful reef break, while nearby **Big Rock** churns out gnarly tubes.

» **Huntington Beach** in Orange County may have the West Coast's most consistent waves, with miles of breaks centered on the pier.

Best Breaks for Beginners

The best spots to learn to surf are at beach breaks of long, shallow bays where waves are small and rolling.

» **Leadbetter Beach**, Santa Barbara
» **Pacific Beach**, San Diego

» **Newport Beach**, Orange County

» **Oceanside**, San Diego's North County

» **Santa Monica**, Los Angeles

Rentals & Lessons

You'll find board rentals on just about every patch of sand where surfing is possible. Expect to pay about $20 per half day for a board, with wet suit rental another $10.

Two-hour group lessons for beginners start around $75 per person, while private, two-hour instruction costs over $100. If you're ready to jump in the deep end, many surf schools offer pricier weekend surf clinics and weeklong 'surfari' camps. Stand-up paddle surfing (SUP) is easier than learning how to board surf, and it's skyrocketing in popularity. You'll find similarly priced rentals and lessons all along the coast.

Books & Maps

» Water-resistant *Surfer Magazine's Guide to Southern California Surf Spots* is jam-packed with expert reviews and information.

» Plan a coastal surfing adventure using **Surf Maps** (www.surfmaps.net), which also has information on seasonal weather and water temperatures.

Online Resources

» Browse the comprehensive atlas, live webcams and surf reports at **Surfline** (www.surfline.com) for the lowdown from San Diego to Santa Barbara.

» Orange County–based **Surfer** (www.surfermag.com) magazine's website has travel reports, gear reviews, newsy blogs, videos and a women's section.

» Environmentalist surfers can join up with **Surfrider** (www.surfrider.org), a nonprofit organization that aims to protect the coastal environment.

» If you're a kook, bone up on your surf-speak so the locals don't go aggro and give you the stinkeye. For translations, use the **Riptionary** (www.riptionary.com).

Windsurfing & Kiteboarding

Experienced windsurfers tear up the waves along the coast, while newbies or those who want a mellower ride skim along calm bays and protected beaches. There's almost always a breeze, but the best winds blow from September through November. Wet suits are a good idea year-round.

Best Places to Windsurf & Kiteboard

Basically, any place that has good windsurfing also has good kiteboarding. Look for the people doing aerial acrobatics as their parachute-like kites yank them from the water. In wide open spaces devoid of obstacles like piers and power lines, you won't have to worry about unexpected flights that could slam you into concrete.

» In San Diego, beginners should check out **Santa Clara Point** in Mission Bay.

» Santa Barbara's **Leadbetter Beach** is another good spot for beginners to learn.

» In LA, you'll see lots of action off **Belmont Shores** near Long Beach and **Point Fermin** near San Pedro.

Rentals & Lessons

The learning curve in windsurfing is steeper than other board sports – imagine balancing on a fast-moving plank through choppy waters while trying to read the wind and angle the sail just so. At most windsurfing hot spots, you'll spend about $75 to $110 for a half-day beginner's lesson.

Although it's harder to get started kiteboarding, experts say it's easier to advance quickly once the basics are down. Beginner kiteboarding lessons ($175 to $400) usually last a few days. The first day is spent learning kite control on the beach and the second day gets you into the water.

Windsurfing gear rentals start at around $50 per day for a beginner's board, plus $15 to $25 for a wet suit and harness. Most windsurfing shops at least dabble in kiteboarding, but usually won't rent kiteboarding gear to people who aren't taking lessons.

Online Resources

» Wind reports, weather forecasts, live windcams and active discussion forums are available at www.iwindsurf.com.

» Aspiring and experienced kiteboarders should check out www.ikitesurf.com and www.kitebeaches.com for primo locations, wind reports and more.

Surf Sites–Santa Barbara to San Diego

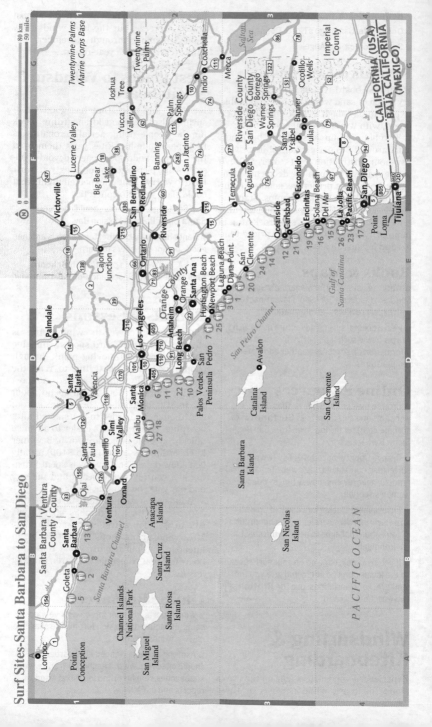

» You'll find more coastal kayaking in **Malibu**, in the coves of Orange County's **Laguna Beach** and around **Gaviota** near Santa Barbara.

43

Surf Sites ✈

Kayaking

Few water-based sports are as accessible and fun for the whole gang as kayaking, and most people manage to get paddling along quickly with minimal instruction. Whether you're looking for adventure and exploring sea caves or just serenely paddling along coastal bluffs, opportunities abound along the SoCal coast.

Best Places to Kayak

» Sea kayaking is fabulous in the **Channel Islands National Park**, offshore from Ventura, and **Catalina Island**, closer to LA. Both are ideal overnight getaways for experienced paddlers too.

» Day trips are equally rewarding, especially for beginners who paddle the calm, protected waters of San Diego's **Mission Bay** or **Dana Point** in Orange County.

» You can explore sea caves while floating above the kelp forests and reefs of **La Jolla Underwater Park Ecological Reserve** in San Diego.

Rentals & Tours

Most outfitters offer a choice between sit-upon (open) kayaks and sit-in (closed-hull) ones, and the latter usually require some training before you head out. Kayak rentals average $35 to $50 for the day, and you'll usually have a choice between single and tandem. Whatever kind of kayak you get, a reputable outfitter will make sure you're aware of the changing tide schedule and wind conditions of your proposed route.

Many kayaking outfitters give lessons (from $50) and lead half-day ($45 to $75) or daylong (starting over $100) trips. Some offer kayak/hike combos or thrilling full-moon paddles. There's nothing quite like seeing the reflection of the moon and stars glittering on the water and hearing the gentle splash of water on your kayak's hull. Small group tours led by local guides with natural history knowledge are best.

Whether you're taking a guided trip or renting kayaks, try to make reservations at least a day before.

Online Resources

» For dozens of links to local kayaking outfitters, schools and organizations, plus handy advice for beginning to expert paddlers, log on to **Kayak Online** (www.kayakonline.com/california.html).

» **California Kayak Friends** (www.ckf.org) offers lots of information about everything from safety and popular paddling destinations to recent trip reports and upcoming events.

Snorkeling & Scuba Diving

Not surprisingly, Southern California has some excellent underwater playgrounds – from rock reefs to shipwrecks to kelp forests – suited for all skill and experience levels. Just don't expect crystal-clear waters like in Hawaii or the Caribbean, as local dive spots can be murky. Ocean waters are warmest between July and September. That said, wet suits are recommended year-round.

Top Diving & Snorkeling Spots

» Great places, especially for first-time divers, are **La Jolla Underwater Park Ecological Reserve** in San Diego and **Casino Point Marine Park** on Catalina Island. Both are accessible right from shore and feature fertile kelp beds teeming with critters close to the surface.

» More experienced divers might want to steer towards **Crystal Cove State Park** just south of Newport Beach, **Divers Cove** in Laguna Beach and San Diego's **Mission Beach**, where you can explore a WWII military shipwreck.

» Many popular dive spots are also good for snorkeling, for example, **Channel Islands National Park**. Guided dive boats and combo kayaking-and-snorkeling trips to the islands leave from Ventura.

Rentals, Lessons & Tours

Local dive shops are your best resources for equipment, guides, instructors and dive-boat trips. To explore California's deep waters, you must have an open-water certificate from the Professional Association of Dive Instructors (PADI) or another recognized organization. Rental dive outfits (including one tank of oxygen) and one-tank boat dives cost about $65 to $110 – it's wise to reserve at least a day in advance.

If you just want to dabble in diving, look for outfitters offering beginner courses that include basic instruction, followed by a shallow beach or boat dive, for about $100 to $150. If you're serious about learning and have the time and money, sign up for a multi-day open-water certificate course, which cost around $300 to $500.

Snorkelers will find mask, snorkel, fin and even wet suit rentals (around $20 for a set) widely available from beach concessionaires near snorkeling sites. Think you'll be taking the plunge more than twice? Buy your own set – it's cheaper and often higher-quality. When heading out snorkeling, don't go alone, don't touch anything and don't forget to wear sunblock!

Books, Magazines & Online Resources

» **LA Diver** (www.ladiver.com) has exhaustive listings of dive sites and shops, certification programs, safety resources and weather conditions for the Los Angeles area, with links for San Diego, Santa Barbara and Orange County, too.

» Lonely Planet's *Diving & Snorkeling Southern California & the Channel Islands* by David Krival is a hands-on guide to happy encounters with garibaldi, sheephead, calico bass and other offshore creatures in SoCal's waters.

» **Scuba Diving** (www.scubadiving. com) and **Sport Diver** (www.sportdiver. com), both magazines published by PADI, have comprehensive websites dedicated to underwater adventures.

Whale-Watching

Every summer 18,000 gray whales feed in the Arctic waters between Alaska and Siberia, and every fall they start moving south down the Pacific Coast of Canada and the US to sheltered lagoons in the Gulf of California off Baja California. In spring these whales turn around and head back to the Arctic. During their 12,000-mile round-trip, the whales pass just off the California coast, typically between late December and early April.

And it's not only gray whales that make appearances. Blue, humpback and sperm whales and schools of dolphins can be seen swimming offshore through the summer and fall, but these spottings are not as predictable as the grays.

To find out more about SoCal's marine mammals, see p447.

On Land vs at Sea

You can try your luck while staying ashore – it's free, but you're less likely to see whales and you'll be removed from all the action. **Point Vicente** on the Palos Verdes Peninsula in LA and San Diego's **Point Loma** are two well-known whale-watching spots, but you could get just as lucky somewhere else.

Just about every SoCal port town worth its salt offers more-thrilling **whale-watching boat tours**, especially during winter. Don't forget your binoculars! Half-day whale-watching boat trips (from $30 to $45 per adult, $15 to $25 per child) last from 2½ to four hours; all-day trips average $65 to $100, and sometimes include meals. Make reservations at least a day in advance, and look for whale-watching tours that limit the number of people and have a trained naturalist or marine biologist on board. Some tour-boat companies will let you go on a second trip for free if you don't spot any whales on your first trip.

Hiking

Got wanderlust? With fabulous scenery, Southern California is perfect for exploring on foot. That's true no matter whether you've got your heart set on peak-bagging 10,000-footers, trekking to palm-tree oases, hiking among fragrant pines or simply going for a wander on the beach accompanied by the booming surf. During spring and early summer, a painter's palette's worth of wildflowers bloom on shaggy hillsides, in mountain meadows on damp forest floors and most famously, in desert sands.

Best Places to Hike

No matter where you find yourself in Southern California, you're never far from a trail, even in the metropolitan areas. The best trails are often in the jaw-dropping scenery of national and state parks, national forests, recreation areas and other public lands. You'll find the gamut of routes, from easy strolls negotiable by wheelchairs and baby strollers to multiday backpacking routes through rugged wilderness.

» In Los Angeles you can hike for miles in **Griffith Park**, one of America's largest urban parks.

» Outside LA the **Santa Monica Mountains** and **Big Bear Lake** are both cooler escapes during summer.

» The **Santa Ynez Mountains** beckon in Santa Barbara, especially during the more temperate spring and fall.

» Offshore, more rugged trails crisscross the **Channel Islands**.

» Palm Springs delivers fantastic hiking in summer atop its aerial tramway in the shadow of **Mt San Jacinto** and in winter in **Indian and Tahquitz Canyons**.

» For spectacular spring wildflower displays, head deeper into the Mojave and Sonoran Deserts to **Anza-Borrego Desert State Park**, **Death Valley National Park** and **Joshua Tree National Park**.

» Although San Diego and Orange County are heavily developed, you can hike year-round through nature preserves, along coastal bluffs like **Torrey Pines State Reserve** and **Crystal Cove State Park**, or in the canyons above **Laguna Beach**.

Safety Tips

» Pay attention on the trail and be aware of potential dangers. Even a minor injury such as a twisted ankle can be life-threatening, especially if you're alone.

» Always let someone know where you're going and how long you plan to be gone. When available, use sign-in boards at trailheads or ranger stations.

» Always carry extra water, snack food and extra layers of clothing. For tips on avoiding dehydration, see p456.

» Don't rely on your cell phone: service is spotty or nonexistent in many areas, especially in the mountains and canyons.

» Weather can be unpredictable. Afternoon summer thunderstorms, for instance, are quite common in the deserts. Check the forecast before heading out.

» Encounters with mountain lions and bears are extremely rare but possible. Rattlesnakes and spiders also present potential dangers. Watch your step!

» For warning signs and symptoms of heat exhaustion, heatstroke and hypothermia, see p456.

Fees

» Most California state parks charge a daily parking fee of $5 to $15; there's often no charge if you walk or bike into these parks.

LEAVES OF THREE, LET IT BE! ✳

Watch out for western poison oak in forests throughout California, especially in areas below 5000ft elevation. It's a shrub most easily identified by its shiny reddish-green tripartite leaves, which turn crimson in the fall, and its white berries. In the winter months, when the plant has no leaves, it looks brown and twiggy, but can still cause a serious allergic reaction. If you brush against poison oak, scrub the affected area immediately with soap and warm water or an over-the-counter remedy such as Tecnu, a soap specially formulated to remove the plant's itchy urushiol oils.

PARK	FEATURES	ACTIVITIES	BEST TIME TO VISIT	PAGE
Anza-Borrego Desert State Park	badlands, canyons, fan-palm oases, hot springs, caves; bighorn sheep, birds	4WD, stargazing, hiking, horseback riding, birding	Nov-Mar	p358
Channel Islands National Park	rocky islands with steep cliffs; elephant seals, sea lions, otters, foxes	snorkeling, diving, kayaking, hiking, birding	Apr-Oct	p405
Crystal Cove State Park	beach, woodland, marine park, tide pools, historic cottages; wildflowers, bobcats	hiking, diving, biking, horseback riding	year-round	p254
Death Valley National Park	unique geology, sand dunes, canyons, volcanic craters; wildflowers, desert tortoise, bighorn sheep, bats	hiking, 4WD, horseback riding, mountain biking, birding	Oct-Apr	p363
Joshua Tree National Park	rocky desert, fan-palm oases; Joshua trees, cacti, wildflowers, desert tortoise, bighorn sheep, coyotes, snakes	rock climbing, hiking, 4WD, mountain biking, birding	Sep-May	p351
Los Padres National Forest	steep canyons, chaparral-covered foothills, mountain forests, waterfalls, hot springs; California condors, mule deer, coyotes, black bears	hiking, birding, wildlife-watching, mountain biking, swimming	Apr-May & Sep-Oct	p389
Mt San Jacinto Wilderness State Park	alpine mountains, forests, meadows, aerial tramway; wildflowers, deer, mountain lions, foxes	hiking, cross-country skiing, snowshoeing, birding	year-round	p337
Upper Newport Bay Nature Preserve	estuary, beach, salt marsh, mud flats, sand dunes, coastal scrub grasslands; birds	birding, kayaking, fishing, biking, horseback riding, hiking	Oct-Apr	p247
Santa Monica Mountains National Recreation Area	tree- and chaparral-covered coastal range; wildflowers, lizards, mountain lions, bobcats, snakes, raptors	hiking, mountain biking, birding	year-round	p142
Torrey Pines State Reserve	coastal lagoon, beaches, salt marsh; pine trees, coastal sage, seals, sea lions, foxes, birds	hiking, birding, tide pooling		p315

» You'll need a **National Forest Adventure Pass** (NFAP; ☏909-382-2622/2623; www.fs.fed.us/r5/sanbernardino/ap/) for parking in the San Bernardino, Cleveland, Angeles or Los Padres national forests. Passes cost $5 per day or $30 per year. Buy them from USFS ranger stations, some sporting-goods stores and local vendors, or order online or by phone.

» National park entry averages $15 to $20 per vehicle, and is good for seven consecutive days. There's no admission fee for Channel Islands National Park.

» For unlimited admission to national parks, national forests and other federal recreation lands, buy the 'America the Beautiful' annual pass ($80; http://store.usgs.gov/pass). It's free for US citizens and permanent residents with disabilities, $10 for seniors aged 62 and over.

Maps & Information

There are bulletin boards showing basic trail maps and other information at most major trailheads. Some also have dispensers stocked with free trail brochures. Parks and national forests almost always have a visitors center or ranger station with clued-in staff happy to offer route suggestions and trail-specific tips.

For short, well-established hikes in national or state parks, free trail maps handed out at ranger stations and visitors centers are usually sufficient. Occasionally a more detailed topographical map may be necessary, depending on the length and difficulty of your hike. The US Geological Survey (USGS; www.store.usgs.gov) offers its topographic maps as free downloadable PDFs, or you can order print copies online.

Books

» Former *Los Angeles Times* columnist John McKinney's excellent hiking guides, published by Olympic Press, include a *Day Hiker's Guide to California State Parks*, the *New Day Hiker's Guide to Southern California* and *Orange County: A Day Hiker's Guide*.

» Jerry Schad's *Afoot & Afield: San Diego County*, *101 Hikes in Southern California* and *Top Trails: Los Angeles* describe fantastic, locals'-favorite routes in evocative detail with plenty of insider tips.

Online Resources

» Modern Hiker (www.modernhiker.com) is a one-stop newsy blog, hikers' forum and virtual encyclopedia of hiking trails, especially in national forests and recreation areas around LA.

» Visit Trails.com (www.trails.com) to search for descriptions of trails that explore SoCal's mountains, deserts and more; trail summary overviews are free.

» Learn how to minimize your impact on the environment while traipsing through the wilderness by visiting the Leave No Trace Center (www.lnt.org) online.

Cycling & Mountain Biking

Strap on your helmet! Southern California is outstanding cycling territory, no matter whether you're off for a leisurely spin along the beach, an adrenaline-fueled mountain ride or a multiday bike-touring coastal adventure. Avoid the mountains in winter and the desert in summer. Be aware of your skill and fitness level and plan accordingly.

Best Bike-Friendly Cities & Parks

For the inside scoop on the local cycling and mountain biking scene, ask the knowledgeable staff at bicycle shops.

» Southland cities are not terribly bike-friendly, Santa Barbara, Santa Monica and Palm Springs being exceptions.

» Fabulous paved beach trails include: LA's South Bay Trail; between Huntington & Bolsa Chica State Beaches in Orange County or El Capitán & Refugio State Beaches, north of Santa Barbara; and the harborfront cycling path in Santa Barbara.

» Mountain bikers can follow tracks in the Santa Monica Mountains outside LA or in Orange County at Crystal Cove State Park near Newport Beach and Aliso & Woods Canyon Park above Laguna Beach.

» Fat-tire speed freaks also sing the praises of Snow Summit resort park at Big Bear Lake, in the San Bernardino Mountains outside LA.

Road Rules

In national parks, bikes are usually limited to paved and dirt roads and are not allowed on trails or in designated wilderness areas. State parks may be slightly more relaxed with this rule, although most trails are still off-limits to bikes. Most of the national forests and Bureau of Land Management (BLM) lands are open to mountain bikers. Just be sure to stay on already established tracks and do not create any new ones. Always yield to hikers and horseback riders.

For Southern California road rules for cyclists, as well as emergency roadside assistance and how to take your bike on public transportation, see p464.

ACTIVITY	LOCATION	DESCRIPTION	PAGE
Fishing	Big Bear Lake	Catch trout in the mountains northeast of LA	p212
	Dana Point	Popular departure point for sportfishing boats	p263
	Malibu	Fish right from the pier, or take a sportfishing tour	p144
	Marina del Rey	Lots of sportfishing trips, including to Catalina Island	p164
	San Diego	Dangle a rod from public piers, or take a sportfishing trip	p306
Hang-gliding & paragliding	Torrey Pines	Glide at SoCal's gliding capital, near La Jolla	p316
	Santa Barbara	Another good spot to soar near the coast	p376
Hot-air ballooning	Del Mar	SoCal's ballooning capital flies in San Diego's North County	p321
Horseback riding	Santa Monica Mountains	Canter where film stars once shot Westerns on location	p148
Rock Climbing	Joshua Tree	World-class, mostly short technical climbs, and bouldering	p353
Skiing & Snow-boarding	Big Bear Lake	Family-friendly resort is the closest powder to LA	p212
Yoga	Los Angeles	Indoor studios abound, from traditional Hatha and heated Bikram to power and martial-arts styles	various locations

Maps & Online Resources

Local tourist offices can supply you with a variety of cycling route ideas, maps and advice.

» **California Association of Bicycling Organizations** (www.cabobike.org) offers freeway access info for bicyclists, printable e-guides and cycling maps.

» **Los Angeles Bicycle Coalition** (www.labike.org) has links to free downloadable bicycle maps for Santa Monica and Orange County.

» **Santa Barbara Bicycle Coalition** (www.sbbike.org) also offers downloadable do-it-yourself cycling tours, including of Santa Barbara's Wine Country.

» **Adventure Cycling Association** (www.adventurecycling.org) sells long-distance cycling route guides and touring maps, including the Pacific Coast Hwy (PCH).

» **League of American Bicyclists** (www.bikeleague.org) lists bicycle specialty shops, local cycling clubs, group rides and other special events.

» **DirtWorld.com** (http://dirtworld.com) and **MTBR.com** (www.mtbr.com) have online forums and reviews of mountain-biking trails in Southern California.

Golf

The Palm Springs and Coachella Valley area is the undisputed golfing center of Southern California with more than 100 courses, while San Diego and Catalina Island have a couple of notably historic places to play.

Most cities and bigger towns in Southern California have public golf courses with reasonable greens fees, although many of the top-ranked courses are at private golf clubs, where you may have to be invited by a member or get a referral from the pro at your home club. Semiprivate clubs are open to nonmembers, except at peak times like weekend mornings.

Fees

Greens fees vary hugely, from $20 to $250 or more for 18 holes, depending on the course, season and day of the week, and

SPA ME, BABY!

If the road has left you feeling frazzled and achy, an hour or more at a day spa may be just what the doctor ordered. There are literally hundreds of spas throughout the Southland, from simple storefronts in strip malls to sumptuous luxury oases in hoity-toity zip codes of the rich and famous, such as **Palm Springs** (p341).

Every spa has its own 'treatment menu,' usually including a variety of massages such as Thai, shiatsu, deep-tissue, Swedish, tandem (for two people) and hot-stone. Beauty treatments range from elemental facials and botanical wraps to exotic elixir baths and body cocktail scrubs. For a treat, detour to **Glen Ivy Hot Springs** (p233), aka 'Club Mud,' famous for its red-clay mud pool but also offering clear mineral-water tubs and a large swimming pool.

Massage pummeling sessions usually go for at least $80 per hour. Smoothing your skin will likely set you back about $60. By the time you've added a 20% tip, the final tab may be high enough to put that frown right back on your forehead.

that usually doesn't include cart or club rental. Golfers can save money – sometimes as much as 50% – by booking twilight play, when desert courses also happen to be cooler. Book tee times well in advance.

Online Resources

For a searchable directory of golf courses throughout Southern California, go to www.sgca.org. Also search these regional golfing websites:

Coachella Valley (www.golfcoachellavalley.com)

Los Angeles (http://golf.lacity.org)

Orange County (www.playocgolf.com)

Palm Springs (www.palmspringsteetimes.com)

San Diego (www.golfsd.com)

Santa Barbara (www.santabarbara.com/activities/golf)

Travel with Children

Best Regions for Kids

Los Angeles

Theme parks, museums and the Hollywood Walk of Fame.

Orange County

There's a reason Disneyland's the most popular attraction in Southern California. Generations of kids and kids at heart love it, older kids will enjoy the thrill rides at Disney's California Adventure, and there's shopping and dining for everyone at Downtown Disney.

San Diego

From pandas to koalas, flamingos to Elephant Odyssey, San Diego Zoo is paws-down the best zoo in America. There's also Zoo Safari Park, the museums of Balboa Park and seafaring sites along the Embarcadero.

By golly, they're right: it *is* a small world after all. Southern California has got to be one of the most child-friendly vacation spots on the planet. The kids will already be begging to go to the theme parks and celebrity hotspots. Get those over with (you may well enjoy them too) and then introduce them to many other worlds, big and small.

Southern California for Kids

SoCal's 'endless summer' of sunny skies and warm temperatures lends itself to outdoor activities too numerous to mention, but here's a start (big breath): swimming, body-surfing, snorkeling, bicycling, kayaking, hiking (mountain or urban), horseback riding and walking. Many outfitters and tour operators have dedicated kids' tours. And on those rare rainy days – or if you need a break from all that sun – head to one of dozens of top-flight museums.

Sometimes no organized activity is even needed. We've seen kids from Washington, DC, thrill at catching their first glimpse of a palm tree, and 11-year-olds with sophisticated palates in bliss over their first taste of heirloom tomatoes at a farmers market or shrimp dumplings at a dim-sum palace. The bottom line: if the kids are having a good time, their parents are having a good time.

Eating Out

Most SoCal restaurants – not just fast-food places – are easygoing with kids. A good measure is the noise level: the louder, the more kid-friendly. Casual eateries in well-trafficked neighborhoods typically have high chairs available and many have specific children's menus, sometimes printed on a take-home coloring book or placemat – complete with crayons! Even restaurants without kids' menus can usually whip up something your children will call yummy. Generally, earlier (before 6pm) is better for families with young ones.

Theme parks have dozens of ways to get the kids hopped-up on sugar and salt at expensive prices, and many don't permit picnics or food to be brought in. One way to get around this: carry a cooler in the car and have a picnic in the parking lot (though be sure to get a hand-stamp for re-entry).

One place kids are generally *un*welcome is high-end restaurants. Unless the children are exceptionally well behaved, properly dressed and old enough to appreciate the meal, neither the staff nor other diners are likely be charmed.

If all else fails, local supermarket chains like Trader Joe's and Gelson's have pleasing, wholesome takeout.

Children's Highlights
Los Angeles
Theme Parks

» Universal Studios Hollywood – If the kids are old enough to appreciate movies that grownups also like, they'll love this theme park, though there's not too much for the preschool set. The adjacent Universal CityWalk makes a colorful meal stop.

» Six Flags Magic Mountain – Older, coaster-friendly kids will thrill while whirring, whizzing and whooping on some of the best in the west.

» Pacific Park, Santa Monica Pier – Fun for the whole family, and reasonably priced.

Screenland

» Hollywood Walk of Fame – Get the kids' pictures taken beside the star of their favorite star on Hollywood Blvd. Actors dressed as famous characters from Sponge Bob to Michael Jackson roam the Walk of Fame too; tip them a couple bucks if you take their picture with your kids.

» Grauman's Chinese Theater – R2-D2's wheel prints and the hand-, foot- and wand-prints of the young stars of the Harry Potter movies are must-snap sites.

Museum Medley

» Exposition Park Museums – The California Science Center is both great and free, and the Natural History Museum is, among other things, where Peter Parker (aka Spiderman) was first bitten.

» Page Museum at the La Brea Tar Pits – See the cast of *Ice Age* (albeit as their former real-life selves) at this archaeological museum.

» Petersen Automotive Museum – Thrill your (inner) eight-year-old boy.

» Skirball Cultural Center – Climb all over the Noah's Ark exhibit made of found objects.

» Kidspace Children's Museum – This play park near the Rose Bowl in Pasadena boasts a kaleidoscope-like building, climbing tower and places for small fry to run around.

» Aquarium of the Pacific – Sharks! 'Nuff said. In downtown Long Beach.

Multi-culti Kids

» Chinatown – Pick up touristy knickknacks, make a wish on a fountain, chow on dumplings or sip boba (with chewy black pearls of tapioca).

» Olvera St – LA's oldest street mixes Mexi-kitsch with quality eats.

» Little Tokyo – Browse for anime and manga, snack on sushi or ramen, and learn about the Japanese-American experience at the Japanese American National Museum.

Go Out & Play

» Griffith Park – Amusements include the landmark Griffith Observatory, a merry-go-round, hiking to view the Hollywood Sign, Travel Town for younger tykes, and the zoo, though it can't compare to San Diego's.

» Bike at the beach – Rental shops line the 22-mile South Coast Bicycle Trail.

Round Round Get Around...

» Take the subway – For kids who don't regularly ride trains, this will be the cheapest thrill ride of your trip, and maybe your fastest connection between Downtown and Hollywood.

Orange County
Theme Parks & Museums

» Do Disney – There's a reason Disneyland's the most popular attraction in Southern California. Generations of kids and kids at heart love it, older kids will enjoy the thrill rides at Disney's California Adventure, and there's shopping and dining for everyone at Downtown Disney.

TOP FIVE PIERS IN SOCAL FOR KIDS

» Stearns Wharf, Santa Barbara – The west coast's oldest continuously operating pier features the engaging Ty Warner Sea Center.

» Santa Monica Pier – The gem of the LA coast, built in 1908, has its own amusement park on top, an aquarium underneath and dance concerts on Thursdays in summer.

» Balboa Island, Newport Beach – It's not one but two piers, plus a reasonably priced amusement park made famous on TV's *The OC*.

» Crystal Pier, Pacific Beach – If you stay at the Crystal Pier Hotel, the waves lapping beneath your bungalow on the pier are a natural sleep aid.

» Paradise Pier, Disneyland – Granted, it's not technically a pier (it's nowhere *near* the ocean), but who cares when the rides are so good?

» Knott's Berry Farm –This place is more homegrown and more low-key than Disney. Charlie Brown and Lucy sub for Mickey and Minnie, and Camp Snoopy is just the right speed for little kids. It's a definite to-do for their older siblings during October's nighttime Halloween Haunt.

» Discovery Science Center – Journey from beneath the earth (Quake Zone) to outer space (Boeing Rocket Lab) and frozen water (the Science of Hockey) at this super-duper museum in Santa Ana.

» Ocean Institute – Over 110,000 K through 12 students come to Dana Point each year to learn about oceanography, science and California history.

Attention Shoppers

» The Block at Orange – A contempo-cool mall with its own skateboard park.

» The Lab – This 'anti-mall' offers vintage clothing and contemporary art exhibits in Costa Mesa.

Beachy Keen

» Huntington Beach – Surf culture in Surf City.

» Newport Beach – Beloved for its piers, amusement park and upscale vibe, particularly on Balboa Island.

San Diego

All Those Animals

» San Diego Zoo – From pandas to koalas, flamingos to Elephant Odyssey, this is paws-down the best zoo in America.

» SeaWorld – Look for Shamu and pals frolicking, penguins playing and specials and combo tickets to keep your expenses down.

» San Diego Zoo Safari Park – Journey to Africa without leaving North San Diego County.

» Birch Aquarium – La Jolla aquarium that's as entertaining as it is educational, thanks to the Scripps Institute of Oceanography.

A Day In the Park

» Balboa Park – After exploring the zoo, spend an additional day at one of the nation's best collections of museums. The Reuben H Fleet Science Center (with IMAX theater), Model Railroad Museum and Natural History Museum are all tailor-made for kids, the Marie Hitchcock Puppet Theater and Automotive Museum will appeal to particular audiences, and the plazas, fountains and gardens offer plenty of open space for children of all ages to let off some steam.

A Little History

» Old Town State Historic Park – Elementary-schoolers and older will appreciate the historical exhibits here, plus old-time shops, south-of-the-border souvenirs and the Mexican restaurants nearby.

» Cabrillo National Monument – The views here inspire awe, and its old-school museum tells the story of the Spanish explorers who 'discovered' California.

By the Sea

» Mission and Pacific Beaches – Teenagers will be in their element among the array of surfers, bikers, 'bladers and buff bods. Alternatively, go kayaking or ride a paddle wheeler on Mission Bay.

» Midway Museum – Board this decommissioned aircraft carrier and gain an appreciation for our men and women in uniform.

» La Jolla Cove – Snorkel to shipwrecks, sea caves and schools of fish.

» Coronado – Quieter kids will appreciate this calming getaway, featuring the Hotel del Coronado and kid-friendly public library.

Palm Springs & the Deserts
Water In the Desert

» Resorts – Who needs to run around, when swimming pools, tennis courts and, for older kids, golf are great family fun? There's a large assortment Down Valley.

» Knott's Soak City – Splish, splash and slide at this water park.

Get Airborne

» Palm Springs Aerial Tramway – Round gondola-style cars rotate ever so slowly as they ascend 6000 vertical feet up the San Jacinto Mountains. Temperatures at the top are up to 40°F lower than on the desert floor; in cooler months, bring warm clothing and snow gear (the latter can be rented).

» Windmills – Take an up-close-and-personal tour of these green power generators west of Palm Springs.

Outdoor Adventures

» Living Desert Zoo – Fascinating and well-presented exhibitions of desert flora and fauna.

» Hike, hike, hike – Active kids will enjoy hiking Indian and Tahquitz Canyons just outside central Palm Springs, while in the center of the region is Joshua Tree National Park; clear blue skies typically make for glorious hiking, light climbing, nature-watching and star-gazing.

Hollywood & History

» Pioneertown – The main street, Mane St, takes you back to the Old West – it was the set for some classic western TV shows and movies. Go for the comedic shoot-'em-up show.

» Palm Springs Follies – Theatrically minded kids won't get the historical references but will be in awe of former Hollywood and Broadway performers their (great-) grandparents' age hoofing it up like way back when.

» World's Biggest Dinosaurs – Little kids go nuts for this pair of life-size concrete dinos and their animatronic pals off I-10, though grownups may be driven nuts by the Creationist message inside.

» Julian – Pan for gold and watch the weekend Old West show.

Santa Barbara
Seaside Escapes

» Stearns Wharf – Pride of place belongs to the pier in central Santa Barbara, and nearby Arroyo Beach and Leadbetter Beach attract many families.

» Carpinteria State Beach – Said to be the world's safest.

» Get outta town – Escape to El Capitan and Refugio State Beaches, or Ventura County is a less expensive and more family-oriented beach getaway.

» Channel Islands National Park – A natural for families who like their vacations, well, natural: hiking, kayaking, camping, whale-watching and more.

In-town Adventures

» Central Santa Barbara – The lovely mission-style town center boasts a low-key Museum of Natural History and Planetarium and a zoo, and opportunities for cycling, roller-skating, boating, whale-watching and various other activities abound.

» Maritime Museum – Family-friendly spot where you can 'reel in' a fake 45lb marlin.

Signature Tastes

» Santa Barbara Shellfish Company – Both delish and kid-friendly, at the end of Stearns Wharf.

» Aebelskiver – Tiny doughnuts in the Danish-themed village of Solvang.

» Santa Barbara County Fair – Sample lots of local food on a stick, all in one place.

Planning
What to Bring

Sunscreen. Bring sunscreen.

And bringing sunscreen will remind you to bring hats, bathing suits, flip-flops and

---

GETTING IN

Children are often entitled to discounts for everything from museum admissions to bus fares and motel stays. The definition of a 'child' varies – in some places anyone under 18 is eligible, while others put the cut-off at age six. Note that many amusement park rides have minimum height requirements.

goggles. If you like beach umbrellas and sand chairs, pails and shovels, you'll probably want to bring or buy your own; all are readily available at local drugstores. At a fair amount of beaches, you can rent bicycles of all stripes; flick over to the On the Road chapters for surf and other water gear.

For mountain outings, bring hiking shoes, plenty of food and water, and your own camping equipment. These can be purchased or rented from markets and outfitters near desert parks, but remember that the best time to test out shoes, sleeping bags and such is before you take your trip. Murphy's Law dictates that wearing brand-new hiking shoes on a big hike results in blisters.

See p18 for information about weather in Southern California.

Online Resources

www.travelforkids.com Has no-nonsense listings of kid-friendly activities and useful services in LA, San Diego and Orange County (called South Coast).

www.dailycandy.com/kids/los-angeles Offers info on the latest trends for your little trend-setters.

www.losangeles.parenthood.com Provides a detailed calendar of events, festivals and places with activities for kids from ceramic-making to language classes.

www.travelingbabyco.com and **www.lababy gearrental.com** Don't want to schlep a pack 'n' play or high chair from home? Rent them and even more; prices vary according to equipment, duration of rental and potential delivery charges. Traveling Baby Co serves all of Southern California.

Driving

For better or for worse, being on the road is an essential part of the SoCal experience, even if you never leave LA. So is traffic, especially in LA. Getting around always seems to take longer than expected, so be sure to build in time, and plan some in-car distractions in case the kids get fidgety. From LA to all but the most remote destinations in our book, travel time is theoretically within two hours, but can easily multiply in traffic. California law requires all passengers in private cars to wear seat belts, and children under the age of six or weighing less than 60lb must be restrained in a child-safety or booster seat. If you're not traveling with your own car seats, most car-rental firms rent them for about $10/50 per day/week; reserve them in advance.

Rest stops on SoCal freeways are few and far between, and we wouldn't recommend gas-station rest rooms for bathroom breaks (frequently icky). However, you're never very far from a shopping mall, which generally have well-kept rest rooms.

Accommodations

Rule one: if you're traveling with kids, be sure to mention it when booking. We've identified kid-friendly places in this book with a 👶. At other spots you may have a hard time if you show up with little ones in tow. If you need to rent a crib or other special equipment, make sure to ask when booking. Sometimes there's an extra charge.

If you're not staying at a hotel and your hosts can't supply it for you, the **Traveling Baby Company** (☑800-304-4866; travelingbabyco.com) rents equipment, with delivery to Los Angeles, Ventura, Santa Barbara, Orange and San Diego Counties.

Figure on $8/35 per day/week for a Pack 'n' Play (portacot) or car seat, plus a $35 delivery charge; weekly multi-equipment packages are available.

Whichever room type you want, request it on booking. If you wait until you arrive, you might not get what you're after.

Often larger chain hotels offer 'kids stay free' promotions; others include breakfast in the rates. Inquire about these promotions when booking. Some smaller B&Bs don't welcome children.

Larger resort hotels offer activity programs for kids, particularly during summer. Fees can be cheaper than babysitting and everyone may enjoy the change of pace.

regions at a glance

Los Angeles
Shopping ✓✓✓
Culture ✓✓✓
Beaches ✓✓✓

Seeing Stars
Hollywood has its glittering restored movie palaces, its pink-starred Walk of Fame and red-carpet movie premieres. And almost everywhere you go in LA, the cult of celebrity will follow, whether you're star-spotting with the paparazzi in Malibu or joining a live studio audience for a TV show taping in the Valley.

Fashionista Alert
You don't need to see *Project Runway* to know that LA is a fashion capital on par with NYC, Paris or Tokyo. Hit the cutting-edge boutiques along Melrose Ave, Robertson Blvd or Abbot Kinney Blvd in Venice, then shop with A-list stars at revered Fred Segal or Beverly Hills' Rodeo Dr.

Gold Coastin'
Follow any jammed freeway westbound and you'll hit the beach. Soar on the solar-powered Ferris wheel on Santa Monica's pier, meet zany characters along Venice's boardwalk, cycle the South Bay, where surfers and party animals mix, or bring the whole family to Long Beach.

Doing Downtown
Though many tourists sidestep it, downtown packs more punch, block-per-block, than any other place in LA. Gobble up the Central Market, Chinatown and Little Tokyo. Catch a contemporary art show or a live performance at Walt Disney Concert Hall, a sculpted Frank Gehry–designed icon sitting atop the Grand Ave Culture Corridor. Museums abound, both downtown and beyond.

p60

Disneyland & Orange County
Beaches ✓✓✓
Surfing ✓✓✓
Family Fun ✓✓✓

Theme Parks
Bring the kids, grandparents, cousins – heck, just load up everyone in the minivan. Disneyland is just the start of your zany trip through Southern California's theme parks. Then again, the Magic Kingdom and Disney's California Adventure might be reason enough for your whole trip.

'The OC'
You've gawked at Orange County's beautiful beaches and bathers in countless movies and TV shows. Now see the fantasy spring to life along this almost-too-beautiful-for-its-own-good stretch of coastline between LA and San Diego County.

Surf City USA
You'll find SoCal's hang-loose surf culture personified in Huntington Beach, though the OC's waves don't stop there. Territorial locals means you'll need an introduction, or earn your chops with a quickie learn-to-surf class or a wild weekend 'surfari' camp.

p214

San Diego
Beaches ✓✓✓
Mexican Food ✓✓✓
Museums ✓✓✓

Palm Springs & the Deserts
Shopping & Spas ✓✓✓
Outdoors ✓✓✓
Nightlife ✓✓

Santa Barbara
Beaches ✓✓✓
Wine ✓✓✓
Culture ✓✓

Cooling Off
Here it's (almost) always sunny and a perfect 68°F. So, do like locals do and just relax, bro. Take your pick of more than a dozen beach towns, each with its own eclectic personality, then join the buff, bronzed and beautiful on the golden sands.

Chow Town
It should be a crime to visit San Diego and not have at least one fish taco, or maybe six. With SoCal's best Mexican food dished up all over town, SD has more taco shops per capita than LA. You'll find yourself addicted soon enough.

Culture Vultures
Dumb-blond surfer jokes aside, San Diego has a surprising wealth of arts and culture. Wander historic Old Town, then spend an afternoon in the museums of Balboa Park. Don't forget the world-famous zoo!

p266

Retro Modern
The mid-20th century modern hang out of Elvis, the Rat Pack and Hollywood celebs, PS is hip again. Tour the resort's architectural gems, fill your bags with vintage goods or just soak up the sun by the pool in your mod hipster hideaway.

Desert Oases
It's not just PS' spas and hot springs that will rejuvenate you. SoCal's deserts are a nature-loving playground (except during summer – it's just too dang hot then), spreading from Joshua Tree's fan-palm oases to Anza-Borrego's hidden canyon waterfalls and Death Valley's panoramic viewpoints.

Dirty Weekends
When it comes to nightlife in SoCal's deserts, nothing can compete with the neon-lit Strip in Las Vegas, just across the California–Nevada state line. We can't think of many reasons to ever leave SoCal, but 'Sin City' is one.

p331

Vineyards
Forget Napa. Even before the indie flick *Sideways*, Santa Barbara's wine country was beloved – and more importantly, respected – for its delicate pinot noirs. Sip vintages with glam crowds from LA, or search out unpretentious tasting rooms on country back roads.

'American Riviera'
Honestly, that touristy tag line stretches the point only a little. Santa Barbara's sunny coast, with white sands and waving palm trees, can compete with any of SoCal's best, whether you're a beach-bum surfer or want to chill at a luxe oceanfront retreat.

State Street
Rebuilt in Mediterranean style after an earthquake in 1925, Santa Barbara's downtown is awash in red-tiled roofs and white-stucco walls. Climb the *Vertigo*-esque county courthouse bell tower for cinematic views, then go bar hopping and shopping along downtown's main artery.

p368

Look out for these icons:

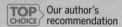 Our author's recommendation

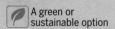 A green or sustainable option

 No payment required

On the Road

Los Angeles

Includes »

Why Go?

LA runs deeper than her blonde beaches, bosomy, celebri-fied hills and beemers-for-days would have you believe. She's a myth. A beacon for countless small-town dreamers, rockers and daredevils, an open-minded angel who encour-ages her people to live and let live without judgment or shame. She has given us Quentin Tarantino, Jim Morrison and Serena and Venus Williams, spawned skateboarding and gangsta rap, popularized implants, electrolysis and spandex, and has nurtured not just great writers, perform-ers and directors, but also the groundbreaking yogis who first brought Eastern wisdom to the Western world.

LA is best defined by those simple life-affirming mo-ments. A cracked-ice, jazz-age cocktail on Beverly Blvd, a hike high into the Hollywood Hills sagebrush, a swirling pod of dolphins off Point Dume, a pink-washed sunset over a thundering Venice Beach drum circle, the perfect burrito. And her night music. There is always night music.

Best Places to Eat

» Gjelina (p168)
» Sushi Ike (p93)
» Mozza (p93)
» Ita Cho (p118)
» Rustic Canyon (p158)

Best Places to Stay

» Figueroa Hotel (p79)
» Hollywood Roosevelt Hotel (p92)
» Chateau Marmont (p116)
» Terranea Resort (p176)
» London (p116)

When to Go

Los Angeles

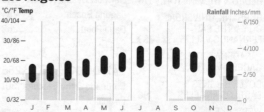

February The red carpet is rolled out for the Academy Awards. Prime time for celeb-spotting.

April & September Most tourists visit when the sun shines the brightest on LA's golden sands.

October–November, January–March The region's two distinct wet seasons.

LA is Now

Now is an exciting time to visit LA. Hollywood, Downtown and Echo Park are in the midst of an unstoppable urban renaissance. An open and experimental climate energizes the art, music and fashion scenes, and innovative chefs have infused LA's eclectic palate with creativity and flavor, while increasing their reliance on local growers who flaunt their earthy goods at hundreds of weekly outdoor farmers markets throughout the city.

DON'T MISS

With so many world-class musicians within LA's orbit, and such spectacular and historic venues, it would be a minor tragedy to leave town without a concert in the bank. The **Hollywood Bowl**, which aside from being the summer home of the LA Philharmonic, has hosted countless legends from Ella to Radiohead. Sitting beneath and among the stars, in a natural bowl tucked into the Hollywood Hills, while music washes over you will make you feel all kinds of glamorous. A second, and only slightly less tasty, summertime venue is the **Greek Theatre** – another nature-cupped outdoor amphitheater, which hosts some tremendous rock and pop acts from MGMT to Wilco.

The music doesn't stop when the weather turns. The **Walt Disney Concert Hall**, the winter base for the LA Phil, is an architectural masterwork and sees its share of intriguing acts, such as jazz giants Sonny Rollins and Keith Jarrett and electro-ambient ambassadors, Air.

Crave the underground? Check into the **Stronghold**, the Venice-based promoter. Though its speak-easy is no more it promotes local up-and-comers in venues across town. Slightly better known acoustic troubadours hold pretour residencies at the **Bootleg Theater** in Silver Lake, and in Lincoln Heights where a handful of DJs have re-imagined dubstep at the weekly club the **Low End Theory**.

LA's Best Beaches

» Westward Beach (p143) is often overshadowed by Zuma to the north, but this wide sweep of sand rambles all the way to Point Dume, and local seals, sea lions and dolphins are frequently glimpsed beyond the break.

» El Matador State Beach (p143) is defined by sandstone rock spires that rise from the swirling azure sea, and its topless-optional ethos.

» Venice Beach (p163) is notable more for its odd pockets of humanity – boardwalk bodybuilders, streetballers, skate rats and hippies old and new peddling goods bizarre, bland and beautiful. The Sunday drum circle is an institution, and the winter sunsets are glorious.

DON'T MISS

Kobe Bryant's pure and true jump shot and Jack Nicholson's dark glasses are on display at the Staples Center when basketball season rocks LA from October to April...or June.

Fast Facts: LA County

» Population: 10,393,000

» Area: 4,060 sq miles

» No of major movie studios: six

» No of unsold screenplays: countless

Planning your Trip

Think about what you want to see and where you want to hang out, and book accommodation accordingly to minimize traffic masochism and maximize joy. We suggest moving around the city, staying for a few nights each in different neighborhoods.

Book your accommodation at http://hotels.lonelyplanet.com

Resources

» www.laweekly.com is the best source for LA news, dining and entertainment listings.

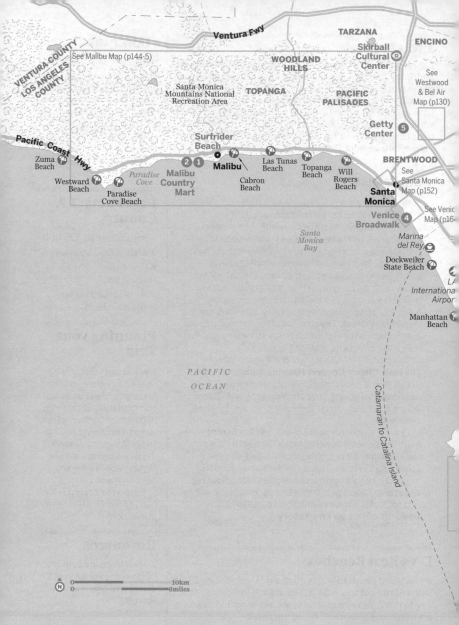

Los Angeles Highlights

❶ Watching surfers carve towering waves at **Surfrider Beach** (p143) in Malibu

❷ Shopping like – and maybe spotting – a star at **Malibu Country Mart** (p150)

❸ Swerving along breathtaking **Palos Verdes Drive** (p170), then hunting for starfish and anemones in the tide pools of **Abalone Cove Shoreline Park** (p175)

❹ Getting your freak on while milling with snake charmers, tarot readers and athletes of all kinds on the **Venice Boardwalk** (p163)

Foothill Fwy 210
See Pasadena Map (p188)
Hollywood Fwy
Golden State Fwy
7 Runyon Canyon
See Hollywood Map (p86)
8 Hollywood
See Los Feliz & Silverlake Map (p100)
See West Hollywood & Mid-City Map (p110-11)
San Bernadino Fwy
10
Downtown 6 Los Angeles
ee Beverly Hills ap (p132-3)
See Downtown Los Angeles Map (p70-1)
Pomona Fwy
605
Los Angeles River
710
SOUTH CENTRAL
San Gabriel River Fwy
Century Fwy 105
WATTS
Harbor Fwy
Long Beach Fwy
5
Santa Ana Fwy
San Diego Fwy
LOS ANGELES COUNTY
ORANGE COUNTY
Pacific Coast Hwy
Hermosa Beach
Artesia Fwy
San Diego Fwy
Long Beach Airport
605
San Gabriel River Fwy
Riverside Fwy
Anaheim
5
Redondo Beach
710
See Long Beach Map (p178)
Palos Verdes Dr:
3 Abalone Cove
See Palos Verdes Peninsula Map (p176)
Long Beach
Outer Long Beach Harbour
Garden Grove Fwy
Abalone Cove
Royal Palms State Beach
San Pedro
White Point
Point Fermin
Outer Los Angeles Harbor
Seal Beach
Sunset Beach
Pacific Coast Hwy
405
Santa Ana River
San Pedro Bay
Ferry to Catalina Island
Bolsa Chica State Beach
Huntington City Beach
Huntington Beach
San Pedro Channel
Huntington State Beach
Newport Beach

5 Feeling your spirits soar surrounded by the fantastic art, architecture, views and gardens of the **Getty Center** (p129)

6 Rubbing shoulders with fashionistas, sipping cocktails in sleek basement lounges and sampling delicious market cuisine in LA's 'new' **Downtown** (p80)

7 Joining the buff, the famous and their canine companions on a hike through **Runyon Canyon** (p116)

8 Hitting the bars and clubs of **Hollywood** (p95) for a night of tabloid-worthy decadence and debauchery

LOS ANGELES IN...

One Day

Fuel up at the **Alcove**, then go star-searching on the **Walk of Fame** along revitalized Hollywood Blvd. Up your chances of spotting actual celebs by hitting the fashion-forward boutiques on paparazzi-infested **Robertson Blvd** and having lunch at the **Ivy**. Take a digestive stroll along **Rodeo Drive** before heading to the lofty **Getty Center**. Wrap up with dinner at **Gjelina**, on **Abbot Kinney Boulevard** in Venice.

Two Days

On the second day, explore rapidly evolving Downtown LA, starting with its roots at **El Pueblo de Los Angeles**, catching up with the present at the dramatic **Walt Disney Concert Hall**, then peeking into the future over a lunch at **Tiara Café** in the emerging fashion district. Check out the funky boutiques in Echo Park and Silver Lake, begin the night early at **El Carmen**, then catch a band at the **Music Box** or the **El Rey** or fall by **La Descarga** for a blast of rum-drenched cool. Still feel like dancing? Hit the floor at **Avalon** and shake it till sunrise.

History

LA's human history begins with the Gabrielino and Chumash, who roamed the chaparral and oak-dotted savannah as early as 6000 BC. Their hunter-gatherer existence ended in the late 18th century with the arrival of Spanish missionaries and Mexican settlers who founded the El Pueblo de la Reina de Los Angeles. This first civilian settlement became a thriving farming community but remained a far-flung outpost for decades.

During the Mexican-American War (1846–48), American soldiers encountered some resistance from General Andrés Pico and other Mexican commanders, but eventually LA came under US rule along with the rest of California. The city was incorporated on April 4, 1850.

A series of seminal events caused LA's population to swell to one million by 1930: the collapse of the Northern California gold rush in the 1850s, the arrival of the railroad in the 1870s, the birth of the citrus industry in the late 1800s, the discovery of oil in 1892, the launch of San Pedro harbor in 1907 and the opening of the LA aqueduct in 1913.

During WWI the Lockheed brothers and Donald Douglas established aircraft manufacturing plants in LA. Two decades later aviation – helped along by billions of federal dollars for military contracts – was among the industries that contributed to a real-estate boom and sparked suburban sprawl. Another, of course, was the film biz, which took root in 1908.

Over the years, LA has had its share of nefarious water barons (William Mulholland), socialist politicians (Gaylord Wilshire), and philanthropic magnates (Colonel Griffith J Griffith). There was a certain filmmaker turned aviation renegade turned agoraphobe (see: Hughes, Howard), a groundbreaking ballplayer (Jackie Robinson), an actress turned studio magnate (Mary Pickford), a newspaper editor turned civil rights activist (Charlotta Spears Bass), a professional raconteur and polyamorous publishing legend who recently saved the Hollywood sign (The Hef) and more than a few celebrity murders, deadly overdoses, divorces and scandals, all of which left their mark on the city. But arguably the biggest impact was made by Detroit's big three automakers who bought, then dismantled the famed LA trolley system after WWII and built freeways – lots of them. While it certainly spurred a massive spike in sales, the insider move has left a once congruous city carved up, and largely defined, by the automobile.

Orientation

As you approach from above, Los Angeles seems as vast and amorphous as anywhere you've ever been, but you'll soon find that the areas of interest to visitors are actually fairly well defined, and that it's easy to concentrate on particular neighborhoods. About 15 miles inland, Downtown LA combines highbrow culture, a growing loft scene and an up-and-coming fashion and arts district, with a touch of midnight grit. Pasadena, to the northeast, is a treasure trove of mid-century residential architecture at the base of the soaring San Gabriel Mountains. Hipster shops and haunts comingle with Mexican bakeries and cevicherias in gentrifying Echo Park northwest of downtown, before bleeding into boho-chic Silver Lake and old-money Los Feliz, the gateway to the Hollywood sign and the large urban playground of Griffith Park. Hip-again Hollywood is a bit further west, but most TV and movie studios are actually in Burbank and Studio City in the San Fernando Valley.

Urban designer chic, fine food, raucous nightlife, lesbigays and a tight knot of Russian émigrés rule West Hollywood, an oddly shaped independent city that segues seamlessly into Mid-City where Museum Row is the main draw. East of here, Wilshire boulevard leads to delicious Koreatown, or head west into ritzy Beverly Hills, then Westwood, home to UCLA and the gateway to Bel Air's estates, and upscale Brentwood where you'll find the hilltop Getty Center. Charming, laid-back Culver City runs parallel to, but a touch south of, this west LA swath, with Sony Pictures as its beating heart.

Santa Monica is the most tourist-friendly beach town, with wide beaches, groovy shopping and some tasty dining. Others include swish Malibu, funky Venice, the South Bay trio of Manhattan Beach, Hermosa Beach and Redondo Beach, and finally, the urban-harbor-surfer stew that is Long Beach.

89.9 KCRW

Based on the campus of **Santa Monica College**, it's more than a public radio station. It's a cultural hub. A vortex of the best music, art and culture this city has to offer. In addition to its solid news coverage and smart talk shows focusing on subjects ranging from food to books to film, the station has the city's best DJs, many of whom moonlight as music supervisors in Hollywood. It broadcasts frequent live performances on radio shows that beam throughout Southern California and are streamed online, and through its iPhone App. KCRW also hosts a stacked calendar of live-music events around town. If you've got nothing on the docket, you probably haven't checked www.kcrw.com.

Getting around is easiest by car, although public transport is usually adequate within specific neighborhoods. See p206 for details.

 Tours

Whether you're interested in the seeds of LA noir, ghost hunting, ethnic nibbling, soaking in neon, architecture or art, or peering at the many sides of the angel city from a road bike, beach cruiser or double-decker bus, we've got you covered.

Esotouric   ECLECTIC
(☏323-223-2767; www.esotouric.com; tours $58) Discover LA's lurid and fascinating underbelly on these hip, offbeat, insightful and entertaining walking and bus tours themed around famous crime sites (Black Dahlia anyone?), literary lions (Chandler to Bukowski) and neglected neighborhoods. Even the snack stops are unique. Nicotine-flavored gelato anyone?

TOP CHOICE **Melting Pot Tours**   WALKING, CULINARY
(☏800-979-3370; www.meltingpottours. com; tours from $49; ☺Wed-Sun) Duck into aromatic alleyways, stroll through fashionable shopping districts, and explore LA landmarks while hunting for and tasting some of the city's best ethnic eats, from Nepalese to Brazilian, Mexican to Japanese. Tours focus on Old Town Pasadena and Mid-City, cover 3 to 3.5 miles and last between three and four hours.

SoCal Bike Tours   CYCLING
(☏310-254-1043; www.socalbiketours.com; tours with/without bike rental from $75/100; ☺May-Sep) Ideal for avid cyclists, and fun for all. Pedal from downtown to Hollywood, swerve 65 miles along Mulholland Dr, coast north or south along the coast, or skirt the studios then pump and sweat up to the top of Mt Hollywood for close-ups of the Hollywood sign and the Griffith Park Observatory. Tours vary in length and difficulty, and are fully supported with a vehicle, fluids, first aid, equipment replacement and optional tour guide.

Dearly Departed   SCANDALOUS LA
(☏800-979-3370; www.dearlydepartedtours.com; tours $40; ☺1pm) This long-running, occasionally creepy, frequently hilarious tour will clue you in on where celebs kicked the bucket, George Michael dropped his trousers, Hugh Grant received certain services and the Charles Manson gang murdered Sharon Tate and co. Not for kids or the prissy.

Neon Cruise
VINTAGE

(☎213-489-9918; www.neonmona.org; 136 W 4th St, Downtown; tours $55; ⊗7:30-10:30pm select Sat) From movie marquees to hotel signs, vintage neon is hot. Start by touring the fabulous Los Angeles Theater, then see LA's best neon art from a genuine London double-decker bus. Tours depart from the Museum of Neon Art (MONA) Downtown. Book early, tours often sell out.

Architecture Tours Los Angeles
ARCHITECTURE

(☎323-464-7868; www.architecturetoursla.com; tours from $68; ⊗tours 9:30am & 1:30pm) If you think LA architecture begins with Frank Lloyd Wright and ends with Frank Gehry, these van tours, six of which focus on particular neighborhoods, will broaden your horizon. Reservation required.

LA River Walks
ECO-URBAN

(☎323-223-0585; www.folar.org; tours $25) Discover the history, mystery and ecology of the LA River as you follow it from Chinatown to Long Beach on these irregularly run tours. Along the way find out why it's not just that ugly concrete channel you've been making jokes about.

FREE Downtown LA Walks
WALKING

(www.downtownlawalks.com) You can get the nitty gritty on downtown history, arts and culture or shopping with these self-guided walking-tour podcasts, ready to be downloaded for free to your MP3 player.

FREE Metro Rail Art Tours
ART

(www.metro.net/about/art/art-tours; ⊗1st Thu, Sat & Sun of month) Some of LA's best contemporary art is not in a museum but in its metro stations. Discover works by such artists as Jonathan Borowsky and Gilbert 'Magu' Lujan on these two-hour tours leaving from the Hollywood/Highland station at 7pm on Thursday and 10am on Saturday, and from Union Station at 10am on Sunday. No reservation required. You can also do it yourself by requesting its art guide via its website.

Perry's Legends Beach Bike Tour
CYCLING

(☎310-939-0000; www.perryscafe.com; tours $35; ⊗May-Sep) The mysteries of Muscle Beach, Jim Morrison's house and Skateboard Mamma all feature on this leisurely 90-minute bike tour of Santa Monica and Venice. The tour charge includes water, a helmet and an additional 90-minute bike rental for self-exploring. Reservation required.

Spirit Dinner Cruises
BOAT

(☎310-548-8080; www.spiritdinnercruises.com) A lovely way to experience LA on a warm day. Activities include harbor tours, dinner cruises, champagne brunch cruises and whale-watching excursions (January to March) from San Pedro and Long Beach.

Hornblower Cruises
BOAT

(☎310-548-8080; www.hornblower.com) Operating from Marina Del Rey and Long Beach, it also offers dinner and brunch cruises in the summertime, including a popular July 4 fireworks cruise.

Los Angeles Conservancy
WALKING

(☎213-623-2489; www.laconservancy.org; tours $10) Downtown LA's intriguing historical and architectural gems – from an art-deco penthouse to a beaux-arts ballroom and a dazzling silent-movie theater – are revealed on 2½-hour walking tours operated by this nonprofit group. To see some of LA's grand historic movie theaters from the inside, the conservancy also offers the Last Remaining Seats film series, screening classic movies in gilded theaters, in summer. Check the schedule and book tickets online or by phone.

Red Line Tours
WALKING

(☎323-402-1074; www.redlinetours.com; tours adult/child $25/15) Learn the secrets of Hollywood on this 'edutaining' walking tour with nifty headsets to cut out traffic noise. Guides use a mix of anecdotes, fun facts, trivia, and historical and architectural data to keep their charges entertained.

Starline Tours
MINIBUS

(☎323-463-333, 800-959-3131; www.starline tours.com; tours from $18) These standard, narrated minibus sightseeing tours are predictably cheesy but not a bad way for first-timers to get oriented. Options include one-hour neighborhood tours, tours of the stars' homes, night tours and trips to theme parks. Buses depart from Hollywood Blvd.

★ Festivals & Events

From the Rose Parade to the Hollywood Christmas Parade, from the Oscars to the *LA Times* Festival of Books, from the progressive, hard-rocking Sunset Junction street fair to the candy colored mayhem of Halloween in WeHo, LA has its share of annual parades, festivals, carnivals and live-music throwdowns.

January & February

Rose Parade
PARADE

(www.tournamentofroses.com) This cavalcade of flower-festooned floats snakes through Pasadena on New Year's Day. Get close-ups of the stunning creations during postparade viewing at Victory Park. Avoid traffic and take the Metro Rail Gold Line to Memorial Park.

Chinese New Year
CULTURAL

(www.lachinesechamber.org, www.chinatownla.com) Colorful celebrations in Chinatown mark the lunar new year, culminating in the Golden Dragon parade, food, floats, and firecrackers. Occurs late January or early February.

Academy Awards
HOLLYWOOD

(www.oscars.org) Ogle your favorite film stars from the Kodak Theatre's red-carpet-adjacent bleachers. Apply in September for one of 600 lucky spots. Held in late February or early March.

March

LA Marathon
SPORT

(www.lamarathon.com) Held in mid-March, this marathon is a 26.2-mile party through the city from Dodger Stadium to the Santa Monica Pier. Rally the 25,000 runners and wheelchair racers. Then wander performance stages and finish-line festivities.

April

Toyota Grand Prix of Long Beach
SPORT

(www.longbeachgp.com) World-class drivers tear up city streets at this weeklong racing spectacle by the sea.

Los Angeles Times Festival of Books
BOOK FAIR

(www.latimes.com/festivalofbooks) It's a bookworm's paradise for one long weekend of reveling in readings, discussions and storytelling at UCLA.

Fiesta Broadway
CULTURAL

(www.fiestabroadway.la; ☺last Sun in Apr) One of the world's largest Cinco de Mayo parties brings out half a million folks to Downtown LA.

May

Incognito Art Fair
ART

(www.smmoa.org) A bustling art auction and fair set in Santa Monica's art-gallery mecca Barnsdall Art Park (p100) on or around May 1.

Cinco de Mayo
CULTURAL

(www.olvera-street.com/fiestas) Celebrates the Mexican victory over the French at the Battle of Puebla (1862); free festivities around Olvera St during early May.

Topanga Banjo Fiddle Contest & Folk Festival
MUSIC

(www.topangabanjofiddle.org) Tasty bluegrass tunes float through Paramount Ranch in the Santa Monica Mountains.

Fiesta Hermosa
STREET FAIR

(www.fiestahermosa.com) Get in the mood for summer at this three-day festival where you can browse for arts and crafts, groove to surf music and tribute bands, and graze an international food court. It's held every Memorial Day and Labor Day weekend.

June

LA Pride
GAY PRIDE

(www.lapride.org) Running since 1970, this three-day festival held in mid-June includes music, exhibitions and a parade down Santa Monica Blvd.

Long Beach Bayou & Blues Festival
MUSIC

(www.longbeachfestival.com; tickets $30) A weekend of Cajun, zydeco and blues music and Creole food against the backdrop of the *Queen Mary*.

Electric Daisy Carnival
MUSIC

(www.electricdaisycarnival.com; tickets from $75) Two days, 80,000 people, five stages. It's one giant party in the Coliseum and Exposition Park, with carnival rides, and performances by 150-plus artists and performers, including many of the best DJs in the world.

July

Independence Day
FIREWORKS

(www.rosebowlstadium.com, www.hollywoodbowl.com, www.beaches.co.la.ca.us) Take a seat for official Fourth of July fireworks extravaganzas held at the Rose Bowl, the Hollywood Bowl or in Marina del Rey. Alternatively, drive up to any hilltop and watch the skies explode.

Central Avenue Jazz Festival
MUSIC

(www.centralavejazz.org) Veteran jazz players perform for free during this weekend-long festival, with music, food, arts and crafts, celebrating the pre-WWII era when Central Ave was a hotbed of West Coast jazz.

August

Nisei Week Japanese Festival CULTURAL
(www.niseiweek.org) This free nine-day festival takes over Little Tokyo with parades, *taiko* (drumming), tea ceremonies, karaoke, food, dancing and crafts.

Long Beach Jazz Festival MUSIC
(www.longbeachjazzfestival.com) This three-day festival features top talents such as Al Jarreau and Poncho Sanchez. Tickets often sell out, so book early.

Sunset Junction Street Fair
MUSIC, STREET FAIR
(www.sunsetjunction.org; admission $15-20) Silver Lake's annual multiblock street party with food, knick-knacks and one of the best live-music line-ups you'll find all year.

September

Leimert Park African Art & Music Festival STREET FAIR
(www.lacountyfair.com) Historic Leimert Park becomes a Labor Day weekend street party with fantastic musicians, delicious food and exceptional African art.

LA County Fair FAIR
(www.lacountyfair.com) A month of horse and pig racing, wine tasting, circus tricks, culinary competitions, monster trucks and rock and roll.

Mexican Independence Festival CULTURAL
(www.olvera-street.com/html/fiestas) On Olvera St, a free mid-September celebration of Mexico's independence from Spain, with live performers and delicious food.

Abbot Kinney Festival STREET FAIR
(www.abbotkinney.org) Soak up the groovy Venice vibe at this annual celebration of local arts, crafts, food and eccentrics, held in late September.

Watts Towers Day of the Drum & Jazz Festival MUSIC
(www.myspace.com/drumnjazz) Two back-to-back events: multicultural beats on Saturday followed by a day of jazz, gospel and blues. Late September.

October

LA Triathlon SPORT
(www.latriathlon.com) It's swim, bike and run in an athletic tour de force that draws some top talent. Includes a spectacular finish at LA Live.

West Hollywood Halloween Carnival
STREET FAIR
(www.westhollywoodhalloween.com) This free rambunctious street fair brings 350,000 revelers – many in over-the-top and/or X-rated costumes – out for a day of dancing, dishing and dating on Halloween.

November

Día de los Muertos CULTURAL
(Day of the Dead; www.olvera-street.com, www.ladayofthedead.com, www.selfhelpgraphics.com; www.festivaldelagente.org) Honor beloved ancestors with dance, face painting, decorated altars and candlelight processions on Olvera St, at Hollywood Forever Cemetery and with the Festival de la Gente along the 6th St Bridge in downtown. Held around November 1.

LADWP Light Festival CHRISTMAS
(www.dwplightfestival.com) Bright lights, no city in this mile-long stretch of enchanting holiday-themed light displays and music in Griffith Park. Walk, drive through slowly or take the shuttle leaving from the zoo on select dates. Runs from early November through until December 26.

Hollywood Christmas Parade PARADE
(www.thehollywoodchristmasparade.com) Celebs ring in the season by waving at fans from flash floats rolling down Hollywood Blvd. Easy access via the Metro Rail Red Line. Held the Sunday after Thanksgiving.

December

Marina del Rey Holiday Boat Parade
PARADE
(www.mdrboatparade.org) Boats decked out in bright, blinking holiday cheer promenade for prizes in the marina. Check it out from Burton Chase Park.

Las Posadas CULTURAL
(www.olvera-street.com/html/las_posadas) Free candlelight processions that re-enact Mary and Joseph's journey to Bethlehem, followed by piñata-breaking and general merriment on Olvera St and around. From December 16 to 24.

Together As One MUSIC
(www.newyearsevela.com; $60-150; ☺7pm-4am) For 10 years running, this has been the place to party on New Year's Eve if you dig electronic music. It's one gigantic rave, set in and around the LA Sports Arena.

DOWNTOWN LOS ANGELES

Downtown Los Angeles is the most historical, multilayered and fascinating part of the city. There's great architecture from 19th-century beaux arts to futuristic Frank Gehry. There's world-class music at the Walt Disney Hall, top-notch art at the Museum of Contemporary Art, superb dining from tiny *taquerias* (taco shops) to hip, health-conscious market cafes to brassy gourmet restaurants. Downtown is a power nexus with City Hall, the courts and the hall of records, and an ethnic mosaic. As recently as 10 years ago it was a relative ghost town at night when it was abandoned to the skid-row tramps and addicts, gangbangers and the ravers who braved the scene for a warehouse or loft party in rickety relics. But today its streets are fertile and alive with creativity.

Thousands of young professionals and artists have snapped up stylish lofts in gorgeously rehabbed art-deco buildings, and the growing gallery district along Main and Spring Sts draws thousands to its monthly art walks. Don't expect Manhattan, but the momentum is undeniably there, and for adventurous urbanites that don't mind a little grit, now is an exciting time to explore.

If you arrive by car, you can save by parking at one of several lots south of Sixth St on Main and Los Angeles, charging only $4 or $5 all day. An excellent way to get around is by DASH shuttle (p210).

◉ Sights

FREE **Walt Disney Concert Hall** VENUE
(Map p70; www.laphil.com; 111 S Grand Ave; ◷10am-2pm; P) A molten blend of steel, music and psychedelic architecture, this iconic concert venue is the home base of the Los Angeles Philharmonic, but also hosts contemporary bands such as Phoenix and classic jazz men like Sonny Rollins. Frank Gehry pulled out all the stops: the building is a gravity-defying sculpture of heaving and billowing stainless-steel walls that conjure visions of a ship adrift in a rough sea. The auditorium, meanwhile, feels like the inside of a finely crafted cello, clad in walls of smooth Douglas fir with terraced 'vineyard' seating wrapped around a central stage. Even seats below the giant pipe organ offer excellent sightlines. forty-five-minute, free, self-guided audio tours narrated by

John Lithgow are available most days, and there are guided tours available, as well, but they won't let you see the auditorium. The best way to experience the hall is to see a show. Parking costs $9.

FREE **Union Station** LANDMARK
(Map p70; 800 N Alameda St) Built on the site of LA's original Chinatown, the station opened in 1939 as America's last grand rail station. It's a glamorous exercise in Mission Revival with art-deco accents. The marble floored main hall, with cathedral ceilings, original leather chairs and grand chandeliers, is breathtaking.

The tiled twin domes north of the station belong to the Terminal Annex, once LA's central post office before it was closed and later reopened as an active postal branch. This is where Charles Bukowski worked for years, inspiring his 1971 novel *Post Office*.

Museum of Contemporary Art MUSEUM
(MOCA; Map p70; www.moca.org; 250 S Grand Ave; adult/student & senior/child under 12 $10/5/free, 5-8pm Thu free; ◷11am-5pm Mon & Fri, to 8pm Thu, to 6pm Sat & Sun; P) A collection that arcs from the 1940s to the present and includes works by Mark Rothko, Dan Flavin, Joseph Cornell and other big-shot contemporary artists is housed in a postmodern building by Arata Isozaki. Galleries are below ground, yet flooded with natural light via pyramidal skylights. Check it out during tours (free with admission) offered at noon, 1pm and 2pm, and don't forget to swing by the bookstore gift shop.

Tickets are also good for same-day admission at Geffen Contemporary at MOCA in Little Tokyo (p75), a quick DASH bus ride away. Catch it at Grand Ave and 1st St.

EL PUEBLO DE LOS ANGELES
Compact, colorful and car-free, this vibrant historic district sits near the spot where LA's first colonists settled in 1781. It preserves the city's oldest buildings, some dating back to its days as a dusty, lawless outpost. More than anything, though, El Pueblo is a microcosm of LA's multi-ethnic heritage and the contributions made by immigrants from Mexico, France, Italy and China. To learn more about this fascinating legacy join a free guided tour leaving from the Old Plaza Firehouse at 10am, 11am and noon Tuesday to Saturday. If you're more the DIY type, you can also pick up a free

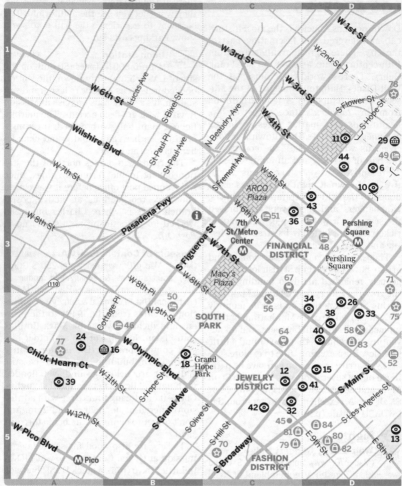

self-guided tour pamphlet at the El Pueblo Visitors Center (p204).

Olvera Street
LANDMARK

(Map p70; www.calleolvera.com; ⊞) This festive Mexican marketplace, with its gaudy decorations and souvenir stalls might scream 'tourist trap,' but there are actually some fairly authentic experiences to be had. You can shop for Chicano art, slurp thick Mexican-style hot chocolate or pick up handmade candles and candy. At lunchtime, construction workers and cubicle drones swarm the little eateries for tacos, *tortas* (sandwiches) and burritos.

Avila Adobe
LANDMARK

(Map p70; E-10 Olvera St; ⊙9am-3pm) The oldest surviving house in LA was built in 1818 by a wealthy ranchero and one-time LA mayor, and later became a boarding house and restaurant. Restored and furnished in heavy oak, it's open for self-guided tours and provides a look at life in the early 19th century.

Italian Hall
LANDMARK

(Map p70; 644-1/2 Main St) A sight notable for its rare rooftop mural called *América Tropical* by David Alfaro Siqueiros, one of Mexico's great early-20th-century mural-

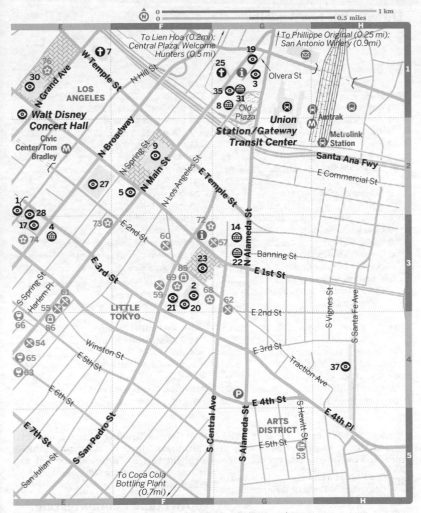

ists. The 1932 work shows a crucified Native American in front of a Mayan pyramid and was so controversial that city fathers ordered it whitewashed immediately. The Getty Conservation Institute recently rehabilitated it.

Old Plaza LANDMARK
(Map p70; Olvera St) El Pueblo's central, magnolia-shaded square has a pretty wrought-iron bandstand. Sleepy during the week, it often turns into a full-blown fiesta zone on Saturdays and Sundays, drawing crooning mariachis, costumed dancers, kissing couples and strolling families. The best time to be here is for one of the many Mexican festivals, like Cinco de Mayo (p67), Día de los Muertos (p68) or the endearing Blessing of the Animals. Dotted around the plaza are statues of such key historical figures as Felipe de Neve, who led the first group of settlers, and King Carlos III of Spain, who financed the venture. The colonists' names are engraved on a nearby bronze plaque.

Pico House LANDMARK
(Map p70; 430 Main St) South of Old Plaza are more historic buildings, including the 1870 home of Pio Pico, California's last Mexican

governor, the city's first three-story building, and later a glamorous hotel with 21 parlors and two interior courtyards.

FREE **Old Plaza Firehouse**   MUSEUM
(Map p70; 134 Paseo de la Plaza; ⊙10am-3pm Tue-Sun) The city's oldest fire station (1884) is now a one-room museum filled with dusty old fire-fighting equipment and photographs.

La Placita   LANDMARK
(Map p70; www.laplacita.org; 535 N Main St; admission free; ⊙7am-7pm) Founded as Iglesia Nuestra Senora Reina De Los Angeles (Our Lady Queen of Angels Church) in 1781, and now affectionately known as 'Little Plaza.' Peek inside for a look at the gilded altar and painted ceiling.

Chinese American Museum   LANDMARK
(Map p70; www.camla.org; 425 N Los Angeles St; adult/student & senior $3/2; ⊙10am-3pm Tue-Sun) Follow the red lanterns to the small

1890 Garnier Building, once the unofficial Chinatown 'city hall'. Changing exhibits highlight various historical, cultural and artistic aspects of the Chinese American experience.

SOUTH PARK & FASHION DISTRICT
This is where fashionistas in minis, knee-high boots and new school cardigans, flaunting just enough sass to make you look twice, wander among crack heads and drunks in neck tattoos and a perma-haze. Here you'll scope fresh-sprayed graffiti art, meet eastside artists, dreadlocked, senior-citizen prophets, and explore the inner sanctums of graystone edifices brushed with the hues of some serene kind of dawn. There's a reason that this corner of the downtown swirl is our favorite.

LA Live   ENTERTAINMENT COMPLEX
(Map p70; 800 W Olympic Blvd) Across the street from the Staples Center and LA Con-

vention Center is this new, extremely corporate entertainment hub which includes the 7100-seat **Nokia Theatre**. There's also the Will I Am and Sheila E–owned **Conga Room**, a megaplex **cinema** for blockbuster action, a dozen restaurants, and a 54-story hotel tower shared by Marriott and the Ritz-Carlton.

Grammy Museum MUSEUM
(Map p70; www.grammymuseum.org; 800 W Olympic Blvd; adult/senior/student $13/12/11; ⏱11:30am-7:30pm Sun-Fri, 10am-7:30pm Sat) Easily the highlight of LA Live. Music lovers will get lost in interactive exhibits, which define, differentiate and link musical genres, while live footage strobes from all corners. You can glimpse GnR's bass drum, Lester Young's tenor, Yo Yo Ma's cello and Michael's glove. Interactive sound chambers allow you and your friends to try your hand at mixing and remixing, singing and rapping.

Staples Center VENUE
(Map p70; ☎213-742-7340; www.staplescenter. com; 1111 S Figueroa St; P) South Park got its first jolt in 1999 with the opening of this saucer-shaped sports and entertainment arena with all the high-tech trappings. It's home turf for the Los Angeles Lakers, Clippers and Sparks basketball teams, and the Kings ice-hockey team. When major headliners – like, say, U2 – are in town, they'll most likely perform at the Staple, where you can glimpse bigger-than-life statues of Magic Johnson and Wayne Gretzky. Parking costs $20.

Grand Hope Park PARK
(Map p70; 9th St) Small, peaceful and designed by Lawrence Halprin (one of the country's foremost landscape architects), this was the first of South Park's beautification projects, and is often filled with students from the adjacent fashion institute. It's located between Grand Ave & Hope Street.

Fashion Institute of Design & Merchandising
FASHION

(FIDM; Map p70; www.fidm.edu; 919 S Grand Ave; ☉10am-4pm Tue-Sat) A private college with an international student body. The gallery has some interesting rotating exhibits, including costumes worn by actors in Academy Award–nominated movies. Bargain hunters should check out the FIDM Scholarship Store, where you can get new but slightly damaged contemporary clothing donated by department stores for just a few dollars.

Fashion District
FASHION

(Map p70; www.fashiondistrict.org) FIDM graduates often go on to launch their own brands or work for established labels in this 90-block nirvana for shopaholics. Bounded by Main and Wall Sts and 7th St and Pico Blvd, the district's prices are lowest in bazaar-like **Santee Alley**, but the styles are grooviest in the **Gerry** and **Cooper buildings**. For a primer on how to get around, see the boxed text LA's Fashion District Demystified (p84).

Flower Market
MARKET

(Map p70; www.laflowerdistrict.com; Wall St; admission Mon-Fri $2, Sat $1; ☉8am-noon Mon, Wed & Fri, 6am-noon Tue, Thu & Sat) Cut flowers at cut-rate prices are the lure here, where a few dollars gets you armloads of Hawaiian ginger or sweet roses, a potted plant or elegant orchid. The market is busiest in the wee hours when florists stock up. Bring cash. It's located in between 7th and 8th streets.

Coca-Cola Bottling Plant
LANDMARK

(1334 S Central Ave) Streamline Moderne doesn't get any sleeker than Robert Derrah's 1937 design, inspired by classic ocean liners. See those portholes, catwalk, cargo doors and bridge? It's in the industrial no-man's land southeast of the Fashion District but worth a quick detour if only to snap a picture of yourself and a giant Coke bottle.

Chinatown
CULTURAL DISTRICT

(Map p70; www.chinatownla.com) As you walk north from El Pueblo, beneath the dragon gates, the aroma of chili and beans gradually gives way to soy and crispy duck. After being forced to make room for Union Station, the Chinese resettled a few blocks north along Hill St and Broadway. Chinatown is still the community's traditional hub, even though most Chinese Americans now live in the San Gabriel Valley.

There are no essential sights here, but the area, a stop on Metro Gold Line, is fun for an aimless wander. Restaurants beckon with dim sum and Peking duck, while shops overflow with curios, culinary oddities (live frogs anyone?), ancient herbal remedies and lucky bamboo.

Of late, parts of Chinatown have received an injection of hipness, no more so than at **Central Plaza** (900 block of Broadway), conceived as an unabashedly kitschy walking mall with outposts of contemporary cool like Welcome Hunters (p83). Across Hill St, the galleries and studios along Chung King Rd bring out art students and aficionados on opening nights. Pick up a self-guided-tour brochure at the **LA Chinatown Heritage & Visitors Center** (www.chssc.org; 411 Bernard St; ☉11am-3pm Wed-Fri, noon-4:30pm Sun).

Dodger Stadium
LANDMARK

(☎866-363-4377; http://losangeles.dodgers.mlb.com/la/ballpark/tours.jsp; 1000 Elysian Park Ave; tours adult/child 4-14yr & senior $15/10; ☉10am & 11:30pm; ℙ) Built in 1962, and one of Major League Baseball's classic ballparks, Dodger Stadium is now offering regular behind-the-scenes tours of the historic stadium. The 90-minute spins cover the press box, the Dodger dugout, the Dugout Club, the field and the Tommy Lasorda Training Center. Since tours are limited to 25 people, reservations are strongly advised. During the season, tours are held almost daily. In the off-season they are less frequent, and there are no tours on day-game days. Of course, the best way to experience the stadium is to go to the ol' ballgame (p82).

FREE Richard Riordan Central Library
LIBRARY

(Map p70; www.lapl.org; 630 W 5th St; ☉10am-6pm Mon, Wed, Fri & Sat, to 8pm Tue & Thu) One of the coolest buildings in town, the Egyptian-flavored 1922 central library was designed by Bertram Goodhue and named for a former mayor. Sphinxes greet you at the 5th St entrance, a colorful 1933 mural showing milestones in LA history swathes a grand rotunda on the 2nd floor, and it's crowned with a stunning Mesoamerican mosaic of the sun.

In the modern **Tom Bradley wing**, escalators cascade down four glass-walled floors through a whimsically decorated glass atrium. Besides 2.1 million books, the library also holds a prized archive of historical photographs, art exhibits, and keeps a dynamic events schedule. One of the best is the **Aloud LA** (www.lfla.org/aloud) series, often featuring major movers and shakers in arts, literature and politics. Recent speakers include Stephen King and Sebastian Junger. It's free but hugely popular, so make online reservations. There are also free tours at 12:30pm on weekdays, 11am and 2pm on Saturday.

Pershing Square & Around   LANDMARK
(Map p70; www.laparks.org) The hub of downtown's historic core, Pershing Sq was LA's first public park in 1866 and is now a postmodern concrete patch enlivened by public art, summer concerts, a holiday-season ice rink and the hulking 1923 Millennium Biltmore Hotel (p80). LA's most illustrious defender of the grand-hotel tradition, it has hosted presidents, kings and celebrities, plus the 1960 Democratic National Convention and eight Academy Awards ceremonies. Its sumptuous interior boasts carved and gilded ceilings, marble floors, grand staircases and palatial ballrooms decorated by White House muralist Giovanni Smeraldi. Afternoon tea is served daily in the rococo-style Rendezvous Court.

Jewelry District   JEWELRY
(Map p70; www.lajd.net; Hill St) South of Pershing Square (btwn 6th & 8th Sts) is the country's second-largest jewelry district after New York. Gold and diamonds are the main currency. One of the marts occupies the historic **Pantages Theatre** (401-21 W 7th St), a hugely popular vaudeville venue in the 1920s. Between Hill St and Broadway, on 7th St, is one of downtown's newest oddities, **St Vincent Court**. The recently restored alleyway is supposed to look like a quaint Parisian street, and is lined with Middle Eastern cafes where clusters of men sip minty tea, and hipsters chow gyro. For details on shopping in the district, see p83.

FREE **City Hall**   LANDMARK
(Map p70; ✆213-978-1995; www.lacity.org; 200 N Spring St; ☺8am-5pm Mon-Fri) Until 1966 no LA building stood taller than the 1928 City Hall, which appeared in the *Superman* TV series and 1953 sci-fi thriller *War of the Worlds*. On clear days you'll have views of the city, the mountains and several decades of downtown growth from the observation deck. Also check out the grand domed rotunda on the 3rd level with a marble floor as intricate as those found in Italian cathedrals. Free, two-hour guided tours leave at 10am Monday to Thursday, but reserva-

tions must be made at least seven days in advance. The public entrance is on Main St.

FREE **Los Angeles Times**   NEWSPAPER
(Map p70; ✆213-237-5757; www.latimes.com; 202 W 1st St; ☺tours 11am & 1:30pm last Tue & Thu of month; P) News junkies can get their fix on a free tour of the nearby *Los Angeles Times* building. Explore either the print works or the editorial offices, learn the paper's history and the publishing process, just don't ask about the murky future of newspapers. Kids under 10 can't come and reservations must be made months in advance.

FREE **Broad Plaza**   LANDMARK
(Map p70; www.dot.ca.gov; 100 S Main St) OK, maybe Caltrans didn't earn their new $150-million digs based on performance alone, but that doesn't change the fact that this floating steel-mesh- and glass-skinned monstrosity is worthy of praise. And you can always take heart from the fact that the 2nd St steps have become a vortex for downtown's skate punks of color. Deal with it, Caltrans! Tours are not available, but it does have a lobby museum open to the public.

FREE **Music Center**   VENUE
(Map p70; www.musiccenter.org; 135 N Grand Ave; P) Disney hall is part of a cultural complex known as the Music Center. Aside from the LA Phil's old home, the **Dorothy Chandler Pavilion**, which is now used for an expanded schedule by the **LA Opera**, it encompasses the **Mark Taper Forum** (p82), the **Ahmanson Theatre** (p82) and a fountain plaza. Guided tours through the four theaters make a brief stop in the Disney hall lobby, last 90 minutes and depart at 10:30am and 12:30pm most Tuesdays to Saturdays. Parking is $9.

Little Tokyo   CULTURAL DISTRICT
(Map p70) Little Tokyo swirls with outdoor shopping malls, Buddhist temples, public art, traditional gardens and some of the most authentic sushi bars, *izakayas* (taverns) and *shabu-shabu* parlors in town. The community can trace its roots back to the 1880s, but only a few historic buildings survive along E 1st St. Stop by the **Little Tokyo Koban** (Map p70; 307 E 1st St; ☺9am-6pm Mon-Sat) for maps and information. There are inexpensive lots and metered street parking on 2nd St east of Central Ave. DASH bus A (DD on weekends) comes through here, and so does the Gold Line on its way to and from Pasadena.

Japanese American National Museum
MUSEUM

(JANM; Map p70; www.janm.org; 369 E 1st St; adult/seniors & students $9/5; ⊘11am-5pm Tue, Wed & Fri-Sun, to 8pm Thu) A great first stop in Little Tokyo, this is the country's first museum dedicated to the Japanese immigrant experience. You'll be moved by galleries dealing with the painful chapter of the WWII internment camps and charmed by such exhibits as George Takei's *Star Trek* suit. Afterwards, relax in the tranquil garden, and browse the well-stocked gift shop. Admission is free on Thursdays from 5pm to 8pm, and all day on the third Thursday of each month.

Geffen Contemporary at MOCA
MUSEUM

(Map p70; www.moca.org; 152 N Central Ave; adult/student & senior/child under 12 $10/5/free, 5-8pm Thu free; ⊘11am-5pm Mon & Fri, to 8pm Thu, to 6pm Sat & Sun) Arty types can pop next door from the Japanese American National Museum to peruse the cutting-edge exhibits at this branch of MOCA Grand Ave. It presents mostly conceptual art and large-scale installations in a police garage converted by Frank Gehry. Tours (free with admission) run at noon, 1pm and 2pm.

Japanese Village Plaza
MALL

(Map p70) The funny-looking tower across 1st St from the JANM is a *yagura*, a traditional fire-lookout tower typically found in rural Japan. It's the gateway to this modern outdoor mall with gift shops, restaurants and good people-watching.

FREE Japanese American Cultural & Community Center
GALLERY

(Map p70; www.jaccc.org; 244 S San Pedro St; ⊘noon-5pm Tue-Fri, 11am-4pm Sat & Sun; P) Little Tokyo's main cultural hub is this gallery spotlighting local artists. There's also a library and a gift shop.

FREE James Irvine Garden
GARDEN

(Map p70; 224 S San Pedro St; ⊘9am-5pm) With bamboo, dwarf pine, magnolias and a gurgling artificial brook, this is a nice chillout spot. Reach it by taking the elevator to the 'B' level and following the signs.

Aratani/Japan America Theater
THEATER

(Map p70; ✆213-680-3700) Next door to the James Irvine Garden, a handmade, peacock-motif silk *doncho* (curtain) from Kyoto dramatically opens the stage for *kabuki*, *no* (stylized dance-dramas), and *bunraku* (puppet shows) performances.

Cathedral of Our Lady of the Angels
CATHOLIC CATHEDRAL

(Map p70; www.olacathedral.org; 555 W Temple St; ⊘6am-6pm Mon-Fri, 9am-6pm Sat, 7am-6pm Sun; P) José Rafael Moneo mixed Gothic proportions with contemporary design for his 2002 Cathedral of Our Lady of the Angels, which exudes a calming serenity achieved by soft light filtering through its alabaster panes. Wall-sized tapestries as intricate and detailed as a Michelangelo fresco festoon the main nave. They depict 135 saints whose gaze is directed towards the main altar, a massive yet simple slab of red marble. Gregory Peck is buried in the beehivelike subterranean mausoleum. Favorite times to visit the cathedral include the 1pm weekday tours and popular organ recitals at 12:45pm on Wednesday, both options free.

FREE Grand Central Market
MARKET

(Map p70; www.grandcentralmarket.com; 317 S Broadway; ⊘9am-6pm) On the ground floor of a 1905 beaux-arts building where architect Frank Lloyd Wright once kept an office. Stroll along the sawdust-sprinkled aisles beneath old-timey ceiling fans and neon signs, past stalls piled high with mangoes, peppers and jicamas, and glass bins filled with dried chilies and nuts. There's even a small pastry factory and plenty of lunch counters for snacking on ceviche, shwarma or chicken soup.

California Plaza & Angels Flight
LANDMARK

(Map p70) MOCA is dwarfed by the soaring California Plaza office tower. The outdoor water-court amphitheatre is host to **Grand Performances**, which is one of the best free summer performance series in the city.

Once again chugging down a steep incline to Hill St and Grand Central Market is **Angels Flight** (per ride 25¢; ⊘6:45am-10pm), a historic funicular billed as the 'shortest railway in the world'. Part novelty act, part commuter train for lazy corporate types who'd rather not climb the stairs, the little trains first started operating in 1901 when this neighborhood was called Bunker Hill and was dotted with Victorians. They were mothballed when the area was redeveloped in the '60s. Nostalgia revived them in the '90s but only until a fatal derailment occurred in 2001. With new safety measures in place, operations resumed in late 2007.

Summer is a great time to visit LA, not in the least because of the free concert series that are offered all over town. Most take place weekly. Check the websites listed here for details.

Some of the biggest crowds come out for the **Twilight Dance Series** (www.santa monicapier.org/twilight; ☉Thu). The eclectic, multicultural line up turns the Santa Monica Pier, and adjacent beaches, into a dance and party zone. In 2010 performances included Ben Lee, Rickie Lee Jones and Dr John.

In keeping with its overall renaissance, Downtown has become a hot spot for concerts. **Pershing Square** (www.laparks.org/pershingsquare/events/downtownStage.htm) hosts live acts on Saturday and Thursday nights. Thursday concerts – curated by Spaceland – have an alternative, hip-hop or world-beat bent. In the Financial District, **Grand Performances** (www.grandperformances.org) brings international music, dance and theater acts to high-rise-flanked California Plaza on Friday and Saturday nights.

Museums also get into the music game. At Los Angeles County Musuem of Art, art and jazz prove an irresistible mix to culture vultures and desk jockeys alike during **Friday Night Jazz** (www.lacma.org), which runs from April to November. The Hammer Museum presents just-about-to-get-big LA and UK bands in a double bill during **Also I Like to Rock** (www.hammer.org; ☉Thu). The Skirball Cultural Center, near the Getty, brings quality world-music acts to a stage surrounded by a lily pond during **Sunset Concerts** (www.skirball.org; ☉Thu), and the Getty's **Saturdays Off the 405** (www.getty.edu; ☉6-9pm Sat May-Oct) offers some of the best acts in the bunch.

FREE | **Bradbury Building**   LANDMARK
(Map p70; 304 S Broadway; ☉9am-6pm Mon-Fri, to 5pm Sat & Sun) This 1893 building is one of LA's undisputed architectural jewels. Its red-brick facade conceals a stunning galleried atrium with inky filigree grillwork, a rickety birdcage elevator and yellow-brick walls that glisten golden in the afternoon light filtering through the tent-shaped glass roof. Location scouts love the place, whose star turn came in the cult flick *Blade Runner*.

The building has a curious genesis. Mining mogul Lewis Bradbury picked not a famous architect but an unknown draftsman named George Wyman to come up with the design. Allegedly, Wyman consulted a Ouija board and accepted the gig after his dead brother told him it would be a success.

FREE | **Broadway Theaters**   THEATER DISTRICT
Until eclipsed by Hollywood in the mid-1920s, Broadway was LA's entertainment hub with no fewer than a dozen theaters built in a riot of styles, from beaux arts to east Indian to Spanish Gothic. Their architectural and historic significance even earned them a spot on the National Register of Historic Places. However, since this area is now a decidedly ungentrified slice of cut-rate retail and gritty urban action,

they're usually closed to the public. The best way to see them is by joining one of the excellent tours offered by the Los Angeles Conservancy (p66).

Million Dollar Theater   THEATER
(Map p70; 307 S Broadway) This was the first theater built by Sid Grauman of Chinese Theatre and Egyptian Theatre fame. Big bands played here in the '40s and, a decade later, it became the first Broadway venue to cater to Spanish speakers. Briefly a church, it's now under restoration.

Los Angeles Theater   THEATER
(Map p70; 615 S Broadway) This 1931 theater is the most ridiculously lavish movie palace on the strip. The soaring lobby is a sparkling hall of mirrors with a three-tiered fountain, crystal chandeliers and a grand central staircase leading to a lavish auditorium where Albert Einstein and other luminaries enjoyed the premiere of Charlie Chaplin's *City Lights*. Restored, it presents special events and screenings.

Palace Theater   THEATER
(Map p70; 630 S Broadway) The exterior of this 1911 building, across the street from the Los Angeles Theater, was inspired by a Florentine palazzo while the interior is French baroque fantasy filled with murals depicting pastoral scenes and garland-draped columns.

State Theater
THEATER

(Map p70; 703 S Broadway) Broadway's biggest entertainment complex (dating from 1921) can seat 2500 people and has a flamboyant ceiling; it's now a Spanish-language church.

Globe Theater
THEATER

(Map p70; 744 S Broadway) This 1913 stage started out as a live theater but, sadly, is now a swap meet.

Tower Theater
THEATER

(Map p70; 802 S Broadway) The world's first talkie, *The Jazz Singer* starring Al Jonson, premiered here in 1927. Its lavish baroque interior is often used for location shoots.

Orpheum Theater
THEATER

(Map p70; www.laorpheum.com; 842 S Broadway) Currently the busiest venue on Broadway is this 1926 theater which was built for vaudeville and has hosted such entertainers as Judy Garland, George Burns and Nat King Cole. It's a truly sumptuous place with silk tapestries, marble pilasters, a gilded, coffered ceiling, still-functioning Wurlitzer organ and an old brass box office. Fully restored, the venerable landmark now presents everything from *American Idol* auditions to Norah Jones concerts to film screenings.

Eastern Columbia Building
THEATER

(Map p70; 849 S Broadway) Across the street from the Orpheum, this strikingly turquoise art-deco tower (1929) originally housed a clothing store and was recently converted into luxury lofts. Note the gilded sunburst pattern above the entrance and on the tower's clock face. One-bedroom apartments rent for $3000 a month; Johnny Depp allegedly bought the penthouse for a cool $2.1 million.

United Artists Theater
THEATER

(Map p70; 818-240-8151; www.drgenescott.com; 933 S Broadway) The construction of this 1927 Spanish Gothic theater was bankrolled by Mary Pickford, Douglas Fairbanks and Charlie Chaplin. It's long been the 'cathedral' of the late televangelist Dr Gene Scott (look for the 'Jesus Saves' sign on the rooftop), now run by his wife Melissa. The only way to get inside is by calling the 'voice of God' to ask for a free reservation for a Sunday service.

Arts District
ARTS DISTRICT

(Map p70) In the gritty, industrial section southeast of Little Tokyo an increasingly lively arts district has sprung up. It's drawn a young, adventurous and spirited crowd of people who live and work in makeshift studios above abandoned warehouses and small factories. There are enough of them here to support a growing number of cafes, restaurants and shops.

Southern California Institute of Architecture
LANDMARK

(Sci-Arc; Map p70; www.sciarc.edu; 960 E 3rd St) The area got a nod of respectability when this institute moved into the former Santa Fe Freight Yard in 2001. It's a progressive laboratory with faculty and students that continually push the envelope in architectural design. You can see some of the results in the **gallery** (admission free; ⊙10am-6pm) or attend a lecture or film screening; see the website for upcoming events.

Brewery Art Complex
ARTISTS COLONY

(www.labrewery.com, www.breweryartwalk.com; 2100 N Main St; P) Northeast, across the LA River, is LA's largest artist colony, housed in a former brewery. Most lofts and studios are generally closed to the public except during the biannual **Artwalks** (usually in spring and fall); check the website for details), though you can wander around to examine the large installations – usually works in progress – scattered throughout.

FREE San Antonio Winery
WINERY

(☎323-223-1401; www.sanantoniowinery.com; 737 Lamar St; ⊙8:30am-7pm Mon-Fri, 9am-7pm Sat & Sun; P) Near the Brewery Art Complex is LA's last remaining historic winery. It was founded in 1917 by Italian immigrant Santo Cambianica, whose descendants still make buttery chardonnay, velvety cabernet sauvignon and other varietals culled from estates in Paso Robles and Napa Valley. Sample them for free in the tasting room, enjoy a meal at the Italian restaurant or learn more about the noble grape at a wine seminar. Free behind-the-scenes winery tours take place at noon, 1pm and 2pm from Monday to Friday, and on the hour from 11am to 4pm on Saturday and Sunday. Reserve ahead.

FREE Wells Fargo History Museum
MUSEUM

(Map p70; www.wellsfargohistory.com; 333 S Grand Ave; ⊙9am-5pm Mon-Fri) Sponsored by the California-based Wells Fargo Bank, this small but intriguing museum chronicles the company's role in the California gold rush. See an original Concord stagecoach, the 27oz gold 'Challenge Nugget', an old bank office and all sorts of other artifacts, or ask the staff to start the 15-minute video.

ST SOPHIA CATHEDRAL

This splendidly opulent **house of worship** (www.stsophia.org; 1324 S Normandie Ave; admission free; ⊙10am-4pm Tue-Fri, to 2pm Sat; P) is the spiritual hub of the local Greek Orthodox community and is as rich and epic as a giant's treasure chest. Financed by the Skouras brothers, Greek immigrants who made it big in Hollywood as studio heads, they hired set designers to swathe the main nave with biblical-themed murals. It's illuminated by muted light streaming through stained-glass windows and emanating from the Bohemian-crystal chandelier. A visit here is easily combined with a plate of gyro at Papa Cristo's (p198).

The exhibits are on the ground floor of the **Wells Fargo Center**, another huge office tower that's filled with public art, including numerous nude sculptures by Robert Graham in the atrium and Jean Dubuffet's cartoonish Le Dandy in the Hope St vestibule.

FREE **US Bank Tower & Bunker Hills Steps** LANDMARK
(Map p70; 655 W 5th St) At 1018ft, the US Bank Tower is the tallest building between Chicago and Taiwan. Film buffs might remember it being attacked by an alien spaceship in *Independence Day*. Of course, the **Deloitte & Tousche Building** nearby is more stunning.

The tower abuts the **Bunker Hill Steps**, a cheesy set-piece staircase that links 5th St with the Wells Fargo Center and other hilltop office complexes. At the top is a small fountain featuring a female nude by Robert Graham. En route you pass **McCormick & Schmick's**, a high-end seafood house famous for its happy hour.

🏃 Activities

TOP CHOICE **Peace Yoga** YOGA
(Map p70; www.peaceyogagallery.com; 903 S Main St; per class $15) A 4000-sq-ft underground studio space all banged together by one bad-ass, eternally creative Ashtanga yogi named Cheri Rae. The bathroom sports reclaimed sinks from barber shops, there are exposed brick walls, DJ decks, massage grottos and more concrete floor space than any other yoga studio in the city. And we haven't even mentioned the raw-food kitchen.

FREE **Downtown Art Walks** ART
(www.downtownartwalk.org; ⊙noon-9pm 2nd Thu of month) A massive, mad swirl of art lovers invades downtown once a month for self-guided, liberally lubricated art walks that link more than 40 galleries and museums across the downtown grid. You'll find most between 3rd and 9th and Broadway and Main. The scene often surpasses the art.

Yoga Circle YOGA
(Map p70; www.yogacircledowntown.com; 400 S Main St; per class $16) Up for some asana? Head to this bright, open blonde-wood studio with exposed fixtures on the ground floor of the historic San Fernando building.

🛏 Sleeping

TOP CHOICE **Figueroa Hotel** BOUTIQUE HOTEL **$$**
(Map p70; ☎213-627-8971; www.figueroa hotel.com; 939 S Figueroa St r $148-194, ste $225-265; P@🛜🏊) It's hard not to be charmed by this rambling owner-operated oasis a basketball toss from Staples. Global-chic rooms blend Moroccan mirrors, Iraqi quilts, and Kurdish grain-sack floor cushions, with paper lanterns from Chinatown. Prince (he's got an all-purple room named for him) is a repeat visitor. Parking costs $8.

Stay HOSTEL **$**
(Map p70; ☎213-213-7829; www.stayhotels.com; 636 S Main St; r with/without bathroom $80/60; P@🛜🏊🍴) Occupying the first three floors of Hotel Cecil, Stay has got the groove factor, what with its marble floors, baby-blue walls and a frosted-glass, faux-flower wall in the wired lobby. Rooms have retro furnishings and bedspreads, iPod docks and safety-orange accent walls. Gleaming shared baths and showers are hewn from marble.

Orchid Hotel BOUTIQUE HOTEL **$$**
(Map p70; ☎213-623-9904; www.ohotelgroup. com; 819 S Flower St; r $109-159, ste $249; P🛜) Also known as 'the O', this hip new boutique nest, with its black-marble lobby, red-lit elevator and relatively modern rooms with berber carpet and charcoal accent walls, is one of the best-value places in the area. Its boomerang of a lobby restaurant-bar, with exposed-brick wall and glass fireplace, offers live music thrice weekly.

Hilton Checkers   HOTEL **$$**
(Map p70; ☎213-624-0000; www.hiltoncheck
ers.com; 535 S Grand Ave; r $210-279; P⊛)
Originally the Mayflower Hotel, when it
was built in 1927, this friendly four-star ad-
dress is understated yet indulgent. Rooms
have all the amenities, with lower prices
on the weekends when the business crowd
vanishes.

Standard Downtown LA   HOTEL **$$$**
(Map p70; ☎213-892-8080; www.standardhotels.
com; 550 S Flower St; r$245-525; ste $1150-1300;
P@⊛≋) This design-savvy hotel in a converted oil-company building was a big hit
when it first opened years ago, and still ap-
peals to a young, hip-ish crowd. Rooms are
mod and minimalist. Hit the rooftop bar for
views. Parking costs $30.

Millennium Biltmore Hotel   HOTEL **$$$**
(Map p70; ☎213-624-1011; www.thebiltmore.
com; 506 S Grand Ave; r $110-300; P@⊛≋)
Drenched in tradition and gold leaf, down-
town's grand dame has bedded stars,
presidents and royalty in modestly sized,
gold-and-blue-hued rooms with all the trap-
pings. The gorgeous art-deco health club
takes the work out of workout. Parking is $40.

Hotel Cecil   HOTEL **$**
(Map p70; ☎213-624-4545; www.thececilhotel.
com; 640 S Main St; r with/without bathroom
$65/55; P⊛) You'll love the grand, old-
school marble lobby with its stained-glass
entry, the young, hip crowd, and the gritty
Main St address. The pastel-brushed rooms
are a touch drab, but the views from the
upper reaches are insane, and the marble
common bathrooms sparkle.

Omni Los Angeles Hotel   HOTEL **$$**
(Map p70; ☎213-617-3300; www.omnihotels.com;
251 S Olive St; r $159-189; P@⊛≋⛐) Omni is
all buttoned-up business during the week
but its lower weekend rates make it an attractive choice for families and culture vultures. Rooms aren't brand new, but they are
bright and spacious and, on clear days, have
views of the city, the Hollywood sign and
the sea. Parking costs $30.

✕ Eating

⭐ **Bottega Louie**   ITALIAN **$$**
TOP CHOICE (Map p70; ☎213-802-1470; www.bottega
louie.com; 700 S Grand; pasta $11, pizzas $16,
mains $18; ⊘breakfast, lunch & dinner; ⛐)
Old-time parlor restaurant meets upscale
Tuscan-market cuisine at this wide and
deep marble bar and dining room, which

has become a magnet for the artsy loft set
and white-collar worker bees alike. The
open kitchen crew – all in chef's whites –
carves deli meats and slices cheese, steams
shellfish in white wine, grills house-made
sausage and wood-fires thin-crust pizza.
So ease into a leather chair, drink in the
alterna-funk-rock soundtrack, order a sec-
ond martini and you may as well wait the
25 minutes for the chocolate soufflé. It does
feel good in here.

Philippe the Original   DINER **$**
(www.philippes.com; 1001 N Alameda St; sand-
wiches $6–7; ⊘breakfast, lunch & dinner; P⛐)
From LAPD hunks to stressed-out attor-
neys to smooching couples, everyone loves
Philippe's, where the French-dip sandwich
was invented over a century ago. Order a
crusty roll filled with meat (we go with the
lamb 'double-dipped'), and hunker down at
communal tables on the sawdust-covered
floor. Cash only.

Gorbals   EASTERN EUROPEAN **$$**
(Map p70; ☎213-488-3408; www.thegorbalsla.
com; 501 S Spring St; dishes $6-43; ⊘lunch & din-
ner) An Eastern European tapas joint set in
the old Alexandria Hotel lobby. Menu main-
stays include latkes with smoked apple
sauce, sublime bacon-wrapped matzo balls
served with pink-hot horseradish mayo,
and lamb ribs braised in white wine and
served with cinnamon-dusted beets.

Sushi Gen   JAPANESE **$$**
(Map p70; ☎213-617-0552; 422 E 2nd St; sushi
$11-21; ⊘lunch & dinner Mon-Sat) When you ask
Little Tokyo locals where to eat the fresh-
est and tastiest sushi, they will point to this
blink-and-you'll-miss-it spot in the Honda
Plaza mini-mall. And if you see them again,
you will thank them profusely.

🌿 **Tiara Café**   ECLECTIC **$$**
(Map p70; www.tiara-cafe-la.com; 127 E 9th
St; mains $11-18; ⊘lunch Mon-Fri; ✍⛐) The
latest from eastside chef Fred Eric is set
in the whimsical ground floor of the New
Mart, with pink walls, soaring ceilings and
thick granite columns. The tables are generally packed with fashionistas, and the
food, like smoked brisket chili, grilled fish
enchiladas, and salads cobbled together
from farmers market produce, is fantastic.

🌿 **Market**   DELI **$**
(Map p70; www.marketrestaurants.com;
862 S Los Angeles St; cupcakes/burgers $3/$9;
⊘lunch Mon-Fri; ✍⛐) Need a quick fix to

sate you through the sample-sale madness? Head here for a pressed Cuban (citrus glazed pork, ham and manchego) or a seared ahi and couscous salad. Eat at common, brushed-metal tables with fellow shoppers and steely-eyed designers. Save room for cupcakes.

Blossom
VIETNAMESE $

(Map p70; ☑213-623-1973; www.blossomrestaurant.com; 426 S Main St; mains $8-11; ⊗lunch & dinner Mon-Sat) This stylish kitchen churns out fresh and tasty Vietnamese food on the cheap. Start with the *goi cuon* (shrimp and pork spring rolls), and follow it with some spicy *pho* (noodle soup) paired with a Southeast Asian pilsner or a bottle of French burgundy ($25).

Lazy Ox Canteen
GASTROPUB $$

(Map p70; ☑213-626-5299; www.lazyoxcanteen.com; 241 S San Pedro; appetizers $4-16, mains $21-21; ⊗lunch & dinner; ⊛) If you'd rather not eat Japanese in Little Tokyo, find these cedar-paneled environs for tapas. Think: pig's ear *chicharon*, grilled squid with garbanzo beans, and brick roast mussels. Pair them with something from the creative beer and wine list. Burgers are sublime, and its nightly family dinners are a big hit.

Maria's Fresh Seafood
MEXICAN SEAFOOD $

(Map p70; www.grandcentralmarket.com; 317 S Broadway; appetizers $4-8, mains $11-23; ⊗breakfast, lunch & dinner) Our favorite counter in the Grand Central Market offers other choices, but you should zero in on the Jalisco-style pescado ceviche ($2.50). It comes piled onto a crisp corn tostada served with a side of hot sauce and a lemon wedge. One's enough. Two are better.

Orochon Ramen
JAPANESE $

(Map p70; 123 S Onizuka St; dishes $10; ⊗lunch & dinner; Ⓟ) On the top floor of the Weller Plaza is the ramen joint of your dreams. Pork and vegetable noodle soups are steeped in three kinds of broth (miso, soy or salt) and tweaked to nine levels of spicy. There's a wall of bravery for those that venture into the top two levels above 'Extreme.'

$.05 Diner
DINER $

(Map p70; www.5cdiner.com; 524 S Main St; dishes $5.50-12.80; ⊗breakfast & lunch Tue-Sun, dinner Tue-Sat) Named for the intersection of 5th & Main, termed 'the Nickel' by nearby skid-row residents who used to come to this corner for their daily meds, this kitschy red-vinyl joint re-imagines American diner fare. Avocados are stuffed with quinoa salad. Burgers piled with poblano chilies, and don't sleep on the maple-glazed bacon donut, one of Jonathan Gold's '99 Things to Eat in LA Before You Die.'

Daikokuya
JAPANESE $

(Map p70; www.daikoku-ten.com; 327 E 1st St; appetizers $3-9, mains $7-13.50; ⊗lunch & dinner; Ⓟ) If you are partial to Japanese noodles, follow your nose to this funky Little Tokyo diner. It serves rice bowls, but noodle soup is king.

Lien Hoa
CHINESE $

(721 N Broadway St; dishes under $10; ⊗lunch & dinner) As funky and flavorful as Chinatown gets, this broke-down deli is deadly serious about its whole, quartered Peking duck and tangy spareribs, which are chopped, weighed and wrapped for carry out.

Pete's Café & Bar
SOUTHERN $$

(Map p70; www.petescafe.com; 400 S Main St; appetizers $8-10, mains $16-28; ⊗lunch & dinner) This hipster favorite is alive with loft dwellers, politicos, journos and artists. Picture windows allow old bank facades to bleed into ambient Americana surroundings. The Southern-edged menu offers pan-roasted pork chops and crispy oyster spoons. The bar gleams with single malt. How's about a 36-year-old Springbank ($95) neat? Open until 2am.

Drinking

TOP CHOICE Las Perlas
BAR

(Map p70; www.lasperlas.la; 103 E 6th St; ⊗7pm-2am Mon-Sat) With a hint of Old Mexico whimsy, a chalkboard menu of over 80 tequilas and mescals, and friendly barkeeps who mix things like egg whites, blackberries and port syrup into new-school takes on the classic margarita, there's a reason we love downtown's best tequila bar. But if you truly want to dig tequila, pick a highland variety and sip it neat.

Association
BAR, LOUNGE

(Map p70; www.theassociation-la.com; 110 E 6th St; ⊗5pm-2am Mon-Fri, 7pm-2am Sat & Sun) This hip basement bar flashes old-school glamour with leather bar stools and lounges tucked into intimate coves. But the bar is the thing. We're talking about dozens of whiskeys, ryes, rums and tequilas. The engaging bartenders muddle and mix like pros. Just don't call them 'mixologists.' They hate that.

Must
PUB

(Map p70; 118 W 5th St; ⏰4pm-midnight Mon-Fri, to 2am Sat & Sun) A hipster pub featuring boutique vintners and craftsmen beers. Sunday game night dusts off the board games you love so well – everything from Scrabble to Connect Four to Jenga. Titties & Wine Tuesdays (aka ladies night) means a DJ and dancing.

Seven Grand
WHISKEY BAR

(Map p70; www.sevengrand.la; 515 W 7th St; ⏰5pm-2am Mon-Wed, 4pm-2am Thu & Fri, 7pm-2am Sat & Sun) A dusky whiskey bar with tongue-in-cheek hunting decor. There are 175 varieties of amber to explore. DJs and smoking patio, too.

Golden Gopher
BAR

(Map p70; www.goldengopherbar.com; 417 W 8th St; ⏰5pm-2am Thu & Fri, 8pm-2am Sat-Wed) Campy gopher lamps give even the pasty-faced a healthy glow at this dark drinking den, favored mostly by techie worker bees and corporate suits, with a smoking patio and in-store liquor store for after-hours revelries.

☆ Entertainment

Villains Tavern
TAVERN

(Map p70; ☎213-613-0766; www.villainstavern.com; 1356 Palmetto St) Restaurateur and interior designer Dana Hollister has turned a rundown deli into a dark-wood and iron den of bluesy cool. There's a salvaged bar top, church-pew seating, high ceilings dangling with vintage chandeliers and a 1600-sq-ft open-air patio where live blues rocks the stage. It has 28 beers on tap (served in iced jars) and the kitchen is creative yet rootsy. Don't miss it.

Edison
CLUB

(Map p70; www.edisondowntown.com; 108 W 2nd St, off Harlem Alley; ⏰5pm-2am Wed-Fri, from 8pm Sat; Ⓟ) *Metropolis* meets *Blade Runner* at this industrial-chic basement boîte where you'll be sipping mojitos surrounded by turbines and other machinery back from its days as a boiler room. Don't worry, it's all tarted up nicely with cocoa leather couches and three cavernous bars. No athletic wear, flip-flops or baggy jeans tolerated.

TOP CHOICE La Cita
CLUB

(Map p70; www.lacitabar.com; 336 S Hill St; ⏰10am-2am) The perfect setting for an afternoon that lasts until midnight or a wild soul-infused dance party, this red-vinyl, Mexican dive bar alternates between a dance club and music venue for downtown hipsters, when DJs whip the crowd into a frenzy with hip-hop, soul, punk and whatever else gets people moving, and a live-band salsa party.

Dodger Stadium
SPORTS

(☎866-363-4377; www.dodgers.com; 1000 Elysian Park; tickets $15-285; Ⓟ) Few clubs can match the Dodgers organization when it comes to making history (Jackie Robinson, Sandy Koufax, Kirk Gibson, and Vin Scully), winning and fan loyalty. The current owners' very messy divorce notwithstanding, the Dodgers still win with flair and fill the ballpark. The season lasts from April to October. Parking costs $15.

Red Cat
THEATER

(Map p70; www.redcat.org; 631 W 2nd St) Downtown's most avante-garde performance laboratory where theater, dance, music, poetry and film merge into impressive exhibitions presented in their own theater and gallery in the Walt Disney Concert Hall complex. The curious name is an acronym for Roy and Edna Disney/Cal Arts Theater. Admission to the gallery is free, theater ticket prices vary.

Mark Taper Forum
THEATER

(Map p70; www.centertheatergroup.org; 135 N Grand Ave; Ⓟ) Part of the Music Center, the Mark Taper is one of the three venues used by the Center Theatre Group, SoCal's leading resident ensemble and producer of Tony-, Pulitzer- and Emmy-winning plays. It's an intimate space with only 15 rows of seats arranged around a thrust stage, so you can see every sweat pearl on the actors' faces.

Ahmanson Theatre
THEATER

(Map p70; www.centertheatregroup.org; 135 N Grand Ave; Ⓟ) Much larger than the Taper, this grand space is another Center Theatre Group venue in the Music Center. It's used primarily for big-time musicals on their way to or from Broadway.

Staples Center
SPORTS, VENUE

(Map p70; www.staplescenter.com; 1111 S Figueroa St; Ⓟ) The **LA Lakers** (☎213-742-7340; www.nba.com/lakers; tickets $15-25,000) were once again crowned the NBA champs at the time of writing. And they still pack all 19,000 seats on a regular basis. Floor seats, like those filled by the ubiquitous Jack Nicholson, cost in excess of $5000 per game. Staples is also home base for the city's other

NBA team, the perennially mismanaged, karmically tainted **LA Clippers** (☑888-895-8662; www.nba.com/clippers; tickets $25-175), and the Candace Parker-led women's team, **LA Sparks** (☑877-447-7275; www.wnba.com/sparks; tickets $10-55). The WNBA season (late May to August) follows the regular men's NBA season (October to April). Tickets are sold online and at the Staples Center box office. Parking at the Staples Center costs $20.

Club Mayan
CLUB, VENUE

(Map p70; www.clubmayan.com; 1038 S Hill St, Downtown; ⊙9pm-3am Fri & Sat, varies Sun-Thu; ℗) Kick up your heels during Saturday's Tropical Nights when a salsa band turns the heat up. Don't know how? Come early for lessons, but there is a dress code. On Fridays it's house and hip-hop, and the club also hosts its share of wrestling events and indie bands with a following.

Los Angeles Theater Center
THEATER

(Map p70; www.thelatc.org; 514 S Spring St; admission $5-20; ⊙gallery noon-6pm Tue-Sat) Housed in the Old Pacific Stock Exchange built in 1915, the downstairs gallery rotates exhibitions curated by the Latino Museum of Art, while the excellent stage shows, produced by the 23-year-old Latino Theater Company, explore culturally diverse material and often feature emerging playwrights.

Nokia Theater
VENUE

(Map p70; www.nokiatheatrelive.com; 777 Chick Hearn Ct) This 7100-seat theater was christened by the Eagles and the Dixie Chicks when it opened in 2007, and has also hosted Neil Young, Anita Baker and Ricky Gervais. Check its website for info on upcoming shows, admission prices vary.

2nd Street Jazz
VENUE

(Map p70; www.2ndstjazz.com; 366 E 2nd St; shows $8; ⊙6:30pm-2am Tue & Thu, 8pm-2am Wed & Fri) An intimate, no-frills music venue offering solid DJ sets, and live hip-hop and jazz in the heart of Little Tokyo.

East West Players
THEATER

(Map p70; www.eastwestplayers.org; 120 N Judge John Aiso St, Little Tokyo; ℗) Founded in 1965, this pioneering Asian-American ensemble seeks to build a bridge between Eastern and Western theatrical styles. Its repertory of Broadway to modern classics takes a backseat to acclaimed premieres by local playwrights. Alumni have gone on to win Tony, Emmy and Academy awards.

Downtown Comedy Club
COMEDY

(Map p70; www.downtowncomedyclub.com; 114 W 5th St; cover $10; ⊙Fri & Sat) *Saturday Night Live* alumnus Garrett Morris is the man behind the curtain of this popular weekend comedy club.

🔒 Shopping

TOP CHOICE Stella Dottir
FASHION

(Map p70; www.stelladotir.com; 430 S Main St) Stella is a dreadlocked, Icelandic fashionista and feline aficionado who crafts one-of-a-kind, 1920s-style black-lace and silk gowns (from $200), with gloves, feathery hats and veils to match. She cuts a mean men's linen suit ($600) too. There's wafting jazz and a leafy entry. Yes, you'd be wise to drop in on the self-professed 'thousand-year-old shopkeeper.' She's special.

Jewelry District
JEWELRY

(Map p70; www.lajd.net; Hill St, Downtown) For bargain bling head to this bustling downtown district, between 6th & 8th Sts, where you can snap up watches, gold, silver and gemstones at up to 70% off retail. The mostly traditional designs are unlikely to be seen on the red carpet, but the selection is unquestionably huge. Quality varies, however.

Hive
ART GALLERY

(Map p70; www.thehivegallery.com; 729 S Spring St; ⊙1-6pm Wed-Sat) Nestled in a decidedly not-yet-gentrified stretch of Spring is a seemingly small, but surprisingly deep, artist-owned gallery, where the art always delivers and its openings rock.

RIF
SHOES

(Map p70; www.rif.la; 334 E 2nd St; ⊙noon-7pm) A hip-hop spiced consignment shoe store and your one-stop shop for new and used limited edition, imported and old-school sneaks.

Spoke
BIKE SHOP

(Map p70; www.redyourdead.com; 100 W 9th St) Hipsters were once better identified by twiggy, pale legs than tree-trunk quads, but a quick spin around downtown will reveal how pervasive the trend is for tricked-out, fixed-gear and single-speed bikes. This shop markets their Better Red Than Dead brand. They sell powder-coated commuters, and trick bikes where the front wheel spins 360 degrees.

Welcome Hunters
FASHION

(www.welcomehuntersla.com; 451 Gin Ling Way; ⊙noon-7pm Wed-Sun) An evolutionary foray

LA'S FASHION DISTRICT DEMYSTIFIED

Bargain hunters love this frantic, 90-block warren of fashion in southwestern Downtown (also see p72). Deals can be amazing, but first-timers are often bewildered by the district's size and immense selection. For orientation, check out www.fashion district.org, where you can download a free shopping-tour podcast or order a map guide to the area. Power-shoppers hungry for the latest inside scoop can book a custom-guided tour with **Urban Shopping Adventures** (www.urbanshopping adventures.com; tour $36).

Basically, the area is subdivided into several distinct retail areas:

» Women – Los Angeles St between Olympic and Pico Blvds; 11th St between Los Angeles and San Julian Sts

» Children – Wall St between 12th St and Pico Blvd

» Men and bridal – Los Angeles St between 7th and 9th Sts

» Textiles – 9th St between Santee and Wall Sts

» Jewelry and accessories – Santee St between Olympic Blvd and 13th St

» Designer knockoffs – Santee Alley and New Alley (enter on 11th St between Maple and Santee Aves)

Shops are generally open from 10am to 5pm daily, with Saturday being the busiest day by far because that's when many wholesalers open up to the public. Cash is king and haggling may get you 10% or 20% off, especially when buying multiple items. Refunds or exchanges are a no-no, so choose carefully and make sure items are in good condition. Most stores don't have dressing rooms.

Sample Sales

Every last Friday of the month, clued-in fashionistas descend upon the corner of 9th St and Los Angeles St armed with cash and attitude to catfight it out for designer clothes priced below wholesale. Their destination: the hip showrooms at the **Gerry Building** (www.gerrybuilding.com; 910 S Los Angeles St), **Cooper Design Space** (cooperdesignspace.com; 860 S Los Angeles St) and the **New Mart** (Map p70; www. newmart.net/samplesales.htm; 127 E 9th St). They each specialize in contemporary and young fashions – though the Cooper and the Gerry are considered the hippest of the bunch. The **California Market Center** (California Mart; Map p70; www.california marketcenter.com; 110 E 9th St) has a great fashion bookstore on the ground floor and houses both clothing and home-furnishing wholesalers. Open from 9am to 3pm, this is the only time the general public is allowed in these trade-only buildings. Come early and leave your modesty at home, as you'll either be trying things on in front of others or not at all. During Christmas season there are often several sales each week. Check the websites for dates and participating showrooms.

into fashion retail, this shop pairs the styles of up-and-coming local designers with funky art installations. The twice-annual Cheap Monday pop-up store located on the ground floor is always popular.

Last Bookstore in Los Angeles BOOKSTORE (Map p70; www.lastbookstorela.com; 400 S Main St) It's actually one of the newest bookstores in LA, stocked with nothing but used books. There's feminist lit, Beat poetry, pop-star biographies, obscure pulp fiction and a few marbled leather classics.

HOLLYWOOD

America loves a comeback, and old Hollywood's was long overdue. For decades the neighborhood had been riding on the coattails of its Golden Age, its very name synonymous with the entire movie industry. Never mind that the studios had fled long ago for Burbank and Studio City and that the only 'stars' left were embedded in the sidewalk. Worse, you had to hopscotch around runaways and druggies to see them. No more.

Big, intelligent dollars, along with a touch of smart design have flooded the area, in the form of shiny new clubs, trendy restaurants and luxe boutiques, supplanting the tacky souvenir shops, tattoo parlors and stripper-supply stores of old. Sure, there's a faux Vegas-type glitz here, but there's life on these streets. Even celebs are back. They're attending premieres at Grauman's Chinese Theater and the Oscars at the Kodak Theater, and being interviewed by Jimmy Kimmel at his theater on Hollywood Blvd. And they're carousing at the clubs on Cahuenga, catching just-blooming bands at the Music Box, and sneaking into hole-in-the-wall Thai joints in Thai Town – a 12-block stretch of Hollywood and Sunset Blvds.

If you're relying on public transport, central Hollywood is a convenient base. The Metro Red Line whisks you to Los Feliz, Downtown and Universal Studios in minutes, and DASH buses provide easy links east along Hollywood Blvd and west to the Sunset Strip and Melrose Ave. Parking at Hollywood & Highland costs just $2 for four hours with validation from any merchant or the Hollywood visitors center (p204).

◎ Sights

TOP CHOICE **Hollywood Bowl** LANDMARK VENUE
(www.hollywoodbowl.com; 2301 Highland Ave; ⊙Apr-Sep; ℗) Summers in LA just wouldn't be the same without this chill spot for symphonies under the stars, and big-name acts from Baaba Maal to Sigur Ros to Radiohead to Paul McCartney. A huge natural amphitheater, the Hollywood Bowl has been around since 1922 and has great sound thanks to a new concert shell. Big projection screens give even the folks in the 'nosebleed' sections (tickets $1 to $14) close-ups of the performers. Come early to claim a table in the parklike grounds for a pre-show picnic (alcohol permitted). There are several concessions if you don't want to lug your own grub.

The bowl is the summer home of the LA Philharmonic and the Hollywood Bowl Orchestra. Sneak into free **rehearsals** usually held from 9am to noon on Tuesday, Wednesday and Friday during the season.

Parking is free during the day, but expensive and limited on performance nights. Save yourself the headache and take a shuttle, such as the one running from Hollywood & Highland, which costs $5 to $8 per person round-trip.

FREE **Hollywood Bowl Museum** MUSEUM
(www.hollywoodbowl.com/event/museum. cfm; admission free; ⊙10am-showtime Mon-Sat & 4pm-showtime Sun Jun-Sep, 10am-5pm Tue-Fri Oct-May) It's all about the vibes here. The Soundscape on the bottom floor allows you to sing into a Spectrogram and watch a moving image of your voice, then manipulate sound waves with Visible Effects of the Invisible. The 2nd-floor gallery lets you relive classic bowl moments with still, audio and video footage of the Beatles, the Stones and Jimi Hendrix.

Hollywood Sign LANDMARK

LA's most famous landmark first appeared in the hills in 1923 as an advertising gimmick for a real-estate development called 'Hollywoodland'. Each letter is 50ft tall and made of sheet metal. Once aglow with 4000 light bulbs, the sign even had its own caretaker who lived behind the 'L' until 1939. In 1932 a struggling young actress named Peggy Entwistle leapt her way into local lore from the letter 'H'.

The last four letters were lopped off in the '40s as the sign started to crumble along with the rest of Hollywood. In the late '70s Alice Cooper and Hugh Hefner joined forces with fans to save the famous symbol, and Hef was back at it again in 2010 when the hills behind the sign became slated for a housing development. The octogenarian Playboy donated the last $900,000 of the necessary $12.5 million it took to buy and preserve the land in perpetuity.

Technically, it's illegal to hike up to the sign, but the good viewing spots are plentiful, including Hollywood & Highland, the top of Beachwood Dr and the Griffith Observatory.

Hollywood Walk of Fame LANDMARK

(Map p86; www.hollywoodchamber.net) Big Bird, Bob Hope, Marilyn Monroe and Sting are among the stars being sought out, worshipped, photographed and stepped on day after day along the Hollywood Walk of Fame. Since 1960 more than 2400 performers – from legends to long-forgotten, bit-part players – have been honored with a pink-marble sidewalk star. Follow the Hollywood Blvd galaxy between La Brea Ave and Gower St, and along Vine St between Yucca St and Sunset Blvd. Check the website for upcoming ceremonies, usually held once or twice monthly.

Hollywood

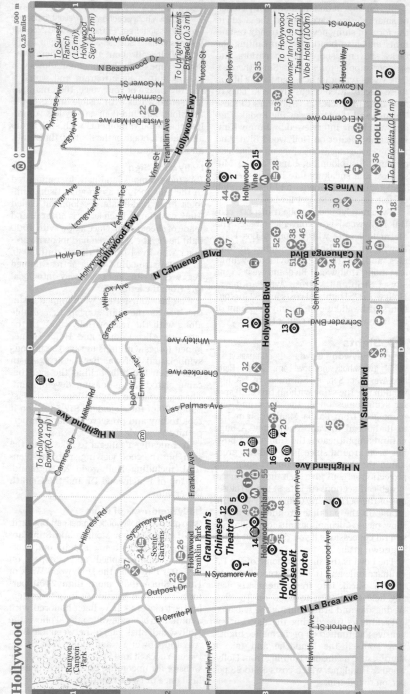

FREE **Grauman's Chinese Theatre**

LANDMARK

(Map p86; www.manntheatres.com; 6925 Holly-wood Blvd) Ever wondered what it's like to be in George Clooney's shoes? Just find his footprints in the forecourt of this world-famous movie palace. The exotic pagoda theater – complete with temple bells and stone heaven dogs from China – has shown movies since 1927 when Cecil B DeMille's *The King of Kings* first flickered across the screen; it's still a studio favorite for star-studded premieres. To see the inside, buy a movie ticket or join a half-hour guided **tour** (adult/child/senior $12.50/8.50/10.50) offered throughout the day. Check in at the gift shop.

Most Tinseltown tourists are just content to find out how big Arnold's feet really are or to search for Jimmy Durante's nose, Betty Grable's legs or Whoopi Goldberg's braids. Douglas Fairbanks, Mary Pickford (who co-owned the theater with Grauman) and Norma Talmadge started the tradition back in 1927 and box-office superstars still get the nod today. Recent honorees have included Matt Damon, Brad Pitt and Daniel

MOVIES UNDER THE STARS

Angelenos love their movies and their fine weather, so it's only logical to combine the two. Screenings under the stars are a popular summer tradition with classic and contemporary flicks spooling off in various locations around town. Come early to stake out a good spot and bring pillows, blankets and snacks.

Cinespia (www.cemeteryscreenings.com; ☉Sat May-Oct; P) has a 'to-die-for' location at Hollywood Forever Cemetery, *the* place of perpetual slumber for a galaxy of old-time movie stars. Classics by Milos Forman, Robert Altman and Alfred Hitchcock are projected onto a mausoleum wall around 9pm, but the hipster crowd starts lining up long before gates open at 7:30pm for picnics and cocktails (yes, alcohol is allowed!) while a DJ spins smooth soundtracks.

If that's too morbid for you, catch the Pacific sea breeze while camping out on the Santa Monica Pier where the **Santa Monica Drive-In at the Pier** (Map p152; www.santamonicapier.org; admission free) presents populist faves every Tuesday in September. Tickets are free but must be picked up at the Santa Monica Visitors Center (p205).

If a day at Universal Studios hasn't left you exhausted, stick around for the **Big Free Outdoor Movie** (www.citywalkhollywood.com; Universal CityWalk; admission free; ☉Thu Jul & Aug).

A more low-key event is **Outdoor Movie Nights** (www.sppreservation.org; 913 Meridian Ave; admission free; ☉dusk Sat Jul & Aug) in South Pasadena, where family-oriented flicks such as *Babe* and *The Wizard of Oz* are beamed onto a tarp hanging from the 1888 Meridian Iron Works. It's close to the Metro Gold Line's Mission St station.

Radcliffe. See www.hollywoodchamber.net for who's up next.

FREE Hollywood Roosevelt Hotel
LANDMARK

(Map p86; www.hollywoodroosevelt.com; 7000 Hollywood Blvd; ☉24hr) Great architecture, rich history and delicious gossip rendezvous at this venerable hotel, where the first Academy Awards ceremony was held in 1929. Following a complete makeover, it briefly became the poolside Hollywood hot spot as tabloid regulars were frequently spotted misbehaving at the velvet-rope Tropicana Bar. Back in her day, glamazon Marilyn Monroe shot her first print ad (for suntan lotion) posing on the diving board of said pool, the bottom of which was later decorated with squiggles by artist David Hockney. And while we're name-dropping: actor Montgomery Clift, who stayed in room 928 while filming *From Here to Eternity,* apparently never checked out; his ghost can still be heard playing the bugle. The Roosevelt itself has made movie appearances aplenty, including in *Catch Me If You Can* and *Charlie's Angels*. See also p92.

El Capitan Theatre
LANDMARK

(Map p86; www.disney.go.com/disneypictures/el_capitan; 6838 Hollywood Blvd) Spanish Colonial meets East Indian at the flamboyant El Capitan movie palace built for live performances in 1926 and now run by Disney. The first flick to show here was *Citizen Kane* in 1941 and it's still a fine place to catch a movie, which is often accompanied by a live show. Before or after, peruse the museum-style exhibits in the lobby related to the current release. Kids love the colorful Disney Soda Fountain downstairs. See also p97.

Egyptian Theatre
LANDMARK

(Map p86; www.egyptiantheatre.com; 6712 Hollywood Blvd; tours $5) The Egyptian, the first of the grand movie palaces on Hollywood Blvd, premiered *Robin Hood* in 1922. The theater's lavish getup – complete with sunburst ceiling, hieroglyphs and sphinx heads – capitalized on the craze for all things Egyptian sparked by the discoveries of archaeologist Howard Carter. (Contrary to popular belief, though, the Egyptian actually opened *before* Carter stumbled upon King Tut's tomb). In its heyday, it had live caged monkeys and usherettes dressed like Cleopatra.

The Egyptian got a royal makeover in the late 1990s and became a shrine to serious cinema when the nonprofit American Cinematheque moved in (p97).

Hollywood & Vine
LANDMARK

(Map p86) If you turned on the radio in the 1920s and '30s, chances were you'd hear a broadcast 'brought to you from Hollywood and Vine'. Before long, though, the fabled intersection went from fab to desperate. But thanks to a recent mega-development splurge in its southeastern corner featuring stores, lofts, a W hotel and a Metro stop, and occasional block parties sponsored by the W hotel and Jimmy Kimmel Live, this revitalized corner deserves to take a bow once more.

FREE Pantages Theater
LANDMARK

(Map p86; www.pantages-theater.com; 6233 Hollywood Blvd) The splendidly restored Pantages Theater is an art-deco survivor from the Golden Age and a fabulous place to catch a play or Broadway musical. Oscars were handed out here between 1949 and 1959 while Howard Hughes owned the building. The uber-noir Frolic Room bar next door was featured in *LA Confidential*.

FREE Capitol Records Tower
LANDMARK

(Map p86; 1750 N Vine St) You'll quickly recognize this iconic 1956 tower, one of LA's great modern-era buildings. Designed by Welton Becket, it resembles a stack of records topped by a stylus blinking out 'Hollywood' in Morse code. Garth Brooks and John Lennon have their stars outside.

Hollywood Museum
MUSEUM

(Map p86; www.thehollywoodmuseum.com; 1660 N Highland Ave; adult/student & senior $15/12; ☉10am-5pm Wed-Sun) Museums on Hollywood Blvd generally fall into the tourist-trap category, but we quite like this slightly musty and convoluted temple to the stars, crammed with kitsch posters, costumes and rotating props. Hannibal Lecter's original jail cell is in the basement and can even be rented for private parties. In fact, LAPD chief William Bratton has held two dinner parties there. Oh yes, but what did he serve?

The museum is housed inside the handsome 1914 art-deco Max Factor Building, where the make-up pioneer once worked his magic on Marilyn Monroe and Judy Garland. The make-up rooms, complete with custom lighting to complement the ladies' complexion and hair color, are still located on the ground floor, along with a wall of Factor's most glamorous clients and the 1965 Silver Cloud Rolls Royce once owned by Cary Grant.

Hollywood Heritage Museum
MUSEUM

(Map p86; www.hollywoodheritage.org; 2100 N Highland Ave; adult/senior/child under 12 $7/5/free; ☉noon-4pm Wed-Sun) Hollywood's first feature-length film, Cecil B DeMille's *The Squaw Man,* was shot in this building in 1913–14, originally set at the corner of Selma and Vine Sts. DeMille went on to cofound Paramount and had the barn moved to the lot in the '20s. Now the Hollywood Heritage Museum, it's filled with a great collection of costumes, projectors and cameras from the early days of moviemaking.

FREE Hollywood Forever Cemetery
CEMETERY

(www.hollywoodforever.com; 6000 Santa Monica Blvd; ☉8am-6pm; P) Next to Paramount, Hollywood Forever Cemetery boasts lavish landscaping, over-the-top tombstones, epic mausoleums and a roll call of dearly departed superstars. Residents include Cecil B DeMille, Rudolph Valentino, femme fatale Jayne Mansfield and punk-rock icons Johnny and Dee Dee Ramone. For a full list of residents, pick up a map ($5) at the flower shop (9am to 5pm).

But these hallowed grounds are anything but dead. Summer brings outdoor movie screenings (p88) and Shakespeare in the Cemetery (www.shakespeareinthecemetery.com), while in November the gates open for Día de los Muertos (Day of the Dead).

Kodak Theatre
THEATER

(Map p86; www.kodaktheatre.com; 6801 Hollywood Blvd; tours adult/child, senior & student $15/10; ☉10:30am-4pm) The Academy Awards are handed out at the Kodak Theatre, which also hosts other big events such as the *American Idol* finals, the Daytime Emmys, the ESPY awards and the Miss USA pageant. On the tour you get to sniff around the auditorium, admire a VIP room and see Oscar up close. Obtaining online discount coupons will help take some sting out of the rather steep admission price.

FREE Hollywood & Highland
MALL

(Map p86; www.hollywoodandhighland.com; 6801 Hollywood Blvd; ☉10am-10pm Mon-Sat, to 7pm Sun) It's apropos that a Disney-fied shopping mall would be the spark for Hollywood Blvd's rebirth. A perfect marriage of kitsch and commerce, the main showpiece is a triumphal arch inspired by DW Griffith's 1916 movie *Intolerance*. Guarded by giant elephants, it frames the Hollywood sign nicely.

Sunset Gower & Sunset Bronson Studios
LANDMARK

(Map p86; www.sgsandsbs.com; Sunset Blvd & Gower Ave, Sunset Blvd & Bronson Ave) Two intersections with a ton of cinematic history. When Nestor Film Company moved to the corner of Sunset and Gower in 1911 it became the Sunset Gower Studios, which eventually birthed Columbia Pictures when the Cohn brothers took it over and hired Frank Capra as their star auteur. Sunset Bronson became a studio when Jack Warner bought an old farm and converted it into his dream location. In fact, it was here after Warner and Zanuck's 1924 success with *Rin Tin Tin*, shot on the lot, that the Warner Brothers franchise was born. Both studios thrived in the 'Golden Age' of cinema then languished as their parent companies moved off the lots. Gene Autry bought Sunset Bronson in 1964 and turned it into indie production space. Sunset Gower languished and became rock rehearsal spaces for guys like Frank Zappa and John Lennon, as well as indoor tennis courts. These days, the two studios are fused and once again offering stage and office space to big-game productions.

Ripley's Believe It or Not!
NOVELTY MUSEUM

(Map p86; www.ripleys.com; 6780 Hollywood Blvd; adult/child $15/9; ⊙10am-midnight) Life's pretty strange and it'll feel stranger still after you've visited Ripley's, where exhibits range from the gross to the grotesque. If shrunken heads, a sculpture of Marilyn Monroe made from shredded $1 bills and a human-hair bikini capture your imagination, this is your place.

Guinness World of Records Museum
MUSEUM

(Map p86; www.guinnessattractions.com; 6764 Hollywood Blvd; adult/child/senior $16/9/14; ⊙10am-midnight; 🏃) You know the drill: the Guinness is all about the fastest, tallest, biggest, fattest and other superlatives.

Hollywood Wax Museum
MUSEUM

(Map p86; www.hollywoodwax.com; 6767 Hollywood Blvd; adult/child/senior $16/9/14; ⊙10am-

---

YOUR 15 MINUTES OF FAME

Come on, haven't you always dreamed of seeing your silly mug on TV or in the movies? Well, LA has a way of making dreams come true, but you have to do your homework before coming to town. Here are some leads to get you started.

Be in a Studio Audience

Sitcoms and game shows usually tape between August and March before live audiences. To nab free tickets, check with **TV Tickets** (www.tvtix.com) or **Audiences Unlimited** (www.tvtickets.com). **CBS** (☎323-575-2624; www.cbs.com; 7800 Beverly Blvd; ⊙9am-5pm Mon-Fri) handles its own ticketing; the office is off Fairfax past the open green gate. For tickets to the *Tonight Show* at **NBC** (www.nbc.com/the-tonight-show; 3000 W Alameda Ave, Burbank), send a request via its website six weeks in advance. Tickets to *Jimmy Kimmel Live*, which conveniently tapes at the **El Capitan Theater** (Map p86; www.1iota.com; 6840 Hollywood Blvd), are available via its website. If you don't have tickets, you may still be able to sneak in just before the 6pm taping. Just ask one of the ushers outside the theater (if they don't ask you first!). Most shows have a minimum age of 18.

Become an Extra

If you'd like to see yourself on screen, check with **Be In a Movie** (www.beinamovie.com) on how to become an extra in a big crowd scene at major film shoots. Most recently the company's supplied the masses for the Steven Soderbergh–directed film *Moneyball*, starring Brad Pitt, Jonah Hill and Philip Seymour Hoffman. There's no money in it, but the behind-the-scenes experience and chance of seeing a big star live and in person should make you a hit back home at the office water cooler.

Become a Game Show Contestant

Jeopardy and *Wheel of Fortune* are among the game shows that tape in LA, but the chances of actually becoming a contestant are greatest on *The Price is Right,* hosted by Drew Carey and taped at CBS. Check www.cbs.com/daytime/price for details.

What to See

If you found David Lynch's 2001 movie *Mulholland Drive* a tad bizarre, perhaps a drive along the road itself will clear things up. The legendary road winds and dips for 24 miles through the **Santa Monica Mountains**, skirting the mansions of the rich and famous (Jack Nicholson's is at No 12850, Warren Beatty's at No 13671) and delivering iconic views of Downtown, Hollywood and the San Fernando Valley at each bend. Named for its creator, California aqueduct engineer William Mulholland, it's especially pretty just before sunset (go west to east, though, to avoid driving into the setting sun) and on clear winter days when the panorama opens up from the snowcapped **San Gabriel Mountains** to the shimmering Pacific Ocean.

At the very least, drive up to the **Hollywood Bowl Overlook** for classic views of the Hollywood sign and the beehive-shaped bowl below. Other pullouts offer hiking-trail access, for instance to **Runyon Canyon** (p116) and **Fryman Canyon**. Note that pulling over after sunset is verboten and may result in a traffic ticket.

Time & Route

Driving the entire route takes about an hour, but even a shorter spin is worth it. Mulholland Dr runs from the US-101 Fwy (Hollywood Fwy; take the Cahuenga exit, then follow signs) to about 2 miles west of the I-405 (San Diego Fwy). About 8 miles of dirt road, closed to vehicles but not to hikers and cyclists, links it with Mulholland Hwy, which continues a serpentine route through the mountains for another 23 miles as far as Leo Carrillo State Beach.

midnight Sun-Thu, to 1am Fri & Sat; 👪) Starved for celeb sightings? Don't fret: at this museum Angelina Jolie, Halle Berry and other red-carpet royalty will stand still – very still – for your camera. This retro haven of kitsch and camp has been around for over 40 years. There are lots of new monsters in the horror exhibit, and Matrix stars in the sci-fi room. Combo tickets with the Guinness World of Records Museum cost $18/11/16 per adult/child/senior.

Madame Tussaud's   MUSEUM
(Map p86; www.madametussauds.com; 6933 Hollywood Blvd; adult/child/senior $25/18/20; ☉10am-10pm; 👪) A rich woman's wax museum. It's newer and a touch more glamorous than the old stalwart, but they've got a similar story. Here you can find motionless movie stars (Salma Hayek, Samuel L Jackson, Messrs Depp and Washington), icons (Clark Gable, Audrey Hepburn etc), movie characters like Hugh's Wolverine from *X-Men*, legendary pop stars and all-time great directors too.

FREE **Jim Henson Studios**   STUDIO
(Map p86; www.henson.com; 1416 N La Brea Ave) If you have a soft spot for muppets, the tramp or general Hollywood history, you'll want to pay your respects to this Tudor compound that was built by Charlie Chaplin in 1917 (he filmed the classics *Gold Rush* and *The Great Dictator* here) and later became the creative stomping ground of the late great Jim Henson.

Janes House   LANDMARK
(Map p86; 6541 Hollywood Blvd) The last remaining Victorian home on Hollywood Blvd, built in 1903, and the former site of Miss Janes' School, which was attended by the children of old Hollywood icons Cecil B De Mille, Douglas Fairbanks and Charlie Chaplin. Now? Um, it's a down-market mini-mall occupied by a Thai massage joint and a taqueria.

🏃 Activities

Golden Bridge Yoga   YOGA
(Map p86; www.la.goldenbridgeyoga.com; 6322 De Longpre Ave; per person per class $16; P) Gurmukh, a longtime Kundalini yogi to the stars, was an early student of Yogi Bhajan's (p147). She built her Golden Bridge brand on the strength of her unparalleled prenatal yoga classes based on Bhajan's teachings. Her Hollywood center offers 100 classes a week, workshops, a cafe and wellness center. When in town, the strong, wise and joyful guru teaches three times weekly.

Sunset Ranch Hollywood
OUTDOORS

(Map p86; ☎323-469-5450; www.sunsetranch hollywood.com; 3400 Beachwood Dr; 1/2hr rides $25/40; P⚙) Rides through Griffith Park, plus famous Sunset Rides ($60), and Dinner Rides (per person $75 to $105) to a Mexican restaurant in Burbank. Advanced reservations are highly recommended. Families will appreciate its '2 for 1 Tuesdays.' Download the coupon from its website. Lessons (Western or English riding) start at $85 per hour.

Musicians Institute
MUSIC

(Map p86; www.mi.edu; 6752 Hollywood Blvd; P) Crave music lessons? Need recording chops or industry knowhow? Then join the young international droves at this urban temple to all things rock. Its six-day summer seminars are popular. Apply online.

Lucky Strike
BOWLING

(Map p86; www.bowlluckystrike.com; 6801 Hollywood Blvd; ☺3pm-midnight Mon-Wed, noon-2am Thu & Fri, 11am-2am Sat & Sun; P) These 12 lanes are as stylish as bowling gets. There's a DJ booth, projection screens, bottle service and leather seating.

🛏 Sleeping

TOP CHOICE Elaine's Hollywood B&B
BED & BREAKFAST $

(☎323-850-0766; www.elaineshollywoodbedandbreakfast.com; 1616 N Sierra Bonita Ave; r $90-145; 🛜) This B&B offers four rooms in a lovingly restored 1910 bungalow on a quiet street. Your outgoing hosts Avik, a longtime Hollywood foreign-press reporter (he has pictures with luminaries past and present), and Elaine speak several languages, make a mean breakfast and will happily help you plan your day. Cash only.

Hollywood Roosevelt Hotel
HISTORIC HOTEL $$

(Map p86; ☎323-466-7000, 800-950-7667; www.hollywoodroosevelt.com; 7000 Hollywood Blvd; r $125-171; P@🛜🏊) It's no longer the place to be for weekly poolside parties, but it still gets plenty of action. The cabanas are the way to go if you're looking for a splurge, or just grab a room in the tower and relax into one of the daybeds in the sun. Also see p88. Parking is $30.

W Hollywood
HOTEL $$$

(Map p86; ☎323-798-1300; www.starwoodhotels.com; 6250 Hollywood Blvd; r $379-619; P@🛜) Rooms live up to the hype generated by your red-carpet arrival. Cool Corner Suites have circular white leather sofas, and triangular glass bedrooms. The more basic Marvelous Suites are just big hotel rooms with a sexy lace curtain separating the bed from the sofa. No matter the category, marble bathrooms are huge with rain showers and soaker tubs. Bands like Groove Armada and Depeche Mode perform at the hotel's monthly Happenings, and the lobby buzzes with Hollywood movers and fakers.

Highland Gardens Hotel
HOTEL $$

(Map p86; ☎323-850-0536; www.highlandgardenshotel.com; 7047 Franklin Ave; r $99-360; P@🏊🐾🛜) This '50s residential-style motel is retro without even trying, but the lobby is more glamorous than the rooms. Have a look before checking in. The sweetest room, pimped out by Antonio Ballatore for HGTV, has black-wood floors, a black-granite kitchen and a looming pink rhino. Brad Pitt stayed here when he first arrived in Hollywood and wore a chicken suit for nearby El Pollo Loco. Janis Joplin overdosed in room 105.

Hollywood Hills Hotel & Apartments
HOTEL $$

(Map p86; ☎323-874-5089, 323-8510800; www.hollywoodhillshotel.com; 7025 Franklin Ave; r $134-159; P🏊) Breathtaking city views, a curvy pool guarded by a pagoda, and roomy digs with balcony and kitchen are among the assets at this older but well-kept property. Check in at the Magic Castle Hotel (p93). Parking costs $10. No children allowed.

Vibe Hotel
MOTEL $

(☎323-469-8600; www.vibehotel.com; 5920 Hollywood Blvd; r $69-99; P@🛜) A funky motel with a hostel-like vibe. No dorms here, however, only private rooms with mod furnishings. There's no communal kitchen, but there is a garage TV lounge, a young, happening international crowd, and a tiled tiki garden splashed with afternoon sun.

Hollywood Historic Hotel
HOTEL $

(☎323-378-6312; www.hollywoodhistorichotel.com; 5162 Melrose Ave; r $49-79; P@🛜) One of the best-value budget offerings in the city, this recently restored brick relic from 1927, with ornate moldings inside and out, is located in the real, gritty Hollywood. Rooms are decent sized, have fresh paint and wood furnishings. It's secure, well lit and very well run, but you'll need a car to stay here.

USA Hostels Hollywood
HOSTEL $

(Map p86; ☎323-462-3777; www.usahostels.com; 1624 Schrader Blvd; r $30-40; P@🛜) This sociable hostel puts you within steps of the Hollywood party circuit. Private rooms are a bit cramped, but making new friends is easy during staff-organized barbecues, comedy nights and $25 all-you-can-drink limo tours. Freebies include a cook-your-own-pancake breakfast.

Best Western Hollywood Hills Hotel
MOTEL **$$**

(Map p86; ☑323-464-5181; www.bestwestern california.com; 6141 Franklin Ave; r $140-180; P@🅟🛜❄) Not all rooms are created equal at this family-run hotel with colorful retro touches. For more space and quiet get one in back facing the sparkling pool. Self-caterers will welcome the refrigerator and microwave, although the on-site coffee shop serves some pretty good comfort food and is open late; service, though, can be glacial.

Hollywood Downtowner Inn
MOTEL **$**

(☑323-464-7191; www.hollywooddowntowner.com; 5601 Hollywood Blvd; r $89-109; P@🅟🛜❄) You'll dig the bougainvillea on the railings, that historic neon sign and the forever groovy Shayla at reception. Rooms are spacious and spotless with exposed-brick walls, sponged walls and high ceilings; some have a kitchenette. Built in the late 1950s, this is the last standing Melrose-style building in Hollywood.

Magic Castle Hotel
HOTEL **$$**

(Map p86; ☑323-851-0800; www.magiccastlehotel. com; 7025 Franklin Ave; r $154-304; P🛜❄🅟) Walls at this perennial pleaser are a bit thin, but otherwise it's a charming base of operation with large, modern rooms, exceptional staff and a petite courtyard pool where days start with fresh pastries and gourmet coffee. Enquire about access to the Magic Castle, a fabled members-only magic club in an adjacent Victorian mansion. Parking costs $10.

✕ Eating

TOP CHOICE **Sushi Ike** JAPANESE **$$**
(Map p86; ☑323-462-9421; 6051 Hollywood Blvd; appetizers $8-14, mains $16-20; ⏲11:30am-11pm Mon-Fri, noon-11pm Sat; 🅟) Sweet and tender scallops are sprinkled with sea salt and squeezed with lemon. The broiled octopus is get-outta-here good, the sashimi comes in thick slabs and always melts in your mouth, the stuffed shitake mushrooms and broiled yellowtail collar are fabulous. Ignore the mini-mall ambience. This fish rocks!

Found a fantastic restaurant that you're longing to share with the world? Disagree with our recommendations? Or just want talk about your most recent trip?

Whatever your reason, head to lonelyplanet.com, where you can post a review, ask or answer a question on the Thorntree forum, comment on a blog, or share your photos and tips on Groups. Or you can simply spend time chatting with like-minded travelers. So go on, have your say.

Mozza
ITALIAN **$$$**

(☑323-297-0100; www.mozza-la.com; 6602 Melrose Ave; appetizers $10-18, mains $17-58; ⏲dinner; 🅟) Osteria Mozza is all about fine dining crafted from market fresh, seasonal ingredients, but being a Mario Batali joint you can expect adventure (think: squid-ink *chitarra freddi* with Dungeness crab, sea urchin and jalapeno) and consistent excellence. Reservations are a must. **Pizzeria Mozza** (☑323-297-0101; www.mozza-la. com; 641 N Highland Ave; ⏲lunch & dinner; 🅟) next door is (much) more laid-back and less expensive, but just as creative. Thin-crust pies come with squash blossoms and mozzarella, eggs and bacon, and stinging nettles and salami.

Providence
NEW AMERICAN **$$$**

(☑323-460-4170; www.providencela.com; 5955 Melrose Ave; appetizers $6-26, mains $40-49; ⏲lunch Fri, dinner daily; 🅟) This sublime dining room with two Michelin stars has long been one of LA's finest. Michael Cimarusti's gourmet creations include foie-gras ravioli with truffles, and spaghetti with *uni* (sea urchin) and English peas. To truly sample the master's talents, splurge for the nine-course tasting menu.

Loteria
MEXICAN **$$**

(Map p86; www.loteriagrill.com; 6627 Hollywood Blvd; tacos $3-9, appetizers $6-12; ⏲breakfast, lunch & dinner; 🅟) The new venture from a long-running, widely loved Farmers Market taco stand of the same name. The menus are quite similar. You can get your cactus tacos, mole burritos and a killer tortilla soup. The big difference is the elegant ambience, and that huge L-shaped bar serving over 80 premium tequilas.

Mercantile
MARKET CAFE **$$**

(Map p86; www.themercantilela.com; 6600 Sunset Blvd; appetizers $7.50-$10.50, mains $13-25; ☺lunch & dinner; **P**) A fun, brick-walled, concrete-floored loft outfitted with a cheese case, a wine bar, shelves of gourmet oils, mustards, jams and more. It also whips up smoked-trout crostinis, foie-gras terrines, Cuban sandwiches and plate lunches.

District
NEW AMERICAN **$$**

(Map p86; ☎323-962-8200; www.districtonsunset.com; 6600 Sunset Blvd; appetizers $3-14, mains $22-25; ☺dinner; **P**) A sleek room marrying gin-soaked yesteryear cocktails served at that magnificent 100-year-old bar, with the progressive present of market-fresh local food. Small plates include shrimp and grits, and rabbit *crepinette*, while mains range from Columbia River salmon to pork belly with an apricot *mostarda*.

Tender Greens
ORGANIC **$**

(Map p86; www.tendergreensfood.com; 6290 Sunset Blvd; dishes $10.50; ☺lunch & dinner; **P**) The concept is a great one. Choose a grilled meat (like herb-brushed seared albacore), and get it on a hot plate with a side salad and mashed potatoes, order it as a sandwich or rest it on a large bowl of salad freckled with golden beets, sprouts and *tatsoi*. Nourishing meals and good vibes aplenty.

🍃 Life Food Organic
RAW **$**

(Map p86; www.lifefoodorganic.com; 1507 N Cahuenga Ave; dishes $5-13; ☺breakfast, lunch & dinner) With recipes gleaned from the wild-souled, raw-powered Dr David Jubbs, this place serves the healthiest fast-food around. Have a chocolate shake made with almond milk, a veggie chili burger with a sesame seaweed salad on the side, and a chocolate cream pie for dessert. You can dine in, but most take it away.

Cheebo
CALIFORNIAN **$$**

(☎323-850-7070; www.cheebo.com; 7533 W Sunset Blvd; salads & pizzas $10-16, sandwiches $12-14; ☺breakfast, lunch & dinner; **P**☎🖶) This funky all-natural, California-chic cafe makes heaping salads, bulging sandwiches and organic pizzas. Kids love the free paper and crayons and special menu in the afternoons. The name, by the way, is a play on the Italian word for food, spelled *cibo*.

Hollywood Farmers Market
MARKET **$**

(Map p86; www.farmernet.com; cnr Ivar & Selma Ave; ☺8am-1pm Sun; 🖶) On the shortlist for the city's best farmers market. This Sunday-morning culinary sprawl unfurls with organic and specialty produce from over 90 farmers, as well as 30 vendors selling tasty prepared food, from smoothies to tamales to crepes to grilled sausages. It's a great event for the family.

Yamashiro Farmers Market
MARKET

(Map p86; www.yamashirorestaurant.com; 1999 N Sycamore Ave; ☺5-9pm Thu; **P**) The best farmers market views in LA are yours from Yamashiro's spectacular perch. In addition to organic produce, expect miso cod tacos, grilled bratwurst, Bulgarian gelato and live music. There's a wine-tasting bar where $8 will allow you to have a full glass of one or a taste of four solid small-batch wines.

Ganda
THAI **$**

(Map p86; 4281 Hollywood Blvd; dishes $6-8; ☺lunch & dinner; **P**) Get a whiff of real Thai street food. Its pick-and-mix steam table has the same selection of stewed, fried and broiled seafood, chicken and veggie dishes as you'd find in any Bangkok night market. It stays open until 2am during the week and 3am on weekends.

Soi 56
THAI **$$**

(Map p86; 1556 N Cahuenga Ave; dishes $3.50-18; ☺lunch & dinner; **P**) Tucked into a gastro mini-mall of sorts, this polished-concrete-floor and raw-wood-paneled dining room serves Thai dishes straight off the *soi* (side street). It serves noodles coated in curry paste with pickled mustard greens and chicken on the bone, barbecued pork noodles and oxtail soup.

Hungry Cat
SEAFOOD **$$**

(Map p86; www.thehungrycat.com; 1535 Vine St; mains $10-27; ☺lunch & dinner; **P**) This kitty is small and sleek and hides out across Sunset from the ArcLight cinemas, making it a handy pre- or postshow stop. It fancies fresh seafood and will have you salivating for hunky lobster roll, portly crab cakes and savory fish-*du-jour* specials. The Pug Burger – slathered with avocado, bacon and blue cheese – is a worthy meaty alternative.

Jitlada
THAI **$$**

(www.jitlada.localthaifood.com; 5233 1/2 Hollywood Blvd; appetizers $5-10, mains $7-10; ☺lunch & dinner; **P**) A transporting taste of southern Thailand. Its wok-fried catfish and *som tum* (spicy papaya salad) are fantastic. It counts

Matt Groenig, Drew Barrymore and Natalie Portman among its loyal, mostly *farang* (European American) customers.

Street
FUSION $$

(☑323-203-0500; www.eatatstreet.com; 742 N Highland Ave; dishes $25; ⊙lunch & dinner; ℗) From Singapore's *kata* toast (a tea cake made from toasted bread, coconut jam and a soft fried egg) to spinach dumplings from the Ukraine to lamb kafta meatballs from Syria, this new hot spot offers global street food in upmarket environs.

🍷 Drinking

La Descarga
LOUNGE

(☑323-466-1324; www.ladescargala.com; 1159 N Western Ave; ⊙8pm-2am Wed-Sat) This tastefully frayed, sublimely sweaty rum and cigar lounge is a revelation. Behind the marble bar are over 100 types of rum from Haiti and Guyana, Guatemala and Venezuela. The bartenders mix and muddle specialty cocktails, but you'd do well to order something aged, and sip it neat as you enjoy the mambo and son sounds bouncing off the walls, and the burlesque ballerina on the catwalk. Reservations are mandatory.

Musso & Frank Grill
RESTAURANT

(Map p86; www.mussoarankgrill.com; 6667 Hollywood Blvd) Hollywood history hangs in the thick air at Musso & Frank Grill, Tinseltown's oldest eatery (since 1919). Charlie Chaplin used to knock back vodka gimlets at the bar and Raymond Chandler penned scripts in the high-backed booths. Star-sightings are still possible today; Mick Jagger and Woody Allen are among the fans of the noir ambience, gentlemen bartenders, and stiff martinis expertly crafted and served in small stems.

Cat & Fiddle
PUB

(Map p86; www.thecatandfiddle.com; 6530 Sunset Blvd; ⊙11:30am-2am; ℗) Morrissey to Frodo, you never know who might be popping by for Boddingtons or Sunday-night jazz. Fortunately, this Brit pub staple with leafy beer garden is more about friends and conversation than faux-hawks and working the deal.

Well
LOUNGE

(Map p86; www.myspace/thewellhollywood; 1536 Argyle Ave; ⊙5pm-2am; ℗) A consistent winner due to its tasty cocktails, rock 'n' roll soundtrack, dark interior, plush booths and sexy staff (of both genders). Bartenders and servers from across town often spend their downtime here.

TOP FIVE LATE-NIGHT NOSH SPOTS

95

» Tofu House (Korea Town, p198)
» Ganda (Hollywood, p94)
» Two Boots (Echo Park, p106)
» Pete's Café & Bar (Downtown, p81)
» Swingers (Mid-City, p119)

Big Wangs
SPORTS BAR

(Map p86; www.bigwangs.com; 1562 N Cahuenga Ave; ⊙11am-1:30am; ℗) Here is a sports bar for the everyman, with polished-concrete floors, booths, tables, bar stools and a pool table, all within view of a flat screen. It has a late-night happy hour, more than a dozen beers on tap, and specializes in chicken wings, tossed in your choice of six sauces, then deep fried.

Tar Pit
LOUNGE

(www.tarpitbar.com; 609 N La Brea Ave; ⊙5pm-2am; ℗) You'll notice the handiwork of co-owner David Silverman (cocreator of *The Simpsons*), but your attention will soon be drawn to the cocktails, divided into three categories: Champagne, aromatics and sours, concocted with syrups, chartreuse and sugar, lime, ginger and smoked cherries.

Beauty Bar
BAR

(Map p86; www.beautybar.com; 1638 N Cahuenga Blvd; ⊙9pm-2am Sun-Wed, 6pm-2am Thu-Sat) Still beautilicious after all these years, this pint-sized, retro cocktail bar is the place for having your nails painted in lurid pink while catching up on gossip and getting liquefied on martinis ($10, 7pm to 11pm Thursday to Saturday).

⭐ Entertainment

Upright Citizens Brigade
COMEDY

(www.ucbtheatre.com; 5919 Franklin Ave; admission $5-8; ℗) Founded in New York by *SNL* alums Amy Poehler and Ian Roberts along with Matt Besser and Matt Walsh, this sketch-comedy group cloned itself in Hollywood in 2005 and is arguably the best improv theater in town. Most shows are $5 or $8 but Sunday's 'Assssscat' is freeeee.

Music Box
VENUE

(Map p86; www.themusicbox.la; 6126 Hollywood Blvd; ℗) The old Henry Fonda theatre has been restored, and remains one of Hollywood's best venues for live music. It's an

JASON BENTLEY: KCRW DJ & MUSIC DIRECTOR

I started at the station the summer after graduating from Santa Monica High School in the late '80s. I've been here 18 years and never get tired of it. I like to think we counteract that Hollywood superficiality that sometimes characterizes the city. We're the substance just beneath the surface.

Favorite Venues Growing Up in LA

I think every generation has their 'British Invasion', and mine was the club music explosion that happened in 1990–91. Downtown LA wasn't like it is now, and I'd go to these underground warehouse parties and hear incredible electronic music.

Favorite Current Venues

The Hollywood Bowl (p85) is a must-do destination for the summer, and in the winter it's the Disney Concert Hall (p69). I saw Air there recently, and it was an incredible show. I also like the El Rey (p121). It's such a great room and they have consistently good line-ups.

Favorite Event

The Electric Daisy Carnival (p67). LA has been the biggest market for electronic music for at least 10 years, and it's happened without being acknowledged or supported by the mainstream. Events like this show that this scene has thrived on its own terms.

intimate, general-admission space with an open dance floor and balcony seating. It books some of the best progressive rock bands (think: Mumford & Sons and Broken Bells) and hosts electronic dance parties most Saturdays. Prices for admission vary.

Hollywood Palladium   VENUE
(Map p86; www.livenation.com; 6215 W Sunset Blvd; P) This art-deco classic, built in 1940 and christened by the Chairman of the Board (Sinatra), has long been a favorite for its open-floor, general-admission intimacy. It has hosted everyone from Hendrix to James Brown to Madonna to Jay Z. Admission prices vary.

El Floridita   LATIN
(Map p86; 323-871-8612; www.elfloridita.com; 1253 N Vine St; cover $10, with dinner free; Mon, Wed, Fri & Sat) *The* place for grown-up *salseros*. Order a mojito and watch the beautiful dancers do their thing (or join in if you feel you've got the moves). The Monday night jams led by Johnny Polanco y su Orquesta Amistad are legendary; make reservations at least a week in advance.

Bardot   CLUB
(Map p86; www.bardothollywood.com; 1735 N Vine St; Mon-Sat; P) Two bars, two floors, blood-red walls, ornate concrete moldings and more dog paintings than seems reason-

able are tucked behind and above Avalon. Monday Nights means **School Night** (www.itsaschoolnight.com), hosted by KCRW's Chris Douridas – a live music club featuring buzzworthy talent.

ArcLight & Cinerama Dome   CINEMA
(Map p86; www.arclightcinemas.com; 6360 W Sunset Blvd; adult/child/senior from $13.50/11.50/12; P) Assigned seats and exceptional celeb-sighting potential make this 14-screen multiplex the best around. If your taste dovetails with its schedule, the awesome 1963 geodesic Cinerama Dome is a must. Bonuses: age 21-plus screenings where you can booze it up, and Q&As with directors, writers and actors. Parking is $3 for four hours.

Improv Olympic West   COMEDY
(Map p86; http://west.ioimprov.com; 6366 Hollywood Blvd; admission $5-10; 8-11pm; P) Second only to the Upright Citizens Brigade in the frequency and quality of shows. It has at least three daily, starting on the hour. The Armando Show ($5) on Monday nights is hosted by a celebrity guest (someone like, say, Drew Carrey) and hinges on suggestions from the audience.

Hotel Cafe   VENUE
(Map p86; www.hotelcafe.com; 1623-1/2 N Cahuenga Blvd; tickets $10-15; P) An anomaly on glittery Cahuenga Corridor, this intimate

venue is the place for handmade music by message-minded singer-songwriters. Big names like Suzanne Vega show up on occasion but mostly it's a stepping stone for newbie balladeers. Get there early and enter from the alley.

Drai's
CLUB
(Map p86; www.draishollywood.com; 6250 Hollywood Blvd; ⊙10pm-3am Tue-Sat; P) The W rooftop is the domain of this classic Vegas after-hours club. And if you dig hip-hop, enjoy the sweaty pulse of a packed dance floor, love gawking at big nightscape views, and can turn a blind eye to tasteless bling and ubiquitous surgical enhancements, you will be in Shangri La. Wednesday and Friday are the big nights.

Club Ecco
CLUB
(Map p86; www.eccohollywood.com; 1640 N Cahuenga Ave; P) This cozy club merits mention because it has used sustainably forested timber, paperless drywall and non-toxic paint during construction, and utilizes LED lighting and green power. Of course, none of that truly matters if the club isn't any fun. It tackles that problem by rotating local and international DJs of note who keep the party bumping.

Colony
CLUB
(Map p86; www.sbe.com/thecolony; 1743 N Cahuenga Blvd; P) Brand-new, hot, and drawing celebs and scenesters on the regular at the time of writing, its going for a Hampton's in Hollywood angle. The indoor-outdoor flow, shutters and boardwalk do feel beachy, and the clientele is mostly young and usually beautiful.

American Cinematheque
CINEMA
(Map p86; www.americancinematheque.com; 6712 Hollywood Blvd; adult/senior & student $11/9) If nonprofits make you yawn, we promise this one won't. Its tributes, retrospectives and foreign films are well curated and presented in two rescued Golden Age venues: the Egyptian Theatre and the Aero Theatre (Santa Monica). Directors, screenwriters and actors often swing by for post show Q&As. Also see p88.

El Capitan Theatre
CINEMA
(Map p86; www.disney.go.com/disneypictures/el_capitan; 6838 Hollywood Blvd; adult/child & senior from $12/9; ⌖) Disney rolls out family-friendly blockbusters at this movie palace, often with costumed characters putting on the Ritz in live preshow routines. The best

seats are on the balcony in the middle of the front row. VIP tickets ($20) allow you to reserve a seat and include popcorn and a beverage. Also see p88.

Grauman's Chinese Theatre
CINEMA
(Map p86; www.manntheatres.com/chinese; 6925 Hollywood Blvd; adult $11.75-15.75, child & senior $9-12) Nowhere in the world are movie premieres as glitzy as at this industry favorite. Make sure you buy tickets for the glam historic theater, not the ho-hum Mann Chinese 6 multiplex next door. Also see p87.

Hudson Theatres
THEATER
(www.hudsontheatre.com; 6539 Santa Monica Blvd; P) This quartet of stages (plus a cute cafe) is a driving force on Hollywood's Theater Row and has catapulted a number of productions to Broadway, TV and the big screen. Nia Vardalos' *My Big Fat Greek Wedding* had its world premiere right here.

MET Theatre
THEATER
(www.themettheatre.com; 1089 N Oxford Ave; tickets $15; P) Holly Hunter and Ed Harris have strutted on the MET's stage and Dustin Hoffman and Angelina Jolie have funneled in some cash. The fare here runs from edgy to traditional and has included the premiere of Sam Sheppard's *Curse of the Starving Class.*

Catalina Bar & Grill
JAZZ
(Map p86; www.catalinajazzclub.com; 6725 W Sunset Blvd; cover $12-35 plus dinner or 2 drinks; P) LA's premier jazz club is now tucked in a ho-hum office building (enter through the garage), but once inside the spacious yet sultry room, all is forgiven. Expect top talent such as McCoy Tyner and Stanley Carke. Two shows nightly; times vary.

Avalon
CLUB
(Map p86; www.avalonhollywood.com; 1735 N Vine St; P) Booking superstar DJs for its electronic 'Avaland' events, this 1400-capacity former theater is in the mix for Hollywood's most energetic weekend dance club. It's the only one with an after-hours permit, so party kids spill onto the sidewalk at daybreak. The more intimate venue is the upstairs **Bardot** (p96).

🔒 Shopping

Amoeba Music
MUSIC
(Map p86; www.amoeba.com; 6400 W Sunset Blvd; ⊙10:30am-11pm Mon-Sat, 11am-9pm Sun; P) Click, click, click...is the sound of

SMALL SCREEN LA

Since the 1950s most TV shows have been made in and around LA. The reasons are simple: studios are based here and union rules make it expensive to move crews very far from the sound stages. Although shows are often filmed in Canada (for tax reasons) or on location (eg New York and New Jersey for *The Sopranos*), Southern California is the location for series such as *CSI: Miami,* which is actually shot in and around Long Beach, possibly an insult to one or the other depending on where you live.

You may recognize the Venice Boardwalk from countless shows (eg the opening of *Three's Company*) but far more humdrum parts of the region are used most often. The number of car chases filmed in and around the workaday environs of Ventura Blvd and Burbank are incalculable, until you note the proximity of Universal Studios and Warner Bros, two of the biggest TV-show producers.

Some LA locations have achieved their own fame through one or several shows. The websites www.tvacres.com and www.seeing-stars.com list oodles of locations in and around LA, but here are a few iconic places you can visit:

Brady Bunch House (11222 Dilling St, Studio City) The bland home of the classic 1970s sitcom family. Although it was prominent in the opening, nothing was actually shot here, leaving Bobby, Cindy and the rest to cavort on Astroturf on a Paramount sound stage. Note that the current owner has added a fence in front to keep warped fans from peeking in the windows in hopes of seeing Marcia in the shower or something.

Torrance High School (2200 W Carson St, Torrance) Buffy Anne Summers (aka *Buffy the Vampire Slayer*) took on the evil subjects of algebra, calculus and chemistry during her day job as a student at Sunnydale High School, set here. The school also did a star turn as West Beverly High in *Beverly Hills 90210*.

Alias Apartment Building (Map p86; 1731 N Sycamore Ave, Hollywood) Only on TV would a grad student live in a posh vintage Hollywood apartment like this. OK, it's Jennifer Garner and the student thing is only a cover for her role fighting evil-doers on the ABC series that ran from 2001 to 2006.

Shooters (6810 Melrose Ave, Hollywood) Hangout for the ever-scheming, ever-copulating gang of *Melrose Place,* this real-life restaurant (named Fellini's) was used for exterior shots. The namesake courtyard apartment building at the center of the intrigue is at 4616 Greenwood Ave in Los Feliz.

Will Rogers State Beach Where Santa Monica Canyon meets the sea, and once the go-to gay-friendly pick-up beach in town, this is where Haselhoff and Pamela saved novice swimmers and stewed in sexual tension in *Baywatch*.

Also worth checking out, and appearing elsewhere in the book:

LA City Hall (p75) *Dragnet*, Daily Planet in the TV version of *Superman*

Bronson Caves (p102) *Lone Ranger,* Bat Cave in the TV *Batman,* countless alien landscapes on *Star Trek* and bandit hideouts on *Bonanza*

Paradise Cove (p154) *Rockford Files*

Malibu Creek State Park (p148) *M*A*S*H*

Ryan Ver Berkmoes

scores of customers flipping through half-a-million new and used CDs, DVDs, videos and vinyl at this granddaddy of music stores. Handy listening stations and its outstanding *Music We Like* booklet keep you from buying lemons. Check the website for free in-store live performances by touring bands.

Mush   GIFTS
(www.m-u-s-h.com; 5651 Hollywood Blvd) An inspiring gift, antique and home-decor boutique filled with color (dig those neon lanterns), style (you'll love the silver jewelry and mod furniture) and soul (stone Buddha anyone?). The music and the owner-operator are warm and groovy.

Bhan Kanom Thai THAI SWEETS
(www.bhankanomthai.com; 5271 Hollywood Blvd; ⊙10am-2am; Ⓟ) Next door to Ganda is a remarkable sweet shop. It has all manner of Thai desserts including candy, dried fruit, gummies, sours, crisps and cakes.

Counterpoint RECORD & BOOKSTORE
(www.counterpointrecordsandbooks.com; 5911 Franklin Ave; ⊙11am-11pm Tue-Sat, 1-9:30pm Sun, 11am-9:30pm Mon) Woodblock stacks are packed high with used fiction, while crude plywood bins are likewise stuffed with vinyl soul, classical and jazz. The real gems (the rare 1st editions and vintage rock posters) are in the collectible wing next door.

Space 1520 MALL
(Map p86; www.space1520.com; 1520 N Cahuenga Blvd; ⊙11am-9pm Mon-Fri, 10am-10pm Sat, to 9pm Sun; Ⓟ) The hippest mini-mall in Hollywood, this designer construct of brick, wood, concrete and glass is home to classic and trendsetting mini-chains like Umami Burger (p118), Hennesy & Ingalls and Free People.

Frederick's of Hollywood LINGERIE
(Map p86; www.fredericks.com; 6751 Hollywood Blvd; ⊙10am-9pm Mon-Sat, 11am-7pm Sun) This famous purveyor gave us the cleavage-enhancing push-up bra and the G-string but, in 2005, competition forced it to abandon its original flagship store and move down the street to Hollywood & Highland. The new, smaller branch still sells everything from chemises to crotchless panties, all tastefully displayed with no need to blush.

LOS FELIZ & GRIFFITH PARK

In the mid-1990s, when *Swingers* mania tore through LA like a proto-hipster storm when more than a few dudes in Dickies, retro slacks and wife-beaters, with their keys chained to their belt loops, fell into bromances as they combed the streets for 'beautiful babies', Los Feliz, (mis)-pronounced *Fee-lez* by the hordes, emerged as LA's next great neighborhood. For it was here, on these clean-swept, tree-lined streets, in the shadow of Griffith Park, north and a touch east of Hollywood, where packs of aspiring actors and writers lived in one-room apartments housed in old Hollywood relics, and gathered in bars and coffeehouses cracking wise, dreaming and flirting big. Of course, what gave it a

depth beneath the sheen of cliché was the fact that Los Feliz has history.

This whole area was once one enormous ranch, called Rancho Los Feliz. In fact, the adobe ranch house, built in the 1830s, still stands. In 1882 Colonel Griffith Jenkins Griffith bought the majority of the ranch and later bequeathed it to the city of LA, forming what became Griffith Park, LA's largest municipal open space. Early movie studios, including Walt Disney's and DW Griffith's, sprouted in the flats in the early 20th century, which is why Los Feliz also has its share of old-money mansions winding into the hills, along with two architectural classics. These days, however, the hipster hub has migrated east, and Los Feliz is forgotten once more. But this neighborhood is still way too cool care.

⊙ Sights

Griffith Park OUTDOORS
(www.laprks.org; admission free; ⊙6am-10pm; Ⓟ🚻) A gift to the city in 1896 by mining mogul Griffith J Griffith, this is a wonderful playground with facilities for all age levels and interests. At five times the size of New York's Central Park, it is one of the country's largest urban green spaces and embraces an outdoor theater, the city zoo, an observatory, two museums, golf courses, tennis courts, playgrounds, bridle paths, 53 miles of hiking trails, Batman's caves and the Hollywood sign.

In May 2007 a devastating fire roared across its chaparral-cloaked hillsides, destroying about 850 acres – or one quarter – of the park and threatening structures and nearby residences. The burnt areas will remain closed long-term, but other hiking trails have reopened, though note that trails close at dusk.

Access to the park is easiest via the Griffith Park Dr or Zoo Dr exits off I-5 (Golden State Fwy). Parking is plentiful and free. For information and maps stop by the Griffith Park Ranger Station (📞323-665-5188; 4730 Crystal Springs Dr).

FREE **Griffith Observatory**
LANDMARK, MUSEUM
(www.griffithobservatory.org; 2800 Observatory Rd; planetarium shows adult/child $7/3; ⊙noon-10pm Tue-Fri, 10am-10pm Sat & Sun; 🚻) This landmark 1935 observatory opens a window onto the universe from its perch on the southern slopes of Mt Hollywood. Its planetarium boasts the world's most advanced

star projector, and astronomical displays touch on the evolution of the telescope, and the ultraviolet x-rays used to map our solar system. We loved the camera obscura on the main floor.

For more tangible thrills, weigh yourself on nine planetary scales (weight-watchers should go for Mercury), generate your own earthquake or head to the rooftop to peek through the refracting and solar telescopes housed in the smaller domes. The sweeping views of the Hollywood Hills and the gleaming city below are just as spectacular, especially at sunset. The public is also welcome to peer into the **Zeist Telescope** on the east side of the roof, and after dark staff wheel additional telescopes out to the front lawn for star gazing if you can't be bothered to wait in line for the Zeist.

You'll definitely want to grab a seat in the **Planetarium** – the aluminum-domed ceiling becomes a massive screen where lasers are projected to offer a tour of the cosmos, while another laser-projection show allows you to search for water, and life, beyond earth.

The observatory has starred in many movies, most famously *Rebel Without a Cause* with James Dean. Outside, have your picture snapped beside the actor's bust with the Hollywood sign caught neatly in the background. The carless can hop on the LADOT Observatory Shuttle (35 minutes, 25¢) from the Red Line station on Vermont and Sunset Blvd.

Barnsdall Art Park LANDMARK
(Map p100; www.barnsdallartpark.com; 4800 Hollywood Blvd) This promontory of a park, with views northwest to the Hollywood sign and northeast to the Griffith Observatory, makes a fine urban sunbathing spot. But the crown jewel is Frank Lloyd Wright's **Hollyhock House** (Map p100; www. hollyhockhouse.net; adult/student/child $7/3/

LOS FELIZ & GRIFFITH PARK SIGHTS

free; ⊙tours hourly 12:30-3:30pm Wed-Sun; P). It's a prime example of Wright's California Romanza style, typified by an easy flow between rooms, courtyard and gardens. Commissioned in 1919 by oil heiress and art nut Aline Barnsdall, its walls, carpets and furniture are awash in abstract hollyhocks, her favorite flower. Guided tours take you into the stunning living room with its moated fireplace.

Barnsdall envisioned her house to be part of a cutting-edge theater colony but, as eccentrics are prone to do, abruptly abandoned the idea in 1927. Instead, she donated the house and grounds to the city of LA with the proviso that they become a public park. There is a **Municipal Art Gallery** (Map p100; admission free; ⊙noon-5pm Thu-Sun; P) with a sculpture garden and a theatre. It also sells Hollyhock House tour tickets.

Los Angeles Zoo & Botanical Gardens
ZOO
(www.lazoo.org; 5333 Zoo Dr; adult/child/senior $13/8/10; ⊙10am-5pm; P⛹) The Los Angeles Zoo, with its 1100 finned, feathered and furry friends from over 250 species, rarely fails to enthrall the little ones. What began in 1912 as a refuge for retired circus animals now brings in over a million visitors each year. Undisputed crowd-pleasers include swinging gibbons, frolicking sea lions, posturing chimpanzees, cuddling koalas, and, according to the zoo's director, anything currently defecating. Tots gravitate to **Adventure Island** with its petting zoo and hands-on play stations as well as the **Children's Discovery Center**.

The zoo also participates in over 20 conservation projects, including the recovery program of the endangered condor; some 126 chicks have hatched here since the '80s.

Museum of the American West
MUSEUM
(www.autrynationalcenter.org; 4700 Western Heritage Way; adult/child/student & senior $9/3/5; ⊙10am-4pm Tue-Fri, to 5pm Sat & Sun; ⛹) Want to know how the West was really won? Then mosey over to this excellent museum – its exhibits on the good, the bad and the ugly of America's westward expansion rope in even the most reluctant cowpokes.

Start downstairs, where a soundscape of music, hooves and whinnying leads you through a frontier village to a nymph-festooned saloon with some interesting cheating devices used in gambling. Nearby, the Wyatt brothers take on their adversaries in the infamous 1881 shoot-out at the OK Corral, re-enacted here in an animated diorama. A glass case holds the original gun used by Doc Holliday, one of the fight's participants, and a precious collection of Colt firearms. Annie Oakley's gold-plated pistols are also on display. Other galleries test the romantic myths of the Old West against its harsher realities, deal with the clashes between conquerors and Native Americans and examine the roles played by successive waves of immigrants.

Kids can pan for gold, explore a stagecoach, or get a hands-on history lesson about Chinese family life in 1930s LA. Year-round gallery talks, symposia, film screenings and other cultural events further spur the imagination. In summer a popular music series is held outside on Thursdays.

FREE **Travel Town** MUSEUM
(www.traveltown.org; 5200 W Zoo Dr; ◎10am-4pm Mon-Fri, to 5pm Sat & Sun; P ♿) This delightful rail yard displays dozens of vintage railcars and locomotives, the oldest from 1864. Kids are all smiles imagining themselves as engineers, clambering around the iron horses. A huge hall holds historic fire engines and a model-train network, which a dedicated local hobby club operates, usually on weekends from 10am to 4pm. Travel Town is open one hour longer during daylight saving time.

Los Angeles Live Steamers TRAINS
(www.lals.org; 5202 Zoo Dr; suggested donation $3; ◎11am-3pm Sun; P ♿) Just east of Travel Town, this is a group of local folks with a passion for scale-model locomotives. On Sunday afternoons they offer rides on their one-eighth-size model trains.

Griffith Park Southern Railroad TRAINS
(4400 Crystal Springs Dr; adult & child/senior $2.50/2; ◎10am-4:15pm Mon-Fri, to 4:30pm Sat & Sun Oct-Apr; P ♿) If that's still not enough train stuff for you, head to the small fleet of miniature trains that has ferried generations of children around a 1-mile loop past pony rides, a Native-American village and an old Western town since 1948. It's open 30 minutes later during daylight savings time.

FREE **Forest Lawn Memorial Park –**
Hollywood Hills CEMETERY
(www.forestlawn.com; 6300 Forest Lawn Dr; ◎8am-5pm; P) Pathos, art and patriotism rule at this humongous cemetery next to Griffith Park. A fine catalog of old-time celebrities – including Lucille Ball, Bette Davis and Stan Laurel – rests within the manicured grounds strewn with paeans to early North American history. Look out for the giant *The Birth of Liberty* mosaic, Boston's re-created Old North Church and bronze statues of Washington, Jefferson and Lincoln, or watch a movie about the American Revolution. Staff isn't helpful in locating stars' graves but you can download guides from the internet (www.seeing-stars.com). More dead stars are at the original Forest Lawn in nearby Glendale (p184).

🏃 Activities

Bronson Canyon HIKING
(www.laparks.org; 3200 Canyon Dr; ◎5am-dusk; P) Although most of the pretty people prefer to do their running, walking and hiking in Runyon Canyon, we always preferred Bronson. With its wide fire road that rises to a lookout point and links to the Hollywood sign, Griffith Park, and the famed **Bronson Caves** – where scenes from *Batman* and *The Lone Ranger* were shot, many a local consider this rather green canyon, shaded by oaks and sycamores and ribboned by a seasonal stream, their own personal recreation center. Celebrity sightings happen.

Head north on Canyon Dr and park in the last lot before the locked gate at Hollywoodland Camp. Walk back south, then turn left and head past a gate and up the fire road. For the Bronson Caves then turn left when the trail forks and the caves will be right there. The trail continues on the other side of the caves.

Griffith Park Merry-Go-Round ATTRACTION
(Griffith Park center; rides $1; ◎11am-5pm daily May-Sep, Sat & Sun Oct-Apr; ♿) The richly festooned 1926 amusement park ride was brought to its current home in 1937. It has 68 beautifully carved and painted horses sporting real horsehair tails.

Griffith Park CYCLING
(www.laparks.org; 4730 Crystal Springs Rd; ◎1-7pm Mon-Fri, 10:30am-dusk Sat & Sun) Directly adjacent to the Crystal Springs picnic area, close to a baseball diamond and the freeway, is the park's only bike-rental concession

(bikes per hour/day $8/25). It has mountain bikes, low-riders and tandems of varying quality, with and without baby seats.

Mineral Wells
PICKNICKING

(www.laparks.org; Griffith Park Dr; ⊙6am-dusk) This is one of our favorite picnic spots in Griffith Park. Near the Wilson Harding golf course, rustling sycamores lean and recline onto a wide lawn enjoyed by mostly immigrant families who barbecue and celebrate birthdays around the public picnic tables. If you've been looking for the real LA, you'll find it here.

Griffith Park
GOLFING

(☑Wilson Harding 323-663-2555, Roosevelt 323-665-2011; 4730 Crystal Springs Dr; greens fees $31-39; ⊙dawn-dusk) The **Wilson Harding golf complex** is actually two 18-hole courses with par 3s, 4s and 5s, and electric golf carts ($24) available for rent. Or play a short round at the nine-hole **Roosevelt Municipal Golf Course**, which slopes down the mountain on the other side of the park, near the Greek Theatre and the Observatory. Golf clubs are available for rent at the Wilson Harding pro shop.

✗ Eating

TOP CHOICE **Umami Burger**
BURGERS $$

(Map p100; www.umamiburger.com; 4655 Hollywood Blvd; burgers $9-17; ⊙lunch & dinner; P⸬) With a spacious brick interior framed by rusted iron, this is by far the grooviest Umami in the fledgling empire. It does the staples everyone loves (the Umami, the SoCal and the Truffle), as well as a *carnitas* (Mexican braised pork) and a Jurky (jerk turkey) burger. The wine bar offers $4 craftsmen drafts or glasses of wine, and $5 'smash burgers' at happy hour (3pm to 7pm).

Alcove
CAFE $$

(Map p100; www.thealcovecafe.com; 1929 Hillhurst Ave; mains $11-18; ⊙breakfast, lunch & dinner; P⸬) Hillhurst's choice breakfast hangout, this sunny cafe spills onto a multilevel, streetside brick patio. It's housed in a restored 1897 Spanish-style duplex, and the food is ridiculously good. There's crab cake benedict, bison chili omelettes, and crepes stuffed with espresso-infused cream.

Little Dom's
ITALIAN $$

(www.littledoms.com; 2128 Hillhurst Ave; pizza $11, mains $15-41; ⊙breakfast, lunch & dinner; P) An understated, yet stylish, Italian deli and restaurant with deep booths, marble tables and wood floors. It does a dynamite kale salad

and good thin-crust pizza. But it's beloved for its antipasti and sandwiches – especially the fried oyster po'boy. If you don't want full service, pop into its deli next door.

Yuca's
TAQUERIA $

(www.yucasla.com; 2056 Hillhurst Ave, Los Feliz; tacos $1.75-2, burritos $2.50-4, tortas $3.50; ⊙lunch & dinner Mon-Sat; P) Location, location, location...is definitely not what lures people to this parking-lot snack shack. It's the tacos, stupid! And the *tortas,* burritos and other Mexi faves that earned the Herrera family the coveted James Beard Award in 2005.

Vermont
NEW AMERICAN $$$

(Map p100; ☑323-661-6163; www.vermontrestaurantandbar.com; 1714 N Vermont Ave; mains $15-30; ⊙lunch & dinner, bar to 1am; P) This is a smart, grown-up spot in the antiquated Pastry Cakes building, with a dining room punctuated by pillars and palmetto palms. The American contemporary food is smart and satisfying and reminds you of the simple goodness of slow-cooked pork, seared halibut or braised duck.

Fred 62
DINER $

(Map p100; www.fred62.com; 1850 N Vermont Ave; dishes $6-$11; ⊙24hr; P⸬) A re-imagined, modern take on diner fare serving polyethnic sandwiches, salads and noodles for young blood on small budgets.

♟ Drinking

TOP CHOICE **Tiki Ti**
BAR

(Map p100; www.tiki-ti.com; 4427 W Sunset Blvd; ⊙4pm-2am Wed-Sat) This garage-sized tropical tavern packs in grizzled old-timers and young cuties for sweet and wickedly strong drinks (try a Rae's Mistake, named for the bar's founder). The under-the-sea decor is surreal. Cash only.

Good Luck Bar
LOUNGE

(Map p100; www.myspace.com/good_luck_bar; 1514 Hillhurst Ave; ⊙7pm-2am Mon-Fri, 8pm-2am Sat & Sun; P) The clientele is sexy, the music loud and the drinks strong at this red-velvet watering hole with all the lascivious seductiveness of a Chinese opium den. Order a baby-blue Yee Mee Loo.

☆ Entertainment

TOP CHOICE **Greek Theatre**
VENUE

(www.greektheatrela.com; 2700 N Vermont Ave; ⊙May-Oct; P) A more intimate version of the Hollywood Bowl, this 5800-seat outdoor amphitheater tucked into a woodsy hillside of Griffith Park is much beloved for its vibe and variety – Imogen Heap to Erykah Badu to Willie Nelson. Parking is stacked, so plan on a postshow wait.

Vista Theatre
CINEMA

(Map p100; 4473 Sunset Blvd; adult/senior & child under 12 $9.50/5.50, matinees $6.50; ⊙1-9:45pm Sat-Thu, to midnight Fri) Charming, historic and one of the last remaining single-screen theatres in Los Angeles. Built back in 1923, it generally plays first-run blockbusters like *Iron Man 2*. It also does weekly midnight screenings of '80s classics like *Ghostbusters* on Fridays at midnight.

Dresden
JAZZ

(Map p100; ☑323-665-4294; www.thedresden. com; 1760 Vermont Ave; ⊙9pm-1:15am Tue-Sat; P) Marty and Elayne have been a Los Feliz fixture since 1982 when they first brought their quirky Sinatra style to the Dresden's lounge. He rumbles on the drums and the upright bass. She tickles the ivories and plays the flute. Both sing. She scats too. They made a brief appearance in the film *Swingers*.

🛍 Shopping

Oou
VINTAGE

(Map p100; www.ooushop.com; 1764 Vermont Ave) Fantastic half-vintage, half-new designer clothing for women that blends the sophisticated with the casual. The 1940s handbags are special, so are the belts and moccasins, and if you can rock it, look into the skimpy rompers from the '60s and '70s.

Skylight Books
BOOKSTORE

(Map p100; 1818 Vermont Ave; ⊙10am-10pm) Like moths to the skylight, folks are drawn to this loftlike indie bookstore focusing on local, nontraditional and foreign authors. It also hosts several book groups and runs meet-the-author events. Its adjacent **Skylight Theater** (www.beverlyhillsplayhouse.com) is run by the Beverly Hills Playhouse.

Vacation
VINYL

(Map p100; www.vacationvinyl.com; 4679 Hollywood Blvd; ⊙11am-9pm Mon-Sat, noon-7pm Sun) It's nice to find crate after crate of vinyl ranging from soul to jazz to rock to gospel in this digitized world.

Wacko
COLLECTIBLES

(Map p100; www.soapplant.com; 4633 Hollywood Blvd; ⊙11am-7pm Mon-Wed, to 9pm Thu-Sat, noon-6pm Sun) Billy Shire's giftorium of camp and kitsch has been a fun browse for over three decades. Pick up dashboard Jesuses, or a Frida Kahlo mesh bag. It has a great selection of comics, and in back is La Luz de Jesus, one of LA's top lowbrow art galleries.

American Vintage
VINTAGE

(Map p100; www.americanvintageclothing.com; 1750 Hillhurst Ave) This cozy stucco-and-brick cottage is stuffed with leather (boots, skirts, jackets, and, god help us, pants), bow ties, Izod shirts and 1920s babydoll dresses and hats. Eras are not stocked separately, so it's a rummage, but a worthwhile one.

SILVER LAKE & ECHO PARK

For decades devout Eastsiders have maintained the coolest, hippest place to be in Los Angeles is Silver Lake, and when Beck burst onto the Spaceland stage with his quirky take on hip-hop, funk and vintage sport coats in the '90s, Silver Lake's cultural capital crystallized, and hipsters and artists poured into a neighborhood that was then mostly Latino, frequently smoggy and often crime-blanched. Eventually the Silver Lake ideal – revitalized modernist homes, groovy bistros, coffeehouses and boutiques patronized by a real community of upwardly mobile, progressive creatives – began to take hold. Which is to say Silver Lake gentrified faster than you can say Casey Affleck lives here. Rents soared, working-class Latino families were pushed out and yuppie babies came along with gaggles of Eastside soccer moms pushing jogger strollers around the reservoir. Point is, Silver Lake lost its edge, and these days saying this place is hip, would be something like worshipping baby-boomer rock stars in 2010. OK, it's not *that* bad, and truth be told, Silver Lake's terrific shopping and dining, and relatively free-thinking locals are all worthy of praise. But gone is the grit, and gone is the funk.

Which is exactly why, if you dig the uneasy interface of edgy urban art, music and culture in multi-ethnic neighborhoods, if you like your rents cheap and historic homes somewhat rickety, and if Silver Lake has cured your insomnia, you'll love Echo Park. One of LA's oldest neighborhoods is punctuated by a serene lake featured in Polanski's *Chinatown*, and for decades has been home to poor, working-class Latinos. Well, the artists and hipsters have

BEST FOR...

Architecture Downtown (p69)

Bargains Downtown (p83)

Beach Scene Hermosa Beach (p172)

Channeling Your Inner Hippie
Venice (p163)

Families Santa Monica (p151)

Gardens Pasadena & San Gabriel
Valley (p187)

Gay and Lesbian West Hollywood
(p108)

Glamour Shopping Beverly Hills
(p129)

History Downtown (p69)

Hot Dining West Hollywood (p118)

Museums Mid-City (p108)

Nightlife Hollywood (p95)

Star-spotting West Hollywood
(p108)

arrived, but not in Silver Lake numbers; leaving the panaderias and cevicherias, swap-meet shopping and lively streets so far untouched, even if you can leaf through used Bukowski and buy triple-milled soap on the same block. Here's hoping it stays that way.

⊙ Sights

Echo Park Lake PARK
(www.laparks.org; 751 Echo Park Ave; P) Surrounded by shingled craftsmen homes that rise with the steep streets and looming hills to the north, and blessed with keyhole downtown views to the south, this fountain lake park is patronized by cool rockers, laid-back vatos, and flocks of ducks and crows, and home to wild, wind-rustled palms. When Nicholson's Gittis was on the tail of Mr Mulray and his young lover, he snapped incriminating photos from a canoe on this very lake. Unfortunately, the paddleboat concession has been closed indefinitely, but some locals still fish the stock from shore. And on sunny summer days, when that geyser of a fountain gushes to the sky, and the lotus flowers are in bloom, the lake glimmers with a beauty undeniable.

John Marshall High School LANDMARK
(Map p100; www.johnmarshallhs.org; 3939 Tracy St) A 1931 historic brick-and-stone beauty with peaked windows, exterior moldings and a fantastic athletic field visible from the street.

🏃 Activities

 826 LA Time Travel Mart VOLUNTEER
(www.826la.org; 1714 W Sunset Blvd; noon-8pm Mon-Fri, to 6pm Sat & Sun) There's a strange and beautiful light glowing in these cages, from these shelves. At first glance, this is a convenience store for time travelers, stocked with anything a time traveler might need. There are products from the past and from the future. You know, like whale oil (not really) and spice rubs (really). There are suction-cup clocks and coolers filled with robot milk and ostrich eggs. But, in all actuality, it's just a front for a drop-in tutoring program specializing in homework help and writing workshops. All the proceeds are funneled into the program, the brainchild of author, screenwriter, and McSweeny's founder, Dave Eggers. Volunteers are always welcome.

Silver Lake Reservoir WALK
(Map p100; www.Silver Lakereservoirs.org; Silver Lake Blvd; P) Fenced in and sitting in a concrete bowl (truly excellent work, City of LA), the neighborhood's wind-kissed namesake shimmers in the late-afternoon sun, when walkers, joggers and cyclists descend to circle it. And even if you can't touch the shore, you will enjoy the views as the lake sits on a plateau surrounded by hills dotted with posh homes, with keyhole vistas of the massive Angeles Crest on clear days. At the southern edge you'll find plenty of street parking, a postage-stamp dog park and some outdoor basketball courts.

Silver Lake Conservatory of Music
MUSIC LESSONS
(Map p100; ☎323-665-3363; www.silverlakeconservatory.com; 3920 Sunset Blvd; per lesson $25; ⊙11am-9pm Mon-Fri, 10am-6pm Sat & Sun) Cofounded by the uber-famous and talented Flea, and the less famous but absurdly skilled Keith Barry (who runs the joint), this quirky storefront music school offers classes for every instrument, every level and all ages.

Raven Spa SPA
(☎323-644-0240; www.theravenspa.com; 2910 Rowena Ave; 60/90min $70/100; ⊙10am-9pm) Stroll through the teak door, beneath the suspended parasols and lanterns and relax into one of LA's sweetest massage spots.

Fountains gurgle, the scent of cedar wood is discernable and an all-Thai staff delivers authentic Thai massage on floor beds in a group space just like in the motherland.

Yas
YOGA
(Map p100; www.go2yas.com; 1932 Hyperion Ave; classes $17; ⊙7:15am-8:15pm Mon-Thu, to 6pm Fri-Sun) It's all about yoga and spinning at this carbon copy of the Venice original (p166).

✗ Eating

TOP CHOICE Café Stella
FRENCH BISTRO $$
(Map p100; ☑323-666-0265; www.cafe stella.com; 3932 W Sunset Blvd; mains $20-34; ⊙lunch & dinner; P) As charming as it gets, here is a cloud of clinking glasses, red wine, good jazz and classic French bistro cuisine under a tented patio and rambling into an antiquated dining room. Artful and reasonable, it bustles at lunch and is packed for dinner. There's a reason.

Barbrix
TAPAS $$
(Map p100; ☑323-662-2442; www.barbrix.com; 2442 Hyperion Ave; mains $6-17; ⊙dinner; P) As stylish and laid-back as Silver Lake, this wine and tapas bar with its horseshoe wine bar, exposed beams and open kitchen has plenty of room inside and out. Go cold with hamachi crudo and one of a dozen kinds of charcuterie, or get hot with veal meatballs, seared scallops and blistered shisito peppers.

Flore
VEGAN $
(Map p100; www.florevegan.com; 3818 W Sunset Blvd; sandwiches $9-11, mains $10-11; ⊙lunch & dinner; P🐾) If you're more hippie than hipster, you'll want to sink into a reclaimed diner booth and feast on tofu scrambles, raw jicima or cooked seitan tacos served in stone-ground corn tortillas. Or will it be a tofu club with tempeh bacon and daikon sprouts? Don't be idle about those cupcakes.

Celaya
MEXICAN BAKERY $
(1630 Sunset Blvd; baked goods $10; ⊙6am-8pm) A proper *panaderia* (Mexican bakery) is always a beautiful thing. Get your warm pan *dulce* (sweet bread), *panales* (pastries stuffed with flavored cream cheese), *pasteles* (cakes), donuts and some special tamales.

Gingergrass
VIETNAMESE $
(www.gingergrass.com; 2396 Glendale Ave; appetizers $5-7.50, mains $12-16; ⊙lunch & dinner; P) Pressed-bamboo tables are scattered on polished-concrete floors in this stylish neighborhood cafe where the chalkboard is filled with daily specials. The buzz on the ground was about its sandwiches, only available at lunch. Choose chicken, beef, pork or tofu stuffed into a crispy baguette topped with pickled veggies, herbs and chilies.

Bulan
VEGETARIAN, THAI $
(Map p100; www.bulanthai.com; 4114 Santa Monica Blvd; appetizers $5-8, mains $7-12. ⊙lunch & dinner; P🐾) Nothing fancy here, just healthy and hearty veggie Thai food off Sunset Junction. Terrific-value lunch specials start at just $8, or choose from among a long list of classic Thai soups, salads and curries with meat substitutes.

El Cochinito
CUBAN $
(Map p100; 3508 W Sunset Blvd; dishes $6-27; ⊙lunch & dinner; P) This 12-table hole-in-the-wall 'little pig' is family-run, neighborhood-adored and serves traditional 'pre-Castro' Cuban at its finest. The *tostones* are thin and crispy and the roasted pork is melt-in-your-mouth tender.

Lamill Coffee
ECLECTIC $$
(Map p100; www.lamillcoffee.com; 1636 Silver Lake Blvd; dishes $10-17; ⊙breakfast, lunch & dinner; ⊚) A neighborhood gem hidden in plain sight on the road to the reservoir. You'll love the red booths and faux-alligator-skin seats, the black-and-white murals and marble bar. It has a Japanese take on the Caesar salad, *burrata* baguettes, arctic char tartar and barbecued eel served over *kim chi*.

Two Boots
PIZZA $
(www.twoboots.com; 1818 W Sunset Blvd; pizzas $6.50-26; ⊙lunch Fri-Sun, dinner daily) It's always a good sign when the Dude is your front man. This rockstar of a storefront pizza joint merges the flavors of New Orleans with the thin-crust goodness of NY pizza. Its signature pie, the Bayou Beast, comes with shrimp, crawfish, Andouille sausage and jalapenos, and it's open late.

Masa
PIZZA $$
(www.masaofechopark.com; 1800 W Sunset Blvd; mains $13-17; ⊙lunch & dinner; P) Chicago deep-dish pizza (where the locally sourced toppings are piled high in a cradle of hand-rolled, house-baked dough, then hidden beneath a layer of cheese) served in whimsical environs that recall the wild, colorful swirl of New Orleans, right down to the swing music.

🍸 Drinking

⭐ City Sip
TOP CHOICE
WINE BAR

(www.citysipla.com; 2150 W Sunset Blvd; ☺5:30-11pm Tue-Thu, to midnight Fri, 5pm-midnight Sat, 6-11pm Sun) A wine bar that grew organically out of the living-room wine tastings of owner Nicole Daddio (you can call her Daddio). She offers classes (she calls it Wine Edjumacation), and pours new- and old-world wines at affordable prices. On Sundays glasses from all open bottles are half price.

Gold Room
BAR

(1558 W Sunset Blvd; ☺noon-2am) Latino soccer freaks linger by day. Hipsters pack the joint by night. It's a cozy, divey room just sketchy enough to have street cred, and those free tacos (not a misprint) keep the good people coming. Of course, according to one of the bartenders, 'the meat quality is not gourmet.'

4100 Bar
BAR

(Map p100; www.4100bar.com; 4100 W Sunset Blvd; ☺7pm-2am; P) Past the bouncer and the thick velvet curtain awaits this good-looking bar with an unpretentious crowd, a jukebox heavy on alt-rock and bartenders who've been around the block once or twice.

Intelligentsia
COFFEEHOUSE

(Map p100; www.intelligentsiacoffee.com; 3920 W Sunset Blvd; ☺6am-8pm Sun-Wed, to 11pm Thu-Sat; 🛜) While there is some spillover into the hip patio of Café Stella, it's hard not to notice that this craftsman coffeehouse, with its sidewalk patio, minimalist interior and outstanding fair-trade joe, attracts younger, decidedly less-groomed boys and girls.

Good
MICROBREW

(Map p100; www.goodmicrobrew.com; 3920 W Sunset Blvd; ☺11am-10pm Mon-Thu, to 11pm Fri, 9am-11pm Sat, to 10pm Sun; P) Think: 500 microbrews from California, Belgium, Brazil, the Czech Republic. It serves flights, tableside draft towers and on Wednesday it's Mystery Beer night. The bartender will pour the beer of his choosing for just $3.

☆ Entertainment

⭐ Echo
TOP CHOICE
VENUE

(www.attheecho.com; 1822 W Sunset Blvd; P) Eastsiders hungry for an eclectic alchemy of sounds pack this funky-town dive that's basically a sweaty bar with a stage and a smoking patio. It books indie bands such as Black Rebel Motorcycle Club, and also has regular club nights.

Bootleg Theater
VENUE

(www.bootlegtheater.org; 2220 Beverly Blvd; P) Part progressive-rock and folk venue, part theater space, part multidisciplinary arts foundation and laboratory. This restored 1930s warehouse hosts one-off shows and long-term residencies for edgy indie bands (like Hot Hot Heat). It also supports spoken word, dance and dramatic artists pushing boundaries.

Spaceland
VENUE

(Map p100; www.clubspaceland.com; 1717 Silver Lake Blvd) Beck and the Eels played early gigs at what is still one of LA's best places for indie and alt-sounds from noise pop to punk-folk to mash-ups. Big-name talent has been known to pop by for quick and dirty impromptu sets. Mondays are free, admission varies at other times.

Little Temple
CLUB

(Map p100; www.littletemple.com; 4519 Santa Monica Blvd; ☺9pm-2am Wed-Sun) This Buddha-themed lounge still brings global grooves to the people via live acts and local DJs. Fans of good reggae, funk, and Latin rhythms shake their collective ass here. Admission prices vary.

🛍 Shopping

Matrushka Construction
FASHION

(Map p100; www.matrushka.com; 3822 W Sunset Blvd, Silver Lake) Who says fashion has to be superficial? Lara Howe crafts her sublime, tailored designs from remnant fabrics personally and locally sourced by the owner-operator. The fabrics are still top notch, they are simply either vintage or discarded by large corporate manufacturers. Expect fitted tees, slinky silk, cotton and, dare we say, lycra dresses, pants and skirts.

Stories
BOOKSTORE

(www.storiesla.com; 1716 W Sunset Blvd; ☺8am-8pm Sat-Thu, to 10pm Fri; 🛜) Bob your head to dub on the hi-fi while you wander through a maze of new and used literature. It has an LA section, plays, short stories, graphic novels and Carl Jung. Brainy types congregate in the back-end cafe, which is wired and has a patio enlightened by a graff-art bodhisattva.

Bobbie
VINTAGE, FASHION

(www.bobbieboutique.com; 2213 W Sunset Blvd) Affordable, sexy, breezy, this boutique has something stylish for women of all ages from mostly local designers. The lace gowns and floral dresses are especially sweet, and there's a vintage rack too. It's owned and operated by a sassy 22-year-old rockabilly entrepreneur and Jacksonville refugee brimming with good vibrations.

Spitfire Girl
GIFTS

(www.spitfiregirl.com; 2203 W Sunset Blvd) The grooviest gift store in the district, if not the city. Here are gift books spanning from cannabis coloring books to Francis Bacon coffeetable tomes to a Russian-criminal tattoo-art encyclopedia. There are stuffed gnomes and kazoos, naked people action figures, organic and aromatic candles scooped into recycled beer bottles, and luscious triple-milled soap from France.

Rockaway Records
RECORD STORE

(www.rockaway.com; 2395 Glendale Blvd; ⊘11am-7pm; P) Rockaway buys, sells and trades all types of great music. Used CDs are fairly priced and there are plenty of booths for prepurchase listening. Collectors can forage through the rare-music section or stock up on posters, magazines and memorabilia. It has a terrific DVD selection too.

Mohawk General Store
VINTAGE, FASHION

(www.mohawkgeneralstore.net; 1102 Mohawk St; ⊘noon-7pm Tue-Sat, 1-6pm Sun) Zen meets the Old West in this tragically hip hybrid boutique. Shoes range from leather to canvas to elegant heels, and those vintage hunting vests are special too. Even though prices are high, this owner-operated boutique will make you smile.

Clover
GIFTS

(Map p100; www.cloversilverlake.com; 2756 Rowena Ave; ⊘11am-7pm) This store has everything from cuddly stuffed toys for baby to designer waste baskets, bamboo salad bowls, alluring fragrances and designer jeans made downtown for mom and dad. There is also some outstanding locally designed gold and silver jewelry. It's one big blast of hippie-chic groovy.

Driftwood
VINTAGE

(Map p100; www.driftwoodla.com; 3938 W Sunset Blvd; ⊘noon-8pm Sun-Wed, 11am-9pm Thu-Sun; P) It doesn't have the largest vintage selection in Silver Lake, but it gets bonus points for panache. Old-school desks and filing cabinets, Linda Ronstadt records, Princeton T-shirts, old worn leather boots, and some new denim are all artfully arranged in an environment suffused with virtuoso garage rock.

Bar Keeper
MIXOLOGY

(Map p100; www.barkeepersilverlake.com; 3910 W Sunset Blvd; ⊘noon-6pm Mon-Thu, 11am-7pm Fri & Sat, 11am-6pm Sun) Eastside mixologists now have their dream habitat. Here are all manner of stemware, absinthe fountains, shakers, mixers and vessels needed to pour fine cocktails.

WEST HOLLYWOOD & MID-CITY

Upscale and low-rent (but not that low), gay fabulous and Russian-ghetto chic, this is a bastion of LA's fashionista best and home to some of the trashiest shops known to womankind (see: Avenue, Melrose). Here you can find macrobiotic vegan cooking, bright market cafes and dark-edged tequila bars. Rainbow flags fly proudly over Santa Monica Blvd, and the set piece Sunset Strip, with its classic rock clubs and iconic hotels overlooking a sea of twinkling lights, still attracts Hollywood glitterati wannabes, especially on weekends when the boulevard swells with suburbanites. When real stars come here to rave, they're usually hidden away in a house party high in the hills. Welcome to West Hollywood (WeHo), an independent city that packs more personality (some might say, frivolity) into its 1.9-sq-mile frame than LA's larger barrios.

To the south and east of WeHo is an amorphous area we have called Mid-City. It encompasses the groovy Fairfax District with the Farmers Market, Miracle Mile with Museum Row and old-money Hancock Park with its grand mansions.

Street parking codes in West Hollywood can only be described as fascist, but you'll find two hours of free parking at 8383 Santa Monica Blvd. Mid-City areas usually have plenty of street parking. DASH buses (p210) serve the area on the Fairfax Route and the Hollywood/West Hollywood Route.

◉ Sights

TOP CHOICE Farmers Market & Around
FOOD, ENTERTAINMENT

(Map p110; www.farmersmarketla.com; 6333 W 3rd St, Fairfax District; admission free; ⊘9am-9pm Mon-Fri, to 8pm Sat, 10am-7pm Sun; P⛟) Long before the city was flooded with farmers markets, there was the Farmers Market. From apples to zucchinis, cheeses to blinis – you'll find them at this 1934 landmark.

Casual and kid-friendly, it's a fun place for a browse, snack or for people-watching. From late May to mid-September it holds the **Summer Music Series** (☉7-9pm). On Thursday nights it's all jazz, and on Fridays the bands can range from zydeco to pop.

Los Angeles County Museum of Art
ART MUSEUM

(LACMA; Map p110; www.lacma.org; 5901 Wilshire Blvd; adult/senior & student/child $12/8/free, after 5pm & 2nd Tue of each month free, ☉noon-8pm Mon, Tue & Thu, noon-9pm Fri, 11am-8pm Sat & Sun; 🖥) LA's premier art museum, LACMA is an Aladdin's cave of paintings, sculpture and decorative arts stretching across ages and borders. Yet, somehow, so far, it just hasn't quite got the respect it deserves. Sure, galleries are stuffed with all the major players – Rembrandt, Cézanne, Magritte, Mary Cassat, Ansel Adams, to name a few – plus several millennia worth of ceramics from China, woodblock prints from Japan, pre-Columbian art, ancient sculpture from Greece, Rome and Egypt and lots of other treasures; the depth and wealth of the collection here is stunning, and the two-phase Renzo Piano 'Transformation' will finally bring a sense of design worthy of the art on the 20-acre LACMA campus.

Phase I is already complete. It includes a new surreal light post entry pavilion and the **Broad Contemporary Art Museum**, presenting part of the personal collection of developer Eli Broad, including seminal works by Jasper Johns, Roy Lichtenstein and Andy Warhol. Some of the buildings and their gifts remain off-limits during phase II.

LACMA also hosts headlining touring exhibits and frequent movie screenings, readings and other events, including a popular Friday-night jazz series (p77).

Grove
MALL

(Map p110; www.thegrovela.com; 189 The Grove Dr) Next door to the Farmers Market is a faux-European yet attractive outdoor shopping mall built around a central plaza with a musical fountain (nicest after dark, almost magical at Christmas time).

CBS Television City
TV STUDIO

(Map p110; www.cbs.com; 7800 Beverly Blvd) North of the Farmers Market is CBS, where game shows, talk shows, soap operas and other programs are taped, often before a live audience (for tickets, see Your 15 Minutes of Fame, p90).

Melrose Ave
COMMERCIAL DISTRICT

(Map p110; Melrose Ave) A popular shopping strip as famous for its epic people-watching as it is for its consumer fruits. On the streets you'll see hair (and people for that matter) of all shades and styles, bizarro takes on the art of piercing and ink, Hasidic pilgrims on their way to shul, and everything from gothic jewels to custom sneakers to medical marijuana to stuffed porcupines to Tiger Woods sex dolls is available for a price. The strip is located between Fairfax & La Brea.

Sunset Strip
ENTERTAINMENT DISTRICT

(Map p110; Sunset Blvd) A visual cacophony of billboards, giant ad banners and neon signs, the sinuous stretch of Sunset Blvd running between Laurel Canyon and Doheny Dr has been nightlife central since the 1920s. Mobster Bugsy Siegel and his posse hung out at such clubs as Ciro's (now the Comedy Store; p122); Marilyn Monroe had her first date with Joe DiMaggio at the **Rainbow Bar & Grill** (Map p110; 9015 Sunset Blvd), which later became the preferred late-night hub of Guns N' Roses. The **Whisky A Go-Go** (p122) gave birth to both the Doors and go-go dancing, and Led Zeppelin raced motorcycles in the Andaz Hotel, formerly the Hyatt, and henceforth known as the 'Riot House'. Then, in the late '90s, the strip recaptured the limelight with the **House of Blues** (HOB; p122), the ultraposh Sky Bar at the Mondrian hotel (p116) and the sexy **Standard Hollywood** (p116).

These days, though, it seems to be coasting on its fabled legacy. The young, hip and fickle have moved on, leaving it to mostly buttoned-down, cashed-up suburbanites.

Hancock Park & Larchmont Village
NEIGHBORHOOD

(Map p110; Larchmont Blvd; 🅿) LA has gorgeous homes galore, but there's nothing quite like the old-money mansions flanking the tree-lined streets of Hancock Park, a genteel neighborhood roughly bounded by Highland and Rossmore and Melrose and Wilshire. LA's founding families, including the Dohenys and Chandlers, hired famous architects to build their pads in the 1920s, and to this day celebrities such as Melanie Griffith, Antonio Banderas and Keifer Sutherland make their homes here. It's a lovely area for a stroll or a drive, especially around Christmas when houses sparkle.

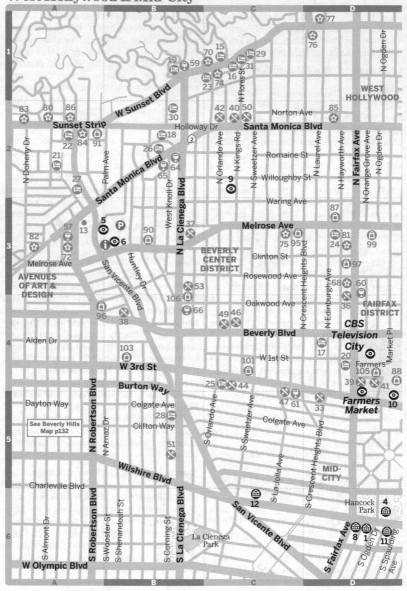

Wrap up your visit here with a cappuccino and a browse through tiny Larchmont Village, the neighborhood's small-town-America-style commercial strip. Keep an eye out for celebs – Paramount Studios is just up the street.

Page Museum & La Brea Tar Pits

PALEONTOLOGY MUSEUM

(Map p110; www.tarpits.org; 5801 Wilshire Blvd; adult/child/student & senior $7/2/4.50; ☺9:30am-5pm; P🚼) Did you know that Manfred the mammoth, Sid the sloth and Diego the

the world's most fecund and famous fossil sites. Thousands of Ice Age critters met their maker between 40,000 and 10,000 years ago in gooey crude oil bubbling up from deep below Wilshire Blvd. Animals wading into the sticky muck became trapped and were condemned to a slow death by starvation or suffocation. A life-size drama of a mammoth family outside the museum dramatizes such a cruel fate. Parking costs $6.

Petersen Automotive Museum MUSEUM (Map p110; www.petersen.org; 6060 Wilshire Blvd; adult/child/senior & student $10/3/5; ⊙10am-6pm Tue-Sun; P) A four-story ode to the auto, the Petersen Automotive Museum is a treat even to those who can't tell a piston from a carburetor. Start by ambling along a fun streetscape that reveals LA as the birthplace of gas stations, billboards, strip malls, drive-in restaurants and drive-in movie theaters. Then head upstairs where it's shiny cars galore, from vintage wheels to hot rods, movie cars to celebrity-owned rarities, presented in rotating exhibits. Want to know how a combustion engine works? Find out one more floor up in the kid-oriented **Discovery Center**, where little ones also get to climb inside a 1910 Model T and pose as a motorcycle cop. And don't miss the **Alternative Power** exhibit on the 2nd floor where future motor-vehicle technology (think: electric, hybrid and fuel cell) is informed by the past. Parking $6.

Sadly, in 1997, the great gangsta rapper Notorious B.I.G. was gunned down in his car outside the museum after leaving a Soul Train Music Awards party.

FREE **Pacific Design Center & Around**
DESIGN
(PDC; Map p110; www.thepacificdesigncenter. com; 8687 Melrose Ave; ⊙9am-5pm Mon-Fri; P) Design is big in WeHo, with around 130 trade-only showrooms at the Pacific Design Center and dozens more in the surrounding **Avenues of Art & Design** (Beverly Blvd, Robertson Blvd & Melrose Ave). PDC showrooms generally sell only to design pros, but often you can get items at a mark-up through the Buying Program.

The PDC itself is an architectural landmark by Cesar Pelli of Petronas Twin Towers (Kuala Lumpur) fame. Best viewed from a Runyon Canyon (p116) trail or a hotel rooftop, the three glass buildings, one each in race-car red, forest green and cobalt blue, bear a rather striking footprint. The West

saber-toothed cat used to roam around LA in prehistoric times? Even if you're not a fan of the *Ice Age* animated film trilogy, you'll likely have a ball at the unique Page Museum, an archaeological trove of skulls and bones unearthed at La Brea Tar Pits, one of

Hollywood tourist office is on the mezzanine level of the blue building.

FREE **MOCA Pacific Design Center** DESIGN (Map p110; www.moca.org; 8687 Melrose Ave; ⏰11am-5pm Tue, Wed & Fri, to 8pm Thu, to 6pm Sat & Sun; P) Standing a bit forlorn amid the glassy behemoths is the small satellite branch of Downtown's Museum of Contemporary Art. Exhibits usually have an architectural or design theme.

Schindler House LANDMARK (Map p110; www.makcenter.org; 835 N Kings Rd; adult/senior & student $7/6, 4-6pm Fri free; ⏰11am-6pm Wed-Sun) The former home and studio of Vienna-born architect Rudolph Schindler (1887–1953) offers a fine primer on the modernist elements that so greatly influenced mid-century California architecture. The open floor plan, a flat roof and glass sliding doors, while considered avant-garde back in the 1920s, all became design staples after WWII. Today Schindler's old pad houses the **MAK Center for Art and Architecture**, which gives tours on weekends, supports innovative foreign-born artists in residence, and hosts exhibitions, lectures, performances and workshops.

Zimmer Children's Museum MUSEUM (Map p110; www.zimmermuseum.org; suite 100, 6505 Wilshire Blvd; adult/child 5-12 $8/5; ⏰12:30-5pm Tue, Thu, Sun, 10am-5pm Wed, Thu & Sun, 10am-12:30pm Fri; P) In the Jewish Federation Center, this charming museum brims with interactive exhibits that gently teach kids about tolerance, generosity and community spirit. Kids 'fly' to exotic lands, become ambulance drivers, work the newsroom and take other fun journeys.

Craft & Folk Art Museum   MUSEUM
(Map p110; www.cafam.org; 5814 Wilshire Blvd; adult/student & senior/under 12yr $5/3/free, 1st Wed of month free; ⊙11am-5pm Tue-Fri, noon-6pm Sat & Sun; ⊛) Zulu ceramics, Japanese *katagami* paper art, Palestinian embroidery – cultural creativity takes infinite forms at this well-respected museum where exhibits change every few months. Also check for upcoming kid-oriented workshops and storytelling sessions, usually on Saturdays. The gift store is one of the best in town.

FREE **Wall Project**   MUSEUM
(Map p110; www.wallproject.org; 5900 Wilshire Blvd) Some rather artistic slabs of the old Berlin Wall are on display on the lawn of a Wilshire high-rise across the street from LACMA as part of the global Wall Project. Salivating goblins, space-age graffiti and profiles of JFK and Reagan are a few of the images you'll see, but it's the feeling you won't be able to shake.

A+D Museum   MUSEUM
(Map p110; www.aplusd.org; 6032 Wilshire Blvd; adult/senior & student $5/2.50; ⊙10am-6pm Tue-Fri, 11am-5pm Sat & Sun) A small Getty-

GAY & LESBIAN LOS ANGELES *ANDREW BENDER*

LA is one of the country's gayest cities (see p425 for the city's contributions to gay culture). Your gaydar may well be pinging throughout the county, but the rainbow flag flies especially proudly in Boystown, along Santa Monica Blvd in West Hollywood (WeHo), flanked by dozens of high-energy bars, cafes, restaurants, gyms and clubs. Most cater to gay men, although there's plenty for lesbians and mixed audiences. Thursday through Sunday nights are prime time.

Beauty reigns supreme among the buff, bronzed and styled of Boystown. Elsewhere, the scene is considerably more laid-back and less body-conscious. The crowd in Silver Lake runs from cute hipsters to leather-and-Levi's and an older contingent. Venice and Long Beach have the most relaxed, neighborly scenes.

If nightlife isn't your scene, there are plenty of other ways to meet, greet and engage. Outdoor activities include the **Frontrunners** (www.lafrontrunners.com) running club and the **Great Outdoors** (www.greatoutdoorsla.com) hiking club. There's gay theater all over town, but the **Celebration Theatre** (Map p110; www.celebrationtheatre.com; 7051 Santa Monica Blvd, West Hollywood) ranks among the nation's leading stages for LGBT plays. The **Cavern Club Theater** (www.cavernclubtheater.com; 1920 Hyperion Ave, Silver Lake) pushes the envelope, particularly with uproarious drag performers including Chico's Angels and Jackie Beat; it's downstairs from Casita del Campo restaurant (p115). If you are lucky enough to be in town when the **Gay Men's Chorus of Los Angeles** (www.gmcla.org) is performing, don't miss out: this amazing group may change your notion of what a chorus can do. For more ideas, check the freebie magazines (such as *Frontiers* and *IN Los Angeles*), which contain up-to-date listings and news about the community and gay-friendly establishments around town. The website www.westholly wood.com is another good source.

The **LA Gay & Lesbian Center** (☎323-993-7400; www.laglc.org; 1625 Schrader Blvd, Hollywood; ☺9am-8pm Mon-Fri, to 1pm Sat) is a one-stop service and health agency, and its affiliated **Village at Ed Gould Plaza** (www.laglc.org; 1125 N McCadden Pl, Hollywood; ☺6-10pm Mon-Fri, 9am-5pm Sat) offers art exhibits and theater programs around a leafy courtyard.

The festival season kicks off in late May with the **Long Beach Pride Celebration** (www.longbeachpride.com) and continues with the three-day **LA Pride** (www.lapride.org) in mid-June with a parade down Santa Monica Blvd. On **Halloween** (October 31; p68), the same street brings out 350,000 outrageously costumed revelers of all persuasions.

WeHo

Abbey   CLUB, RESTAURANT

(Map p110; www.abbeyfoodandbar.com; 692 N Robertson Blvd; mains $9-13; ☺8am-2am) From its beginnings as a humble coffeehouse, the Abbey has developed into WeHo's bar/club/restaurant of record. Always cool and fun, it has so many different flavored martinis and mojitos that you'd think they were invented here, plus a full menu of pub grub and desserts. Match your mood to the many different spaces, from outdoor patio to goth lounge to chill room. On weekend nights, they're all busy.

Micky's   CLUB

(www.mickys.com; 8857 Santa Monica Blvd) Recently reopened after a fire, Micky's is the quintessential WeHo dance club, with go-go boys, expensive drinks, attitude and plenty of eye candy.

Marix Tex Mex   RESTAURANT

(Map p110; 1108 N Flores St; mains $8-16; ☺11:30am-11pm) It should be stamped on airline tickets: every gay or lesbian WeHo visitor has to go here at least once. Year-in, year-out the open-air Marix has patios for kick-ass margaritas and lots of meeting and greeting, plus great fish tacos, fajitas, salads and other Tex-Mex faves.

Factory/Ultra Suede
CLUB

(Map p110; www.factorynightclub.com; 652 La Peer Dr) This giant double club has an edgy New York feel, and sports different stripes every night. On Friday night, the Girl Bar (at Ultra Suede) is the preferred playground of fashion-forward femmes, while male hot bods strut their stuff on Saturdays.

Palms
LESBIAN BAR

(Map p110; 8572 Santa Monica Blvd) This staple has been keeping lesbians happy for over three decades and even gets the occasional celebrity drop-in, as in Melissa Etheridge or Ellen DeGeneres. Beer is the beverage of choice and the Beer Bust Sundays are perfect for those who don't want the weekend to end.

Eleven
RESTAURANT

(www.eleven.la; 8811 Santa Monica Blvd; mains $13-29; ⊗6-10pm Tue-Sun, 11am-3pm Sat & Sun) This glam spot occupies a historic building, serves New American cuisine and offers different theme nights from musicals to high-energy dance parties; check the website for club nights.

Fiesta Cantina
BAR

(www.fiestacantina.net; 8865 Santa Monica Blvd) Extra-long happy hours, reasonably priced nachos and a busy sidewalk patio are the draw for a vibrant crowd of 20-something revelers. Nothing fancy, but always busy.

Beyond WeHo

Akbar
BAR

(Map p100; www.akbarsilverlake.com; 4356 W Sunset Blvd, Silver Lake) Best jukebox in town, Casbah-style atmosphere, and a great mix of people that's been known to change from hour to hour – gay, straight, on the fence or just hip, but not too hip for you.

Casita Del Campo
RESTAURANT

(www.casitadelcampo.com; 1920 Hyperion Ave, Silver Lake; mains lunch $8, dinner $14-17; ⊗11am-11pm; P) What's not to love about this Mexican cantina? It's cozy, it's fun, and you might even catch a drag show in the tiny Cavern Club Theater.

Faultline
BAR

(Map p100; www.faultlinebar.com; 4216 Melrose Ave, Silver Lake; ⊗5pm-2am Tue-Fri, 2pm-2am Sat & Sun) Indoor-outdoor venue that's party central for manly men, with nary a twink in sight. Take off your shirt and join the Sunday-afternoon beer bust (it's an institution), but get there early or expect a long wait.

MJ's
CLUB

(Map p100; www.mjsbar.com; 2810 Hyperion Ave, Silver Lake) Popular contempo hangout for dance nights, porn-star events and cruising. Attracts a young but diverse crowd.

Other Side
PIANO BAR

(Map p100; www.flyingleapcafe.com; 2538 Hyperion Ave, Silver Lake) Old-school piano bar where the crowd skews older and you can actually hear yourself talk. Friday nights tend to be rowdiest; otherwise it's pretty mellow. Prices are reasonable, and the attached Flying Leap Café does reasonably priced Cal-American cuisine.

Roosterfish
BAR

(Map p164; www.roosterfishbar.com; 1302 Abbot Kinney Blvd, Venice; ⊗11am-2am) The Westside's last gay bar standing is a friendly kind of place that's still current and cool. Go on Friday for the busiest night, or go for the laid-back Sunday-afternoon barbecue.

sponsored space that keeps its finger on the pulse of emerging trends, people and products in the design and architecture community from its new base near the Petersen Automotive.

✻ Activities

Dancing Shiva   WELLNESS
(Map p110; www.dancingshiva.com; 7466 Beverly Blvd; classes $15; ⊙9am-7:30pm) Mas Vidal, a former sprinter and longtime yogi, has been the force behind one of LA's most authentic Hatha Yoga habitats for nearly a decade. He offers group yoga classes (one to four daily) and a full Ayurveda (Vedic medicine) clinic in the studio next door.

Balliamos   DANCE
(Map p110; ☎323-855-9855; www.balliamos.com; 8936 Santa Monica Blvd; classes $20) The mother of *Dancing with the Stars'* Mark Ballas owns this stylish studio, with its suspended wood floor, exposed-brick walls and black-wrapped chandeliers. You can take one-off group or private lessons here. Thursday's popular group-salsa class is followed by a dance party. Call ahead to reserve your space.

Runyon Canyon   HIKING
(Map p86; www.lamountains.com; 2000 N Fuller Ave; ⊙dawn-dusk) A chaparral-draped cut in the Hollywood Hills, this 130-acre public park is as famous for its beautiful, bronzed and buff runners, as it is for the panoramic views from the upper ridge. Follow the wide, partially paved fire road up, then take the smaller track down the canyon where you'll pass the remains of the Runyon estate.

🛏 Sleeping

TOP CHOICE London   BOUTIQUE HOTEL $$$
(Map p110; ☎323-854-1111; www.thelondonwesthollywood.com; 1020 San Vicente Blvd; r $349-649; P❋ᐧ⊛) A sleek, grand and relatively new all-suite property on the doorstep of the Sunset Strip is favored by the young, hip and upwardly optimistic. The lobby's pearl-toned mosaic motif migrates to guestrooms where there's berber carpeting, marble desks, silver washbasins and sophisticated fleur-de-lis wallpaper. South-facing views are massive.

Sunset Tower Hotel   BOUTIQUE HOTEL $$$
(Map p110; ☎323-654-7100; www.sunsettowerhotel.com; 8358 W Sunset Blvd; r $295-325, ste $345-2500; P@ᐧ⊛) Connect to the magic of yesterday when Errol Flynn, Truman

Capote and Marilyn Monroe resided at this art-deco marvel. Fully renovated, this classy boutique hotel with a historic pedigree spells romance in soothing rooms, a flirty bar (in Bugsy Siegel's former apartment) and a top-notch spa with Turkish *hammam* (steam bath). Parking is $30.

Chateau Marmont   HOTEL $$$
(Map p110; ☎323-656-1010; www.chateaumarmont.com; 8221 W Sunset Blvd; r $415, ste $500-875; P❋ᐧ) Its French-flavored indulgence may look dated, but this faux castle has long lured A-listers with its five-star mystique and legendary discretion. Howard Hughes used to spy on bikini beauties from the same balcony suite that today is Bono's favorite. The garden cottages are the most romantic, but the superstitious might want to steer clear of No 2 where John Belushi set his final speedball in 1982. Parking is $28.

Mondrian   HOTEL $$$
(Map p110; ☎310-650-8999; www.mondrianhotel.com; 8440 W Sunset Blvd; r $295-375, ste $405-495; P@ᐧ⊛) Like Ron Burgundy, this elegant tower is staying classy. Even during ever-so-slight renovations, the lobby looked sleek and billowy white. Rooms have wood floors, dangling chandeliers, tinted orange and pink glass accents, rain showers and down duvets. It's been the place to be since its attached Sky Bar's '90s heyday.

Sunset Marquis Hotel & Villas   HOTEL $$$
(Map p110; ☎310-657-1333; www.sunsetmarquishotel.com; 1200 N Alta Loma Rd; r $250-365, ste $445-1175; P@ᐧ⊛) 'Rock-and-roll retreat' may sound like an oxymoron, but not at this quiet, secluded, tropical-garden hideaway that often checks in visiting music royalty including Mick Jagger and Eric Clapton (there's even a recording studio onsite). Being a guest lets you hobnob at the exclusive Whiskey Bar. Parking is $30.

Standard Hollywood   HOTEL $$
(Map p110; ☎323-650-9090; www.standardhotel.com; 8300 W Sunset Blvd; r $165-250, ste $350-550; P@ᐧ⊛) Kind of yesterday's news but still a good standby, this Sunset Strip haunt has you shacking up in sizable shagadelic rooms with silver beanbag chairs, orange-tiled bathrooms and Warhol poppy-print curtains. South-facing rooms have the massive views. Parking costs $29.

Andaz
HOTEL $$$

(Map p110; 323-656-1234; www.westholly wood.andaz.hyatt.com; 8401 W Sunset Blvd; r $240-415; P@🖥🛜🏊) The famed Hollywood Hyatt House (aka Riot House) has been reopened as an Andaz, Hyatt's mod urban brand. The staff is swathed in wardrobe crafted by local designers, the art comes from local painters, and the rooms have flat screens, marble baths, and complimentary snacks and nonalcoholic drinks. The infamous John Bonham party tore up the 6th floor.

Le Montrose Hotel
HOTEL $$

(Map p110; 310-855-1115; www.lemontrose. com; 900 Hammond St; ste $189-399; P@🛜🏊) It's a hop, skip and jump from anything that matters, yet this stylish hideaway still manages to feel like a cocoon of quiet and sophistication. The spruced-up suites are sheathed in an easy-on-the-eye palette of earth tones and lavender, and are popular with clued-in industry folk. Bonus: the rooftop pool and tennis court. Parking costs $30.

Farmer's Daughter Hotel
MOTEL $$

(Map p110; 323-937-3930; www.farmers daughterhotel.com; 115 S Fairfax Ave; r $219-269; P@🛜🏊🐶) Denim bedspreads and rocking chairs give this flirty motel a groovy farmhouse vibe. Long before the renovation, a young and devastating Charlize Theron stayed here with mom when they were hunting for a Hollywood career. Adventurous lovers should ask about the No Tell Room.

Best Western Sunset Plaza Hotel
HOTEL $$

(Map p110; 323-654-0750; www.sunsetplaza hotel.com; 8400 W Sunset Blvd; r $175-209; P🛜🏊🐶) There's more elegance and class at this Mediterranean-inspired chateau than one would expect from the brand. Rooms have crown moldings, rambling bougainvillea twisting around the wrought-iron window treatments, iPod docks and flat screens. Nothing hip about it, but it's nice value. Parking costs $14, and continental breakfast is free.

Orbit Hotel & Hostel
HOSTEL $

(Map p110; 323-655-1510; www.orbithotel. com; 7950 Melrose Ave; r $17-75; P@🛜) Fun-seekers should thrive at this retro-styled hostel within staggering distance of hip shopping, boozing and dancing. Staff-organized movie nights, Sunday barbecues and club shuttles are ideal for meeting up with fellow-minded travelers. Dorms sleep six in full-size beds and have lockers, while private rooms come with TV and bathroom.

San Vicente Inn
GUESTHOUSE $

(Map p110; 323-854-6915; www.thesanvicente inn.com; 845 N San Vicente Blvd; r $89-200; P🛜🏊) There's no boys-only rule, but it feels like it's raining men at this WeHo party-people compound. It doesn't look like much from the front, but you'll soon discover charming and clean powder-blue rooms and cottages, which spill onto a pool, hot tub and tropical garden.

SLS Hotel
HOTEL $$$

(Map p110; 310-247-0400; www.slshotels.com; 465 S La Cienega Blvd; r $369-509; P🛜🏊) A somewhat gaudy, somewhat sleek, centrally located habitat, sprinkled with Phillipe Starck furnishings, lush linens, marble desks and terrazzo soaker tubs. The lobby is more like a rambling lounge with indoor nooks and outdoor patio seating.

Beverly Laurel Hotel
MOTEL $

(Map p110; 323-651-2441; 8018 Beverly Blvd; r $159-192; P🛜🏊) Ride the retro wave on the (kind of) cheap at this slicked-up 1950s motel near the Farmers Market. Rooms wrap around a tiny pool and are just above basic, but framed photographs and diamond-patterned bedspreads add a stylish touch. The attached Swingers hipster diner (p119) does tasty food. There are kitchens in the corner units.

Orlando
BOUTIQUE HOTEL $$

(Map p110; 323-658-6600; www.theorlando. com; 8384 W 3rd St; r $169-229; P@🛜🏊) This fashionista favorite is smack-dab on the boutique-lined W 3rd St and just a five-minute walk from the Beverly Center mall. Natural woods, earth tones and votive candles provide a soothing antidote to an exhausting shopping spree, as do the heated saltwater pool and pocket-sized gym. Nearby chic eateries abound. Parking is $29.

Chamberlain West Hollywood
BOUTIQUE HOTEL $$$

(Map p110; 310-657-7400; www.chamberlain westhollywood.com; 1000 Westmount Dr; r $260-290; P@🛜🏊) Trendy, design-minded travelers dig these 112 gadget-filled studios and suites draped in icy blues and dusky grays, with balcony and sumptuous bedding perfect after a night of cavorting on the nearby Sunset Strip. There's a nice rooftop pool, too. Parking costs $24.

Ramada Plaza HOTEL **$$**

(Map p110; ☎310-652-6400; www.ramadaweho
.com; 8585 Santa Monica Blvd; r $139-399;
P@🅰🌊) Yes, it's a chain, but it's also a
simple, clean three-star choice with ame-
nities in the heart of the action. Parking
is $27.

✖ Eating

TOP CHOICE **Ita Cho** JAPANESE **$$**

(Map p110; ☎323-938-9009; www.ita
chorestaurant.com; 7311 Beverly Blvd; dishes $4-
16; ☺lunch Mon-Fri, dinner Mon-Sat; P) Simply
put, some of the best Japanese available
in Los Angeles, which places it high in the
running for tastiest nationwide. Stock up
on small plates, and don't miss the *nasu
miso* (eggplant coated in sweet miso sauce),
the buttery *enoki,* the broiled *unagi,* and
anything sashimi.

Angeli Caffé ITALIAN **$$**

(Map p110; ☎323-936-9086; www.angeli
caffe.com; 7274 Melrose Ave; dishes $3.50-14.50;
☺lunch & dinner Tue-Sat) Long before it was
en vogue to be doing it slow, fresh, local,
seasonal and organic, Evan Kleinman, the
chef and host of KCRW's *Good Food*, was
doing it all very well at Angeli. At month-
ly family-style dinners (per person $40)
guests join one another at long tables and
pass heaping platters of goodness.

Dan Tana's ITALIAN **$$$**

(Map p110; ☎310-275-9444; www.dantanas
restaurant.com; 9071 Santa Monica Blvd; mains
$22-29; ☺dinner; P) There are three reasons
this 46-year-old exclusive, yet somehow
still laid-back Italian chop house remains
packed with Hollywood celebrities and
sports stars on a near nightly basis: the
steaks, the service, and the hours. It serves
late supper until 1:30am.

Terroni ITALIAN **$$**

(Map p132; ☎323-954-0300; www.terroni.ca;
7605 Beverly Blvd; pasta $15-18, pizza $12-16;
☺lunch & dinner) Traditional Southern Ital-
ian cuisine, by way of, um...Toronto? Facts
is facts, and you will love the *carpaccio
di tonno*; and the *calamari alla griglia,*
the thin-crust *pizze* and pasta dishes are
likewise fantastic. Just don't expect pizza
cutters or substitutions. It doesn't change
nuthin' for nobody! But do demand those
awesome, vinegary, fiery red chilies.

Umami Burger BURGERS **$**

(Map p110; www.umamiburger.com; 850 S La Brea
Ave; burgers $9-11; ☺lunch & dinner; P) This is
where Japanese flavor (Umami is Japanese
for the fifth taste) and the American burger
first collided. The namesake comes topped
with a shitake shroom, oven-dried tomato,
caramelized onions and a parmesan crisp.
Then there are the fresh-cut fries, tempu-
ra onion rings and Japanese pickles. In a
word: outstanding!

M Café MACROBIOTIC **$**

(Map p110; www.mcafedechaya.com; 7119
Melrose Ave; sandwiches $9-15; ☺breakfast,
lunch & dinner; P🌿) Meals are mostly vege-
tarian and all macrobiotic, which means
no meat and no refined sugar. It does of-
fer seared tuna and wild-salmon dishes,
as well as plenty of tasty salads (we love
the M chopped) with sprouts and seeds
and pickled radishes, tempeh bacon and
glazed tofu.

Dominick's CONTINENTAL **$$**

(Map p110; ☎323-652-2335; www.dominicks
restaurant.com; 8715 Beverly Blvd; dishes $8-
38; ☺dinner; P) A Rat Pack staple when it
opened in 1948, this place has effortlessly
held onto that martini-era cool. The brick
patio is a great spot for a long summer's
dinner and the interior bar is ideal for a
discreet cocktail. The menu, mostly broiled
seafood and steaks, is likewise understated
yet satisfying.

Mandarette CHINESE **$$**

(Map p110; www. mandarettecafe.com; 8386 Bev-
erly Blvd; mains $11-13 ☺lunch & dinner; P) We
love the tangy spicy chicken (sliced and
spiced white meat seared and presented on
a bed of Chinese broccoli) at this refined
neighborhood joint decorated with framed
silk robes on the high walls. The food is
classic Chinese that's not too heavy or
greasy, and it's beloved by Hollywood types.

Little Door FRENCH **$$$**

(Map p110; ☎323-951-1210; www.thelittledoor.
com; 8164 W 3rd St; appetizers $14-50, mains
$34-44; ☺dinner; P) When the rich and fa-
mous go out for a fine celebratory meal,
many of them come to this stunning garden restaurant hidden away amid the 3rd St
buzz. There's seared foie gras, black-olive-
tapenade-coated and grilled fillet mignon,
the service is impeccable, and the veggies
are plucked from local farmers markets. It's
an LA classic, but it is pricey, so you may
choose to dine from the all-organic menu of
homemade croissants, terrines and quiches
at the cute **Little Next Door**. Which is...
next door.

Comme Ca

FRENCH $$

(Map p110; ☎310-782-1178; www.commecarestaurant.com; 8479 Melrose Ave; appetizers $9-16, mains $17-29; ⏱lunch & dinner; ⓟ) The dining is French bistro classic. Think: roasted meats (leg of lamb and pork chops), braised pork short ribs, roasted beet salads and bouillabaisse, served in white-leather booths as jazz wafts over you in the sleek throwback space. Oh, and that bar. Cocktails do not get much better (see p120).

AOC

ITALIAN $$$

(Map p110; ☎323-653-6359; www.aocwinebar.com; 8022 W 3rd St; mains $14-18; ⏱dinner; ⓟ) At this jewel of a wine bar, chef Suzanne Goin and sommelier/owner Caroline Styne feed a feistily flavored small-plate menu to friends, lovebirds and trendy families. Over 50 wines can be ordered by the glass. All the better to find the perfect match for the artisanal cheeses, homemade terrines, braised lamb cheeks and other richly nuanced morsels.

Café Midi

CAFE $$

(Map p110; www.cafemidi.com; 148 S La Brea Ave; mains $13.50-16; ⏱brunch & lunch; ⓟ) Let the bossa nova grooves flow at this ever-so-cute French cafe set in the American Rag complex. There are tables on the sidewalk, but we like the sofa lounges and throwback vibe inside. Pouty model types tend to gather to eat quiche and sip espresso off-peak hours.

Matsuhisa

JAPANESE $$$

(Map p110; ☎323-659-9639; www.nobumatsuhisa.com; 129 S La Cienega; dishes $5-36; ⏱lunch Mon-Fri, dinner Mon-Sun) Long before he was a household name, chef Matsuhisa alchemized some of the best and most imaginative cooked food on the planet in this dining room. Robert De Niro couldn't live without the flavor and together they opened Nobu in New York, and then things got all corporatey.

TOP FIVE VEGETARIAN PICKS

» Real Food Daily (Santa Monica, p120)
» Raw (Santa Monica, p158)
» Flore (Silver Lake, p106)
» Bulan (Silver Lake, p106)
» Fatty's & Co (Eagle Rock, p203)

Kings Rd Café

CAFE $$

(Map p110; www.kingsroadcafe.com; 8361 Beverly Blvd; dishes $5-11; ⏱breakfast, lunch & dinner; ⓟ) A hip sidewalk cafe fluttering with pretty girls and boys, with terrific coffee, a damn good Niçoise salad and a deep newsstand immediately adjacent. It closes at 8pm on weekdays and 6:30pm on weekends.

Swingers

DINER $

(Map p110; www.swingersdiner.com; 8020 Beverly Blvd; dishes $4-10; ⏱6:30am-4am; ⓟ) Americana with a dollop of Hollywood is the ammo of this genuine retro diner where booths are red and servers wear fishnet stockings. Join the kool kids combating hunger pangs or hangovers with juicy burgers, awesome fries and other all-American faves while Little Richard heats up the jukebox.

Canters

DELI $

(Map p110; www.cantersdeli.com; 419 S Fairfax Ave; sandwiches $9.50-13, dishes $13-16; ⏱24hr; ⓟ) This sprawling deli, founded in the 1940s, has been the late-night hang of counterculturalists and rockers since the 1960s. Its dive bar, the **Kibitz Room**, once hosted regular Tuesday-night jams attended by luminaries like Jackson Browne and Slash (at the height of his fame). The food is fair. The late-night scene is grand.

🌿 Hugo's

ORGANIC $$

(Map p110; www.hugosrestaurant.com; 8401 Santa Monica Blvd; dishes $6.85-18.15; ⏱breakfast, lunch & dinner; ⓟ🌿) Hugo's blipped onto the Hollywood radar in the early-aughts when Harvey Weinstein was a morning regular. Famous for its terrific frittatas and omelettes (try the Bulgarian – with roasted sweet peppers, spinach and goat cheese), smoothies and a sustainability ethos, you'll want to come back too.

🌿 Green Leaves

VEGAN $

(Map p110; www.glvegan.com; 8351 Santa Monica Blvd; dishes $4.55-7.55; ⏱lunch & dinner; ⓟ🌿) A stylish diner with an all-vegan, all-the-time ethos and a profound Southeast Asian and Mexican confluence in the kitchen.

Joan's On Third

CAFE $$

(Map p110; www.joansonthird.com; 8350 W 3rd St; sandwiches $9-12.50, salads $10-14; ⏱breakfast, lunch & dinner; 🌿🚼) One of the first market cafes in the LA area is still one of the best. The coffee and pastries are absurdly good. The deli churns out tasty gourmet sandwiches and salads and the recent expansion has just meant more, fresh baked, thinly sliced flavor for all. Joan's closes at 8pm.

Real Food Daily
VEGAN $$

(Map p110; 414 N La Cienega Blvd; mains $13-14.30; ☉lunch & dinner; ☑) No need to drive to Santa Monica to enjoy Ann Gentry's famous vegan cuisine. See p159 for full review.

Village Idiot
PUB $$

(Map p110; ☎323-655-3331; www.villageidiotla.com; 7383 Melrose Ave; dishes $6-15; ☉11:30am-2am Mon-Fri, 9am-2am Sat & Sun; ℗) Fantastic gastropub fare with great fish and chips and other comfort food for a smart but still plenty boisterous crowd. This is a pub after all. Kitchen stays open until midnight. Drinks flow until 2am, and it has all the football matches on the telly.

Blu Jam
CAFE $$

(Map p110; www.blujamcafe.com; 7371 Melrose Ave; mains $7-15; ☉breakfast & lunch; ℗☑☝) Yes, it serves lunch, but you should come for the all-day breakfast with organic coffee and tea; there are two pages of mains that include four kinds of Benedict.

Jones
ITALIAN $$

(Map p110; ☎310-850-1726; 7205 Santa Monica Blvd; pizzas & pasta $10.75-18.50; ☉noon-2am Mon-Fri, 6pm-2am Sat & Sun; ℗) If you want good food late in the evening with a rock vibe and a pretty bar crowd, this joint's been doing it since the late '90s. Slip into a booth, get the fried calamari, some kind of pizza, a beverage, and stick around awhile.

Campanile
ITALIAN $$$

(Map p110; ☎323-938-1447; www.campanilerestaurant.com; 624 S La Brea Ave; meals $40-55; ☉brunch Sat & Sun, lunch Mon-Fri, dinner Mon-Sat; ℗) In a gorgeous building commissioned by Charlie Chaplin, owner-chef Mark Peel has been turning market-fresh ingredients into beautiful dishes for over 15 years. Loyal locals practically mob the place on Mondays for $40 three-course dinners and on Thursdays for Grilled Cheese Night.

The **Farmers Market** (Map p110; www.farmersmarketla.com; 6333 W 3rd St; ☉9am-9pm Mon-Fri, 9am-8pm Sat, 10am-7pm Sun; ℗☝) is a great spot for a casual meal any time of day, especially if the rug rats are tagging along. Favorite belly-filling stations include the following:

Lotería! Grill
MEXICAN $

(www.loterigriall.com; tacos, burritos & tostadas $3-8.50) Back-to-basics, authentic, regional Mexican food, which makes it gourmet.

Gumbo Pot
CAJUN, CREOLE $

(www.gumbopotla.com; mains $7.50-10) Southern food so finger-lickin' good, Blanche Dubois would approve.

Singapore's Banana Leaf
SOUTHEAST ASIAN $

(mains $8-9.50) Southeast Asian noodles, satay and stir-fries perfumed with peanut, mango and tamarind.

Pink's Hot Dogs
HOT DOGS $

(Map p110; www.pinkshollywood.com; 709 N La Brea Ave; hot dogs $3.30-4.90; ☉9:30am-2am Sun-Thu, to 3am Fri & Sat) Landmark doggeria with glacially moving lines. Chili dog worth the wait? You be the judge.

Astro Burger
BURGERS $

(Map p110; 7475 Santa Monica Blvd; burgers $2.40-5.60, hot dogs $2-4.25; ☉7am-midnight Mon-Thu, to 1am Fri & Sat, 9am-midnight Sun; ℗☑) Because the city's best damn late-night veggie burger deserves some ink. The shakes don't suck either.

🍷 Drinking

For gay and lesbian bars, see the boxed text on p115.

Roger Room
BAR

(Map p110; 370 N La Cienega Blvd; ☉6pm-2am Mon-Fri, 7pm-2am Sat, 8pm-2am Sun; ℗) Cramped but cool. Too cool even to have a sign out front. When handcrafted, throwback cocktails first migrated west and south from New York and San Fran, they landed here. Expect nothing but the best in speakeasy environs.

Comme Ca
BAR

(Map p110; www.commecarestaurant.com; 8479 Melrose Ave; ☉5:30-11pm; ℗) The brainy barmen serve prohibition-era cocktails – meaning they only use what was available during the 1920s and 1930s. No tropical fruits and, as one particularly surly barman says, 'no fucking cranberry juice.' Penicillin blends scotch with ginger, honey and lemon strained over block ice, and the Mexican Maid mixes tequila, muddled lime and mint, finished with sliced cucumber.

TOP CHOICE El Carmen
TEQUILA BAR

(Map p110; 8138 W 3rd St; ☉5pm-2am Mon-Fri, 7pm-2am Sat & Sun; ℗) A pair of mounted bull heads and *lucha libre* (Mexican wrestling) masks create an over-the-top 'Tijuana North' look and pull in an industry-heavy crowd at LA's ultimate tequila and mezcal tavern (over a hundred to choose from).

Bar Marmont
BAR

(Map p110; ☑323-650-0575; 8171 Sunset Blvd; ⊙6pm-2am; ℗) Elegant, but not stuck up. Been around, yet still cherished. With high ceilings, molded walls and terrific martinis, the famous, and wish-they-weres, still flock here. If you time it right you might see Tom Yorke, or perhaps Lindsey Lohan? Come midweek. Weekends are for amateurs.

Bar Lubitsch
BAR

(Map p110; www.barlubitsch.com; 7702 Santa Monica Blvd; ⊙6pm-2am Mon-Fri, 8pm-2am Sat & Sun; ℗) Would you seriously consider venturing into the Russian wing of West Hollywood and leaving without sipping potato vodka? Remember, a crisp martini on a summer evening can be very good for you. This spare yet stylish brick house of a vodka bar will keep you lubricated.

Beverly Hills Juice Club
JUICE BAR

(Map p110; 8382 Beverly Blvd; ⊙7am-6pm Mon-Fri, 10am-6pm Sat; ℗) This hippie classic, and the first on the LA health-food, raw-power bandwagon, started out on Sunset when Tom Waits and Rickie Lee Jones used to stumble in between shows. It still attracts an in-the-know crowd craving wheatgrass shots and banana-manna shakes. Get yours with a shot of algae. No, seriously.

FREE Foundry
LOUNGE

(Map p110; ☑www.thefoundryonmelrose.com; 7465 Melrose Ave; ⊙5:30pm-2am) Live jazz and absinthe anyone? Granted the lounge is cramped and the restaurant's layout ain't winning any design awards, but you have to patronize a place that brings in live bands regularly, and jazz combos every Thursday night, when absinthe is the cocktail of choice. The music rolls on from 9:30pm to 1am and it's free.

Mexico Barra y Restaurante
RESTAURANT, BAR

(Map p110; www.gogomexico.com; 8512 Santa Monica Blvd; ⊙5pm-12:30am Sun-Thu, to 1:30am Fri & Sat; ℗) In the 1970s this building, known as the Doors Workshop, is where Jim Morrison and the boys recorded *LA Woman*. These days it's cotton-candy pink, strung with Christmas lights and piñatas and drenched in hand-squeezed margaritas at happy hour.

Formosa Cafe
BAR

(Map p110; 7156 Santa Monica Blvd; ⊙4pm-2am Mon-Fri, 6pm-2am Sat & Sun; ℗) Humphrey Bogart and Clark Gable used to knock 'em back at this bat cave of a watering hole so authentically noir that scenes from *LA Confidential* were filmed here. Skip the Chinese food.

Dime
BAR

(Map p110; www.thedimela.com; 442 N Fairfax Ave; ⊙7pm-2am; ℗) Yes, it can be too dark, cramped, loud and overheated, but it does rotate in some good hip-hop DJs, and when most of town is dead, the Dime usually offers some life.

☆ Entertainment

TOP CHOICE Largo at the Coronet
VENUE

(Map p110; www.largo-la.com; 366 N La Cienega Blvd; tickets $20-35; ⊙Mon-Sat) This longtime progenitor of high-minded pop, culture (most recently it nurtured Zach Galifinakis to stardom) has moved to the Coronet Theatre complex. It's still bringing edgy comedy (Sarah Silverman), and nourishing night music (Brad Meldau and his jazz piano to Andrew Bird's acoustic ballads).

El Rey
VENUE

(Map p110; www.theelrey.com; 5515 Wilshire Blvd; ℗) This is one gorgeous venue, an old art-deco dance hall decked out in red velvet and chandeliers and flaunting an awesome sound system and excellent sightlines. Although it can hold 800 people, it feels quite small. Performance-wise, it's popular with indie bands and the rockers who love them.

Mint
VENUE

(www.themintla.com; 6010 W Pico Blvd; cover $5-18; ℗) Built in 1937, Mint is an intimate, historic venue. Legends such as Ray Charles and Stevie Wonder played here on the come up and recent classic crooner Ben Harper made his start here too. Expect a packed slate of terrific jazz, blues and rock shows and sensational sound, and you'll never be more than 30ft from the performance stage.

Troubadour
VENUE

(Map p110; www.troubadour.com; 9081 Santa Monica Blvd; tickets $12-20; ⊙Mon-Sat; ℗) The celebrated 1957 rock hall launched a thousand careers, those of James Taylor and Tom Waits included. It's still a great spot for catching tomorrow's headliners and appeals to beer-drinking music aficionados that keep attitude to a minimum. Come early to snag a seat on the balcony. No age limit.

Groundlings
COMEDY

(Map p110; www.groundlings.com; 7307 Melrose Ave; tickets $14-18; P) This improv school and company has launched Lisa Kudrow, Will Ferrell, Maya Rudolph and other top talent. Their sketch comedy and improv can be belly-achingly funny, especially on Thursdays when the main company, alumni and surprise guests get to riff together in 'Cookin' with Gas.'

Voyeur
CLUB

(Map p110; www.voyeur7969.com; 7969 Santa Monica Blvd; ⊙10:30pm-2am Wed-Sat) From the dimly lit neo-Gothic interior to the pumping music and bustier-clad, whip-carrying dancing girls, to the rich and famous clientele who pay up to $1200 for bottle service, it's all very *Eyes Wide Shut* in here. But that's not necessarily a bad thing. There's a list and a velvet rope, so make arrangements in advance.

Roxy
VENUE

(Map p110; www.theroxyonsunset.com; 9009 W Sunset Blvd; P) A Sunset fixture since 1973, the Roxy has presented everyone from Miles Davis to David Bowie to Jane's Addiction, was central to John Lennon's famous lost weekend in 1973, and still occasionally manages to book music that matters today. It's a small venue, so you'll be up close and personal with the bands.

House of Blues
VENUE

(Map p110; www.houseofblues.com; 8430 W Sunset Blvd; ⊙5:30pm-2am Mon-Sat, 10am-2am Sun; P) Frankly, there ain't much blues playing these days at this faux Mississippi Delta shack but at least its small size and imaginative decor make it a neat place to catch bands of all stripes: headliners and up-and-comers, rock, reggae or hip-hop.

Comedy Store
COMEDY

(Map p110; www.thecomedystore.com; 8433 W Sunset Blvd; P) There's no comedy club in the city with more street cred than Sammy and Mitzi Shore's Comedy Store on the strip. Sammy launched the club, but Mitzi was the one who brought in hot young comics such as Richard Pryor, George Carlin, Eddie Murphy, Robin Williams and David Letterman. These days her son, Pauly, runs it. And gifted, battle-tested comics still prowl.

Improv
COMEDY

(Map p110; www.improv.com; 8162 Melrose Ave; tickets $10-15; ⊙Thu-Sat) The launch pad for countless stand-up comics from Richard Pryor to Jerry Seinfeld to Ellen DeGeneres to Dave Chapelle. Improv still gets the odd headliner, but it's mostly up-and-comers these days. Tuesday evenings at 5pm anyone can grab the open mic.

Bang.
COMEDY

(Map p110; www.bangstudio.com; 457 N Fairfax Ave; tickets $5-15; ⊙Thu-Sun) Another Improv and stand-up lab with a slate of classes and shows, and the occasional celeb cameo. Recent guest stars include Jeff Garlin (*Curb Your Enthusiasm*), Rainn Wilson (*The Office, USA*), and Sarah Silverman (the bomb!...er, the *Sarah Silverman Show*). Their popular Streep Tease show features Meryl Streep monologues performed by an all-male company.

Trousdale
CLUB

(Map p110; ☎310-274-7500; 9229 W Sunset Blvd; P) The first Brent Bolthouse joint since he went indie. Think of a Mafioso rec room and fill it with the scantily clad, well coiffed and comely. At the time of writing, this was brand new, and the place to be on Tuesdays and Fridays.

Laugh Factory
COMEDY

(off Map p110; www.laughfactory.com; 8001 W Sunset Blvd; P) The Marx Brothers used to keep offices at this longstanding club with multicultural programming: Chocolate Sundays and Latino Night on Mondays. It's mostly up-and-comers here but it does get some big names. Kevin Nealon had a residency at the time of writing.

Whisky A Go-Go
VENUE

(Map p110; www.whiskyagogo.com; 8901 W Sunset Blvd, West Hollywood; P) Like other aging Sunset Strip venues, the Whisky coasts more on its legend status than current relevance. Yup, this was where the Doors were the house band and go-go dancing was invented back in the '60s. These days the stage usually belongs to long-shot hard rockers.

Viper Room
VENUE

(Map p110; www.viperroom.com; 8852 W Sunset Blvd; P) Another longtime Sunset cave where young bands frequent the stage. The late River Phoenix overdosed at this venue and passed away on the sidewalk out front shortly after.

Laemmle's Sunset 5
CINEMA

(Map p110; www.laemmle.com; 8000 W Sunset Blvd; adult/child & senior $11/8; P) The West Hollywood branch of LA's beloved art-house empire has all the current indie and foreign-language offerings.

Acme Comedy Theatre
COMEDY

(Map p110; www.acmecomedy.com; 135 N La Brea Ave; tickets $10-15; ☉Thu-Sat) Not the most famous sketch-comedy theatre, but big names like Adam Corolla, Joel McHale and Russell Brand have appeared on stage. There are shows almost every weekend, but the calendar fills up haphazardly.

Zephyr Theatre
THEATRE

(Map p110; www.goldstar.com; 7456 Melrose Ave; tickets $10-25) An easy-to-miss, intimate black-box theatre with amphitheatre-style seating and fun, original productions.

New Beverly Cinema
REVIVAL CINEMA

(Map p110; www.newbevcinema.com; 7165 W Beverly Blvd; adult/senior/child $7/5/6) Serious filmophiles and megaplex foes put up with the worn seats and musty smell of this beloved double-feature revival house that started out as a vaudeville theater in the '20s and went porno in the '70s. In 2007 Quentin Tarantino, who has been coming to this cinema since 1982, held the world premiere of *Grindhouse* here, shortly before the cinema's longtime owner passed away suddenly. Then with the cinema on the verge of closure, Tarantino bought it just to keep the doors open. 'It was going to be turned into a Super Cuts,' he said.

Pacific Theatres at the Grove
CINEMA

(Map p110; www.pacifictheaters.com; 189 The Grove Dr; adult/senior/child $13/9/9.50; ☑) This is a fancy all-stadium, 14-screen multiplex with comfy reclining seats, wall-to-wall screens and superb sound. The Monday Morning Mommy Movies series (11am) gives the diaper-bag brigade a chance to catch a flick with their tot but without hostile stares from nonbreeders.

Silent Movie Theatre
CINEMA

(Map p110; www.cinefamily.org; 611 N Fairfax Ave; tickets $12) One of the last silent movie theaters in the country just went all talkie. But the vintage 1942 art-deco theater has been restored beautifully and is still a revival house where you can snuggle up on leather sofas and watch early John Waters and David Lynch. Check the website for upcoming shows and events.

🛍 Shopping

Fahey/Klein Gallery
GALLERY

(Map p110; www.faheykleingallery.com; 148 S La Brea Ave; ☉10am-6pm Tue-Sat) The best in vintage and contemporary fine-art photography by icons like Annie Leibovitz, Bruce Weber and the late, great rock 'n' roll shutterbug, Jim Marshall. It even has his lesser-known civil rights catalog in its vast archives.

Voila!
GALLERY

(Map p110; www.voilagallery.com; 518 N La Brea Ave; ☉10am-5pm Mon-Fri, noon-7pm Sat) Another La Brea gallery with eye-popping contemporary photography, paintings and mixed-media work, but it also sells rare decorative collectibles, like French clock-tower faces, glove molds and antique print work. It's a fascinating place to burn some time.

Louder
FASHION

(Map p110; www.1louder.com; 7664 Melrose Ave; ☉11am-7pm Mon-Fri, to 8pm Sat & Sun) A groovy boutique featuring underground labels like Atticus T-shirts and Vestal shades. It partners with underground bands on the rise, has bright-colored belts, black skinny jeans; basically anything a disaffected rocker might be wearing. And it has Hensley, the dog. And a damn fine dog he is.

Bodhi Tree
BOOKSTORE

(Map p110; www.bodhitree.com; 8585 Melrose Ave; ☉10am-11pm) For 40 years Southern California seekers have flocked to this cozy converted home, piled with books from all the spiritual traditions (including several you've never heard of), and self-help gurus. There's a lecture space and used-book annex too. Sadly, the Bodhi Tree will close its doors in the fall of 2011. Pay your respects before it does.

Melrose Trading Post
VINTAGE, GIFTS

Here you'll find threads, jewelry, housewares and other offbeat items proffered by over 100 purveyors. It's held in the Fairfax High parking lot and proceeds help fund school programs.

Palmetto
BEAUTY

(Map p110; 8321 W 3rd St) Jane Kennedy's all-natural beauty emporium lets you indulge all your femme pampering needs, from prettily packaged potions to Julie Hewitt's LA-based make-up line and Commando invisible underwear.

Slow
VINTAGE

(Map p110; www.slow7474.com; 7474 Melrose Ave) Worth a stop for vintage shoppers. There's specs and hats, sun dresses from the '60s, band-leader coats and ragged old army threads. It specializes in one-of-a-kind pieces and leather goods. Prices are reasonable.

Fred Segal
FASHION

(Map p110; www.fredsegal.com; 8100 Melrose Ave; ☻10am-7pm Mon-Sat, noon-6pm Sun) Celebs and beautiful people circle for the very latest from Jet, Jill Stewart and McQ at this warren of high-end boutiques under one impossibly chic but slightly snooty roof. The only time you'll see bargains (sort of) is during the two-week blowout sale in September.

Book Soup
BOOKSTORE

(Map p110; www.booksoup.com; 8818 Sunset Blvd) A bibliophile's indie gem, sprawling and packed with entertainment, travel, feminist and queer studies, and eclectic and LA-based fiction, plus appearances by big-name authors.

Polkadots & Moonbeams
BOOKSTORE

(Map p110; www.polkadotsandmoonbeams.com; 8367 W 3rd St; P) Like a burst of sunlight on a cloudy day, this whimsical yet exceptional vintage women's wear shop, stocked with affordable designer dresses, shades, scarves and hats, will make you smile. There's another branch with some new labels a few doors down, but the vintage shop is where it's at.

American Rag Cie
VINTAGE

(Map p110; www.amrag.com; 150 S La Brea; ☻10am-9pm Mon-Sat, noon-7pm Sun; P) This industrial-flavored warehouse-sized space has kept trend-hungry stylistas looking fabulous since 1985. Join the vintage vultures in their hunt for second-hand leather, denim, T-shirts and shoes. It also has some new gear. It's not cheap, but it is one hell of a browse. We particularly enjoyed the period homewares in the Maison Midi wing.

Keep
SHOES

(Map p110; www.keepcompany.com; 523 N Fairfax Ave; ☻noon-7pm Tue-Sat) Are your feet vegetarian? Keep offers funky colors and designs of high- and low-top cloth shoes. All with a hip, urban feel, and none of the bad karma. The kicks are made in LA from mostly sustainable materials.

Guy Hepner Gallery
GALLERY

(Map p110; www.guyhepner.com; 300 N Robertson Blvd; P) Fans of high-fashion photography, pop and street art will love the eye-popping, glittering canvasses of Marilyn and Mao on display at this small but sleek and groovy gallery.

Taschen
BOOKSTORE

(Map p110; www.taschen.com; 6333 W 3rd St; ☻9am-9pm Mon-Sat, 10am-7pm Sun; P) Benedikt Taschen publishes some of the hippest photography books under the sun. He loves vintage landmarks, and swooped when the Farmer's Market Clock Tower became available. In keeping with the image, the interior, though, is all Philippe Starck postmodern.

Undefeated
SHOES

(Map p110; www.undftd.com; 112 1/2 S La Brea Ave) The Mid-City branch of LA's top limited-edition and imported sneaker store offers the smoothest kicks this side of Tokyo.

Harveys
FASHION

(Map p110; www.seatbeltbags.com; 7955 Melrose Ave) Eco-stylish handbags, wallets, laptop sleeves and beach bags made entirely out of recycled seatbelts sourced from junked GM cars. This has to be the most innovative environmental response coming out of Detroit in decades.

Trashy Lingerie
LINGERIE

(Map p110; www.trashy.com; 402 N La Cienega Blvd; ☻10am-7pm Mon-Sat, noon-5pm Sun) Those who worship at the altar of hedonism should check into this cluttered store, stocked with burlesque-inspired corsets, cat masks, school-girl outfits and whatever else girls and boys with imagination might need for a night of naughtiness. To keep out lookyloos, you must pay $5 for an 'annual membership' at the door.

Pleasure Chest
EROTICA

(Map p110; www.thepleasurechest.com; 7733 Santa Monica Blvd; ☻10am-midnight Sun-Wed, to 1am Thu, to 2am Fri & Sat) LA's kingdom of kinkiness is filled with sexual hardware catering to every conceivable fantasy and fetish. Please, who doesn't need a penis beaker and a blow-up doll? Yeah, there's more of the naughty than the nice here.

Agent Provocateur
LINGERIE

(Map p110; www.agentprovocateur.com; 7961 Melrose Ave; ☻Mon-Sat) As sexy as it is expensive (read: very, very), you'll love the sweet and naughty burlesque sheers, lace and

Los Angeles is often touted as kid-unfriendly, but that's a myth. Looking around Rodeo Dr, the Sunset Strip and Grand Ave, you might think that LA's children have been banished to a gingerbread cottage in the woods. But they're here, trust us – you've just gotta know where to look.

With miles of beaches, mountain trails, urban parks and museums dedicated to them, there are countless activities at your disposal and several restaurants fit the kid-friendly bill quite happily.

As far as beaches go Santa Monica (p151), Zuma (p143) and Manhattan Beach (p171) are the best for kids, with wide sweeps of golden sand, and long shallows perfect for wading. Zuma can be a bit more treacherous than the others when the rip tides strike, however.

Pacific Park at the Santa Monica Pier (p151) was made for kids. With a carousel, roller coasters and old school arcades, hours can be spent in hyper-smiling reverie.

At Griffith Park there's the Southern railroad (p102) and the Observatory (p99), as well as horse stables, trails and shady fields where kids can run and spin and play while mom and dad picnic happily.

La Brea Tar Pits (p110) is a must for dino-philes, and what kid isn't in love with dinosaurs?

And the California Science Center (p200) and the Zimmer Children's Museum (p112) are educational diversions disguised as fun.

Then there's the Santa Monica Mountains. All the trails in the Santa Monicas are suitable for and doable with kids – even the trail to Sandstone Peak (p147). We're not saying they won't whine, but kids do love searching for critters, sniffing sage and spotting wildflowers in the chaparral-draped mountains that define the city.

The city's best shops catering to kids include the following:

» Puzzle Zoo (p162)
» Whimsic Alley (p126)
» American Girl Place (p126)
» Lola Et Moi (p142)

For a meal the whole family will enjoy, try these eateries:

» Bob's Big Boy (San Fernando Valley, p186)
» Farmers Market (Mid-City, p108)
» Mama D's (Manhattan Beach, p172)
» San Pedro Fish Market & Restaurant (San Pedro, p181)
» Uncle Bill's Pancake House (Manhattan Beach, p172)

See the Travel with Children chapter (p50) for more family-friendly ideas.

silks that will work quite well with those thigh highs or the slender pumps, and could potentially coexist with that sharp, studded bustier if, you know, the occasion calls for it.

Break Your Neck SHOES
(Map p110; www.byncustoms.com; 7552 Melrose Ave; ☉11am-7pm) Pimp your shoes at this creative sneaker emporium with graffiti art and hip-hop roots, where you can get your basic Nikes, Levis or Converse sneaks illustrated, in-laid and layered. Step out in shoes ($80 to $500) like no other.

Mystery Pier Books BOOKSTORE
(Map p110; www.mysterypierbooks.com; 8826 W Sunset Blvd; ☉11am-7pm Mon-Sat, noon-5pm Sun) An intimate, hidden-away courtyard shop that specializes in selling signed shooting scripts from past blockbusters, and first editions from Shakespeare ($2500 to $4000), Salinger ($21,000) and JK Rowling ($30,000 and up).

Traveler's Bookcase
BOOKSTORE
(Map p110; www.travelersbookcase.com; 8375 W 3rd St; P) It's cool to support indie booksellers, especially ones catering to unrepentant nomads. Its maps, travel guides, fiction and photography books are geared to whet the appetite of wanderlust.

Crossroads Trading Company
VINTAGE
(Map p110; www.crossroadstrading.com; 7409 Melrose Ave; ☺noon-8pm Mon-Sat, to 7pm Sun) One of the most affordable and contemporary of the vintage shops in the area, it offers premium denim labels.

Whimsic Alley
TOYS
(Map p110; www.whimsicalley.com; 5464 Wilshire Blvd) Muggles love LA's own Diagon Alley, where Harry Potter and friends seem to wait just one portkey away. Flip through Hogwarts sweaters and capes at Haber & Dasher, find your favorite wand at Phoenix Wands, or poke around nooks overflowing with Harry Potter memorabilia and like-minded literature on piratology, dragons and wand making.

American Girl Place
DOLLS
(Map p110; www.americangirl.com; 189 The Grove Dr, Grove Mall; ☺9am-9pm Mon-Sat, to 7pm Sun; P) Little girls go gaga for this make-believe toy land where they can take their plastic friends to lunch or afternoon tea at the cafe or a revue-style show, get photographed for a mock American Girls magazine cover at the photo studio or give them a makeover in the doll hair salon.

Meltdown Comics & Collectibles
COLLECTIBLES
(Map p110; www.meltcomics.com; 7522 Sunset Blvd; ☺11am-9pm Thu-Tue, 10am-10pm Wed) LA's coolest comics store beckons with indie and mainstream books, from Japanese manga to graphic novels by Daniel Clowes of *Ghost World* fame. Also here is the kid-oriented store-within-a-store called **Baby Melt**, with a great selection of offbeat books, clothing and toys.

CULVER CITY & MAR VISTA

A few years ago Culver City bloomed from its bland, semisuburban studio-town roots into a stylish yet unpretentious destination for fans of art, culture and food. Hipsters flocked here. Local media raved at such an out-of-nowhere success story, and best of all, it happened organically. It wasn't imagineered by some hot-shot developer or urban planning board. Then the recession happened, and Culver City (like so many other parts of town – namely Santa Monica's Montana Ave) took a hit. Some galleries couldn't make it through. The Jazz Bakery – a horn-blowing, Helms Bakery (p128) institution – closed its doors. Layoffs hit Sony Pictures, which tightened the belts of local eateries, and the optimism waned a bit.

Still, the roots of groovy remain. There are some terrific restaurants and art galleries, the wonderful Kirk Douglas Theatre and the venerable Culver Hotel, where the Munchkins from *The Wizard of Oz* once slept within the city limits. And they still make motion pictures here. Hard times or no, it's clear Culver City will not be ignored.

Neither will Mar Vista. A flowering of laid-back Venice cool and Culver City charm can be found sprouting on Venice Boulevard, something of an asphalt bridge between the two.

⊙ Sights

Arts District
ART
(www.ccgalleryguide.com; La Cienega) The Helms complex marks the beginning of Culver City's vital new arts district, which runs east along Washington to La Cienega and up one block to Venice Blvd. In 2003 art-world movers and shakers Blum & Poe relocated their gallery here from Santa Monica, drawn by cheap rents and airy, malleable spaces in old warehouses. Since then, more than two-dozen galleries have piggybacked on their success.

Museum of Jurassic Technology
MUSEUM
(MJT; www.mjt.org; 9341 Venice Blvd; suggested donation adult/student & senior/under 12yr $5/3/free; ☺2-8pm Thu, noon-6pm Fri-Sun) Arguably LA's most intriguing exhibition space. Nope, it has nothing to do with dinosaurs and even less with technology. Instead, you'll find madness nibbling at your synapses as you try to read meaning into displays about Cameroonian stink ants, a tribute to trailer parks and a sculpture of the Pope squished into the eye of a needle. It may all be a mind-bending spoof, an elaborate hoax or a complete exercise in ironic near-hysteria by founder David Wilson. Maybe. But one thing's certain: the

MJT will challenge the way you look at museums. For an entertaining read about the place, pick up *Mr Wilson's Cabinet of Wonder* by ex–*New Yorker* staff writer Lawrence Weschler.

FREE | Museum of Design Art and Architecture MUSEUM

(www.spfagallery.com; 8609 Washington Blvd; admission free; ⏲9am-6pm Mon-Fri) A private museum curated by artist and architect Judit Meda Fekete, and underwritten by the renowned Studio Pali Fekete Architects. Exhibitions range from paintings to sculpture to architectural design, all with a modern, minimalist slant.

Hayden Tract ARCHITECTURE

(3500 block of Hayden Ave) Architecture fans gravitate to the block where Eric Owen Moss has turned a worn-out industrial compound into eye-popping offices.

🏃 Activities

Massage Garage WELLNESS

(☎310-202-0082; www.themassagegarage.com; 3812 Main St; massages 30/60/90min $32/48/74, facials from $45; ⏲10am-9pm) Feeling as rundown as your '97 Honda? Why not pull in for a 'test drive' (30 minutes), a 'tune-up' (60 minutes) or an 'overhaul' (90 minutes) at this industrial-flavored yet comfortable day spa? Choose from five massage treatments, including shiatsu and Swedish massage.

🛏 Sleeping

Culver Hotel HOTEL $$

(☎310-558-9400; www.culverhotel.com; 9400 Culver Blvd; r $159-179; ⓟ@⛶) The Munchkins bunked in this 1924 heritage hotel in downtown Culver City while filming the *Wizard of Oz*. A mahogany-paneled lobby gives way to rooms with antique furnishings and marble bathrooms but surprisingly few amenities. Although there is live music (7:30pm to 10:30pm) here six nights a week, including the popular Bluegrass Night on Wednesdays.

Rodeway Inn MOTEL $

(☎310-398-1651; www.rodewayinn.com; 11933 W Washington Blvd; r $74-89; ⓟ@⛶) Everything you could want in a budget motel. Rooms are sunny and sparkling with new bedspreads, granite washbasins, fridge and microwave. Some have flat screens. There's no pool, but hummingbirds love the adobe-style fountain gushing on their patch of

grass out front. You're closer to Venice than Culver's main drag if you stay here.

127

🍴 Eating

TOP CHOICE | Curious Palate CAFE $

(www.thecuriouspalate.com; 12034 Venice Blvd; dishes $10-15; ⏲breakfast, lunch & dinner Mon-Sat, breakfast & lunch Sun) A humble, but special Mar Vista kitchen cafe where the chalkboard menu offers sinful sandwiches like the Sloppy Giuseppe (slow-braised lamb shoulder piled into a brioche). They cure their own pastrami, make fresh soups, sell organic chocolates, and toss tasty, fresh and filling salads. Oh, and breakfasts are superb too.

Akasha NEW AMERICAN $$

(☎310-845-1700; www.akasharestaurant.com; 9543 Culver Blvd; mains $8-22; ⏲lunch & dinner Mon-Fri, dinner Sat & Sun; ⏵) The classic building was restored to its original steel, concrete and brick arches with a modern flair, and the kitchen takes all-natural ingredients and turns them into tasty small plates – like bacon-wrapped dates stuffed with chorizo and big ones like the Zinfandel braised short rib.

Ford's Filling Station GASTROPUB $$

(☎310-202-1470; www.fordsfillingstation.net; 9531 Culver Blvd; mains $12-26; ⏲lunch & dinner) The 'Ford' in question is Ben Ford (son of Harrison) and he'll fill you up in his lively gastropub favored by a chatty, boozy crowd. The Filling Station's flatbreads are toasted to perfection, the fish and chips have a tempura lightness, and the vegetarian polenta cake is a symphony of textures and flavors.

Tender Greens CALIFORNIAN $

(www.tendergreensfood.com; 9523 Culver Blvd; mains $10.50; ⏲lunch & dinner; ⏵) The original Culver City branch of the popular Hollywood market cafe (p94).

India Sweets & Spices INDIAN $

(www.indiasweetsandspices.us; 9409 Venice Blvd; dishes $3-9; ⏲lunch; ⏵⏵) A curry-infused, saffron-brushed South Indian deli and market, where you can pick and mix tasty vegetarian mains. The samosas are excellent and so are the milk cakes made with almonds and cashews.

Versailles CUBAN $

(www.versaillescuban.com; 10319 Venice Blvd; mains $11-15; ⏲lunch & dinner; ⓟ⏵) We'll always have a soft spot for the Cuban-style

CULVER CITY & MAR VISTA ACTIVITIES

roast lemon chicken and succulent roast pork doled out to everyone from college kids to grizzled grips. Plates are served with beans, rice, fries and salad, and the service is impeccable.

🍴 Drinking

Saints & Sinners
BAR

(www.saintsnsinnersbar.com; 10899 Venice Blvd; ⏰5pm-2am) No, Mar Vista's favorite neighborhood bar is not into S&M, although the velvet walls, fireplace and naughtily named cocktails have a certain '70s-porn feel – in a good way. DJs usually play a wicked mix of indie, '80s and punk.

Venice Grind
COFFEEHOUSE

(www.venicegrind.com; 12224 Venice Blvd; ⏰6am-10pm; P🛜) Classic roots reggae blends with the steam-engine whir of a top-end espresso machine and mingles with the locally roasted aroma of the world's favorite caffeine-delivery system. Spare and industrial but still inviting – dig those signed Obey prints and classic skate decks on the walls.

Ugo
WINE BAR

(www.facebook.com/ugowinebar; 3865 Cardiff Ave; ⏰4-11pm Sun-Thu, to 1am Sat) This brickwall jazz-washed wine den is notable for $4 glasses of the good stuff (old world and new) at happy hour (4pm to 7pm), and its digitasting terminals. Purchase wine cards ($10 minimum) and taste away. Wine is priced and delivered by the ounce.

⭐ Entertainment

El Baron
CLUB

(www.myspace.com/ebrnc; 8641 Washington Blvd; cover $10; ⏰9am-11pm Mon-Fri, 8am-late Sat & Sun) This humble stucco cottage nightclub has tasty tequila at good prices, and a wide dance floor and bandstand featuring top-shelf musicians playing the pan-Latin spectrum for an almost exclusively working-class Latino crowd. Salsa classes sprout on Monday night, and tango on Wednesday. Show up at 8pm and move.

Kirk Douglas Theatre
THEATER

(www.centertheatregroup.org; 9820 Washington Blvd) An old-timey movie house has been recast as a 300-seat theater, thanks to a major cash infusion from the Douglas family. Since its opening in 2004, it's become an integral part of Culver City's growing arts scene. It's primarily a showcase of terrific new plays by local playwrights.

Zabumba
CLUB

(www.zabumba.com; 10717 Venice Blvd; cover $3-8; ⏰8pm-2am Thu-Sun) See if you can keep your hips from moving when being doused with bossa nova, jazz, *axé*, samba, salsa and reggae at this Brazilian-themed restaurant-bar-club. Every Thursday and Sunday it's salsa night. It serves Brazilian food too.

Actors' Gang
THEATER

(www.theactorsgang.com; Ivy Substation, 9070 Venice Blvd) The 'Gang' was founded in 1981 by Tim Robbins and other renegade UCLA acting-school grads. Its daring and offbeat reinterpretations of classics have a loyal following, although it's the bold new works pulled from ensemble workshops that make this socially mindful troupe one to watch.

🔒 Shopping

Gregg Fleishman Studio
GALLERY

(www.greggfleishman.com; 3850 Main St; ⏰11am-7pm Wed-Sat) Like Eames on acid, Fleishman puts the 'fun' in functional with his ingenious, solid-birch plywood furniture bent, carved and spiraled into springy forms. Lumbar support never looked or felt so... mind opening. And if you think the modular playhouses are cool, dig the automobile bound for Burning Man.

Helms Bakery District
FURNITURE

(www.helmsbakerydistrict.com; 8800 Venice Blvd) From points north, this charming 1932 artdeco bakery is the gateway to Culver City. Sadly the great Jazz Bakery is no more, but these warehouses and studios are packed with one of the most stylish collections of furniture galleries in the city. There are a few restaurants here too, including a Culver City branch of Santa Monica's beloved Father's Office (p160).

Haro Gallery
GALLERY

(www.theharogallery.com; 3825 Main St) Eclectic and deep, brash and vibrant, this expansive gallery has remarkable sculpture, carvings and basketry. There's a blowfish made from recycled bolts, flowers fashioned from steel and blown glass, and enormous freestanding vases lathed from a single log.

Blum & Poe
GALLERY

(www.blumandpoe.com; 2727 S La Cienega Blvd; ⏰10am-6pm Tue-Sat) Major player and juggernaut of the Culver City arts district; reps such international stars as Takashi Murakami, Sam Durant and Sharon Lockhart.

BEVERLY HILLS, BEL AIR, BRENTWOOD & WESTWOOD

With its reputation for old-Hollywood glamour, top-end couture and posh dining still circulating in the collective consciousness, Beverly Hills remains impressive to those who stroll Beverly Blvd and Rodeo Dr for the first time. But if you take a closer look, you might see some slippage. Most if not all of the downtown Beverly Hills shopping is of the corporate variety. The names are here – Prada, Gucci – but most of it is designer in label only (the best shopping is actually on N Robertson). The architecture is also feeling a bit dated, and aside from a few talent agencies and restaurants that still draw power lunchers, Hollywood doesn't have such a heavy footprint here anymore either. That's not to say that Beverly Hills is without her charms, it's just not the scene it was in Dean Martin's day. Still, there remain more Ferraris per capita here than anywhere else, along with 111 gardeners per sq mile, and the median home value comes in at a cool $1.8 million.

Some stars are holed up in the hills and canyons north of Sunset Blvd, but Beverly Hills' wealth is mostly new money, brought by Iranian immigrants who've been settling here since the Shah's fall some 30 years ago. In March 2007, the city elected its first Iranian-born mayor, Jimmy Delshad.

Downtown, several city-owned garages offer two hours of free parking, including one at 9510 Brighton Way. For two hours of free valet parking, head to the garage underneath Two Rodeo (enter from Dayton Way).

West of Beverly Hills, past the mini-downtown of Century City, a commercial district created and named for the 20th Century Fox Studio, is a college town plopped into the middle of a big city. Westwood is practically synonymous with UCLA, the huge campus of which is hemmed in by Sunset Blvd and the Westwood Village. The village is pedestrian-friendly but it's increasingly vacant these days as the charming, but aging, movie theaters continue to lose traffic to nearby multiplexes, and LA nightlife pulls students out into the wider world. A farmers market along Weyburn Ave livens things up on Thursday afternoons. You can snag an hour of free parking in the public garage at 1036 Broxton Ave.

North of Westwood, Bel Air is a favorite hideaway of stars whose sybaritic homes are generally hidden behind security gates and dense foliage, among them the great Quincy Jones' estate and Hef's Playboy Mansion.

Brentwood, west of the I-405 (San Diego Fwy), is just as exclusive and home to one of LA's big attractions, the hilltop Getty Center. Despite a high celeb quotient (Spielberg lives here), it's pretty low-key, and young professionals like the location, close to Santa Monica and only 20 minutes from the Sunset Strip. Marilyn Monroe died in her home at 12305 5th Helena Dr, but more recently Brentwood made global headlines when Nicole Simpson and her friend Ron Goldman were murdered at 875 Bundy Dr. In the subsequent criminal trial, her husband OJ Simpson was (in)famously acquitted.

◉ Sights

FREE **Getty Center**   MUSEUM
(www.getty.edu; 1200 Getty Center Dr; ⊙10am-5:30pm Tue-Fri, 10am-9pm Sat, to 5pm Sun; P ♿) In its billion-dollar, in-the-clouds perch, high above the city grit and grime, the Getty Center presents triple delights: a stellar art collection (everything from Renaissance to David Hockney), Richard Meier's cutting-edge architecture, and the visual splendor of seasonally changing gardens. On clear days, you can add breathtaking views of the city and ocean to the list. A great time to visit is in the late afternoon after the crowds have thinned. Sunsets create a remarkable alchemy of light and shadow and are especially magical in winter, when the orange orb drops straight into the Pacific.

Even getting up to the 110-acre 'campus' aboard a driverless tram is fun. From the sprawling arrival plaza, a natural flow of walkways, stairs, fountains and courtyards encourages a leisurely wander between galleries, gardens and outdoor cafes. Five buildings hold collections of manuscripts, drawings, photographs, furniture and decorative arts and a strong assortment of pre-20th-century European paintings. Must-sees include Van Gogh's *Irises*, Monet's *Wheatstacks*, Rembrandt's *The Abduction of Europa* and Titian's *Venus and Adonis*. Don't miss the lovely **Cactus Garden** on the remote South Promontory for those amazing city views.

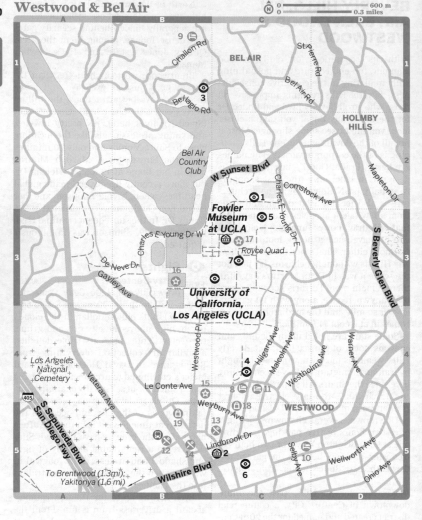

Tours, lectures and interactive technology, including audioguides ($3), help make the art accessible to all. Children can take a Family Tour, visit the interactive Family Room, borrow a kid-oriented audioguide or browse the special kid bookstore. Concerts, lectures, films and other cultural events are another way they keep things dynamic for locals. Most are free but some require reservations (or try standby). The free (almost weekly) summertime Saturday-evening concert series, 'Off The 405', brings some tremendous progressive pop (Meyer Hawthorne, the Antlers) and world music (Bomba Estéreo) acts to the Getty gardens.

Admission is free as well, but parking is $15 (free after 5pm); both Metro Bus 761 and the Big Blue Bus 14 stop at the Getty.

Skirball Cultural Center   MUSEUM
(Map p132; www.skirball.org; 2701 N Sepulveda Blvd; adult/under 12yr/student & senior $10/5/7, Thu free; ⊘noon-5pm Tue-Fri, 10am-5pm Sat & Sun; 🖽) Although it's, technically speaking, the country's largest Jewish museum and cultural center, the Skirball has something for all. The preschool set can board a gigantic wooden **Noah's Ark** while grownups gravitate to the permanent exhibit, an engagingly presented romp through 4000

Westwood & Bel Air

years of history, traditions, trials and triumphs of the Jewish people. This includes displays explaining Jewish holidays, a replica mosaic floor from an ancient synagogue, and Hitler's racist rant *Mein Kampf*.

A busy events schedule features celebrities, Hollywood moguls and fine thinkers in panel discussions, lectures, readings and performances. And while you may be less interested in some of the rotating exhibits, like the quirky 'Jews on Vinyl,' it does lure world-music acts for the occasional summer concert (p77).

FREE University of California, Los
Angeles (UCLA)   UNIVERSITY
(Map p130; ✈tours 310-825-8764; www.ucla.edu; 405 Hilgard Ave; ℗) Founded in 1919, UCLA ranks among the nation's top universities, with five Nobel Prize winners on its faculty

and four alumni laureates. UCLA is also the alma mater of Jim Morrison, Kareem Abdul Jabbar, Jackie Robinson and LA mayor Antonio Villaraigosa.

The campus is vast: walking briskly from one end to the other takes at least 30 minutes; free tours (reservations required) are offered at 10:30am and 1:30pm. It makes for a most lovely saunter, along manicured, sycamore-shaded lawns, profuse gardens and past replicas of Italian Renaissance churches on historic Royce Quad. One of them, the Powell Library, harbors the **UCLA Film and TV Archive** (Map p130; www.cinema. ucla.edu; admission free; ◷9am-5pm Mon-Fri), the country's second-largest after the Library of Congress, with more than 220,000 movies and TV shows. It's only open to researchers, but regular screenings take place at the state-of-the-art Billy Wilder Theater in the Hammer Museum (p132).

Garden retreats include the **Murphy Sculpture Garden** (Map p130) northeast of Royce Quad, with more than 70 stunning works by Rodin, Moore, Calder and other American and European artists set amid jacaranda and coral trees. The latest addition is a ginormous torqued ellipse by Richard Serra in the plaza of the new **Broad Art Center** (Map p130). Designed by Richard Meier, it houses the UCLA visual-arts programs and an MFA student gallery.

In the campus' southeastern corner, the **Mildred E Mathias Botanical Garden** (Map p130; www.botgard.ucla.edu/bg-home. htm; admission free; ◷8am-5pm Mon-Fri, to 4pm Sat) has more than 5000 native and exotic plants and flowers. Enter on Tiverton Ave. On winter weekdays gates close an hour earlier. It's only open by reservation for self-guided 50-minute tours, but the lovely **Hannah Carter Japanese Garden** (Map p130; ✆310-794-0320; www.japanesegarden.ucla.edu; 10619 Bellagio Rd; admission free; ◷10am-3pm Tue, Wed & Fri; ℗) is well worth the trouble. Strolling through this gem, inspired by the terraced gardens of Kyoto, is an instant escape from city life. Call at least 10 days in advance. It's about one mile north of campus.

FREE Fowler Museum at UCLA   MUSEUM
(Map p130; www.fowler.ucla.edu; ◷noon-5pm Wed & Fri-Sun, to 8pm Thu) Near the Film & Television Archive in UCLA, this museum presents sometimes intriguing, sometimes baffling ethno-exhibits. A recent one

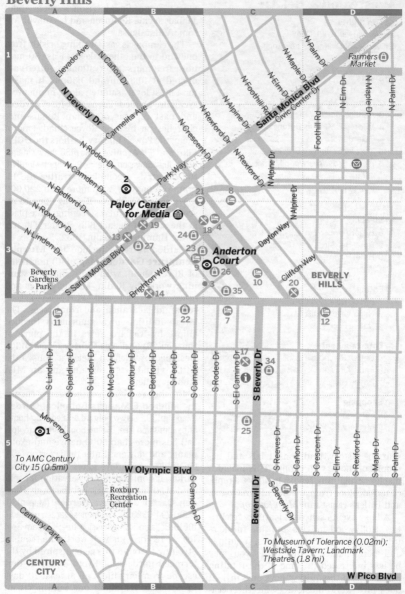

featured the stunning Retalbo-inspired paintings of Mexico's David Mecalco, who sold his quirky devotional art at a humble Mexico City Thieves' Market stall for two decades. Another featured the art and soundscapes of (the other) Nick Cave.

Hammer Museum   ART MUSEUM
(Map p130; www.hammer.ucla.edu; 10899 Wilshire Blvd; adult/senior/under 17yr $5/3/free; ⊙11am-7pm Tue, Wed, Fri & Sat, to 9pm Thu, to 5pm Sun; ℙ) Once a vanity project of the late oil tycoon Armand Hammer, his eponymous mu-

hibits featuring local, under-represented and controversial artists. As an intellectual forum, it presents incredibly diverse, high-caliber and often free readings, lunchtime art talks, screenings, happenings, discussions, lectures and summer concerts (we love the Also I Like To Rock concert series, p77), and the entire museum is free to all on Thursdays. Parking costs $3.

Rodeo Drive
SHOPPING DISTRICT

(Map p132) It's pricey and pretentious, but no trip to LA would be complete without a saunter along Rodeo Dr, the famous three-block ribbon of style where sample-size fembots browse for Escada and Prada. The latter's flagship store at No 343 is a Rem Koolhaas–designed stunner lidded by a pitched glass roof. Most people gravitate to Euro-flavored **Via Rodeo** (cnr Rodeo Dr & Wilshire Blvd), a cobbled lane lined with outdoor cafes for primo people-watching. Tip: if Rodeo price tags make you gasp, head one block over to the more down-to-earth boutiques and chic chains (Lululemon to Jigsaw London) along Beverly Dr.

For Frank Lloyd Wright fans, there's the 1953 **Anderton Court** (Map p132; 322 N Rodeo Dr), a zany zigzag construction, although clearly not his best work. Also check out the 1988 **O'Neill House** (Map p132; 507 N Rodeo Dr), a few blocks north. It doesn't have a famous architect, but the free-form art-nouveau design in the tradition of Catalán master Antonio Gaudí is definitely one of the more imaginative structures in the area.

Paley Center for Media
MUSEUM

(MTR; Map p132; www.paleycenter.org; 465 N Beverly Dr; suggested donation adult/child/student & senior $10/5/8; ☉noon-5pm Wed-Sun) Bye, bye Museum of TV & Radio and hello Paley Center for Media. This industry institution renamed itself in 2007, 'cause, well, this is the digital age after all. Behind the scenes, though, not much has changed. For visitors, the main lure is still the mind-boggling archive of TV and radio broadcasts going back to 1918. The Beatles' US debut on the *Ed Sullivan Show*? The moon landing? The *Ugly Betty* pilot? All here, docs to day-soaps, cartoons to sitcoms, available for your listening and viewing pleasure at private consoles. Plus, two theaters for screenings, live broadcasts and discussions with the casts of shows like *Desperate Housewives* and *How I Met Your Mother*. Getty Center architect Richard Meier designed the crisp, gleaming-white building.

seum has long since graduated to a widely respected art space. Selections from Hammer's personal collection include relatively minor works by Monet, Van Gogh and Mary Cassat, but the museum really shines when it comes to cutting-edge contemporary ex-

Beverly Hills

FREE **Beverly Hills Hotel** LANDMARK (Map 134; www.beverlyhillshotel.com; 9641 Sunset Blvd) Affectionately known as the 'Pink Palace,' the Beverly Hills Hotel has served as unofficial hobnobbing headquarters of the industry elite since 1912.

In the 1930s, its Polo Lounge was a notorious hangout of Darryl F Zanuck, Spencer Tracy, Will Rogers and other lords of the polo crowd. Marlene Dietrich had her very own 7ft-by-8ft bed installed in Bungalow 11, and Howard Hughes, the billionaire recluse, went progressively off his nut during 30 years of delusional semiresidence. Elizabeth Taylor bedded six of her eight husbands in various bungalows. While filming *Let's Make Love*, Yves Montand and Marilyn Monroe were probably doing just that; Marilyn is also reported to have 'bungalowed' both JFK and RFK here.

Alas, by the '70s, the grande dame had lost her luster and the stars went elsewhere. It took 20 years for a 'knight in shining armor' to rescue her from oblivion. The Sultan of Brunei coughed up almost $300 million to make her regain her blush, lurid wink and ability to seduce the power players. Scripts are once again read and deals cut by the pool, in the Polo Lounge, the Fountain Coffee Shop and the hip new Bar Nineteen12. If you'd like to stay here, see p137 for details.

Virginia Robinson Gardens GARDEN (☎310-276-5367; www.robinsongardens.org; 1008 Elden Way; tour adult/5-12yr/student & senior/$11/4/6; ⊙10am & 1pm Tue-Fri) Beverly Hills' ultimate 'secret' garden is tucked among the manicured estates north of Sunset Blvd. Virginia Robinson, wife of department-store mogul Harry Robinson, had a passion for plants and devoted much of her life to creating this sloping six-acre symphony of trees and flowers that can only be experienced on guided tours. You'll also get to peek inside the Robinsons' magnificent beaux-arts mansion, where Fred Astaire, Ronald Reagan and other Hollywood royalty used to pop by for a game of bridge and a stiff whiskey. Make reservations at least two weeks in advance, and even further ahead in spring.

Museum of Tolerance MUSEUM (Map p132; ☎information 310-553-8403; www.museumoftolerance.com; 9786 W Pico Blvd; adult/child/student & senior $15/12/11; ⊙10am-

5pm Mon-Thu, to 3:30pm Fri, 11am-5pm Sun; P (wheelchair)) Run by the Simon Wiesenthal Center, this museum uses interactive technology to make visitors confront racism and bigotry, with particular focus given to the Holocaust. You can study various Nazi-era memorabilia, including letters by Anne Frank, a bunk bed from the Majdanek camp and Göring's dress-uniform cap.

A renovation in 2007 added a new history wall that celebrates diversity, exposes intolerance and champions rights in America. You can also cast your opinion on current issues in a poll booth with the results tabulated instantly for all to see. The 2nd floor has been converted into a creative space for interactive children's programs. The last entry is 2½ hours before closing, and reservations are suggested.

A separate exhibit called **Finding Our Families, Finding Ourselves** (adult/under 12yr & student/senior $8/6/7; ⊙10am-5pm Mon-Thu, to 3:30pm Fri, 11am-5pm Sun) examines the diversity of American society and what it means to be an American. It includes the participation of famous American athletes like Kareem Abdul Jabbar and Michelle Kwan, poet Maya Angelou, and musician Carlos Santana.

Greystone Mansion & Park   MANSION
(www.greystonemansion.org; 905 Loma Vista Dr; ⊙10am-6pm Apr-Oct, to 5pm Nov-Mar; P) Gloomy and gothic, this 1928 castlelike mansion seems better suited for foggy Scottish moors than shiny Beverly Hills. In 1929 its owner, oil heir Ned Doheny, was found with a bullet in his head along with his male secretary in an alleged murder-suicide – a mystery that remains unsolved to this day.

Nobody's lived here since but the mansion has appeared in countless movies and TV shows, including *Spider-Man 3*, *Indecent Proposal* and *Alias*. It's empty and closed except for special events, but you're free to peer through the dusty windows and explore the surrounding park, which has an odd melancholic air about it. Views from the top are quite impressive (drive up to the parking lot).

Pierce Bros Westwood Memorial Park
CEMETERY
(Map p130; 1218 Glendon Ave; admission free; ⊙8am-dusk; P) This little cemetery packs more old-Hollywood star power per square foot than any other in town. Best of all, the staff is happy to have you here and will even help you locate your favorite six-foot-under resident. Lipstick prints usually decorate Marilyn Monroe's crypt next to one reserved for Hugh Hefner, and Natalie Wood, Burt Lancaster, Truman Capote and Jack Lemmon aren't far either. Rodney Dangerfield is finally getting some respect in his spot on the park's south side. Enter via the driveway immediately to your left as you turn south on Glendon Ave.

Activities

Yoga West   WELLNESS
(www.yogawestla.com; 1535 S Robertson Blvd; classes $17; ⊙9am-9pm Mon & Thu, to 9:30pm Tue & Wed, 7am-8:30pm Fri, 8:30am-2pm Sat, 10am-6:30 Sun) Yogi Bhajan (p147) began teaching Kundalini yoga in a dusty antique shop on Robertson. Eventually, he found a permanent location and Yoga West was born. One of his first students, Guru Singh, is based here, and there's no better teacher in all of LA.

Beverly Hills Trolley   TOUR
(Map p132; cnr Rodeo Dr & Dayton Way; adult/under 12yr $10/5; ⊙11am-4pm Tue-Sun Jul, Aug, Nov & Dec, Sat & Sun Sep, Oct & Jan-Jun) A quick, narrated spin around Beverly Hills aboard an open-air trolley.

See Where the Stars Live   TOUR
One could debate the merits of spending precious hours gawking at celebrity spoils from outside a fence or fencelike substance, but if you must see where Leo and Jake G spend their downtime, buy a map to the stars' homes at **Linda Welton's Star Maps** (cnr Sunset Blvd & Baroda Dr), or join a tour (p191).

Sleeping

TOP CHOICE **Hotel Palomar**   HOTEL $$
(Map p130; ☎310-475-8711; www.hotel palomar-lawestwood.com; 10740 Wilshire Blvd; r $209-289; P☎) Hip and eco-funky, the mother-of-pearl mosaic at reception belies the Kimpton chain's green ethos. They compost, recycle and use nontoxic cleaners exclusively, but such earnest leanings have no bearing on the stylish rooms with faux-snakeskin dressers, floating day beds and 42in plasmas. South-facing nests have views of the Mormon Temple and beyond.

W   HOTEL $$$
(Map p130; ☎310-208-8765; www.starwood hotels.com; 930 Hilgard Ave; r $289-609; P@☎) This is where Larry David stole silverware

FAMOUS ALUMNI

They may not be like the rest of us, but even celebs once studied math and science. Our list shows you who went where.

Beverly Hills High School (Map p132; 241 S Moreno Dr, Beverly Hills) Nicolas Cage, Jamie Lee Curtis, Angelina Jolie, Lenny Kravitz, Rob Reiner, David Schwimmer and Alicia Silverstone.

Buckley School (3900 Stansbury Ave, Sherman Oaks) This illustrious private school nurtured Laura Dern, Paris Hilton, Alyssa Milano, Matthew Perry and Nicole Richie.

Fairfax High (Map p110; 7850 Melrose Ave, Mid-City) Home to the cool Melrose Trading Post flea market at the weekend (see p123), this school taught algebra to David Arquette, Flea, Anthony Kiedis and all of the original Red Hot Chili Peppers, James Elroy, Al Franken, Demi Moore and Slash.

Hollywood High School (Map p86; 1521 N Highland Ave, Hollywood) Brandy, Carol Burnett, Laurence Fishburne, Judy Garland and Lana Turner are alumni depicted in the big mural on Highland Ave, but there are literally hundreds more, including James Garner and Sharon Tate.

Immaculate Heart High School (5515 Franklin Ave, Hollywood) No boys are allowed at this Catholic school once attended by Tyra Banks, Natalie Cole and Mary Tyler Moore.

John Marshall High School (Map p100; 3939 Tracy St, Silver Lake) Leonardo DiCaprio's alma mater doubled as Sunnydale High in the 1992 big-screen version of *Buffy the Vampire Slayer*.

Notre Dame High School (13645 Riverside Dr, Sherman Oaks) Rachel Bilson, Kirsten Dunst and Dave Navarro.

Polytechnic High (1600 Atlantic Ave, Long Beach) Cameron Diaz, Snoop Dogg, Marilyn Horne, Spike Lee.

Santa Monica College (1900 Pico Blvd, Santa Monica) Schwarzenegger studied English, and Dustin Hoffman honed his acting chops at this community college that also counts Buzz Aldrin, James Dean and Hillary Swank as alumni.

Santa Monica High School (Map p152; 601 Pico Blvd, Santa Monica) Robert Downey Jr, Rob Lowe, Sean Penn, Emilio Estevez and Charlie Sheen undoubtedly caused trouble at this public school near the beach.

University High School (11800 Texas Ave, near Santa Monica) Marilyn Monroe dropped out of Uni High; Jeff Bridges, James Brolin, Bridget Fonda, Nancy Sinatra and Elizabeth Taylor graduated.

University of California, Los Angeles (UCLA; Map p130; 405 Hilgard Ave, Westwood) Carol Burnett, James Dean, Francis Ford Coppola, Heather Locklear, Jim Morrison and Tim Robbins.

University of Southern California (USC; 3535 S Figueroa St, Downtown) Neil Armstrong, Frank Gehry, Ron Howard, George Lucas, Tom Selleck, OJ Simpson, John Wayne and Robert Zemeckis.

and was forced into a walk of shame. It's where smooth poolside cabanas are the Westside spot for sun-drenched weekend brunches and midweek power lunches. Like all Ws, public spaces are wallpapered in ambient and modern rock music, most rooms are suites and blessed with mod furnishings.

Avalon Hotel　　　　HOTEL **$$**
(Map p132; ☏310-277-5221; www.avalonbeverly hills.com; 9400 W Olympic Blvd; r $228-370; P@☎⚛) Midcentury modern gets a 21st-century spin at this fashion-crowd fave, which was Marilyn Monroe's old pad in its days as an apartment building. The beautiful, moneyed and metrosexual now vamp it

up in the chic restaurant-bar overlooking a sexy hourglass-shaped pool. Rooms facing the other direction are quieter. Parking costs $30.

Beverly Terrace Hotel HOTEL **$$**

(Map p132; ☎310-274-8141; www.hotelbeverlyterrace.com; 469 N Doheny Dr; r $139-199; P 📶 🏊) This older, but high-value, Euro-style property dances on the border with West Hollywood and puts you close to the Santa Monica Blvd fun zone. Rooms are cramped but recently redone in mid-century style with soothing greens, crisp blues and bright reds. The rooftop sundeck is blessed with beautiful views of the Hollywood Hills.

Crescent HOTEL **$$**

(Map p132; ☎310-247-0505; www.crescentbh.com; 403 N Crescent Dr; r $175-235; P @ 📶) The buzzy fireside lounge out front attracts a crowd from time to time, and though the Dodd Mitchell–designed rooms are more minimalist than fancy, they do feel good. Single rooms are a tight squeeze, but Queen rooms are spacious and good value. Parking costs $28.

Beverly Wilshire HOTEL **$$$**

(Map p132; ☎310-275-5200; www.fourseasons.com/beverlywilshire; 9500 Wilshire Blvd; r $495-545, ste $695-1795; P @ 📶 🏊 👪) Now part of Four Seasons, it has corked Rodeo Dr since 1928. The amenities are very much up-to-the-minute, both in the original Italian Renaissance wing and in the newer addition. And yes, this is the very hotel from which Julia Roberts first stumbled then strutted in *Pretty Woman*, and where Warren Beatty kept a suite for 10 years. Parking costs $33.

Beverly Hills Hotel HOTEL **$$$**

(☎310-276-2251; www.beverlyhillshotel.com; 9641 Sunset Blvd; r $530-655, ste $950-2800; P @ 📶 🏊 👪) If the walls of this belle hotel could talk, the tales would make you laugh, blush, cry and cringe. Staying here means dwelling in the utmost of luxury. Parking costs $33.

Montage HOTEL **$$$**

(Map p132; ☎310-860-7800; www.montagebeverlyhills.com; 225 N Cañon Dr; r $550-775, ste $850-1750; P @ 📶 🏊) With new construction in Italian Renaissance style, rooms are spacious and elegant with powder-blue walls, marble foyer, leather martini shakers, sofas and mountain views from the upper reaches. The lobby sprawls with plenty of nooks to relax into, and there's a rooftop pool. Of course, the real attraction is Thomas Keller's new restaurant, Bouchon (p138).

Mosaic Hotel HOTEL **$$$**

(Map p132; ☎310-278-0303; www.mosaichotel.com; 125 Spalding Dr; r $350-700; P @ 📶 🏊) This relatively new and updated 49-room boutique hotel splashed throughout with exotic fabrics offers soothing quarters after a day of power shopping and star-watching. Rooms exude a classic, timeless feel, while the Frette linens, Bulgari soaps and rainforest showerheads feed luxury cravings. Parking costs $30.

Luxe Hotel HOTEL **$$$**

(Map p132; ☎310-273-0300; www.luxehotelrodeodrive.com; 360 N Rodeo Dr; r $150-1550; P @ 📶) Hidden among the fabulous flagships on Rodeo Dr, the rooms here are a bit dark, but they're also elegant, with huge picture mirrors framed in gold leaf, lush linens, frosted-glass desks and iHomes in every room. West-facing rooms have the most light and overlook Rodeo Dr.

Thompson Hotel HOTEL **$$**

(Map p132; ☎310-273-1400; www.thompsonhotels.com; 9360 Wilshire Blvd; r $209-239; P @ 📶) There's a case for style over substance at this new nest, where black-wood floors and a touch of space-age decor have been mounted on old bones. Nevertheless, the rooftop pool bar, the youngish, hippish crowd, affordability, and the Thompson pedigree have made it a bit of a hot spot, in spite of the rattling elevator.

Hilgard House Hotel HOTEL **$$**

(Map p130; ☎310-208-3945; www.hilgardhouse.com; 927 Hilgard Ave, Westwood; r $184-189; P 📶) There's something comfortably stuffy about this 55-room, Euro-style hotel near UCLA. It's an unflashy, unpretentious abode with smallish rooms but the high ceilings make them feel airy, and the antiques offer a classy kiss.

Hotel Bel-Air HOTEL **$$$**

(Map p130; ☎310-472-1211; www.hotelbelair.com; 701 N Stone Canyon Rd, Bel Air; P @ 📶 🏊) One of LA's iconic properties, this Bel Air hideaway favored by royalty – Hollywood and otherwise – is a classy Spanish Colonial estate where white swans preen in romantic gardens and pink stucco rooms come with private entrances and French furnishings. It was undergoing a major renovation at research time and scheduled to reopen in mid-2011.

✖ Eating

TOP CHOICE Yakitoriya
JAPANESE $$

(☑310-479-5400; 11301 W Olympic Blvd, West LA; dishes $2.50-27; ⊘dinner; 🖶) Simple and real, this chef-owned and family-operated *yakitori* (Japanese grilled chicken) joint crafts the most tender and savory grilled-chicken skewers you can imagine. It's one of several tasty Japanese spots north of Olympic on Sawtelle. We love the wings, the neck, chicken skin, meatballs and the minced chicken bowl topped with quail egg.

Nate 'n Al
DELI $$

(Map p132; www.natenal.com; 414 N Beverly Dr; dishes $6.50-13; ⊘breakfast, lunch & dinner; 🖶) Dapper seniors, chatty girlfriends, busy ex-ecs and even Larry King have kept this New York–style nosh spot busy since 1945. The huge menu brims with corned beef, lox and other old-school favorites, but we're partial to the pastrami, made fresh on-site.

Bouchon
FRENCH $$$

(Map p132; ☑310-279-9910; www.bouchonbistro.com; 235 N Cañon Dr; mains $17-36; ⊘lunch & dinner; 🅿) Quiche and salad, oysters on the half-shell or mussels steamed opened in white-wine sauce, steak frittes or roast leg of lamb with artichoke, Thomas Keller's newest branch of his growing Bouchon empire brings you classic French bistro cuisine in classy, but not stuffy environs. You can sneak a taste for a discount at Bar Bouchon downstairs.

Bombay Palace
INDIAN $$

(Map p132; www.bombaypalace.com; 8690 Wilshire Blvd; dishes $7.50-28; ⊘lunch & dinner; 🖉) Our favorite Indian dining room in all of LA. There's nothing fusion or experimental about it, just tasty curry pot, clay-oven cooking from the old country. Munch auspiciously as Hindu gods look down approvingly from their little nooks in the wall. It has a full bar.

Westside Tavern
GASTROPUB $$

(www.westsidetavernla.com; 10850 W Pico Blvd, Westwood; appetizers $9-13, mains $6-21; ⊘lunch & dinner; 🅿🖶) Set in the ground floor of the Westside Pavilion shopping mall, this gastropub sports clean lines and gets creative in the kitchen. Think: pulled pork and leek flatbreads, a tri-tip sandwich piled with arugula and brushed with mustard-horseradish sauce. The most popular dish, the one folks order to go, after they've eaten? Hummus.

Newsroom
ORGANIC $$

(120 N Robertson Blvd; sandwiches $8-10, burgers $8.50-9.50; ⊘breakfast, lunch & dinner; 🅿🖉🖶) Before organic, veggie cuisine became de rigueur for so many, there was the Newsroom – a concept restaurant with a fully stocked newsstand upfront. It's still packed thanks to a creative juice bar, appetizers like the flame-grilled artichoke, and tasty breakfasts (we dig the Cajun catfish and eggs).

Katsuya
JAPANESE $$$

(☑310-207-8744; www.sbe.com/katsuya; 11777 San Vicente Blvd, Brentwood; sushi $5-17, meals $25-70; ⊘lunch & dinner; 🅿🖶) A minimalist Philippe Stark masterpiece with blonde-wood floors and walls, white leather loveseat booths, and sensational (and sensationally pricey) Japanese cuisine. There's a glam-spiced scene here on Saturday nights when the usually dormant backroom becomes the 'Dragon Bar,' with happy hour prices from 10:30pm to 2am.

Tavern & Larder
NEW AMERICAN $$

(www.tavernla.com; 11648 San Vicente Blvd, Brentwood; mains $11-39; ⊘lunch & dinner; 🅿) Two restaurants in one, there's a brick-walled atrium dining room in back, connected to a cool, dark-wood lounge in the middle. This is the Tavern. The market counter up front, the Larder, is open for lunch and brunch only and offers gourmet sandwiches, salads, cheeses and pastries.

John O'Groats
GASTROPUB $$

(www.ogroatsrestaurant.com; 10516 W Pico Blvd, Westwood; mains $12-15; ⊘breakfast & lunch daily, dinner Wed-Sat; 🅿🖶) Come for breakfast, and tuck into Mediterranean scrambles, or the famed huevos O'Groats (a tortilla made with biscuit dough topped with black beans, salsa, onions and peppers and an over-medium egg smothered with cheese).

Ivy
SOUTHERN $$$

(Map p132; ☑310-274-8303; www.theivyla.com; 113 N Robertson Blvd; mains $12-32; ⊘lunch & dinner; 🅿🖶) With a long history of celebrity power-lunches, this is where Southern comfort food (like fried chicken and crab cakes) have been elevated to haute cuisine, service is refined and impeccable, and paparazzi etiquette (among one another and their prey) is a fluid, dynamic beast.

Mako
JAPANESE $$

(Map p132; ☑310-288-8338; 225 S Beverly Dr; mains $9-20; ⊘lunch Tue-Fri, dinner Tue-Sat; 🅿)

STAR-STRUCK

For born-and-raised or long-time locals, seeing stars around town isn't new. Still, depending upon the celeb, it can be exciting. However, the odds of actually seeing a star in or around what may or may not be their primary residence isn't very high – you're more likely to bump into them at Coffee Bean. Even views of the homes themselves are often obscured. But if you have time to kill and feel like doing the paparazzi prowl, grab a star map (p135), join a tour (p184), or try your luck with a meal at one of the top five restaurants for celebrity-spotting:

» AOC (Mid-City, p119)
» Ivy (Beverly Hills, p138)
» Little Door (West Hollywood, p118)
» Nobu Malibu (Malibu, p149)
» Gjelina (Venice, p168)

Champion chef Makoto Tanaka trained with Wolfgang Puck and now supplies the faithful at his own minimalist restaurant. At lunch most order the bento box filled with whatever inspires Makoto that day.

Native Foods VEGAN $
(Map p130; ☎310-209-1055; www.native foods.com; 1110-1/2 Gayley Ave, Westwood; dishes $8-10; ☺lunch & dinner; ☑) Pizzas, burgers, sandwiches, salads – the menu reads like those at your typical diner with one notable difference: no animal products will ever find their way into this vegan haven. Don't come for ambience but do try the Bali surf burger and chili fries.

Napa Valley Grille CALIFORNIAN $$
(Map p130; www.napavalleygrille.com; 1100 Glendon Ave, Westwood; dishes $7-32; ☺breakfast, lunch & dinner; ☑☑) Preppy, but not stuffy, this is the spot for good, honest California cuisine. It grills Sonoma lamb, Catalina Island swordfish, and pan-roasts diver scallops. The grilled salmon club on sourdough is also a great choice. Pair your meal with a glass or flight of wine from the all-Cali wine list.

Elysee Bakery & Cafe FRENCH CAFE $
(Map p132; www.elyseebakery.com; 1099 Gayley Ave, Westwood; dishes $6-14; ☺breakfast, lunch & dinner; ☑☑☑) Westwood Village's

favorite breakfast table since 1979, with delicious coffee, fresh-baked pastries, fluffy omelettes and a wonderful Mediterranean Benedict where bacon is replaced with Kalamata olives, tomatoes, red peppers and feta. Order at the counter and eat in the sunny interior or on the sidewalk.

Crumbs BAKERY $
(Map p132; www.crumbs.com; 9465 S Santa Monica Blvd; cupcakes under $7; ☺lunch & dinner; ☑☑☑) America's most famous pedestrian pastry billowed into a full-blown fad in the early aughts thanks to this small shop where you can choose among dozens of gourmet cakes in cups. You will love them. You will curse them. You will be back for more.

Sham Shiri PERSIAN $$
(www.shamshiri.com; 1712 Westwood Blvd, Westwood; appetizers $4-16, mains $13-24; ☺lunch & dinner; ☑☑) One of a string of Persian kitchens, these guys bake their own pita which they use to wrap chicken, beef and lamb shwarma, kebabs and falafel served with a green, *shirazi* or tabouli salad. They also do broiled lamb and seafood platters, and vegan stews. Come for one of their great-value lunch specials.

Coral Tree Cafe CAFE $
(www.coraltreecafe.com; 11645 San Vicente Blvd, Brentwood; salads, sandwiches & pasta $9-13; ☺lunch; ☑☑) Probably the most popular lunch spot in Brentwood, where spinach salads are served in deep bowls and grilled Portobello burgers are devoured in the open wood-floor interior or on the shady patio. They pour organic coffee, teas and mix mimosas ($6). When we visited, Jessica Alba was lunching. Paparazzi hovered in bushes out front.

Kate Mantilini AMERICAN $$
(Map p132; www.katemantilinirestaurant.com; 9101 Wilshire Blvd; dishes $4-12; ☺breakfast, lunch & dinner; ☑) Restaurants that vacillate from deli to pasta to roast chicken and seafood rarely get anything right. This classic LA spot, a stylish glass box named for the world's first female boxing promoter, is the exception. It bustles best at lunch and happy hour, but breakfast rocks too and the kitchen stays open late.

M Café MACROBIOTIC $$
(Map p132; www.mcafedechaya.com; 9433 Brighton Way; salads & sandwiches $8-10; ☺breakfast, lunch & dinner; ☑☑) Another macrobiotic

shoot off the Melrose original. You won't find meat, refined sugar or dairy here, but there are fish (grilled and raw), salads with radish sprouts and seaweed, and an assortment of brown-rice bowls.

Spago Beverly Hills
FUSION $$$

(Map p132; ☑310-385-0880; www.wolfgangpuck. com; 176 N Cañon Dr; mains $43-150; ⊙lunch Mon-Sat, dinner daily; P) Spago has long been an essential California kitchen, the one that pioneered the designer pizza and made Wolfgang Puck a household name. Book early if you want to scan the power-crowd for famous faces while noshing on the legendary smoked-salmon pizza or other frightfully pricey fusion fare.

Papa Jakes
SANDWICHES $

(Map p132; Santa Monica Blvd; mains $8.50-10; ⊙lunch Mon-Sat) This greasy hole-in-the-wall is a longtime Beverly Hills classic, famous for its Philly-cheese steaks made with thinly sliced rib eye or, if you must, chicken breast. Papa Jakes promises 'the best 12-inches you'll ever put in your mouth.' Um, yeah.

Greenleaf
SALADS $

(Map p132; www.greenleafchopshop.com; 9671 Wilshire Blvd; salads $8.50-12.50; ⊙lunch Mon-Sat; P🞖) A sleek interior with photography and decor dedicated to the almighty leafy green. After all, salads are what this self-proclaimed 'gourmet chop shop' does best. Build your own from the dozens of specialty veggies, legumes, meats, cheeses and dressings on offer.

🍷 Drinking

TOP CHOICE Nic's Beverly Hills
BAR

(Map p132; www.nicsbeverlyhills.com; 453 N Cañon Dr; ⊙5-11:30pm Mon-Wed, to 1:30am Thu-Sat) Martinis for every palate lure the cocktail crowd to upscale but fun-loving Nic's, the only decent watering hole in all of Beverly Hills, where the libations and crowd range from the colorful and sassy to the no-frills and classy.

Polo Lounge
LOUNGE

(www.beverlyhillshotel.com; 9641 Sunset Blvd; ⊙7am-1:30am) With its mix of tennis whites, business suits and chichi dresses, this swanky, wood-paneled watering hole has the feel of a Hollywood country club. Isaac Mizrahi to George Hamilton to David Arquette, you never know who you'll see murmuring in the perpetually reserved, dark booths. It's part of the Beverly Hills Hotel (p134).

☆ Entertainment

UCLA Basketball
SPORTS

(uclabruins.com; tickets $15-150; ⊙Nov-Feb; P) In all of American sports, it would be hard to find a more dominant team than the UCLA squads under the late, great John Wooden. A mastermind of team basketball, the coach, known as 'the wizard of Westwood' cultivated the genius and piqued the intellectual leanings of Kareem Abdul Jabbar (then Lew Alcindor) and Bill Walton, and led his teams to 10 national titles in 12 years (including seven straight), and at one point owned an 88-game winning streak. The Bruins, who play on campus in **Pauley Pavilion** (Map p130), remain a competitive bunch feeding young guards like Oklahoma City's Russell Westbrook into the NBA.

Royce Hall
VENUE

(Map p130; uclalive.org; UCLA; tickets from $22; P) An exceptional theater housed in UCLA's historic heart. The brick building reeks of academia, but **UCLA Live** have been known to bring in authors like David Sedaris and Anthony Bourdain for lively readings, and spectacular musicians like the great Cape Verdian vocalist Cesaria Evora, tabla master Zakir Hussain, and recent indie faves Edward Sharpe and the Magnetic Zeroes.

Laemmle Music Hall
CINEMA

(www.laemmle.org; 9036 Wilshire Blvd; adult/child & senior $11/8; P) Cinephiles will dig this dated three-in-one art-house cinema playing second-run arty and foreign-language flicks. It's the anti-multiplex. Even though, you know, it is a multiplex.

Geffen Playhouse
THEATRE

(Map p130; www.geffenplayhouse.com; 10886 Le Conte Ave, Westwood) David Geffen forked over $17 million to get his Mediterranean-style playhouse back into shape. Boy, is it gorgeous, and the perfect venue to show off his Hollywood clout. A recent lineup included *Love, Loss, and What I Wore*, cowritten by Nora Ephron and starring Rita Wilson (Mr Hanks' better half), and the biographical Thurgood Marshall drama *Thurgood*, starring Laurence Fishburne.

Nuart Theatre
CINEMA

(www.landmarktheaters.com; 11272 Santa Monica Blvd, Westwood; adult/senior & child $10.50/8) This hip art and revival house presents the best in offbeat and cult flicks, including a highly interactive screening of

The Rocky Horror Picture Show supported by an outrageous live cast at midnight on Saturdays. Bring glow sticks and toilet paper.

Landmark Theatres　　　　CINEMA
(www.landmarktheatres.com; 10850 W Pico Blvd, Westwood; adult/child & senior $12.50/9.50) 'Art house' and 'multiplex' in the same breath? That's the cocktail at the recently refurbished Landmark with its dozen deluxe stadium-style screening rooms. The supremely comfortable leather chairs, gourmet snack menu, wine bar and free parking don't hurt. It screens blockbusters too.

AMC Century City 15　　　　CINEMA
(www.amctheatres.com; Westfield Century City, 10250 Santa Monica Blvd; adult/child/senior $13.50/10.50/12.50) Since being expanded and updated, this mall-based multiplex – the best west of the ArcLight, can now host up to 3000 people in 15 theatres, with blockbuster movies on wall-to-wall screens, stadium-style 'loveseats' with lifting armrests and top-notch sound.

Vibrato Grill & Jazz　　　　JAZZ
(www.vibratogrilljazz.com; 2930 Beverly Glen Circle, Bel Air) Trumpet-legend Herb Alpert is the man behind this posh Bel Air supper club, and he's got the pull to bring in big-name acts. There's usually no cover with dinner or a two-drink minimum; all ages.

🔒 Shopping
While Downtown Beverly Hills and Rodeo Dr still get most of the shopping hype, the best boutiques are hidden in plain sight on Robertson, between Beverly Blvd and Burton Way.

Undrest　　　　LINGERIE
(www.undrest.com; 110 S Robertson Blvd) From laid-back supina, silk and satin loungewear to sexy French lace and chiffon, to cashmere knit underthings inspired by the '20s this designer label boutique (the first of its kind) manufactures its goods in LA. It even has blindfolds and garter belts, and Barbie dolls dressed by Undrest.

Coppola Art Exchange　　　　GALLERY
(Map p132; www.coppolaartexchange.com; 315 S Beverly Dr) Yes, the owner's a Coppola. No, she's not Hollywood royalty. But she has amassed one hell of a collection of fine and pop-art oils and lithographs, as well as some phenomenal rock-and-roll photography by the great Richard E Aaron.

Barneys New York　　　　DEPARTMENT STORE
(Map p132; www.barneys.com; 9570 Wilshire Blvd; ☺10am-7pm Mon-Wed, Fri & Sat, to 8pm Thu, noon-6pm Sun; P) When Vince and his Entourage go shopping together (and, seriously, how butch is that?), they explore these four floors of chic. Prices are steep, so keep any eye out for one of its twice-annual warehouse sales for some cheap threads.

Kitson　　　　FASHION
(Map p132; www.shopkitson.com; 115 S Robertson Blvd; ☺10am-7:30pm Mon-Sat, 11am-6pm Sun) Paris and her crew made it famous, and high-energy tunes keep cover girls fast-flipping through up-to-the-second hoodies, purses, shoes and jeans. It's a routine stop for celebs before or after lunch at the Ivy (p138). Guys should check the goods at **Kitson Men** (Map p132; 146 N Robertson Blvd).

Lisa Kline　　　　FASHION
(Map p132; www.lisakline.com; 143 S Robertson Blvd; ☺11am-7pm Mon-Sat, to 6pm Sun) Lisa Kline was a style-maker on Robertson long before it became a fashion runway. She stocks plenty of denim plus all the hot labels you see on LA starlets and also does her own line. She has **Lisa Kline Kids** (Map p132; 123 S Robertson Blvd; ☺9am-5pm Mon-Sat, to 4pm Sun) up the block.

Cheese Store of Beverly Hills　　　　FINE FOOD
(Map p132; www.cheesestorebh.com; 419 N Beverly Dr; ☺Mon-Sat) Mimolette and Raclette are not characters in a French opera but just two of the hundreds of handcrafted bries, blues, goudas and other cheeses temptingly displayed at this delectable *fromagerie* along with the world's finest olive oils, wines, pâtés and pestos.

American Tea Room　　　　FINE FOOD
(Map p132; www.americantearoom.com; 401 N Cañon Dr) If you consider fine tea one of life's great pleasures, you'll find kindred spirits at this exquisite boutique. Friendly staff will gladly help you find a new favorite from among the 250 varieties of quality teas from the Amazon to north China, each with its own distinctive character.

Mystery Bookshop　　　　BOOKSTORE
(Map p130; www.mystery-bookstore.com; 1036-C Broxton Ave, Westwood; ☺10am-7pm Mon-Thu, to 9pm Fri & Sat, 11am-4pm Sun) If you crave whodunits, if you like a sniff of whiskey and a perplexing crime scene, and if you like to meet crime authors up close and personal, this place is for you. From noir to screwball, if there's a case to be solved, it's here.

Compartes of California   CHOCOLATIER

(www.compartes.com; 912 S Barrington Ave, Brentwood) Compartes has supplied mouth-watering truffles, toffees and chocolates to Frank Sinatra, Nicole Kidman and other chocophiles for more than half a century. Its specialty, though, is hand-dipped fruits. Try the apricots drenched in rich dark chocolate.

K Chocolatier   CHOCOLATIER

(Map p132; www.dianekronchocolates; 9606 S Santa Monica Blvd) Dark mints to Viennese marzipan, Diane Krön's chocolate creations are truly decadent. This goes especially for the K Sensuals line made with Chinese herbs that supposedly work like Viagra for women.

Lola Et Moi   CHILDREN

(Map p132; www.lolaetmoi.com; 238 1/2 S Beverly Dr) OK, the prices are absurd. After all, kids' clothes were always destined to be the canvas of chocolate ice cream and cranberry juice stains. But with an emphasis on 1960s flower-child style, they are damned cute, and with prices frequently slashed by 50%, they're affordable. If a bit unreasonable.

You're guaranteed superior quality, with corresponding price tags, at any of the jewelry shops on Rodeo Dr in Beverly Hills. For those of us who failed to triple our net worth during that Vegas side trip, even a pair of tiny diamond stud earrings may remain elusive at $4000. But, hey, there's no cost for oohing and aahing at the trio of treasure chests listed below.

Tiffany   JEWELRY

(Map p132; www.tiffany.com; 210 N Rodeo Dr)

Cartier   JEWELRY

(Map p132; www.cartier.us; 370 N Rodeo Dr)

Harry Winston   JEWELRY

(Map p132; www.harrywinston.com; 310 N Rodeo Dr) The ultimate diamond purveyor to the stars.

MALIBU & PACIFIC PALISADES

Malibu enjoys near-mythical status thanks to its large celebrity population, and the incredible beauty of its coastal mountains, pristine coves, wide sweeps of golden sand and epic waves. Stretched out for 27 miles, there are several small commercial strips, but the heart of town is at the foot of Pepperdine where you'll find the Malibu Country Mart and the Malibu Civic Center.

Malibu has been celebrity central since the 1930s when money troubles forced landowner May Rindge to lease out property to her famous Hollywood buds. Clara Bow and Barbara Stanwyck were the first to stake out their turf in what would become the Malibu Colony (Map p144). Privacy-seeking A-listers, including Leo, Britney, Jennifer and many others are or have been residents, owning or renting houses for as much as $25,000 per month. While it's impossible to get past the gate without a personal invitation from a resident, you could always join the paparazzi on the beach – just stay below the high-tide mark. For photogenic birds'-eye views of the colony, head a little up the coast to Malibu Bluffs Park.

Despite its wealth and star quotient, the best way to appreciate Malibu is through its natural assets, so grab your sunscreen and a towel and head to the beach. Westward Beach, Zuma and El Matador are especially nice and teem with tight bods on summer weekends. You may strike gold and find free parking on the Pacific Coast Hwy (PCH; check signs for restrictions), but otherwise lots charge between $6 and $10. On summer weekends they often fill up by midday.

During the cooler months, hitting the trails of the Santa Monica Mountains National Recreation Area, including Malibu Creek, Sycamore Canyon and La Jolla Canyon State Parks is a ticket to sanity for many locals.

South of Malibu, Pacific Palisades, founded by Methodists in the 1920s, is another upscale neighborhood with a small-town feel, high celebrity quotient and the Getty Villa blockbuster sight. Strolling along Sunset Blvd and its side streets you may spot local residents Tom Hanks or Hillary Swank.

In the 1930s the Palisades' gorgeous setting and Mediterranean charm lured numerous European exiles, including writers Thomas Mann and Lion Feuchtwanger – who escaped a Nazi work camp. In the early 1980s it became known more for its overprivileged, cocaine-driven teens whose antics resembled those detailed in Brett Easton Ellis' brilliant 1985 novel *Less Than Zero*. These days it's a mellow, moneyed slice of suburbia with a sniff of seawater in the air.

Malibu's locals, famous for their love of privacy, don't want you to know this, but you're actually free to be on any beach as long as you stay below the high-tide line. That means you can walk, swim, beach comb or whatever right on Carbon Beach, Broad Beach, Little Dume and wherever the famous like to frolic. You may get nasty looks from security guards, but there's nothing they can legally do to stop you from being there. Driving along Pacific Coast Hwy, keep an eye out for the brown Coastal Access signs. Locals have been known to take them down and put up 'Private Beach' or 'No Trespassing' signs; don't be deterred. For the full scoop and 'secret' access points, download the handy map and guide from www.laurbanrangers.org.

◉ Sights

El Matador State Beach   OUTDOORS

(32215 Pacific Coast Hwy; P) Arguably Malibu's most stunning beach, where sandstone rock towers rise from emerald coves, topless sunbathers stroll through the tides, and dolphins breech the surface beyond the waves. Spectacular.

Zuma & Westward Beach   OUTDOORS

Zuma (30000 Pacific Coast Hwy); Westward (6800 Westward Rd; P) Zuma is easy to find, and thanks to the wide sweep of blonde sand that has been attracting valley kids to the shore since the 1970s, it gets busy on weekends and summer afternoons. But we prefer Westward Beach. That same wide stretch of sand winds south of Zuma and wraps halfway around hulking Point Dume. Here the surf thunders and rip currents can be strong, but the water is crystal clear, and sea lions, seals and dolphins are frequent visitors. If you get here early you should find free parking on Westward Rd. Point Dume State Beach begins once you pass through the parking gate south of The Sunset restaurant.

Surfrider Beach   OUTDOORS

(26000 Pacific Coast Hwy; P) Surf punks descend in droves to this sandy and rocky point that shapes some of the best waves on earth. There are several breaks here. The first is well formed for beginners and long boarders, the second and third breaks demand short boards and advanced-level skill. Whichever way you ride, know your etiquette before paddling out.

Topanga Canyon State Park   OUTDOORS

(Map p144; www.parks.ca.gov; Entrada Rd; per vehicle $10; ☺8am-dusk; P) There are 36 miles of trails in this scenic 11,529-acre state park that wind through grass savannah and aromatic chaparral, duck beneath shady live oaks, reach peaks and skirt cliffs with ocean views. Most link with the Santa Monica Mountains' contiguous **Backbone Trail**, which means you can hike north and south from here to other canyons and parks. A quick day hike from park headquarters leads 2.2 miles south to a waterfall along the Santa Ynez trail. The **Eagle Rock Trail** (2 miles) leads to a picnic area surrounded by contoured ridges.

FREE Getty Villa   MUSEUM

(Map p144; www.getty.edu; 17985 Pacific Coast Hwy; P) Although self-described as the Getty Villa Malibu, this famous museum in a replica 1st-century Roman villa is actually in Pacific Palisades. It's a stunning 64-acre showcase for exquisite Greek, Roman and Etruscan antiquities amassed by oil tycoon J Paul Getty. When it reopened in 2006 after a seven-year renovation, the institution immediately found egg on its face when allegations of illegally obtained treasures surfaced. Although dozens of items have since been returned to Italy, there's plenty left. You'll see wine goblets, beads and pendants culled from Partha tombs, and cut, blown and colored glass from the 1st century. The geometric configurations in the **Hall of Colored Marble** will bend your brain. Then there's the **Temple of Herkales**, and who doesn't love an action hero? The upper balcony has the best view of the lovely courtyard garden – a spare yet attractive quilt of Mediterranean and native herbs framed by palms and roses and surrounding a reflecting pool. Don't miss the oft-ignored **East Garden**, which abuts a wooded hillside and sports a champagne-glass fountain surrounded by grasses and lilies.

Admission is theoretically free, and available by timed ticket, which can be reserved online, but parking costs $15, and there are

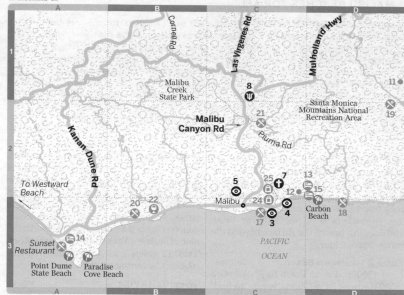

no drop-offs or walk-ins allowed unless you arrive by public bus and ask the driver to hole-punch your villa ticket.

FREE **Self-Realization Fellowship Lake Shrine**
SPIRITUAL
(Map p144; www.lakeshrine.org; 17190 Sunset Blvd; ⊙9am-4:30pm Tue-Sat, 12:30-4:30pm Sun; P) An oasis of Jah-love in the Pacific Palisades. No matter your religious persuasion, any negative vibes just seem to disappear while strolling these uplifting meditation gardens. Paths meander around a spring-fed, artificial lake and past clumps of flowers and swaying palms to a windmill turned chapel where George Harrison's memorial was held, and back to a shrine containing some of the ashes of Mahatma Gandhi. Sprinkled throughout are quotes from Hindu and Christian saints. The gold-lotus peaked sanctuary situated on the hillside is where meditation services and lectures are held by resident monks and nuns on Friday evenings at 7:30pm and Sundays at 6:30pm, and are open to the public. The fellowship was founded in 1925 by charismatic yogi Paramahansa Yogananda, one of the first yogis to come to the West from India. His teachings blend traditions and stories from the five major religions.

Malibu Pier
LANDMARK
(Map p144; www.malibupiersportfishing.com) The recently restored vintage pier marks the beginning of Malibu's commercial heart. It's open for strolling and license-free pier fishing (note the brackets for your rod and reel) and delivers fine views of surfers riding waves off Surfrider Beach. The two restaurants cater to tourists almost exclusively.

Adamson House & Malibu Lagoon Museum
LANDMARK
(Map p144; www.adamsonhouse.org; 23200 Pacific Coast Hwy; adult/child $5/2; ⊙11am-3pm Wed-Sat; P) Up on a bluff overlooking Surfrider is this gorgeous Spanish-style villa, which used to belong to the Rindge family and is awash in locally made, hand-painted tiles. Check out the 'Persian rug' in the entryway and the tiled dog bath outside. To learn more about Malibu's arc of history – Chumash to glamourtown – pop into the adjacent Malibu Lagoon Museum. The last tour leaves at 2pm. From here it's a pleasant stroll through the marsh to Surfrider Beach.

Serra Retreat
CATHOLIC RETREAT
(Map p144; www.serraretreat.com; 3401 Serra Rd; admission free; ⊙9am-4:30pm) Another for-

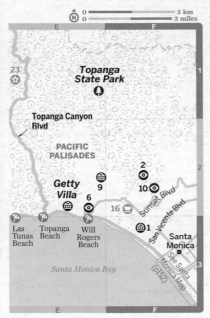

Malibu Lagoon State Beach OUTDOORS

(www.parks.ca.gov; P) This salty marsh is where Malibu Creek meets the ocean, attracting migratory birds and their human admirers. Bring a picnic and binoculars and grab a spot in the sand or at a picnic table near Malibu Creek Bridge. Unfortunately, the water quality is usually terrible, so swimmers should push on further north.

Pepperdine University UNIVERSITY

(Map p144; www.pepperdine.edu; 24255 Pacific Coast Hwy; admission free; P) Self-assuredly holding court atop a grassy slope where deer graze at sundown, this private institution affiliated with the Church of Christ has views of the Pacific and the mountains and is easily one of the world's most beautiful campuses. Ken Starr, the independent investigator who revealed to the world where Bill Clinton put his cigars, was the dean of the law school here from 2004 to 2010. Art fans should check out the latest show at the university's **Frederick R Weisman Museum of Art** (www.pepperdine.edu/arts/museum; admission free; ☉11am-5pm Tue-Sun; P), which has some pretty edgy works created by contemporary American artists.

Will Rogers State Historic Park

MONUMENT, OUTDOORS

(Map p144; www.parks.ca.gov; 1501 Will Rogers State Park Rd; ☉8am-sunset; P🛜) Rugged but small, this park sprawls across ranch land once owned by Will Rogers (1875–1935), an Oklahoma-born cowboy turned humorist, radio-show host and movie star (in the early 1930s he was the highest paid actor in Hollywood). In the late '20s he traded his Beverly Hills manse for a 31-room **ranch house** (☉tours 11am, 1pm & 2pm Thu & Fri, hourly 10am-4pm Sat & Sun) and lived here until his tragic 1935 death by plane crash. Following extensive renovations free guided tours allow you to again nose around the Western art and Native American rugs and baskets and marvel at the porch swing right in the living room. Parking costs $7.

The park's chaparral-cloaked hills, where Rogers used to ride his horses, are laced with trails and offer an easy escape from the LA hubbub. The best time for a ramble is late in the day when the setting sun delivers golden views of the mountains, city and ocean from **Inspiration Point**. They're yours after an easy-to-moderate 1.5-mile trek. Trails continue along the Backbone Trail into Topanga State Park.

mer Rindge home is now a religious sanctuary. Martin Sheen, a longtime Malibu mainstay, is known to visit with the Franciscan friars in the lovely ocean-view gardens. You're free to walk around and enjoy the flowers and the views, but respect the tranquil, hushed ambience. The Serra Rd turnoff is about a quarter mile west of the Malibu Pier (look for the sign and tell the guard you're going to the retreat). The road winds through another celebrity enclave where Britney unloaded her home for a cool $12 million in 2007.

Sri Venka Teswara Swamy Temple

HINDU TEMPLE

(Map p144; 1600 Las Virgenes Canyon Rd; admission free; ☉9am-noon & 5-8pm Mon-Fri, 9am-8pm Sat & Sun, to 7pm Nov-Mar; P) This house (or, more precisely, these houses) of Hindu gods sneaks up on you as you drive up Malibu Canyon, but you won't miss the ivory towers located 6.5 miles north of Pepperdine. Temple grounds are shaped and dappled like a big blissful sandcastle and include a series of shrines to various deities such as Laxmi and Saraswati. Visitors are welcome any time, but it's best to visit on a Hindu holiday when colorfully robed flocks descend with fruit, flowers and smoldering incense in hand. Kick your shoes off at the entrance.

Malibu

A big polo fan, Will Rogers built his own field to yee-haw it with such famous buddies as Spencer Tracy, Gary Cooper and Walt Disney. The **Will Rogers Polo Club** (www.willrogerspolo.org; admission free; ☺2pm Sat, 10am Sun late Apr–early Oct) still plays in the park on what is the city's only remaining polo field.

Eames House & Studio MONUMENT
(Map p144; ☎310-459-9663; www.eamesfoun dation.org; 203 Chautauqua Blvd; suggested donation $5; ☺10am-4pm Mon-Fri, to 3pm Sat; ℙ) The striking Eames House & Studio, built in 1949 by Charles and Ray Eames, resembles a Mondrian painting in 3-D. It's still used by the Eames family, but with at least 48-hour advance reservations you can study the exterior, walk around the garden, which was a natural meadow preserved by the Eames, and peek through the window into the kitchen and living room. Visitors

are allowed inside the home if they become members of the Eames Foundation.

While here also have a look at the adjacent 1949 **Entenza House** (Map p144; 205 Chautauqua Blvd). Termite infested, torn down and rebuilt almost exactly as it was designed by Charles Eames and Eero Saarinen, it can be seen peeking elegantly behind that modern monstrosity. The best view is across the wall from the Eames House garden. Richard Neutra designed the nearby **Bailey House** (Map p144; 219 Chautauqua Blvd), which was built from 1946 to 1948.

FREE Villa Aurora CULTURAL
(Map p144; ☎310-454-4231; www.villa -aurora.org; Paseo Miramar) High in the hills above Sunset Blvd, Lion Feuchtwanger's old home, complete with a 1927 pipe organ (yes, there is an organ room), thick timber-beamed ceilings and miraculous sea views, was once a gathering place for European

artists and intellectuals in exile. Folks like Bertholt Brecht, Charles Chaplin and Thomas Mann were part of Feuchtwagner's loose network and buzz-worthy salons. It stands to reason then that it is now a German-American art and cultural center hosting visiting artists, musicians, film-makers and writers in residence. It hosts occasional concerts, screenings and events here too. In fact, there was a pre-Oscar reception for *Inglorious Busterds*' Best Sup porting Actor Christoph Waltz here. Tours are free but must be arranged in advance.

Malibu Canyon   SCENIC DRIVE
(Map p144; Malibu Canyon Rd) One of the most beautiful drives through the Santa Monica Mountains starts right next to Pepperdine on Malibu Canyon Rd, which cuts through Malibu Creek State Park, bisects Mulholland Hwy (beyond which it's called Las Virgenes Rd) and joins with the 101 (Ventura Fwy) near Agoura Hills.

Topanga Canyon   SCENIC DRIVE
(Map p144; Topanga Canyon Rd) Take this sinuous road from the sea and climb into a primordial cut deep in the Santa Monica Mountains, one that lays bare naked boulders and reveals jagged chaparral-covered peaks from every hairpin turn. The road is shadowed by lazy oaks and glimmering sycamores and the whole thing smells of windblown black sage and 'cowboy cologne' (artemisia). About halfway to the pass, a cute country town sprouts on both sides of the highway where you'll find several restaurants, including **Inn of the Seventh Ray** (p150) and the always special **Will Geer Theatricum Botanicum** (p150).

🏃 Activities

TOP CHOICE **Mishe Mokwa Trail & Sandstone Peak**   HIKING
(www.nps.gov/samo; 12896 Yerba Buena Rd; P) On warm spring mornings when the snowy blue *ceonothus* perfumes the air with honeysuckle, the Santa Monica Mountains are green and striped with wildflowers, there's no better place to be than this 6-mile loop trail that winds through a red-rock canyon dotted with climbers, through the oak oasis at **Split Rock** and up to the tallest mountain in the Santa Monica Mountains, Mount Allen, aka Sandstone Peak. With a

---

SWAMIS, HIPPIES & HOLLYWOOD

Los Angeles enjoys one of the richest and deepest yoga traditions in the West, because this was where the gurus first brought forth their peaceful warrior wisdom from the ashrams of India. Parmanahansa Yogananda was one of the first to make the Stateside sojourn, when he came straight from Ranchi, India to address a religious conference in 1920. He could barely speak English. Three years later the *Los Angeles Times* reported on 'the extraordinary spectacle of thousands...being turned away an hour before the advertised opening of [his] lecture with the 3,000-seat [LA Philharmonic Hall] filled to its utmost capacity.' In October 1925 he established the Self Realization Fellowship (p203) at a vacant Mt Washington hotel. Yogananda felt his success lay in the fact that he offered something the religious establishment did not, a physical experience of God. In his *Autobiography of a Yogi* he wrote, 'The universal appeal of yoga is its approach to God through a daily usable scientific method, rather than a devotional fervor that, for the average man, is beyond his emotional scope.'

Another powerful guru, Yogi Bhajan, a devout Sikh, arrived here during the second wave, when the US streets were alive with revolution and free love. He showed up with next to no money, and began teaching immediately. His classes filled up quickly, especially those at a dusty antique shop on Robertson Blvd, where every night 80 to 90 hippies emerged from packed vans to take the class. Yogi Bhajan told his obviously experimental students, 'Do Kundalini yoga. You can get higher, it's legal and there are no side effects.' Two of his original students, Guru Singh and Gurmukh still teach in town at Yoga West (p135) and Golden Bridge Yoga (p91). Yogi Bhajan went on to found Yogi Teas and Peace Cereals, and taught until his death in 2004.

But it's Hatha yoga that keeps most of LA om-ing and sweating in studios from Long Beach to the Valley, from Santa Monica to Pasadena. LA's original Hatha pioneer was the Russian-born, India-educated Indra Devi. She opened her Hollywood studio in 1947, and taught the first in a long line of celebrities how to do a down dog properly.

spectacular perch overlooking the sea and the West Valley, with golden eagles and red-tail hawks riding the thermals, this is what silence sounds like.

Take PCH past Trancas to Yerba Buena Rd (look for Neptune's Net). Make a right on Yerba Buena and follow it to the ranger station at Circle X Ranch. Maps and trail conditions are available at the ranger station, but it's usually only staffed on weekends. You can also download a map online. The trailhead is actually a mile past the station on left. Hike for 800m up the fire road (spoiler alert – this steep yet wide trail leads directly to the peak in 1.5 miles) before verging onto the Mishe Mokwa connector trail, a spur that will lead you to the gorgeous Mishe Mokwa trail. Picnic beneath the oaks then keep humping up to the peak, you won't be able to miss it. After enjoying the view, don't double back on Mishe Mokwa. Keep hiking down the fire road all the way to the parking lot. Come during the week. It gets crowded on weekends.

Pt Mugu State Park HIKING, BIKING
(www.parks.ca.gov; 9000 Pacific Coast Hwy; per vehicle $8; P) With 70 miles of trails connecting two canyons, shaded by hulking oak and sycamores, laced with seasonal creeks and blanketed with blooming chaparral in the upper reaches, there is plenty of excellent hiking and mountain biking to be had. The park has 5 miles of coastline too, but the beaches are better elsewhere.

Malibu Outfitters WHALE-WATCHING, FISHING
(Map p144; www.malibupier.com; 23000 Pacific Coast Hwy; adult/child $45/35; P) Located at the far end of the pier, Malibu Outfitters offers half-day whale-watching and open fishing trips in the bay. Expect to see dolphins, sea lions and flocks of brown pelicans, and during the whaling season you'll likely spot migrating grey and pilot whales.

Malibu Creek State Park HIKING, SWIMMING
(Map p144; www.parks.ca.gov; Las Virgenes/Malibu Canyon Rd) Another beautiful spot in the Santa Monica Mountains; *M*A*S*H* and *Planet of the Apes* were shot here. Laced by a creek with swimming holes in the spring, this park has excellent hiking, with trails leading past craggy oaks and stately sycamores. The park is about 5 miles north of the PCH via Malibu Canyon Rd.

Malibu Surf Shack SURFING
(Map p144; www.malibusurfshack.com; 22935 Pacific Coast Hwy; kayaks per day $30-50, surf boards per day $25, surf lessons per person $100; ⏲10am-6pm) This barefoot surf shop rents (and sells) kayaks and surfboards. Surf lessons take place on Surfrider beach, last 90 minutes and include a full day's rental of the board and wetsuit. The paddling between here and Point Dume is excellent, with frequent dolphin and sea-lion sightings.

Malibu Long Boards SURFING
(☎310-467-6898; www.malibulongboards.com; per lesson per person $75-99) Private lessons in Malibu given by college-level surf instructors; email them for a free surf video.

Los Angeles Horseback Riding OUTDOORS
(Map p144; www.losangeleshorsebackriding.com; 2623 Old Topanga Canyon Rd, Topanga Canyon; 1hr ride $55, sunset rides $80, full-moon rides $125, gratuity mandatory & not included) Day and full-moon rides along the Santa Monica Mountains Backbone Trail with fabulous views all around, and beach rides on the Ventura county coast (four to five hours total travel time). Western-style only, group size limited to six people, reservations required.

Sleeping

TOP CHOICE Malibu Beach Inn INN $$$
(Map p144; ☎310-456-6444; www.malibubeachinn.com; 22878 Pacific Coast Hwy; r $325-385, ste $725-1075; P 📶) If you want to live like a billionaire, stay with one. Hollywood mogul David Geffen has given this intimate hacienda the four-star treatment. It's right near his private house on Carbon Beach and has 47 superdeluxe ocean-facing rooms sheathed in soothing browns and outfitted with fireplaces, a handpicked wine selection and Dean & Deluca goodies.

Malibu Country Inn INN $$
(Map p144; ☎310-457-9622; www.malibucountryinn.com; 6506 Westward Beach Rd; r $165-250; P 📶) Perched above the highway and overlooking Westward Beach is this somewhat humble shingled inn with an array of fairly large rooms drenched in corny florals. But they all have sun patios and some have massive sea views.

Pt Mugu State Park Campground CAMPING $
(☎800-444-7275; www.reserveamerica.com; 9000 Pacific Coast Hwy; campsite $34 P) You have two choices here: the creekside campsites shaded by gnarled, native sycamore and oak, or the windswept beachside spots

that are visible (and well within earshot) of the highway. All are within walking distance of flush toilets and coin-operated hot showers.

Leo Carrillo State Park Campground
CAMPING $

(☎800-444-7275; www.reserveamerica.com; 35000 W Pacific Coast Hwy; campsite $35; ☎📶) This kid-friendly campground sits on a famous 1.5-mile stretch of beach. Offshore kelp beds, caves, tide pools, plus the wilderness of the Santa Monica Mountains create a natural playground. There are 140 sycamore-shaded sites, flush toilets and coin-operated hot showers. Bookings for summer weekends should be made six months in advance.

Malibu Motel
MOTEL $$

(Map p144; ☎310-456-6169; www.themalibumotel.com; 22541 Pacific Coast Hwy; r $139-219; 📶🚭📶) This 18-room motel has been redone in retro-on-the-cheap. Beds are comfy and draped in crisp linen but amenities are limited to a minifridge and wall-mounted Vizios. Light sleepers should gear up with earplugs to combat PCH traffic noise. Still, not-bad value for the area and the beach is just across the highway.

Casa Malibu Inn on the Beach
MOTEL $$$

(Map p144; ☎310-456-2219; 22752 Pacific Coast Hwy; r $130-470; 📶📶) It feels more like a vintage motel than an inn. Beachfront rooms come with beamed ceilings, gas fireplaces and bathtubs, private patios and rattan furnishings. And even if it is owned by Oracle's Larry Ellison, and Lana Turner did once use it as her own personal beach getaway, it's still overpriced.

✗ Eating

TOP CHOICE **Malibu Seafood** SEAFOOD $$
(Map p144; www.malibuseafood.com; 25653 Pacific Coast Hwy; dishes $5-14; ⊘lunch & dinner; 📶📶) A hole-in-the-highway beloved by Malibu locals, this seafood market and fish grill offers tasty, simply prepared fresh plate lunches of snapper, ahi, sea bass, scallops, halibut and trout. It has fried seafood baskets and sandwiches too. It closes at 7:30pm.

Taverna Tony
GREEK $$

(Map p144; ☎310-317-9667; www.tavernatony.com; 23410 Civic Center Way; appetizers $8-17; mains $13-38; ⊘lunch & dinner; 📶) This lively spot fronted by a flowery terrace feeds both the soul and belly. At lunchtime the baby lamb sandwich is divine, but for a serious indulgence loosen your belt and order the Greek Feast ($33 per person; two-person minimum), and indulge in 15 different dishes. Dinner reservations are advised.

John's Garden
DELI $

(Map p144; www.johnsgardenmalibu.com; 3835 Cross Creek Rd; sandwiches $5.50-10, salads $6.50-11; ⊘lunch; 📶) Malibu's favorite lunch counter, where you can order fresh daily soups like curry tomato lentil and Louisiana gumbo, salads culled from the gardens of Greece, Italy, Cape Cod and Korea, and tasty sandwiches, such as the Woody (corned beef and swiss on rye) or the Surfer Princess (turkey and avocado).

Coogies Beach Café
DINER $$

(Map p144; www.coogies.malibu.menuclub.com; 23755 Malibu Rd; mains $7-15; ⊘breakfast, lunch & dinner; 📶📶) Locals can't resist Coogie's famous wholewheat pancakes packed with fresh strawberries and bananas. A great place to hit before or after the beach, it serves breakfast until 3pm, has tasty sandwiches and salads for lunch and fresh fish for dinner.

Sunset
ITALIAN, SEAFOOD $$

(www.thesunsetrestaurant.com; 6800 Westward Rd; dishes $9-22; ⊘lunch & dinner Jun-Sep, dinner Oct-May; 📶📶) A converted white-washed beach house with fresh oysters on the halfshell, terrific flatbreads (we're partial to the chorizo and artichoke) and a popular weekend brunch. It's the perfect oasis after a day at the beach.

Duke's
SEAFOOD $$

(Map p144; www.dukesmalibu.com; 21150 Pacific Coast Hwy; mains $9-29; ⊘lunch & dinner; 📶📶) Named for Duke Kahanamoku (the 'founding father of surfing'), this Malibu seaside classic deserves mention not for its overpriced seafood dinners, but for Taco Tuesdays, when Pepperdine students and Malibu locals descend for $2.50 grilled, fried and Cajun-spiced fish tacos served in the Barefoot Bar. Pair it with a Pacifico.

Nobu Malibu
JAPANESE $$$

(Map p144; ☎310-317-9140; www.noburestaurants.com; Suite 18a, 3835 Cross Creek Rd; sushi $5.50-18, mains $9-30; ⊘dinner; 📶) Tucked into the Malibu Country Mart, Nobu, while still plenty tasty, is starting to coast on its fame and famous clientele. Still, most will enjoy the creative Japanese fare (remember: it's the cooked food, not the sushi, that made the brand). And the stargazing, especially on the dimly lit patio, can't be beat.

Inn of the Seventh Ray
ORGANIC $$$
(Map p144; ☑310-455-1311; www.innofthe seventhray.com; 128 Old Topanga Canyon Rd; mains $24-55; ⊘lunch & dinner; P☑) If you've lived through the '60s, you might experience flashbacks at this New-Agey hideaway in an impossibly idyllic setting in Topanga Canyon. All of the food is organic, much is raw, most of it meat-free and some rather esoteric. Crispy vegan duck anyone?

Saddle Peak Lodge
FINE DINING $$$
(Map p144; ☑818-222-3888; 419 Cold Canyon Rd; appetizers $14-32, mains $29-52; ⊘brunch Sun, dinner Wed-Sun; P) As rustic as a Colorado mountain lodge, this rural oasis tucked into the Santa Monica Mountains serves up elk, venison, buffalo and other game in a setting watched over by mounted versions of the same. This is fine dining so don't come here after a day on the trail. Reservations are recommended.

Guido's
ITALIAN $$$
(Map p144; ☑310-456-1979; www.guidosmalibu. com; 3874 Cross Creek Rd; appetizers $10-15, mains $12-24; ⊘lunch Mon-Fri, dinner Mon-Sun; P) A hidden Malibu institution overlooking the mouth of Malibu Creek, where guests sink into turquoise-tinted vinyl booths, and munch tasty pizza and pasta, chicken picatta and osso bucco on pressed white linens by candlelight.

Café Vida
CALIFORNIAN $$
(Map p144; ☑310-573-1335; 15317 Antioch St, Pacific Palisades; dishes $8.75-17; ⊘breakfast, lunch & dinner) Get your California comfort food at this sunny seafront cafe serving everything from 'Green Grass Alkalizing Smoothies' to chicken soft tacos. Eclectic? Sure. It's also fresh and delicious.

TOP FIVE ROMANTIC SPOTS

» Inn of the Seventh Ray (Malibu, above)

» Little Door (West Hollywood, p118)

» Bar Chloe (Santa Monica, p160)

» Sandstone Peak (Malibu, p147)

» Yamashiro Farmers Market (Hollywood, p94)

Drinking

Rosenthal Vineyard
WINERY
(Map p144; www.rosenthalestatewines.com; 26023 Pacific Coast Highway; ⊘1-6pm Thu, 11am-6pm Fri-Sun; P) Malibu's only vintner doesn't offer public tours of its 250-acre Newton Canyon estate where grapes are grown, crushed and barreled, but the cozy wine room right on PCH sells its wine, sauces and tapenades, and it offer tastings of the estate's finest.

☆ Entertainment

Will Geer Theatricum Botanicum
THEATRE
(Map p144; www.theatricum.com; 1419 N Topanga Canyon Blvd, northwest of Santa Monica; P) TV's Grandpa Walton founded this beloved theater as a refuge for blacklisted actors like himself during the 1950s McCarthy years. The woodsy setting is a perfect backdrop for such classic crowd-pleasers as Shakespeare's *A Midsummer Night's Dream* and Bram Stoker's *Dracula*. The season runs from June to early October. To get there, head north on Pacific Coast Hwy, turn inland on Topanga Canyon Blvd and proceed for 6 miles; the theater will be on your left.

Shopping

TOP CHOICE Malibu Country Mart
MALL
(Map p144; 3835 Cross Creek Rd; P) Across from Surfrider Beach, this mall spans both sides of Cross Creek Rd. Which is why it's affectionately known as Cross Creek by the sweet, sexy, sun-kissed local beach girls and boys who gather on this high-end outdoor shopping mall to flirt, grub and shop. There are some stunning, creative and casual designer boutiques such as Ron Herman (☑310-317-6705; www. ronherman.com) and Free City (☑310-456-5651; www.freecitysupershop.com), and you may glimpse a celebrity soccer mom or dad as they sip coffee or watch their toddlers scramble around the courtyard playground. There's a cinema here too.

Village Books
BOOKSTORE
(Map p144; www.palivillagebooks.com; 1049 Swarthmore Ave, Pacific Palisades; ⊘10am-8pm Mon-Fri, to 6pm Sat & Sun) Sweet, inviting and indie, the concrete floors, handwritten staff recommendations, obscure and mainstream titles, alluring clutter and overstuffed stacks make this a bookworm's paradise, and we mean that in the best way possible.

Lumberyard
MALL

(Map p144; www.themalibulumber.com; 3939 Cross Creek Rd; P 🛜) Steps west of the Malibu Country Mart is the sleekest and newest shopping center in town, set on the site of Malibu's longtime lumber yard. The highlights here are the refined longboard of a boutique that is **James Perse** (www.jamesperse.com), and **Kitson Malibu** (www.shopkitson.com).

Intemperantia
CHOCOLATE

(Map p144; www.intemperantia.com; 15324 Antioch St, Pacific Palisades) A boutique chocolatier, where organic, dark, vegan and white-chocolate truffles are crafted with love, and the French hot chocolate is legendary.

SANTA MONICA

Here's a place where real-life Lebowskis sip white Russians next to martini-swilling Hollywood producers, celebrity chefs dine at family-owned taquerias, and soccer mom's and career bachelors shop shoulder to shoulder at abundant farmers markets. It's a small city with forward-thinking social and environmental ideals and fascist parking codes. Here, you'll navigate a landscape of surf rats, skate punks, string bikinis, yoga freaks, psychics, street performers and a prodigious homeless population. Most, if not all, of which can be found along a stretch of sublime coastline that cradles the city to the west, and laps at the heels of an undulating mountain range that defines the entire LA area to the north. This is Santa Monica – LA's cute, alluring, hippie-chic little sister, its karmic counterbalance and, to many, its salvation.

Cooler than Los Angeles in the summer and warmer in the winter, Santa Monica's sweetness lies in its tendency to blend the natural with the urban. Its sagebrush-and-oak draped hills, freckled with wildflowers in the spring, are ribboned with canyons, seasonal streams and hiking trails, mere minutes from downtown. The bay's smooth, sandy bottom and gentle, rolling break is tailor-made for the virgin surfer, and barefoot strolls in the tide or lazy rides on the beachfront bike path can soothe the city from your soul quicker than you can say 'om'.

But Santa Monica is no sleepy resort town. Well within the Hollywood sphere of influence, production companies, post-production studios and record labels lend it a certain buzz. Shoppers patrol three distinct shopping districts, rummage through thrift stores and dress up in refined boutiques. At night you can choose from sprawling outdoor cafes, chic hotel lounges, dance clubs, and casual wine bars. There's live blues, salsa and world music almost every night of the week, and Santa Monica cuisine spans the globe with something for every wallet. As the sun drops, however, there is really only one place you'll want to be. That's the wide golden beach that put Santa Monica on the map in the first place.

⊙ Sights

FREE **Santa Monica Pier**
LANDMARK

(Map p152; www.santamonicapier.org; ⊙24hr; P 🚻) Dating back to 1908, the Santa Monica Pier is the city's most compelling landmark. There are arcades, carnival games, a vintage carousel, a Ferris wheel, a roller coaster, and an aquarium, and the pier comes alive with free concerts (Twilight Dance Series, p77) and outdoor movies (p88) in the summertime. There are also a number of bars and restaurants, but the thing here is the view: extending almost a quarter mile over the Pacific, you can stroll to the edge, hang out among the motley anglers, and lose yourself in the rolling blue-green sea.

Kids get their kicks at **Pacific Park** (Map p152; www.pacpark.com; ⊙11am-9pm Sun-Thu, to midnight Fri & Sat Jun-Aug, shorter hrs Sep-May; 🚻), a small amusement park with a solar-powered Ferris wheel, kiddy rides, midway games and food concessions. Rides cost between $3 and $5 each; a day of unlimited spins costs $21.95/15.95 (over/under 42in tall); check the website for discount coupons.

Near the pier entrance, nostalgic souls and their offspring can giddy up the beautifully hand-painted horses of the 1922 **merry-go-round** (Map p152; rides adult/child $2/1; ⊙11am-5pm Mon, Wed & Thu, to 7pm Fri-Sun Sep-Jun, to 7pm Mon, Wed & Thu, to 9pm Fri-Sun Jul-Aug; 🚻) featured in the movie *The Sting*.

Peer under the pier – just below the carousel – for Heal the Bay's **Santa Monica Pier Aquarium** (Map p152; www.healthebay.org/smpa; suggested/minimum donation $5/3, under 12yr free; ⊙2-6pm Tue-Fri, 12:30-6pm Sat & Sun; 🚻). Sea stars, crabs, sea urchins and other critters and crustaceans scooped from the bay stand by to be petted – ever so gently, please – in their adopted touch-tank homes.

South of the pier is the **Original Muscle Beach** (Map p152), where the Southern California exercise craze began in the mid-20th century, and new equipment now draws a new generation of fitness fanatics. Closeby, the search for the next Bobby Fischer is on at the **International Chess Park** (Map p152). Anyone can join in. Following the **South Bay Bicycle Trail**, a paved bike and walking path, south for about 1.5 miles takes you straight to Venice Beach. Bike or in-line skates are available to rent on the pier and at beachside kiosks.

TOP 10 LA BEACHES

Long before the Beach Boys brought surf culture to the masses, Southern California was an American dream destination because of one thing: the beach. With miles of golden sand, swaying palms and wide beaches hemmed in by ragged, towering bluffs, and gentle rolling surf that serves beginners but can get big enough to charge up old sea dogs, LA remains an epic beach destination. And this year, thanks to the soulful and visionary Portraits of Hope project, the lifeguard towers look as bright and wild as a perfect wave at sunset.

The following beaches are listed north to south. For access to Malibu's hidden beaches, see boxed text, p143.

El Matador This small, remote hideaway is a popular filming location thanks to superscenic battered rock cliffs and giant boulders, but the surf is wild and clothing is optional.

Westward Beach Around the bend from Point Dume and just south of Zuma, Malibu locals favor this wide, blonde beach for crystal water and resident dolphins. The shallows aren't made for kiddies though.

Zuma Two miles of pearly sand. Mellow swells make for perfect body surfing. Come early on weekends to snag parking.

Paradise Cove The site of a kitschy (but not bad) restaurant and an upscale mobile-home park (only in Malibu), the beach is close enough to Point Dume to get set-piece rock formations and mellow waves. Eating at the restaurant cuts the $25 parking fee down to $3. Walk-ins are $5.

Leo Carrillo Families love this summer-camp-style beach with enough stimulating tide pools, cliff caves, nature trails and great swimming and surfing to tire out even the most hyperactive kids.

Santa Monica Wide slab of sand where beach-umbrella-toting families descend like butterfly swarms on weekends to escape the inland heat. Water quality is poor right by the pier but OK a few hundred yards south.

Venice Beach Get your freak on at the Venice Boardwalk. During Sunday's drum circle, the bongos crescendo and dancers turn to silhouettes as the sun dips into the ocean. Plus, the wide beaches south of the Venice Pier are an undiscovered gem with excellent bodysurfing and swimming.

Manhattan Beach Brassy SoCal beach with a high flirt factor and hard-core surfers hanging by the pier for, like, totally epic waves. Families can check out marine life in the Roundhouse Marine Studies Lab & Aquarium (p171).

Hermosa Beach LA's libidinous, seemingly neverending beach party with hormone-crazed hard bodies getting their game on over beach volleyball and in the raucous pubs along Pier Ave. If you have nothing happening on July 4, come here.

Malaga Cove This crescent-shaped, cliff-backed shoreline is the only sandy Palos Verdes beach easily accessible by the hoi polloi. Blends into rocky tide pools and has excellent rolling waves for surfers (at Haggerty's), but no lifeguards.

Main Street　　　　　SHOPPING DISTRICT

(Map p152) Retail therapy gets a fun twist along Main St, which is lined with owner-run boutiques and galleries that are light years from chain-store conformity. As you browse around, keep an eye out for Frank Gehry's playful **Edgemar Center for the Arts** (p161), a former ice factory turned sculptural complex and cultural venue.

California Heritage Museum　　　MUSEUM

(Map p152; www.californiaheritagemuseum.org; 2612 Main St; adult/student & senior/under 12yr $5/3/free; ☺11am-4pm Wed-Sun; ℗) For a trip back in time, check out the latest exhibit at this museum housed in one of Santa Monica's few surviving grand Victorian mansions – this one built in 1894. Curators do a fine job presenting pottery, colorful tiles, Craftsman furniture, folk art, vintage surfboards and other fine collectibles in as dynamic a fashion as possible. To see locals at play, come during the Sunday morning farmers market in the museum's parking lot.

Jadis
MUSEUM

(Map p152; 2701 Main St; per person $1; ⊙noon-4pm Sun) Don't miss this homespun museum crammed with old antiques clocks, planes, globes, lights and gear madness – most of which were old film props. The prized piece is the robot from the famed 1927 film *Metropolis*.

Third Street Promenade
MALL

(Map p152) Stretching for three long blocks sprawled between Broadway and Wilshire Blvd, Third Street Promenade is a case study in how to morph a dilapidated, dying main street into a dynamic and happening strip. It offers carefree and car-free strolling accompanied by the sound of flamenco guitar or hip-hop acrobatics courtesy of street performers. You can grab a bite to eat, catch a movie and browse the Gap or Zara. And every Wednesday and Saturday, hobby cooks and professional chefs jostle for the freshest foods at the farmers market.

Santa Monica Place
MALL

(Map p152; www.santamonicaplace.com; 395 Santa Monica Place, 10am-9pm Mon-Thu, to 10pm Fri & Sat, to 8pm Sun) The old indoor mall at the southern end of the Third Street Promenade has been cracked open into the sunlight, styled up and contoured, and is now a high-end mall with couture boutiques, Macy's Bloomingdale's, Tiffany & Co and more. The top-floor Dining Deck comes with Pacific Ocean views, and there are occasional live concerts and DJ sets in the summer months. There's free two-hour parking.

Santa Monica Museum of Art
MUSEUM

(www.smmoa.org; Bldg G1, Bergamot Station; suggested donation $5; ⊙11am-6pm Tue-Sat; ℗) A saucy and irreverent home of edgy art and community events, this small museum gives exposure to both local and national artists working with new and experimental media. It's part of the **Bergamot Station Arts Center**, a cluster of galleries, studios and shops set in a former railyard. Don't miss the annual Incognito Art Fair and auction held in early May.

Gehry House
MONUMENT

(1002 22nd St) In his creative life before the Walt Disney Concert Hall, Frank Gehry was primarily known as that crazy guy who sculpted houses from chain-link fencing, plywood and corrugated aluminum. A great place to see the 'early Gehry' is his 1979 private home, a deconstructivist postmodern collage that architecture-critic Paul Heyer called a 'collision of parts.' Neighbors were none too pleased at first, but that was before Gehry had claimed his spot in the pantheon of contemporary architects.

🏃 Activities

Santa Monica Mountains
HIKING

(www.nps.gov/samo/planyourvisit/parksites) A haven for hikers, trekkers and mountain bikers, the northwestern-most stretch of the Santa Monica Mountains is where the nature gets bigger and wilder, with jaw-dropping red-rock canyons, and granite outcrops with sublime sea views. Of course, the best trails are in Pacific Palisades, Topanga and Malibu. The **Backbone Trail** is the longest trail in the range, linking – and accessible from – every state park. It's 68 miles all told, running from Will Rogers to Pt Mugu State Park, and can be completed in a few days.

South Bay Bicycle Trail
BIKING

(Map p152) Dodge the in-line skaters, power walkers, lollygaggers, surfers and volley-balls as you pedal the South Bay Bicycle Trail, which parallels the sand for most of the 22 miles between Will Rogers Beach near Santa Monica and Torrance Beach. Weekends get jammed and there are sections where you must push your bike.

ANNENBERG COMMUNITY BEACH HOUSE

Like a beach club for the rest of us, this sleek and attractive public **beach club** (www.beachhouse.smgov.net; 400 Pacific Coast Hwy; adult/child $10/4; ⊙8:30am-8:30pm Jun-Sep) built on actress Marion Davies' estate (she had a thing with William Randolph Hearst), has a lap pool, lounge chairs, yoga classes, beach volleyball, a fitness room, photo exhibits and even poetry readings. There's a cafe nearby, and it's set on a sweet stretch of Santa Monica Beach.

DON'T MISS

HIKING LA

If hiking doesn't feel like an indigenous LA activity, you may need to reassess. This town is hemmed in and defined by two mountain ranges and countless canyons. In the **San Gabriel range**, trails wind from Mt Wilson (p190) into granite peak wilderness, once the domain of the Gabrielino people and the setting for California's last grizzly bear sighting. The Chumash roamed the **Santa Monicas**, which are smaller, but still offer spectacular views of chaparral-draped mountains with stark drops into the Pacific. The Backbone Trail (p143) spans the range, but our favorite hike is to Sandstone Peak (p147). Day hikes in Topanga Canyon State Park (p143), Malibu Canyon (p147), Point Mugu and Leo Carillo state parks are also recommended. And if you only have an hour or two check out Runyon (p116) or Bronson (p102) canyons in Hollywood. For more advice about trails in and around Southern California check out www.trails. com, or buy these two tomes: *Top Trails: Los Angeles* (Wilderness Press) and *60 Hikes Within 60 Miles* (Menasha Ridge Press), which was published in 2009.

Bike Attack

BIKE RENTAL

(Map p152; www.bikeattack.com; 2400 Main St; cruisers per hr/day $15/30, mountain bikes per day $50; ☺9:30am-5:30pm) A terrific resource for mountain bikers, this laid-back shop rents the best beach cruisers and mountain bikes in Santa Monica. They know the top mountain-bike trails in Southern California, and can repair your bike if necessary. Tell them you're a club member and get 10% to 15% off all merchandise.

Perry's Café & Rentals

OUTDOORS

(Map p152; ☎310-939-0000; www.perryscafe. com; Ocean Front Walk; cruisers per hr/day $10/25, bodyboards per hr/day $8/17; ☺9:30am-5:30pm) With several locations on the bike path, they rent bikes and skates or perhaps you'll grab a body board and ride the foaming rollers in the wide Santa Monica Bay. They offer a unique beach butler service too, but only accept cash.

Santa Monica Skate Park

SKATING

(www.socalskateparks.com; cnr 14th St & Olympic Blvd; daily pass adult/child $6.50/5) Skate rats will love the 20,000 sq ft of vert, street and tranny terrain in Memorial Park.

Santa Monica Power Yoga

YOGA

(Map p152; www.poweryoga.com; admission by donation; ☺5:30am-10:45pm Mon-Thu, 8am-8pm Fri-Sun) Studio West (1410 2nd St); Studio East (522 Santa Monica Blvd) You'll sweat, you'll tone, you'll meditate, you'll feel great. The renowned and oh-so-physical Bryan Kest still teaches at the funky space on Santa Monica Blvd that he made famous by packing in hard bodies. The recommended donation is $14, but give what you can.

Yoga Works

YOGA

(Map p152; www.yogaworks.com; 2215 Main St, 1426 Montana Ave; per class $22; ☺7am-9pm) Dozens of classes per week, for all levels of expertise, plus one- and two-day intro courses. These were the studios that started the Southern California Hatha yoga boom.

Tao Healing Arts

WELLNESS

(Map p152; ☎310-396-4877; www.thaconline.com; 2309 Main St; ☺9am-8:30pm) Classes and clinicians are available at this longtime purveyor of Eastern wisdom. Learn acupuncture or shiatsu, or simply drop by for budget-priced treatments from the master's apprentices.

Urban Craft Center

ARTS & CRAFTS

(Map p152; www.theurbancraftcenter.com; 2433 Main St; class $65-80; ☺10am-6pm) Whether it's sewing or silk screening, soap making or jewelry making, you can learn how to do it in a simple one-session class, or just rent studio space and work on your own. The groovy retro fabrics are sold by the quarter yard.

Duganne Ateliers

ARTS & CRAFTS

(Map p152; ☎310-314-0050; www.duganne.com; 2651 Main St; per class $60) A professional print shop, this romantically rickety studio and gallery space hidden in plain sight on Main St offers three-hour mono print-making, photography and pottery classes by appointment.

Beaches

SWIMMING, SURFING

Water temperatures become tolerable by late spring and are highest (about 68°F or 20°C) in August and September. Water quality varies; for updated conditions check the **Beach Report Card** (www.healthebay.org).

The waves in Santa Monica are gentle and well shaped for beginner surfers, as well as bodyboarders and bodysurfers. The best swimming beaches are Will Rogers State Beach on the border of Pacific Palisades, and south of the pier.

Learn to Surf LA SURFING
(☎310-663-2479; www.learntosurfla.com; per lesson per person $90-120) Great for beginners, in Santa Monica, it guarantees you'll get up on the board on your first lesson. Lessons last one hour and 45 minutes.

Surf Academy SURFING
(☎310-372-2790; www.surfacademy.org; per lesson per person $65-75) Founded by a US surfing champion, it offers lessons up and down the coast. Lessons last from 75 minutes to two hours.

🛏 Sleeping

TOP CHOICE **Huntley** BOUTIQUE HOTEL $$$
(Map p152; ☎310-394-5454; www.the huntleyhotel.com; 1111 2nd St; r $489-579, ste $699-750; @🛜🏊♿) Santa Monica's newest and most stylish boutique nest offers olive-green rooms with chocolate-wood furnishings, lush linens and designer suites with mid-century style seating, a window-side daybed and two flat screens. The cool-factor follows you from the lobby to the rooftop restaurant, 'The Penthouse' where you can sit side by side with industry players and marvel at the Santa Monica Mountains tumbling into sea.

Shutters HOTEL $$$
(Map p152; ☎310-458-0030; www.shutterson thebeach.com; 1 Pico Blvd; r $425-950, ste $1195-2195; P@🛜♿) Bringing classic Cape Cod charm to the Pacific Coast, the best rooms, which were recently done by Obama's White House designer, Michael Smith, have a beach-cottage feel with marble baths, wood floors, spectacular ocean views, and whitewashed shutters, of course. The in-house seafood cafe is hip and delicious, and the upscale signature restaurant gets great reviews too.

Viceroy HOTEL $$$
(Map p152; ☎310-260-7500, 800-622-8711; www.viceroysantamonica.com; 1819 Ocean Ave; r $370-670; P@🛜🏊) Starving for some LA glam by the sea? With porcelain hounds at the door, frosted glass and white-vinyl lounges in the lobby, and shag carpet in the library, the mod-meets-regency design works. Rooms are so slick even the marble

bathroom is hip. Ambient electronic music wallpapers public spaces, there's a flashy bar scene, and it's a block from the beach.

Shangri-La BOUTIQUE HOTEL $$$
(Map p152; ☎310-394-2791; www.shangrila -hotel.com; 1301 Ocean Ave; r $305-1050; @🛜♿♿) Stylish enough to be alluring but not too stuck up or intimidating, this art-deco classic, built across the avenue from the bluffs in 1932, sports paint jobs and apartments with funky paint jobs and wallpaper, marble baths, wood floors, and kitchenettes, and they all have at least a sliver of a sea view.

🌿**Ambrose** BOUTIQUE HOTEL $$
(☎310-315-1555; www.ambrosehotel.com; 1255 20th St; r $225-269; P@🛜) This sustainable boutique hotel beautifully blends Craftsman and Asian aesthetics and goes the extra mile when it comes to being green. Standard amenities in the spick-and-span rooms – some with balconies and fireplaces – include recycling containers and a composting program alongside the gamut of electronic gadgets. Breakfast is an organic gourmet affair.

Embassy Hotel Apartments BOUTIQUE HOTEL $$
(Map p152; ☎310-394-1279; www.embassy hotelapts.com; 1001 3rd St; r $169-390) This hushed hideaway is embraced by gardens and delivers 1920s charm by the bucket. A rickety elevator takes you to light-flooded units oozing old-world flair. There's no air-con but rooms are equipped with modern kitchens. The relative paucity of hotel services makes this place better suited for do-it-yourselfers. The best deals can be found online.

Channel Road Inn B&B BED & BREAKFAST $$
(☎310-459-1920; www.channelroadinn.com; 219 W Channel Rd; r $235-395; P@🛜♿) This frilly home in leafy Santa Monica Canyon mixes Cape Cod colonial with West Coast Craftsman and has romantic rooms facing the ocean or the lovely garden. Breakfast is a gourmet affair. There are also convivial afternoon teas, evening wine receptions with fellow guests, and a Jacuzzi out back. Free bike rentals.

Casa Del Mar HOTEL $$$
(Map p152; ☎310-581-5533; www.hotecasa delmar.com; 1910 Ocean Way; r $425-1275, ste $1695-3000; P@🛜♿) A historic brick hotel built beachside in 1926. A touch stodgy for

some, the powder-blue rooms have a wood-floor entry, four-poster beds and marble bathrooms with soaker tubs. The lobby bar gets a good crowd in both summer and winter when the fireplace roars. You'll get the best price if you book online.

Georgian Hotel HOTEL **$$$**
(Map p152; ☎310-395-9945, 800-538-8147; www.georgianhotel.com; 1415 Ocean Ave; r $255-405; P@☎) This eye-catching art-deco landmark with its snug veranda for breakfast and sunset lounging has decor so *Great Gatsby*-esque that wearing a straw boater wouldn't feel out of place. The rooms, in soothing earth tones, are surprisingly modern. Cute factor: the rubber duckie in the tub.

HI-Los Angeles/Santa Monica HOSTEL **$**
(Map p152; ☎310-393-9913; www.lahostels.org; 1436 2nd St; r $26-30; @☎) Near the beach and Promenade, this hostel has a location that's the envy of much fancier places. Its 200 beds in single-sex dorms and bed-in-a-box doubles with shared bathrooms are clean and safe, and there are plenty of groovy public spaces to lounge and surf, but those looking to party are better off in Venice or Hollywood.

Sea Shore Motel MOTEL **$$**
(Map p152; ☎310-392-2787; www.seashoremotel.com; 2637 Main St; r $125-150, ste $250-270; P☎) These friendly, family-run lodgings put you just a Frisbee toss from the beach on happening Main St (expect some street noise). The tiled rooms are basic but attractive enough, and families can stretch out comfortably in the modern suites with kitchen and balcony in a nearby building.

Hotel Carmel BOUTIQUE HOTEL **$$**
(Map p152; ☎310-451-2469; www.hotelcarmel.com; 201 Broadway Ave; r $135-195; P☎) Charming historic façade aside, there's nothing fancy about this boutique hotel around the corner from the Promenade. Despite the weathered carpeting, rooms are fairly bright and have ceiling fans, wood furnishings, new bathroom tile and some have sea views. Walk-ins can sometimes snag a room for $109.

✕ Eating

TOP CHOICE Rustic Canyon CALIFORNIAN **$$**
(Map p152; ☎310-393-7050; www.rucanyonwinebar.com; 1119 Wilshire Blvd; mains $31-50; ☺dinner) Almost all the ingredients come from local organic producers, which means the menu shifts with availability, but count on two handmade pasta dishes, and an assortment of stunning small plates. Think: grilled wild boar sausage, mussels steamed in white wine, chili and thyme, and crispy, garlicky baby artichokes. And the burger. There is always the burger: a world-class mound of mouth-melting meat on a buttered bun that eats like culinary soft-porn. Pair it with a California burgundy from its superb cellar.

Bay Cities ITALIAN DELI **$**
(Map p152; www.baycitiesitaliandeli.com; 1517 Lincoln Blvd; ☺9am-7pm Tue-Sat, to 6pm Sun) Not just the best Italian deli in LA, this is arguably the best deli, period. With sloppy, spicy godmothers (piled with salami, mortadella, coppacola, ham, prosciutto, provolone, and pepper salad), house-roasted tri-tip, tangy salads, imported meats, cheeses, breads, oils and extras. Get your sandwich with the works. And, yes, it's worth the wait.

Tacos Por Favor MEXICAN **$**
(1406 Olympic Blvd; dishes $4.50-11; ☺breakfast, lunch & dinner) This is a no-nonsense taco joint, a dingy hole-in-the-wall, smoky, hot and crowded. It also happens to serve the best shrimp, chicken and carne asada tacos and burritos in town. Hence, the lunchtime crush.

Huckleberry CAFE **$$**
(Map p152; www.huckleberrycafe.com; 1014 Wilshire Blvd; mains $9-12; ☺breakfast, lunch & dinner) Zoe Nathan devises some of the most exquisite pastries available in the city. Think: crostatas bursting with fruit, maple bacon biscuits, and pumpkin and ginger tea cakes. Later in the day the crowds keep coming for the much-lauded BBQ pork sandwich, the brisket plate or any number of deli salads. We call it yuppie soul food.

Santa Monica Seafood SEAFOOD **$$**
(Map p152; www.santamonicaseafood.com; 1000 Wilshire Blvd; appetizers $6-12, mains $9-12; ☺lunch & dinner) The best seafood market in Southern California now offers a tasty oyster bar and market cafe, where you can sample delicious chowder, salmon burgers and albacore melts, oysters on the half shell, and pan-roasted halibut.

Raw RAW **$$**
(Map p152; www.planetraw.com; 609 Broadway Ave; appetizers $4-10, mains $6-16; ☺lunch & dinner; ☎) The first, and still arguably the best, raw cafe in town is owned by the

brilliant, if temperamental, Juliano, who dehydrates, liquefies and reimagines Thai, Mexican, Sushi and Italian dishes sans fire. Their salads, soups and strawberry smoothies rock too.

Euphoria Loves Rawvolution   RAW $$
(Map p152; www.euphorialovesrawvolution. com; 2301 Main St; appetizers $2-11, mains $10-13; ⊙lunch & dinner; ✍) The scent of sprouts and seaweed permeates the premises, which is patrolled and patronized by perma-smiling descendents of California groovy. But they aren't here, beneath the lotus flower ceiling fans, to navel-gaze. They've come to create and chow mock tuna tacos, green monster burgers on spirulina bread and to swill dynamite nut-milk smoothies.

Latitude   THAI $
(Map p152; www.latitiudethai.com; 2906 Lincoln Blvd; dishes $5-10; ⊙lunch & dinner; ✍) It's easy to miss this humble Thai joint as you speed down the Lincoln corridor, but if you crave rich coconut curries, hot basil stir-fry and spicy lemongrass prawns cooked and served by Bangkok natives, you shouldn't.

JiRaffe   CALIFORNIAN-FRENCH FUSION $$$
(Map p152; ☎310-917-6671; 502 Santa Monica Blvd; appetizers $11-16, mains $28-38; ⊙dinner; ℗) Raphael Lunetta knows his waves and his kitchen. The avid surfer who studied cooking in France is a wizard when it comes to Cal-French compositions: pork chops are caramelized and paired with cider sauce; glazed salmon comes with saffron lemon couscous and artichokes. It's elegant, complex and supremely satisfying.

Chinois   ASIAN FUSION $$$
(☎310-392-9025; www.wolfgangpuck.com; 2709 Main St; appetizers $16.50-27.75, mains $25-46; ⊙lunch Wed-Fri, dinner Mon-Sun; ℗) Wolfgang Puck's Asian fusion masterwork. It's been around since 1983, so it can (and does) seem dated, but you'll dig the open kitchen and stylish turquoise table tops. Don't miss the sizzling catfish in ponzu sauce – recently tabbed by Jonathan Gold as one of his '99 Things To Eat In LA Before You Die'.

Le Pain Du Jour   FRENCH $
(www.lepaindujour.com; Suite 2, 828 Pico Blvd; dishes $5-16; ⊙7:30am-2pm) Flat out the best croissants and baguettes in LA, which is why this wholesale bakery makes its mint selling its goods to high-end restaurants throughout Southern California. Thankfully there's plenty left for us. And do not pass on the oozing sweetness of the almond croissant, a buttery path to gastro-enlightenment.

La Grande Orange   CALIFORNIAN $$
(Map p152; www.lagrandeorangesm.com; 2000 Main St, dishes $10-20; ⊙breakfast, lunch & dinner; ℗) Choose from a menu that conjures farmers market produce and all natural ingredients into miso-glazed salmon rolls, rib eye and swordfish tacos, veggie-nut and green chili burgers. It's a market-style cafe on weekdays, with full service on weekends and plenty of outdoor seating.

Fig   BISTRO $$
(Map p152; ☎310-319-3111; www.figsantamonica. com; 101 Wilshire Blvd; mains lunch $13-24, dinner $18-32; ⊙breakfast daily, lunch Mon-Sat, dinner Tue-Sat, brunch Sun) Set poolside at the historic Miramar hotel, and conceived with a coastal organic ethos, Fig leans heavily on local growers – most of what is served here is sourced from the twice-weekly farmers market down the street. We love the corn and kale veggie burger, the BLT (with quarter-inch thick slab of bacon), the beef salad and the *torta de lengua* (tongue sandwich) at lunch. Dinnertime features stars such as the short rib and pancetta meatloaf, shellfish cooked in a jalapeno and tequila broth and a bone-in halibut chop. Its beer and wine rock too.

Bravo Pizzeria   CALIFORNIAN $
(Map p152; www.bravosantamonica.com; 2400 Main St; pizzas $15-23; ⊙lunch & dinner) On the shortlist for best pizza in LA, this place makes sublime thin-crust pies, and sensational meatball and chicken parm subs too. Oh, and those chocolate-dipped canolis are flown in from New York City for a reason.

Real Food Daily   VEGAN $$
(Map p152; www.realfood.com; 514 Santa Monica Blvd; appetizers $9-11, mains $13-15; ⊙lunch & dinner; ✍) New World vegancooking guru Ann Gentry gives meat and dairy substitutes an interesting inflection. The lentil-walnut pâté is a complex starter and classics like the Salisbury seitan (a wheat gluten-based dish) and tempeh tacos feed the body and soul.

Border Grill   MEXICAN $$
(Map p152; ☎310-451-1655; www.bordergrill.com; 1445 4th St; dishes $7.50-30; ⊙lunch & dinner) Dressed-up Mexican nouveau done to perfection, with four kinds of ceviche, and a

terrific lamb tostada. Compared to most of LA's Mexican joints, it isn't cheap, but you get what you pay for here. If you can't make the restaurant, look for its food truck.

Father's Office
PUB $

(1018 Montana Ave; dishes $6-16; ⊙5pm-1am Mon-Thu, 4pm-2am Fri, noon-2am Sat, noon-midnight Sun) This elbow-to-elbow gastropub is famous for its burger: a dry-aged-beef number dressed in smoky bacon, sweet caramelized onion and an ingenious combo of Gruyère and blue cheese. Pair it with fries served in a mini shopping cart and a mug of handcrafted brew chosen from the three dozen on tap. No substitutions tolerated.

Lares
MEXICAN $$

(www.laresrestaurant.com; 2909 Pico Blvd; dishes $6-11; ⊙breakfast, lunch & dinner; P ⚍) There's nothing trendy about this family-run Mexican neighborhood favorite with subdued Spanish Colonial furnishings that make it feel more festive than fiesta. The slow-cooked *carnitas* – juicy, fall-apart pork – are a specialty, as are the sizzling fajitas. Just don't OD on the smoky chipotle salsa. Good margaritas, too.

R&D Kitchen
CONTINENTAL $$

(www.hillstone.com; 1323 Montana Ave; dishes $14-20; ⊙lunch & dinner; P ⚍) The sceniest spot on Montana Ave, this bar-restaurant's clean lines and chestnut interior open wonderfully onto the street attracting the yuppies from all corners for its tasty burgers, salads and pastas, and the full bar, of course.

Library Alehouse
PUB $$

(Map p152; www.libraryalehouse.com; 2911 Main St; mains $9-23; appetizers $7-13, mains $12-20; ⊙11:30am-midnight) Locals gather for the food as much as the beer at this wood-paneled gastropub with a cozy outdoor patio in the back. Angus burgers, fish tacos and hearty salads sate the 30-something postwork regulars while 29 handcrafted microbrews keep 'em hanging around till midnight.

Gate of India
INDIAN $

(Map p152; 117 Santa Monica Blvd; appetizers $3.50-8, mains $12-18; ⊙lunch & dinner; ⚎) Funky and friendly, with Indian tapestries tacked to the ceiling, hand-carved arches and doors inlaid with mother of pearl, this is the perfect atmosphere to dine on aromatic curries and chicken, lamb and prawns broiled to perfection in a clay oven. Vegetarian options abound.

Kafe K
CALIFORNIAN $

(Map p152; www.kafekcalifornia.com; 2209 Main St; sandwiches $8.50-11; ⊙breakfast & lunch) Cheerful and stylish, this hip little owner-operated indie cafe serves fresh-squeezed orange and pomegranate juice, creative salads (like the appetizing wild arugula and pear), organic egg dishes, tasty sandwiches and a daily quiche.

Santa Monica Farmers Markets
MARKET $

(Map p152; www01.smgov.net/farmers_market; ⊙8:30am-1pm Wed, 9:30am-1pm Sun) You haven't really experienced Santa Monica until you've explored one of its weekly outdoor farmers markets stocked with organic fruits, vegetables, flowers, baked goods and fresh-shucked oysters. The Wednesday market begins on 3rd and Arizona and winds along three blocks, and is the biggest and arguably the best for fresh produce, which is why it's so often patrolled by local chefs, but the Sunday morning market on Main St is more of a community scene. There's live music, pony rides, and a half-dozen stalls cooking up omelettes, tamales, crepes and grilled corn. Just hand your bicycle to the valet (um, yes, we know, but it is free), and relax with the locals on the luscious green lawn.

🍷 Drinking

Copa d'Oro
TOP CHOICE
LOUNGE

(Map p152; www.copadoro.com; 217 Broadway Ave; ⊙6pm-2am Mon-Fri, 8pm-2am Sat & Sun; P) The cocktail menu was created by the talented Vincenzo Marianella – a man who knows his spirits, and has trained a team to concoct addictive cocktails from a well of top-end liquors and a produce bin of fresh herbs, fruits, juices and a few veggies too. The rock tunes and the smooth, dark ambience don't hurt.

Bar Chloe
LOUNGE

(Map p152; www.barchloe.com; 1449 2nd St) Cozy, dark and elegant with dangling chandeliers, twinkling candles, intimate booths, crisp white tablecloths, and a lavender gimlet that has earned rave reviews. The tapas and sliders are decent too.

Flying Saucers
COFFEEHOUSE

(Map p152; www.flyingsaucersla.blogspot.com; 312 Pico Blvd; ⊙7am-5pm; P 🛜) Small batches of locally roasted fair-trade beans are ground, soaked and steamed into first-rate espresso drinks at this boho spot, where pain du jour pastries are served and the works of local artists are flaunted on the brick walls. It's a great way to kick your corporate coffee addiction.

Rick's Tavern
BAR

(Map p152; ☎310-392-2772; 2907 Main St; ⊙11am-2am) When everywhere else on Main is dead, this reasonably priced, friendly sports bar has a pulse. Late night? Midday? There's always a fun vibe, a ballgame on the flat screen, and it serves a mean bar burger too.

Circle Bar
BAR

(Map p152; www.thecirclebar.com; 2926 Main St; ⊙9pm-2am) A long-running 'meet market'. Strong drinks, loud music and seductive red-on-black decor further loosen inhibitions, but waiting in line to get past the bouncers can be a turnoff.

If you like bars with booze history, pop into **Chez Jay** (Map p152; www.chezjays.com; 1657 Ocean Ave) or the **Galley** (Map p152; www.thegalleyrestaurant.net; 2442 Main St), both low-key, classic watering holes with campy nautical themes.

☆ Entertainment

TOP CHOICE **Harvelle's**
BLUES

(Map p152; www.harvelles.com; 1432 4th St; cover $5-10) This dark blues grotto has been packing 'em in since 1931 but somehow still manages to feel like a well-kept secret. There are no big-name acts here, but the quality is usually pretty high. Sunday's Toledo Show mixes soul, jazz and cabaret, and the crowd is usually a mix of grizzled old-timers, skate punks and Hollywood types.

Zanzibar
CLUB

(Map p152; www.zanzibarlive.com; 1301 5th St; cover $7-10; ⊙Tue-Sun) Beat freaks will be in heaven at this groovetastic den dressed in a sensuous Indian-African vibe with a shape-shifting global DJ lineup that goes from Arabic to Latin to African depending on the night. The crowd is just as multiculti.

McCabe's Guitar Shop
ACOUSTIC

(www.mccabes.com; 3101 Pico Blvd; tickets $8-22; ⊙8pm Fri & Sat, 11am & 7pm Sun) Sure, this mecca of musicianship sells guitars and other instruments, but you want to come for concerts in the postage-stamp-sized back room where the likes of Jackson Browne and Liz Phair have performed live and unplugged. It hosts a popular Matinee Kids' Show every Sunday at 11am.

Laemmle's Monica 4
CINEMA

(Map p152; www.laemmle.com; 1332 2nd Street; adult/child $11/8; ⊙11am-1am) Art-house films in old-school multiplex environs. The only frills here are good-sized screens and current, tasteful cinema.

Bar Copa
CLUB

(Map p152; www.barcopa.com; 2810 Main St; cover Fri & Sat $5; ⊙9pm-2am Wed-Sat) There's a tantalizing underground vibe at this pint-sized, signless dancing den where drinks are reasonable, the crowd attitude-free and DJs spin a mix of dancehall, R&B, soul and hip-hop. Get there before 10pm to avoid the queue.

Broad Stage
THEATER

(Map p152; www.thebroadstage.com; 1310 11th St) A 499-seat, state-of-the-art theater is the anchor of SMC's striking new modernist performing-arts complex, which is a satellite campus on its own; 2010 was the stage's inaugural season, and it featured vocal performances, and one-man shows by Placido Domingo and Alan Cumming.

Magicopolis
MAGIC

(Map p152; ☎310-451-2241; www.magicopolis.com; 1418 4th St; tickets $22-27; ⊙8pm Fri & Sat, 2pm Sat & Sun; ⊛) Not only aspiring Harry Potters will enjoy the comedy-laced sleight-of-hand, levitation and other illusions performed by Steve Spills and cohorts in this intimate space. Escapes from reality last about 90 minutes, and there's even a small shop for all your wizard supplies.

Edgemar Center for the Arts
THEATER

(Map p152; www.edgemarcenter.org; 2437 Main St) There are two stages and a gallery, and the Edgemar also provides a platform for crossover collaborations between playwrights, musicians, actors, dancers and performance artists. It also has an acting school.

Highways Performance Space & Gallery
THEATER

(☎310-315-1459; www.highwaysperformance.org; 1651 18th St) Provocative and experimental performance art is what socially progressive artists cook up in Highways Performance Space, a cutting-edge lab of creativity. This results in a multicultural, all-embracing mosaic of cabaret, music, readings, dance recitals, mixed-media shows and plays that continually push the envelope of expression.

Bay Shore Lanes
BOWLING

(Map p152; www.amf.com; 234 Pico Blvd; per person per game $5.75-7; ⊙9am-midnight; P) With its kitschy red-vinyl lounge, greasy spoon diner and 24 shimmering lanes, this is where 'The Dude' rolled so well. Just don't flash your piece out on the lanes.

🛍 Shopping

TOP CHOICE Paris 1900
VINTAGE

(Map p152; www.paris1900.com; 2703 Main St) An exquisite collection of vintage French fashion from 1900 to 1930, and a few new vintage-inspired garments. Expect the finest jewelry and lace with an emphasis on period bridal. Look for the Montmartre-inspired art-nouveau entry.

Planet Blue
FASHION

(Map p152; www.shopplanetblue.com; 2940 Main St) Everyone from moneyed hipsters to soccer moms to Hollywood royalty peruses the racks at this expansive and stylish boutique stocked with tremendous denim and contemporary casual collections from designers like Gypsy 05, as well as high-end beauty essentials and some sexy silver too. There is also a location on Montana Ave.

Great Labels
FASHION

(Map p152; www.greatlabels.com; 1126 Wilshire Blvd) Sensational secondhand couture and designer hand-me-downs from celebrity consigners. There's Oscar and Golden Globe gowns, elegant handbags, shoes and accessories from Pucci, Prada, Jimmy Choo and Dior. If you've ever wanted to pay $250 for a four-figure dress, you'll come here.

Free People
FASHION

(Map p152; www.freepeople.com; 2925 Main St) Hippie-chic women's gear with a dash of retro cool. SM's pretty, pouty, and upscale flower children get dressed here.

Wine Expo
WINE & SPIRITS

(www.wineexpo.com; 2933 Santa Monica Blvd) LA's best nightlife generally sprouts at house parties. When you get your invitation, stop here to grab wine, champagne, whiskey or tequila from the best small producers and distilleries in the world. There are always great deals on great bottles to be had. Ask the knowledgeable staff for guidance.

Fred Segal
FASHION, JEWELRY

(Map p152; www.fredsegalfun.com; 500 Broadway; ⊙10am-7pm Mon-Sat, noon-6pm Sun; P) Celebs and beautiful people circle this impossibly chic but slightly snooty warren of high-end boutiques that straddles 5th St and dominates an entire block.

REI
OUTDOORS, ADVENTURE

(Map p152; www.rei.com; 402 Santa Monica Blvd; ⊙10am-9pm Mon-Sat, 11am-7pm Sun) This 'cathedral to outdoor gear' makes it easy to stock up on everything from wool socks to speed-dry underwear, rolling backpacks to Everest-capable sleeping bags. The staff is friendly and knowledgeable. REI also rents camping equipment.

Undefeated
SHOES

(Map p152; www.undeftd.com; 2654b Main St; ⊙10am-7pm Mon-Sat, 11am-6pm Sun) Get your kicks at this slammin' sneaker store specializing in vintage and limited editions, hand selected from the manufacturer by the manager. When new shipments arrive, expect sidewalk campouts as seen on Entourage.

Puzzle Zoo
GAMES

(Map p152; www.puzzlezoo.com; 1413 Third St Promenade; ⊙10am-9pm Sun-Thu, to 11pm Fri & Sat) Those searching galaxywide for the caped Lando Calrissian action figure, look no more. Puzzle Zoo stocks every imaginable Star Wars figurine this side of Endor. There's also an encyclopedic selection of puzzles, board games and toys.

Clouds
CANDLES

(Map p152; www.cloudsonmain.com; 2719 Main St) Affordable and aromatic, this handmade candle depot has the best selection in the area. You know, if you have a special night planned back at the suite...or the hostel.

Aura Shop
NEW AGE

(Map p152; www.aurashop.com; 2914 Main St) Well, you are in California. You may as well get your aura read. Yes, auras do exist (it's that heat energy radiating off your skin) and the color trails they leave behind signify... something, or so we're told. Just get the aura photo and the reading and believe it or not. Also sells books, candles and crystals.

Crossroads Trading Co
VINTAGE

(Map p152; www.crossroadstrading.com; 1449b 4th St) Sift, seek and find desirable denim, slinky dresses and all manner of footwear at this branch of America's popular vintage chain. Deals aren't hard to find and they'll buy your old gear too.

Hennessey & Ingalls
BOOKSTORE

(Map p152; www.hennesseyingalls.com; 214 Wilshire Blvd; ⊙10am-8pm) LA's best art and architecture bookstore features work from Matisse, Renzo Piano and all the giants of architecture, as well as lesser known volumes on sustainable design and graffiti. All in a cavernous and stylishly spare warehouse space with exposed beams patrolled by staff who have forgotten more about design than most will ever learn.

Marie Mason Apothecary   BEAUTY
(www.mariemasonapothecary.com; 225 26th St; P) The baby-blue walls, white shelves and antler chandeliers exude the feel of an intimate beach bungalow, and create a breezy setting for the exclusive beauty goods available at this Brentwood Country Mart boutique. Look for hard-to-find Trilogy from Australia and local Sage body lotions.

Natural High Lifestyle   FASHION
(Map p152; www.naturalhighlifestylestore.com; 2400 Main St) Because you thought organic cotton, bamboo, tencel (recycled wood pulp) and hemp clothing would never be this well tailored, because it's all sourced and made in LA and the flagship Santa Monica store is a fine place to browse and buy.

VENICE & MARINA DEL REY

If you were born too late, and have always been a little jealous of the hippie heyday, come down to the Boardwalk and inhale an incense-scented whiff of Venice, a boho beach town and longtime haven for artists, New Agers, road-weary tramps, freaks and free spirits. This is where Jim Morrison and the Doors lit their fire, where Arnold Schwarzenegger pumped himself to stardom and the place the late Dennis Hopper once called home.

SoCal's quintessential bohemian playground is the legacy of Abbot Kinney (1850–1920). A tobacco mogul by trade and a dreamer at heart, Kinney dug canals and turned fetid swampland into a cultural and recreational resort he dubbed the 'Venice of America'. For nearly two decades, crowds thronged to this 'Coney Island on the Pacific' to be poled around by imported gondoliers, walk among Renaissance-style arcaded buildings and listen to Benny Goodman tooting his horn in clubs. But time was not kind to Kinney's vision.

Most of the canals were filled and paved over in 1929 and Venice soon plunged into a steep decline until its cheap rents and mellow vibe drew first the beatniks, then hippies in the '50s and '60s. A few years later Venice turned 'Dogtown' as modern skateboarding hit the big time. These days, there are expanding pockets of gentrification, but overall it's still a low-key enclave with a strong sense of community. Think indie boutiques instead of cookie-cutter malls and local coffeehouses instead of Starbucks. There's plenty of innovative architecture and public art but, besides the Boardwalk, no traditional attractions, making the area great for independent exploring. Abbot Kinney Blvd has street parking, while parking lots on and near the beach charge between $6 and $12.

Follow the coast south of Venice and you'll come to Marina del Rey, which has nearly as many boats as residents. Some 5300 vessels bob in what is one of the largest artificial small-craft harbors in the country. Wrested from coastal wetlands in the '60s, the surrounding neighborhood consists mostly of generic concrete towers and has that disjointed, sterile feel typical of urban planning during the Modernist era. As an architectural case study, the Marina has its appeal, but the rest of us are really here to get active in what is truly an aquatic playground.

South of the Marina is the laid-back beach enclave of Playa Del Rey, where beachside fire pits are legal and the last swath of the Ballona wetlands still blooms.

◉ Sights

Venice Boardwalk   LANDMARK
(btwn Venice Pier & Rose Ave; ⊙24hr; ⊛) Life in Venice moves to a different rhythm and nowhere more so than on the famous Venice Boardwalk, officially known as Ocean Front Walk. It's a freak show, a human zoo and a wacky carnival, but as far as LA experiences go, it's a must. This is where to get your hair braided, your karma corrected or your back massaged qi gong–style. Encounters with budding Schwarzeneggers, hoop dreamers, a Speedo-clad snake charmer and a roller-skating Sikh minstrel jamming like Hendrix are pretty much guaranteed, especially on hot summer days. The Sunday-afternoon drum circle draws hundreds of revelers for tribal jamming and spontaneous dancing on the grassy mounds (sometimes beats migrate to the sand, as well). If the noise doesn't show you the way there, just follow your nose towards skunky cigarettes, which

are sold over the counter at several canna-bis clubs. And don't miss those tagged up towers and the free-standing concrete wall, forever open to aerosol Picassos to curb vandalism.

Venice Canals NEIGHBORHOOD
(Map p164) Even many Angelenos have no idea that just a couple of blocks away from the Boardwalk madness is an idyllic neigh-borhood that preserves 3 miles of Kinney's canals. The **Venice Canal Walk** threads past eclectic homes, over bridges and water-ways where ducks preen and locals lollygag in little rowboats. It's best accessed from either Venice or Washington Blvds, near Dell Ave.

Abbot Kinney Boulevard SHOPPING DISTRICT
(Map p164) Kinney would probably be de-lighted to find that one of Venice's most individualistic streets bears his name. Sort of a seaside Melrose with a Venetian

flavor, the mile-long stretch of Abbot Kin-ney Blvd between Venice Blvd and Main St is chockablock with unique boutiques, galleries, lofts, vintage clothing stores and sensational restaurants, including **Gjelina** (p168), **Joe's** (p168) and humble **Abbot's Pizza** (p168). In late September, the **Abbot Kinney Festival** (p68) draws thousands of revelers, as does the now-institutionalized **First Friday** art walk, when the galleries and shops stay open late and you'll roam all night with the tramps, hippies, weirdos, fashionistas, yuppies and squares.

Fisherman's Village SHOPPING DISTRICT
(www.visitmarinadelrey.com; 13755 Fiji Way) Most boats, including a daily ferry to Catalina Is-land (p210), party fishing boats and winter whale-watching tours leave from this kitschy strip of candy-colored cottages filled with tacky gift shops and forgettable restaurants. North of here, the small **Burton Chace Park** is a good spot for a picnic, flipping a Frisbee,

flying a kite or watching the parade of boats sailing through the Main Channel. In July and August there's a free concert series on Thursday and Saturday evenings. The same months also see the **WaterBus** in operation, a fun way to get around the Marina. It makes six strategic stops, including at Fisherman's Village and the park, and costs $1 per boarding or $5 for a day pass.

Mother's Beach   OUTDOORS
At the easternmost end of the Marina there is a decent stretch of sand that spills into the murky channel where boats bob in their slips and everything is bathed in golden light at sunset. There are no waves, and we wouldn't suggest swimming here, even if there are lifeguards on duty in the summertime.

Ballona Wetlands   OUTDOORS
Wetlands are the unsung heroes of the natural world. They clean silty rivers before the water trickles into the sea, provide shelter and hatcheries for birds and fish and are extremely difficult to restore and protect in an increasingly urbanized world. These last remaining wetlands in LA County are home to at least 200 migrating and resident bird species, including the great blue heron. Their habitat, however, has shrunk significantly since Playa Vista, a much-debated custom-planned luxury community for about 11,000 residents, took root across Lincoln. But the developers, via the **Friends of the Ballona Wetlands** (www.friendsofballona. org), get points for restoring and expanding the healthiest intact marsh, which has seen increasing bird activity in recent years.

Dockweiler State Beach   OUTDOORS
With jumbo jets soaring overhead, sailboats bobbing beyond the rolling surf, bonfires raging in the pit, and a waxing moon rising high, summer nights on Dockweiler – a 3.5-mile stretch of open beach – are always a good time.

South Venice Beach OUTDOORS

(Map p164) South of Washington Boulevard, the throng dissipates, and the golden sands unfurl in a more pristine manner. Waves roll in consistently and are ideal for bodysurfing, and volleyball games erupt at a moment's notice. Parking is an issue, which makes it a mostly local scene. Go ahead and crash it.

Activities

Venice Beach Skate Park SKATE PARK

(Map p164; 1800 Ocean Front Walk; ☺dawn-dusk) Long the destination of local skate punks, the concrete has now been molded and steel-fringed into 17,000 sq ft of vert, tranny and street terrain with unbroken ocean views. The old-school-style skate run and the world-class pool are most popular for spectators.

YAS WELLNESS

(Map p164; ☎310-396 6993; www.go2yas.com; 1101 Abbot Kinney Blvd; per class $15; ☺7am-7.30pm Mon-Thu, to 6pm Fri, 8.30am-6pm Sat & Sun) This studio offers the yin and yang of workouts, combining 30 minutes each of yoga and spinning, to put both your body and mind into a state of bliss. Also popular is the Yoga for Athletes classes. Weekends get busy, so preregister.

Exhale WELLNESS

(Map p164; www.exhalespa.com; 245 S Main St; per class $22, community class $11; ☺6:30am-9:30pm Mon-Fri, 7:15am-8pm Sat, 8:45am-8pm Sun) Just over the border from Venice, Exhale has two spacious studios, a gifted teacher roster, and a loyal (and attractive) dogtown crowd.

Gold's Gym GYM

(Map p164; www.goldsgym.com; 360 Hampton Dr; per class/day/week $10/20/70; ☺4am-midnight Mon-Fri, 5am-11pm Sat & Sun) Channel your inner Schwarzenegger at the hallowed original branch of Joe Gold's Pumping Iron empire.

Muscle Beach GYM

(Map p164; www.musclebeach.net; 1800 Ocean Front Walk; per day $10; ☺8am-7pm May-Sep, to 6pm Oct-Apr) Gym rats with an exhibitionist streak can get a tan and a workout at this famous outdoor gym right on the Venice Boardwalk where Arnold and Franco Columbo once bulked up.

Marina Boat Rentals BOAT RENTAL

(☎310-574-2882; www.boats4rent.com; 13719 Fiji Way) If you're feeling the call of the ocean, you can come here where vessels, everything from powerboats (per hour $65 to

---

VENICE ART WALK

Who needs galleries when you've got great outdoor art? Venice has plenty of both, so keep your eyes open as you stroll around town (and let us know your favorite finds!). A leisurely tour might start at the corner of Rose Ave and Main St where Jonathan Borofsky's 30ft tutu-clad **Ballerina Clown** (1989; Map p164) offers up a surreal presence. One block south, Frank Gehry's **Chiat/Day building** (Map p164) is fronted by massive binoculars by Claes Oldenburg and Coosje van Bruggen.

But Venice's real strength is its murals. Fine specimens along the Venice Boardwalk include **Chagall Returns to Venice Beach** (1996; Map p164; 201 Ocean Front Walk at Ozone Ave) by Christina Schlesinger, and **Venice Reconstituted** (1989; 25 Windward Ave) by Rip Cronk. The latter is a parody of Botticelli's *Venus in the Halfshell* and a cacophony of figures, many of them real Venetians. As you walk around, you'll find lots more Cronk murals. His **Homage to a Starry Night** (1990; Map p164; Ocean Front Walk at Wavecrest Ave) was inspired by the Van Gogh original. The same artist also created the epic 30ft-high portraits of one-time Venice resident **Jim Morrison** (Morning Shot; 1991; Map p164; 1881 Speedway) and of city-founder **Abbot Kinney** (2004; Map p164; N Venice at Pacific Ave).

With such a strong mural tradition, it only makes sense that the nonprofit **Social & Public Art Resource Center** (SPARC; www.sparcmurals.org; 685 S Venice Blvd; admission free; ☺10am-6pm Mon-Fri), which promotes, preserves and produces public murals throughout LA, is based in Venice. Its gallery and bookstore are well worth a look.

Each May the Venice Family Clinic sponsors an art auction and studio tour also known as the **Venice Art Walk** (www.venicefamilyclinic.org; tickets $50). With the ticket you receive a map and pass that grants entry into dozens of local studios featuring hundreds of original pieces whether you plan on bidding or not.

California voters approved the state's medical marijuana law in 1996, but it wasn't until 2002 when the first **'cannabis clubs'** (medical marijuana dispensaries) began sprouting on public streets. Those bold storefront 'cafes' were in a dilapidated section of Oakland, California and quickly earned the moniker, '**Oaksterdam**'. Police raids soon followed and by 2004, with the application of the law very much in flux, most cannabis clubs in LA were hush-hush affairs, where stoner intellectuals offered top-grade weed and spectacular edibles packaged like throwback Gen-X candy (think: Reefers Peanut Butter Cups) to a string of daring customers who'd seen the 'doctor', and skulked into heavily guarded, under-the-radar shops, usually set in run-down environs with no sign. It all felt like a house of cards. Fast forward just a few years later, and suddenly by 2009 there were over 500 cannabis clubs operating freely and openly in the city of LA, serving a steady stream of customers who paid their $70 to $150 for a prescription. All seemed eerie.

Then word began to trickle out of an alleged spike in violent crime and tax evasion associated with the, usually, very-profitable clubs. Worse, none of this income seemed to be flowing to the state at a time when the coffers were dry and school funding was threatened, which may be why the City of LA recently passed legislation limiting the number of clubs to 70. At the time of wiritng the law was on the verge of implementation, meaning several clubs were about to be shut down.

In November 2010 California voters will consider another marijuana initiative to fully legalize the ganja bush, trashing the medical ruse altogether. If it passes, one can only hope the city and state can figure a way to use the potential windfall to public benefit.

$25), to small sailing skiffs (per hour $45-75) to jet skis (two hours $160), to kayaks (per hour $15), and paddle boards (per hour $25) are sea worthy and available for rent by the hour and half day.

🛏 Sleeping

TOP CHOICE Inn at Playa del Rey B&B

BED & BREAKFAST **$$**

(✆310-574-1920; www.innatplayadelrey.com; 435 Culver Blvd, Playa del Rey; r $185-450; [P][@][✶][🛉]) A gorgeous rambling cottage, this quiet and impeccably run inn has clean, canary-yellow rooms with a contemporary feel (all with bathtubs and iPod docks, some with balcony or fireplace) and directly overlooks the state-protected Ballona Wetlands. It has free bike rental, and serves sensational breakfasts too.

Venice Breeze Suites BOUTIQUE HOTEL **$$**

(Map p164; ✆310-566-2222; www.venicesuites.com; 2 Breeze Ave; r $135-260; [P][✶]) A classy beachfront property with stylish studios and suites boasting wood floors and exposed-brick walls, floating beds, rain showers, frosted-glass desks and wall-mounted flat screens. Suites have full-sized kitchens and there's a fantastic communal barbecue area on the rooftop. Parking included.

Venice Beach Suites & Hotel

BOUTIQUE HOTEL **$$**

(Map p164; ✆310-396-4559; www.venicebeachsuites.com; 1305 Ocean Front Walk; r $119-235; [P][✶]) This good-value place right on the Boardwalk scores big for its bend-over-backwards staff, and bevy of beach toys for rent. There are exposed-brick walls, kitchenettes, wood floors and built-in closets. It's ideal for long stays. Kitchen suites are big enough for dinner parties. Parking is $20.

Hotel Erwin BOUTIQUE HOTEL **$$**

(Map p164; ✆310-452-1111; www.hotelerwin.com; 1697 Pacific Ave; r $209-439; [P][✶]) Venice's entry in the chic boutique hotel movement sweeping LA, this 23-year-old motor inn has been dressed up, colored and otherwise funkified in retro style. Think: eye-popping oranges, yellows and greens, framed photos of graffiti art, flat screens, and ergo sofas in the spacious rooms. Book online for the best deals.

Venice Beach Apartment Hotel HOSTEL **$**

(Map p164; ✆310-452-3052; 1515 Pacific Ave; r $129-349; [✶]) It's not exactly new, but the oddly configured dorms and rooms are clean and bright despite the party-animal, crash-pad aura that hovers around the joint's common spaces. It has free pancakes and waffles in the morning and it's in the heart of the Venice Beach scrum.

Inn at Venice Beach
MOTEL **$$**

(Map p164; ☎310-821-2557; www.innatvenice beach.com; 327 Washington Blvd; r $129-270; ☑☏) Close to the beach, the Venice canals, bars and restaurants, this Oaxacan-themed motel sports brightly hued rooms with a good range of amenities. All wrap around a central courtyard perfect for munching your free breakfast in the morning. Parking costs $7. It's good value when you can get the walk-in rate of $129.

Venice Beach House
BED & BREAKFAST **$$**

(Map p164; ☎310-823-1966; www.venicebeach house.com; 15 30th Ave; r $150-340; ☑☏) Close to the more pristine south end of Venice, this ivy-draped B&B in a 1911 Craftsman bungalow is a genteel retreat from the Boardwalk hubbub, which is a mere block away. If early-20th-century vintage living appeals, you won't mind the slightly faded elegance of the nine rooms, some with shared bathrooms.

Su Casa
BOUTIQUE HOTEL **$$**

(Map p164; ☎310-452-9700; www.sucasavenice. com; 431 Ocean Front Walk; r $150-365; ☑☏) Another in the string of boho boardwalk studio and apartment hotels overlooking the Boardwalk. These are fairly large with new wood floors, wall-mounted flat screens, humidifiers and air-con, and framed black and whites of old-school surfers. There is a three-day minimum.

✖ Eating

TOP CHOICE Gjelina
ITALIAN **$$$**

(Map p164; ☎310-450-1429; www.gje lina.com; 1429 Abbot Kinney Blvd; dishes $8-25; ☻lunch & dinner; ☑) Whether you carve out a slip on the communal table between the hipsters and yuppies, or get your own slab of wood on the elegant, tented stone terrace, you will dine on delicious and imaginative small plates (think chanterelles and gravy on toast or raw yellowtail spiced with chili and mint and drenched in olive oil and blood orange), and sensational thin crust, wood-fired pizza. They serve until midnight.

Axe
ASIAN FUSION **$$**

(Map p164; ☎310-664-9787; www.axerestaurant. com; 1009 Abbot Kinney Blvd; ☻lunch & dinner Wed-Fri, brunch & dinner Sat & Sun; ☑) One of our favorite kitchens in Venice suffered a fire in August 2010. It should re-open at some point in 2011 but at press time we didn't have a date. It's worth looking into for fans of Asian fusion.

Joe's
CAL-FRENCH **$$$**

(Map p164; ☎310-399-5811; www.joe'srestaurant. com; 1023 Abbot Kinney Blvd; mains $13-17; ☻lunch & dinner Tue-Sun; ☑) Joe's was one of the first restaurants on Abbot Kinney's restaurant row and, like a fine wine, only seems to get better with age. It's casual yet stylish with gimmick-free Cal-French food. The best deal here is the fabulous three-course, prix-fixe lunch for $18. No cell phones allowed!

Leomonade
MARKET CAFE **$**

(Map p164; www.leomonadela.com; 1661 Abbot Kinney Blvd; dishes $5-15; ☻lunch &dinner; ☑) An imaginative market cafe with a line-up of tasty salads (think: watermelon radish and chili or tamarind pork and spicy carrots), stockpots bubbling with lamb and stewed figs or miso-braised short ribs, and it has six kinds of lemonade augmented with blueberries and mint or watermelon and rosemary.

Abbot's Pizza
PIZZA **$**

(Map p164; www.abbotspizzaco.com; 1407 Abbot Kinney Blvd; slices $2.50-3, pizzas $9.50-16; ☻11am-11pm; ☑) Join the flip-flop crowd at this shoebox-sized pizza kitchen for habit-forming bagel-crust pies tastily decorated with tequila-lime chicken, Portobello mushrooms, goats cheese and other gourmet morsels served up at tummy-grumbling speed.

J's Kitchen
VEGAN **$**

(Map p164; www.jskitchen.com; 1239 Abbot Kinney Blvd; dishes $3-11; ☻11am-6pm; ☑) This sunny corner cafe promises organic, macrobiotic and vegan dishes. The bento boxes came with a root veggie salad, seitan chicken, pickles, tempeh and miso, and they do vegan chili fries and tofu scrambles too.

Mao's Kitchen
CHINESE **$**

(Map p164; www.maoskitchen.com; 1512 Pacific Ave; dishes $1-10; ☻lunch & dinner Sun-Thu) Cheap and cheerful, Mao's feeds the local proletariat with country-style Chinese prepared with SoCal flair (read: fresh ingredients, no MSG). Reliable menu picks include the orange-ginger chicken and the onion pancakes. Savvy eaters take advantage of the bargain lunches served until 5pm, and it's open till the wee hours (3am) on weekends.

EDDIE LIN: LA'S FOOD TRUCK BOOM

Eddie Lin writes for the LA food blog, **Deep End Dining** (www.deependdining.com) and is the author of Lonely Planet's *Extreme Cuisine*. He has appeared on the Travel Channel and is heard regularly on KCRW's *Good Food*.

The Origins

The Kogi truck started it all with its popular fusion of Korean BBQ meat and Mexican tacos. With the perfect-storm combination of a major downturn in the economy and a foodie fanaticism for a unique Korean fusion twist on the ubiquitous LA taco truck, the success of Kogi was only a glimpse of a major food revolution. Throw in the power of social media tools like Twitter and soon eating on the sidewalk became the new white tablecloth.

Single Best Truck Bite

Kogi's short rib taco. Kogi is king.

Top Three Trucks

» **Kogi** (www.kogibbq.com, http://twitter.com/kogibbq)

» **Grilled Cheese Truck** (www.thegrilledcheesetruck.com, http://twitter.com/grlldcheesetruk)

» **Dim Sum Truck** (www.thedimsumtruck.com, http://twitter.com/dimsumtruck)

How to Find Them

The website www.trucktweets.com is the single best way to keep track of the trucks.

Rose Café CAFE **$**
(Map p164; www.rosecafe.com; 220 Rose Ave; dishes $5.50-13.50; ⊙breakfast & lunch; P) Laptop-toting writers, ponytailed artists and beefcakes from nearby Gold's Gym dig this Euro-style cafe-bakery with two hedge-framed patios to slurp your latte or scarf up tasty salads and frittatas. Order at the market counter, or head for the hostess stand. Before leaving, browse for unique knick-knacks in the little gift store.

Hal's Bar & Grill CONTINENTAL **$$$**
(Map p164; 310-396-3105; www.halsbarandgrill.com; 1349 Abbot Kinney Blvd; mains $9-32; ⊙lunch & dinner) The name may evoke brass and wood, but Hal's Bar & Grill is an all-cool industrial loft brightened by revolving artworks from local artists who treat the dining room like it's an extended living room. The food menu is sourced from farm-fresh ingredients and changes seasonally. There's free jazz on Sunday and Monday, and the stylish bar serves drinks until 2am.

Fig Tree's Café CALIFORNIAN **$$**
(Map p164; www.figtreescafe.com; 429 Ocean Front Walk; appetizers $8-11, mains $12-16; ⊙breakfast, lunch & dinner) The best eats on the boardwalk. Here you can munch shitake omelettes made with organic eggs, ginger noodles, or a pesto-brushed, arugula-dressed salmon sandwich. The veg-heads will appreciate the spinach nut burger. Meals come with complementary sea views.

Shack PUB **$**
(185 Culver Blvd; dishes $5.25-9.25; ⊙lunch & dinner; P) A Playa Del Rey classic, with a knotted-wood bar, flatscreen TVs strobing sports and porthole windows inside, as well as a sunshine patio out back. But the crowds are here for the famed Shack Burger (a beef patty topped with a butterflied Louisiana sausage). It's a slightly intimidating, spicy, savory thing of artery-clogging beauty.

Chaya Venice ASIAN FUSION **$$$**
(Map p164; 310-39-1179; 110 Navy St; appetizers $7.15, mains $18.35; ⊙lunch Mon-Fri, dinner daily; P) The Venice branch of Tachibe's off-Robertson classic. It's a happy-hour hot spot for savory sushi and icy martinis, and the full menu is well worth exploring. It serves a reasonably priced late supper until 11:30pm on weeknights and midnight on weekends.

Drinking

Brig BAR

(Map p164; www.thebrig.com; 1515 Abbot Kinney Blvd; ⊙6pm-2am; P) Old-timers remember this place as a divey pool hall owned by ex-boxer Babe Brandelli (that's him and his wife on the outside mural). Now it's a bit sleeker, and attracts a trendy mix of grown-up beach bums, arty professionals and professional artists. On First Fridays, the parking lot attracts a fleet of LA's famed Food Trucks.

Intelligentsia COFFEEHOUSE

(Map p164; www.intelligentsiacoffee.com; 1331 Abbot Kinney Blvd; ⊙6am-8pm Mon-Wed, to 11pm Thu & Fri, 7am-11pm Sat, 7am-8pm Sun; P�) In this hip, industrial, minimalist monument to the coffee gods, skilled baristas – who roam the circle bar and command more steaming machines than seems reasonable – never short you on foam or caffeine, and the Cake Monkey scones and muffins are addictive too.

☆ **Entertainment**

TOP CHOICE **Stronghold** SPEAKEASY

(Map p164; www.facebook.com/the stronghold; 1625 Abbot Kinney Blvd; ⊙varies; P) The Stronghold had a brief life as a killer newschool speakeasy set in a loft above the Stronghold leather shop. It was famous for a consistent lineup of some of LA's best local musicians trying out their new material between gigs. Sadly, The Man shut them down, so now it's taken its ethos on the road, and is promoting the same kind of gigs at venues in Venice, the Marina and beyond. Check its Facebook page for details.

Air-Conditioned CLUB

(Map p164; www.airconditionedbar.com; 625 Lincoln Blvd; ⊙7pm-2am; P) It calls itself a supper club, but few of its patrons dine here. Most come for live indie rock and rotating DJs sans attitude.

🔒 **Shopping**

TOP CHOICE **LFrank** JEWELRY

(Map p164; www.lfrankjewelry.com; 1116 Abbot Kinney Blvd) If you are a fan of original and imaginative gold and silver jewelry made with everything from African trade beads to South Sea pearls to conflict-free rose and rough-cut diamonds, you should check out Liseanne Frankfurt's work, which is worn by stars such as Demi Moore, Gwyneth Paltrow and Alanis Morissette.

Strange Invisible APOTHECARY

(Map p164; www.siperfumes.com; 1138 Abbot Kinney Blvd) Ancient and organic perfumes are crafted from wild and natural ingredients and blended into intoxicating perfumes with names like Aquarian Rose and Urban Lilly. It sells dark chocolate too.

Ten Women GALLERY

(Map p164; www.tenwomengallery.com; 1237 Abbot Kinney Blvd) This bright, whimsical gallery is actually a collective of two-dozen female artists and craftswomen who paint, weave wire, blow glass and create beautiful material magic. They all do time behind the counter, which means you can meet one or two of the artists.

99 High Art Collective ART GALLERY

(Map p164; www.99collective.com; 1108 Abbot Kinney Blvd ⊙10am-10pm) Psychedelic lightbox art draws in the seekers of higher planes, especially on First Fridays when DJs, percussionists and sitar masters jam and the wafting essence of medicinals permeates the proceedings from the backroom cannabis club. But the art is for sale too.

Surfing Cowboys VINTAGE

(Map p164; www.surfingcowboys.com; 1624 Abbot Kinney Blvd) A blast of Beach Boys–era California, with vintage and vintage-style T-shirts and hoodies, wall sized Frankie and Annette posters and wall-mounted early-days surf and skateboards.

Luna Garcia GALLERY

(Map p164; www.lunagarcia.com; 201 San Juan Ave; ⊙10am-5pm Mon-Sat) An artist-owned pottery gallery where elegantly curved vases, platters, bowls, cups and sake bottles are thrown and glazed in earthly hues.

SOUTH BAY BEACHES

When you've had all the Hollywood ambition, artsy pretention, velvet ropes and mind-numbing traffic you can take, head south of the airport, where, like a whole new hemisphere, this string of beach towns will soothe that mess from your psyche in just one sunset. It all starts with Manhattan Beach, just 15 minutes from the airport. This increasingly tony town has its share of high-end shopping and dining, but the homes are stacked high on these steep streets because of the sublime stretch of sand and sea that made all of that possible. USC frat boys and sorority girls, financially challenged surfers and the beautiful boys and girls who love them, call Hermosa Beach home. The rents are lower here, and the scene trashier, but that's part of the charm. And if you prefer a cool, casual distance from the Pier Ave fracas, just belly up to one of the town's epic dives. As the coast winds to the south end of Santa Monica Bay you can follow it to diverse Redondo Beach, which bleeds into Torrance, which leads to the stunning Palos Verdes Peninsula.

MANHATTAN BEACH

A bastion of surf music and the birthplace of beach volleyball, Manhattan Beach has gone chic. Its downtown area along Manhattan Beach Blvd has seen an explosion of trendy restaurants, boutiques and hotels. Many of them cluster around the sleek Metlox Plaza (Manhattan Beach Blvd & Valley Dr), a small and upscale outdoor mall built on the site of a former pottery. Besides the Greek restaurant Petros and a **True Religion** premium denim flagship store, there's Shade, the South Bay's first designer boutique hotel whose bar often spills over with starlets streaming in from the nearby Raleigh Studios where *Boston Legal* and *CSI Miami* are shot.

Yet, even with this Hollywood-ification, Manhattan is undeniably a seaside enclave with plenty of beach and surf action around the pier.

There's a Friday **farmers market** (⊘noon-4pm Fri) near city hall, metered parking at the base of the pier and a public parking garage on Valley Dr between Manhattan Beach Blvd and 13th St.

◉ Sights

Manhattan Beach Open   VOLLEYBALL
(www.avp.com) Every August thousands of bad-ass babes in sport bikinis and trunks take to the sacred sand during the the world's oldest and most prestigious volleyball tournament (played since 1960). Go to Marine Ave to see them practice year-round.

Roundhouse Marine Studies Lab & Aquarium   AQUARIUM
(www.roundhouseaquarium.org; suggested donation $2; ⊘3pm-sunset Mon-Fri, 10am-sunset Sat & Sun; ⊛) Family fun awaits at this compact aquarium at the end of the 928ft-long pier. Pet a slimy sea cucumber, see Nemo the clownfish up close and check out the new deep-ocean tank with its anemones, baby sharks and sunflower starfish.

🏃 Activities

Sun Bums Beach Rentals   BEACH RENTAL
(1116 Manhattan Ave; ⊘10am-5pm Mon-Thu, to 6pm Fri, to 7pm Sat & Sun) Anything you need to complete your dream beach day – a cruiser with a babyseat (per hour/day $10/21), a long, short, or bodyboard (per hour/day $10/30), a pair of in-line skates (per hour/day $6.50/19), or just a really good chair – is here for the renting.

Sand Dune Park   OUTDOORS
(www.citymb.info; cnr 33rd & Bell Ave; ⊘7:30am-9pm Apr-Oct, 6am-8pm Nov-Mar; P⊛) When we visited, the long, deep, 100ft-high, natural sand dune was closed for maintenance, but the wooded trails are lovely, even if the suburban smoke stack views aren't your thing. And if it has reopened when you visit, your kids will love hurling themselves down the dunes again, and again, and again.

🛏 Sleeping

Shade Hotel   BOUTIQUE HOTEL **$$$**
(☎310-546-4995; www.shadehotel.com; 1221 N Valley Dr; r $295-595; P@⊛) Manhattan Beach goes Hollywood where mod luxury rooms are jammed with lifestyle essentials (iPod docking stations, margarita blender) and even have color-therapy spa tubs big enough for two. The service is inspired, the beach is just three blocks away and the Zinc Lounge bar is buzzy with cool sea-urchin chandeliers.

Sea View Inn   MOTEL **$$**
(☎310-545-1504; www.seaview-inn.com; 3400 N Highland Ave; r $130-275; P⊛⊛⊛) This motel spans Highland Ave with luxurious, ocean-facing rooms on the west side, and basic but still nicely appointed rooms on the east side. All of them are a steep trek back from the beach, but otherwise this friendly property has a lot going for it, including free bikes, beach chairs and boogie-board rentals.

Manhattan Beach Hotel   MOTEL **$**
(☎310-545-9020; 4017 N Highland Ave; r $60-90; P⊛) Eleven clean but basic rooms in an owner-operated motor inn with a top floor sun deck and unobstructed views as far as Anacapa and Catalina. No kids allowed, but the wi-fi, longboards and beach cruisers are free to guests. Weekly rates range from $385 to $539.

Eating

North End Caffe
CAFE $$
(3421 N Highland Ave; dishes $8-13; ☺breakfast, lunch & dinner; P ⛺) Tasty market sandwiches (like roast beef with horseradish or prosciutto with brie and parm), fresh soups and entrée salads at lunch and early dinner (it closes at 8pm), plus breakfast done a dozen different ways (try the *huevos divorciados*, even if you're still hitched). Dishes come with a side of ocean views.

Mama D's
ITALIAN $$
(☎310-456-1492; 1125 Manhattan Ave; dishes $5-8; ☺lunch & dinner; ⛺) This neighborhood Italian joint fits like a well-worn shoe and puts the 'heap' into 'cheap'. The thin-crust pizzas, homemade ravioli, tangy cioppino and freshly baked bread, all served with a smile, keep regulars coming back for more. Expect a wait.

El Gringo
MEXICAN $
(www.elgringo.com; dishes $6.50-10; ☺lunch & dinner; ⛺) Hermosa Beach (2620 Hermosa Ave); Manhattan Beach (921 N Sepulveda Blvd; P); Redondo Beach (821 Torrance Blvd; P) Mini-mall dives usually make the best Mexi-fare and this tri-city mini-chain definitely delivers. Authentic charm is doled out with as much abandon as the delish dishes. Skip the standards in favor of *machaca* (shredded beef) burritos, *pollo negro* (blackened chicken) salads and flavor-packed *xcholti* (pronounced 'soul-chee') soup. Most locals favor the fish tacos.

Uncle Bill's Pancake House
DINER $
(www.unclebills.net; 1305 N Highland Ave; dishes $7-12.50; ☺breakfast & lunch; ⛺) Grab a stool, a booth or better yet an ocean-view table at this greet-the-day South Bay institution. Sexy surfers, tottering toddlers and gabbing girlfriends – everybody's here for the famous pancakes and big fat omelettes (try the 'Istanbul' made with turkey). Put your name on the list – the wait's worth it.

Rock'n Fish
SEAFOOD $$
(www.rocknfishmb.com; 120 Manhattan Beach Blvd; appetizers $11-13; mains $7-19; ☺lunch & dinner; P) If you're the type who likes to pair fresh shucked oysters, barbecued shrimp or oak-grilled seafood with a day at the beach, then come to this classy yet laid-back brick house and dine well.

Petros
GREEK $$
(☎310-545-4100; www.petrosrestaurant.com; 451 Manhattan Beach Blvd; appetizers $8-14, mains $6-20; ☺lunch & dinner; P) Finally, a Greek restaurant for the 21st century. Petros is all about class and substance as evidenced in dishes like feta-encrusted rack of lamb or the smoky eggplant and walnut dip. Grab a seat on the people-watching patio or lose the baseball cap for a dress-code-worthy experience indoors.

Drinking

Ercole's
DIVE BAR
(1101 Manhattan Ave; ☺10am-2am) A nice counterpoint to the HD-inundated, design-heavy sports bars on Manhattan Beach Blvd. This hole is dark and well irrigated. The tile is chipped and faded, and the barn door has been open to everyone from salty barflies to yuppie pub crawlers to volleyball stars and wobbly coeds since 1927.

Simmzy's Pub
SPORTS PUB
(www.simmzys.com; 229 Manhattan Beach Blvd; ☺11am-1am) For a more civilized view of the big game, relax into this stylish, if a bit cramped, sports pub where the microbrews are listed on the blackboard, and the HD screens are never far from view. The menu is simple yet tasty and it does wine flights and holds 'Sangria Saturdays' here too.

HERMOSA BEACH

Strolling down Hermosa Beach's **Pier Ave** on a summer weekend, you're immediately struck by two things: everybody's wearing flip-flops, tiny tees and a tan, and they all seem to be having way too much fun. The short, car-free strip is party central in a small town (within a big town) that's always lived the easy life. Once home to long-haired hippies and underground punk bands like Black Flag, it's now solidly ruled by hormone-crazed surfer dudes and the chicks that dig 'em. The beach is indeed *muy hermosa* (Spanish for 'beautiful') – long, flat and dotted with permanent volleyball nets. Go to 16th St to see local pros bump, set and spike in preparation for the **AVP Hermosa Open** (www.avp.com) in July.

Hermosa is one of several towns claiming to be the birthplace of surfing and even has its own **Surfers Walk of Fame**, but in 2006 the official nod went to Huntington Beach.

Every Memorial Day and Labor Day weekend Hermosa's three-day **Fiesta Hermosa** (www.fiestahermosa.com), with music, food, kiddy rides and a huge arts-and-crafts fair, attracts large throngs of revelers.

Activities

Hermosa Cyclery
BIKE RENTALS
(www.hermosacyclery.com; 20 13th St; ☺10am-5pm; P) Get your cruisers, six-speeds, boogie boards and beach chairs by the hour or day. Rates are competitive and quality is high.

Sleeping

Beach House at Hermosa
BOUTIQUE HOTEL **$$$**
(☑310-374-3001; www.beach-house.com; 1300 The Strand, Hermosa Beach; r $219-419; P @ �)
This sparkling beachfront inn epitomizes California's laid-back lifestyle. Open the balcony door of your lofty ocean-view suite to let in the ocean breezes, soak in a deep, warm tub or fall asleep to the soft crackling of a wood-burning fireplace. The paved bikeway is right outside and restaurants and nightlife are a quick stroll away. No kids allowed.

Sea Sprite Motel
MOTEL **$$**
(☑310-376-6933; www.seaspritemotel.com; 1016 The Strand; r $119-279; P ☺ ☀) The rooms here aren't fancy, but they are superclean, come with minifridge, microwaves and wood furnishings, and the location – right on the beach, overlooking the bustling strand – could not be better.

Surf City Hostel
HOSTEL **$**
(☑310-798-2323; www.surfcityhostel.com; 26 Pier Ave; r $25-70; @ ☺) Steps from the sand, the halls of this convivial hostel are splashed with cool murals of cartoon hall-of-famers. It's mostly co-ed four- and six-person dorms here and even the private rooms have shared baths. If you're looking to spend your days beaching and your nights partying, this is your place.

Eating

Martha's 22nd St Grill
DINER **$**
(25 22nd St; dishes $6.50-13; ☺breakfast & lunch;) Locals swear by the eggs at this unassuming beachside patio joint. It does sandwiches and salads too, but the eight varieties of Benedictine eggs and omelettes, stuffed with veggies and havarti, avocado, bacon and cheddar or hummus, sundried tomatoes and goats cheese, are the draw.

Big Mike's
SANDWICHES **$**
(1499 Hermosa Ave; dishes $5-14; ☺lunch & dinner) Because health-crazed California demands a counterpoint. Because hoagies (sandwiches) and Philly cheesesteaks (hoagies stuffed with thinly sliced rib eye, onions, peppers and cheese) are the perfect beach-blanket meal. Because grease + spice = hangover cure. Because it stays open after the bars close on weekends.

Drinking

Barnacle's
DIVE BAR
(www.myspace.com/barnaclesbarandgrill; 837 Hermosa Ave; ☺9-2am) Nestled thankfully off the Pier Ave crush, this decidedly grungy neighborhood joint has friendly (not bubbly) blondes behind the bar, boards (snow, skate, surf) in the rafters, Credence on the stereo and ball games on the flatscreens. On Saturdays it offers $4 drafts and $8 author-tested bloodies (spicy and delectable they are), and you may as well wander outside to the sun patio to gaze at the big blue sea.

Mermaid
DIVE BAR
(11 Pier Ave; ☺10am-10:30pm) The bad old granddad of the Hermosa strand, this divey classic with black-vinyl booths, and a circle bar patrolled by grizzled vets, is the perfect antidote to the varying degrees of fromage found beyond its grimy windows. Who needs an ocean view when you can have a martini in a joint like this?

Entertainment

Saint Rocke's
VENUE
(www.saintrocke.com; 142 Pacific Coast Hwy; ☺from 5pm Mon-Fri, from 6pm Sat & Sun; P)
The South Bay's best live-music venue lies within this dated brick house with nightly live bands ranging from the kitschy (think: dueling pianos) to the up-and-coming (White Buffalo) to the past-their-prime and still doing it well (Toots and the Maytalls). Thursday night is Reggae Night.

Cafe Boogaloo
BLUES
(www.boogaloo.com; 1238 Hermosa Ave) This relaxed joint offers up a mixed musical bag that might include zydeco one night, blues the next, followed by American roots. A welcome escape from the usual Hermosa Beach frat-pack madness, Boogaloo also serves wicked cocktails, two dozen microbrews and a Cajun menu.

Shore
LOUNGE
(www.theshorerestaurantandlounge.com; 1320 Hermosa Ave; ☺5:30pm-1am Mon-Fri, from 2pm Sat & Sun; P) Live music and comedy right on the Hermosa strip. It has something going almost every night and offers bottle service and sushi. But that doesn't mean you should eat it.

🛍 Shopping

TOP CHOICE **Bo Bridges Photography & Spit Studio** GALLERY
(www.bobridges.com; 1246 Hermosa Ave; ⊙11am-5pm Sat & Sun, varies Mon-Fri) One of the best, if not the best, photo galleries in Southern California. Bridges made his name as a surf photographer, but has since branched into general sport and commercial as well as pop art. Check out dramatic shots of glacier surfers in Alaska, Kelly Slater barreling Pipeline, profiles of Derek Jeter and Serena Williams, and several of prominent rockers, skaters and other jocks in their element. Get your prints framed or glazed onto a skate or surfboard.

REDONDO BEACH & TORRANCE

Redondo Beach is a working-class beach town, it's also largest in the South Bay, and the most ethnically diverse, as it wanders inland and bleeds into neighboring Torrance. Its heart is at King's Harbor, where the dated pier is still an excursion-worthy detour on your way south to the most absurdly beautiful coastal stretch in all of LA.

👁 Sights

Redondo Beach Pier LANDMARK
Arching from the bottom of Torrance Blvd all the way to **Kings Harbor**, this classic 1960s multilevel beast is either aesthetically challenged or unpretentious and cool, depending upon your point of view. Regardless, it is the Redondo hub with a weekly Thursday **farmers market** (⊙7am-1pm), and plenty of pierside anglers, restaurants and watering holes to keep you nourished and entertained.

Redondo & Torrance Beaches OUTDOORS
These beaches, which technically join in one contiguous stretch of sand, have their beauty and charms, but the middle section thins out, exposing drain pipes and breakwaters at low tide. It's best to stick to the northern stretch of Redondo (which is actually south of the pier and boasts a thick manicured blanket of sand and volleyball nets aplenty), and the southern edge of Torrance Beach along the Palos Verdos bluffs where it's all naturally gorgeous.

🏃 Activities

Marina Bike Rentals OUTDOORS
(505 Harbor Dr, Redondo Beach; ⊙10am-5pm; P🚻) Can you really contemplate that winding concrete bike path stretching north from Kings Harbor through Hermosa and Manhattan Beach and not rent a cruiser? Is that seriously possible?

Seaside Lagoon POOL
(www.redondo.org/seasidelagoon; 200 Portofino Way at Harbor Dr; adult/child $4.50/3.25; ⊙10am-5:45pm late May–early Sep; P🚻) Geared to the little ones, this large, shallow saltwater outdoor pool with a slide and cascading fountain usually teems with an ethnic potpourri of families frolicking in the sand or picnicking in the grass. Parking costs $3 with validation.

Sea D Sea DIVING
(www.seadsea.com; 1911 S Catalina Ave, Redondo Beach; ⊙10am-6pm) This neighborhood dive center offers six dive trips per year to Catalina (three dives per day, per person $90-130). If you're certified you can rent gear and gather tips here and explore the wild Palos Verdos coast as long as you have a buddy in tow. Remember, this is cold-water diving even in the summer.

🛏 Sleeping

Redondo Inn & Suites MOTEL **$**
(☎310-540-1888; www.redondoinnandsuites.com; 711 S Pacific Coast Hwy, Redondo Beach; r $59-119; P🛜🚻) Rooms aren't huge at this humble motor hotel, but the carpet is fresh, the bathroom tiles sparkling, there are crown moldings and an attractive, sponged paint job, plus a minifridge and microwave, and it's just two blocks from the beach. Superb value all around.

Miyako Hybrid Hotel BOUTIQUE HOTEL **$$**
(☎310-212-5111; www.miyakohybridhotel.com; 21381 S Western Ave, Torrance; r $189-350; P🛜) A slice of Tokyo in downtown Torrance. The location here is best suited for the suits headed to Honda and Toyota's US headquarters nearby, but it deserves mention because of its sustainable ethos (recycled wallpaper, recyclable carpeting and solar power) as well as the only-in-Japan touches like deep-soaking tubs and robo-toilets.

Portofino Hotel & Yacht Club HOTEL **$$**
(☎310-379-8481; www.hotelportofino.com; 260 Portofino Way, Redondo Beach; r $210-357, ste $1080-1344; P@🛜🏊) This '60s oceanfront property next to the Redondo Pier blends urban sophistication with nautical lightheartedness. Get an ocean-view room with a balcony for watching the sunset and an adorable sea-lion colony. Marina-facing views overlook not only boats but

also a power plant, partly hidden behind a Wyland whale mural. Parking is $22.

✕ Eating

🌱 Green Temple
VEGAN $
(www.greentemple.net; 1700 S Catalina Ave, Redondo Beach; appetizers $7-9.50, mains $8-11; ◷lunch & dinner; 🖋) Sit in the flowery courtyard or amid funky Asian artwork at this sanctuary where meat is a no-no and organic, local produce is plentiful. Salads, including the tasty Sproutada, come with a slice of delicious homemade bread and there's also an entire page of Mexican options. Waist-watchers can ask for the 'junior' portions.

TOP CHOICE Christine
FUSION $$
(📞310-373-1952; www.restaurantchristine.com; 24530 Hawthorne Blvd, Torrance; mains $16-29; ◷lunch Mon-Fri, dinner daily; P) This top pick in the South Bay is more about substance on the plate than the cheesy Mediterranean decor and dressed-up clientele. Chef Christine finds inspiration in the feisty flavors of Provence, Tuscany and the Pacific Rim, all expertly woven together in such dishes as *char sui*–glazed filet mignon.

Wildflower Café
CAFE $$
(821 Torrance Blvd; dishes $5.50-11; ◷breakfast & lunch; 🚼) Locally beloved for hearty, healthy sandwiches (like the grilled eggplant and mozzarella with arugula), omelettes with broccoli, tomato and basil, fresh bagels and, of course, banana-walnut pancakes. Eat in the cozy interior or on the heated patio.

Yellow Vase
CAFE $$
(www.yellowvase.com; 1805 S Catalina Ave, Redondo Beach; dishes $7-13.50; ◷breakfast & lunch; 🚼) One of the most fun, sunniest and colorful spots in the South Bay, this flower-shop-meets-California-cafe is where pastries and cakes are plentiful and freshly baked, panini are grilled to melting, salads are organic and filling, and blossoms are sold by the stem.

El Indio
MEXICAN $
(📞310-370-0038; 2523 Artesia Blvd, Torrance; dishes $4.10-10.50; ◷breakfast, lunch & dinner; P🚼) Family-owned and -operated since 1960, El Indio loyalists venture into Torrance for carne asada burritos, *carnitas* tacos, and especially for its unparalleled tamales. Sweet and spicy, they come in one flavor: pork. Just like in old Mexico.

☆ Entertainment

Brixton
VENUE
(www.brixtonsouthbay.com; 100 Fishermans Wharf; ◷from 9pm Thu-Sun; P) A basement rock and reggae club on the Redondo pier mainlining frayed classics like the Crash Test Dummies, Dramarama and Fishbone, as well as a Springsteen tribute band.

PALOS VERDES PENINSULA

We're not talking about Malibu or Santa Monica here, but the little-known Palos Verdes Peninsula, or PV as it is affectionately known. Here is a revelation of sand-swept silver bays and Catalina shadows whispering through a fog rising from the cold Pacific blue. There are long, elegant and perfectly manicured lawns bearing sprawling mansions. And to the north, south and east there's nothing but layered jade hills forming the headland that cradles the southernmost reach of the great Santa Monica Bay.

◉ Sights

Wayfarers Chapel
SPIRITUAL
(Map p176; www.wayfarerschapel.org; 5755 Palos Verdes Dr S; ◷8am-5pm; P) The most stunning non-natural attraction on Palos Verdos was built by Lloyd Wright (son of Frank) in 1951, and no matter where you stand among the great saints (Jesus, Buddha, Krishna, Muhammad, Moses or Yahweh), this place will touch your soul. It's a glass church cradled by soaring redwood trees. Not surprisingly, it's an insanely popular spot to tie the knot, so avoid coming on weekends.

Abalone Cove Shoreline Park
OUTDOORS
(Map p176; www.palosverdes.com; Palos Verdes Dr; ◷9am-4pm; P🚼) The best place to hunt for starfish, anemones and other shoreline critters is in and around this rock-strewn eco-preserve. The walk down to the beach gets pretty steep in some sections, so watch your footing. Parking costs $5.

FREE Point Vicente Lighthouse
LANDMARK
(Map p176; www.palosverdes.com/pv light; P) Watch the earth curve and the sea crash on the Point Vicente bluffs while leaning against the gleaming-white 1926 lighthouse, which was staffed until 1971. These days electronic sensors activate the foghorn, which you can hear bellow on the wings of the wind. You can peek inside from 10am to 3pm on the second Saturday of the month.

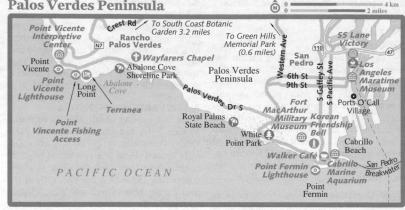

Point Vicente Interpretive Center

VIEWPOINT

(Map p176; 31501 Palos Verdes Dr W; donations appreciated; ☺10am-5pm; ⓟ☒) Binocular-toting whale-watchers gather north of the adjacent lighthouse between December and April when the Pacific gray whales embark on their fascinating and arduous migration from Alaska to Mexico. Inside are fun exhibits for boning up on the specifics. Picnic beneath palm trees and stroll along the blufftop trail.

South Coast Botanic Garden   GARDEN

(Map p176; www.southcoastbotanicgarden.org; 26300 Crenshaw Blvd; adult/5-12yr/student $8/3/6; ☺9am-5pm; ⓟ) It's hard to believe that this flowering and fruiting, sprouting and sprawling blast of life (we're talking around 2000 species of life) was reclaimed from a former landfill. Plant shows and sales take place year-round. Admission is cash only.

PV Peninsula   SCENIC DRIVE

(Map p176; Palos Verdes Dr, Palos Verdes; ☒) Start at Point Fermin Park in San Pedro, and cruise north along Palos Verdes Dr at sunset for awesome eyefuls of stunning shoreline. Steep cliffs tumble down to rocky shores and secluded coves as the roadway ribbons past rambling multi-million-dollar mansions. Catalina Island looms hazily across the sparkling Pacific.

🛏 **Sleeping**

TOP
CHOICE
Terranea   RESORT $$$

(Map p176; ☎310-265-2800; www.terranea.com; 100 Terranea Way, Palos Verdes; r $300-450, ste $655-2850; ⓟ@☞☒☒) Once

the domain of trick sea mammals, the old Marineland property is now LA's best five-star beach resort. Rooms are flooded with natural light, and have been designed in classic California style, with blonde-wood furnishings, picnic-table desks, berber carpeting and stone and marble baths – 92% of them have ocean views. Trails wrap the property, skirt the wild coast and are open to the public, as are the five restaurants and nine-hole golf course. Parking and access to the beach is free and guests have free access to kayaks, mountain bikes and paddleboards.

LONG BEACH, SAN PEDRO & WILMINGTON

Long Beach has come a long way since its working-class oil and navy days. Over the past decade or so, LA's southernmost seaside town has quietly reinvented its gritty downtown and, recent recession-related vacancies notwithstanding, made it an attractive place to live and party. On any Saturday night the restaurants, clubs and bars along lower **Pine Ave** are abuzz with everyone from buttoned-down conventioneers to the testosterone-fuelled frat pack. Additional eateries line a new waterfront boardwalk linking the Aquarium of the Pacific with **Shoreline Village**, the departure point for boat cruises.

Despite the name, the beach isn't such a big draw here. In fact, the water tends to be rather polluted thanks to the proximity of the giant Port of Los Angeles, the country's busiest (it ranks 13th worldwide). And those palm-studded mini-islands you see offshore? They're actually disguised oil rigs. If you want to hit the water locally, do it in Belmont Shores, about 2 miles east of downtown.

The stress-free way to get to Long Beach is by riding the air-conditioned Metro Rail Blue Line. Once downtown you can walk or catch the red Passport buses, which swing by all the museums and other points of interest, including Belmont Shore (free within downtown; $1.25 otherwise, exact change required). From June to mid–September, the AquaBus links the aquarium and the *Queen Mary*, as does the high-speed Aqua-Link, which also goes out to Alamitos Bay (Naples).

Just northwest of Long Beach, the port town of San Pedro (San Pee-dro) is a working-class harbor town and a bedroom community, charming and just rough enough to be real without losing its sweetness. Expect old wooden homes, wind-ravaged bluffs, and cold, salty blasts of sea. The Pedro time warp is so pervasive that many of the dive bars where Charles Bukowski probably ruined his liver are still open. LA's late, great bad-boy poet now rests in **Green Hills Memorial Park** (plot 875, 27501 S Western Ave; Ocean View; **P**).

'San Pedro is real quiet,' Bukowski once observed. That's still true today, except for the distant clanging of containers being hoisted on and off gigantic cargo vessels. LA's own 'Golden Gate', the 1500ft-long suspended Vincent Thomas Bridge, links San Pedro with Terminal Island.

The father of the harbor, Phineas Banning, lived in adjacent Wilmington; his 1864 Greek Revival remains, along with Southern California's original Civil War–era barracks.

◉ Sights

TOP CHOICE **Aquarium of the Pacific**   AQUARIUM
(Map p178; www.aquariumofpacific.org; 100 Aquarium Way; adult/child/senior $24/12/21; ⊙9am-6pm; **P** ⊞) Long Beach's most mesmerizing experience, the Aquarium of the Pacific is a vast, high-tech indoor ocean where sharks dart, jellyfish dance and sea lions frolic. More than 12,000 creatures inhabit four re-created habitats: the bays and lagoons of Baja California, the frigid northern Pacific, the coral reefs of the tropics and local kelp forests. Parking costs $8.

Among the many not-to-be-missed exhibits is the **Shark Lagoon** where you can pet young sharks in a touch pool and go nose-to-nose – through a window – with their adult-sized cousins patrolling a larger tank. The teeth on the bull shark are the stuff that'll give you *Jaws*-style nightmares. The best time to be here is during the daily feeding sessions (check the schedule online or in the lobby).

Elsewhere, you'll be entertained by the antics of sea otters, spooked by football-sized crabs with spiny 3ft-long arms, and charmed by Seussian-looking sea dragons. It's a wondrous world that'll easily keep you enthralled for a couple of hours. On weekdays, avoid the field-trip frenzy by arriving around 2pm; on weekends beat the crowd by getting here as early as possible.

For an extra fee, the aquarium offers behind-the-scenes tours and, from late May to early September, ocean boat trips.

Point Fermin Park & Around   PARK, LANDMARK
(Map p176) Locals come to this grassy community park on the bluffs to jog, picnic, watch wind- and kitesurfers, cool off in the shade of spreading magnolias, wonder at never-ending waves pounding a rugged crescent coastline or to enjoy live jazz on balmy summer Sundays. Ostensibly the main visitor attraction is the restored 1874 Victorian **Point Fermin Lighthouse** (Map p176; www.pointferminlighthouse.org; 807 Paseo Del Mar; ⊙1-4pm Tue-Sun), one of the oldest in the West. The first keepers of the light were trailblazing sisters Mary and Ellen Smith, but eventually the author, George Bernard Shaw took their place. After the tour stop by the geriatric biker bar, **Walker Cafe** (p182).

Just north of Point Fermin, in Angels Gate Park, is the **Fort MacArthur Military Museum** (Map p176; www.ftmac.org; 3601 S Gaffey St; donations appreciated; ⊙noon-5pm Tue, Thu, Sat & Sun), an LA harbor defensive post until 1945. Unless you're a total pacifist, bring your kids to this outdoor museum to scale the gun batteries and search for secret tunnels. But even more impressive is the **Korean Friendship Bell** (Map p176; www.kccla.org; 3601 S Gaffey St; ⊙10am-6pm; **P** ⊞). A gift from South Korea to the US government, this huge, cast-iron, low-slung oval chime and its green-tiled shrine dominates the hillside and makes for a fantastic lookout point. The nearby exhibition hall holds various Korean cultural totems.

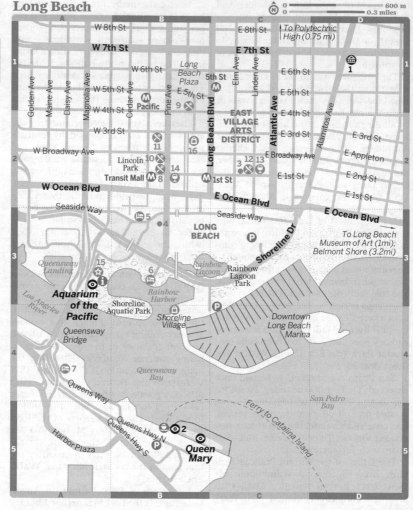

Belmont Shore & Naples

COMMERCIAL, COASTAL DISTRICT

If downtown Long Beach feels urban and corporate, Belmont Shore exudes quintessential SoCal laid-back-rity. It has a fine beach with a pier for fishing and sunsets, and keeps it real along a buzzy four-block-long strip of mostly indie boutiques, cafes filled with surfers and students, and busy restaurants like **Bono's** (p181).

Naples, just south of here, is Long Beach's most exclusive neighborhood. It's a canal-laced borough, not coincidentally created in 1903 by Arthur Parsons, a contemporary of Venice's Abbot Kinney. It's best explored on a gondola ride.

Drum Barracks Civil War Museum MUSEUM (www.drumbarracks.org; 1052 N Banning Blvd; suggested donation $5; ☉tours 10am & 11:30am Tue-Thu, 11:30am & 1pm Sat & Sun; Ⓟ) This is the only surviving Civil War-era US army structure in Southern California. It's filled with artifacts from the years 1861–66 when this was a training center and supply depot for battlegrounds in Southern California, Arizona and New Mexico, and it's run by a proper history lover who has cobbled together modest resources to find

Long Beach

FREE **West Coast Choppers** SHOWROOM
(www.westcoastchoppers.com; 1200 West Coast Choppers Pl; ⊙9am-5pm Mon-Fri, to 4pm Sat; P) The iron-gated compound straddling both sides of 'West Coast Choppers Place' belongs to marital outlaw Jesse James. This is where sleek, impossibly angular choppers are custom-made by burly, goatee-sporting LBC locals. The showroom is small but worth a peek, and the gift shop sells shirts and memorabilia, but all those German crosses (on the webbed gates, on the chrome, in the lights) look pretty ominous.

FREE **East Village Arts District**
COMMERCIAL DISTRICT
(Map p178; www.eastvillagelive.com; East Long Beach) Don't get overly excited just because the words East Village and Arts happen to appear in the same sentence. Still, this rather small corner of Long Beach (between Ocean Blvd and 7th St) does have a funky feel with some groovy cafes, restaurants and boutiques to explore.

Queen Mary LANDMARK
(Map p178; www.queenmary.com; 1126 Queens Hwy; adult/child/senior from $23/12/20; ⊙10am-6pm; P) Long Beach's 'flagship' attraction is this grand and supposedly haunted British luxury liner. Larger and more luxurious than even the *Titanic,* she transported royals, dignitaries, immigrants, WWII troops and vacationers between 1936 and 1964. Today the sad air of a tourist trap hangs over her bow, but once you've studied the memorabilia on display you might well be able to envision dapper gents escorting ladies in gowns to the art-deco lounge for cocktails or the sumptuous Grand Salon for dinner.

Basic admission includes the hokey **Ghosts & Legends** special-effects tour, which features strange apparitions in the 1st-class swimming pool and the boiler room. Various other tours and packages are also available and combination tickets with the aquarium cost $35/19 per adult/child. If you'd like to spend the night, see p181. On Saturdays midnight screenings of *The Rocky Horror Picture Show* draw a rowdy party crowd. Parking costs $10, and opening hours can vary according to the season; check the website for times before you visit.

The Cold War–era Soviet submarine **Scorpion** (adult/child $11/10) is moored alongside the *Queen.* As you scramble around, imagine how 78 crew shared 27 bunks and two bathrooms, often for months at a time; definitely not for the claustrophobic.

and display a Gatling gun, and an original 34-star flag from the battle of Vicksburg, and prepare exhibits on how the Civil War led to warfare innovations including such 'advances' as mines, submarines and torpedoes, aerial surveillance (via hot-air balloon) and the telegraph. California gold, by the way, paid for 25% of the Union's war effort.

White Point Park BEACH
(Map p176; 628 Alamitos Ave) There's a baseball field up top, and wind-blasted pebble shoals down low where daredevil kitesurfers ride gales and catch air along the bluffs as gulls ride the thermals. It's also the high-school hangout. Low tide leaves small pools between the rocks south of the lifeguard tower.

Museum of Latin American Art   MUSEUM

(Map p178; www.molaa.org; 628 Alamitos Ave; adult/student & senior/under 12yr $9/6/free; ⊙11:30am-5pm Wed & Fri-Sun, 11am-9pm Thu; P) This gem of a museum presents a rare survey of Latin American art created since 1945. Cecilia Míguez' whimsical bronze statuettes, Eduardo Kingman's wrenching portraits of indigenous people and Arnaldo Roche Rabel's intensely spiritual abstracts are among the many outstanding pieces in the permanent collection, selections of which rotate every six months. There are a few works by Botero, Tamayo and Cuevas, but the focus is really on artists who are megastars in their home countries but haven't yet hit the big time internationally. Some of the best pieces are in the sculpture garden.

Long Beach Museum of Art   MUSEUM

(www.lbma.org; 2300 E Ocean Blvd; adult/student & senior/under 12yr $7/6/free, Fri free; ⊙11am-5pm Tue-Sun) The beachfront location is breathtaking, and the restaurant in a nicely detailed 1912 Craftsman mansion serves tasty lunches, but exhibits in the adjacent two-room pavilion can be a bit hit-and-miss. The museum's permanent collections boast pop art, midcentury pieces and some contemporary work. Among the rotating exhibitions we've seen amazing enamelware sharing exhibit space with ghastly watercolors and sophomoric sculpture. Check the schedule before forking over the admission or visit on free Fridays. Most of the art is by contemporary regional artists.

Cabrillo Marine Aquarium   AQUARIUM

(Map p176; www.cabrillomarineaquarium.org; 3720 Stephen White Dr; suggested donation adult/child $5/1; ⊙noon-5pm Tue-Fri, 10am-5pm Sat & Sun; P ♿) This city-owned aquarium is the smaller, older, less frantic and high-tech cousin of Long Beach's Aquarium of the Pacific. It's also a lot lighter on your wallet and probably less overwhelming for small children. Spiky urchins, slippery sea cucumbers, magical jellyfish and other local denizens will bring smiles to even the most PlayStation-jaded youngster. Naturalists lead rambles around the rocky tidepools and salt marshes and organize all sorts of other educational programs, including the grunion watches (April to July). The curvaceous rocky breakwater, swatch of golden sand and deep, green sea out front isn't bad either.

Los Angeles Maritime Museum & Around   MUSEUM

(Map p176; www.lamaritimemuseum.org; Berth 84; adult/child & senior $3/1; ⊙10am-5pm Tue-Thu & Sat, noon-5pm Fri; P ♿) For a salty introduction to the area, visit this endearing but notoriously short-staffed museum. Galleries set up in a historic ferry building tell the story of LA's relationship with the sea and display enough ship models (including an 18ft cutaway of the *Titanic*), figureheads and navigational equipment to keep your imagination afloat for an hour or so.

If you enjoy clambering around old ships, head a mile north to the **SS Lane Victory** (Map p176; www.lanevictory.org; Berth 94; adult/child $3/1; ⊙9am-3pm), a museum vessel that sailed the seven seas from 1945 to 1971. Self-guided tours take in the engine room and the cargo holds. See the website for directions.

Further south, you'll be besieged by shrieking gulls and excited children at **Ports O'Call Village** (Map p176; Berth 77; admission free; ⊙11am-10pm). Skip the trinket stores and fill up on fresh fish and shrimp at the raucous **San Pedro Fish Market & Restaurant** (p181). Afterwards, hop on a port cruise or join a whale-watching trip (January to March).

Banning Residence Museum   MUSEUM

(www.banningmuseum.org; 401 East M St; suggested donation adult/child $5/1; ⊙hourly tours 12:30-2:30pm Tue-Thu, 12:30-3:30pm Sat & Sun; P) Built in 1864, the original home of Phineas Banning, father of the LA Harbor, is stacked with a trove of gorgeous antiques and set in a rugged yet bland south LA suburb. It offers an intriguing glimpse into the daily lives of well-heeled 19th-century Angelenos.

🏃 Activities

LA Harbor Sportfishing   BOATING

(Map p176; ☎310-547-9916; www.laharborsportfishing.com; 1150 Nagoya Way, Berth 79; whale-watching adult/child $20/15, sport fishing adult/child $38/28, harbor tours adult/under 11yr $13/free; P ♿) Whether you love dropping a line or making like Melville and spotting the biggest mammal of them all, this humble shop is your gateway to the blue Pacific. Trips head from this harbor six to seven miles out in the open ocean. The best time to spot blue and humpback whales is between October and April. Open boat fishing trips are available year-round. It does 45-minute harbor tours too.

SS Lane Victory Catalina Cruise AQUATIC
(Map p176; ☑310-519-9545; www.lanevictory.org;
Berth 94; adult/child $130/115) It's one thing
to clamor around this old warship, but it's
quite another to ride this retired WWII
merchant vessel on the open sea. Five times
each summer, the old girl makes the day-
long haul to Catalina. On the way back into
harbor you'll receive a fireboat escort and
have to duck as vintage planes dive and attack, just like in (great) granddad's day.

Clay ARTS & CRAFTS
(Map p178; www.clayonfirst.com; 406 E 1st Street;
🅿🚺) If you know how to throw, then come
and get your hands wet and dirty at this
storefront ceramics studio for just $90 per
month. Otherwise, take the time and learn
how (six classes, $90, by reservation).

🛏 Sleeping

Hotel Maya BOUTIQUE HOTEL $$
(Map p178; ☑562-435-7676; www.hotelmaya
longbeach.com; 700 Queens Way; r $159-189;
🅿@🌐🏊) West of the *Queen Mary*, this
reclaimed Hilton hits you with hip imme-
diately upon entering the rusted-steel and
glass lobby, and continues in the rooms
(think: coral tile, river-rock headboards),
which are set in four 1970s-era hexagons
with views of downtown Long Beach. The
floating poolside cabanas aren't bad either.

Avia Hotel BOUTIQUE HOTEL $$$
(Map p178; ☑562-436-1042; www.aviahotels.com;
285 Bay St; r $127-279; 🅿@🌐🏊) A hip urban
all-suite hotel in the Pike Center complex, a
short walk from the aquarium. Rooms have
sleek modern furnishings, purple-papered
accent walls, flat screens, and small sitting
areas.

Hotel Queen Mary HISTORIC HOTEL $$
(Map p178; ☑562-435-3511, 800-437-2934; www.
queenmary.com; 1126 Queens Hwy; r $110-395;
🅿@🌐) There's an irresistible romance to
ocean liners like the *Queen Mary,* a nos-
talgic retreat that time-warps you to a
long-gone, slower-paced era. The 1st-class
staterooms are nicely refurbished and brim
with original art-deco details, but they're
rather small. Avoid the cheapest cabins on
the inside – claustrophobic! Parking costs
$15 to $19.

Dockside Boat & Bed BED & BREAKFAST $$
(Map p178; ☑562-436-3111, 800-436-2574; www.
boatandbed.com; Rainbow Harbor, Dock 5, 316 E
Shoreline Dr; r $220-375; 🅿🌐) Get rocked to
sleep by the waves aboard your own private

yacht with retro '70s charm, galley kitchens
and high-tech entertainment centers. Boats
are moored right along the newly expanded
waterfront fun zone in downtown Long
Beach, so expect some noise. Breakfast is
delivered to your vessel.

🍴 Eating

TOP CHOICE **San Pedro Fish Market &
Restaurant** SEAFOOD $$
(www.sanpedrofishmarket.com; 1190 Nagoya Way,
San Pedro; meals $13.50; ⊙breakfast, lunch & din-
ner; 🅿🚺) Seafood feasts don't get any more
rootsy and decadent than at this family-
run, harbor-view institution. Pick from the
day's catch, have it spiced and cooked to
order with potatoes, tomatoes and pep-
pers, lug your tray to a picnic table, fold up
your sleeves and devour meaty crabs, plump
shrimp, slimy oysters, melty yellowtail and
tender halibut. Don't forget to order some
buttery garlic bread and a pile of extra nap-
kins. You can save a buck or two next door at
Crusty Crab, a relative newcomer doing the
same exact work with slightly less selection.

Claire's at the Museum CALIFORNIAN $$
(www.lbma.org/café; 2300 Ocean Ave, Long
Beach; mains $13-22; ⊙lunch Mon-Fri, breakfast
& lunch Sat & Sun; 🅿) Set in a 100-year-old
Craftsman masterpiece (the original home
of the Long Beach Art Museum next door),
this brunch cafe serves tasty Californian
cooking with exquisite views.

King's Fish House SEAFOOD $$
(Map p178; ☑562-432-7463; www.kingfishhouse.
com; 100 W Broadway Ave, Long Beach; mains
$16-26; ⊙lunch & dinner; 🅿) A fun, casual,
downtown fish house where the fresh catch
(think: Mississippi catfish, Tahitian ono,
Baja yellowtail) is charbroiled, steamed or
skillet- or kettle-fried. Most eat on the pa-
tio, but the dining room has loads of charm
and blues on the stereo.

Downtown Long Beach Farmers Market
MARKET
(Map p178; www.farmernet.com; CityPlace Center,
N Promenade & E 4th St; ⊙9:30am-3:30pm Fri;
🅿🚺) One of the two best markets in south
LA gets points for its 21 farmers selling
fresh, mostly organic produce. Crowds swell
for the vendors who deal in smoked ribs and
chicken, pecan pie and pralines, and sweet
corn – roasted or kettle popped.

Bono's CALIFORNIAN $$
(www.bonoslongbeach.com; 4901 E 2nd St, Long
Beach; appetizers $10-14, mains $19-32; ⊙lunch

& dinner; P) Sonny Bono's daughter Christy presides over this upbeat, beachy lair right on Belmont Shore's buzzy 2nd St. The menu is strongest on light yet flavor-packed salads and sandwiches – the lobster, avocado and papaya salad is a standout.

Alegria
PERUVIAN, MEXICAN $$

(Map p178; ☏562-436-3388; www.alegriacocina latina.com; 115 Pine Ave, Long Beach; appetizers $5-11, mains $7-20; ⊘lunch & dinner; P) The trippy, technicolor mosaic floor, an eccentric art-nouveau bar and trompe l'oeil murals form an appropriately spirited backdrop to Alegria's fresh and vivid Latino cuisine. The tapas menu is great for grazers and the paella a feast for both eyes and stomach. There's even live flamenco on some nights.

Omelette Inn
DINER $

(Map p178; www.omeletteinn.com; 318 Pine Ave, Long Beach; dishes $10; ⊘breakfast & lunch; 🖷) From clerks to cops to city-council members, *every*body's got a soft spot for this unassuming joint where breakfasts and sandwiches are served in belt-loosening portions. Build up your own omelettes from more than 40 ingredients or pick from tried-and-true menu favorites such as the Sicilian or Grecian Formula.

Utopia
ECLECTIC GLOBAL $$

(Map p178; www.utopiarestaurant.net; 445 E 1st St, Long Beach; meals $10-45; ⊘lunch & dinner; 🖷) Here are original canvasses on the wall, tablecloths and fresh flowers on the tables and an eclectic kitchen melding Caribbean, Cajun and Himalayan flavors, which may in fact be the necessary ingredients for an actual utopia.

🍸 Drinking

TOP CHOICE Fuego
TEQUILA BAR

(Map p178; www.fuegolongbeach.com; 700 Queens Way, Long Beach; ⊘10am-11pm Mon-Thu, to 1am Fri-Sun; P) Fuego is the place to be for Sunday brunch, Happy Hour or whenever you're thirsty. Here are 30-plus tequila labels, seven firepits and cushioned Balinese day beds on the tiki-themed patio. Then there's sweet, funny, old-school Linda. She's usually got a story and is always pouring something promising.

House of Hidden
BAR

(Map p178; 421 E 1st St, Long Beach; ⊘noon-2am) A sleek and tough rock-and-roll surf bar in downtown LBC with antique long boards in the rafters, Christmas-light skulls on the

exposed-brick wall, a rock-stocked juke-box and a pool table, but there's no sign out front.

Madison
BAR

(Map p178; www.themadisonrestaurant.com; 102 Pine Ave, Long Beach; ⊘11:30am-11pm; P) This converted, historic bank with its weighty granite bar, crystal chandeliers, burly wooden columns, masterfully painted ceiling and regular jazz combos demands a martini.

Basement
LOUNGE

(Map p178; www.thebasementloungelb.com; 149 Linden Ave, Long Beach; ⊘6pm) Like the name says, it is a lounge in a basement of a historic, arched, brick edifice in the East Village Arts District. It's one of those places where the comely, young, hip people go, and, yes, several have facial hair. LB's best DJs spin here.

Belmont Brewing Company
GASTROPUB

(www.belmontbrewing.com; 25 39th Pl, Belmont Shore) This bustling gastropub has a great outdoor deck overlooking the Belmont Pier (perfect for watching sunsets), fresh and handcrafted brews (try the Long Beach Crude stout or Top Sail ale), and a well-priced menu that goes far beyond pub grub.

Riley's
SPORTS BAR

(5331 E 2nd St, Belmont Shore; ⊘11am-midnight Sun-Thu, to 2am Fri & Sat) Local sports freaks and sun worshippers collide here for big games where ice-cold beer is poured into massive goblets, the pub grub is decent and the outdoor patio is almost always packed full.

Aroma Di Roma
CAFE

(www.aromadiroma.com; 5327 E 2nd St; ⊘5:30-10:30pm Mon-Thu, to 11pm Fri & Sat, 6-10pm Sun) Belmont's more staid, dare we say intellectual, crowd hangs out at the common table on the patio beneath the turquoise umbrellas with their laptops and chessboards in tow. Aside from the exceptional espresso and poetic gelato, it also does pasta and serves quaffable table reds at reasonable prices.

Walker Cafe
DINER

(Map p176; 700 Paseo del Mar; ⊘10am-9pm) A biker bar on Medicare, Bessie Walker started selling sandwiches here in 1943 and the place has hardly changed a lick. Great Americana, greasy burgers, cold beers, and it's been featured in *Chinatown*.

☆ Entertainment

Laugh Factory Long Beach COMEDY
(Map p178; www.laughfactory.com; 151 S Pine Ave,
Long Beach; ☺8pm & 10pm Wed-Sat) The Long
Beach shingle of Hollywood's comedy clas-
sic features both stand-up veterans and up-
and-comers.

🛍 Shopping

TOP
CHOICE **$1 Bookstore** BOOKS
(Map p178, www.odbstore.com, 248 Pine
Ave; ☺10am-9pm Sun-Thu, 9am-10pm Fri, 10am-
10pm Sat) A creative antidote to gargantuan
corporate, online booksellers (not that
there's anything wrong with that). This
groovy warehouse stacks fiction and non,
comics, text books and piles of old *National
Geographic*. And, yes, everything is $1.
Stock up on your road reading here.

**Long Beach Outdoor Antique &
Collectible Market** FLEA MARKET
(Veteran's Memorial Stadium, 4901 E Conant
St; admission $5; ☺6:30am-3pm 3rd Sun of
month; P) Bargains abound at this sprawling market with over 800 stalls hawking
everything from vintage postcards to pottery, fur to furniture near the Long Beach
Airport.

BURBANK, UNIVERSAL CITY & THE SAN FERNANDO VALLEY

Despite being home to most of LA's major
movie studios – including Warner Bros,
Disney and Universal – much of the sprawling grid of suburbia known as 'the Valley'
is an exercise in bleakness. It also has the
dubious distinction of being the original
world capital of porn, memorably captured
in Paul Thomas Anderson's 1997 *Boogie
Nights*. Car culture was also basically invented in the Valley, which claims to have
given birth to the mini-mall, the drive-in
movie theater, the drive-in bank and the
drive-in restaurant.

Attractions are few and scattered about;
Burbank has the studios, and North Hollywood, west of here, is home to a growing
arts scene. Studio City, west of Universal,
has some superb sushi on Ventura Blvd. At
last count there were 21 sushi bars within
a six-block radius, which is why some call
it, LA's Sushi Row. Studio City's grooviest
shopping and cafe strip can be found on

Tujunga Blvd, which is also where you'll
find Vitello's restaurant, where Robert
Blake's wife was killed by a gunshot wound
in 2001.

Note that temperatures here are usually
20°F (11°C) higher – and pollution levels
worse – than in areas further south. But
it's not all bad. In fact, with lower-cost
housing and the lack of congestion, the
Valley is more laidback and down to earth
than elsewhere in the city. This is where
LA gets real. For studio tours, see the
boxed text on p184.

⦿ Sights

**Universal Studios Hollywood &
CityWalk** THEME PARK
(www.universalstudioshollywood.com; 1000 Universal Center Dr; admission over/under 48in $69/59,
annual pass $84; P) One of the world's old-
est continuously operating movie studios,
Universal presents an entertaining mix
of fairly tame – and sometimes dated –
thrills, live action shows and a tram ride.
It is a working studio, but the chances of
seeing any action, let alone a star, are slim
to none.

Try to budget a full day, especially in
summer. To beat the crowds, get there before the gates open or invest in the Front of
Line Pass ($129) or the deluxe guided VIP
Experience ($239). Some rides have mini-
mum height requirements. The Southern
California CityPass and the Go Los Angeles
Card (see p455) are valid for general admission. Buying online tickets usually yields
discounts and coupons.

First-timers should head straight for the
45-minute narrated **Studio Tour** aboard a
rickety tram that drives around the soundstages in the front lot, then heads to the
back lot past the crash site from *War of the
Worlds*, vehicles from *Jurassic Park*, the
spooky Bates Motel from *Psycho* and – with
any luck – Wisteria Lane from *Desperate
Housewives*. Also prepare to brave a flash
flood, survive a shark attack, a spitting
dino and an 8.3-magnitude earthquake, before facing down King Kong in a new 3-D
exhibit created by Peter Jackson. It's a bit
hokey, but fun.

The best thrill ride is **Jurassic Park**, a
gentle float through a prehistoric jungle
with a rather 'raptor-ous' ending. **Revenge
of the Mummy** is a short, but satisfying,
indoor roller-coaster romp through 'Imho-
tep's Tomb' that at one point has you going

BEHIND THE CURTAIN: MOVIE MAGIC UNMASKED

Did you know it takes a week to shoot a half-hour sitcom? Or that you rarely see ceilings on shows because the space is filled with lights and lamps? You'll learn these and other fascinating nuggets of information about the make-believe world of film and TV while touring a working studio. Star-sighting potential is better than average, except during 'hiatus' (May to August) when studios are pretty deserted. Reservations are required and so is photo ID.

Paramount (☎323-956-1777; www.paramount.com; 5555 Melrose Ave; tours $40; ☺tours hourly 10am-2pm Mon-Fri) *Star Trek, Indiana Jones* and *Shrek* are among the blockbusters that originated at Paramount, the longest operating and the only movie studio still in Hollywood proper. Two-hour tours through the backlots and sound stages are available year-round and are led by passionate, knowledgeable guides.

Sony (☎310-244-8687; 10202 W Washington Blvd, Culver City; tours $33, minimum age 12; ☺tours 9:30am, 10:30am, 12:30pm, 1:30pm & 2:30pm Mon-Fri; P) This two-hour tour includes visits to the sound stages where *Men in Black*, *Spider-Man*, and *Charlie's Angels* were filmed. Munchkins hopped along the Yellow Brick Road in the *Wizard of Oz*, filmed when this was still the venerable MGM studio.

Warner Bros (☎818-972-8687; www.wbstudiotour.com; 3400 Riverside Dr, Burbank; tours $45, minimum age 8; ☺8:30am-4pm Mon-Fri, longer hr Mar-Sep; P) This tour offers the most fun, yet authentic, look behind the scenes of a major movie studio. The 2¼-hour romp kicks off with a video of WB's greatest film hits (*Rebel Without a Cause, Harry Potter* etc) before a tram whisks you to sound stages, backlot sets and technical departments, including props, costumes and the paint shop. Tours conclude at the studio museum, a treasure trove of props and memorabilia, including Hogwarts' famous Sorting Hat. Tours leave roughly every half hour.

backwards. A new ride based on **The Simpsons** sends guests rocketing along with the Simpson family to experience a side of Springfield previously unexplored.

Of the live shows, **Terminator 2: 3-D** combines live-action stunts with digital imaging technology and stars the Governator himself. **Spider-Man Rocks** is a cutesy, fast-paced musical show with dance numbers and aerial acrobatics. The movie may have bombed, but the **Water World** show is a runaway hit with mind-boggling stunts that include giant fireballs and a crash-landing seaplane. **Shrek 4-D** takes you from Lord Farquaad's dungeon into a theater where you'll don Ogre-vision 3-D glasses and become immersed in the action as you head out on an adventure with the *Shrek* crew touching all the senses with moving seats, wind and mist.

Snack food and drinks, including beer and margaritas, are available throughout the park, although you'll have more choices at the adjacent **Universal CityWalk**, a promenade of restaurants, shops, bars and entertainment venues. Be sure to get your hand stamped for re-entry. Parking costs $5 to $14, opening hours vary by season.

Forest Lawn Memorial Park – Glendale
CEMETERY
(www.forestlawn.com; 1712 S Glendale Ave; admission free; ☺9am-5pm; P) This sprawling cemetery is the final home of such Golden Age superstars as Clara Bow, Humphrey Bogart and Jimmy Stewart. Alas, many of their graves are in mausoleums and off-limits to the public. It doesn't help that cemetery staff strongly discourage star seekers. You can download maps from the internet (for example www.seeing-stars.com), but be discreet or risk having them confiscated. The grounds are still worth a visit if only to marvel at the country-club feel of the place and oddly impressive art such as a stained-glass version of Leonardo da Vinci's *Last Supper*.

Americana at Brand
MALL
(www.americanaatbrand.com; 889 Americana Way) If you dig The Grove in Mid-City, then you'll enjoy this narrow, set-piece shopping mall that feels like an extended walking street, developed by the same folks. And it really is just as popular. There's an 18-screen multiplex, 19 restaurants, including a Katsuya and some very good, albeit very corporate, shopping, including an af-

fordable Barney's Co-op. It has a dancing fountain and light show too.

🛏 Sleeping

TOP CHOICE **Hotel Amarano** BOUTIQUE HOTEL **$$**
(☑818-842-8887; www.hotelamarano.com; 322 N Pass Ave; r $245-585; P@🛜) There are several classes of rooms in this boutique business hotel, but even the basic superior rooms are large and sunny, with fresh berber carpeting, stylish blonde-wood furnishings, soft bedding and a slate-blue accent wall. Step up in class and you can have a kitchenette and a huge flat-screen TV.

Embassy Suites HOTEL **$$**
(☑818-550-0828; www.embassysuites.com; 800 N Central Ave; r $198-279; P@🛜🏊) Ignore the oh-so-corporate moniker. This tower hotel with the frosted-glass facade has class and value. All rooms are suites, there's a lap pool on the 2nd floor ledge, a full fitness center, and a free full breakfast for up to four people. It's set in downtown Glendale and within walking distance to the Americana mall.

Annabelle Hotel HOTEL **$$**
(☑818-845-7800; www.coasthotels.com; 2011 W Olive Ave; r $179-263; P@🛜🏊) The stucco atrium doesn't look like much from the outside, but standard rooms are spacious with high ceilings, wood furnishings and flat screens, and it get high marks for friendly staff. The pool is shared with the Safari Inn.

Safari Inn MOTEL **$**
(☑818-845-8586; www.safariburbank.com; 1911 W Olive Ave; r $89-156; P🛜🏊) This 1950s motel boasts a vintage neon sign, beds are draped in boldly colored patterned spreads, and framed poster art adds charm to rooms that are otherwise on the small and darkish side. The breakfast is rather lacking, but the pool is nice, the staff professional, and you'll be close to the studios.

🍴 Eating

TOP CHOICE **Daichan** JAPANESE **$$**
(11288 Ventura Blvd; dishes $3.50-16; ⊙lunch & dinner Mon-Sat; P) Stuffed with knickknacks, pasted with posters, staffed by the sunny and sweet owner-operator, this offbeat Japanese diner offers the best (and one of the tastiest) deals on sushi row. The fried seaweed tofu gyoza are divine and so are the bowls – especially the *negitoro* bowl, where fatty tuna is served over rice, lettuce and seaweed.

Kazu Sushi JAPANESE **$$$**
(☑818-763-4836; 11440 Ventura Blvd; dishes $10-19; ⊙lunch Mon-Fri, dinner Mon-Sat; P) Stuck in a cramped and otherwise nondescript minimall is one of the best-kept secrets among LA's sushi aficionados. Inside are bamboo furnishings, oversized *kabuki* masks and some of the best sushi in the city. It's Michelin rated, very high-end, has a terrific sake selection, and is absolutely worth the splurge.

Kiwami JAPANESE **$$$**
(☑818-763-3910; www.katsu-yagroup.com/kiwami; 11920 Ventura Blvd; appetizers $4-16, mains $5-20; ⊙lunch & dinner Mon-Sat, dinner Sun; P) Chef Katsuya, a man whose very name has become synonymous with excellent sushi, still serves here. Just choose a selection from his crammed dry-erase board or opt for cultural fusion like Cajun seared tuna or mango scallops with caviar. The best deals are the set sushi ($15) and sashimi ($16) lunches.

Sushi Nozawa JAPANESE **$$$**
(☑818-508-7017; www.sushinozawa.com; 11288 Ventura Blvd; sushi $2.50-7.50; ⊙lunch & dinner Mon-Fri; P) What would Sushi Row be if it didn't have an honest-to-goodness sushi Nazi. You know, the kind that tells you what you've ordered and does not tolerate insurrection in the slightest. Just sit quietly, subserviently even, and munch gratefully.

Baklava Factory MIDDLE EASTERN **$**
(www.baklavafactory.com; 17450 Ventura Blvd; ⊙9:30am-7:30pm) Hidden in the Encino sprawl, it's easy to miss this tiny pastry shop, but if you enjoy sweet, light, nutty, syrupy, crunchy desserts, you shouldn't. These folks do baklava right, all-natural with pistachios and walnuts, some rolled, others sliced into squares. You can buy it by the pound or by the piece. Just...wow!

Dr Hogly Wogly's Tyler Texas Bar-B-Que
BARBECUE **$$**
(www.hoglywogly.com; 8136 N Sepulveda Blvd; mains $14-28; ⊙lunch & dinner; P) A tiny Tudor shack leaking smoky sweetness into the Valley streets. Its slabs of spare and beef ribs, Texas hot links and chicken amount to the best Texas-style barbecue this side of Dallas. Years ago we were feasting here, and in walked the late great Wilt Chamberlain. Barefoot and smiling, he walked out with two slabs of ribs and a pot of sauce.

Bob's Big Boy
DINER $

(www.bboy.com; 4211 Riverside Dr; burgers & sandwiches $7-9; ⏰24hr; P🚗) Bob, that cheeky pompadoured kid in red-checkered pants, hasn't aged a lick since serving his first double-decker in 1936. This Wayne McAllister–designed Googie-style 1950s coffee shop is the oldest remaining Big Boy's in America. On Friday nights hot-rods roar in the parking lot, while the car-hop service (5pm to 10pm) brings in families and love doves in droves on Saturdays and Sundays.

Gelato Bar & Espresso Cafe
GELATO $

(www.gelatobar-la.com; 4342 Tujunga Ave; gelato $3.50-16; ⏰breakfast, lunch & dinner; P🚗) A cheery cafe with multihued walls, terracotta floor and a case of tasty, creamy gelato (we like the dark chocolate) and sorbetto (blood orange anyone?), and some outstanding fair-trade coffee.

Artisan Cheese Gallery
CHEESE $$

(www.artisancheesegallery.com; 12023 Ventura Blvd; cheeses $7.75-13; ⏰10:30am-7pm Mon-Sat, 9am-5pm Sun; P) You don't have to be a cheese head to enjoy a meal here, but it sure helps. Inside the gallery are wood blocks stacked with wheels and wedges of the stinky stuff. They put together platters and will pair them with wine and beer for you, or you could opt for a gourmet sandwich.

⭐ Entertainment

Baked Potato
JAZZ, BLUES

(www.thebakedpotato.com; 3787 Cahuenga Blvd; cover $10-25 plus 2 drinks; ⏰7pm-2am) Near Universal Studios a dancing spud beckons you to come inside this diminutive jazz-and-blues hall where the schedule mixes no-names with big-timers. The recently passed master *conguero*, Francisco Aguabella was a frequent performer. Drinks are stiff, and actual baked potatoes (priced from $6.50 to $15) are optional.

Noho Arts Center Ensemble
THEATER

(www.thenohoartscenter.com; 11136 Magnolia Blvd; tickets $25; ⏰shows 8pm Fri & Sat, 3pm Sun) The crown jewel of North Hollywood's budding theater scene offers some terrific reimagined classic and new cutting-edge theater.

Pacific 18
CINEMA

(www.pacifictheaters.com; 322 Americana Way; adults/child/senior $12/9/10; ⏰shows 10:30am-10:30pm) It has all the attributes of the Grove branch: the cushy seats, the amphitheater arrangement, leg room for days, and Monday Morning Mommy Movies at 11am.

Gibson Amphitheatre
VENUE

(www.livenation.com; 100 Universal City Plaza) This indoor amphitheatre is a major venue for headlining pop acts from Toby Keith to

---

LOCAL KNOWLEDGE

ANDY LIPKIS: ENVIRONMENTALIST

For nearly 30 years TreePeople founder Andy Lipkis and his team have been leading tree plantings in neighborhoods, on school campuses and in the mountains around LA. These days he's focused on solving LA's massive water problem.

Biggest Success

We convinced the county to invest $250,000 into the Sun Valley watershed, instead of spending $50,000 on a storm drain. Now floodwaters, which pour past auto yards and were carrying pollutants to the sea, filter through permeable asphalt, soil and gravel and back into the water table.

Most Visible Project

We developed a **Green Street** (Bicknell St btwn Main & Pacific) with the city of Santa Monica. We ripped out asphalt and replaced it with permeable concrete, doubled the parkway and now rainwater which was pooling in the street flows into mulched swails and filters directly to the roots of nearby palms.

Favorite Leafy Street

I love Pasadena's live oaks, and the way the camphors on Maple Dr (Map p132) in Beverly Hills form a canopy over the street. They are huge, sculptural, beautiful.

OUR FAVORITE FLEA MARKETS

Flea markets are like urban archaeology: you'll need plenty of patience and luck when sifting through other people's trash and detritus, but oh the thrill when finally unearthing a piece of treasure! Arrive early, bring small bills, wear those walking shoes and get ready to haggle. These are the best of the best:

» Rose Bowl Flea Market (p196)

» Pasadena City College Flea Market (p196)

» Melrose Trading Post (p123)

Tony Bennett. Lately it has been bringing in some of the biggest names in Latin pop, as well.

🛍 Shopping

Psychic Eye   NEW AGE
(☏818-906-8263; www.pebooks.com; 13435 Ventura Blvd; readings 15/30/60min $20/30/50; ☺10am-10pm Mon-Sat, to 8pm Sun; ℗) A long-time pipeline of psychics and astrologers, amulets and idols, pentacles, books, candles and potions. If there's a spell you'd like to cast or break, if you need intuitive advice or would otherwise like to peer into the past or the future, find this strange vortex of the occult.

It's A Wrap   USED CLOTHING
(www.itsawraphollywood.com; 3315 Magnolia Blvd; ☺10am-8pm Mon-Fri, to 6pm Sat & Sun) Here are fashionable, postproduction wares worn by TV and film stars. What that means to you is this: great prices on mainstream designer labels, including racks of casual and formal gear. The suits are a steal, and so is the denim. New arrivals are racked by show affiliation.

PASADENA & THE SAN GABRIEL VALLEY

One could argue that there is more blue-blood, meat-eating, robust Americana in Pasadena than in all other LA neighborhoods combined. Here is a community with a preppy old soul, a historical perspective, an appreciation for art and jazz and a slightly progressive undercurrent. The Rose Parade (p67) and Rose Bowl football game may have given Pasadena its long-lasting fame, but it's the progressive spirit of this genteel city and its location beneath the lofty San Gabriel Mountains that make it a charming and attractive place year-round. Its immaculate streets, shaded by gnarled, native oaks, may conjure visions of Wisteria Lane (of *Desperate Housewives* fame), but there are also plenty of grand old Craftsman mansions, mid-century modern apartment buildings, fine-art museums, extraordinary gardens and a lively Old Town, which give it depth and charm. Sure, it can be hazy in the mornings, and smoggy in the summertime, but how those gorgeous mountains loom when the sky clears.

The main fun zone is Old Pasadena, a bustling 20-block shopping and entertainment district set up in successfully restored historic brick buildings along Colorado Blvd west of Arroyo Parkway. The best California bungalows and old Victorians can be found along Grand Ave and Arroyo, while stunning mid-century apartment complexes are strung like a strand of Betty Draper's pearls off South Lake Ave, a largely corporate shopping district with some decent eateries near Cal Tech University.

South Pasadena is Main St USA meets Southern California, and a land where free parking still exists (hell, it's encouraged), old brick and wood edifices still stand, people-moving trains still roll through downtown, and shoppers and neighbors still smile at one another when crossing paths.

The San Gabriel Valley, where you'll find the San Gabriel Mission, actually predates the city of LA, and though it boasts the art-deco Santa Anita race track and the LA County Arboretum, these days it's best known for thousands of native Chinese residents who have turned this string of communities into one of the great dim-sum destinations in the US.

Pasadena is served by the Metro Rail Gold Line from Downtown LA. Pasadena ARTS buses (fare 75¢) plough around the city on seven different routes.

👁 Sights

Rose Bowl Stadium & Brookside Park
     LANDMARK, PARK
(www.rosebowlstadium.com; 1001 Rose Bowl Dr) One of LA's most venerable landmarks, the 1922 Rose Bowl Stadium can seat up to

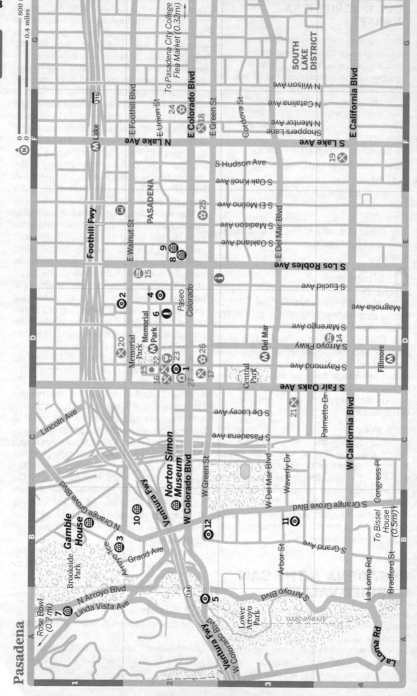

Pasadena

0   0   800 m
0   0.4 miles

To Pasadena City College
Flea Market (0.32mi)

SOUTH
LAKE
DISTRICT

E Foothill Blvd

E Union St

24

E Colorado Blvd

18

E Green St

N Wilson Ave

N Catalina Ave

Cordova St

N Mentor Ave

Shoppers Lane

E California Blvd

S Lake Ave

N Lake Ave

M Lake

19

S Hudson Ave

S Oak Knoll Ave

S El Molino Ave

S Madison Ave

S Oakland Ave

E Del Mar Blvd

25

PASADENA

E Walnut St

Foothill Fwy

9

8

S Los Robles Ave

S Euclid Ave

Magnolia Ave

i

Memorial
Park

2

M Park

4

6

Paseo
Colorado

15

S Marengo Ave

S Arroyo Pkwy

14

M Del Mar

S Del Mar

20

13

16   22

23

1

27   17

26

Central
Park

S Raymond Ave

Fillmore

M

S Fair Oaks Ave

21

S De Lacey Ave

S Pasadena Ave

W California Blvd

Palmetto Dr

Lincoln Ave

Norton Simon
Museum

Gamble
House

W Colorado Blvd

10

W Green St

W Del Mar Blvd

Waverly Dr

W Orange Grove Blvd

To Bissel
House
(0.5mi)

Congress Pl

N Orange Grove Blvd

Ventura Fwy

3

Arroyo Tce

Grand Ave

12

11

S Grand Ave

Arbor St

La Loma Rd

Bradford St

Rose Bowl
(0.7mi)

Brookside
Park

N Arroyo Blvd

Linda Vista Ave

7

5

Lower
Arroyo
Park

S Arroyo Blvd

Arroyo Seco

La Loma Rd

W Colorado Blvd

Ventura Fwy

93,000 spectators and has its moment in the sun every New Year's Day when it hosts the famous Rose Bowl postseason college football game, or the spotlight glows a few nights later if it's hosting the BCS National Championship game that year. At other times, the UCLA Bruins play their home games here and the occasional concert or special event also brings in the masses. As does a monthly flea market. In 2006 *American Idol* held its Los Angeles auditions here.

The Rose Bowl is surrounded by **Brookside Park**, which is a nice spot for hiking, cycling and picnicking. Families should check out the excellent **Kidspace Children's Museum** (Map p188; www.kidspacemuseum.org; 480 N Arroyo Blvd; admission $10; ⊙9:30am-5pm Mon-Fri, from 10am Sat & Sun; ⓟⓗ), and architecture nuts the palatial 1903 **Vista del Arroyo Hotel** (Map p188; 125 S Grand Ave), now home to the Ninth Circuit Court of Appeals. It's open to the public, and worth stepping into the law library to see the old, stopped Chicago clock on the south wall and sensational views of the gracefully arched 1913 **Colorado St Bridge** (Map p188).

Huntington Library, Art Collections & Botanical Gardens   MUSEUM, GARDENS
(www.huntington.org; 1151 Oxford Rd; adult/5-11yr/student/senior Mon & Wed-Fri $15/6/10/12, Sat & Sun $20/6/10/15; ⊙10:30am-4:30pm Wed-Mon; ⓟⓗ) Unwind in the Zen-like tranquility of a Japanese Garden? Study the jaunty pose of Thomas Gainsborough's *The Blue Boy*? Linger over the illuminated vellum of a 1455 Gutenberg Bible? It's hard to know where to start exploring this genteel country estate, the legacy of railroad tycoon Henry Huntington and one of the most delightful and inspirational spots in LA. It's lovely year-round but best on a weekday in spring, as summers get very hot and weekends are busy.

Set aside at least an hour to admire the 18th-century French and British paintings and **rare and ancient books**, then leave another hour for romping around the **Japanese Garden** with its sunken bridge and water-lily pond, the charming **Desert Garden** with Seussian-shaped, organ-pipe cacti and giant blue agave, or the **Rose Garden**, which is at its redolent best from April to August. For kids, the interactive **Children's Garden** yields lots of tactile surprises.

The classic way to cap off a visit to the Huntington is with afternoon tea in the **Rose Garden Tea Room** (☎626-683-8131; adult/4-8yr $25/12.50). It's hugely popular, so make advance reservations or else pick up some sandwiches in the adjacent self-service cafeteria.

FREE **El Molino Viejo** HISTORIC MILL
(Old Mill; www.oldmill.org; 1120 Old Mill Rd; ☺1-4pm; P) While in the Huntington Library area, make a quick detour to this transporting brick-and-adobe structure with creaky wood floors and exposed timbers in the rafters. It houses Southern California's first water-powered gristmill built in 1816 for the San Gabriel Mission. The displays here are nothing special, but the building is worth the trip.

Norton Simon Museum ART MUSEUM
(Map p188; www.nortonsimon.org; 411 W Colorado Blvd; adult/senior/under 18yr & student $8/4/free; ☺noon-6pm Wed-Mon, to 9pm Fri; P) Rodin's *The Thinker* is only a mind-teasing overture to the full symphony of art in store at this exquisite museum. Norton Simon (1907–93) was an entrepreneur with a Midas touch and a passion for art who parlayed his millions into a respectable collection of Western art and Asian sculpture. The highly accessible, user-friendly galleries teem with choice works by Rembrandt, Renoir, Raphael, Van Gogh, Botticelli and Picasso, as well as an outstanding array of paintings and sculpture by Degas. Asian sculpture is in the basement, while Western sculpture graces the gorgeous garden inspired by Monet's at Giverny, France.

Angeles National Forest OUTDOORS
(www.fs.fed.us/r5/angeles) The San Gabriel mountain range that hems in the northern edge of Pasadena, and all of urban LA, is part of the Angeles Crest, the creeks, canyons and campgrounds of which provide quick city getaways year-round. It's particularly pretty during the spring wildflower season and even gets lovely fall color. Note that visiting the Angeles National Forest requires a National Forest Adventure Pass. Pick one up in La Cañada at the start of the Angeles Crest scenic drive (p192) at **Sport Chalet** (920 Foothill Blvd) or **Jay's Shell Station** (4530 Angeles Crest Hwy).

FREE **Mt Wilson Observatory** LANDMARK
(www.mtwilson.edu; Red Box Rd; ☺10am-4pm Apr-Oct) As you drive into the Angeles National Forest take the Red Box Rd turn-off which, 5 miles later, dead-ends atop 5715ft Mt Wilson. Operating since 1904, this was the world's top astronomical research facility in the early 20th century and is still in use today. You can walk around the grounds (download a handy self-guided tour from the website) and visit the museum. Free guided tours run at 1pm on Saturdays and Sundays. The website also has details on how to schedule a viewing session for the 1908 60-inch telescope (half-/full night $900/1700 for groups of up to 25 people). The observatory was severely threatened when it was surrounded by wildfires in summer 2009 (see p193). It's closed in bad weather.

Gamble House LANDMARK
(Map p188; www.gamblehouse.org; 4 Westmoreland Pl; adult/student & senior/child $10/7/free; ☺noon-3pm Thu-Sun; P) It's the exquisite attention to detail that impresses most at the Gamble House, a 1908 masterpiece of Craftsman architecture built by Charles and Henry Greene for Proctor & Gamble heir David Gamble. The entire home is a work of art, its foundation, furniture and fixtures all united by a common design and theme inspired by its Southern California environs. Note sleeping porches, iridescent stained glass and subtle appearances of the Gamble family's rose and crane crest.

Other Greene and Greene homes, including Charles Greene's former private **residence** (368 Arroyo Tce), line nearby Arroyo Tce and Grand Ave. Pick up a self-guided walking-tour pamphlet at the Gamble House bookstore.

Descanso Gardens BOTANICAL GARDEN
(www.descanso.com; 1418 Descanso Dr; adult/5-12yr/student & senior $7/2/5; ☺9am-5pm; P) Another set of lovely gardens, Descanso puts on a dazzling show all year, but especially in January and February when some 34,000 camellias brighten the LA winter, some as tall as 20ft. In spring lilacs perfume the air, followed by roses in summer. It's easy to spend a whole day amid the greenery, waterways and bird sanctuary. The gardens are in La Cañada-Flintridge, about 6 miles northwest of Pasadena at the foot of the Angeles Crest Scenic Byway (see p192).

FREE **Art Center College of Design**
COLLEGE
(☎tour reservations 626-396-2373; www.artcenter.edu; 1700 Lida St) Overlooking the Arroyo Seco from its ridgetop perch is this world-

WORTH A TRIP

MISSION SAN FERNANDO REY DE ESPAÑA

It's a long drive out to the northern San Fernando Valley, but history and architecture buffs will likely enjoy this haunting old **Spanish mission** (www.missiontour.org; 15151 San Fernando Mission Rd, Mission Hills; adult/7-15yr & senior $4/3; ⊘9am-4:30pm; P), the 17th of 21 missions built in California. And so will fans of Bob Hope who, in 2003, was buried in a special garden adjacent to the main building. Singer Richie 'La Bamba' Valens, who died in the 1959 plane crash that also killed Buddy Holly, rests in the cemetery behind the mission.

renowned arts campus. Free tours are offered during the school year at 2pm Monday to Friday; reservations are required. To see what students and alumni have been up to, check out the latest exhibit at the **Williamson Gallery** (www.artcenter.edu/Williamson; ⊘noon-5pm Tue-Sun, to 9pm Fri).

FREE **California Institute of Technology (Caltech)** UNIVERSITY
(www.caltech.edu; 551 S Hill Ave; P) With 31 Nobel laureates among its faculty and alumni, it's no surprise that Caltech is regarded with awe in academic circles. Earthquake studies were essentially pioneered here in the 1920s with the inventions of the seismograph and the Richter scale, and to this day Caltech scientists are usually the first experts to be consulted whenever a shaker strikes.

The hallowed campus is dotted with century-old buildings and shady old oaks. Free student-led **tours** (☏626-395-6341; ⊘11:15am year-round, 2:15pm Mar, Apr, Jul & Aug) depart from the **Office of Undergraduate Admissions** (355 S Holliston). Alternatively, pick up a self-guided tour booklet at the office or download one from the website.

Caltech also operates the **Jet Propulsion Laboratory** (JPL; ☏tours 818-354-9319; www.jpl.nasa.gov; 4800 Oak Grove Dr), NASA's main center for robotic exploration of the solar system, about 3.5 miles north of campus. It's possible to visit JPL during public lectures in the annual open house (usually in May) or by requesting a free tour well in advance.

San Gabriel Mission LANDMARK
(www.sangabrielmission.org; 428 S Mission Dr; adult/6-17yr/senior $5/3/4; ⊘9am-4:30pm; P ♿) In 1781, a small group of settlers set out from this mission to found El Pueblo de Los Angeles in today's Downtown area. Set about 3 miles southeast of Pasadena in the city of San Gabriel, it's the fourth in the chain of 21

missions in California and one of the prettiest. Its church boasts Spanish Moorish flourishes, a copper baptismal font, carved statues of saints and a 1790 altar made in Mexico City. On the grounds you'll discover the cemetery, original soap-and-tallow vats and fountains. The small museum has historic Bibles, religious robes and Native American artifacts.

The mission surroundings are also well worth a quick stroll. Following Mission Dr takes you past the 1927 Civic Auditorium, the Civic Center, a historical museum and galleries.

Los Angeles County Arboretum & Botanic Garden GARDEN
(www.arboretum.org; 301 N Baldwin Ave; adult/5-12yr/student & senior$8/3/6, 3rd Tue of month free; ⊘9am-4:30pm). It's easy to spend hours amid the global vegetation, waterfalls, spring-fed lake and historic buildings of this fantastic, rambling park. Originally the private estate of real-estate tycoon Elias 'Lucky' Baldwin, it's so huge, there's even a tram to haul those who are foot-weary. The grounds are often used in filming, for instance standing in for the African jungle in *African Queen* and as Central Park in *End of Days*. It's in Arcadia, about 5 miles east of central Pasadena, right by the Santa Anita Park racetrack.

Santa Anita Park SPORT
(www.santaanita.com; 285 W Huntington Dr, Arcadia; admission general $5, clubhouse $8.50, turf club $20, under 17yr free; ⊘racing season Christmas–mid-Apr, late Sep–early Nov) Home of the legendary Seabiscuit, the stunning art-deco thoroughbred racetrack is the oldest and one of the most prestigious in Southern California. Free **tram tours** (☏626-574-6677; ⊘8:30am & 9:45am Sat & Sun) taking you to Seabiscuit's barn, filming locations, the jockey's room and other sites are offered during racing seasons.

The track opened in 1934 and pioneered the use of the automated starting gate, the photo finish and the electrical timer. Stars who kept and raced their horses here have ranged from Bing Crosby and Errol Flynn to Mark McGrath (of Sugar Ray), Alex Trebek and Burt Bacharach. The only stain on its legacy happened during WWII when it served as a Japanese-American detention camp.

Pasadena Civic Center Area   LANDMARK
Pasadena's Civic Center, built in the 1920s, is a reflection of the great wealth and local pride that have governed the city since its early days. Highlights include the Spanish Renaissance–style City Hall (Map p188; 100 N Garfield Ave) and the Central Library (Map p188; 285 E Walnut St). Nearby, the Jackie & Mack Robinson Memorial (Map p188; cnr Garfield & Union Sts) honors the Georgia-born, but Pasadena-reared athletic brothers. The often overshadowed Matthew 'Mack' Robinson was a former world-record holder and won an Olympic silver in the 200m sprint in the 1936 Olympics in Berlin (he finished 0.4 seconds behind Jesse Owens). In 1945 his youngest brother, Jackie, became the first African American to be signed to a major-league baseball team. He became a perennial all-star, World Series champion, and hall-of-famer for the Brooklyn (now LA) Dodgers.

Pacific Asia Museum   MUSEUM
(Map p188; www.pacificasiamuseum.org; 46 N Los Robles Ave; adult/student & senior $9/7; ⊙10am-6pm Wed-Sun; P) A block east of the Civic Center, a re-created Chinese palace that was once the home of local art dealer and Asia-phile Grace Nicholson is now nine galleries, which rotate ancient and contemporary art and artifacts from Asia and the Pacific Islands. From Himalayan Buddhas to Chinese porcelain and Japanese costumes, the quality and range of Nicholson's collection is stellar.

Pasadena Museum of California Art   MUSEUM
(Map p188; www.pmcaonline.org; 490 E Union St; adult/student & senior/child $7/5/free, 1st Fri of month free; ⊙noon-5pm Wed-Sun; P) A progressive gallery dedicated to art, architecture and design created by California artists since 1850. Shows change every few months and have included masterpieces by Maynard Dixon, collages by Beatnik artist Jess, and vinyl toys by Gary Basemen, David Gonzales and other artists. Also swing

by the Kosmic Kavern, which is what this former garage has become thanks to spray-mural pop artist Kenny Scharf.

FREE Tournament House & Wrigley Gardens   LANDMARK
(Map p188; www.tournamentofroses.com; 391 S Orange Grove Blvd; tours ⊙2pm & 3pm Thu Feb-Aug) Chewing-gum magnate William Wrigley spent his winters in the elegant Italian Renaissance–style mansion where the Tournament of Roses Association now masterminds the annual Rose Parade. When they're not busy, you can tour the rich interior and inspect Rose Queen crowns and related memorabilia. Feel free to nose around the rose garden any time.

Pasadena Museum of History   MUSEUM
(Map p188; www.pasadenahistory.org; 470 W Walnut St; suggested donation adult museum/house tour/combination $5/4/7, child free; ⊙noon-5pm Wed-Sun, tours 1:30pm Wed-Fri, 1:30pm & 3pm Sat & Sun; P) A palatial beaux-arts mansion that once housed the Finnish consulate, this interesting museum now presents changing exhibits on some facets of the culture, history and art of Pasadena and its neighboring communities. If you want to see the precious antiques and furnishings of the house itself, you'll need to join a tour. The admission price also lets you sneak a peek inside a shedlike structure housing folk art from Finland.

39 Raymond   MUSEUM
(Map p188; 39 Raymond Ave) This no-name gallery displays modern paintings, sculpture, and architectural plans and schemes through the windows of a defunct downtown corner car dealership. It all comes courtesy of Art Center College of Design alumni and can be easily glimpsed from the sidewalk.

Angeles Crest   SCENIC DRIVE
(Hwy 2; www.byways.org/explore/byways/10245/travel.html) The two-lane Angeles Crest Scenic Byway treats you to fabulous views of big-shouldered mountains, the Mojave Desert and deep valleys on its 55-mile meander from La Cañada to the resort town of Wrightwood. The road skirts LA County's tallest mountain, officially called Mt San Antonio (10,064ft) but better known as Old Baldy for its treeless top. You'll pass ranger stations along the way, but the main Chilao Visitors Center (www.fs.fed.us; ⊙8am-4pm Sat & Sun mid-Apr–mid-Oct) with natural exhibits and trails is about 27 miles from the turnoff.

🏃 Activities

Kenyon Devore Trail
HIKING

(www.fs.fed.us; Mount Wilson Observatory, Red Box Rd) Named after a longtime San Gabriel Mountain man, this trail begins a quarter mile from the Mt Wilson summit on Red Box Rd and drops down the mountain through stunning oak and pine habitat, meandering on both sides of the year-round Strayns Creek. It's stunning countryside, especially in the spring – when wildflowers pop – and the fall when valley and black oaks turn gold and drop their spinning leaves. Follow the trail for 4 miles to West Fork Campground, before turning back. It's a moderate 9-mile round-trip.

Switzer Falls
HIKING

(www.fs.fed.us; Switzer Picnic Area, Hwy 2) This easy 4-mile round-trip leaves from the Switzer Picnic Area (signposted 10.5 miles from La Cañada on Hwy 2). Follow the trail down the canyon, boulder hopping along the way. When you reach Switzer Trail Camp follow the trail as it climbs out of the canyon (do not follow the stream below the camp – there's a steep vertical and rocky drop), and make a left at the unmarked junction with the Arroyo Seco Trail (if you go right, you'll be hiking to the Rose Bowl), dropping back into the gorge. When you reach the creek, follow it back upstream for a quarter mile to reach the falls.

Armory Center for the Arts
CRAFTS

(Map p188; www.armoryarts.org; 145 Raymond Ave; ⊙gallery noon-5pm Tue-Sun) Set in a magnificent old armory, this space has been gutted to the rafters and filled with printing presses and drumming studios, dark rooms, mixed-media sculpture and crafts classes of all kinds for all ages and backgrounds. There's a groovy, modern-edged gallery too. For class schedules and description check the website.

🛏 Sleeping

Langham
RESORT $$$

(☎626-568-3900; www.pasadena.langhamhotels.com; 1401 S Oak Knoll Ave; r $150-259, ste $509-1300; P@🅿🛜🏊) Opened as the Huntington Hotel in 1906, it spent the last several decades as the Ritz Carlton before recently donning the robes of Langham. But some things don't change and this incredible 23-acre, palm-dappled, beaux-arts country estate – complete with rambling gardens, giant swimming pool and covered picture bridge – has still got it. Langham's 380 rooms and cottages have sensational marble baths, though some of the heavy drapery and patrician furniture will be updated once renovations are complete. The Sunday brunch ($55), featuring a chocolate fountain, remains a pricey but memorable treat.

Bissell House B&B
BED & BREAKFAST $$

(☎626-441-3535; www.bissellhouse.com; 201 S Orange Grove Blvd; r $155-255; P🛜🏊) Antiques, hardwood floors and a crackling fireplace make this secluded Victorian B&B on 'Millionaire's Row' a bastion of warmth and romance. The hedge-framed garden feels like a sanctuary, and there's a big pool for cooling off on hot summer days. The top-floor Bridal Suite has a double Jacuzzi.

Artists' Inn & Cottage B&B
BED & BREAKFAST $$

(☎626-799-5668, 888-799-5668; www.artistsinns.com; 1038 Magnolia St; r $135-225; P) Just three blocks from a Metro Gold Line station, this lovely Victorian farmhouse built in 1895 has 10 artist-inspired rooms, some with fireplaces and canopy beds. If you don't like frilly Laura Ashley, ask for the Van Gogh. It comes with high ceilings and manic depression. Smoking is verboten. Check in is from 3pm to 6pm.

FIRE!

Late 2009 was one of the worst fire seasons in California history – 63 wildfires were active between July and November devouring 336,020 acres (525 sq miles), destroying hundreds of structures and killing two people. The largest was the Station Fire. Sparked by arson, it burned 160,577 acres and threatened or swallowed parts of La Cañada, Glendale, La Crescenta, Altadena, Sunland and Tujunga. It even licked Mt Wilson. Thankfully, the observatory and its astronomical tools were mostly unharmed. Additional fires raged in San Bernardino, Ventura and Orange counties. Throughout the summer, sun was obscured by ash, which, at times, rained down. The burn lit up the night and multiple blazes on completely different ranges were visible from a single viewpoint, and, as karma would have it, from area freeways.

RONALD REAGAN LIBRARY & MUSEUM

No matter how you feel about Ronald Reagan (1911–2004), his **presidential library** (www.reaganlibrary.com; 40 Presidential Dr; adult/teen/senior $12/6/9; ☉10am-5pm; P) is really quite fascinating. Galleries cover the arc of the man's life from his childhood in Dixon, Illinois, through his early days in radio and acting to his years as governor of California, although the focus is obviously on his stint as president (1980–88) in the waning years of the Cold War. The museum features re-creations of the Oval Office and the Cabinet Room, Reagan family memorabilia, gifts from heads of state, a nuclear cruise missile and even a graffiti-covered chunk of the Berlin Wall. His grave is on the grounds as well. Get there via the I-405 (San Diego Fwy) north to the 118 (Ronald Reagan Fwy) west; exit at Madera Rd South, turn right on Madera and continue straight for 3 miles to Presidential Dr.

Westin HOTEL $$$
(Map p188; ☏626-792-2727; www.westin.com; 191 N Los Robles Ave; r $189-925; P@☎⛱) Pasadena's newest sleep is a large, modern, Spanish-style complex with comfortable rooms and all the amenities in a central old-town location. A nice choice.

Saga Motor Hotel MOTEL $
(☏626-795-0431; www.thesagamotorhotel.com; 1633 E Colorado Blvd; r $79-135; P☎⛱) This peach-tinted, palm-shaded motel isn't fancy or as cool as that sign makes it look, but even if some of the beds are saggy and carpet faded, rooms are clean, have tubs and showers and some homey touches – like shutters on the window and books on the shelves. There are plans to renovate soon.

Pasadena Inn MOTEL $
(Map p188; ☏626-795-8401; www.oldpasadenainn.com; 400 S Arroyo Pkwy; r $89-109; P@☎⛱) This older property won't be featured on the pages of *House Beautiful,* but it offers shut-eye at a modest tariff. In the morning drag your coffee and Danish out to the pool area. At night the adjacent Thai restaurant makes a decent curry if you don't feel like hoofing it to Old Pasadena, a 15-minute walk away.

✕ Eating

Sea Harbour CHINESE $$
(☏626-288-3939; 3939 Rosemead Blvd; dishes $10-30; ☉lunch & dinner; P⛊) When Eddie Lin (p169) craves dim sum, he comes to where classic dumplings have been modernized. Not that a novice would notice. Because when we see shredded pork wrapped in sticky rice and a lotus leaf, or shrimp folded into thick flat noodles and soaked in sweet soy, all we do is eat.

NBC Seafood CHINESE $$
(☏626-282-2323; 404 S Atlantic Blvd; dishes $5-15; ☉breakfast, lunch & dinner; P⛊) Grand and bright, Chinese droves descend here for dim sum at breakfast and lunch, and to binge on tasty Chinese seafood dishes when night falls. It's part of the Monterey Mall.

Yujean Kang's CHINESE FUSION $$
(Map p188; www.yujeankangs.com; 67 N Raymond Ave; appetizers $3-5, mains $8-10; ☉lunch & dinner) An almost unnoticeable Old Town haunt – with somewhat dated decor – that serves up Chinese cuisine with a twist. Beef noodles are stir-fried with sun-dried tomatoes. Polenta and risotto dishes are stirred with pork, black mushrooms and Chinese greens. Fish fillets are fried crispy, spiced liberally and doused with fresh tomato sauce.

Yun Cha Café CHINESE $
(www.yunchacafe.com; 1635 S San Gabriel Blvd; dim sum $1-3.40; ☉breakfast, lunch & dinner; P⛊) Set in a mini-mall, this classic Cantonese cheapie is where roast duck and slabs of roast pork are chopped and wrapped to go. It also does a tremendous noodle soup with barbecued pork (just $1.39) and various concoctions of *congee* (rice porridge) with ingredients like pork blood, intestine or preserved egg.

101 Noodle Express CHINESE $
(1408 E Valley Blvd; dishes $5-10; ☉lunch & dinner; P⛊) Tablecloths and wood furnishings can't dress up this mini-mall greasy spoon famous for one dish and one dish only: the beef roll. Think: thin slices of marinated beef with chopped cilantro, green onions, and sweet bean sauce rolled into lightly crisp tortilla-like pancake. Nice!

Bistro 45
CONTINENTAL $$$

(Map p188; ☎626-795-2478; www.bistro45.com; 45 Mentor Ave; dishes $10.50-23.50; ⊘lunch & dinner Tue-Sun; P) Touted as the best fine-dining in the 'dena, this pink-and-green, art-deco dining room is elegant yet not stiff. It's the kind of place top Central Californian winemakers choose if they're hosting a dinner for potential buyers. The seafood, steaks and chops are all seriously good.

Akbar
INDIAN $$

(Map p188; www.akbarcuisineofindia.com; 44 N Fair Oaks Ave; mains $10-16; ⊘lunch Mon-Thu, dinner Sat-Thu) Cozy without being cramped, this tiny saffron-scented dining room with an open kitchen bakes bread and broils meat in a tandoori oven, and stir up all the curries too.

Saladang Song
THAI $$

(Map p188; www.saladangsong.com; 383 S Fair Oaks Ave; dishes $10-18; ⊘breakfast, lunch & dinner; P☗) Traditional Thai is served in contemporary environs at this pseudo-industrial outpost hemmed in by artfully rendered concrete walls. It has simple curries, vermicelli with fish balls steamed in green curry, and real deal Thai breakfasts (think: rice porridge and muddy coffee), which are often hard to find this side of Bangkok.

Mi Piace
ITALIAN $$

(Map p188; www.mipiace.com; 25 E Colorado Blvd; pizzas & pasta $9-15; ⊘breakfast, lunch & dinner; ☗P) A midrange Italian kitchen that gets packed with Pasadena's business crowd on weekdays, and shoppers on weekends. There's a shady sidewalk patio, a Sinatra soundtrack and popular thin-crust pizza.

Marston's
DINER $

(Map p188; www.marstonsrestaurant.com; 151 E Walnut St; mains $16-26; ⊘breakfast & lunch daily, dinner Wed-Sat; P☗) Marston's serves lunch and dinner, but it's the prospect of the scrumptious all-American breakfasts that helps us get out of bed. But no matter when you get there, this diminutive cottage with its sunny porch is likely to be packed.

Burger Continental
ECLECTIC $

(Map p188; www.burgercontinental.com; 535 S Lake Ave; mains $9-14; ⊘breakfast, lunch & dinner; P☗) What sounds like a patty-and-bun joint is in reality a high-energy (mostly) Middle Eastern nosh spot (think: kebabs, shishk, gyros) with a taco bar. Um,

yeah, but it works, especially for families. The all-you-can-eat Sunday brunch buffet is popular, and it hosts live jazz in the terracotta courtyard on Wednesday nights.

Mike & Anne's
NEW AMERICAN $$

(☎626-799-7199; www.mikeandannes.com; 1040 Mission St; appetizers $6-13, mains $16.50-26; ⊘breakfast, lunch & dinner Tue-Sun; P) Right on the Mission St drag in South Pasadena, Mike & Anne's is a sweet and unhurried jewel with mostly local patrons clamoring for the clever but unfussy food à la the 'red flannel hash' for breakfast, barbecued short rib sandwich at lunch and miso-and-sake-braised cod at dinner time.

Bar Celona
SPANISH $$

(Map p188; www.barcelonapasadena.com; 46 E Colorado Blvd; tapas $6-24; ⊘lunch & dinner; P) Rioja-tinted walls offer a fiery backdrop for the seafood paellas and wine-braised steaks streaming from the kitchen into the candlelit dining room. Grazers can pick their way around the tapas menu, while sangria-sipping scenesters wind down the night in the adjacent lounge, which has live music on Tuesday nights.

🍷 Drinking

Heritage Wine Company
WINE BAR

(Map p188; 155 N Raymond Ave; ⊘11am-10pm Tue & Wed, to 11pm Thu-Sat, 3-9pm Sun) More of a laid-back, brick-and-wood wine bar with some tasty tapas, and an affordable and sensational wine selection geared to take-home clientele. Day or night, you can create your own flights here.

Vertical Wine Bistro
WINE BAR

(Map p188; www.verticalwinebistro.com; 70 N Raymond Ave; ⊘Tue-Sun; P) Although it's a sophisticated wine bar dressed in cocoa and candlelight, don't worry if you can't tell your pinot noir from your pinot grigio. Tapas come with a wine recommendation and you can sample 2oz tastes from most of the over 400 bottles in the cellar.

☆ Entertainment

Red White & Bluezz
JAZZ

(Map p188; www.redwhitebluezz.com; 70 S Raymond Ave; ⊘10:30am-9pm Sun, from 11am Mon-Wed, 11am-11pm Thu, to midnight Fri & Sat; P) It's a wine shop, a wine bar, a restaurant and a terrific jazz club all rolled into one. Jazz blows nightly, so belly up to that fine marble bar and enjoy some of the best area talent doing their thing.

Ice House COMEDY

(Map p188; www.icehousecomedy.com; 24 N Mentor Ave, Pasadena; P) Dana Carvey, Lily Tomlin and Billy Crystal have honed their chops at this former ice warehouse. Today's lineup includes Latino funnyman Rudy Moreno and vets like Joe Rogan and Harland Williams. Drinks are disappointing, the show – usually – not. Over 18s only.

Pasadena Playhouse THEATER

(Map p188; www.pasadenaplayhouse.org; 39 S Molino Ave; P) Since 1917 actors good and bad, the well known and the lesser, have infused this attractive, adobe-style complex with drama (and some musical comedy too). There are actually two theaters here, but recently the complex had slipped into Chapter 11. It should emerge with new productions soon – check the website for updates.

🔒 Shopping

Rose Bowl Flea Market VINTAGE, GIFTS

(www.rgcshows.com/rosebowlfleamarket; 1001 Rose Bowl Dr; adult/under 12yr $8/free; ⊙9am-3pm 2nd Sun of the month) California's Marketplace of Unusual Items descends upon the football field bringing forth the rummaging hordes. There are over 2500 vendors and 15,000 buyers here every month, and it's always a great time.

Vroman's BOOKSTORE

(Map p188; www.vromansbookstore.com; 695 E Colorado Blvd; ⊙9am-9pm Mon-Thu, to 10pm Fri & Sat, 10am-9pm Sun) Southern California's oldest bookstore (since 1894) is still a favorite with local literati for browsing and frequent author appearances. Vroman's have everything from greeting cards to candles and bath products, and its attached coffee shop serves the good strong stuff.

Pasadena City College Flea Market

VINTAGE, GIFTS

(www.pasadena.edu; 57 E Colorado Blvd; ⊙9am-3pm 2nd Sun of each month) Another Pasadena rummage blooms on the second Sunday of every month, on this decidedly stylish and spare art-deco campus. There are about 450 vendors here, with some particularly good vinyl music to be discovered. Proceeds help fund scholarships and student activities.

Neo 39 SHOES

(Map p188; www.neo39footwear.com; 39 E Colorado Blvd; ⊙10am-9pm Sun-Thu, to 10pm Fri, to 11pm Sat) In the thick of the Old Town Pasadena shopping district is this smart sneaker depot sporting rare, imported and generally colorful and stylish high tops, low tops and skate shoes. It even sells eco-chic Tom's.

Distant Lands BOOKS & TRAVEL

(Map p188; www.distantlands.com; 56 S Raymond Ave) Anything and everything you could possibly need to keep you safe, sane and entertained while you're on the road – from travel guides and travelogues to money belts, maps and roller bags.

BOYLE HEIGHTS & EAST LOS ANGELES

The Los Angeles River is a bit like the US–Mexican border without the wall and the minutemen. Beyond the concrete gulch lies the oldest and largest Mexican community outside of Mexico. It's been the breeding ground for musicians like Los Lobos, athletes like boxer Oscar de la Hoya and actors like Anthony Quinn.

Life in the barrio is tough but lively. Stroller-pushing moms stop for *pan dulce* (sweet bread) and gossip at local *panaderías* (bakeries), and pick up dinner at the *carnicería* (butcher shop) and fresh tortillas straight from the factory. On summer nights, makeshift grills pop up at street corners, *taquerías* (taco shops) get packed with families, and laborers chill with a cold *cerveza* (beer) after another hard day's work.

But there's more than Mexican-American roots beneath the concrete. Developer Andrew Boyle purchased the river bluffs in 1858. Within 40 years the suburb had water and sewage services and became known as the Ellis Island of Los Angeles, when newly arrived immigrants from Europe (including the author's ancestors) flocked here after reading of clear blue skies and river views while suffering in Chicago and New York tenements. By 1939 Boyle Heights was predominantly Jewish, but along with the original Canter's Deli, there were also several Japanese stores and Buddhist temples in the mix.

There aren't any major stops on the tourist track out here, but even a quick drive or stroll, and perhaps a bite in one of several excellent restaurants, will deepen your understanding of this complex city. Access has been made much easier since completion of the Metro Rail Gold Line extension.

You should step off at **Mariachi Plaza** (cnr Boyle Ave & 1st St), where traditional Mexican musicians in fanciful suits and wide-brimmed hats troll for work in the old-school *zócalo* (public square) on one side and B-boys and skate punks gather, spin and grind out front of the futuristic metro station on the other.

East of here, a nondescript building houses the **Hollenbeck Youth Center** (www.hollenbeckpbc.org; 2015 E 1st St), where Oscar 'Golden Boy' de la Hoya punched himself into shape for his 1992 Olympic gold medal. Just past a giant cemetery is **El Mercado** (www.elmercadodelosangeles.com; 3425 E 1st St & Lorena), a colorful indoor market, with its faux Mayan temple on the 3rd-floor food court where locals come for homemade *mole* (sauce), *dulce de leche* (caramel), toys and tortilla presses. On weekends, it's a scene and a half when 'dueling' mariachi bands entertain families and kissing couples.

If you're hungry for something a little less loud, head northwest from here, past countless murals and front-yard gardens to savory **La Parilla** (www.laparillarestaurant.com; 2126 Cesar Chavez Ave; ☺breakfast, lunch & dinner), where you can snack on fresh guacamole prepared tableside and spiced to order, along with steaming, freshly made corn tortillas. And if you have time, stop at **Self-Help Graphics & Art** (www.selfhelpgraphics.com; 3802 Cesar E Chavez Ave at Gage Ave). It's been nurturing and promoting Latino art for the past three decades. Despite recent budget issues, the staff still puts on the Southland's best and largest Día de Los Muertos (Day of the Day) celebration on November 1. The **mural** on the eastern wall (above Super Taco) is a re-creation of David Alfaro Siqueros' controversial 1932 *América Tropical* on Olvera St (p70).

WESTLAKE & KOREATOWN

Until relatively recently, historic Westlake, just west of Downtown, was the go-to zone for scoring rock cocaine or a fake drivers' license. Slowly, though, the area is cleaning up its act and even toying with gentrification. Crime is down and families have returned to **MacArthur Park** (cnr Wilshire Blvd & Alvarado St) for picnics and paddling around a spring-fed lake, at least in the daylight hours. So have the skaters (they grind in benign packs) and the world beats. The restored Levitt Pavilion band shell is the place for the park's **summer concert series** (www.levittla.org). And yes, this is the park that 'melts in the dark' in the eponymous Jimmy Webb song made famous by Donna Summer. The park is at its best north of Wilshire. It's still pretty trashy south of the lake. Though still largely a working-class Latino neighborhood, artists, hipsters and young professionals are trickling into the neighborhood with bars, eateries and cultural spaces following in their tracks. Just get off at the Wilshire/MacArthur Park stop of the Red Line subway and see for yourself.

Westlake spills seamlessly into Koreatown, a vast, amorphous area that can feel more like Seoul than LA. Korean immigrants began settling here in the 1960s and still form a very tight-knit community. Many signs are in Korean and some shopkeepers and servers speak only a few words of English. All this makes for an interesting experience, especially when it comes to food and day spas. Of late, Koreatown has also developed a nightlife scene. A good place for *soju* (similar to vodka) cocktails and Hite beer is the eccentric Prince.

Wilshire Blvd is the most attractive thoroughfare, lined with striking historic churches and other buildings harkening back to the time when this area was a wealthy business and residential district known as Wilshire Center.

◉ Sights & Activities

Grier Musser Museum   MUSEUM
(www.griermussermuseum.org; 403 S Bonnie Brae St; adult/child/student & senior $10/5/7; ☺noon-4pm Wed-Sat by reservation; Ⓟ) Fans of Victoriana will get their fill inside this beautiful Queen Anne home with intricate woodwork and luscious stained glass. It's stuffed with antiques and yesteryear's knickknacks, including a neat 1909 windup Victrola phonograph that still works. To keep things dynamic, the dedicated staff puts together monthly exhibits usually revolving around a holiday theme. The Christmas one is famous.

Bullocks Wilshire   ARCHITECTURE
(www.swlaw.edu/bullockswilshire; 3050 Wilshire Blvd) This 1929 art-deco gem was the country's first department store designed for shoppers arriving by car. Unfortunately, it closed in 1992 and is now a law school rarely open to the public.

Aroma Wilshire Center · MALL

(www.aromaresort.com; 3680 Wilshire Blvd; P) These days shopping around here is done at slick malls such as this new one near the Metro Red Line Wilshire/Western station. Pick through Korean groceries, cosmetics, music, books, stationery and all sorts of fun imports, get a workout at the golf-driving range or work out the kinks at the fancy fitness center.

Century Sports Club & Day Spa · SPA

(www.centurydayspa.com; 4120 W Olympic Blvd; 6am-10pm Mon-Fri, 7am-10pm Sat & Sun; P) If you want to do some serious spa time you'll need to find this place, where for just $20 you can get a deep steam in wet and dry, clay, wood and marble saunas, enjoy a belching vichy, dip into some seriously hot tubs and get your sinuses clear with a cold plunge. It offers a range of massage treatments (including Korean-style shiatsu) and has golf and fitness facilities, as well.

Beverly Hot Springs · SPA

(www.beverlyhotsprings.com; 308 N Oxford Ave; per person Mon-Thu $30, Fri-Sun $40; 9am-9pm; P) If you want less marble and more grotto, you'll do your soaking at this place where the water is geothermically heated 2200ft below the city streets.

FREE Korean American Museum · MUSEUM

(www.kamuseum.org; Suite 400, 3727 W 6th St; admission free; 11am-6pm Wed-Fri, to 3pm Sat) To connect with local Korean culture, pop into this museum which has changing art exhibits and cultural events. It sometimes closes between rotating exhibits. Call before you come by.

✕ Eating & Drinking

Soot Bull Jeep · KOREAN $$

(213-387-3865; 3136 W 8th St; dishes $15-25; lunch & dinner; P) Korean barbecue does not get more authentic than this smoky diner, with real charcoal grills sunk into the Formica tables. The waitress will grill thinly sliced marinated steak and short rib, shrimp and squid, or tongue as you snack on bowls of daikon, seaweed salad and kim chi (spicy pickled cabbage).

Tahoe Galbi · KOREAN $

(www.tahoegalbi.com; 3986 Wilshire Blvd; meals $10-18; lunch & dinner; P) A K-town classic that attracts blue-haired locals, suits and stoners for all-you-can-eat Korean barbecue. For $10 you'll get brisket, pork belly

and chicken to grill tableside along with ample soup, salad and kim chi.

Tofu House · KOREAN $

(www.bcdtofu.com; 3575 Wilshire Blvd; dishes $9-16; 24hr; P) Sure, it's called the Tofu House, but it still serves 'small intestine of cattle.' More to the point, these worn wooden floors are patrolled by no-nonsense Korean maidens and madams who herd diners with absolute authority and serve ceramic bowls of steaming tofu soup and curry, spicy raw crab, and sizzling skillets of thinly sliced beef.

Langer's · DELI $$

(www.langersdeli.com; 704 S Alvarado St; sandwiches $2-9, grill $15.50-23; breakfast & lunch Mon-Sat;) Since 1947, generations of smoked-meat lovers have flocked to this old-school Jewish deli famous for its juicy hot pastrami sandwiches (No 19 with coleslaw and Swiss cheese is the bestseller) and fresh chopped liver. The Metro Red Line subway station is right outside.

Papa Cristo's · GREEK $$

(www.papacristos.com; 2771 W Pico Blvd; appetizers $2-9, mains $7-15; breakfast, lunch Tue-Sun, dinner Tue-Sat;) Like a blast of Greek sunshine, this frenzied market bistro is deeply nourishing. The gyros are super, the rack of lamb is a steal. Gather your posse and come for the Big Fat Greek Thursday Night Dinner ($19) at 6:30pm, when tables bend with nibbles and belly dancers shake it.

Mama's Hot Tamales Café · MEXICAN $

(www.mamashottamales.com; 2124 W 7th St; dishes $6-9; breakfast & lunch) Pan-American tamales (a stuffed cornmeal patty) are served at this cheerful nosh spot, right beside MacArthur Park and the vortex of a robust job-training program. Try chicken-potato from Oaxaca, spicy beef from Acapulco or spinach-mushroom from Peru. They're so good, you'll want to pick some up for later in the attached mercado (market).

R Bar · LOUNGE

(213-387-7227; www.myspace.com/4rbar.com; 3331 8th St; 6pm) The K-Town hipster hangout of the moment when we rolled through. The jukebox is stocked with classics and neo-classics, and you have to know the password to get past the gate-keeper. Seriously. Call for the password, it's always changing. Wednesday night is Karaoke time.

Prince   BAR
(3198 W 7th St, Koreatown; ☺4pm-midnight; P)
In the movie *Chinatown*, Faye Dunaway
meets with Jack Nicholson at this campy
joint that defies any categorization. It's
a former hotel lounge with colonial-era
British-pub looks (check out the wacky sol-
dier lamps) and *soju* and Hite beer on the
menu. The crowd is a potpourri of ethnicities united by a penchant for stiff drinks at
civilized prices.

Brass Monkey   KARAOKE
(www.cafebrassmonkey.com; 3440 Wilshire Blvd;
2-drink minimum or cover $15; ☺10am-2am; P)
Belt out your best Madonna or Michael at
this 1930s bank vault turned kooky karaoke
joint. *American Idol* wannabes can pick
from 60,000 songs in six languages. Those
in the know usually come early to stake out
a good spot before the action starts at 9pm
(4pm on Friday). Enter through the back.

Taylor's   STEAKHOUSE, BAR
(www.taylorssteakhouse.com; 3361 8th St; ☺lunch
& dinner; P) Some consider it an LA institution for the decent steaks at affordable
prices. We like the dark-leather booths, the
dim lights, and the oak bar, which holds up
a martini glass just fine.

☆ Entertainment

Wiltern Theatre   THEATER
(www.wiltern.com; 3790 Wilshire Blvd) A 1931
movie theater (*Westside Story* premiered
here) turned epic concert venue struts its
stuff in a glorious turquoise mantle right
at the intersection of Wilshire and Western
Blvds (get it?). Neil Young, Bob Dylan, the
National and Massive Attack are among the
artists who've played here recently. If you
find a show you like, do not miss it. This
stage has a way about bringing out the best
in a performer.

SOUTH CENTRAL & EXPOSITION PARK

South Central LA burst into global consciousness with the rat-a-tat-tat rhythm
and rhyme of some of hip-hop's greatest
pioneers. With infectious beats and sharp
tongues, folks like Ice T, Ice Cube, Eazy E
and Dr Dre, and later Tupac Shakur brought
gangsta life to the suburbs and beyond. The
notoriety was a double-edged blade. In one
sense, awareness is the first step to healing, on the other hand, South Central was
suddenly defined by its gangs, drugs, poverty, crime and drive-by shootings, which,
though not entirely undeserved, never told
the whole story.

After WWII over five million African
Americans left what at the time was still a violently racist South and moved to northern
cities like Chicago, Philadelphia and NYC for
manufacturing jobs, in what has been called
the Second Great Migration (nearly two
million moved in the first migration, which
took place between 1910 and 1930). Some of
those families moved west, from Mississippi,
Louisiana and Texas to Los Angeles. They
found manufacturing jobs, bought property
and built fully functioning working-class
neighborhoods south of downtown. They
brought a thriving Central Ave jazz scene
with them, and though life wasn't perfect,
it was a step up. Fast-forward 30 years and
suddenly the high-wage manufacturing jobs
dried up, drug addiction soared, families
fell apart, guns became accessible, gang violence bloomed, and South Central began to
earn its reputation. But recent investment
of time, money and vision from the likes
of Magic Johnson and Ted Watkins, an expanded rail service and fantastic Exposition
Park museum complex, has helped turn the
tide somewhat. Sure, much of South Central
still feels bleak and foreboding, but there's
also a lot of spirit here, especially in the
thriving cultural hub of Leimert Park, and
around the Watts Towers, which are not to
be missed. And lest we forget, this is the
neighborhood of the University of Southern
California, where the Trojans play football,
George Lucas studied film, and Will Ferrell
became, well, Will Ferrell.

◉ Sights

Leimert Park   NIGHTLIFE, CULTURAL DISTRICT
(Degnan Blvd & 43rd St) The soft lilt of a saxo-
phone purrs from a storefront. Excited
chatter streams from a coffeehouse. The
mingling aroma of barbecue and seafood
gumbo wafts into the steamy noontime
air. Welcome to Leimert (luh-*mert*) Park,
the old-school cultural hub of LA's African
American community. About 2.5 miles west
of Exposition Park, the mostly residential
neighborhood was designed by the Olm-
sted brothers of New York Central Park
fame and has been nicknamed 'the black
Greenwich Village' by filmmaker and local
resident John Singleton (*Boyz n the Hood*).

Here, bongo freaks gather in the park for Sunday afternoon drum circles. Nearby, the World Stage is a destination for jazz aficionados, while blues lovers head around the corner to the historic Babe & Ricky's. Check out the **Sankofa Passage** (Leimert Park's walk of fame) paying homage to local figures like LA jazz legends Horace Tapscott, Dexter Gordon and Buddy Collette.

Natural History Museum of LA County
MUSEUM
(www.nhm.org; 900 Exposition Blvd; adult/child/senior & student $9/2/6.50; 9:30am-5pm; P) Dinos to diamonds, bears to beetles, hissing roaches to African elephants – this museum will take you around the world and back millions of years in time. It's all housed in a beautiful 1913 Renaissance-style building that stood in for Columbia University in the first *Spider-Man* movie – yup, this was where Peter Parker was bitten by the radioactive arachnid.

The special exhibits usually draw the biggest crowds, but don't miss out on a spin around the permanent halls to see such trophy displays as a tyrannosaurus rex skull and a megamouth, one of the world's rarest and creepiest sharks. Historical exhibits include prized Navajo textiles, baskets and jewelry in the **Hall of Native American Cultures**. If diamonds are your best friend, head to the **Gem & Mineral Hall** with its walk-through gem tunnel and a Fort Knox-worthy gold collection. Summers see the opening of the **Pavilion of Wings** (adult/5-12yr/senior & student$3/1/2; mid-Apr–early Sep) on the South Lawn, an enchanting landscape where some 30 species of butterflies roam freely.

Kids will have plenty of ooh and aah moments in the spruced-up **Discovery Center**, where they can make friends with Cecil the iguana and Peace, a 9ft boa; dig for dinosaur fossils; handle bones, antlers and minerals; and get close to tarantulas, scorpions and other creepy-crawlies.

For grown-ups, the museum turns up the volume during its First Fridays event series, which combines a lecture with guided tours and a party (with booze and hip live music) in the African Mammal Hall. Check the website for upcoming dates.

FREE **California Science Center** MUSEUM (www.californiasciencecenter.org; 39th & Figueroa St; 10am-5pm;) A simulated earthquake, baby chicks hatching and a giant techno-doll named Tess bring out the kid in all of us at this multimedia museum with plenty of buttons to push, lights to switch on and knobs to pull.

The enormous space is divided into three themed areas. Upstairs on the left, **World of Life** focuses mostly on the human body. You can 'hop on' a red blood cell for a computer fly-through of the circulatory system, ask Gertie how long your colon really is, watch open-heart surgery, and learn about homeostasis from Tess, billed as '50ft of brains, beauty and biology.' Tots may have trouble understanding the science, but they will remember Tess.

On the right, **Creative World** is all about the ingenious ways humans have devised to communicate with each other, transport things and build structures. Meet a family of crash-test dummies, fly a virtual hovercraft and get all shook up during a fake earthquake.

Aircraft and space travel take center stage in the **Sketch Foundation Gallery**, in an adjacent Frank Gehry building (yes, he's everywhere). Spirits will soar at the sight of a pioneering 1902 Wright glider; the original *Gemini XI* capsule flown by US astronauts in 1996; and a replica Soviet *Sputnik*, the first human-made object to orbit the earth in 1957.

Ecosystems, the museum's newest addition, takes visitors through a variety of habitats: desert, river, island, urban, and forest. There are plans to add a living Southeast Asian rainforest indoors, but for now you'll have to make do with the kelp forest tunnel. It's all good educational fun but, we're sad to say, in this fast-moving tech-age some of the exhibits that were cutting edge only a few years ago already seem oddly dated.

But that **IMAX theater** is right on time. If the Hubble 3-D film is on, see it.

Exposition Park
LANDMARK
A quick jaunt south of Downtown LA by DASH bus (p210), the family-friendly Exposition Park began as an agricultural fairground in 1872, then devolved into a magnet for the down-and-out, and finally emerged as a patch of public greenery in 1913. It contains three quality museums, a robust and rambling **Rose Garden** (8:30am-sunset Apr-Dec) and the 1923 **Los Angeles Memorial Coliseum** (www.lacoliseum.com; 3939 S Figueroa St). The latter hosted the 1932 and 1984 Summer Olympic Games, the 1959 baseball World Series and two Super Bowls, and is the home stadium for USC Trojans

(American) football team. The adjacent indoor **Los Angeles Memorial Sports Arena** dates from 1959 and is used for rock concerts (we saw the Grateful Dead play here way back when), ice shows, the circus, USC basketball and even the occasional rodeo. Parking costs $6, and it only takes cash.

FREE **University of Southern California**
UNIVERSITY
(USC; ☎213-740-6605; www.usc.edu; Exposition Blvd & Figueroa St) George Lucas, John Wayne and Neil Armstrong are among the famous alumni of this well-respected private university, founded in 1880, just north of Exposition Park. Free 50-minute, student-led tours touch on campus history, architecture and student life and leave on the hour from the Admissions Center midweek. Reservations are strongly recommended.

Harris Hall is the home of **USC Fisher Gallery** (www.fishergallery.org; 823 Exposition Blvd; ⊙noon-5pm Tue-Sat Sep-May), which presents changing selections from its ever-expanding collection of American landscapes, British portraits, French Barbizon School paintings and modern Mexican masters such as Salomón Huerta and Gronk (Glugio Nicandro).

Watts Labor Community Action Committee
MUSEUM, COMMUNITY CENTER
(WLCAC; ☎323-563-5639; www.wlcac.org; 10950 S Central Ave; tours adults/child $5/free; ⊙8:30am-5pm) Watts was the epicenter of two sets of LA riots – 1965 and 1992 – when this vibrant community and cultural center was burned to the ground. The neighborhood is still teeming with large numbers of kids growing up poor and angry, but there are pockets of improvements thanks in part to such groups as this. Founded by Ted Watkins and run by his son, Timothy, their headquarters doubles as a cultural theme park. A huge bronze sculpture of a black woman called *Mother of Humanity* dominates the campus. Nearby, **Mudtown Flats** is a facade re-creating iconic black LA historic sites and is often used for movie shoots, and the **Cecil Ferguson Gallery** rotates exhibits of LA's best African American artists like Willie Middlebrook and Michael Massenburg. The most powerful exhibit, though, is the **Civil Rights Museum**, only available by guided tours that must be booked at least a day in advance. Guides take you through the hull of the *Amistad* (the actual façade used in the Spielberg film), a body-filled slave ship, and along the

Mississippi Delta Rd to displays about Martin Luther King, the Black Panther Party and the 1960s Civil Rights Movement. On the last Friday of the month big-name jazz and blues acts amble up to the front porch of the **Mississippi Delta House** and put on public concerts ($15-25). When we visited a new and expansive skate park was under construction. It will soon give South Central's growing crew of skaters a place to freelance and grind.

Watts Towers
LANDMARK
(www.wattstowers.us; 1761-1765 E 107th St; adult/under 12yr/teen & senior $7/free/$3; ⊙10am-4pm Wed-Sat, noon-4pm Sun; P) The fabulous Watts Towers rank among the world's greatest monuments of folk art. In 1921 Italian immigrant Simon Rodia set out 'to make something big' and then spent 33 years cobbling together this whimsical freeform sculpture from a motley assortment of found objects – from green 7-Up bottles to sea shells, rocks to pottery. You can admire it any time, but to get inside you have to join a half-hour tour. The adjacent **Watts Towers Art Center** sponsors workshops, performances and classes for the community, hosts art exhibits and organizes the acclaimed Watts Towers Day of the Drum and Jazz Festival in September (p68). Its volunteers also lead tours through the park and around the spires from 10am to 3pm Thursday through Sunday.

Central Avenue
HISTORIC DISTRICT
From the 1920s to the 1950s, Central Ave was the lifeblood of LA's African American community, not by choice but because segregation laws kept black people out of other neighborhoods. It was also a hotbed of jazz and R&B, a legacy commemorated every July with the Central Avenue Jazz Festival (p67) held outside the 1928 **Dunbar Hotel** (4225 S Central Ave). Duke Ellington once maintained a suite at what was LA's only 1st-class hotel for African Americans. It's now a low-income seniors center and, like much of the street, a rather drab sight.

FREE **African American Firefighter Museum**
MUSEUM
(www.aaffmuseum.org; 1401 S Central Ave; ⊙10am-2pm Tue & Thu, 1-4pm Sun) It has the usual assortment of vintage engines, uniforms and an 1890 hose wagon set in a restored 1913 fire station that, until 1955, was one of only two in town that employed black firefighters.

FREE **California African American Museum** MUSEUM

(www.caamuseum.org; 600 State Dr; ⏰10am-5pm Tue-Sat, 11am-5pm Sun; P) This museum does an excellent job of showcasing African American artists, such as the great John T Scott, whose woodblock prints are full of expression and shadow. They don't, on the other hand, spend much time explaining how and when African Americans moved to California. There's an old bill of sale from the slavery days, photos of Tom Bradley and Ella Fitzgerald, and a few informative paragraphs here and there in the lone historical gallery (like how blacks made up over half the population of the original pueblo), but it doesn't come together to tell the overall story.

✖ Eating & Drinking

Phillip's Barbecue BARBECUE $
(4307 Leimert Blvd; mains $10.50-22; P 🍴) The pork and beef ribs are fall-off-the-bone tender and the sauce smoky at this soulful hole-in-the-wall that perfumes the whole block in tasty goodness. The sauce comes with various degrees of heat, so go easy. The 7-Up cake makes for an unusual finish. Cash only.

Vieux Carré CREOLE $$
(www.novieuxcarre.com; 4317 Degnan Blvd; mains $15-25; P 🍴) From the jazz soundtrack to the Micalopoulos New Orleans prints to the hospitality, this is a fantastic find for those who love Creole cooking. The gumbo is peppery and stocked with sausage, chicken and crab. It also has red beans and rice, seven kinds of po' boys (including fried oyster), and hearty fried seafood dinners.

☆ Entertainment

World Stage JAZZ
(www.theworldstage.org; 4344 Degnan Blvd) Founded by the late hard-bop drummer Billy Higgins, this place doesn't serve food or drink, just good music from some of the best emerging talents in jazz. The Thursday jam session has people grooving until 2am. And on Sundays, the women-only (performers that is) jazz jam hums till midnight. There's drum, writing and vocal workshops too.

Babe & Ricky's BLUES
(4339 Leimert Blvd; ⏰Thu-Mon) This legendary blues joint is great any day, but Monday is Jam Night – $10 gets you all the music and soul-food you'll need.

🛍 Shopping

TOP CHOICE **Sika** FOLK ART
(4330 Degnan Blvd) It would be hard to find a better collection of antiques, masks, clothes and jewelry outside of West Africa than those found in this owner-operated treasure chest. It cosponsors a three-day Labor Day Music, Food & Art Festival in the lot next door.

Eso Won Books BOOKSTORE
(www.esowonbookstore.com; 4331 Degnan Blvd; ⏰10am-7pm Mon-Sat, noon-5pm Sun) Twenty-four years in business and still doing it in an Amazon world, this store focuses on African American literature, fiction and nonfiction. Luminaries like Maya Angelou, BB King, and Kareem Abdul Jabbar have held book signings here, and Bill Clinton and President Obama have both stopped by to pay their respect.

Africa by the Yard FABRICS
(4319 Degnan Blvd) If you can't make it to the motherland, but still crave colorful West African fabrics, drop in. Maybe there's a *dashiki* in your future?

Zambezi Bazaar FOLK ART, MUSIC
(6383 Degnan Blvd) It truly is a bazaar in the sense that the stock is eclectic and changing. Everything from beauty products to jewelry and clothes to out-of-print African American literature and vintage jazz LPs are available here.

EAGLE ROCK, HIGHLAND PARK, MOUNT WASHINGTON & LINCOLN HEIGHTS

Once you cross that picturesque Colorado St Bridge, the conservative, old California vibration that permeates Pasadena fades into a groovy nook of working-class LA. There are some renovated and downright tony Spanish-style homes and California bungalows tucked into a bowl that rests between the last gasp of the Santa Monicas and the stark rise of the San Gabriel foothills, but for the most part Eagle Rock is about left-leaning Occidental college, and the regular Dodger-loving, Laker-rooting masses. Tough yet laid-back, cool in a completely unpretentious way, Eagle Rock is low on sights but worth checking out if you're doing the Pasadena museum disco.

The best thing you can do here is eat pizza at **Casa Bianca** (☎323-256-9617; 1650 Colorado Blvd; ☺dinner Tue-Sat; 🖶). LA food scribe Jonathan Gold has this square-cut, thin-crust pie, originally conceived in 1955, as one of his '99 Things to Eat in LA Before You Die.' He suggests ordering yours topped with fried eggplant and sweet-and-spicy homemade sausage. Casa Bianca is open until midnight midweek, until 1am on weekends, and there's usually a wait. Nearby **Fatty's & Co** (☎323-254-8804; 1627 Colorado Blvd; ☺dinner Thu-Sun;✎ 🖶) is a far trendier, all-vegetarian wine and foodie place.

Mt Washington and Highland Park wrap around the Arroyo Seco, a rocky riverbed running from the San Gabriel Mountains to Downtown LA. It was flooded with artists and architects in the early 20th century, but lost its idyllic setting with the arrival of I-110 (Pasadena Fwy) in 1940. Of late, though, there's been an artistic revival and the area is slowly becoming the go-to place for contemporary Latino art. About two-dozen galleries now belong to the **Northeast Los Angeles Arts Organization** (NELAart; www.nelaart.com). They keep their doors open late during Gallery Night every second Saturday of the month. Galleries are too scattered to be explored on foot, so plan on driving or hop on a bicycle for the free **Spoke(n) Art Tour** (http://bikeoven. com/spokenart).

Other area attractions spotlight pre-metropolitan LA. Eight Victorian beauties saved from the wrecking ball were airlifted here to become the **Heritage Square Museum** (www.heritagesquare.org; 3800 Homer St; adult/6-12yr/senior $10/5/8; ☺noon-4pm Fri-Sun), just off the Ave 43 exit of I-110 (Pasadena Fwy). You're free to walk around the grounds for close-ups of several impressive residences, including the way-cool Octagon House, a Methodist church and a carriage barn. The interiors of five of the eight structures can only be seen on tours offered on Saturday and Sunday on the hour from noon to 3pm (included in the admission price).

Another oldie is the 1910 **Lummis House** (www.socalhistory.org; 200 E Ave 43 at Carlota Blvd; admission free; ☺noon-4pm Fri-Sun), the former home of writer, librarian and Arts and Crafts pioneer Charles Lummis. It was built largely by hand using local boulders and old rails. Inside is a small exhibit on Lummis, who also founded LA's oldest museum, the nearby **Southwest Museum of the American Indian** (www.southwest museum.org; 234 Museum Dr; 🅿🖶), which rests on the shoulders of steep, leafy Mt Washington. It was recently undergoing massive restoration and remains closed to the public. The exhibits, which include British Colombian totem poles, petroglyph shards and 250 varieties of basketry, were currently living at the Autry Museum of the American West.

But there is still one massive highlight on that hill. When Parmanhansa Yogananda first came to LA in the 1920s to spread his yoga love and multi-denominational light, he set up shop at the original **Self Realization Fellowship** (www.yogananda -srf.org; 3880 San Rafael Ave; ☺9am-5pm; 🅿🖶) in Mt Washington. It remains a working monastery, with plenty of sitting areas in the garden, which offer stunning views of the downtown skyline. The house doors are also open. Peek into the library where you'll find a number of books by 'yogiji', as he's affectionately called, his old specs, robe and tablas, as well as tomes from great philosophers and poets from Plato and Dostoevsky to Gandhi (one of his contemporaries). The meditation chapel is open to all comers, and it is said that if you sit in an area where Yogananda sat for a prolonged period, you may feel his calming vibration. Word is that every night before bed he sipped tea on that sofa by the fireplace.

Lincoln Heights is another historically working-class neighborhood wedged on either side of the LA River north of Chinatown, with a main drag on Broadway. You'll notice a touch of the Highland Park art scene here, but these days this Lincoln Heights is best known for the collective of experimental DJs who are bridging the gap between improvisational jazz and psychedelic dubstep at the weekly **Low End Theory** (www.lowendtheoryclub.com; 2419 N Broadway Ave; 18 & over cover $10; ☺10pm-2am Wed) club at the Airliner. But don't expect jazzanova remixes of late great horn blowers. Here, jazz is an idea, a mode of thought, a way of mashing industrial and harmonic sounds. The club was founded by resident DJs Daddy Kev and Gaslamp Killer, and has recently gained notoriety for launching the great Flying Lotus into the international limelight.

❶ Information

Emergency

Emergency (☎911) For police, fire or ambulance service.

Police (☎877-275-5273) For nonemergencies within the city of LA.

Rape & Battering Hotline (☎800-656-4673; ⊗24hr)

Internet Access

For general information about internet access, see p457. Internet cafes in LA seem to have the lifespan of a fruit fly, but dozens of cafes and restaurants around town offer free wi-fi.

Libraries

There are public libraries everywhere, but the ones we've listed here are the largest and best. All of them offer free internet and wi-fi access, carry international periodicals, have special reading rooms for kids' and host readings and cultural events.

Beverly Hills Library (www.bhpl.org; 444 N Rexford Dr; ⊗10am-9pm Mon-Thu, to 6pm Fri & Sat, noon-5pm Sun; ℗⊛)

Hollywood Library (www.lapl.org; 1623 Ivar Ave, Hollywood; ⊗10am-8pm Mon-Thu, to 6pm Fri & Sat, 1-5pm Sun; ℗⊛)

Richard Riordan Central Library (www.lapl. org; 630 W 5th St, Downtown; ⊗10am-8pm Mon-Thu, to 6pm Fri & Sat, 1-5pm Sun; ℗⊛) Also see p204.

Santa Monica Library (www.smpl.org; 601 Santa Monica Blvd, Santa Monica; ⊗10am-9pm Mon-Thu, to 5:30pm Fri & Sat, 1-5pm Sun; ℗⊛)

Media

KCRW 89.9 FM (www.kcrw.com) LA's cultural pulse, the best station in the city beams National Public Radio (NPR); eclectic and indie music, intelligent talk, and hosts shows and events throughout Southern California. Also see p96.

KPFK 90.7 FM (www.kpfk.org) Part of the Pacifica radio network; news and progressive talk.

La Opinión (www.laopinion.com) Spanish-language daily.

LA Weekly (www.laweekly.com) Free alternative news, terrific live music and entertainment listings, and the mothership for Jonathan Gold – the only food critic ever to win a Pulitzer.

Los Angeles Downtown News (www.down-townnews.com) It has its finger on the cultural, political and economic pulse of the booming downtown district.

Los Angeles Magazine (www.losangeles magazine.com) Glossy lifestyle monthly with a useful restaurant guide.

Los Angeles Sentinel (www.losangeles sentinel.com) African American weekly.

Los Angeles Times (www.latimes.com) Major daily newspaper.

Medical Services

Cedars-Sinai Medical Center (☎310-423-3277; www.csmc.edu; 8700 Beverly Blvd, West Hollywood; ⊗24hr emergency room; ℗)

LA County/USC Medical Center (☎323-226-2622; www.doctorsofusc.com; 1200 N State St, Downtown; ⊗24hr emergency room; ℗)

Rite Aid Pharmacies (☎800-748-3243; www. riteaid.com)

Ronald Reagan UCLA Medical Center (☎310-825-9111; www.uclahealth.org; 757 Westwood Plaza, Westwood; ⊗24hr emergency room; ℗)

Venice Family Clinic (☎310-392-8636; www. venicefamilyclinic.org; 604 Rose Ave, Venice) Good for general health concerns, with payment on a sliding scale according to your means.

Women's Clinic (☎310-203-8899; www. womens-clinic.org; Suite 500, Century City, 9911 W Pico Blvd; ℗) Fees are calculated on a sliding scale according to your capacity to pay.

Money

American Express (☎310-659-1682; 8493 W 3rd St; ⊗9am-6pm Mon-Fri, 10am-3pm Sat)

Travelex Santa Monica (☎310-260-9219; www.travelex.com; 400 Wilshire Blvd; ⊗9am-5:30pm Mon-Fri); West Hollywood (☎310-659-6093; US Bank, 8901 Santa Monica Blvd; ⊗9am-5:30pm Mon-Fri, to 1pm Sat)

Post

Call ☎800-275-8777 for the nearest post office branch.

Tourist Information

Beverly Hills (Map p132; www.lovebeverly hills.org; 239 S Beverly Dr; ⊗8:30am-5pm Mon-Fri)

Downtown LA (Map p70; www.discover losangeles.com; 333 S Hope St; ⊗8:30am-5pm Mon-Fri)

El Pueblo Visitors Center (www.lasangelitas. org; Sepulveda House, 622 N Main St; ⊗10am-3pm)

Hollywood (Map p86; ☎323-467-6412; Hollywood & Highland complex, 6801 Hollywood Blvd; ⊗10am-10pm Mon-Sat, to 7pm Sun) In the Kodak Theatre walkway.

Long Beach (Map p178; www.visitlongbeach. com; 3rd fl, One World Trade Center; ⊗11am-7pm Sun-Thu, 11:30am-7:30pm Fri & Sat Jun-Sep, 10am-4pm Fri-Sun Oct-May)

Marina del Rey (www.visitthemarina.com; 4701 Admiralty Way; ⊙10am-4pm)

Pasadena (Map p188; www.visitpasadena.com; 300 E Green St; ⊙8am-5pm Mon-Fri, 10am-4pm Sat)

Santa Monica (www.santamonica.com) Information Kiosk (Map p152; 1400 Ocean Ave; ⊙9am-5pm Jun-Aug, 10am-4pm Sep-May); Visitors Center (Map p152; 1920 Main St; ⊙9am-6pm) Roving information officers patrol the promenade on Segways too!

West Hollywood (Map p110; www.visitwesthollywood.com; Suite M-38, Pacific Design Center blue bldg, 8687 Melrose Ave; ⊙8:30am-5:30pm Mon-Fri)

Websites

www.at-la.com Web portal to all things LA.

www.blacknla.com Online directory for LA's African American community.

www.dailycandy.com Little bites from the stylish LA scene.

www.deependdining.com An LA foodie blog with street cred.

www.discoverlosangeles.com Official Convention and Visitors' Bureau website.

www.experiencela.com Excellent cultural calendar packed with useful public-transportation maps and trips.

www.gridskipper.com/travel/los-angeles Urban travel guide to the useful, offbeat, naughty and nice.

www.hiddenla.com A quirky blog with a tremendous Facebook page where LA locals post their favorite hidden jewels.

www.kcrw.com LA's public-radio beacon of good taste, real news and great music. It hosts several local live shows and events each month.

www.la.com Hip guide to shopping, dining, nightlife and events.

www.lalmanac.com All the facts and figures at your fingertips.

www.latinola.com Plugs you right into the Latino arts and entertainment scene.

www.laweekly.com LA's longtime alternative news source and the most comprehensive arts and entertainment listings available.

www.lonelyplanet.com/usa/los-angeles Lonely Planet's dedicated Los Angeles page offers lots of links and inspiration.

ⓘ Getting There & Away

Air

The main LA gateway is **Los Angeles International Airport** (LAX; www.lawa.org), a U-shaped, bilevel complex with nine terminals linked by the free **Shuttle A** leaving from the lower (arrival) level. Cabs and hotel and car-rental shuttles stop here as well. A free minibus for disabled people can be ordered by calling ☎310-646-6402. Ticketing and check-in are on the upper (departure) level. The hub for most international airlines is the Tom Bradley International Terminal.

Domestic flights operated by Alaska, American, Southwest, United and other major US airlines also arrive at **Bob Hope/Burbank Airport** (www.burbankairport.com), which is handy if you're headed for Hollywood, Downtown or Pasadena.

To the south, on the border with Orange County, the small **Long Beach Airport** (www.longbeach.gov/airport) is convenient for Disneyland and is served by Alaska, US Airways and Jet Blue.

Bus

The main bus terminal for **Greyhound** (www.greyhound.com; 1716 E 7th St) is in a grimy part of Downtown, so try not to arrive after dark. Take bus 18 to the 7th St subway station or bus 66 to Pershing Square Station, then hop on the Metro Rail Red Line to Hollywood or Union Station with onward service around town. Some Greyhound buses go directly to the terminal in **Hollywood** (Map p86; 1715 N Cahuenga Blvd) and a few also pass through **Pasadena** (Map p188; 645 E Walnut St) and **Long Beach** (1498 Long Beach Blvd).

Car & Motorcycle

If you're driving into LA, there are several routes by which you might enter the metropolitan area.

From San Francisco and Northern California, the fastest route to LA is on I-5 through the San Joaquin Valley. Hwy 101 is slower but more picturesque, while the most scenic – and slowest – route is via Hwy 1 (Pacific Coast Hwy, or PCH).

From San Diego and other points south, I-5 is the obvious route. Near Irvine, I-405 branches off I-5 and takes a westerly route to Long Beach and Santa Monica, bypassing Downtown LA entirely and rejoining I-5 near San Fernando.

From Las Vegas or the Grand Canyon, take I-15 south to I-10, then head west into LA. I-10 is the main east–west artery through LA and continues on to Santa Monica.

Train

Amtrak trains roll into Downtown's historic **Union Station** (Map p70; 800 N Alameda St). Interstate trains stopping in LA are the *Coast Starlight* to Seattle, the *Southwest Chief* to Chicago and the *Sunset Limited* to Orlando. The *Pacific Surfliner* travels daily between San Diego and Santa Barbara via LA.

① Getting Around

To/From the Airport

All services mentioned below leave from the lower terminal level. Practically all airport-area hotels have arrangements with shuttle companies for free or discounted pick-ups. Door-to-door shuttles, such as those operated by **Prime Time** (☏800-733-8267; www.primetimeshuttle. com) and **Super Shuttle** (☏800-258-3826; www.supershuttle.com), charge $15, $26 and $16 for trips to Santa Monica, Hollywood or Downtown, respectively.

Curbside dispatchers will be on hand to summon a taxi for you. The flat rate to Downtown LA is $42, while going to Santa Monica costs around $30, to Hollywood around $45 to $50 and to Disneyland $90.

Public transportation has become a lot easier since the arrival of **LAX FlyAway** (www.lawa. org; ⏱5am-1am). These buses travel nonstop to Downtown's Union Station ($7, 45 minutes), Van Nuys ($7, 45 minutes), and Westwood Village near UCLA ($5, 30 minutes). To get to Hollywood, connect to the Metro Red Line subway at Union Station ($5.25; 1¼ hours).

For Santa Monica or Venice, catch the free Shuttle C bus to the **LAX Transit Center** (96th St & Sepulveda Blvd), then change to the Santa Monica Rapid 3 (75¢, one hour). The center is the hub for buses serving all of LA. If you're headed for Culver City, catch Culver City bus 6 ($1, 20 minutes). For Manhattan or Hermosa Beach, hop aboard Beach Cities Transit 109 ($1), which also stops at Lot G. For Redondo Beach head to Lot C and hop the Metro Local 232. Trip-planning help is available at www.metro.net.

The **Disneyland Resort Express** (☏714-978-8855; http://grayline anaheim.com/airport_info.html) travels hourly or half-hourly from LAX to the main Disneyland resorts for $20 one way or $30 round-trip for adults. Round-trips for families are $99.

Bicycle

Most buses have bike racks, and bikes ride for free, although you must securely load and unload them yourself. Bicycles are also allowed on Metro Rail trains except during rush hour (6:30am to 8:30am and 4:30pm to 6:30pm Monday to Friday).

BEDDING DOWN BEFORE TAKEOFF

If you get into LAX late or have to catch an early flight, you'll probably want to stay near the airport. But how to avoid generic, beige-box blandness? We've cased the area and found these stylish shut-eye zones. All have free shuttle buses to the airport.

Custom Hotel
HOTEL $$

(☏310-645-0400; www.customhotel.com; 8639 Lincoln Blvd; r $99-179; P@☎☒) This hip new kid in town occupies a mid-century tower by Welton Beckett (who also drafted the crafty Capital Records Tower in Hollywood). The streamlined design scheme and poolside tapas bar might just radiate enough urban poshness to appeal to the style patrol, and it throws Sunday pool parties too. Parking costs $25.

Renaissance Montura Hotel
HOTEL $$

(☏310-337-2800; www.mariott.com; 9620 Airport Blvd; r $115-239; P@☒) Old-world European sophistication and grace combine with American amenities at this reasonably stylish and ultracomfy haven. Rooms aren't huge, but they have granite desks and end tables and seriously lush bedding. Parking is $24.

Sheraton Gateway
HOTEL $$$

(☏310-642-1111, 800-325-3535; www.sheratonlosangeles.com; 6101 W Century Blvd; r $179-265; P@☎) There's way more style here than you could ever expect from the brand name and blocky exterior, but this self-contained resort, with its eye-candy design, intimate, boutique-style service and above-average eateries, makes an ideal setting for that bout of agoraphobia that sometimes strikes at the start of a long journey. Parking costs $30.

Belamar Hotel
HOTEL $$

(☏310-750-0300; www.thebelamar.com; 3501 Sepulveda Blvd, Manhattan Beach; r $179-329; P☎☒) If it were in Hollywood, this designer hotel would be hipster central. But it's five minutes from Manhattan Beach and 10 minutes from the airport, so it's often overlooked. Still, a decent rate buys stylish digs, superb beds and easy access to a nature trail to the beach for jogging off your jet lag.

Angelenos live and die by their freeways and sooner or later you too will end up part of this metal cavalcade. It helps to know that most freeways have both a number and a name, which corresponds to where they're headed. However, to add to the confusion, freeways passing through Downtown LA usually have two names. The I-10, for instance, is called the Santa Monica Fwy west of the central city and the San Bernardino Fwy east of it. The I-5 heading north is the Golden State Fwy, heading south it's the Santa Ana Fwy. And the I-110 is both the Pasadena Fwy and the Harbor Fwy. Generally, freeways going east–west have even numbers, those running north–south have odd numbers. Except for the 110 that is. Hmmm...

Car & Motorcycle

Unless time is no factor – or money is extremely tight – you're going to want to spend some time behind the wheel, although this means contending with some of the worst traffic in the country. Avoid rush hour (7am to 9am and 3:30pm to 6pm).

Parking at motels and cheaper hotels is usually free, while fancier ones charge anywhere from $8 to $30 for the privilege. Valet parking at nicer restaurants and hotels is commonplace with rates ranging from $3.50 to $10.

For local parking suggestions, see the introductions to individual neighborhoods.

The usual international car-rental agencies have branches at LAX and throughout LA (see p466 for toll-free reservation numbers) and there are also a couple of companies renting hybrid vehicles. If you don't have a prebooking, use the courtesy phones in the arrival areas at LAX. Offices and lots are outside the airport, but each company has free shuttles leaving from the lower level.

For Harley rentals, go to **Eagle Rider** (☎888-600-6020; www.eaglerider.com; 11860 S La Cienega Blvd, Hawthorne; ☺9am-5pm), just south of LAX, or **Route 66** (☎310-578-0112, 888-434-4473; www.route66riders.com; 4161 Lincoln Blvd, Marina del Rey; ☺9am-6pm Tue-Sat, 10am-5pm Sun & Mon). Rates start from $140 per day, and there are discounts for longer rentals.

Public Transportation

Most public transportation is handled by **Metro** (www.metro.net), which offers trip-planning help through its website.

The regular base fare is $1.50 per boarding or $6 for a day pass with unlimited rides. Weekly passes are $20 and valid from Sunday to Saturday. Monthly passes are $75 and valid for one calendar month.

Single tickets and day passes are available from bus drivers and vending machines at each train station. Weekly and monthly passes must be bought at one of 650 locations around town, including Ralphs, Vons and Pavilions supermarkets (call or see the website for the one nearest you).

METRO BUSES Metro operates about 200 bus lines, most of them local routes stopping every few blocks. Metro Rapid buses stop less frequently and have special sensors that keep traffic lights green when a bus approaches. Commuter-oriented express buses connect communities with Downtown LA and other business districts and usually travel via the city's freeways.

METRO RAIL This is a network of five light-rail lines and two subway lines, with five of them converging in Downtown. A sixth light-rail line, the Expo Line linking Exposition Park and Downtown LA with Culver City, is expected to open by summer 2011, with an extension reaching the beach in Santa Monica by 2015.

Red Line The most useful for visitors! It's a subway linking Downtown's Union Station to North Hollywood (San Fernando Valley) via central Hollywood and Universal City; connects with the Blue Line at the 7th St/Metro Center station in Downtown and the Metro Orange Line express bus at North Hollywood.

Blue Line Downtown to Long Beach; connects with the Red Line at 7th St/Metro Center station and the Green Line at the Imperial/Wilmington stop.

Gold Line East LA to Chinatown and Pasadena via Union Station, Mt Washington and Highland Park; connects with the Red Line at Union Station.

Green Line Norwalk to Redondo Beach; connects with the Blue Line at Imperial/Wilmington.

Purple Line Subway between Downtown LA and Koreatown; shares six stations with the Red Line.

Orange Line Links Downtown and Hollywood with the west San Fernando Valley; connects with the Red Line in North Hollywood.

Silver Line Links USC and Exposition Park with Downtown LA, where it connects with the Red Line at Union Station.

Metro Rail System

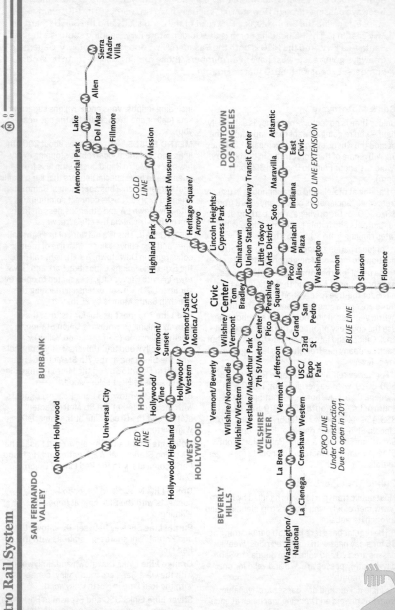

10 km
6 miles

SAN FERNANDO VALLEY

BURBANK

North Hollywood

Universal City

RED LINE

HOLLYWOOD

WEST HOLLYWOOD

Hollywood/Highland

Hollywood/Vine

Hollywood/Western

Vermont/Sunset

Vermont/Santa Monica/LACC

Vermont/Beverly

Vermont/Western

Wilshire/Normandie

Wilshire/Western

WILSHIRE CENTER

Westlake/MacArthur Park

7th St/Metro Center

Wilshire/Vermont

Civic Center/Tom Bradley

BEVERLY HILLS

Washington/National

La Cienega

La Brea

Crenshaw

Western

Vermont

USC/Expo Park

Jefferson

23rd St

Grand

Pico

San Pedro

Pershing Square

*EXPO LINE
Under Construction
Due to open in 2011*

BLUE LINE

DOWNTOWN LOS ANGELES

Memorial Park

Lake

Del Mar

Allen

Fillmore

Sierra Madre Villa

Mission

GOLD LINE

Southwest Museum

Highland Park

Heritage Square/Arroyo

Lincoln Heights/Cypress Park

Chinatown

Union Station/Gateway Transit Center

Little Tokyo/Arts District

Pico/Aliso

Mariachi Plaza

Soto

Indiana

Maravilla

East Civic

Atlantic

GOLD LINE EXTENSION

Washington

Vernon

Slauson

Florence

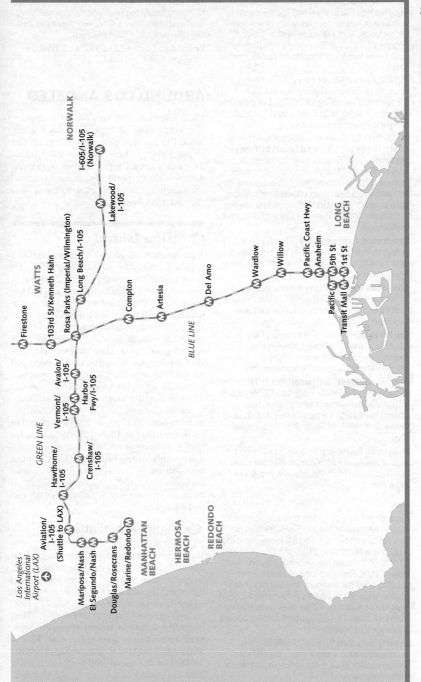

MUNICIPAL BUSES Santa Monica-based **Big Blue Bus** (BBB; www.bigbluebus.com) burns clean fuel and serves much of western LA, including Santa Monica, Venice, Westwood and LAX (75¢). Its express bus 10 runs from Santa Monica to Downtown ($1.75, one hour).

The **Culver CityBus** (www.culvercity.org) provides service throughout Culver City and the Westside, including LAX (75¢). **Long Beach Transit** (www.lbtransit.com) serves Long Beach and surrounding communities.

DASH BUSES These small clean-fuel shuttle buses, run by the **LA Department of Transportation** (LADOT; www.ladottransit.com), operate along 33 routes serving local communities (25¢ per boarding), but only until 7pm and with limited services on weekends. Many lines connect with other DASH routes; see the website for details. Here are some of the most useful lines:

Beachwood Canyon Route (Monday to Saturday) Useful for close-ups of the Hollywood sign; runs from Hollywood Blvd and Vine St up Beachwood Dr.

Downtown Routes (daily) Six separate routes hit all the hot spots, including Chinatown, City Hall, Little Tokyo, the Financial District and Exposition Park.

Fairfax Route (Monday to Saturday) Makes a handy loop past the Beverly Center mall, the Pacific Design Center, western Melrose Ave, the Farmers Market/Grove and Museum Row.

Hollywood/West Hollywood Route (Monday to Saturday) Connects Hollywood & Highland with the Sunset Strip, the shopping zone around the Pacific Design Center, the Beverly Center and south of Beverly on Robertson Blvd.

Hollywood Route (daily) Covers Hollywood east of Highland Ave and links with the short Los Feliz Route (daily) at Franklin Ave & Vermont Ave.

Taxi

Because of LA's size and its traffic, getting around by cab will cost you. Cabs are best organized over the phone, though some prowl the streets late at night, and they are always lined up at airports, train stations, bus stations and major hotels. Fares are metered and vary depending upon the company and the city they're registered in. In the city of LA, rates are $2.85 at flagfall plus about $2.70 per mile. Cabs leaving from LAX charge a $2.50 airport fee. For details, check www.taxicabsla.org.

Beverly Hills Cab (☎800-273-6611; www.beverlyhillscabco.com) A solid, dependable company, with good rates to the airport and a wide service area.

Taxi Taxi (☎310-444-4444; www.santamonicataxi.com) Easily the best and most professional fleet available. They'll drive you anywhere, but can only pick up in Santa Monica.

Yellow Cab (☎877-733-3305; www.layellowcab.com) If all else fails.

AROUND LOS ANGELES

Make like Jack Kerouac, ditch the congestion, crowds and smog, and use LA as a hub to all the natural glory of California. Get an early start to beat the commuter traffic (or catch a ferry, Greyhound bus or ride the Amtrack rails), point the compass across the ocean, up into the mountains or into the vast and imposing desert.

Catalina Island

Mediterranean-flavored Catalina Island is a popular getaway for harried Angelenos, but sinks under the weight of day-trippers in summer. Stay overnight, though, and feel the ambience go from frantic to romantic. Catalina has a unique ecosystem and has gone through stints as a hangout for sea-otter poachers, smugglers and Union soldiers. It was snapped up by chewing-gum magnate William Wrigley Jr (1861–1932) in 1919, and for years he sent his Chicago Cubs baseball team here for spring training. Today most of it is owned by the Santa Catalina Island Conservancy. Commercial activity is concentrated in Avalon, small enough to be explored in an hour or two, so there's plenty of time for hiking, swimming and touring.

The only other settlement, even tinier than Avalon, is Two Harbors in the remote backcountry, which has only a general store, a dive and kayak center, a snack bar and a lodge.

☉ Sights & Activities

It's a nice stroll along the waterfront to the 1929 art-deco **Casino** (1 Casino Way), which has well-done murals, a movie theater with a twinkling ceiling and a fabulous upstairs ballroom; the last can only be seen on guided one-hour tours (adult/child $31/23). Tickets also include admission to the modest but insightful **Catalina Island Museum** (www.catalinamuseum.org; adult/child/senior $5/2/4; ☉10am-4pm Oct-May, to 5pm Jun-Sep closed Thu Jan-Mar) in the same building. Continuing past the casino takes you to the privately owned **Descanso Beach**, where you can fork over $2 to lie in the grass or sand, get sloshed at the bar, or go snorkeling. There's good snorkeling at **Lovers' Cove** and at **Casino Point Marine Park**, a marine reserve that's also the best shore dive. Another way to escape the throngs is by kayaking to the quiet coves along Catalina's rocky coastline. **Descanso Beach Ocean Sports** (www.kayakcatalinaisland.com; rentals per hr/day from $18/64) rents snorkeling gear and kayaks, and also runs guided kayaking tours and kayak camping trips.

About 1.5 miles inland from Avalon harbor is the peaceful **Wrigley Memorial & Botanical Gardens** (☎310-510-2595; 1400 Avalon Canyon Rd; adult/child $5/free; ⊗8am-5pm), where you'll enjoy sweeping garden views from a monument awash in colorful local tile. Wrap up the day with a luxurious massage, facial or mud wrap at **A Touch of Heaven** (☎800-300-8528; www.hotel-metropole.com).

To get into the protected backcountry, hop on the **Safari Bus** (☎310-510-2800; tickets $10-30; ⊗mid-Jun–early Sep), which goes all the way to Two Harbors. You must book in advance and get a permit (and maps) from the **Catalina Conservancy** (☎310-510-2595; www.catalinaconservancy.org; 125 Claressa Ave, Avalon; biking/hiking $35/free) if you're going to be hiking or mountain biking. There are 200 miles of scenic trails (including the 37.2-mile Trans-Catalina trail), but very little shade, so bring a hat, sunscreen and plenty of water.

Alternatively, you could just hop on an air-conditioned tour bus and let someone else show you around. Both **Catalina Adventure Tours** (www.catalinaadventuretours.com; adult/child from $17/13.25) and **Discovery Tours** (www.visitcatalina.com; adult/child from $43/33) operate historical Avalon itineraries, and jaunts further out with memorable views of the rugged coast, deep canyons and sandy coves, and possible encounters with eagles and a herd of bison left behind after a 1924 movie shoot. Discovery Tours also offers a new California Zip Line Eco Tour (two hours, per person $92.50), leading you from an altitude of 500ft down to sea level in five zips – including a 1045ft line that will have you humming at 45mph.

Certified scuba divers should find **Catalina Dive Shop** (www.catalinadiveshop.com; Lovers Cove; per trip $89-119) to glimpse local shipwrecks and kelp forests. It rents snorkel gear here too. **Two Harbors Dive and**

Recreation Center (www.visitcatalinaisland.com; 1/2 tanks $59/89) accesses pristine dive sites off the island's less-developed coast.

🛏 Sleeping

Rates soar on weekends and between May and September, and at other times are about 30% to 60% lower than what's listed below. For camping information, see www.visitcatalinaisland.com/avalon/camping.php.

Hotel Metropole   BOUTIQUE HOTEL **$$$**
(☎800-300-8528; www.hotel-metropole.com; 205 Crescent Ave; r $249-849) The newest and grooviest spot in Avalon. Ocean Front rooms are huge with wood floors, fireplaces, soaker tubs and spectacular blue sea views. Design is more classic California than edgy, and that works perfectly on this island.

Villa Portofino   INN **$$$**
(☎310-510-0555; www.hotelvillaportofino.com; 111 Crescent Ave; r $448-912) Comfortable and kissed with a touch of Mediterranean elegance. The suites are the smart play here. There are gas fireplaces and bay-view sundecks.

La Paloma & Las Flores   INN **$$**
(☎310-510-0737, 800-310-1505; www.lapalomalasflores.com; 328 Sunny Lane; r $79-249; 🐾) Choose from Old Catalina cottages or newer, pricier apartments with two-person spas and balconies. Most are bright and cheery.

Hermosa Hotel & Cottages   INN **$**
(☎877-453-1313; www.hermosahotel.com; 131 Metropole St; r $75-250) Central, clean, tidy – your only budget pick on the island.

🍴 Eating

Catalina Country Club Restaurant
                      CALIFORNIAN FUSION **$$$**
(☎310-510-7404; www.visitcatalina.com; 1 Country Club Dr; appetizers $8-15, mains $21-31; ⊗dinner Thu-Mon) The Country Club name implies a certain pressed-tablecloth, ironed-shirt formality. The dining is more free-wheeling, ranging from ahi towers to a daily risotto to bone-in New York steaks.

M   NEW AMERICAN **$$**
(☎310-510-8404; www.hotel-metropole.com; Metropole Marketplace; appetizers $7-10, mains $16-29; ⊗lunch & dinner) The newest joint in town crafts creative plates – such as zucchini risotto or duck breast and oyster mushrooms coated in blood orange molasses – from fresh, seasonal and local ingredients.

Cottage DINER $
(www.menu4u.com/thecottage; 603 Crescent
Ave; sandwiches & burgers $8-11; ☺breakfast,
lunch & dinner) Huge breakfasts, sandwiches and American, Italian and Mexican favorites are served here.

Casino Dock Café CAFE $$
(www.casinodockcafe.com; 1 Casino Way;
appetizers $6-12, sandwiches, burgers & hot
dogs $4-10; ☺breakfast & lunch) Casual
waterfront hangout, good for a beer and a
simple meal.

❶ Information

Tourist office (www.catalina.com) On the
Green Pier.

❶ Getting There & Away

The following companies operate ferries to
Avalon and Two Harbors. Reservations are rec-
ommended in the summer.

Catalina Express (www.catalinaexpress.com;
adult/child round-trip $67/51) Ferries to Avalon
from San Pedro, Long Beach and Dana Point
in Orange County and to Two Harbors from
San Pedro. It takes one to 1½ hours, with up to
three ferries daily.

Catalina Marina del Rey Flyer (www.catalina
ferries.com; adult/under 12yr round-trip
$83/64) Catamaran to Avalon and Two Harbors
from Marina del Rey in LA (one to 1½ hours).

Catalina Passenger Service (www.catalina
info.com; adult/child round-trip $68/51). Cata-
maran to Avalon from Newport Beach in Orange
County (1¼ hours, once daily).

Six Flags Magic Mountain & Hurricane Harbor

About 30 miles north of LA, right off the I-5
(Golden State Fwy), velocity is king at Six
Flags Magic Mountain (www.sixflags.com/
parks/magicmountain; 26101 Magic Mountain
Parkway, Valencia; adult/child under 4ft & seniors
$60/33; P☺), a daredevil roller-coaster
park that has had its own financial ups and
downs lately and almost got sold off to land
developers in 2006. Fortunately, operators
decided to hang on to it, so for now you can
still go up, down and inside out faster and
in more baffling ways than anywhere else
besides a space shuttle. Parking is $15.

Teens and college kids get their jollies
on the 16 bone-chilling roller coasters, in-
cluding the aptly named **Scream**, which
goes through seven loops, including a zero-
gravity roll and a dive loop, with you sitting

in a floorless chair. If you've got a stomach
of steel, don't miss **X2**, where you ride in
cars that spin 360 degrees while hurtling
forward and plummeting all at once. Note
that many rides have height restrictions
ranging from 36in to 58in. However, fami-
lies need not worry as there are plenty of
tamer rides for the elementary-school set,
plus shows, parades and concerts to keep
everyone entertained.

Still, on hot summer days, little ones
might be more in their element next door
at **Six Flags Hurricane Harbor** (www.six
flags.com/parks/hurricaneharborla; 26101 Magic
Mountain Parkway; adult/child under 4ft & senior
$30/20; ☺). At this jungle-themed 22-acre
water park you can chill in a tropical lagoon,
brave churning wave pools and plunge down
wicked high-speed slides with names like
Reptile Ridge and Taboo Tower.

Check the website for packages or dis-
counts and for opening hours, which vary
throughout the year. If you don't have your
own vehicle, look for organized tour flyers
in your hotel.

Big Bear Lake

Big Bear Lake is a low-key and family-
friendly mountain resort (elevation 6750ft)
about 110 miles northeast of LA. Snowy
winters lure scores of ski bunnies and
boarders to its two mountains, while sum-
mers bring hikers, mountain bikers and
water-sports enthusiasts wishing to escape
the stifling heat down in the basin. Even
getting here via the spectacular, curvy and
panorama-filled **Rim of the World Drive**
(Hwy 18) is a treat.

🏃 Activities

Big Bear's two ski mountains are jointly
managed by **Big Bear Mountain Resorts**
(www.bigbearmountainresorts.com; adult lift ticket
Mon-Fri half/full-day $39/49, Sat & Sun $50/62).
The higher of the two, **Bear Mountain**
(8805ft) is nirvana for freestyle freaks with
over 150 jumps, 80 jibs, and two pipes in-
cluding a 580ft in-ground superpipe. **Snow
Summit** (8200ft) is more about traditional
downhill and has trails for everyone. Alto-
gether the mountains are served by 14 lifts
and crisscrossed by over 31 runs. Ski and
boot rentals are about $30. After a day on
the slopes, prevent muscle fatigue with an
expert massage by **Mountain Mobile Mas-
sage** (☎909-800-8103; www.bigbearmassage.

com; 30/60min $55/85); a therapist will come to you.

In summer Snow Summit issues its siren call to mountain bikers. Several pro and amateur races take place here each year. The nine-mile **Grandview Loop** is great for getting your feet in gear. The **Scenic Sky Chair** (one way/day $12/25; ⊘May–start of ski season) provides easy access to the top. Maps, tickets and bike rentals are available from **Bear Valley Bikes** (www.bvbikes.com; 40298 Big Bear Blvd; bikes per hr incl helmet $10-20, per day $40-70). It charges higher rates for full suspension.

Hiking is another major summer activity, as are swimming, jet skiing, kayaking, boating and fishing. Boating rentals are available along the lakeshore.

To get off the beaten track, take your car for an off-road spin along the **Gold Fever Trail**, a 20-mile self-guided romp on a graded dirt road around an old gold-mining area. If you prefer to let someone else do the driving, contact **Big Bear Off-Road Adventures** (☑909-585-1036; www.offroadadventure. com) for its tour schedule.

🛌 Sleeping & Eating

Knickerbocker Mansion   BED & BREAKFAST **$$**
(☑909-878-9190, 877-423-1180; www.knicker bockermansion.com; 869 Knickerbocker Rd; r $145-240; P@) A classy, ornate B&B in a hand-built 1920s log home, secluded from the tourist fray. It has great breakfasts, tasty Friday- and Saturday-night dinners, and asks a two-night minimum stay on weekends.

Castlewood Theme Cottages   CABINS **$$**
(☑909-866-2720; www.castlewoodcottages.com; 547 Main St; cabins $199-299; P@�

) Bored with bland motel rooms? Your fantasies can go wild in these well-crafted, clean and amazingly detailed cabins, complete with Jacuzzi tubs and costumes. Let your inner Tarzan roar, fancy yourselves Robin and Marian or Antony and Cleopatra, or cavort amongst woodland fairy-folk or an indoor waterfall. It's cheesy, wacky and, oddly, fun. Kids are not allowed.

Grey Squirrel Resort   CABINS **$$**
(☑909-866-4335,   800-381-5569; www.grey squirrel.com; 39372 Big Bear Blvd; cabins $78-375; P�

≋) Set amid the pines, here's a clump of delightful cabins, some with a fireplace, sundeck and Jacuzzi.

Big Bear Hostel   HOSTEL **$**
(☑909-866-8900; www.adventurehostel.com; 527 Knickerbocker Rd; r $24-49; P@�

) Clean and friendly hostel on the edge of the village run by people happy to clue you in about the best trails, runs and all things extreme. Linens are provided, but BYOT (towel).

Grizzly Manor Cafe   DINER **$**
(41268 Big Bear Blvd; dishes $10; ⊘breakfast; P[+]) One-man grillmeister Jayme makes bear-sized breakfasts for quirky locals and the tourists who love them.

Kujo's   CAFE **$**
(www.kujosrestaurant.com; 41799 Big Bear Blvd; dishes $5-15; ⊘breakfast, lunch & dinner; P�

[+]) Soul- and energy-restoring pit stop with 30 varieties of homemade quiche, ginormous sandwiches and a killer Roquefort burger. It has a wine bar too.

Peppercorn Grille   AMERICAN **$$**
(☑909-866-5405; www.peppercorngrille.com; 553 Pine Knot Ave; mains $8.95-15.95; ⊘lunch & dinner) Locals and visitors alike swear by the Italian-inspired American fare for a fancy meal in the village.

ℹ Information

Big Bear Blvd (Hwy 18), the main road, runs south of the lake, skirting the pedestrian-friendly village with cutesy shops, galleries, restaurants and the **visitors center** (www.big bear.com; 630 Bartlett Rd; ⊘8am-5pm Mon-Fri, 9am-5pm Sat & Sun). The ski resorts are east of the village. Quiet N Shore Dr (Hwy 38) provides access to campgrounds and trails.

If you're driving, pick up a National Forest Adventure Pass, available at the **Big Bear Discovery Center** (www.bigbeardiscoverycenter.com; 40971 N Shore Dr, Fawnskin; ⊘8am-4:30pm, closed Wed & Thu mid-Sep–mid-May) on the North Shore.

ℹ Getting There & Away

Big Bear is on Hwy 18, an offshoot of Hwy 30 in San Bernardino. A quicker approach is via Hwy 330, which starts in Highland and intersects with Hwy 18 in Running Springs. If you don't like serpentine mountain roads, pick up Hwy 38 near Redlands, which is longer but easier on the queasy. **Mountain Area Regional Transit Authority** (Marta; ☑909-878-5200; www.marta. cc) buses connect Big Bear with the Greyhound and Metrolink stations in San Bernardino ($2.50, 1¼ hours).

Disneyland & Orange County

Best Places to Stay

» Shorebreak Hotel (p240)

» Disney's Grand Californian Hotel & Spa (p222)

» Montage (p257)

» Bay Shores Peninsula Hotel (p248)

» Crystal Cove Cottages (p254)

Best Places to Eat

» Walt's Wharf (p236)

» Napa Rose (p224)

» 242 Cafe Fusion Sushi (p258)

» Bear Flag Fish Co (p249)

» Filling Station (p232)

Why Go?

Never underestimate the power of the boob tube. With the successes of Bravo's *Real Housewives*, MTV's *Laguna Beach* and Fox's *The OC*, Orange County has gone from humdrum to hip. Glamorous teens, gorgeous beaches and socialite catfights have forced King Mickey to share the OC's spotlight. But the mouse isn't worried. He knows today's trash-watching teens will soon grow up, get married and bring their kiddies to Disneyland too.

Today three million people and 34 independent cities jostle for space in Orange County's 789 sq miles, a huge swath of real estate stretching south from LA to San Diego. And while there's a whiff of truth to those stereotypical images of life behind the 'Orange Curtain' – big, boxy mansions, fortress-like shopping malls, conservatives tossing Happy Meals out of their Humvees – there are deep pockets of individuality, beauty and open-mindedness keepin' the OC 'real.'

When to Go

Anaheim

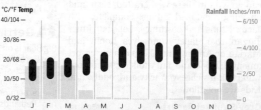

May Visitation dips after spring break until Memorial Day. Mostly sunny days, balmy temperatures.

July & August Summer vacation and beach season peak. Surfing and art festivals by the coast.

September Blue skies, cooler temperatures inland, fewer crowds. Tall Ships Festival at Dana Point.

DISNEYLAND & ANAHEIM

POP 337,900

Mickey is one lucky mouse. Created by animator Walt Disney in 1928, this irrepressible rodent caught a ride on a multimedia juggernaut (film, TV, publishing, music, merchandising and theme parks) that rocketed him into a global stratosphere of recognition, money and influence. Plus, he lives in the 'Happiest Place on Earth,' a slice of 'imagineered' hyper-reality where the streets are always clean, the employees – called 'cast members' – are always upbeat and there are parades every day of the year.

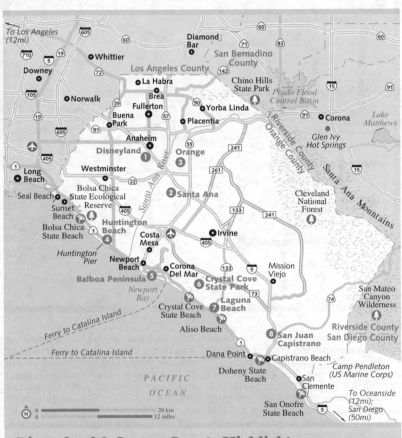

Disneyland & Orange County Highlights

1 Meeting Mickey and screaming your head off on Space Mountain at **Disneyland** (p215), then catching the fireworks show

2 Fighting outrageous bed hair inside the eye of a hurricane at the **Discovery Science Center** (p231)

3 Shopping for vintage treasures and slurping milkshakes from a soda fountain in **Old Towne Orange** (p232)

4 Building a beach bonfire after a day of surfing killer waves at **Huntington Beach** (p238)

5 Cycling past the as-seen-on-TV sands of Newport Beach's **Balboa Peninsula** (p245)

6 Falling asleep to the sound of the surf inside an oceanfront cottage at **Crystal Cove State Beach** (p254)

7 Watching the sun dip below the horizon from the bluff-tops of art-filled **Laguna Beach** (p254)

8 Being awed by the Spanish colonial history and the beauty of **Mission San Juan Capistrano** (p261)

DISNEYLAND & ORANGE COUNTY DISNEYLAND & ANAHEIM

It would be easy to hate the guy, but since opening his Disneyland home in 1955, he has been a pretty thoughtful host to millions of guests. There are a few potholes on Main St – every ride seems to end in a gift store, prices are sky-high and there are grumblings that management could do more about affordable housing and health insurance for employees – but even the most determined grouch should find something to warrant a grin. For the more than 14 million kids, grandparents, honeymooners and international tourists who visit every year, Disneyland remains a magical experience.

For a guide to planning your Disneyland trip, including tips on saving money, beating the lines, accommodating people with disabilities and general advice, see p34.

History

Having celebrated its 55th anniversary, Disneyland still aims to be the 'Happiest Place on Earth,' an expression coined by Walt Disney himself when the 'theme park' (another Disney-ism) first opened on July 17, 1955. Carved out of Anaheim's orange and walnut groves, the park's construction took just one year. Disneyland's opening day was a disaster, however. Temperatures over 100°F melted asphalt underfoot, leaving women's high heels stuck in the tar. There were plumbing problems: all of the drinking fountains quit working. Hollywood stars didn't show up on time, and more than twice the number of expected guests – some 28,000 by day's end – crowded through the gates, some holding counterfeit tickets. But none of this kept eager Disney fans away for long, as more than 50 million tourists visited in its first decade alone.

During the 1990s, Anaheim, the city surrounding Disneyland, undertook a staggering $4.2 billion revamp and expan-

Disneyland & Anaheim

sion, cleaning up run-down stretches and establishing the first police force in the US specifically to guard tourists (they call it 'tourist-oriented policing'). The cornerstone of the five-year effort was the addition of a second theme park in 2001, Disney's California Adventure (DCA). Adjacent to the original Disneyland, the amusement park was designed to pay tribute to the state's most famous natural landmarks and cultural history. More recently added was Downtown Disney, an outdoor pedestrian mall. The ensemble is called the Disneyland Resort.

Meanwhile, access roads near the parks were widened, landscaped and given the lofty name of Anaheim Resort. In 2008, Anaheim GardenWalk opened just east of the parks. This outdoor mall, though lacking personality, creates more options for sit-down dining and entertainment in the Disney-adjacent neighborhood.

◉ Sights & Activities

Both parks are open 365 days a year. During peak summer season, Disneyland's hours are usually 8am to midnight; the rest of the year, 10am to 8pm or 10pm. DCA closes at 10pm or 11pm in summer, earlier in the off-season.

One-day admission to *either* Disneyland or DCA currently costs $76 for adults and $68 for children aged three to nine. To visit *both* parks in one day costs $101/91 per adult/child. An entry ticket includes admission to all of the parks' individual rides and attractions. For more information on buying tickets, discounts and deals, as well as the best times to go, see p34.

DISNEYLAND PARK

While the 'Happiest Place on Earth' designation is debatable, it's hard to deny the perceptible change in atmosphere as you're whisked by tram from the outside world into the heart of the resort. Wide-eyed children lean forward with anticipation while stressed-out parents sit back, finally relaxing. Uncle Walt's in charge, and he's taken care of every possible detail.

Walk through the gates of Disneyland and along the red-brick path – suggestive of a red carpet – a floral Mickey Mouse blooms before you. A sign above the nearby archway reads 'Here you leave today and enter the world of yesterday, tomorrow and fantasy.' It's an apt but slightly skewed greeting that's indicative of the upbeat, slightly skewed 'reality' of the park itself – a reality that's an undeniable delight to the millions of children who visit every year. This is their park, but adults who can willingly suspend disbelief and give in to the 'magic of Disney' may have just as much fun.

Main Street USA   RIDES, ATTRACTIONS

Fashioned after Walt's hometown of Marceline, Missouri, bustling Main St, USA resembles the classic turn-of-the-20th-century all-American town. It's an idyllic, relentlessly upbeat representation, complete with barbershop quartet, penny arcades, ice cream shops and a steam train. The music playing in the background is from American musicals, and there's a flag-retreat ceremony every afternoon. There's plenty of shopping here too.

One Day

Get to **Disneyland** early. Stroll **Main Street USA** toward **Sleeping Beauty's Castle**. Enter **Tomorrowland** to ride **Space Mountain**. In **Fantasyland** don't miss the classic **It's a Small world** ride. Race down the **Matterhorn Bobsleds** or take tots to **Mickey's Toontown**. Grab a Fastpass for the **Indiana Jones Adventure** or **Pirates of the Caribbean** before lunching in **New Orleans Square**. Plummet down **Splash Mountain**, then visit the **Haunted Mansion** before the **fireworks** and **Fantasmic!** shows begin.

Two Days

At **Disneyland's California Adventure**, take a virtual hang-gliding ride on **Soarin' Over California** and let kids tackle the **Redwood Creek Challenge Trail** before having fun at **Paradise Pier**, with its roller coaster, Ferris wheel and carnival games. Watch the Pixar Play Parade, then explore **Cars Land** or cool off on the **Grizzly River Run**. After dark, drop by the **Twilight Zone Tower of Terror** and **World of Color** show.

Three Days

Escape the mouse house for more thrills-a-minute at **Knott's Berry Farm** theme park or educational family fun at the **Discovery Science Center**. Sans kids, take a spa day at **Club Mud**, then go vintage shopping in **Old Towne Orange**, appreciate art at the **Bowers Museum** or eat your way through **Little Saigon**.

Great Moments with Mr Lincoln, a 15-minute audio-animatronic presentation on Honest Abe, sits inside the fascinating **Disneyland Story** exhibit. Oh, and it's air-conditioned. Take time out to watch the video of comedian Steve Martin narrating Disneyland's history with vintage film footage. Nearby, kids love seeing old-school Disney cartoons like *Steamboat Willie* inside **Main Street Cinema**.

Main St ends in the **Central Plaza**. Lording over the plaza is **Sleeping Beauty Castle**, the castle featured on the Disney logo. Inside the iconic structure (fashioned after a real 19th-century Bavarian castle), dolls and big books tell the story of Sleeping Beauty. As if you didn't know it already.

Tomorrowland   RIDES, ATTRACTIONS

How did 1950s imagineers envision the future? As a galaxy-minded community filled with monorails, rockets and Googie-style architecture, apparently. In 1998 this 'land' was revamped to honor three timeless futurists – Jules Vern, HG Wells, and Leonardo da Vinci – while major corporations like Microsoft and HP sponsor futuristic robot shows and interactive exhibits in the **Innoventions** pavilion.

The retro high-tech **monorail** glides to a stop in Tomorrowland, its rubber tires traveling a 13-minute, 2.5-mile round-trip route to Downtown Disney. Right away, kiddies will want to shoot laser beams on **Buzz Lightyear's Astro Blaster** adventure. Then jump aboard the **Finding Nemo Submarine Voyage**. Look for Nemo from within a refurbished submarine and rumble through an underwater volcanic eruption.

The recently reimagineered **Star Tours** clamps you into a Starspeeder shuttle for a wild and bumpy 3D ride through the desert canyons of Tatooine on a space mission with several alternate storylines, so you can ride it again and again. **Space Mountain**, Tomorrowland's signature attraction and one of the USA's best roller coasters, hurtles you into complete darkness at frightening speed. Another classic is **Captain EO**, a special-effects tribute film, starring none other than Michael Jackson.

Fantasyland   RIDES, ATTRACTIONS

Behind Sleeping Beauty Castle, Fantasyland is filled with the characters of classic children's stories. If you only see one attraction in Fantasyland, visit **It's a Small World**, a boat ride past hundreds of creepy animatronic children from different cultures all singing the annoying theme song in an astounding variety of languages, now joined by Disney characters. Another classic, the **Matterhorn Bobsleds** is a steel-frame roller coaster that mimics a bobsled ride down a mountain. Fans of old-school attractions will also get a kick out of the *Wind in the Willows*-inspired **Mr Toad's Wild Ride**, a loopy jaunt in an open-air jalopy through London. Younger kids love whirling around the **Mad Tea Party** teacup ride and **King Arthur Carousel**, then cavorting with characters in nearby **Mickey's Toontown**, a topsy-turvy minimetropolis where kiddos can traipse through Mickey and Minnie's houses.

Frontierland RIDES, ATTRACTIONS
Arrgh matey! Captain Jack Sparrow and his pirate crew have hijacked an American classic. Frontierland's Tom Sawyer Island – the only attraction in the park personally designed by Uncle Walt - has been reimagined in the wake of the *Pirates of the Caribbean* movies. Renamed the **Pirate's Lair on Tom Sawyer Island**, the island now honors Tom in name only. After a raft ride to the island, wander among roving pirates, cannibal cages, ghostly apparitions and buried treasure. Or just cruise around the island on the **Mark Twain Riverboat**, a Mississippi-style paddle wheel boat, or the 18th-century replica **Sailing Ship Columbia**. The rest of Frontierland gives a nod to the rip-roarin' Old West with a shooting gallery and **Big Thunder Mountain Railroad**, a mining-themed roller coaster.

Adventureland RIDES, ATTRACTIONS
Adventureland loosely derives its jungle theme from Southeast Asia and Africa. The hands-down highlight is the safari-style **Indiana Jones Adventure**. Enormous Humvee-type vehicles lurch and jerk their

---

IS IT A SMALL WORLD AFTER ALL?

Pay attention to the cool optical illusion along Main Street USA. As you look from the entrance up the street toward Sleeping Beauty Castle, everything seems far away and bigger-than-life. When you're at the castle looking back, everything seems closer and smaller – a technique known as forced perspective, a trick used on Hollywood sets where buildings are constructed at a decreasing scale to create an illusion of height or depth. Welcome to Disneyland.

---

way through the wild for spine-tingling encounters with creepy crawlies and scary skulls in re-creations of stunts from the famous film trilogy. Nearby, little ones love climbing the stairways of **Tarzan's Treehouse**. Cool down with a **Jungle Cruise**, as exotic animatronic animals from the Amazon, Ganges, Nile and Irrawaddy Rivers jump out and challenge your boat's skipper. Even if you don't stay for the South Seas show, at least walk into the vintage **Enchanted Tiki Room** to look at the carvings of Hawaiian gods and goddesses.

New Orleans Square RIDES, ATTRACTIONS
Adjacent to Adventureland, New Orleans Square has all the charm of the French Quarter but none of the marauding drunks. New Orleans was Walt's and his wife Lillian's favorite city, and Walt paid tribute to it by building this stunning square. **Pirates of the Caribbean** is the longest ride in Disneyland (17 minutes) and provided 'inspiration' for the popular movies. Real human skeletons from the UCLA Medical Center were used as props when the attraction first opened in 1967 because Disney's versions didn't look real enough. Today you'll float through the subterranean haunts of tawdry pirates, where dead buccaneers perch atop their mounds of booty and Jack Sparrow pops up occasionally. Over at the **Haunted Mansion**, 999 'happy haunts' – spirits, goblins, shades and ghosts – appear and evanesce while you ride in a cocoonlike 'Doom Buggy' through web-covered graveyards of dancing skeletons.

DISNEYLAND FASTPASS ATTRACTIONS

» Autopia (Tomorrowland)

» Big Thunder Mountain Railroad (Frontierland)

» Buzz Lightyear Astro Blasters (Tomorrowland)

» Indiana Jones Adventure (Adventureland)

» Roger Rabbit's Car Toon Spin (Mickey's Toontown)

» Space Mountain (Tomorrowland)

» Splash Mountain (Critter Country)

DON'T MISS

THE WHAMMY

Have you gotten the Disneyland whammy yet? Don't worry, it's not a hex that cast members put on you for cutting in line. It's what fanatics call riding all three of Disneyland's 'mountain' rides – Splash Mountain, Space Mountain and the Big Thunder Mountain Railroad – in one day. Overachievers can jump on the Matterhorn Bobsleds for extra credit.

Critter Country   RIDES, ATTRACTIONS

Tucked behind the Haunted Mansion, Critter Country's main attraction is **Splash Mountain**, a flume ride that transports you through the story of Brer Rabbit and Brer Bear, based on the controversial 1946 film *Song of the South*. Right at the big descent, a camera snaps your picture. Some visitors lift their shirts, earning the ride the nickname 'Flash Mountain,' though R-rated pics are destroyed. Just past Splash Mountain, hop in a mobile beehive on **The Many Adventures of Winnie the Pooh**. Nearby on the Rivers of America, you can paddle **Davy Crockett's Explorer Canoes** on summer weekends.

DISNEY'S CALIFORNIA ADVENTURE

Across the plaza from Disneyland's monument to fantasy and make-believe is Disney's California Adventure (DCA), an ode to Californian geography, history and culture – or at least a sanitized G-rated version. DCA, which opened in 2001, covers more acres than Disneyland and feels less crowded, even on summer weekend afternoons. If the original theme park leaves you feeling claustrophobic and jostled – or gasp! bored – you'll like this park better, with its more modern rides and attractions.

DCA's entrance was designed to look like an old-fashioned painted-collage postcard. After passing under the Golden Gate Bridge, you'll arrive at **Sunshine Plaza**, where a 50ft-tall sun made of gold titanium 'shines' all the time (heliostats direct the rays of the real sun onto Disney's version). In 2012, Sunshine Plaza will be replaced by an homage to a 1920s Los Angeles streetscape, complete with a red trolley running down the street into what will be renamed 'Hollywoodland.'

Hollywood Pictures Backlot
                                      RIDES, ATTRACTIONS

California's biggest factory of dreams is Tinseltown, presented here in miniature, complete with soundstages, movable props, and – of course – a studio store. If you arrive early in the day, you'll have an unobstructed look at the forced-perspective **mural** at the end of the street, a sky-and-land backdrop that looks, at least in photographs, like the street keeps going. Very cool.

The big attraction, however, is the **Twilight Zone Tower of Terror**, a 13-story drop down an elevator chute situated in a haunted hotel – one eerily resembling the historic Hollywood Roosevelt Hotel in Los Angeles. From the upper floors of the tower, you'll have views of the Santa Ana mountains, if only for a few heart-

---

DISNEYLAND FIREWORKS, PARADES & SHOWS

Magical, the fireworks spectacular above Sleeping Beauty's Castle, happens nightly around 9:30pm in summer. (In winter, artificial snow falls on Main Street USA after the fireworks.) The extremely short **Celebrate! A Street Party** parade down Main Street USA is forgettable, though.

At the **Princess Fantasy Faire** in Fantasyland, your little princesses and knights can join the Royal Court and meet some Disney princesses. Storytelling and coronation ceremonies happen throughout the day in summer. Younglings can learn to harness 'The Force' at Tomorrowland's **Jedi Training Academy**, which accepts Padawans several times daily in peak season.

Fantasmic!, an outdoor extravaganza on Disneyland's Rivers of America, may be the best show of all, with its full-size ships, lasers and pyrotechnics. Arrive early to scope a spot – the best are down front by the water – or reserve balcony seats in New Orleans Square. Book reserved seating (☎714-781-4400, adult/child $59/49) up to 30 days in advance.

pounding seconds. Less brave children can navigate a taxicab through 'Monstropolis' on the **Monsters, Inc: Mike & Sulley to the Rescue!** ride heading back toward the street's beginning.

Hot enough for ya? Slip into the cool air-conditioned **Muppets 3D** theater for a special-effects film. Then learn how to draw like Disney in the **Animation Academy**, discover how cartoon artwork becomes 3D at the Character Close-Up or simply be amazed by the interactive Sorcerer's Workshop, all housed inside the **Animation Building**.

Expect some changes when this theme-park area is reimagineered as 'Hollywoodland' in 2012.

Golden State RIDES, ATTRACTIONS

Just off Sunshine Plaza, Golden State is broken into sections highlighting California's natural and human achievements. **Condor Flats** recognizes the aerospace industry. Its main attraction, **Soarin' Over California**, is a virtual hang-gliding ride using Omnimax technology that lets you float over landmarks such as the Golden Gate Bridge, Yosemite Falls, Lake Tahoe, Malibu and, of course, Disneyland itself. Enjoy the light breeze as you soar, keeping your nostrils open for the smell of the sea, orange groves and pine forests blowing in the wind. **Grizzly River Run** takes you 'rafting' down a faux Sierra Nevada river – you *will* get wet, so come when it's warm. While fake flat-hatted park rangers look on, kids can tackle the **Redwood Creek Challenge Trail**, with its 'Big Sir' redwoods, wooden towers and lookouts, and rock slide and climbing traverses. Tamer attractions include tours of the **Boudin Bakery** and **Mission Tortilla Factory** and behind-the-scenes looks at what's in the works next for Disneyland's theme parks inside **Walt Disney Imagineering Blue Sky Cellar**.

Paradise Pier RIDES, ATTRACTIONS

If you like carnival rides, you'll love Paradise Pier, designed to look like a combination of all the beachside amusement piers in California. The state-of-the-art **California Screamin'** roller coaster resembles an old wooden coaster, but it's got a smooth-as-silk steel track: it feels like you're being shot out of a cannon. Awesome. Just as popular is **Toy Story Mania**, a 4D ride with lots of old-fashioned arcade games. Want a bird's-eye view of the park? Head to **Mickey's**

DCA FASTPASS ATTRACTIONS

» California Screamin' (Paradise Pier)

» Grizzly River Run (Golden State)

» Soarin' Over California (Golden State)

» Twilight Zone Tower of Terror (Hollywood Pictures Backlot)

» World of Color (Paradise Pier)

Fun Wheel, a 15-story Ferris wheel where gondolas pitch and yaw (unless you've requested one of the stationary ones). Nearby, **Silly Symphony Swings** is a hybrid carousel with tornado-like chair swings, while **Goofy's Sky School** is a cute, cartoon-themed coaster ride.

Cars Land RIDES, ATTRACTIONS

Look for this brand-new area of DCA, designed around the popular Pixar movie *Cars* and expected to open sometime in 2012. Take a tractor ride through **Mater's Junkyard Jamboree**, steer your bumper car through **Luigi's Roamin' Tires** or ride along with the wacky **Radiator Springs Racers**. Route 66–themed gift shops and diners will take on that special glow of nostalgia underneath neon lights in the evening.

🛏 Sleeping

For valuable tips on picking the right hotel for your Disney experience, see p37. If you want a theme-park hotel for less money, try Knott's Berry Farm (p230).

DISNEYLAND RESORT

Each of the resort's **hotels** (☑reservations 714-956-6425, 800-225-2024; www.disneyland. com) has a swimming pool with a water-slide, kids' activity programs, a fitness center, restaurants and bars, and a business center with internet-connected computers, and offers valet and a complimentary self-parking area for registered guests. Every standard air-con room can accommodate up to five guests and has a mini-refrigerator and a coffeemaker. Staying at one of Disney's resort hotels may also get you early admission to the parks. To save money, book a vacation package that includes theme-park admission tickets online at www.disneyland.com.

ℹ FLYING SOLO

If you're here alone, ask the staff at the entrance to park rides if a single-rider line is available, where you wait in a separate, shorter line. Availability may depend on the size of the crowd – and also on how that particular cast member is feeling that day, so be nice! Disneyland's single-rider attractions include the ever-popular Indiana Jones Adventure and Splash Mountain. At DCA, look for single-rider lines at Soarin' Over California, California Screamin' and the Grizzly River Run.

TOP CHOICE Disney's Grand Californian Hotel & Spa   HOTEL $$$

(☎714-635-2300; www.disneyland.com; 1600 S Disneyland Dr; r $265-745; @🛜🏊♿) Soaring timber beams rise above the cathedral-like lobby of the six-story Grand Californian, Disney's homage to the Arts and Crafts architectural movement. Rooms have cushy amenities, such as triple-sheeted beds, down pillows, bathrobes and all-custom furnishings. Outside there's a faux-redwood waterslide into the pool. At night, kids wind down with bedtime stories by the lobby's giant stone hearth. For a little adult pampering, your coconut rub and milk ritual wrap awaits at the Mandara Spa. Even if you're not staying here, a brief respite in the astounding lobby is a must (and totally acceptable). Enter from DCA or Downtown Disney.

Disney's Paradise Pier Hotel   HOTEL $$$

(☎714-999-0990; www.disneyland.com; 1717 S Disneyland Dr; r $250-370; @🛜🏊♿) Sunbursts, surfboards and a giant superslide are all on deck at the Paradise Pier Hotel, the cheapest, but maybe the most fun, of the Disney hotel trio. Kids will love the beachy decor, not to mention the rooftop pool and the tiny-tot video room filled with mini Adirondack chairs. Rooms are just as spotlessly kept as at the other hotels and are decorated with colorful fabrics and custom furniture. The hotel connects directly to DCA. Request a room overlooking Paradise Bay's World of Color show.

Disneyland Hotel   HOTEL $$$

(☎714-778-6600; www.disneyland.com; 1150 Magic Way; r $210-395; @🛜🏊♿) Built in 1955, the year Disneyland opened, the park's original hotel seems in need of a dash of bibbidi-bobbidi-boo. Staff seem a little less happy-go-lucky here, and the rooms – though good-sized – are more tired than inspired. But this 990-room convention-friendly hotel hasn't turned into a pumpkin yet; it's redeemed by the best swimming pool of the three Disney hotels, plus cartoon character–themed Signature Suites. The monorail to Tomorrowland stops right outside, just a short walk from Downtown Disney.

ANAHEIM

Anaheim gets the most business from Disneyland tourism, but it's also a year-round convention destination. Room rates spike accordingly, so rates quoted below fluctuate. Most motels and hotels offer packages

---

DON'T MISS

DCA SHOWS & PARADES

DCA's premier show is **World of Color,** a dazzling nighttime display of lasers, lights and animation projected over Paradise Bay. It's so popular, you'll need a Fastpass ticket (see p228). Otherwise, reserved seating (☎714-781-4400, per person $15) includes a picnic meal; make reservations up to 30 days in advance. Tip: If you're here in summer and have a park-hopper ticket, see World of Color first, then head over to Disneyland for the fireworks and to catch the later show or Fantasmic!

During the day, don't miss the **Pixar Play Parade**, led by hot-rodder Lightning McQueen from *Cars* and featuring energetic, even acrobatic appearances by characters from other popular animated movies like *Monsters, Inc, The Incredibles, Ratatouille, Finding Nemo* and *Toy Story*. Be prepared to get squirted by aliens wielding water hoses.

DCA's other live entertainment includes minimusical extravaganzas like *Aladdin* and *Toy Story*, based on movies. Check out what's playing at the **Hyperion Theater** on the Hollywood Studios Backlot. Arrive 30 to 60 minutes early to get good seats.

including tickets to Disneyland or other local attractions. Ask about family-friendly suites that sleep five or more people. Some hotels offer free Disneyland shuttles, or you can ride Anaheim Resort Transit's frequent shuttles from many area hotels.

Candy Cane Inn
MOTEL $$

(☎714-774-5284, 800-345-7057; www.candycaneinn.net; 1747 S Harbor Blvd; r $95-179; ☎☀) You'll find more than candy canes at this oh-so-cute motel, with welcoming grounds bursting with gorgeous blooms. Rooms have all mod cons, plus down comforters and plantation shutters. The hotel is adjacent to Disneyland's main gate, so you can zip back after lunch for a swim and a nap. It's a top value choice and booking a year in advance is advised.

⭐ TOP CHOICE Hotel Ménage
BOUTIQUE HOTEL $$

(☎888-462-7275; www.hotelmenage.com; 1221 S Harbor Blvd; r $75-130; @☎☀) Who cares that it's in the shadow of the freeway? This stylish hotel pulls off a sophisticated vibe that's perfect after a day of running around the mouse house. Earth-tone sofas, leather headboards, plasma TVs and sunflower showerheads all make this your personal oasis – it's worth splurging on high-ceilinged 'studio loft' rooms and a poolside cabana. The hotel's trendy K'ya Restaurant serves globally spiced street food.

Alpine Inn
MOTEL $$

(☎714-535-2186, 800-772-4422; www.alpineinnanaheim.com; 715 W Katella Ave; r $60-190, ste $95-300; ☎☀) Connoisseurs of kitsch will hug their Hummels over this snow-covered chalet sporting an A-frame exterior and icicle-covered roofs – framed by palm trees, of course. Right on the border of DCA, the inn also has Ferris wheel views. Air-con rooms are aged but clean.

Anabella
HOTEL $$

(☎714-905-1050, 800-863-4888; www.anabellahotel.com; 1030 W Katella Ave; r $89-155, ste $99-169; @☎☀) Formerly three separate motels, this 7-acre complex has the feel of a laid-back country club, complete with trams that carry guests effortlessly from the lobby to their buildings. Air-con rooms have a whisper of Spanish Colonial style, with extras like minifridges and TV entertainment systems. Bunk-bedded kids' suites have Disney-inspired decor. Grab a 'Tangerita' cocktail on the poolside patio. Parking is $11.

YOU SAY IT'S YOUR BIRTHDAY...

If you're visiting on a special day and want to embrace the Disney experience whole-mouse, stop by Main Street USA's **City Hall** to pick up some ornamental flair in the form of oversize buttons celebrating birthdays, anniversaries, 'Just Married' and more.

Ayres Hotel
HOTEL $$

(☎714-634-2106, 800-595-5692; www.ayreshotels.com; 2550 E Katella Ave; r $120-140; @☎☀) Orange County's minichain of business hotels delivers solid-gold value. Air-con rooms possess a modicum of French country style, with velvet curtains, mahogany furnishings and pillowtop mattresses, and rates include a full breakfast. It's about a 10-minute drive east of Disneyland, near the train station.

Camelot Inn & Suites
MOTEL $$

(☎714-635-7275, 800-828-4898; www.camelotanaheim.com; 1520 S Harbor Blvd; r $110-179, ste $190-269; @☎☀🛏) Looking a bit like King Arthur's castle from the outside, this five-story motel has minifridges and microwaves in every air-con room, plus on-site laundry, a small wading pool and hot tub, and a kids' game room and video arcade. You can walk to Disneyland in 10 minutes. Some top-floor rooms have fireworks views.

Carousel Inn & Suites
MOTEL $$

(☎714-758-0444, 800-854-6767; www.carouselinnandsuites.com; 1530 S Harbor Blvd; r $119-139; @☎☀) Just over the wall from Disneyland, this four-story air-con motel makes an effort to look good, with upgraded furnishings, pillowtop mattresses and flowerpots hanging from the exterior corridors' wrought-iron railings. The rooftop pool has great views of Disneyland's fireworks.

Park Vue Inn
MOTEL $$

(☎714-772-3691, 800-334-7021; www.parkvueinn.com; 1570 S Harbor Blvd; r $105-149; @☎☀) This two-story motel looks worn due to the rotating hordes of families. But standard rooms come with air-con, microwaves and minifridges, and downstairs there's an outdoor pool and hot tub. It's almost opposite Disneyland's main gate.

TOP FIVE THEME-PARK AREAS FOR YOUNG KIDS

» Fantasyland (Disneyland)
» Mickey's Toontown (Disneyland)
» Critter Country (Disneyland)
» Paradise Pier (DCA)
» Cars Land (DCA)

HI Fullerton
HOSTEL $$

(☎714-738-3721, 800-909-4776; www.hi hostels.com; 1700 N Harbor Blvd, Fullerton; dm $22-25; ☺mid-Jun–mid-Sep; @🛜) Situated on a former dairy farm six miles north of Disneyland, this two-story hacienda houses 20 beds in three variations of air-con dorms (male, female, mixed), as well as all the usual youth-hostel amenities. Rates include continental breakfast and parking. Public transportation available.

Best Western Stovall's Inn
MOTEL $

(☎714-778-1880, 800-780-7234; www.bestwest ern.com; 1110 W Katella Ave; r $90-130; @🛜🏊) Remodeled contemporary motel rooms sparkle; all have air-con, a microwave and minifridge. Walk to Disneyland in 15 minutes. Parking $8. Another Best Western motel nearby, the Pavilions, is cheaper, but it's slightly further away from Disneyland.

Hotel Pepper Tree
MOTEL $

(☎714-774-7370, 877-888-5656; www.hotel peppertree.com; 2375 W Lincoln Ave; r $79-129, ste $119-159; 🛜🏊) A 15-minute drive northwest of Disneyland, this three-story extended-stay motel offers modest studio and one-bedroom suites with full kitchens and hand-carved wooden furniture. Outdoor heated pool. Weekly and monthly rates.

✗ Eating

For tips on dining with Disney, including making reservations, character meals and what you can bring into the parks, see p38. By driving just a couple of miles or so away, the variety improves – in retro Old Towne Orange (p232) or Little Saigon (p234), for starters. Or go exploring the Middle Eastern kebab shops and bakeries of Anaheim's Little Arabia, along Brookhurst St north of Ball Rd, a short drive west of Disneyland.

DISNEYLAND PARK

In the park itself, each 'land' has several places to eat, mostly fast-food stands and family-style restaurants. Don't expect miracles – all are overpriced, jam-packed and alas, the food's not great.

Blue Bayou
SOUTHERN $$$

(☎714-781-3463; New Orleans Square; mains $22-40; ☺lunch & dinner) Surrounded by the 'bayou' inside the Pirates of the Caribbean attraction, this is the top choice for sit-down dining in Disneyland Park and is famous for its Creole and Cajun specialties at dinner. Order fresh-baked pecan pie topped by a piratey souvenir for dessert.

Café Orleans
SOUTHERN $$

(New Orleans Square; mains $14-20; ☺lunch & dinner) The next best thing to Blue Bayou is this Southern-flavored restaurant, which is famous for its Monte Cristo sandwiches at lunch. Breakfast served seasonally.

Plaza Inn
AMERICAN $$

(Main Street USA; mains $13-16, breakfast buffet adult/child 3-9yr $28/14; ☺breakfast, lunch & dinner) Finger-lickin' good fried chicken platters come with mashed potatoes, buttermilk biscuits and veggies at this 1950s original. Fun breakfast buffet with Disney characters.

Carnation Cafe
AMERICAN $$

(Main Street USA; mains $9-12; ☺breakfast, lunch & dinner) Classic ice-cream parlor near the Disneyland entrance serves OK sandwiches, chicken pot pie, Matterhorn sundaes and Mickey-shaped breakfast waffles.

DISNEY'S CALIFORNIA ADVENTURE

Again, no surprise: it's mostly high-priced, low-quality theme-park fare. Look for new eateries opening along DCA's 'reimagineered' streetscape entrance in 2012.

Napa Rose
TOP CHOICE
CALIFORNIAN $$$

(☎714-781-3463; Grand Californian Hotel, 1600 S Disneyland Dr; mains $32-45; ☺dinner) Soaring windows, high-back Arts and Crafts–style chairs, leaded-glass windows and towering ceilings befit the Disneyland Resort's top-drawer restaurant. On the plate, seasonal 'California Wine Country' (read: NorCal) cuisine is as impeccably crafted as Sleeping Beauty's Castle. Kids' menu available. Reservations essential. Enter the hotel from DCA or Downtown Disney.

Wine Country Terrace   CALIFORNIAN **$$**
(Golden State, DCA; mains $13-17; ⊙lunch &
dinner) If you can't quite swing the Napa
Rose, this sunny Cal-Italian terrace res-
taurant is a fine backup. Fork into Italian
pastas, salads or veggie paninis. Decent
wine list.

Pacific Wharf Cafe   AMERICAN **$$**
(Golden State, DCA; mains $9-12; ⊙breakfast,
lunch & dinner) At least the hearty soups in
sourdough bread bowls, farmers-market
salads and deli sandwiches are pretty
filling.

DOWNTOWN DISNEY

The quarter-mile-long pedestrian mall that
is Downtown Disney feels longer than it
really is, mostly because it's packed with
stores, restaurants, entertainment venues
and, in summer, hordes of people. Most
restaurants are chains that accommodate
crowds. Call ahead for reservations.

For more bars and live-music venues that
also serve food, see p226.

Steakhouse 55   AMERICAN **$$$**
(☎714-781-3463; Disneyland Hotel, 1150 Magic
Way; mains $30-40, 3-course prix-fixe menu
$35; ⊙dinner) Nothing at Disneyland is ex-
actly a secret, but this grown-up hideaway
comes pretty darn close. Dry-rubbed bone-
in rib eye, Australian lobster tail, heirloom
potatoes and green beans with applewood-
smoked bacon uphold a respectable chop-
house menu. Kids' menu available. Good
wine list. The hotel is near the monorail,
at the far end of Downtown Disney.

Catal   CALIFORNIAN **$$$**
(☎714-774-4442; www.patinagroup.com; dinner
mains $18-40; ⊙breakfast & dinner) The chef
cooks up a fusion of Californian and Mediterranean cuisines (squid-ink pasta with
lobster, grilled ahi with curry sauce) at this
airy two-story restaurant decorated in a
sunny Mediterranean-Provençal style with
exposed beams and lemon-colored walls.
Sit on the balcony.

Compass Books Café   AMERICAN **$**
(snacks $3-8; ⊙7am-10pm Sun-Thu, 7am-11pm
Fri & Sat) Cozy bookstore has a take-out
counter serving light sandwiches, pastries, hot and iced espresso drinks, cookies, cheesecake and more.

Jamba Juice   TAKE-OUT **$**
(snacks $4-8; ⊙7am-11pm Sun-Thu, 7am-
midnight Fri & Sat) It's the fairest deal in all
of Disneyland: powerful fresh-fruit juices,

smoothies and frozen blends will lift your
sunburned spirit. Healthy snacks and
fruit-topped hot oatmeal for breakfast, too.

ANAHEIM

Most restaurants on the streets surrounding Disneyland are chains, like at the outdoor mall **Anaheim GardenWalk**. The mall
may be a long walk from Disneyland with
little ones (take the ART shuttle), but since
there are few other options in the vicinity,
we won't complain.

Tusca   CAL-ITALIAN **$$**
(☎714-750-1234; Hyatt Regency Orange
County, 11999 Harbor Blvd, Garden Grove; mains
$11-24; ⊙6:30am-2pm & 5-10pm) Anaheim's
cuisine scene is so bleak that we recom-
mend you dine inside a chain hotel. Bear
with us, though, because crispy handmade
pizzas, seasonally inspired pastas like
whole-wheat penne with wild mushrooms,
and succulent pork chops with roasted
lemon – all prepared by a northern Italian
chef – justify the detour. Fresh herbs and
veggies are even grown on the hotel's own
rooftop. Meanwhile, lobby-level **OC Brew-
house** pours California microbrews. Free
parking with restaurant validation.

Bangkok Spice   THAI **$**
(☎714-777-1583; 5031 E Orangethorpe Ave, cnr
Lakeview Ave; mains $7-13; ⊙11am-9:30pm Mon-
Sat) It's a 20-minute drive northeast of Dis-
neyland, but if you crave Thai food made
just like in the Land of Smiles, you've got to
visit this friendly strip-mall mom-and-pop
shop for rich curries, fresh savory salads
and strong iced coffee. It's about 2 miles off
Hwy 91 east of Anaheim (exit Lakeview Ave
northbound). Call if you get lost.

ⓘ TIRED TOOTSIES?

The miniature bio-diesel **Disneyland
Railroad** chugs in a clockwise circle
around Disneyland, stopping at Main
Street USA, New Orleans Square,
Mickey's Toon Town and Tomorrow-
land, taking about 20 minutes to make
a full loop. Between the Tomorrowland
and Main Street USA stations, look
out for **dioramas** of the Grand Canyon
and a Jurassic-style 'Primeval World.'
From Tomorrowland, you can catch
the zero-emissions monorail directly
to Downtown Disney.

TOP 10 RIDES FOR TEENS

» Indiana Jones Adventure (Adventureland)

» Space Mountain (Tomorrowland)

» Twilight Zone Tower of Terror (Hollywood Pictures Backlot, DCA)

» Splash Mountain (Critter Country)

» California Screamin' (Paradise Pier, DCA)

» Soarin' Over California (Golden State, DCA)

» Big Thunder Mountain Railroad (Frontierland)

» Grizzly River Run (Golden State, DCA)

» Matterhorn Bobsleds (Fantasyland)

» Buzz Lightyear Astro Blasters (Tomorrowland)

🍷 Drinking & Entertainment

DISNEYLAND RESORT

You can't buy any alcohol in Disneyland, but you can at DCA, Downtown Disney and Disney's trio of resort hotels. Too tired to venture too far from the mouse house? Downtown Disney offers bars, live music, a 12-screen cinema and more.

Uva Bar WINE BAR
(www.patinagroup.com; Downtown Disney) Named after the Italian word for grape, this bar resembling a Paris metro station is Downtown Disney's best outdoor spot to tipple wine, nibble Cal-Mediterranean *tapas* and people-watch. There are 40 wines available by the glass. Come for happy hour.

ESPN Zone SPORTS BAR
(www.espnzone.com; Downtown Disney) Show up early and score a personal leather recliner at this sports and drinking emporium with 175 TVs – flat-screens even hang above the men's-room urinals. Ball-park food and couch-potato classics make up an all-American menu. Families gravitate toward the virtual-reality and video-game arcade upstairs.

House of Blues NIGHTCLUB
(📞714-778-2583; www.houseofblues.com; Downtown Disney) HOB occasionally gets some heavy-hitting rock, pop, jazz and blues concerts. Call or check online for showtimes and tickets. Make reservations for Sunday's fun gospel brunch. But come for the music, not the food.

Golden Vine Winery BAR
(Disney's California Adventure) Centrally located terrace is a great place for relaxing and regrouping in DCA. Nearby at Pacific Wharf, walk-up window Rita's Margaritas whips up frozen cocktails.

Napa Rose Lounge LOUNGE
(Disney's Grand Californian Hotel) Raise a glass to Napa as you nosh on pizzettas, artisan cheese plates and Scharffen Berger chocolate truffle cake.

Ralph Brennan's New Orleans Jazz Kitchen BAR
(http://rbjazzkitchen.com; Downtown Disney) Hear live jazz combos on the weekends and piano weeknights at this resto-bar. Food quality is erratic.

AMC Downtown Disney 12 CINEMA
(📞888-262-4386; Downtown Disney) Every theater has stadium seating and shows new Hollywood releases. Free parking with theater validation.

AROUND ANAHEIM

Disney's cocoonlike atmosphere can make you forget there's a thriving city outside its walls where you can catch major-league sports games and live touring bands.

Grove of Anaheim CONCERT HALL
(📞714-712-2700; www.thegroveofanaheim.com; 2200 E Katella Ave) At this indoor 5000-seat venue, headliners from the Magnetic Zeros to Last Comic Standing appear, plus 'locally grown' rock bands. Sightlines are great. Call or check online for showtimes and tickets. Parking $10.

Honda Center STADIUM
(📞800-745-3000; www.hondacenter.com; 2695 E Katella Ave) The 2007 Stanley Cup winners, the Anaheim Ducks, play hockey from October to April at this indoor venue, formerly called Arrowhead Pond. Professional rodeo events, fight nights and megaconcerts round out the schedule. Tickets prices vary. Parking $15 to $20.

Angel Stadium STADIUM
(📞714-940-2000, 888-796-4256; www.angelsbaseball.com; 2000 Gene Autry Way) The controversially (and oh-so-awkwardly) named Los Angeles Angels of Anaheim play major-league baseball here from May to October. Single-game tickets start at $12. Parking $8.

Anaheim GardenWalk MALL

(☑714-635-7410; www.anaheimgardenwalk. com; 321 W Katella Ave) This dining, shopping and entertainment complex just east of Disneyland (take the ART shuttle) has a family-friendly bowling alley, cineplex and adults-only wine bar.

Block at Orange CINEMA, MALL

(☑714-769-4001; www.simon.com; 20 City Blvd W, Orange; ☎) Another megamall with a cineplex, Dave & Buster's video game arcade, Vans skate park and cool Lucky Strike Lanes for a round of beers, bowling and billiards. There's free wi-fi in the mall.

🔒 Shopping

DISNEYLAND PARK & DISNEY'S CALIFORNIA ADVENTURE

Each 'land' has its own shopping, appropriate to its particular theme, whether the Old West, Route 66 or a seaside amusement park. The biggest theme-park stores – Disneyland's **Emporium** (Main Street USA) and **Greetings from California** (DCA) have a mind-boggling variety of souvenirs, clothing and Disneyana, from T-shirts to mouse ears. Girls go wild at the **Bibbidi Bobbidi Boutique** (reservations ☑714-781-7895; Fantasyland), where princess makeovers – including hairstyle, makeup and gown – don't come cheap. For collectors, **Disney Gallery** (Main Street USA) and **Off the Page** (DCA) sell high-end art and collectibles like original sketches and vintage reproduction prints.

You don't have to carry your purchases around all day; store them at the Newsstand (Main Street USA), Star Trader (Tomorrowland), Pioneer Mercantile (Frontierland) or Engine Ear Toys (DCA). If you're staying at Disneyland, have packages sent directly to your hotel.

DOWNTOWN DISNEY

Most shops in Downtown Disney open and close with the parks.

Vault 28 CLOTHING, GIFTS

(Downtown Disney) From distressed T-shirts with edgy Cinderella prints to black tank tops patterned with white skulls, the hipster inventory is discombobulating. They stock a few familiar brands like Harajuku Lovers and Betsey Johnson, but it's the Disney-only boutique lines – Kingdom Couture and Disney Vintage – that really intrigue.

D Street CLOTHING, GIFTS

(Downtown Disney) Even wannabe gangstas, skate rats and surfers get their own store at Disney. If you've got tweens or teens, resistance is futile. Retro comic-book hero, Japanimation-style and graffiti-art tees hang on the racks next to urbanized Western wear and rockabilly dresses.

Island Charters CLOTHING, GIFTS

(Downtown Disney) Images of Earhart and Lindbergh come to mind wandering this travel-minded store complete with Tilly hats, bomber jackets, Tommy Bahama shirts and model planes.

World of Disney SOUVENIRS

(Downtown Disney) Pirates and princesses are hot at this minimetropolis of mouse-related merchandising. Don't miss the special room dedicated to Disney's villains – gotcha, Evil Queen! Grab last-minute must-haves here.

Compass Books BOOKS

(Downtown Disney) Decorated in the style of an old-school NYC Explorers' Club, high adventure feels nigh. Until then, browse best sellers, manga paperbacks and travel tomes from an independent local bookseller.

Kitson Kids CHILDREN

(Downtown Disney) An offshoot of the main store in LA, with heaps of clever T-shirts, shoes, books and toys (and few Disney logos, whew!).

ℹ️ Information

Before you arrive, consult our Disneyland Trip Planner (p37). For more help and up-to-date information about the parks, contact the **Disneyland Resort** (☑recorded info 714-781-4565, live assistance 714-781-7290; www.disneyland. com).

Internet Access

There's no internet access inside the theme parks.

FedEx Office (☑714-703-2250; 700 W Convention Way, Anaheim Convention Center, Anaheim Marriott; per min 20-30¢; ☺7am-10pm Mon-Fri, 9am-5pm Sat & Sun) Self-service online computer workstations.

Internet Resources

MousePlanet (www.mouseplanet.com) One-stop resource for all things Disney, with news updates, podcasts, trip reports, reviews and discussion boards.

LA Times Daily Deal Blog (http://travel.la times.com/daily-deal-blog) Browse the 'Theme Parks' category for breaking news about Disneyland and Anaheim travel.

FASTPASS

Even if you don't have a smartphone app (p229) to update you with current wait times at the theme parks' rides and attractions, you can still significantly cut your time in line with Fastpass.

» Walk up to a Fastpass ticket machine – located near the entrance to select theme park rides – and insert your park entrance ticket or annual passport. You'll receive a slip of paper showing the 'return time' for boarding (it's always at least 40 minutes later).

» Then show up within the window of time printed on the ticket and join the ride's Fastpass line, where a cast member will check your Fastpass ticket. There'll still be a wait, but it's shorter (typically 15 minutes or less). Hang on to your Fastpass ticket until you board the ride, just in case another cast member asks to check it.

» Even if you're running late and miss the time window printed on your Fastpass ticket, you can still try joining the Fastpass line. Cast members are rarely strict about enforcing the end of the time window, although showing up before your Fastpass time window is a no-no.

You're thinking, what's the catch, right? When you get a Fastpass, you will have to wait at least two hours before getting another one (check the 'next available' time printed at the bottom of your ticket). So, make it count. Before getting a Fastpass, check the display above the machine, which will tell you what the 'return time' for boarding is. If it's much later in the day, or doesn't fit your schedule, a Fastpass may not be worth it. Ditto if the ride's current wait time is just 15 to 30 minutes.

Some Disneyland fans have developed strategies for taking advantage of the Fastpass system. For example, for now there's nothing to prevent you from simultaneously getting Fastpasses at both parks. As long as you have a park-hopper ticket and don't mind doing a *lot* of walking between the two parks, you can bounce back and forth between a dozen or so of the most popular rides and attractions all day long.

Lonely Planet (www.lonelyplanet.com/usa/california/disneyland-and-anaheim) For planning advice, author recommendations, traveller reviews and insider tips.

Theme Park Insider (www.themeparkinsider.com) Newsy blog, travel tips and user reviews of Disneyland rides, attractions and lodging.

ScreamScape (www.screamscape.com) Independent views on theme-park news, developments and rumors.

Kennels

Kennels (☑714-781-7290; per animal per day $20) Just outside the theme parks' main entrance, indoor day-boarding (no overnights) for cats and dogs with proof of vaccinations.

Lockers

Self-service lockers with in-and-out privileges cost $7 to $15 per day. You'll find them on Main Street USA (Disneyland), in Sunshine Plaza (DCA) and at the picnic area just outside the theme park's main entrance, nearby Downtown Disney.

Lost & Found

Lost & Found (☑714-817-2166) Look for the office steps just east of DCA's main entrance.

Medical Services

You'll find first-aid facilities at Disneyland (Main Street USA), DCA (Pacific Wharf) and Downtown Disney (next to Ralph Brennan's Jazz Kitchen).

Anaheim Urgent Care (☑714-533-2273; 2146 E Lincoln Ave, Anaheim; ⊙8am-8pm Mon-Fri, 10am-6pm Sat & Sun) Walk-in nonemergency medical clinic.

Western Medical Center (WMC) (☑714-533-6220; 1025 S Anaheim Blvd, Anaheim; ⊙24hr) 24-hour hospital emergency room.

Money

Disneyland's City Hall offers foreign-currency exchange. In DCA, head to the guest relations lobby. Multiple ATMs are found in both theme parks and at Downtown Disney.

Travelex (☑714-502-0811; Downtown Disney; ⊙10am-4pm Mon-Fri) Also exchanges foreign currency.

Post

Holiday Station (www.usps.com; 1180 W Ball Rd, Anaheim) Full-service post office.

Smoking

Check theme-park maps for specially designated smoking areas, which are few and far between. At Downtown Disney, smoking is allowed outdoors.

Strollers & Wheelchairs

Rental strollers and wheelchairs may be used in the theme parks, but not Downtown Disney. Strollers cost $15 per day. Nonmotorized wheelchairs rent for $12 per day; an Electronic Convenience Vehicle (ECV) costs $50. Rentals may be sold out during busy times, so it's better to bring your own. For more tips on visiting Disneyland with children, see p36. For tips for travelers with special needs, see p37.

Tourist Information

For information or help inside the parks, just ask any cast member or visit Disneyland's City Hall or DCA's guest relations lobby.

Anaheim/Orange County Visitor & Convention Bureau (www.anaheimoc.org; 800 W Katella Ave, Anaheim Convention Center; ◷8am-5pm Mon-Fri) Offers information on countywide lodging, dining and transportation. Parking $12 to $15.

ⓘ Getting There & Away

AIR You can avoid always-busy Los Angeles International Airport (LAX) by flying into the easily navigated **John Wayne Airport** (SNA; ☑949-252-5200; www.ocair.com; 18601 Airport Way) in Santa Ana. International travelers craving duty-free shopping should stick to LAX, but for get-in, get-out domestic travel, SNA is ideal. The airport is 8 miles inland from Newport Beach via Hwy 55, near the junction of I-405 (San Diego Fwy). **Long Beach Airport** (LGB; ☑562-570-2600; www.longbeach.gov/airport; 4100 E Donald Douglas Dr), just across the LA County line, is another handy alternative. See p462 for domestic and international airlines serving these regional airports.

BUS Southern California Gray Line/Coach America (☑714-978-8855, 800-828-6699; www.graylineanaheim.com; one-way/round-trip to LAX $20/30, SNA $15/25) runs Disneyland Resort Express buses from LAX and Orange County's John Wayne Airport (SNA) to Disneyland-area hotels every 30 minutes to one hour from 7:30am until 10pm. Reservations aren't required, except if you want to take advantage of money-saving family passes.

Greyhound (☑714-999-1256, 800-231-222; www.greyhound.com; 100 W Winston Rd, Anaheim) has several daily buses to/from Downtown LA ($8 to $15, 45 minutes) and San Diego ($14 to $27, 2¼ hours). The bus station is a half mile east of the Disneyland Resort, accessible via taxi or the ART shuttle (see Getting Around, p230).

The **Orange County Transportation Authority** (☑714-560-6282; www.octa.net) operates buses serving towns throughout the county. The fare is $1.50 per ride, or $4 for a day pass. Both types of tickets are sold on board (cash only, exact change).

CAR & MOTORCYCLE Anaheim's Disneyland Resort is just off I-5 (Santa Ana Fwy), about 30 miles southeast of Downtown LA.

Arriving at Disneyland and DCA is like arriving at an airport. Giant, easy-to-read overhead signs indicate which ramps you need to take for the theme parks, hotels or Anaheim's streets.

TRAIN All trains stop at the depot next to Angel Stadium, a quick ART shuttle or taxi ride east of Disneyland. **Amtrak** (☑714-385-1448, 800-872-7245; www.amtrak.com; 2150 E Katella Ave) has almost a dozen daily trains to/from LA's Union Station ($12, 45 minutes) and San Diego ($25, two hours). Less frequent **Metrolink** (☑800-371-5465; www.metrolinktrains.com) commuter trains connect Anaheim to LA's Union Station ($8.25, 50 minutes), Orange ($5, 10 minutes), San Juan Capistrano ($8, 40 minutes) and San Clemente ($9, 50 minutes).

ⓘ Getting Around

Downtown Disney is just a short walk from the main entrance to the theme parks, Disneyland and DCA, directly opposite each other across a small pedestrian plaza. All resort transportation options listed below are wheelchair-accessible.

CAR & MOTORCYCLE All-day parking costs $15 ($20 for oversize vehicles). Enter the 'Mickey & Friends' parking structure from southbound Disneyland Dr, off Ball Rd. Walk outside and follow the signs to board the free tram to Downtown Disney. The parking garage opens one hour before Disneyland does.

GET SMART

If you've got a smartphone, make sure you bring it with you fully charged (with an extra battery) to Disneyland. The fierce market for Disney-specific smartphone apps means that you can easily download all the details you need – restaurant menus, insider 'Hidden Mickey' tips, live webcams, park opening hours and show schedules and, most importantly, current wait times at rides and attractions – into your handheld mobile device. Some of the best apps are free, so check out app user reviews before spending any money. For iPhones, try Disneyland Mouse Wait (http://app316.com).

Downtown Disney parking is reserved for diners, shoppers and movie-goers. It has a different rate structure, with the first three hours free. Downtown Disney also offers drive-up valet parking in the evenings for an additional $6 plus tip (cash only).

SHUTTLE Anaheim Resort Transit (ART; ☏714-563-5287, 888-364-2787; www.rideart. org) operates frequent shuttles between Disneyland and area hotels, convention centers and malls, saving traffic jams and parking headaches. Shuttles typically start running an hour before Disneyland opens, operating from 7am to midnight daily during summer.

An all-day ART pass costs $3 per adult ($1 per child aged 3 to 9) and must be bought before boarding with a credit card or cash (exact change) at one of over a dozen kiosks near ART shuttle stops or online in advance; otherwise the fare is $3 (cash only) each trip. Discounted multiday passes available.

Many hotels and motels offer their own free shuttles to Disneyland and other area attractions; ask when booking.

TRAM & MONORAIL A free **tram** connects the Disneyland Resort's main parking garage and Downtown Disney, a short walk from the theme parks' main entrance. Trams operates from one hour before Disneyland opens until one hour after the park closes.

If you've got an admission ticket to Disneyland, you can ride the **monorail** between Tomorrowland and the Disneyland Hotel, at the far end of Downtown Disney. It sure beats walking both ways along crowded Downtown Disney.

AROUND DISNEYLAND

Disneyland's not the only game in town. Within 10 easy miles of the mouse house you'll find a big scoopful of sights and attractions worth a visit in their own right. Anaheim's streets are laid out in an easy-to-navigate grid. So get out, explore, expand your horizons. It *is* a small world, after all.

Knott's Berry Farm

They bring 'em in by the busloads to America's oldest **theme park** (☏714-220-5200; www.knotts.com; 8039 Beach Blvd, Buena Park; adult/child 3-11yr & senior $55/24; ◷10am-6pm, to 10pm summer; ♿). Knott's is smaller and less frenetic than Disneyland, but it can be more fun, especially for thrill-seeking teens, roller coaster fanatics and younger kids who love the *Peanuts* gang.

KNOTT'S SCARY FARM

Every year, Knott's Berry Farm puts on SoCal's best and scariest Halloween party. On select days from late September through October 31, the park closes around 5:30pm or 6pm, reopens at 7pm as **Knott's Scary Farm** and stays open until 1am or 2am. Horror-minded thrills include creepy mazes like Club Blood, monster-themed shows and terrifying scare zones, not to mention thousands of restless young ghouls roaming the park. For tips, news and updates, visit the official Facebook page for Knott's Scary Farm or the unofficial website **Ultimate Haunt** (www.ultimatehaunt.com).

The park opened in 1932, when Mr Knott's boysenberries (a blackberry-raspberry hybrid) and Mrs Knott's fried-chicken dinners attracted crowds of local farmhands. Mr Knott built an imitation ghost town to keep them entertained, and eventually hired local carnival rides and charged admission. Mrs Knott kept frying the chicken, but the rides and Old West buildings became the main attraction.

Today Knott's keeps the Old West theme alive and thriving with a variety of shows and demonstrations at **Ghost Town**, but it's the thrill rides that draw the big crowds. The **Sierra Sidewinder** roller coaster rips through banks and turns while rotating on its axis. Nearby, the suspended, inverted **Silver Bullet** screams through a corkscrew, a double spiral and an outside loop. From the ground, look up to see the dirty socks and bare feet of suspended riders who've removed their shoes just for fun. **Xcelerator** is a 1950s-themed roller coaster that blasts you, as if from a cannon, from 0mph to 82mph in under 2½ seconds; there's a hair-raising twist at the top. For tamer rides, **Camp Snoopy** is a kiddy wonderland populated by the *Peanuts* characters.

If it's too darn hot, the park's **Perilous Plunge** whooshes at 75mph down a 75-degree angled water chute that's almost as tall as Niagara Falls.

Opening hours vary seasonally, so call ahead, and check the website for discounts and deals: online savings can be substantial (eg $10 off adult admission for buying print-at-home tickets). Manual/motorized wheelchair rentals cost $15/45 per day. Minimum height restrictions apply for many rides and attractions, so check the theme park's website in advance to avoid disappointment.

Next door to Knott's Berry Farm is the affiliated water park **Soak City Orange County** (☏714-220-5200; www.knotts.com; 8039 Beach Blvd, Buena Park; adult/child 3-11yr & senior $31/20, after 3pm all $20; ☺10am-5pm May-Sep; ♿), boasting a 750,000-gallon wave pool and dozens of high-speed slides, tubes and flumes. You must have a bathing suit without rivets or metal pieces to go on some slides. Bring a beach towel and a change of dry clothes.

The park is open from Memorial Day to Labor Day (till 7pm during peak summer season), plus additional May and September weekends. For small discounts off adult admission, buy tickets online. Rental lockers ($7 to $22 per day) and private cabanas (from $99) are available.

🛏 Sleeping & Eating

Conveniently adjacent to the theme park, **Knott's Berry Farm Resort Hotel** (☏714-995-1111, 866-752-2444; www.knottshotel.com; 7675 Crescent Ave, Buena Park; r $80-190; @🛜🏊♿) is a contemporary high-rise with bland air-con rooms and ho-hum housekeeping. Perks include an outdoor pool, fitness center and tennis and basketball courts. For young Charlie Brown fans, ask about Camp Snoopy rooms, where kids will be treated to *Peanuts*-themed decor, telephone bedtime stories and a goodnight 'tuck-in' visit from Snoopy himself. Shuttle service to Disneyland is complimentary. Parking costs $10.

You're only allowed to bring small bottles of water and sports drinks, plus soft-sided shoulder coolers with baby food, into the theme park. The park has plenty of carnival-quality fast food, but the classic meal is the button-busting fried chicken and mashed potato dinner at the nuthin'-fancy **Mrs Knott's Chicken Dinner Restaurant** (mains $16-20). In a hurry? Grab a bucket from **Chicken-to-Go** and slices of pie from **Knott's Berry Farm Bakery**. All three eateries are open daily (hours vary) in the California Marketplace, a shopping mall outside the park's main gate.

ⓘ Getting There & Away

Knott's Berry Farm is about 6 miles northwest of Disneyland, off the I-5 Fwy or Hwy 91 (Artesia Fwy). All-day parking costs $12. There's free three-hour parking for California Marketplace visitors only.

Medieval Times Dinner & Tournament

Hear ye, hear ye! All those who have sired knights-to-be and future princesses, gather ye clans and proceed forthwith to **Medieval Times** (☏714-523-1100, 866-543-9637; www.medievaltimes.com; 7662 Beach Blvd, Buena Park; adult/under 12yr $58/36; ♿) for an evening-long medieval feast and performance. Yep, it's completely over-the-top but in a harmless, party-like-it's-1099 sort of way. Dinner guests root for various knights as they joust, fence and show off their horsemanship on real Andalusian horses to protect the honor of the kingdom and the beautiful princess. The food is alright – roast chicken and spare ribs that you eat with your hands (vegetarian options available) – but the show's the thing. Make reservations, show up 90 minutes early (seating is not guaranteed, even with reservations) and accept that you'll be wearing a cardboard crown for the evening. The mock castle is about a half mile north of Knott's Berry Farm. Buy discounted tickets online.

Discovery Science Center

Follow the giant 10-story cube – balanced on one of its points – to the doors of the best educational kiddie attraction in town, the **Discovery Science Center** (☏714-542-2823; www.discoverycube.org; 2500 N Main St, Santa Ana; adult/3-17yr $13/10, incl Dino Quest & 4D movie $21/18; ☺10am-5pm; ♿), about 5 miles southeast of Disneyland via the I-5. More than 100 interactive displays await in exhibit areas with names such as Discovery Stadium, Dino Quest and more. Step into the eye of a hurricane – your hair will get mussed – or grab a seat in the Shake Shack to virtually experience a magnitude 6.4 quake. Warning: parents may be tempted to nudge their kids aside for a turn at many of the interactive displays. Special science-themed exhibits like 'Grossology' are fun too.

Bowers Museum & Kidseum

Gliding under the radar like a stealth bomber, the small, little-known **Bowers Museum** (☎714-567-3600, special-exhibition tickets 877-250-8999; www.bowers.org; 2002 N Main St, Santa Ana; adult/6-17yr & senior $12/9, special-exhibit surcharge varies; ⊗10am-4pm Tue-Sun) explodes on to the scene every year or two with a remarkable exhibit that reminds LA-centric museum-goers that the Bowers is a power player on the local and national scenes too. The museum's permanent exhibits are impressive, with a rich collection of pre-Columbian, African, Oceanic and Native American art. Docent-guided gallery tours are given every afternoon. For lunch, the atmospheric cafe **Tangata** (mains $10-20; ⊗11am-3pm Tue-Sun) serves fresh soups, salads and sandwiches, as well as California wines by the glass.

General admission tickets to the Bowers Museum include entry to the family-focused **Kidseum** (☎714-480-1520; 1802 N Main St, Santa Ana; admission $3, under 3yr free; ⊗10am-3pm Tue-Fri, 11am-3pm Sat & Sun; ⊕), two blocks further south. Hands-on arts and cultural exhibits will keep the preschool and early-elementary school set entertained.

The museums are 6 miles southeast of Disneyland, off I-5 in Santa Ana. Admission is free on the first Sunday of each month. Public parking in nearby lots costs $2.

Old Towne Orange

Settlers began arriving en masse in Orange County after the Civil War, responding to the lure of cheap land and fertile fields. Rumor had it that almost anything could be grown in the rich soil, and many crops (such as oranges, apricots, corn, lemons, pumpkins, peaches and walnuts) did indeed thrive despite occasional irrigation and drought issues. Today the city of Orange, 7 miles southeast of Disneyland, retains its charming historical center. It was originally laid out by Alfred Chapman and Andrew Glassell, who in 1869 received the 1-sq-mile piece of real estate in lieu of legal fees. It became California's only city laid out around a central plaza, making it pleasantly walkable, even in the 21st century. Antique hounds, SoCal nostalgia fans and food lovers needing to escape Anaheim will all find it worth a detour.

✖ Eating

Stroll around Old Towne Orange's traffic circle, then north along Glassell St to take your pick of more than a dozen cafes, restaurants, wine bars and brewpubs.

Felix Continental Cafe   LATIN AMERICAN $$$
(☎714-633-5842; www.felixcontinentalcafe.com; 36 Plaza Sq; mains $7-17; ⊗11am-10pm Mon-Fri, 8am-10pm Sat & Sun) Longtime downtown favorite serves spiced-just-right Caribbean, Cuban, and Spanish dishes, most accompanied by a hefty serving of plantains, black beans and rice. Paella is the house specialty. Scope out a patio table if you can. Lunch served until 5pm.

TOP CHOICE | **Filling Station**   DINER $
(www.fillingstationcafe.com; 201 N Glassell St; mains $5-12; ⊗7am-3pm) For breakfast, nothing beats this former vintage gas station now serving haute pancakes, chorizo scrambles, Cobb salads and patty melts instead of unleaded. Check out the vintage SoCal photographs on the walls. Sit on the outdoor patio (which is dog-friendly), or grab a shiny counter stool or booth inside. Breakfast is served till 2pm, lunch from 11am.

Rutabegorz   CALIFORNIAN $$
(www.rutabegorz.com/orange; 264 N Glassell St; mains $9-14; ⊗11am-9pm Mon-Sat) Known by locals as just 'Ruta's,' this flowering bower north of the plaza puts a healthy spin on breakfast or lunch. Cal-Mexican, vegetarian and Middle Eastern snacks all jostle on the tables alongside comfort-food sandwiches, wraps, salads, soups and fruit smoothies. Kids' menu available.

Waston Drug   DINER $
(116 E Chapman Ave; mains $6-15; ⊗7am-9pm Mon-Sat, 8am-6pm Sun) Old-fashioned soda-fountain treats such as egg creams, milkshakes and sundaes, as well as burgers and all-day breakfast burritos, set inside a turn-of-the-20th-century pharmacy.

Citrus City Grille   BISTRO $
(☎714-639-9600; http://citruscitygrille.com; 122 N Glassell St; mains lunch $10-18, dinner $17-33; ⊗11am-10pm Mon-Thu, 11am-11pm Fri & Sat, 9:30am-10pm Sun) Sophisticated yet casual Cal-American bistro cooks creative modern classics like wild-mushroom meatloaf, Angus beef tacos or blackened salmon over penne in tomato-cream sauce. House-made rosemary bread, yum.

DON'T MISS

CLUB MUD

Nicknamed 'Club Mud' for its famous red-clay mineral mud bath, **Glen Ivy Hot Springs & Day Spa** (✆888-453-6389; www.glenivy.com; 25000 Glen Ivy Rd, Corona; admission Mon-Thu $39, Fri-Sun & holidays $52; ⊙9:30am-5pm daily, till 6pm Apr-Oct) has no fewer than 19 pools and spas filled with naturally heated mineral water, surrounded by acres of bougainvillea blooms and eucalyptus and palm trees.

You can wallow in the water, lounge in the saunas or steam rooms, take an aqua-aerobics class, swim laps in a swimming pool or treat yourself to a massage (for an extra fee). The minimum age for entry is 16. It gets busy in summer, so arrive early if you want a chair.

For lunch, try a fresh salad, panini or stuffed calzone at the spa's **Café Solé** (mains $7-14) or head back toward the freeway to stock up on fresh fruits, artisan cheeses and old-fashioned candy at **Tom's Market** (✆951-277-4422; www.tomsfarms.com; 23900 Temescal Canyon Rd, Corona), which also serves tasty tacos at **Senor Tom's** (mains $6-18).

The spa is in Corona, just east of Orange County. To get here, exit off I-15 at Temescal Canyon Rd, turn right and drive 1 mile to Glen Ivy Rd, then take another right and go straight to the end. If traffic isn't too bad, it's about a 45-minute drive from Old Towne Orange.

🛍 Shopping

Shops line up primarily north and south but also east and west of Old Towne's **plaza** (cnr Chapman Ave & Glassell St), where you can find the OC's most concentrated collection of antiques, collectibles, and vintage and consignment shops. It's fun to browse, but real bargains are rare and unscrupulous dealers may try to pass off fakes as authentic. Unlike stuffier antiques minimalls, indie **Woody's Antiques** (173 N Glassell St) feels like walking on to a *Mad Men* set, with mid-century modern and art-deco furnishings and accent pieces galore. A hipsters' love affair for both sexes, **Elsewhere Vintage** (www.elsewherevintage.com; 133 W Chapman Ave) hangs 1950s bowling shirts and sundresses next to hats, leather handbags and fabulous costume jewelry. Whimsical **Dragonfly Shops & Gardens** (www.dragonflyshopsandgardens.com; 260 N Glassell St) sells native California plants, garden-minded gifts and beaded jewelry inside a white-picketed cottage.

ℹ Getting There & Away

You can drive here from Anaheim in under 20 minutes: take I-5 south to Hwy 22 east, then drive north on Grand Ave, which becomes Glassell St, for just over a mile. Both **Amtrak** (✆800-872-7245; www.amtrak.com) and **Metrolink** (✆800-371-5465; www.metrolinktrains.com) commuter trains stop at Orange's **train station** (191 N Atchison St), a few blocks west of the plaza.

Richard Nixon Library

About 10 miles northeast of Anaheim, the reformed bad boy of presidential libraries recently got a reality check. Long maligned because of inaccuracies in the Watergate exhibit room, the **Richard Nixon Presidential Library & Birthplace** (✆714-993-5075; www.nixonfoundation.org; 18001 Yorba Linda Blvd, Yorba Linda; adult/7-11yr/student/senior $12/4/6/7; ⊙10am-5pm Mon-Sat, 11am-5pm Sun) was transferred in 2007 to federal control with oversight by the National Archives. The old Watergate exhibit – which called the scandal a 'coup' instigated by Nixon's rivals and provided favorably edited White House tapes – was completely torn out. It was a bold move, considering that 'Tricky Dick' and First Lady Pat Nixon lie buried just outside. In exchange, the library received 42 million pages of the president's papers and over 4000 hours of tapes. Today, the museum offers a fascinating walk though America's modern history. Noteworthy exhibits include excerpts from the Nixon and Kennedy debates, a full-size replica of the White House's East Room, audiotapes of conversations with Apollo 11 astronauts while on the moon and access to the ex-presidential helicopter, complete with wet bar and ashtrays. To get here, take Hwy 57 north and exit east on Yorba Linda Blvd, then continue straight and follow the signs.

Crystal Cathedral

You needn't be a fan of Christian televangelist Robert H Schuller's original *Hour of Power* to appreciate the architecture of the **Crystal Cathedral** (☎714-971-4000; www.crystalcathedral.org; 12141 Lewis St) in Garden Grove, about 3 miles southeast of Disneyland. The skyscraping cathedral is built in the shape of a four-pointed star, with over 10,000 windows, seating for 2700 and a 16,000-pipe organ. Designed by the late Cleveland-born Philip Johnson, International Style architect turned postmodernist, the church anchors a vast campus of gardens, reflecting pools, fountains and sculpture. Explore on your own or take a free 30-minute tour (usually offered between 9am and 3:30pm Monday to Saturday). You can also just take a gander from the parking lot, which has a specially reserved section for Sunday morning 'drive-in' church services.

ORANGE COUNTY BEACHES

It's true you'll find gorgeous sunsets, prime surfing and just-off-the-boat seafood when traveling the OC's sun-kissed coast. But it's also the unexpected, serendipitous discoveries you'll remember long after you've left this blissful 42 miles of surf and sand behind. Whether you're learning to surf the waves in Seal Beach, playing Frisbee with your pooch in the surf at Huntington Dog Beach, piloting your own boat around Newport Harbor, wandering around eclectic art displays on a bluff-top trail in Laguna Beach, or spotting whales on a cruise out of yacht-filled Dana Point harbor – you'll discover that each beach town has its own brand of quirky charm.

Your mission, should you choose to accept it, is to find out which beach town

---

WORTH A TRIP

LITTLE SAIGON

Ready for a break from big-eared mice and boysenberry pie? Head to Little Saigon in suburban Westminster, about 7 miles southwest of Anaheim. The strip-mall neighborhood lies south of Hwy 22 (Garden Grove Fwy) and east of the I-405 (San Diego Fwy). Vietnamese immigrants began arriving here after the end of the Vietnam War in the early 1970s, carving out their own vibrant commercial district, starting around the intersection of Bolsa Ave and Brookhurst St. A short drive further west takes you to the **Asian Garden Mall** (9200 Bolsa Ave), a behemoth of a structure packed with scores of food shops, boutiques, herbalists and jade jewelers.

The best reason to visit Little Saigon is the food. Newbies can start at the mall's **Lee's Sandwiches** (www.leessandwiches.com; 9200 Bolsa Ave, Suite 305; sandwiches from $4; ☺8am-7pm; 🛜) or just west of the mall at **Ba Le** (9152 Bolsa Ave; sandwiches from $4; ☺8:30am-6:30pm), both fast-growing chains serving budget-friendly Vietnamese sandwiches on French baguette rolls. The traditional toppings on these belly-fillers provide a delish, not-too-spicy kick – try the pork. Another great, inexpensive casual eatery at the Asian Garden Mall is **Pho 79** (9200 Bolsa Ave, Suite 117; mains from $6; ☺8am-7:30pm), which dishes up a variety of noodle and vegetable dishes. The *pho ga* (chicken noodle soup) has a hearty broth.

For a real treat (involving some DIY navigation) visit **Brodard** (☎714-530-1744; www.brodard.net; 9892 Westminster Ave; mains $7-14; ☺8am-9pm Wed-Mon), known for its *nem nuong cuon* – rice-paper spring rolls wrapped tightly around spamlike grilled pork patties and served with a tangy sauce. It's oddly addictive. Here are the directions: drive to the strip mall at the corner of Brookhurst Ave and Westminster Ave, continue to the back of the 99¢ Only store, turn right, drive past the dumpsters and park near the red awning-covered entrance.

Cheat sheet: *pho* is soup, *ga* is chicken, *tom* is shrimp and *bo* is beef. Enjoy.

Wait, you're vegetarian? Little Saigon hasn't forgotten about you. But you've been exiled north of Hwy 22 to Garden Grove, where family-owned **Hoa Sen** (12180 Brookhurst St; mains $7-10; ☺10am-9pm Wed-Mon; 🌱) makes fresh salads, noodle soups, rice bowls, clay pots and more with vegan mock meats like seitan. Its name means 'lotus' in Vietnamese. Although service sure ain't flowery and the surroundings are kinda drab, the savory flavors are right on.

suits your personality best. Starting near the LA County line, Seal Beach is the OC's northernmost beach town. From there, you can crawl along Route 1, aka the Pacific Coast Hwy (PCH), south along the ocean for more than 40 miles, passing through Sunset Beach, Huntington Beach, Newport Beach, Laguna Beach, Dana Point and San Clemente just before reaching San Diego County. The drive takes at least an hour, but with bumper-to-bumper beachfront traffic, especially on summer weekends, expect it to take two or three times that long. But don't worry: it's almost always worth it.

Seal Beach

POP 24,238

In the SoCal beauty pageant for pint-size beach towns, Seal Beach enjoys an unfair advantage over the competition: 1.5 miles of pristine beach sparkling like an already-won crown. And that's without mentioning three-block Main St, a stoplight-free zone bustling with mom-and-pop restaurants and indie shops that are low on 'tude and high on charisma. But truth be told, Seal Beach's lasting small-town allure may owe a debt to the Scylla and Charybdis lurking: Leisure World ('Seizure World' to the non-PC), a sprawling retirement community looming north of town via Seal Beach Blvd, and the huge US Naval Weapons Station (look for grass-covered bunkers) crouching to the east. But thoughts of shuffleboard and apocalypse aside, Seal Beach is one of the last great California beach towns and a refreshing alternative to the more crowded coast further south.

◉ Sights & Activities

In the morning or afternoon, amble Main St and check out the laid-back local scene – barefoot surfers trotting toward the beach, friendly shopkeepers opening their doors and silver-haired foxes scoping the way-too-young beach bunnies. Where Main St ends, walk out onto **Seal Beach Pier**, extending 1865ft over the ocean. The 1906 original fell victim to winter storms in the 1930s and has since been rebuilt three times with a wooden boardwalk. It's splintery in places, so wear shoes (no heels!). Snap a picture of the playful bronze seal standing guard at the pier's east entrance – he may be the only one you see.

On the **beach**, which faces south here, families spread out on blankets, build sand castles and play in the water. Though there's a hideous oil derrick just off shore, if you put on dark sunglasses and focus on what's immediately in front of you, it's lovely. The gentle waves make it a great place to learn to surf. Newbies should stick close to the pier. Surfers and boogie boarders are segregated; read the signs or ask a lifeguard. For surf conditions, look for the sign on the sand between the parking lots. The ocean here is also popular with stingrays, attracted to the warm water flowing in with the San Gabriel River from the north.

Learn to surf with **M&M Surfing School** (☏714-846-7873; www.surfingschool.com), which offers five-day surf intensives from $250, or three-hour group lessons for $65 per person, which includes surfboard and wet suit rental. You can rent a soft (foam) board for $25 per day. Look for their van in the parking lot just north of the pier, off Ocean Ave at 8th St.

🛏 Sleeping

There are no budget accommodations in Seal Beach. Either head inland or south along the Pacific Coast Hwy.

Pacific Inn MOTEL **$$**
(☏562-493-7501, 866-466-0300; www.pacific inn-sb.com; 600 Marina Dr; r $150-180; @🐾🛜🏊) The only motel near town that's within walking distance of the beach has recently renovated rooms with extras such as down comforters and comfy mattresses. The property could still use a little TLC, but a sunny central pool and hot tub, a workout room, free wi-fi and complimentary guest shuttle around town make up for that. Bicycle rentals available. Pet fee $50.

CHEAP(ER) SLEEPS

In summer the OC's beach accommodations get booked out far in advance, room rates rise, and some places require minimum two- or three-night stays. You can often save money by staying multiple nights in one beach town and just taking day trips to the others. Otherwise, look inland to chain motels and hotels closer to I-405 and I-5 Fwys – for example, in Costa Mesa, Santa Ana or Irvine.

✖ Eating

Walt's Wharf SEAFOOD, STEAKHOUSE **$$$**
(☎562-598-4433; www.waltswharf.com; 201 Main St; mains lunch $11-18, dinner $20-45; ⊙11am-3:30pm & 4-9pm) Everybody's favorite for fresh fish (some drive in from LA), Walt's packs them in on weekends. You can't make reservations for dinner (though they're accepted for lunch), but it's worth the wait for the oak fire–grilled seafood and steaks. Otherwise, eat at the bar. Don't be overwhelmed by the long menu or the huge selection of wines by the glass – knowledgeable waitstaff are happy to share their expertise.

Crema Café BAKERY, CAFE **$**
(322 Main St; mains $5-9; ⊙6:30am-3pm Mon-Thu, 6:30am-4pm Fri & Sat, 7am-4pm Sun) Service can be harried at this breezy, open-air cafe, but all is forgiven after a bite of their 'simple' French crepe covered with cinnamon sugar, whipped cream and caramel sauce. Add strawberries and bananas for an extra splash of flavor. In a hurry? Made-from-scratch pastries and muffins are fab, as are garden-fresh salads and toasted panini sandwiches.

Nick's Deli DELI **$**
(223 Main St; mains $5-8; ⊙7am-7pm Mon-Fri, to 4pm Sat & Sun) Don't be fooled by the extensive hand-scrawled menu hanging over the counter at Nick's, a local joint where traditional deli fare is served alongside Mexican specialties. The crowds flock here for one thing: the mad breakfast tortilla stuffed with scrambled eggs, chorizo, bacon, potatoes and cheese – basically, a heart attack on a plate. Ask for it toasted.

Beachwood BBQ BARBECUE **$$**
(☎562-493-4500; www.beachwoodbbq.com; 131½ Main St; mains $9-17; ⊙11:30am-9:30pm) Downtown's barbecue hut ropes in regulars with fried pickles, buffalo sloppy joe sandwiches, applewood-smoked beef brisket with blue-cheese grits on the side, and a cool selection of microbrews (check out the website's 'Hop Cam'). For beach picnics, order takeout.

Mahe FUSION **$$$**
(☎562-431-3022; www.eatatmahe.com; 1400 Pacific Coast Hwy; mains $20-50; ⊙5-10pm Mon-Sat, 4-9pm Sun, bar till midnight or 1am) Raw-fish fans gather barside at this surfboard-chic sushi bar for $25 all-you-can-eat deals offered some weeknights. Spicy scallop and shrimp wonton-chip nachos, baked salmon bombs with avocado and mango *maki* (rolls) all hang out on the Cal-Japanese menu.

Ruby's DINER **$**
(900a Ocean Ave; mains $5-12; ⊙7am-9pm Sun-Thu, to 10pm Fri & Sat; ⓘ) At the end of the pier, this red-and-white '40s-themed diner whips up pretty good burgers, chili and hot-fudge sundaes. Oh, the ocean views are fantastic too.

♟ Drinking & Entertainment

Jazz, folk and bluegrass bands play by the pier at the foot of Main St from 6pm to 8pm every Wednesday during July and August for the annual **Summer Concerts in the Park**.

Bogart's Coffee House CAFE
(www.bogartscoffee.com; 905 Ocean Ave; ⊙6am-9pm Mon-Thu, 6am-10pm Fri, 7am-10pm Sat, 7am-9pm Sun; ⓐ) Sip espresso on the leopard-print sofa and play Scrabble by the beach view as you watch the surf roll in. Bogart's sometimes hosts live music, psychic readings, book clubs and morning meditations by the sea.

Main Street Wine Cellar BAR
(http://mainstreetwine.com; 302 Main St; ⊙closed Mon) For California wines and European cheeses and charcuterie plates, grab a stool at this popular wine-shop bar that's perfect for solos or small groups. Wednesday evening wine-tasting flights are 2-for-1.

Bay Theatre CINEMA
(☎562-431-9988; www.baytheatre.com; 340 Main St; adult/under 13yr $8/5, senior & student $6) Historic 1947 cinema screens indie foreign flicks and revives much-loved classics on the big screen, from the Marx Brothers to *Goonies*. Movies start on time – there are no previews.

🔒 Shopping

Be sure to walk the full three blocks of Main St and browse all of the eclectic shops.

Harbour Surfboards OUTDOORS
(www.harboursurfboards.com; 329 Main St) It's not just about computer-designed boards, but also the surf-and-skate lifestyle, man. Eavesdrop on local surfers talking about their wax as you pillage the racks of hoodies, wet suits, beach Ts and beanie hats. Across the street, **Alternative Surf** is bodyboarding central.

Endless Summer CLOTHING
(124 Main St) Teenie Wahine, Roxy and Billabong jostle for attention at this bustling store for girly tweens to college-age beach babes. It's packed to the rafters with bikinis, beach bags, shades and loads more.

Up, Up & Away GIFTS
(http://upupandawaykites.com; 139½ Main St) In addition to kites in every color of the rainbow, you'll find tons of decorative flags. Lighthouses, sailboats, frogs wearing sunglasses – if you want it waving in front of your house, there's a flag for it. Badass beach kites are at the back.

Seal Beach Music MUSIC
(118 Main St; ⊘closed Sun) Eclectic music lovers will dig this old-fashioned small-town music shop that carries new and used vinyl, memorabilia and vintage musical instruments from around the world. You know, just in case the ocean inspires you to strum a ukulele.

Knock Knock Toy Store TOYS
(www.knockknocktoystore.com; 219½ Main St) Thoughtfully chosen, fun and educational toys line the shelves here, from name brands to quirky one-off products like wind-up space robots. Afterward, duck down the street to **Raspberry & Sage**, stocking clothing, gifts and accessories for newborns, tots and hip moms.

❶ Information

Mary Wilson Library (www.ocpl.org; 707 Electric Ave; ⊘noon-8pm Mon & Tue, 10am-6pm Wed & Thu, 10am-5pm Sat) Free one-hour walk-in guest internet access.

Post Office (221 Main St; ⊘9am-5pm Mon-Fri) Three blocks inland from the beach.

❶ Getting There & Around

OCTA (☏714-560-6282; www.octa.net) bus 1 connects Seal Beach with the OC's other beach towns and LA's Long Beach every hour; the one-way fare is $1.50 (exact change).

There's two-hour free parking along Main St between downtown Seal Beach and the pier, but it's difficult to find a spot in summer. Public parking lots by the pier cost $3 per two hours, $6 all day. Free parking along residential side streets is subject to posted restrictions.

Sunset Beach

A 1-mile strip of coastal real estate between genteelly retro Seal Beach and gentrifying punk Huntington Beach, this tiny community spits in the face of Orange County conformity. With a high concentration of dive bars, ratty motels and beach bum 'tude, it's a great place to surf, kayak and drink, but you might not want to, um, live here.

◎ Activities

Kayak the calm waters of **Huntington Harbor** for an up-close look at ritzy homes and tricked-out yachts. **OEX Sunset Beach** (☏562-592-0800; www.oexsunsetbeach.com; 16910 Pacific Coast Hwy) rents kayaks (single/double $15/25 for two hours) and stand-up paddle (SUP) surfboard sets (per hour/half day $15/35) and offers lessons and tours. Surfers can rent hard and soft boards from **Bruce Jones Surfboards** (☏562-592-2314; www.brucejones.com; 16927 Pacific Coast Hwy) from $20 per half day (wet suit $10 to $15). A local icon since the 1960s, **Katin Surf Shop** (☏562-592-2052; www.katinsurf.com; 16250 Pacific Coast Hwy) is known for their canvas board shorts, but nowadays they sell all kinds of surfwear, swimsuits and beach gear.

🛏 Sleeping & Eating

Best Western Harbour Inn & Suites MOTEL $$
(☏562-592-4770, 800-546-4770; www.bestwestern.com; 16912 Pacific Coast Hwy; r $139-199; @🛜🐾) Just a short walk from the beach, this reliable roadside chain boasts an outdoor hot tub and workout room. Spacious, spick-and-span rooms have a dash of tropical flair, with lime-green accent walls and aloha-print comforter covers. Families can rent DVD players, video-game consoles and board games to keep kiddos entertained. Small pets welcome.

Sanatra Inn MOTEL $$
(☏562-592-1993, 866-726-2872; www.sanatrainn.com; 16555 Pacific Coast Hwy; r $110-180; 🛜) Don't kid yourself: what you're paying for is proximity to the beach, not ocean views or fancy towels and bed linens. Standard rooms with coffeemakers, minifridges and microwaves will do for a night; suites have full kitchens.

Harbor House Café DINER $$
(www.harborhousecafe.com; 16341 Pacific Coast Hwy; mains $7-19; ⊘24hr) High-school skaters, 30-something beach bums and old-timers mix easily under ramshackle walls slathered with movie posters at this classic neon-lit roadside diner. The menu is long, portions huge and waitstaff downright

friendly. Breakfast served around the clock, but cheese fries are your best bet after midnight.

Roman Cucina   ITALIAN $$
(☑562-592-5552; www.romancucina.com; 16595 Pacific Coast Hwy; mains $13-20; ☺dinner) For hearty Italian fare, follow the twinkling lights to this trattoria, known as much for its thick slices of bruschetta, baked meatball mozzarella and huge pasta bowls as for the ripped waiters serving the food. Don't miss $5 Martini Mondays.

 Drinking

Sunset Beach is the unofficial capital of SoCal dive bars. For a wood-paneled, trapped-in-the-captain's-hold vibe, try **Turc's** (16321 Pacific Coast Hwy); it's the ivy-covered building at the corner of PCH and Anderson St in the shadows of the water tower–like house. Just south is tiny but raucous biker bar **Mother's Tavern** (16701 Pacific Coast Hwy), in the red building with Harleys out front, just past the barber shop. On a lazy Sunday, you might catch a rockabilly band there. Gals will be invited to tack their bra to the wall or ceiling, so look out.

If you're a fan of seriously kitschy tiki bars, **Don the Beachcomber** (16278 Pacific Coast Hwy) will knock you over the head with its 'Vicious Virgin' and 'Missionary's Downfall' drinks. Zombie cocktail limit: 2. For more civilized pours, drop by the bar at **Brix NY Deli** (16635 Pacific Coast Hwy; ☺noon-8pm Sun-Tue, noon-9pm Wed, noon-10pm Thu-Sat), which has more than 20 craft beers on tap plus West Coast wine flights. Weekday happy hours get jam-packed.

Huntington Beach

POP 202,480

Hawaiian-Irish surfing star George Freeth, after being hired by railroad magnate and real-estate developer Henry Huntington, gave demonstrations in Huntington Beach (HB) in 1914, and the city has been a surf destination ever since. In recent years, its surfing image has been heavily marketed, city politicos even getting legally aggressive in ensuring HB's exclusive rights to their now-trademarked nickname 'Surf City, USA' (Santa Cruz lost that fight, sorry). The moniker originally came from the 1963 song by singing surf daddies Jan and Dean. But the city does have a reason to protect its surfing turf. The sport is big business,

with buyers for major retailers coming here to see what surfers are wearing, then marketing the look.

At times HB can seem like a teenager with growing pains. Long considered a low-key, not-quite-fashionable beach community, recent uninspired development along Main St has left downtown with a vaguely antiseptic, prefab feel – except for sidewalk-surfing skate rats and hollering late-night barflies. Despite the changes, HB is still a quintessential spot to celebrate the hang-loose SoCal coastal lifestyle. With consistently good waves, surf shops, a surf museum, bonfires on the sand, a canine-friendly beach and a sprinkling of hotels and restaurants with killer views, it's an awesome place for sun, surf and sand.

◉ Sights

Huntington Pier   HISTORIC SITE
(☺5am-midnight) 1853ft-long Huntington Pier has been here – in one form or another – since 1904. The mighty Pacific has damaged giant sections or completely demolished it multiple times since then, though. The current concrete structure was built in 1983 to withstand 31-foot waves or a 7.0 magnitude earthquake, whichever hits HB first. On the pier you can rent a fishing pole from **Let's Go Fishin'** bait and tackle shop.

International Surfing Museum   MUSEUM
(www.surfingmuseum.org; 411 Olive Ave; donations welcome; ☺noon-5pm Mon-Fri, 11am-6pm Sat & Sun) One of the few of its kind in California, this small museum is an entertaining stop for surf-culture enthusiasts. Exhibits chronicle the sport's history with photos, vintage surfboards, movie memorabilia and surf music. For the best historical tidbits, spend a minute chatting with the all-volunteer staff.

Activities

If you forgot to pack beach gear, you can rent umbrellas, beach chairs, volleyballs and other essentials from **Zack's** (www.zacks hb.com) Pier Plaza (☎714-536-0215; 405 Pacific Coast Hwy); Zach's Two (☎714-536-2696; 21579 Pacific Coast Hwy). Just south of the pier on the strand, friendly **Dwight's Beach Concession** (201 Pacific Coast Hwy), around since 1932, rents bikes, boogies boards, umbrellas and chairs.

Huntington City Beach   BEACH
(⊘5am-midnight) One of SoCal's best beaches, the sand surrounding the pier at the foot of Main St gets packed on summer weekends with surfers, volleyball players, swimmers and families. Bathrooms and showers are located north of the pier at the back of the snack-bar complex.

In the evening, volleyball games give way to beach bonfires. If you want to build one or have a barbecue, stake out one of the 1000 cement fire rings early in the day, especially on holiday weekends, when you should plan to arrive when the beach opens. To indicate that it's taken, surround the ring with your gear. You can buy firewood from concessionaires on the beach.

Surfing

Surfing in HB is competitive. Control your longboard or draw ire from local dudes who pride themselves on being 'aggro.' If you're a novice (or need a bodyguard), it's a good idea to take lessons. Surf north of the pier.

Zack's (see above) Offers one-hour lessons ($75 to $100) at the beach that include

GIMME MORE!

Want even more surf and sand? Further south of the pier, **Huntington State Beach** (www.parks.ca.gov; ⊘6am-10pm) extends 2 miles from Beach Blvd (Hwy 39) to the Santa Ana River and Newport Beach boundary. All-day parking costs $15. Meanwhile, dogs can romp in the surf at **Huntington Dog Beach** (www.dogbeach.org; ⊘5am-10pm), between Goldenwest St and Seapoint Ave, north of Huntington City Beach. Nearly a mile long, it's a postcard-perfect place to play with your pooch. Parking meters cost 25¢ every 10 minutes.

HUNTINGTON BEACH FOR CHILDREN   239

If you want a break from the beach scene but don't want to drive too far, **Huntington Central Park** (www. ci.huntington-beach.ca.us; 18000 Goldenwest St; 🚻), 3 miles north of downtown, is a green suburban retreat with a disc-golf course, a down-and-dirty adventure playground featuring a rope bridge and a cable slide, and two little lakes with walking paths. Parking lots are along Goldenwest St and at the library off Talbert Ave. For a thoughtful examination of local flora and fauna, including abundant bird life, stop by **Shipley Nature Center** (www.shipleynature.org; 17851 Goldenwest St; ⊘9am-1pm Mon-Sat; 🚻), which has kid-friendly exhibits on conservation efforts and a self-guided wetlands nature trail.

all-day board and wet suit rental. For board rentals, you'll pay $12/35 per hour/day, plus $5/15 each for bodyboards and wet suits.

Dwight's Beach Concession (see above) Also rents surfboards, bodyboards and wet suits at competitive rates.

Huntington Beach Surf & Sport (☎714-841-4000; 300 Pacific Coast Hwy) Megastore at the corner of PCH and Main St rents surfboards for $10/30 per hour/day (wet suit $8/15).

Cycling & Skating

Explore the coast while cycling or skating along the 8.5-mile **paved recreational path** running from Huntington State Beach in the south to Bolsa Chica State Beach. Rent beach cruisers ($10/30 per hour/day) or tandem bikes ($18/50) at Zack's Pier Plaza. Dwight's Beach Concession also rents cruiser bikes at similar rates – ask for a copy of the owner's hand-drawn map of the bike path showing distances from the pier.

Frisbee

Throw a disc back and forth for hours on the beach, or test your skills at the **Huntington Beach Disc Golf Course** (Huntington Central Park, 18381 Goldenwest St; admission per person $1-2). Aim for baskets at this scenic

WORTH A TRIP

LITTLE POCKET, BIG REWARDS

A 3-mile-long strip of sand favored by surfers, volleyball players and fishers, **Bolsa Chica State Beach** (www.parks.ca.gov; Pacific Coast Hwy; ⏲6am-10pm) stretches alongside PCH (between Seapoint and Warner Aves), between Huntington Dog Beach to the south and Sunset Beach to the north. Even though it faces a monstrous off-shore oil rig, Bolsa Chica (meaning 'little pocket' in Spanish) gets mobbed on summer weekends. All-day parking costs $10. You'll find picnic tables, fire rings and beach showers, plus a bike path running north to Anderson Ave in Sunset Beach and south to Huntington State Beach.

At the park's small **visitors center** (☎714-377-5691; ⏲9am-4pm; 📶) you can check out the views through telescopes pointed at the beach or inland at **Bolsa Chica Ecological Reserve** (http://bolsachica.org; ⏲sunrise-sunset), on the other side of PCH. The reserve may look desolate, but its restored salt marsh is an environmental success story and teems with more than 200 species of bird. Over 1200 acres were saved by a band of determined locals from numerous development projects over the years. Sadly, it's also one of the last remaining coastal wetlands in SoCal – over 90% have already succumbed to development. A 1.5-mile loop trail starts from the footbridge near the south parking lot right on PCH. A mile north, the **Bolsa Chica Wetlands Interpretative Center** (3842 Warner Ave; ⏲10am-4pm Tue-Fri, 9am-noon Sat, 12:30pm-3:30pm Sun) sits in the north parking lot, near other walking trails.

18-hole course, downhill from the sports complex. Newbies and seasoned players welcome. The on-site pro shop sells discs.

Festivals & Events

Car buffs, get up early on Saturday mornings for the **Donut Derelicts Car Show** (www.donutderelicts.com), a weekly gathering of woodies, beach cruisers and pimped-out street rods at the corner of Magnolia St and Adams Ave, 2.5 miles inland from PCH.

4th of July (www.hb4thofjuly.org) Expect big crowds when the city closes sections of Main St and PCH for its Independence Day parade. The daylong celebration ends with evening fireworks over the pier.

US Open of Surfing (www.usopenofsurfing.com) In late July and early August, this six-star competition lasts several days and draws more than 600 world-class surfers. Festivities include beach concerts, motocross shows and skateboard jams.

Huntington Harbor Cruise of Lights (www.cruiseoflights.org) If you're here for the Christmas holidays, don't miss the evening boat tour past harborside homes twinkling with holiday lights. Ticket sales support nonprofit school programs.

Sleeping

There aren't many budget options in HB, especially during summer beach season when nothing-special motels hike their prices to ridiculous levels. Head inland along mind-numbing Hwy 39 toward the I-405 (San Diego Fwy) to find cheaper cookie-cutter motels and hotels.

TOP CHOICE **Shorebreak Hotel** BOUTIQUE HOTEL **$$$**
(☎714-861-4470, 877-744-1117; www.shorebreakhotel.com; 500 Pacific Coast Hwy; r $249-469; @📶) Stow your surfboard (lockers provided) as you head inside HB's newest and hippest hotel, a stone's throw from the pier. The Shorebreak spruces things up with a surf concierge, a fitness center and yoga studio, bean bag chairs in the lobby and rattan and hardwood furniture in geometric-patterned air-con rooms (some pet-friendly). Have sunset cocktails on the upstairs deck at Zimzala.

Hilton Waterfront Beach Resort RESORT **$$$**
(☎714-845-8000, 800-445-8667; www.waterfrontbeachresort.hilton.com; 21100 Pacific Coast Hwy; r $279-390; @📶🏊👪) The sprawling, lounge-filled poolside is reminiscent of Vegas, but then you see the backdrop: miles and miles of gorgeous deep-blue sea. This 100% nonsmoking hotel has a giant tower that stands in blatant disregard of the town's low rooflines, but if you want an ocean view from up high, this is the only place. Air-con rooms are plush but tempered with smart, beach-casual style. Bicycle rentals available. Parking $24.

Hyatt Regency Huntington Beach Resort & Spa
RESORT $$$

(☎714-698-1234, 800-492-8804; 21500 Pacific Coast Hwy; www.huntingtonbeach.hyatt.com; r $320-400; @🛜🏊♿) It looks like an ersatz Spanish-style condo complex on steroids, but all of the deluxe air-con rooms are inviting and impeccably maintained. There's also an outdoor lagoon swimming pool with grottoes, two tennis courts, a decent day spa and direct access to the beach via a pedestrian bridge, plus Camp Hyatt activities for kids. Parking $25.

Sun 'N Sands Motel
MOTEL $$

(☎714-536-2543; www.sunnsands.com; 1102 Pacific Coast Hwy; r $129-269; 🛜) Rates spike absurdly high in summer at this nothing-special, mom-and-pop motel, but its location across from the beach lets them get away with it. Potato chips, toothpaste, contact solution and other sundries are for sale in the lobby. It can get loud at night.

Huntington Surf Inn
MOTEL $$

(☎714-536-2444; www.huntingtonsurfinn.com; 720 Pacific Coast Hwy; r $159-209; 🛜) You're paying for location at this two-story motel just south of Main St and across from the beach. Air-conditioned rooms are clean, if well worn, and there's a small common deck area with a beach view. Don't ask for a refund if you've made a reservation, but change your mind once you see the place – you won't get your money back.

Best Western Regency Inn
MOTEL $$

(☎714-962-4244, 800-780-7234; www.best western.com; 19360 Beach Blvd; r $110-160; @🛜♿) Air-con rooms are relatively quiet if you're facing away from the highway. Continental breakfast included. The other BW near the beach costs twice as much, yet isn't half as nice.

Comfort Suites
MOTEL $$

(☎714-841-1812; 877-424-6423; www.comfort suites.com/hotel/ca102; 16301 Beach Blvd; r $100-170; @🛜♿) Hot breakfast items make this 100% smoke-free chain motel with bland but comfy air-con rooms more special. It's closer to I-405 than the beach.

✖ Eating

Sugar Shack
CAFE $

(www.hbsugarshack.com; 213 Main St; mains $5-10; ☺6am-4pm Mon, Tue & Thu, to 8pm Wed, to 5pm Fri-Sun) Expect a wait at this HB institution, or get here early to see surfer dudes don their wet suits. Breakfast is served all day on the bustling Main St patio and inside, where you can grab a spot at the counter or a two-top. Photos of surf legends plastering the walls raise this place almost to shrine status.

Bodhi Tree
VEGETARIAN $$

(www.bodhitreehb.com; 501 Main St; mains $8-16; ☺11am-10pm; ✔) Just north of downtown, this 100% vegetarian and vegan pan-Asian joint has a huge and varied menu, including mock-meat delights like *pho* noodle soup and Thai curries with fake 'chicken' and 'beef.' Vietnamese baguette sandwiches and wok-fried garlic 'shrimp' are also tasty.

Duke's
SEAFOOD $$

(☎714-374-6446; www.dukeshuntington.com; 317 Pacific Coast Hwy; mains lunch $9-15, dinner $17-30; ☺11:30am-2:30pm Tue-Fri, 10am-2pm Sun, 5-9pm Tue-Sun) It may be touristy, but this Hawaiian-themed restaurant – named after surfing legend Duke Kahanamoku – is a kick. With unbeatable views of the beach, a long list of fresh fish and a healthy selection of sassy cocktails, it's a primo spot to relax and show off your tan. For just drinks and appetizers, step into the Barefoot Bar (open from 3:30pm daily).

Cucina Alessá
ITALIAN $$

(☎714-969-2148; www.cucinaalessa.com; 520 Main St; mains lunch $9-13, dinner $12-25; ☺11am-10pm Mon-Thu, to 11pm Fri & Sat, breakfast Sat & Sun) Every beach town needs its favorite go-to Italian kitchen. Alessa wins hearts and stomachs with classics like Neopolitan lasagna, butternut squash ravioli and chicken marsala. Lunch brings out panini, while weekend breakfasts include frittata and 'illegal' French toast.

Park Bench Cafe
AMERICAN $

(www.parkbenchcafe.com; 17732 Goldenwest St; mains $8-11; ☺7:30am-2pm Tue-Fri, 7:30am-3pm Sat & Sun; 🐾) Sometimes Fido likes to order off the menu too. In a dog-friendly setting with shady outdoor picnic tables, try this casual outdoor restaurant in Huntington Central Park. Order an avocado-topped omelet or BLT sandwich for yourself and a juicy 'Hound Dog Heaven' beef patty for your four-legged friend.

Chronic Tacos
CAL-MEXICAN $

(www.eatchronictacos.com; 328 11th St; mains $5-10; ☺9am-10pm Mon-Fri, 8am-10pm Sat, 9am-9pm Sun) Mosey into this sticker-covered shack and request a made-to-order 'Fatty

TOP FIVE CHEAPO BREAKFASTS BY THE BEACH

» Sugar Shack (p241), Huntington Beach

» Nick's Deli (p236), Seal Beach

» Harbor House Café (p237), Sunset Beach

» Cappy's Café (p249), Newport Beach

» Orange Inn (p258), Laguna Beach

Taco.' With the Dead playing on the stereo, a couple of surf bums chillin' by the pool tables, and the talkative staff, you might never leave. It could be way cleaner, though.

Spark Woodfire Grill CALIFORNIAN **$$**
(☎714-960-0996;www.sparkwoodfiregrill.com; 300 Pacific Coast Hwy; mains $10-35; ◎dinner) Come before dark to this 2nd-floor Cal-Mediterranean restaurant and watch the sun set over the water while forking into fairly decent fire-grilled steaks, chops and seafood or crispy-thin pizzas from the wood-burning oven. An over-30 crowd habituates themselves at the bar with tasty appetites.

Mother's Market & Kitchen TAKE-OUT **$**
(19770 Beach Blvd; mains $5-10; ◎8am-10pm Mon-Sat, to 8pm Sun; ✏ ✿) Get your organic, health-conscious groceries here. A deli and take-out cafe caters to all diets (eg vegetarian, vegan, gluten-free, nondairy). Juice bar open till 8pm daily.

John's Philly Grille SANDWICH SHOP **$**
(20379 Beach Blvd; mains $5-8; ◎10:30am-9pm) Oh, yeah. Authentic cheesesteaks so lip-smackin' good, you won't mind the drive from the beach. Get 'The Works' or South Philly–style with marinara sauce.

Azteca's Fine Mexican Food TAKE-OUT **$**
(17491 Beach Blvd; mains $5-11; ◎9am-10pm Mon-Sat) Take-out taco shop worth a detour inland for huge, pillowy homemade tamales.

♟ Drinking

It's easy to find a bar in HB. Walk up Main St and you'll spot them all. For dives, look inland along Beach Blvd.

Hurricanes Bar & Grill BAR
(www.hurricanesbargrill.com; 2nd fl, 200 Main St) Two words: meat market. But then again, any strip of beach bars worth its margarita

salt needs at least one. DJs nightly, ocean-view patios, a laser-light dance floor, 22 beer taps and loads of special cocktails – if you're not slurping body shots by midnight, you have no one to blame but yourself.

Killarney Pub & Grill BAR
(www.killarneypubandgrill.com; 209 Main St) It bills itself as an Irish pub, but the profusion of plasma TV screens makes it more like a sports bar with leprechaun green–painted walls. Rollicking good fun for beer-drinking Wii Sports fans. DJs and dancing, live bands or howlin' karaoke after dark.

Huntington Beach Beer Co BAR
(www.hbbeerco.com; 2nd fl, 201 Main St; ☎) Cavernous brewpub specializes in ales and has over a half dozen giant, stainless-steel kettles brewing all the time. Alas, the pub grub is better than the beer. DJs and dancing on weekend nights.

Main Street Wine Company WINE BAR
(www.mainstreetwinecompany.com; 301 Main St; ◎11am-9pm Tue-Thu, 11am-10pm Fri, noon-10pm Sat, noon-7pm Sun) Boutique California-wine shop with a sleek bar, generous pours and meet-your-(wine)maker nights.

Zimzala LOUNGE
(www.restaurantzimzala.com; Shorebreak Hotel, 2nd fl, 500 Pacific Coast Hwy; ◎11am-11pm Mon-Thu, 10am-midnight Fri & Sat, 10am-11pm Sun) With a long, lazy afternoon happy hour, this happening hotel lounge has 2nd-floor ocean-view perches surrounding fire pits. Sexy cocktails, microbrews and California wines. So-so food.

Shopping

About halfway up Huntington Beach Pier, you'll find two tiny stores. **Surf City HB** is the only shop in town officially licensed to use the name 'Surf City' on its merchandise – pick up a beach hoodie or T-shirt. Across the way, **Kite Connection** vends single-line and deluxe spinner kites.

Huntington Beach Surf & Sport
SPORTS, CLOTHING
(www.hsssurf.com; 300 Pacific Coast Hwy) Towering behind the statue of surf hero Duke Kahanamoku at the corner of PCH and Main St, this massive store supports the Surf City vibe with vintage surf photos, concrete handprints of surf legends and lots of tiki-themed decor. You'll also find rows of surfboards, beachwear and surfing accessories.

American Vintage Clothing CLOTHING
(201c Main St) Thrift and vintage hounds check out this small but jam-packed store. Boots, Jim Morrison T-shirts, earrings and loads of dresses arranged by decade. Enter off Walnut Ave.

Carmen Parks Boutique CLOTHING
(www.carmenparks.com; 201d Main St) If you've grown weary of surf fashion, stop by this surprisingly glam, high-end women's boutique. Independent designers' labels include Velvet, Twisted Heart and Michael Stars.

Electric Chair ALTERNATIVE
(www.electricchair.com; 410 Main St) Get pierced at this subversive shop for screw-the-man accessories. You'll find skull and vampire couture, alternative fetish fashion, punk stretch jeans and one lonely 'I Love Elvis' tee.

ⓘ Information

Beach Center post office (316 Olive Ave; ◎9am-5pm Mon-Fri)

Central Library (www.hbpl.org; 7111 Talbert Ave; internet terminals per hr $5; ◎1-9pm Mon, 9am-9pm Tue-Thu, 9am-5pm Fri & Sat; @🛜) Main branch in Huntington Beach Central Park; free wi-fi.

Huntington Beach Hospital (☎714-843-5000; www.hbhospital.com; 17772 Beach Blvd; ◎24hr) 24-hour emergency room.

Main St Library (www.hbpl.org; 525 Main St; internet terminals per hr $5; ◎10am-7pm Tue-Fri, 9am-5pm Sat; @🛜) Small but just five blocks from the beach; free wi-fi.

Visitors bureau (800-729-6232; www.surfcityusa.com) Main St (☎714-969-3492; 2nd fl, 301 Main St; ◎9am-5pm); Pier Plaza (◎11am-7pm) Hard-to-spot upstairs office on Main St provides maps and information, but the Pier Plaza center is more convenient.

ⓘ Getting There & Around

The Pacific Coast Hwy runs alongside the beach. Main St intersects PCH at the pier. Heading inland, Main St ends at Hwy 39 (Beach Blvd), which connects north to I-405.

Public parking lots by the pier and beach – when you can even get a spot – are 'pay and display' for $1.50 per hour, $15 daily maximum. Self-service ticket booths scattered across the parking lot take dollars or coins. More municipal lots alongside PCH and around downtown cost at least $15 per day in summer, typically with an evening flat rate of $5 after 5pm. On-street parking meters cost $1 per 40 minutes.

OCTA (☎714-560-6282; www.octa.net) bus 1 connects HB with the rest of OC's beach towns every hour; one-way fare is $1.50 (exact change). At press time, a free **Surf City Downtown Shuttle** (☎714-536-5542) operates from 10am until 8pm on weekends during summer, making a 3.5-mile loop around downtown to the pier, starting from the free public parking lot at **City Hall** (2000 N Main St).

Newport Beach

POP 86,252

Primetime soap *The OC* may be over, but the angst-ridden adventures of its glamorous teens have given a hipper, youthful sheen to the city's longstanding image as a paradise for wealthy yachtsmen and their trophy wives. Small-screen fame aside, the city's basics haven't changed too much: seafood lovers still flock to the harbor for just-off-the-boat seafood, boogie boarders still brave human-eating waves at The Wedge, and the ballet of yachts in the harbor still captivates the imagination. Just inland, more lifestyles of the rich and famous revolve around Fashion Island, a posh outdoor mall that's one of the OC's biggest shopping centers.

⊙ Sights

Balboa Fun Zone AMUSEMENT PARK
(www.thebalboafunzone.com; per ride $2-3; ◎11am-9pm Sun-Thu, 11am-10pm Fri & Sat; 👶) On the harbor side of Balboa Peninsula, the Fun Zone has delighted locals and visitors since 1936. There's a small Ferris wheel (where Ryan and Marissa shared their first kiss on *The OC*), carousel, arcade games, touristy shops and restaurants, and frozen banana stands (just like the one in the TV sit-com *Arrested Development*). Nearby the landmark 1905 **Balboa Pavilion** is beautifully illuminated at night. The Fun Zone is also the place to catch a harbor cruise, fishing or whale-watching excursion, or the ferry to Balboa Island just across the channel.

Newport Harbor Nautical Museum MUSEUM
(☎949-675-8915; www.nhnm.org; 600 E Bay Ave, Balboa Fun Zone; adult/4-12yr $4/2; ◎11am-6pm Sun-Thu, to 7pm Fri & Sat) With new digs in the Balboa Fun Zone, this museum's exhibits document the region's maritime heritage through old-time photographs, paintings and memorabilia. There's a kid-friendly touch tank and an awesome big-screen video of Laird Hamilton surfing monster

Newport Beach

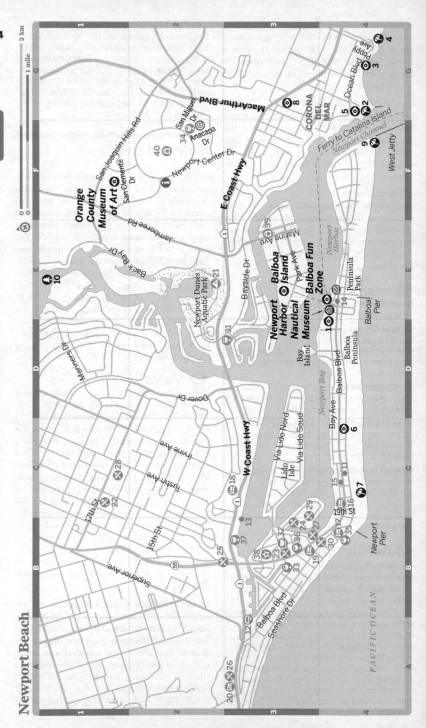

0   1 mile
0   2 km

Orange County Museum of Art

San Joaquin Hills Rd

San Miguel Dr

34

Anacapa Dr

San Clemente Dr

Newport Center Dr

40

MacArthur Blvd

CORONA DEL MAR

Ocean Blvd

Poppy Ave

4

3

2

5

9

8

West Jetty

Ferry to Catalina Island

Newport Channel

E Coast Hwy

Jamboree Rd

Back Bay Dr

Newport Dunes Aquatic Park

21

31

Bayside Dr

Marine Ave

Park Ave

Balboa Island

Newport Harbor Nautical Museum

Balboa Fun Zone

Peninsula Park

Balboa Pier

Bay Island

Balboa Blvd

Balboa Peninsula

Newport Bay

39

14

1

W Coast Hwy

Dover Dr

Mariners Dr

Irvine Ave

Tustin Ave

17th St

15th St

Via Lido Nord

Lido Isle

Via Lido Soud

Bay Ave

6

18

28

22

13

29

24

27

15

11

19th St

16

7

Superior Ave

55

Balboa Blvd

Seashore Dr

12

20

26

25

37

38

23

32

36

33

19

30

35

Newport Pier

PACIFIC OCEAN

10

waves. It's free to browse the museum's model ship pavilion, which includes a fully rigged 1950s Snowbird sailboat.

Orange County Museum of Art   MUSEUM
(☏949-759-1122; www.ocma.net; 850 San Clemente Dr; adult/student & senior $12/10, child under 12yr free, 2nd Sun free; ⏱11am-5pm Wed-Sun, till 8pm Thu) Less than a half mile from Fashion Island, this engaging museum highlights California art and cutting-edge contemporary artists, with exhibitions rotating through two large spaces. Recent exhibitions have included 'Birth of the Cool: Art, Design and Culture at Midcentury' and '15 Minutes of Fame: Portraits from Ansel Adams to Andy Warhol.' There's also a sculpture garden, eclectic gift shop and theater screening classic, foreign and art-related films. On the third Thursday of the month, stop by for behind-the-scenes gallery tours, films and videos, and even live music and DJs.

🏃 Activities

Balboa Peninsula   BEACHES
Four miles long but less than a half mile wide, the Balboa Peninsula has a white-sand beach on its ocean side and countless stylish homes, including the 1926 **Lovell Beach House** (1242 W Ocean Front). Designed by Rudolph Schindler, one of SoCal's most prominent modernist architects, it was built using site-cast concrete frames shaped like figure eights. It's just inland from the paved beachfront **recreational path**, across from a small **playground**.

BALBOA ISLAND

For a quick pleasure trip across Newport Harbor, the **Balboa Island Ferry** (www.balboaislandferry.com; adult/5-11yr $1/50¢, car/motorcycle/bicycle $1/50¢/25¢; ☺6:30am-midnight Sun-Thu, 6:30am-2am Fri & Sat, to 2am daily in summer) leaves from the Balboa Fun Zone about every 10 minutes. It's tiny, holding just three cars packed single file between open-air seats. The distance covered is only 800ft, and the trip lasts less than five minutes.

The ferry lands at Agate Ave, a half mile west of Marine Ave, the main drag on **Balboa Island** (www.balboa-island.net). It's lined with beachy boutique shops, cafes and restaurants, and old-fashioned ice cream shops vending Balboa bars (vanilla ice cream dipped in chocolate, peanuts, sprinkles and crushed Oreo cookies on a stick). Fido won't feel left out at **Barneys Barkery** (http://barneysbarkery.com; 322 Marine Ave), a 'bow-wow boutique' selling yummy treats like frosted 'pupcakes.'

For close-ups of the island's beautiful, well-maintained homes, take a stroll along its shoreline. It's only about 1.5 miles around. Then catch the ferry back. You can also reach Balboa Island by driving south of PCH along Jamboree Rd to Marine Ave. But what fun is that?

Hotels, restaurants and bars cluster around the peninsula's two famous piers: **Newport Pier** near the western end and **Balboa Pier** at the eastern end. The two-mile oceanfront strip between them teems with beachgoers, and people-watching is great. Near Newport Pier, several shops rent umbrellas, beach chairs, volleyballs and other necessities. For swimming, families will find a more relaxed atmosphere and calmer waves at 10th St and 18th St. The latter beach, also known as **Mothers Beach**, has a lifeguard, restrooms and a shower.

At the very tip of Balboa Peninsula, by the West Jetty, the **Wedge** is a bodysurfing, bodyboarding and knee-boarding spot famous for its perfectly hollow waves that can swell up to 30ft high. The waves are shore-breakers that crest on the sand, not out to sea, so you can easily slam your head. There's usually a small crowd watching the action. This is *not* a good place for learning how to handle the currents. Newcomers should head a few blocks west. Park on Channel Rd or E Ocean Blvd and walk through tiny West Jetty View Park.

Surfing

Surfers flock to the breaks at the small jetties surrounding the Newport Pier between 18th and 56th streets. Built in the 1960s after a storm destroyed much of the beach, the jetties are so prized by local surfers that they successfully protested the city's attempt to fill the spaces between them. Word of warning: locals can be territorial.

For lessons, try Huntington Beach or Laguna Beach instead.

15th Street Surf Shop (☎949-673-5810; www.15thstreetsurfshop.com; 103 15th St) Rents all kinds of surfing gear, including surfboards (per day $20), boogie boards ($8), wet suits ($7.50) and fins ($5).

Paddle Power (☎949-675-1215; www.paddlepowerh2o.com; 1500 W Balboa Blvd) Also near Newport Pier, rents stand-up paddle boards ($20/75 per hour/day) and offers 90-minute SUP lessons (from $45).

Boating

Besides the beach itself, the best thing about Newport Beach is its harbor. Take a boat tour (see p247), or rent your own kayak, sailboat or outboard motorboat. Even better, rent a flat-bottomed electric boat that you pilot yourself, and take a cruise with up to 12 friends. No boating experience required; maps provided.

Duffy Electric Boat Rentals (☎949-645-6812; www.duffyofnewportbeach.com; 2001 W Pacific Coast Hwy) Advance reservations recommended for heated electric boats with canopies (per hour $85/100 on weekdays/weekends). Bring CDs, food and drinks for a fun evening.

Balboa Boat Rentals (☎949-673-7200; http://boats4rent.com; 510 E Edgewater Ave) By the Balboa Fun Zone. Hourly single/double kayak rentals cost $15/25, sailboats $45, powerboats $65 to $90, and electric boats $75 to $95.

Marina Boat Rentals (☎949-673-3372; http://newportbeachboatrentals.com; 600 Edgewater Ave) At the Balboa Fun Zone. Single/double kayaks rent for $18/25 per hour, sailboats $45, motorboats from $65 and electric boats from $85.

Paddle Power (☎949-675-1215; www.paddle powerh2o.com; 1500 W Balboa Blvd) Rents single/double kayaks from $15/20 per hour, or $60/75 per day; 90-minute kaya-king lessons for beginners from $45.

Cycling & Skating

To experience fabulous ocean views, ride a bike along the paved **recreational path** that encircles almost the entire Balboa Peninsula. Inland cyclists like the paved **scenic loop** around Upper Newport Bay Ecological Reserve.

There are many places to rent bikes near Newport and Balboa Piers:

Easyride's Back Alley Bicycles (☎949-566-9850; www.easyridebikes.com; 204b Washington Sat; beach cruisers per day $10, tandem bicycles per hr/day $25/50) On the boardwalk, near Balboa Fun Zone.

15th Street Surf Shop (☎949-673-5810; www.15thstreetsurfshop.com; 103 15th St; beach cruisers per hr/day $5/17, tandem bicycles $6/20) Prices may fluctuate and shop hours are variable, so call ahead to check. Think twice before renting a surrey (with the fringe on top) and pedaling the pier-flanked bike path, as locals have been known to bombard surreys with water balloons!

Diving

There's terrific diving just south of New-port Beach at the underwater park at **Crystal Cove State Park** (see p254), where divers can check out reefs, anchors and an old military plane crash site. For dive-boat trips, stop by **Beach Cities Scuba Center** (☎949-650-5440; www.beachcitiesscuba.com; 4537 W Coast Hwy), where full equipment rental costs $60 per day.

Spas

After power shopping at Fashion Island, indulge yourself at **Spa Gregorie's** (☎949-644-6672; www.spagregories.com; 200 Newport Center Dr, Suite 100). After you've been re-juvenated by the quiet room, a one-hour massage starts around $100 per hour or unwind with a 75-minute signature facial from $110, plus tip.

☞ Tours

Several companies offer narrated tours of glitzy Newport Harbor, departing near the Balboa Fun Zone and Balboa Pavilion. Reserve ahead for the Christmas Boat Parade (p248), when boat tours cost about $26 per adult, less for seniors and children.

Fun Zone Boat Co (☎949-673-0240; www.funzoneboats.com; 600 Edgewater Ave; 45-min cruise per adult/senior/5-11yr $14/7/11) Sea lion–watching and celebrity home tours depart beneath the Ferris wheel in the Fun Zone.

Davey's Locker (☎949-673-1434; www.daveyslocker.com; 400 Main St; 2½hr whale-watching cruise per adult/3-12yr & senior

---

WORTH A TRIP

BACK BAY

Inland from the harbor, where runoff from the San Bernardino Mountains meets the sea, the brackish water of 752-acre **Newport Bay Ecological Reserve** supports nearly 200 bird species. As this is one of SoCal's few estuaries that has been preserved, it's an important stopover on the migratory Pacific Flyway, as well as for nature lovers in Orange County. It's also under the flyway for planes taking off from John Wayne Airport, but this annoyance doesn't overly detract from the wildlife viewing.

Inside the boundaries of the reserve is the **Upper Newport Bay Nature Preserve**. Stop by the **Muth Interpretive Center** (☎949-923-2290; www.ocparks.com/unbic, www.newportbay.org; 2301 University Dr, off Irvine Ave; ☉10am-4pm Tue-Sun; ♿), made from sustainable and renewable materials. Built right into the hillside, it's not visible from the parking lot. Walk past the information kiosk and down a short hill to the center. Inside, you can wander around the kid-friendly exhibits, which explain how the bay is like an egg beater and a sponge, among other scientific fun facts. Before heading out, grab a trail map. Call for schedules of guided sunset strolls.

$30/25, half-day sportfishing trip $40/33) At Balboa Pavilion; offers whale-watching and sportfishing trips.

Gondola Adventures (☎949-646-2067, 888-446-6365; www.gondola.com; 3101 W Coast Hwy; 1hr cruise per couple from $150) Totally cheesy Venetian-esque gondola rides with chocolates and sparkling cider for your sweetie.

★ Festivals & Events

Newport Film Festival (www.newportbeach filmfest.com) Roll out the red carpet in mid-April for screenings of over 350 mostly new independent and foreign films, along with occasional major-studio premieres such as *Crash* and anniversary showings of classics like *Sunset Boulevard*.

Taste of Newport (www.tasteofnewport. com) Flashy food-and-wine fest shows off local restaurateurs, top chefs, prestigious winemakers and brewmasters with live rock concerts staged near Fashion Island in mid-September.

Christmas Boat Parade (www.christmas boatparade.com) The week before Christmas brings thousands of spectators to Newport Harbor to watch a tradition dating back over a century. The 2½-hour parade of up to 150 boats, including some fancy multimillion-dollar yachts all decked out with Christmas lights and holiday cheer, begins at 6:30pm. You can watch for free from the Fun Zone or Balboa Island, or book ahead for a harbor boat tour.

⌂ Sleeping

If you're looking to save some dough, you'll find chain hotels and motels further inland, especially around John Wayne Airport and the triangle junction of Hwy 55 (Costa Mesa Fwy), toll road Hwy 73 and I-405 (San Diego Fwy).

Resort at Pelican Hill RESORT $$$
(☎949-467-6800, 800-315-8214; www.pelican hill.com; 22701 Pelican Hill Rd S; r from $495; @ 🅟 ≋) At this Tuscan-themed resort secluded in the Newport Coast hills, mature trees and Palladian columns line the way to over 300 deluxe air-con bungalows and villas. Pleasures include a circular mosaic-inlaid swimming pool (diameter: 136ft), two 18-hole championship golf courses, a soothing spa, top-notch Northern Italian fare at Andrea restaurant and multilingual concierge staff who define solicitous. Rates are sky high, but the pampering: priceless.

TOP CHOICE **Bay Shores Peninsula Hotel**
HOTEL $$$
(☎949-675-3463, 800-222-6675; www.thebe stinn.com; 1800 W Balboa Blvd; r $190-275; @ 🅟) This three-story, reimagined motel is ready to flex some surf-themed muscle. From *Endless Summer* surfing murals and complimentary fresh-baked cookies to air-con rooms and free rental movies, Bay Shores is beachy, casual and customer-focused. It's also pretty close to Newport Pier, which explains the steep rates. Complimentary parking, beach gear and breakfast buffet. Coin-op laundry available.

Newport Channel Inn MOTEL $$
(☎949-642-3030, 800-255-8614; www.newport channelinn.com; 6030 W Coast Hwy; r $110-160; 🅟) The ocean is just across PCH from this spotless two-story motel. Other perks include large air-con rooms with microwaves and mini-fridges, a big common sundeck and genuinely friendly owners. Enjoy a vacation-lodge vibe under the A-frame roof of Room 219, which sleeps up to seven. Close to Cappy's Café too.

Newport Dunes Waterfront RV Resort & Marina CABINS, CAMPING $$
(☎949-729-3863, 800-765-7661; www.new portdunes.com; 1131 Backbay Dr; campsites from $55, studios/cottages from $150/200; @ 🅟 ≋ 🐾) RVs and tents aren't required for a stay at this upscale campground: two dozen tiny A-frame studios and one-bedroom cottages are available, all within view of Newport Bay. A fitness center and walking trails, kayak rentals and tours, board games, family bingo, ice cream socials, horseshoe and volleyball tournaments, an outdoor pool and playground, and summertime movies on the beach await. Everything is wheelchair-accessible. Pets are allowed at campsites (small surcharge applies).

Doryman's Oceanfront Inn B&B $$$
(☎949-675-7300; www.dorymansinn.com; 2102 W Oceanfront; r $269-399) They leave your room door open until you check in at this 2nd-floor oceanfront B&B decorated with Victorian country flair. Each air-conditioned room is unique, and some boast ocean views, fireplaces and deep soaking tubs. Preferred by older couples and antiques lovers, it has a great location by Newport Pier, although it can get loud. Parking and continental breakfast included.

Holiday Inn Express
MOTEL $$

(☎949-722-2999, 800-308-5401; www.hinew portbeach.com; 2300 W Coast Hwy; r $160-240; @🛜🐾🐾) Air-con motel rooms have up-to-date furnishings and extras like microwaves, mini-refrigerators and work desks. Centrally located on PCH between major attractions. Rates include breakfast buffet.

Little Inn by the Bay
MOTEL $$

(☎949-673-8800, 800-438-4466; www.little innbythebay.com; 2627 Newport Blvd; r $120-180; @🛜) If you're not bothered by street noise, you can walk to the beach from this older motel. There's air-con in half the rooms. Beach gear and bikes to borrow.

✖ Eating

Don't be alarmed to find tasty restaurants tucked into prefab strip malls, especially in adjacent Costa Mesa. This is the OC, after all.

Crab Cooker
SEAFOOD $$

(☎949-673-0100; www.crabcooker.com; 2200 Newport Blvd; mains $11-30; ⊘11am-9pm Sun-Thu, to 10pm Fri & Sat) Expect a wait at this always-busy joint, a landmark since 1951. It serves great seafood and fresh crab on paper plates to an appreciative crowd wearing flip-flops and jeans. Don't miss the delish chowder – it's loaded with clams. If you're in a hurry, saunter up to the fish market counter inside and order your seafood to go.

Buddha's Favorite
JAPANESE $$

(☎949-723-4203; www.buddhasfavorite.com; 634 Lido Park Dr; dishes $4-21; ⊘dinner) Who are we to disagree with the Enlightened One? This sushi joint's Yokohama-born chef crafts creative hot and cold appetizers like sashimi 'candy,' a tuna tower and deep-fried halibut with eel sauce. Snag a table outside on the heated deck and enjoy the twinkling harbor night lights. If you're not a raw-fish fan, try the soba and udon noodles in hot broth or heaping *donburi* rice bowls.

⎡TOP⎤ Bear Flag Fish Co
⎣CHOICE⎦ SEAFOOD $

(www.bearflagfishco.com; 407 31st St; dishes $3-13; ⊘11am-9pm Tue-Sat, to 8pm Sun) Tucked behind Rudy's sports bar, this is *the* place for generously sized, grilled and panko-breaded fish tacos, ahi burritos, spankin' fresh seviche and oysters. Pull up a bar stool and pick out what you want from the ice-cold display cases. Just about the only way this seafood could be any fresher is if you caught and hauled it off the boat yourself!

Bluewater Grill
SEAFOOD $$

(☎949-675-3474; www.bluewatergrill.com; 630 Lido Park Dr; mains $10-35; ⊘11am-10pm Mon-Thu, 11am-11pm Fri & Sat, 10am-10pm Sun) Sit on the wooden deck and watch the boats at this polished harborside restaurant and oyster bar that serves incredibly fresh fish. Great for Bloody Marys and a leisurely lunch – maybe swordfish tacos and coleslaw, beer-battered fish and chips or seared ahi with white-bean hummus. Happy hour and small-plates menu available from 3:30pm to 6:30pm weekdays.

Sabatino's
ITALIAN $$

(☎949-723-0621; www.sabatinoschicagosausage .com; 251 Shipyard Way, Cabin D; mains $9-23; ⊘11am-10pm Mon-Fri, 8:30am-10pm Sat & Sun) The claim to fame of this authentic Italian place is its handmade sausage, blended with Sicilian goat cheese for that cholesterol double-whammy. Family-size deli sandwiches, shrimp scampi and stuffed and baked pastas keep the locals coming back for more. It's hard to find – when you get lost, just call.

Cappy's Café
AMERICAN $

(www.cappyscafe.com; 5930 W Coast Hwy; mains $6-12; ⊘6am-3pm Mon-Fri, to 4pm Sat & Sun) Bright blue diner by the ocean serves monster omelets, crispy bacon, country fried steak, stuffed French toast and other classic blue-plate breakfasts (for the health-conscious, egg substitutes available). Not the place for lunch, though.

TK Burgers
AMERICAN $

(www.tkburgers.com; 2119 W Balboa Blvd; dishes $2-6; ⊘10am-8:30pm Sun-Thu, to 9pm Fri & Sat; 🐾) Beef, turkey and shiitake mushroom burgers, ahi and rib-eye steak sandwiches, and good ol' corn dogs please ravenous crowds of beachgoers. There's limited seating indoors, but why would you want to miss out on the ocean breezes? Cash only.

Taco Rosa
MEXICAN $$

(www.tacorosa.com; 2632 San Miguel Rd; mains $8-17; ⊘11am-10pm; 🐾) Festive, *niños*-friendly Mexican restaurant (at the back of a strip mall) makes thoughtfully prepared dishes a step above everyday taco-beans-rice combos. The blackened-chicken burrito and crab enchiladas are tops, as is the chocolate fountain where kids hover with warm churros. Sunday brunch buffets served from 10am to 1:30pm. Costa Mesa's Taco Mesa (p251) is run by the same family.

Zov's Café
MEDITERRANEAN $$

(www.zovs.com; 21123 Newport Coast Dr, mains $12-25; ⊙11am-9pm Mon-Thu, 11am-9:30pm Fri, 8am-9:30pm Sat, 8am-9pm Sun) Bustling Zov's is the creation of local chef Zov Karamardian, known for her Mediterranean-style dishes prepared with California flair. Discounted prix-fixe lunch and dinner menus.

Cafe Lotus
VIETNAMESE $

(☑949-574-2479; 325 Old Newport Blvd; mains $5-12; ⊙8am-5pm Mon-Sat; ⊛) In the shadow of Hwy 55, this small, family-run spot serves crunchy Vietnamese baguette sandwiches, BBQ-shrimp steamed buns, rich iced coffee and more.

🍷 Drinking & Entertainment

Alta Coffee Warehouse
COFFEEHOUSE

(www.altacoffeeshop.com; 506 31st St; ⊙7am-11pm Sun-Thu, 7am-midnight Fri & Sat) Hidden on a side street, this cozy coffeehouse inhabits a beach bungalow (formerly a bookstore). It lures locals with live music and poetry readings, art on the walls and honest baristas who dish the lowdown on the day's desserts and baked goods. No coffee or food service after 9pm weekdays, 10pm weekends.

Malarky's Irish Pub
BAR

(www.malarkyspub.com; 3011 Newport Blvd; ⊙7:30am-2am) After sunset at the beach, follow the laughing leprechaun to this Balboa Peninsula sports bar where hunky lifeguard bartenders pour pints for sorority girls and their frat-boy suitors from USC. Bring ID – you *will* get carded – and show up early, or wait in line.

Muldoon's
BAR

(www.muldoonspub.com; 202 Newport Center Dr, Fashion Island; ⊙closed Mon) The SoCal Irish tradition continues at upbeat Muldoon's, anchoring a small strip mall across the street from Fashion Island. Decent, if pricey, Irish pub grub, 10 beers on tap and live acoustic sounds on summer Sunday afternoons.

Newport Beach Brewing Company
BREWPUB

(www.newportbeachbrewingcompany.com; 2920 Newport Blvd; ⊙11:30am-11pm Mon-Thu, 11:30am-1am Fri, 9am-1am Sat, 9am-11pm Sun; ⊛) The town's only microbrewery (try their signature blonde or Bisbee's ESB) is a laid-back place to catch the big game or just kick it with your buds after a day at the beach.

Regency Lido
CINEMA

(☑949-673-8350; www.regencymovies.com; 3459 Via Lido) Showing movies since 1938, the Lido screens mostly mainstream Hollywood fare, but some indie flicks too. Fully restored, it has a red velvet waterfall curtain and Italian tile work. It's at the corner of Newport Blvd, just over the bridge on the Balboa Peninsula.

Mutt Lynch
BAR

(www.muttlynchs.com; 2301 West Oceanfront; ⊙7am-midnight) Rowdy dive by the beach offers pool tables, schooners filled with dozens of beers on tap and martinis made with Korean vodka. Best on 'Sunday Fundays.'

Wine Lab
WINE BAR

(www.winelabnewport.com; 2901 W Coast Hwy; ⊙4-9pm Tue-Thu, noon-10pm Fri, 2-10pm Sat, 2-7pm Sun) Friendly wine shop offers New World wine and craft-beer tasting flights, plus small plates of artisan cheeses and charcuterie.

3-Thirty-3 Waterfront
LOUNGE

(www.3thirty3nb.com; 333 Bayside Dr) Sip cocktails with Newport's in-crowd at this upscale lounge with killer views of the yacht-filled harbor. With leopard-spotted lampshades, can you say 'Cougartown'?

Shopping

Fashion Island
MALL

(www.shopfashionisland.com; 401 Newport Center Dr; ⊙10am-9pm Mon-Fri, 10am-7pm Sat, 11am-6pm Sun) A chic outdoor mall that opened in 1967, Fashion Island sits in the middle of a traffic loop known as Newport Center Dr. Anchored by Bloomingdales, Macy's and Neiman Marcus, the mall's breezy, Mediterranean-style walkways are lined with more than 200 specialty stores, upscale kiosks, 40 chain restaurants, two multiplex cinemas and the occasional koi pond or burbling fountain. The miniature train will keep the kiddies amused.

On Balboa Island (p246), Marine Ave is lined with darling shops in an old-fashioned village atmosphere, a good place to pick up something for the kids, unique gifts or beachy souvenirs, or jewelry, art or antiques for yourself.

ℹ Information

For currency exchange, head to Costa Mesa (see p260).

Balboa Branch Library (www.city.newport-beach.ca.us/nbpl; 100 E Balboa Blvd; ⊙9am-

6pm Tue & Thu-Sat, to 9pm Mon & Wed; @奈)
Near the beach; ask for a free internet-terminal
guest pass.

Balboa Post Office (www.usps.com; 204 Main
St; ⊗9am-4pm Mon-Fri) Situated close to the
beach.

Central Library (www.city.newport-beach.
ca.us/nbpl; 1000 Avocado Ave; ⊗9am-9pm
Mon-Thu, 9am-6pm Fri & Sat, noon-5pm Sun;
@奈) Near Fashion Island mall; ask for a free
internet-terminal guest pass.

FedEx Office (www.fedexoffice.com; 230
Newport Center Dr; per min 20-30¢; ⊗7am-
11pm Mon-Fri, 9am-9pm Sat & Sun; @)
Internet access at self-service computer
workstations; free wi-fi.

Hoag Memorial Hospital Presbyterian
(☑949-764-4624; www.hoaghospital.org; 1
Hoag Dr; ⊗24hr) With 24-hour emergency
room.

Newport Walk-in Medical Group (☑949-
760-9222; http://newportwalkin.net; 2075
San Joaquin Hills Rd; ⊗8am-8pm Mon-Fri,
9am-5pm Sat & Sun) Nonemergency urgent-
care clinic.

Visit Newport Beach Inc (www.visitnewport-
beach.com; 1200 Newport Center Dr, Suite 120;
⊗8am-5pm Mon-Fri) On the loop road around
Fashion Island; hands out free brochures and
maps.

ⓘ Getting There & Around

BUS OCTA (☑714-560-6282; www.octa.net)
bus 1 connects Newport Beach and Fashion
Island mall with the OC's other beach towns,
including Corona del Mar just east, every 30
minutes to one hour. From the intersection of
Newport Blvd and PCH, bus 71 heads south
along the Balboa Peninsula to Main Ave every
hour or so. On all routes, the one-way fare is
$1.50 (exact change).

BOAT The West Coast's largest passenger catamaran, the **Catalina Flyer** (☑800-830-7744;
www.catalinainfo.com; round-trip adult/3-12yr/
senior $68/51/63, per bicycle $7), makes a
daily round-trip to Catalina Island (p211), taking
75 minutes each way. It leaves Balboa Pavilion
around 9am and returns before 6pm; check
online for discounts.

CAR & MOTORCYCLE Frequently jammed
from dawn till dusk, Hwy 55 (Newport Blvd) is
the main access road from I-405 (San Diego
Fwy); it intersects with the Pacific Coast Hwy
near the shore. In town, PCH is called W Coast
Hwy or E Coast Hwy, both in mailing addresses
and conversationally by locals.

The municipal lot beside Balboa Pier costs
$0.50 per 20 minutes, or $15 per day. Street
parking meters on the Balboa Peninsula cost
50¢ to $1 per hour (bring coins). Free parking

on residential streets, just a block or two from
the sand, is time-limited and subject to other
restrictions. In summer, expect to circle like a
hawk for a space.

For information on the Balboa Island car ferry,
see p246.

Around Newport Beach

COSTA MESA

If not for South Coast Plaza, a mammoth
shopping complex, Costa Mesa would likely
be considered just another landlocked suburb transected by the I-405. But nearby
Newport Beach and Anaheim won't be
kicking sand in the face of Costa Mesa anytime soon, not as long as the mall – properly
termed a 'shopping resort' – continues to attract 24 million visitors a year.

But Costa Mesa does have other things
going for it besides shopping. Visitors will
find Orange County's cultural heart here,
and suburban strip malls reveal surprisingly tasty cafes and foreign food holes-
in-the-wall, along with some hip bars and
clubs, that make it well worth the short
drive inland. Costa Mesa's chain hotels
and motels can be bargains compared with
Newport Beach.

✖ Eating

Mentatsu Ramen   JAPANESE $
(☑714-979-2755; 688 Baker St; mains $7-10;
⊗lunch & dinner) If you've been missing
those true-blue Tokyo noodle houses, look
no further. The OC's number-one ramen
shop, at the corner of Bristol St, is a casual
affair, where the cook's daughter brings out
piping-hot bowls of *negi-miso* ramen with
green onions and succulent sliced pork,
maybe with steaming hot *gyōza* (pot stick-
ers). Add a bottle of Sapporo or Kirin and
you're in hog heaven. Wait for a table, or
grab a seat at the counter.

Plums Café   CALIFORNIAN $$
(Map p244; ☑949-722-7586; http://plumscafe.
com; 369 E 17th St; mains $10-25; ⊗8am-3pm &
dinner) Raise your breakfast game at this
gourmet caterer's bistro tucked in the cor-
ner of a cookie-cutter strip mall. With its
exposed brick walls and sleek designs,
Plums will have you feeling oh-so-chic as
you nibble roasted hazelnut pancakes with
Oregon pepper bacon on the side or lamb
burgers with feta and couscous. Breakfast
served until 11:30am weekdays, brunch till
3pm on weekends.

Avanti Café
VEGETARIAN $

(Map p244; www.avantinatural.com; 259 E 17th St; mains $7-11; ☺11am-10pm Mon-Fri, 10:30am-10pm Sat, 10:30am-8pm Sun; ☑) A mom-and-pop vegetarian cafe so good, even carnivores will leave feeling sated. It looks like just another strip-mall storefront, but step inside for the creative chef duo's magic like shiitake-artichoke pesto pizza, eggplant sloppy 'Giotto' or smokin' tempeh BBQ. The menu features organic produce from local farms.

Habana
NUEVO LATINO $$

(☎714-556-0176; The Lab, 2930 Bristol St; mains lunch $6-13, dinner $15-36; ☺11:30am-4pm & 5-11pm Sun-Thu, to midnight Fri & Sat) With its flickering votive candles, ivy-covered courtyard and spicy Cuban, Mexican and Jamaican specialties, this sultry cantina whispers rendezvous. Paella, *ropa vieja* (shredded flank steak in tomato sauce) and salmon *al parilla* (grilled) come with plantains and black beans on the side. On weekends, the bar gets jumpin' late-night.

Memphis Café Bar
SOUTHERN $$

(☎714-432-7685; http://memphiscafe.com; 2920 Bristol St; mains lunch $7-12, dinner $12-22; ☺lunch Mon-Fri, 10am-3pm Sat & Sun, dinner daily) Inside a vintage mid-century modern building, this fashionable eatery is all about down-home flavor – think pulled-pork sandwiches, popcorn shrimp, gumbo and buttermilk-battered fried chicken. Happy hour at the bar is best.

Eat Chow
CAFE $$

(Map p244; www.eatchownow.com; 1802 Newport Blvd; mains $8-15; ☺7am-9pm Sun-Wed, to 10pm Thu-Sun) Next to a clothing boutique, a youthful crowd nibbles on parmesan-truffle fries, turkey burgers and contemporary wedge salads. Groovy indie-rock soundtrack.

Taco Mesa
MEXICAN $

(Map p244; www.tacomesa.net; 647 W 19th St; dishes $2-10; ☺7am-11pm) Sister restaurant to Newport Beach's Taco Rosa, this fresh, healthy Mexican hot spot with a salsa bar is consistently pointed out as a local favorite.

Native Foods
CAFE $

(www.nativefoods.com; The Camp, 2937 Bristol St; mains $7-12; ☺11am-10pm; ☑☒) Lunch in a yurt? In Orange County? Them's the digs at this vegan spot serving organic salads, veggie burgers, rice bowls and ooey-gooey desserts.

🍸 Drinking & Entertainment

Kitsch Bar
LOUNGE

(www.kitschbar.com; 891 Baker St; ☺8pm-2am) You won't find pink flamingos or Elvis bobbleheads at this decidedly unkitschy watering hole. Just a low-key, dimly lit lounge where the vibe is self-consciously hip. Enter between not-so-hip State Farm Insurance and Costa Mesa Dentistry. No shorts, baseball caps or flip-flops; no sign outside either.

Orange County Performing Arts Center
THEATER, CONCERT HALL

(☎714-556-2787; www.ocpac.org; 600 Town Center Dr) The ambitious Orange County Performing Arts Center draws international performing-arts luminaries and Broadway shows. Individual venues include the acoustically stunning 1700-seat Renée and Henry Segerstrom Concert Hall and the smaller multifunctional Samueli Theater, which has a wide-ranging calendar.

South Coast Repertory
THEATER

(☎714-708-5555; www.scr.org; 655 Town Center Dr) Started by a band of plucky theater grads in the 1960s, the South Coast Repertory has evolved into an Tony Award–winning company that's managed to hold true to its mission to 'explore the most urgent human and social issues of our time.' It stages groundbreaking, original plays from fall through to spring.

Milk + Honey
CAFE

(The Camp, 2981 Bristol St; ☺8am-10pm Mon-Thu, 8am-11pm Fri & Sat, 10am-10pm Sun; ☎) Fair-trade, shade-grown and organic coffee, chai tea and strong espresso drinks, plus fruit smoothies, frozen blender drinks and seasonal fro-yo flavors.

Detroit
DIVE BAR

(☎949-642-0600; www.detroitbar.com; 843 W 19th St; ☺8pm-2am) A hipster dive bar with a mod vibe and live indie bands almost nightly. Cover is less than $10, sometimes free. Weird strip-mall locale, though.

🛍 Shopping

South Coast Plaza
MALL

(www.southcoastplaza.com, 3333 Bristol St; ☺10am-9pm Mon-Fri, 10am-8pm Sat, 11am-6:30pm Sun) Like any self-respecting SoCal diva, this megamall got a facelift for her 40th birthday. Renovations paved the way for Italian travertine marble flooring in the glamorous Jewel Court and the county's first H&M and Prada stores. But the changes seem superfluous when compared to the mall's already stellar statistics: nearly 300 luxury brand and chain shops, five department stores, five valet stations and 12,750 parking spaces. Grab a map from a concierge booth.

Lab   MALL
(www.thelab.com; 2930 Bristol St) This outdoor, ivy-covered 'anti-mall,' is an in-your-face alternative to South Coast Plaza. Indie-minded shoppers can sift through vintage clothing, unique sneakers and trendy duds for teens, tweens and 20-somethings. For short attention spans, contemporary art exhibitions are displayed in the walk-through trailers of the community ARTery Gallery.

Camp   MALL
(www.thecampsite.com, 2937 Bristol St) Vegans, tree-huggers and rock climbers, lend me your ears. The Camp offers one-stop shopping for all your outdoor and natural-living needs. Patagonia, Cyclewerks, fair-trade Seed People's Market and Bundles & Bumps for moms-to-be are among the stores clustered along a leafy outdoor walkway. The parking lot is painted with inspirational quotes like 'Show Up for Life.'

ℹ Information
Travelex (South Coast Plaza, 1st fl, 3333 Bristol St; ⊙10am-9pm Mon-Fri, 10am-8pm Sat, 11am-6:30pm Sun) Foreign-currency exchange inside the mall, between Sears and Bloomingdale's.

ℹ Getting There & Around
Costa Mesa starts immediately inland from Newport Beach via Hwy 55. South Coast Plaza is off Bristol St, north of the intersection of I-405, toll-road Hwy 73 and Hwy 55, about 6 miles northeast of PCH.

Several **OCTA** (☑714-560-6282; www.octa.net) routes converge on South Coast Plaza, including bus 57 running along Bristol Ave south to Newport Beach's Fashion Island ($1.50, 20 minutes, every half hour).

CORONA DEL MAR
Savor some of SoCal's most celebrated ocean views from the bluffs of Corona del Mar, a chichi community stretching along PCH and hugging the eastern flank of Newport Channel. In addition to stellar lookouts, several postcard-perfect beaches, rocky coves and child-friendly tidepools beckon along this idyllic stretch of coast.

A half mile long, **Main Beach** (aka Corona del Mar State Beach) lies at the foot of rocky cliffs. There are restrooms, fire

TOP 10 BEACHES IN ORANGE COUNTY

» Seal Beach (p235)
» Bolsa Chica State Beach (p240)
» Huntington City Beach (p239)
» Balboa Peninsula (p245)
» Corona del Mar (below)
» Crystal Cove State Beach (p254)
» Aliso Beach County Park (p255)
» Doheny State Beach (p262)
» San Clemente City Beach (p264)
» San Onofre State Beach (p264)

rings (arrive early to snag one) and volleyball courts. All-day parking costs $15, but spaces fill by 9am on weekends. If you're lucky, you may find free parking atop the cliffs behind the beach along Ocean Blvd.

Above the west end of Main Beach, **Lookout Point** (Map p244) sits on Ocean Blvd near Heliotrope Ave. Conceal your chardonnay: technically you can't drink here, though many people do. In fact, some people practically throw cocktail parties, mostly because of the fantastic views overlooking the harbor. Take the nearby stairs off the north end of the Main Beach parking lot down to hideaway **Pirates Cove** (Map p244), a waveless beach that's great for families. Scenes from the classic TV show *Gilligan's Island* were shot here.

Kids also love the tide pools at **Little Corona Beach** (Map p244) just east of Main Beach, but be aware that the pools are being loved to death. Don't yank anything from the rocks and tread lightly; light, oxygen and heavy footsteps can kill the critters. Because there's no parking lot here, crowds may be lighter. Look for street parking on Ocean Blvd near Poppy Ave. Further west near the intersection of Ocean Blvd with Orchid Ave is **Inspiration Point** (Map p244), where the views of surf, sand and sea are impressive.

Downtown along PCH at the **Sherman Library & Gardens** (www.slgardens.org; 2647 E Pacific Coast Hwy; adult/12-16yr $3/1, free admission Mon; ⊙gardens 10:30am-4pm daily, library 9am-4:30pm Tue-Thu), profuse orchids, a rose garden, a koi pond and even a desert garden are worth a wander. The small, non-circulating research library holds a wealth of historical documents from California, Arizona, Nevada and Baja.

CRYSTAL COVE STATE PARK

With 3.5 miles of open beach and over 2300 acres of undeveloped woodland, this state beach (www.parks.ca.gov, www.crystalcovestatepark.com; 8471 N Coast Hwy; ☉6am-sunset) lets you forget you're in a crowded metropolitan area, at least once you get past the parking lot (entry $15) and stake out a place on the sand. Many visitors don't know it, but Crystal Cove is also an underwater park. Scuba enthusiasts can check out two historic anchors dating from the 1800s as well as the crash site of a Navy plane that went down in the 1940s. Alternatively you can just go tide pooling, fishing, kayaking and surfing along the undeveloped shoreline. On the park's inland side, miles of hiking and mountain biking trails await.

Sleeping & Eating

In the park's historic district, you can rent your own little cottage (http://crystalcove beachcottages.org) on the beach. Competition is so fierce that you'll usually need to book on the first day of the month six months before your intended stay, unless you get very lucky with a last-minute cancellation. You can reserve cottages and campsites by contacting ReserveAmerica (☎800-444-7275; www.reserveamerica.com; campsites $25, cottages shared $60-170, private $125-360). Campsites are environmentally friendly and undeveloped (no drinking water or toilets) and are only accessible via a strenuous three-mile hike.

South Carolina has South of the Border, South Dakota has Wall Drug and SoCal has Ruby's Crystal Cove Shake Shack (7703 E Coast Hwy; shakes $5; ☉10am-6pm). Although this been-here-forever wooden shake stand is now owned by the Ruby's Diner chain, at least the ocean views are as good as ever. Don't fear the date shake, it's delish. The shack is just east of the Crystal Cove/Los Trancos entrance to the state park's historic district.

In the district, the atmospheric Beachcomber Café (☎949-376-6900; www.thebeach combercafe.com; 15 Crystal Cove; mains breakfast & lunch $8-16, dinner $18-37; ☉7am-9:30pm) lets you soak up the vintage 1950s beach vibe as you tuck into macadamia-nut pancakes, roasted turkey club sandwiches or more serious surf-and-turf. Sunset is the magic hour for Polynesian tiki drinks by the sea.

Laguna Beach

POP 24,131

It's easy to love Laguna: secluded coves, romantic cliffs, azure waves and waterfront parks imbue the city with a Riviera-like feel. But nature isn't the only draw. From public sculptures and art festivals to free summer shuttles, the city has taken thoughtful steps to promote tourism while discreetly maintaining its moneyed quality of life (MTV's racy reality show *Laguna Beach* being one drunken, shameless exception).

One of the earliest incorporated cities in California, Laguna has a strong tradition in the arts, starting with the 'plein air' impressionists who lived and worked here in the early 1900s. Today it's the home of renowned arts festivals, several dozen galleries, a well-known museum and exquisitely preserved arts and crafts cottages and bungalows that come as a relief after seeing endless miles of suburban beige-box architecture.

Laguna stretches about 7 miles along PCH. Shops, restaurants and bars are concentrated along a short walkable stretch of downtown's 'village,' along three parallel streets: Broadway, Ocean Ave and Forest Ave. Downtown swells with tourists on summer weekends, but away from the downtown village (also the central business district) and Main Beach (where the downtown village meets the shore), there's plenty of uncrowded sand and open water. Bring quarters for the meters. Lots of quarters.

☉ Sights

With 30 public beaches sprawling along 7 miles of coastline, Laguna Beach is perfect for do-it-yourself exploring. There's always another stunning view or hidden cove just around the bend. Although many of the coves are blocked from street view by multimillion-dollar homes, a good local map or sharp eye will take you to stairways leading from PCH down to the beach. Just look for the 'beach access' signs, and be prepared to pass through people's backyards to reach the sand. Unlike its neighbors to the north, Laguna doesn't impose a beach curfew. You can rent beach chairs, umbrellas and boogie boards from Main Beach Toys (150 Laguna Ave; ☉9am-9pm), opposite Main Beach on the corner of South Coast Hwy.

FIRST THURSDAYS

On the first Thursday of the month, downtown Laguna Beach gets festive during the **First Thursdays Gallery Art Walk** (📞949-683-6871; www. firstthursdaysartwalk.com). This free monthly event takes place between 6pm and 9pm, when you can make the rounds of 40 local galleries and the Laguna Art Museum via free shuttles running between Laguna's art gallery districts (see p260).

Laguna Art Museum   MUSEUM
(📞949-494-8971; www.lagunaartmuseum.org; 307 Cliff Dr; adult/under 12yr/student & senior $15/free/12; ⊙usually 11am-5pm, to 9pm on 1st Thu) This breezy museum has changing exhibitions featuring contemporary Californian artists, and a permanent collection heavy on Californian landscapes, vintage photographs and works by early Laguna bohemians. Free guided tours are usually given at 2pm daily, and there's a unique gift shop. Hours may be extended during some exhibitions.

🌿**Pacific Marine Mammal Center**
    NATURE CENTER
(www.pacificmmc.org; 20612 Laguna Canyon Rd; donations welcome; ⊙10am-4pm; 🚸) A nonprofit organization dedicated to rescuing and rehabilitating injured or ill marine mammals, this center northeast of town has a small staff and many volunteers who help nurse rescued pinnipeds – mostly sea lions and seals – before releasing them back into the wild. There are several outside pools and holding pens – but remember, this is a rescue center, not SeaWorld. Still, it's educational and heart-warming. Admission is by donation, and anything you buy in the gift shop (say, a stuffed animal) helps.

🏃 Activities

Central Beaches   BEACHES
Near downtown's village, **Main Beach** has volleyball and basketball courts, a playground and restrooms. It's Laguna's best beach for swimming. Just north at **Picnic Beach**, it's too rocky to surf; tide pooling is best. Pick up a tide table at the visitors bureau. (Tide pool etiquette: tread lightly on dry rocks only and don't pick anything up that you find living in the water or on the rocks.)

Above Picnic Beach, the grassy, bluff-top **Heisler Park** offers vistas of craggy coves and deep-blue sea. Bring your camera – with its palm trees and bougainvillea-dotted bluffs, the scene is definitely one for posterity. Drop down below to **Divers Cove**, a deep, protected inlet popular with snorkelers and, of course, divers. A scenic walkway also connects Heisler Park to Main Beach.

North of downtown, **Crescent Bay** has big hollow waves good for bodysurfing, but parking is difficult; try the bluffs atop the beach. Off Cliff Dr north of Heisler Park before reaching Crescent Bay, **Shaw's Cove** provides the best tide pooling around. Volunteers are often on duty to answer questions and give you tide pooling tips.

Southern Beaches   BEACHES
About one mile south of downtown, secluded **Victoria Beach** has volleyball courts and **La Tour**, a Rapunzel's-tower-like structure from 1926. Skimboarding (at the south end) and scuba diving are popular here. Take the stairs down Victoria Dr; there's limited parking along PCH.

Further south, **Aliso Beach County Park** (www.ocparks.com/alisobeach; 31111 S Coast Hwy; ⊙6am-10pm) is popular with surfers, boogie boarders and skimboarders. With picnic tables, fire pits and a play area, it's also good for families. Pay-and-display parking costs $1 per hour. Or drive south and park on PCH for free.

Jealously guarded by locals, **Thousand Steps Beach** is hidden about 1 mile south of Aliso Beach. Just past Mission Hospital, park along PCH or residential side streets. At the south end of 9th St, more than 200 steps (way less than 1000) lead down to the sand. Though rocky, the beach is great for sunbathing, surfing and bodysurfing.

Diving & Snorkeling

With its coves, reefs and rocky outcroppings, Laguna is one of the best SoCal beaches for diving and snorkeling. One of the most famous spots is **Divers Cove** just below Heisler Park. It's part of the **Glenn E Vedder Ecological Reserve**, an underwater park stretching to the northern border of Main Beach. Also popular is **Shaw's Cove**. Check weather and surf conditions (📞949-494-6573) beforehand, as divers have recently drowned off this coast.

The visitors bureau has tide charts. For rentals or to rinse your gear, stop by **Laguna Sea Sports** (☑949-494-6965; www.lagunaseasports.com; 925 N Coast Hwy) near Shaw's Cove. Check out its website for more info about local dive spots and diving etiquette, as well as classes.

Surfing

Because of Laguna's coves, the surfing here isn't as stellar as it is further north. If you must, try the beaches at Thalia St, Brooks St or St Ann's Dr (but beware of rocks).

Costa Azul Surf Co (☑949-497-1423; www.costaazul.net; 689 S Coast Hwy) Rents surfboards ($30), wet suits ($20) and bodyboards or skimboards ($15). One-hour lessons (including board rental) cost $95 for one person, or $75 each for two to three people.

Stand Up Paddle (SUP) Company (☑949-715-4530; www.supcompany.com; 1099 S Coast Hwy) C'mon, everybody's doing it! It's time to learn to stand-up paddle surf, with group/private lessons costing from $45/90. SUP rentals cost $50 for three hours, $70 for all day.

Kayaking

Take a guided kayaking tour of the craggy coves of Laguna's coast – and you might just see a colony of sea lions – with **La Vida Laguna** (☑949-275-7544; www.lavidalaguna.com; 2hr guided tour adult/under 11yr $70/35). Make reservations.

Cycling & Mountain Biking

Laguna Beach isn't the greatest for road biking. Drivers along always-busy PCH are distracted by the view, so you must pay attention if you head out on that road. Up in the hills, you can have a blast mountain biking. Crystal Cove State Park and **Aliso & Wood Canyons Wilderness Park** (www.ocparks.com/alisoandwoodcanyons; 28373 Alicia Pkwy, Laguna Niguel) are rated highly by locals.

Laguna Cyclery (☑949-494-1522; www.lagunabeachcyclery.com; 240 Thalia St; ☺9am-6pm Mon-Fri, 10am-5pm Sat & Sun) Get trail info here; 24-hour road bike rental costs $65, mountain bikes $50 to $85.

Rainbow Bicycle Co (☑949-494-5806; www.teamrain.com; 485 N Coast Hwy; ☺1-6pm Mon, 10am-6pm Tue-Thu, noon-4pm Fri-Sun) Just north of downtown, 24-hour rentals of road bikes cost $35, full-suspension mountain bikes $40 (helmets included).

Hiking

Surrounded by a green belt – a rarity in SoCal – Laguna has great nature trails for hikes. If you love panoramic views, take the short, scenic drive to **Alta Laguna Park**, a locals-only park up-canyon from town. There, the moderate **Park Avenue Nature Trail**, a 1.25-mile one-way hike, takes you through fields of spring wildflowers. Open to hikers and mountain bikers, the 2.5-mile **West Ridge Trail** follows the ridgeline of the hills above Laguna. Both trails are in-and-out trips, not loops. To reach the trailheads, take Park Ave from town to its end at Alta Laguna Blvd then turn left to the park, which has restrooms and a drinking fountain.

☞ Tours

Stop by the visitors bureau (p260) to pick up brochures detailing self-guided tours on foot and by public bus. The *Heritage Walking Companion* is a tour of the town's architecture with an emphasis on Laguna's many bungalows and cottages, most dating from the 1920s and '30s. Laguna also overflows with public art, from well-placed murals to freestanding sculptures in unlikely locations. The free *Public Art Brochure* has color photos of all of Laguna's public art pieces and a map to help you navigate. Or you can just swing by Heisler Park to see almost a dozen sculptures.

🛏 Sleeping

Lodging in Laguna is on busy PCH, so expect traffic noise; bring earplugs or ask for a room away from the road. For cheaper motels and hotels, head about 10 miles inland to the I-405 (San Diego Fwy) around Irvine.

FIRE!

Like almost anywhere in SoCal, fire is an ever-present danger in and around Laguna Beach, especially on hiking and mountain-biking trails. The canyons act like chimneys and small grass fires can quickly become infernos. Use extreme caution when lighting matches and don't just toss your cigarette butts – extinguish them with water or dirt, and once they're completely out, dispose of them properly.

DON'T MISS

FESTIVALS & THE CITY

With a dramatic canyon backdrop, Laguna's **Festival of Arts** (www.foapom.com; 650 Laguna Canyon Rd; ⊗10am-11:30pm Jul & Aug; adult/student & senior $7/4) is a two-month celebration of original artwork in almost all its forms. About 140 exhibitors display artwork ranging from paintings and handcrafted furniture to scrimshaw. Begun in the 1930s by local artists who needed to drum up buyers, the festival now attracts international patrons. In addition to the art show, there are kid-friendly art workshops and live music and entertainment daily. Across the road, look for the slightly more independent-minded **Sawdust Festival** (www.sawdustartfestival.org; 935 Laguna Canyon Rd; adult/6-12yr/senior $8/3/6; ⊗10am-10pm Jul & Aug).

The most thrilling part of the main festival, an experience that will leave you rubbing your eyes in disbelief, is the **Pageant of the Masters** (☑800-487-3378; www.pageanttickets.com; admission $15-350), where human models blend seamlessly into re-creations of famous paintings. Tickets are hard to get, unless you order them more than six months in advance, but you may be able to snag last-minute cancellations at the gate. Performances usually begin at 8:30pm nightly.

Montage　　　　　　　　RESORT **$$$**
(☑949-715-6000, 866-271-6953; www.montage lagunabeach.com; 30801 S Coast Hwy; d from $525; @⏃☀☲) You'll find nowhere more indulgent on the OC's coast than this over-the-top luxury resort, especially if you hide away with your lover in a secluded bungalow. Even if you're not staying, come for a spa treatment or a cocktail and check out the lobby art and the spectacular sunburst-inlaid swimming pool. At the resort's southern end, there's underground public parking and a public walkway that loops around the grounds atop the bluffs overlooking the sea, and grants access to the sandy shore.

Inn at Laguna Beach　　　　HOTEL **$$$**
(☑949-497-9722, 800-544-4479; www.innat lagunabeach.com; 211 N Coast Hwy; r $210-600; ⏃☲) This three-story white concrete hotel, at the north end of Main Beach, walks the fine line between hip and homey. All air-con rooms have a fresh, clean look, complete with French blinds and thick featherbeds. Some have balconies overlooking the water. Extras include DVD and CD players, bathrobes and continental breakfast delivered to your door. Borrow beach gear. Parking $14.

Casa Laguna Inn & Spa　　　　B&B **$$$**
(☑949-494-2996, 800-233-0449; www.casa laguna.com; 2510 S Coast Hwy; r $300-649; @⏃) Laguna's most romantic B&B is built around a historic 1920s mission revival house surrounded by flowering gardens. Smallish air-con rooms include those inside former artists' bungalows from the 1930s

and '40s. All have fluffy beds and some have Jacuzzis. There's also a full chef-prepared breakfast made with local, organic ingredients and evening wine-and-cheese reception. Some pets OK (fee $25).

TOP CHOICE **Tides**　　　　　MOTEL **$$**
(☑949-494-2494, 888-777-2107; www.tideslaguna.com; 460 N Coast Hwy; r $175-285; ⏃☲) A bargain for Laguna, especially considering its convenient location just three long blocks north of the village. Plush bedding contributes to the two-story motel's upscale vibe. As a fun touch, each room has its own inspirational quote – try to find yours painted somewhere inside. All air-con, some kitchenettes. Pet fee $25.

Laguna Cliffs Inn　　　　HOTEL **$$**
(☑949-497-6645, 800-297-0007; www.laguna cliffsinn.com; 475 N Coast Hwy; r $190-280; ⏃☲) Be it good feng shui, friendly staff or proximity to the beach, something just feels right at this renovated 36-room courtyard inn. From the big earth-tone pillows and hardwood floors to air-con and flat-screen TVs, the decor is contemporary, comfy and clean. Settle into the outdoor heated Jacuzzi with a glass of wine as the sun drops over the ocean.

Surf & Sand Resort　　　　HOTEL **$$$**
(☑949-497-4477, 888-869-7569; www.surfand sandresort.com; 1555 S Coast Hwy; r $505-595; @⏃☲) Be lulled to sleep by the crashing of waves at this sparkling, if cookie-cutter seaside hotel where most rooms have an ocean view. Air-con rooms have ultracomfy beds,

flat-screen TVs, an iPod dock with speakers and soothing natural color schemes. There's also a full-service spa.

Hotel Seven4one
BOUTIQUE HOTEL **$$$**
(☎949-494-6200, 877-741-9283; www.seven4one.com; 741 S Coast Hwy; r $269-399; @🐾🌐🐕) Madly mod digs make a trendy alternative to motels. With just a dozen air-con rooms and one-bedroom suites, decked out in sleek contemporary design, the staff can afford to give you some personal attention. Pluses: energy-efficient, eco-conscious upgrades. Minuses: small rooms with super-thin walls.

Art Hotel
MOTEL **$$**
(☎949-494-6464, 877-363-7227; www.arthotellagunabeach.com; 1404 N Coast Hwy; r $139-179; 🌐🐾🐕) A mile northwest of the village, this easygoing, better-than-average two-story motel charges bargain rates, at least for Laguna. In keeping with the theme, colorful paintings hang throughout the halls. Some pet-friendly rooms, all air-con. Take the shuttle downtown.

✕ Eating

Laguna's dining scene will tickle foodies' fancies. Vegetarians will be happy, too, especially at the weekly **farmers market** (384 Forest Ave; ⊙8am-noon Sat) in the Lumberyard parking lot, near City Hall.

Taco Loco
MEXICAN **$**
(http://tacoloco.net; 640 S Coast Hwy; dishes $3-14; ⊙11am-midnight Sun-Thu, to 2am Fri & Sat) Throw back Coronas with the surfers while watching the passersby on PCH at this Mexican sidewalk cafe across from the beach. Taco, quesadilla and nacho options seem endless: blackened calamari or tofu, swordfish, veggie and shrimp to name a few. Order at the counter, dude.

⬙TOP CHOICE 242 Cafe Fusion Sushi
JAPANESE **$$$**
(www.fusionart.us; 242 N Coast Hwy; mains $18-45; ⊙4:30-10pm Sun-Thu, to 10:30pm Fri & Sat) One of the only female sushi chefs in Orange County, Miki Izumisawa slices and rolls Laguna's best sushi – and it's artfully presented too. The place seats maybe 20 people at a time, so expect a wait or come early. The 'sexy' handroll – spicy ahi, scallops and shrimp with mint, cilantro, avocado and crispy potato – is date-enhancing.

Watermarc
NEW AMERICAN **$$$**
(☎949-376-6272; www.watermarcrestaurant.com; 448 S Coast Hwy; dinner mains $21-38;

⊙lunch & dinner) At this stylish purveyor of New American cuisine, the small-plates menu ($6 to $12) ranges from filet mignon pot pie and clams casino to sizzling shrimp and *chilies fritas*. In fact, appetizers are so good, and the cocktail list so inventive (blueberry-coconut mojito, anyone?), you might decide to skip the classic surf-and-turf dinners. The sleek, not stuffy dining room has glass front doors thrown open to the sidewalk and sea breezes.

Zinc Café & Market
VEGETARIAN **$**
(www.zinccafe.com; 350 Ocean Ave; breakfast & lunch mains $6-13; ⊙market 6am-6pm, cafe 7am-4pm Mon & Tue, to 9:30pm Wed-Sun; 🐾) Ground zero for Laguna's see-and-be-seen vegetarians, this gourmet market has a hedge-enclosed patio where you can munch on tasty vegetarian and vegan meals such as garden-fresh salads and pizzas. If you've been hesitant to order oatmeal at a restaurant, resist no more: Zinc's fresh fruit-covered version is delish. Strong espresso too.

Stand
VEGETARIAN **$**
(☎949-494-8101; 238 Thalia St; dishes $5-10; ⊙7am-7pm; 🐾) With its friendly, indie-spirited vibe comes this tiny tribute to healthy cuisine. From hummus and guac sandwiches to sunflower sprout salads and black-beans-and-rice burritos, the menu is varied and all of it soul-satisfying. Try a smoothie or an all-natural shake. Order at the counter in the red minibarn, then cross your fingers for an outdoor patio table.

230 Forest Avenue
CALIFORNIAN **$$$**
(☎949-494-2545; http://230forestave.com; 230 Forest Ave; mains $16-30; ⊙lunch & dinner) Sleek, contemporary and chatty bistro in the heart of downtown's village is always bustling – not just for its martini bar but more importantly for its fresh seafood like buttermilk calamari, 'bang-bang' rock shrimp, five-spice ahi sashimi or garlic-lemongrass soup with clams and mussels. It may look haute, but you can get away with a dressy swimsuit cover-up at lunch.

Mozambique
AFRICAN FUSION **$$$**
(☎949-715-7777; www.mozambiqueoc.com; 1740 S Coast Hwy; dinner mains $15-55; ⊙3:30pm-midnight Mon-Sat, 11am-midnight Sun) Trendy, half-hearted ode to peri-peri spiced cuisine from southern Africa manages to have fun with its theme – witness the parrot out front and the canopied lounge – while serving sophisticated, exotically spiced dishes. Who knows, you might see a *Desperate*

Housewives cast member hiding out in the clubhouse-y second-floor bar, which has live music on weekends.

Orange Inn
DINER $
(☎949-494-6085; 703 S Coast Hwy; mains $5-8; ⊗6am-5pm) Date shakes, big breakfasts, homemade muffins and deli sandwiches on whole-wheat or sourdough bread. It's where surfers fuel up before hitting the waves.

House of Big Fish & Cold Beer
SEAFOOD $$
(949-715-4500; www.houseofbigfish.com; 540 S Coast Hwy; dishes $8-24; ⊗11:30am-10:30pm) The name says it all. (What else do you need?) Hawaii-style *poke* (marinated raw fish), Baja-style fish tacos, coconut shrimp and the fresh catch o' the day. Make reservations, or wait, like, forever.

Drinking & Entertainment

There are almost as many watering holes in downtown's village as there are art galleries. Most cluster along S Coast Hwy and Ocean Ave, making for an easy pub crawl.

Rooftop Lounge
LOUNGE
(www.rooftoplagunabeach.com; 1280 S Coast Hwy) Perched atop La Casa del Camino hotel, this bar, with its coastal views and friendly vibe, has locals singing hallelujahs. Follow the fashionable crowds through the hotel's lobby and take the elevator to the top. Mango and wild berry mojitos add some spice to the cocktail menu.

Marine Room Tavern
DIVE BAR
(214 Ocean Ave) The party's always rockin' at this lively tavern in downtown's village where the Harley-loving crowd isn't afraid to whoop it up, sometimes right on the sidewalk. Although you won't find food or many marines, there are pool tables and pinball. Live music most nights.

Ocean Brewing Company
BREWPUB
(www.oceanbrewing.com; 237 Ocean Ave) For pub grub and microbrews after a day of surfing. This place lines up copper vats behind the bar and has different DJs and live acoustic acts almost nightly (except when there's karaoke). Kick back on the outdoor patio for primo people-watching.

Las Brisas
BAR
(www.lasbrisaslagunabeach.com; 361 Cliff Dr) Locals roll their eyes at the mere mention of this tourist-heavy resto, but out-of-towners flock here for a reason: the view. You won't soon forget the image of

crashing waves as you sip margaritas on the glassed-in patio on the bluff. Cocktail hour gets packed. Don't come if it's dark outside.

Koffee Klatsch
COFFEEHOUSE
(1440 S Coast Hwy; ⊗6:30am-11pm Sun-Thu, to midnight Fri & Sat) About a mile south of downtown, this cozy coffee shop draws a mixed gay/straight crowd. So does the formerly gay men's bar next door, **Bounce**, a tiny room for mingling and getting down with DJs on weekends.

Laguna Playhouse
THEATER
(☎949-497-2787; www.lagunaplayhouse.com; 606 Laguna Canyon Rd) Orange County's oldest continuously operating community theater stages lighter plays in summer, more serious works in winter.

🛍 Shopping

Downtown's village is a shopper's paradise, with hidden courtyards and eclectic little bungalows that beg further exploration. Forest Ave has the highest concentration of chic boutiques, but south of downtown, PCH has its fair share of fashionable, eclectic and arty shops too.

Hobie Surf Shop
SPORTS, CLOTHING
(www.hobie.com; 294 Forest Ave) Hobart 'Hobie' Alter started his internationally known surf line in his parents' Laguna Beach garage more than 50 years ago. Today, this is one of only a handful of logo retail shops where you can stock up on surfboards and beachwear (love those rainbow flip-flops!) for both babes and dudes.

Laguna Supply
CLOTHING
(210 Beach St) This earth-toned corner shop hits that right pitch for an effortless girlfriends' weekend beach getaway, somewhere in between urban chic and beach preppy, with distressed denim, boyfriend shirts and breezy woven scarves.

Muse Boutique
CLOTHING
(www.myspace.com/museboutiquelagunabeach; 300 Forest Ave) Fans of MTV's *Laguna Beach* will recognize this upbeat gallery where women's beach-chic couture, handbags and jewelry glitter under a sky-blue ceiling dotted with wispy clouds. You'll faint after glimpsing the price tags.

Art for the Soul
GIFTS
(www.art4thesoul.com; 272 Forest Ave) Decorated in big, bold colors, this offbeat craft gallery is the place to fill your bags with

DIY GALLERY WALK

Laguna has three distinct gallery districts: **Gallery Row**, along the 300 to 500 blocks of N Coast Hwy; in **downtown's village**, along Forest Ave and PCH; and further south on **S Coast Hwy** between Oak St and Bluebird Canyon Dr. Pick up an art-walk map at the visitors bureau.

Laguna North Gallery (www.lagunanorthgallery.com; 376 N Coast Hwy; ⊙11am-4:30pm), **Studio 7 Gallery** (www.studio7gallery.com 384b N Coast Hwy; ⊙11am-5pm) and off-the-beaten-path **seven-degrees** (www.seven-degrees.com; 891 Laguna Canyon Rd; ⊙10am-5pm Mon-Fri) further inland are all artists' cooperative galleries. South of downtown, **Bluebird Gallery** (www.bluebirdgallery.net; 1540 S Coast Hwy; ⊙11am-5pm Wed-Sun) exhibits California landscape paintings in Laguna's impressionist *plein-air* style. On First Thursdays (see p255), most participating galleries stay open until 9pm.

surf 'woody' wagon night lights, painted pint glasses, art-glass jewelry and starfish wind chimes.

Pacific Gallery   GIFTS
(www.pacificgallery.net; 228 Forest Ave) Here you'll find art that's whimsical and sometimes irresistible, but no bargains. All of the pieces are handmade – from sculptures and paintings to welded metal and mosaics – some by Laguna artists.

Trashpretty   CLOTHING, GIFTS
(http://trashprettyshop.com; 1103 S Coast Hwy) If you want to run screaming from Laguna's perfectly coiffed movie-star boutiques, head for this alternative universe of outrageous vintage dresses, costume jewelry, funky hats and vinyl records and tapes from decades gone by. Garage and surf-punk bands occasionally play live shows.

ⓘ Information

Bookstores

Barnaby Rudge Bookseller (www.barnaby rudge.com; 1445 Glenneyre St) Wonderful antiquarian bookstore also sells antique maps and SoCal landscape prints.

Laguna Beach Books (www.lagunabeach books.com; 1200 S Coast Hwy, Old Pottery Place) Friendly indie bookshop stocks everything, including surf culture and SoCal local-interest titles.

Latitude 33 (latitude33bookshop.com; 311 Ocean Ave) Crammed floor to ceiling with books, this eclectic shop sponsors children's story time, open-mic nights and author readings.

Internet Access

The **Laguna Beach Visitors & Conference Bureau** (see p260) has free wi-fi and 15-minute internet terminal access.

Laguna Beach Library (www.ocpl.org; 363 Glenneyre St; ⊙10am-8pm Mon-Wed, to 6pm Thu, to 5pm Fri & Sat; @⊚) Free wi-fi and walk-in online computer access.

Internet Resources & Media

Green Laguna Beach (http://greenlaguna beach.com) Green travel ideas, garden tours, hiking trails, eco-events and more tips.

Laguna Beach Coastline Pilot (www.coast linepilot.com) Newspaper covering the dining, arts and culture scenes, with an up-to-date calendar online.

OC Weekly (www.ocweekly.com) Free alternative tabloid and website reviewing nightlife, restaurants and the arts, plus a current events calendar.

Medical Services

Mission Hospital Laguna Beach (☏949-499-1311; www.missionforhealth.com; 31872 Coast Hwy; ⊙24hr) A 24-hour hospital emergency room, 4 miles south of downtown along PCH.

Sleepy Hollow Medical Group (☏949-494-3740; www.andersonwmcmd.com; 364 Ocean Ave; ⊙8am-6pm Mon-Sat, 9am-1pm Sun) Walk-in nonemergency clinic.

Post

Post office (www.usps.com; 350 Forest Ave; ⊙9am-5pm Mon-Fri)

Tourist Information

Laguna Beach Visitors & Conference Bureau (www.lagunabeachinfo.com; 381 Forest Ave; ⊙10am-5pm; @⊚) Helpful staff, bus schedules, restaurant menus and free brochures on everything from hiking trails to self-guided walking tours.

ⓘ Getting There & Away

From I-405, take Hwy 133 (Laguna Canyon Rd) southwest. Hwy 1 goes by several names in Laguna Beach: south of Broadway, downtown's main street, it's called South Coast Hwy; north of Broadway it's North Coast Hwy. Locals also call it Pacific Coast Hwy or just PCH.

OCTA (☎714-560-6282; www.octa.net) bus 1 heading along the coast connects Laguna Beach with Orange County's other beach towns, including Dana Point heading south, every 30 to 60 minutes. The one-way fare is $1.50 (exact change).

❶ Getting Around

Bus Laguna Beach Transit (www.laguna beachcity.net; 375 Broadway) has its central bus depot in downtown's village. Buses operate on three routes at hourly intervals (no service from 12:30pm to 1:30pm or on Sundays or public holidays). Routes are color-coded and are easy to follow. For tourists, the most important bus route runs south of downtown along PCH. Rides cost $0.75 (exact change). All routes are free during July and August. You can pick up an information brochure and bus schedule at the visitors bureau.

CAR Through town, PCH moves slowly in summer, especially on weekends.

Parking lots in downtown's village charge between $10 and $20 per entry; they fill up early in the day during summer. Street parking can be hard to find near the beaches during summer, especially in the afternoons and on weekends – arrive early. Coin-operated meters cost from $1 per hour and pay-and-display lots cost $2 per hour. There's a change machine on Cliff Dr at Jasmine St and a few more scattered around downtown. Alternatively, you can park for free in residential areas, but obey time limits and posted restrictions, or you'll be towed. If you can't find any parking downtown, drive to the north or south ends of town by the beach, then ride the bus.

SHUTTLE To alleviate summer traffic, **free trolley shuttles** travel between downtown and popular festival sites in Laguna Canyon and north–south along PCH. These trolleys make continuous loops every 20 to 30 minutes between 9:30am and 11:30pm daily from late June until late August.

Around Laguna Beach

SAN JUAN CAPISTRANO

Famous for its swallows that fly back to town every year on March 19 (though sometimes they're just a bit early), San Juan Capistrano is also home to the 'jewel of the California missions.' It's a little town, about 11 miles south and inland of Laguna Beach, but there's enough history and charm here to make almost a day of it.

◉ Sights & Activities

Mission San Juan Capistrano

HISTORIC BUILDINGS

(www.missionsjc.com; 26801 Ortega Hwy; adult/4-11yr/senior $9/5/8; ◷8:30am-5pm) Plan on spending at least an hour poking around the sprawling mission's lush gardens, fountains, courtyards and mission structures – including the padre's quarters, soldiers' barracks and the cemetery. Particularly moving are the towering remains of the Great Stone Church, almost completely destroyed by a powerful earthquake on December 8, 1812. The **Serra Chapel** – white-washed outside with restored frescoes inside – is believed to be the oldest building in California. It's certainly the only one still standing in which Junípero Serra gave Mass. Serra founded the mission on November 1, 1776, and tended it personally for many years.

Admission includes a worthwhile free audio tour with interesting stories narrated by locals. The Mission is at the corner of Camino Capistrano.

Los Rios Historic District HISTORIC BUILDINGS
One block southwest of the Mission, next to the Capistrano train depot, this peaceful assemblage of a few dozen historic cottages and adobes now mostly houses cafes and gift shops. To see 1880s-era furnishings and decor, as well as vintage photographs, stop by the tiny **O'Neill Museum** (31831 Los Rios St; ◷9am-noon & 1-4pm Tue-Fri, noon-3pm Sat & Sun). You can pick up a free walking-tour guide of historic San Juan Capistrano at the volunteer-staffed information kiosk off Verdugo St, by the railroad tracks.

✖ Eating & Drinking

There are a lot of restaurants within walking distance of the Mission; the following are a few favorites.

Ramos House Café CALIFORNIAN $$
(www.ramoshouse.com; 31752 Los Rios St; mains $11-17; ◷8:30am-3pm Tue-Sun) Famous for earthy comfort food flavored with herbs from the garden round back, Ramos House is the best spot for breakfast or lunch near the Mission. To find it, walk across the railroad tracks at the end of Verdugo St and turn right. Promptly reward yourself with cinnamon-apple beignets, basil-cured salmon lox or pulled-pork sandwiches with sweet-potato fries.

DON'T MISS

FIESTA DE LA GOLONDRINAS

The famous swallows return to nest in the walls of Mission San Juan Capistrano every year around March 19, the feast of Saint Joseph, after wintering in South America. Their flight covers about 7500 miles each way. The highlight of the town's month-long **Festival of the Swallows** (www.swallowsparade.com) is the big parade and outdoor *mercado* (market), held on a Saturday in mid-March.

Señor Pedro's MEXICAN $
(31721 Camino Capistrano; dishes $3-6; ⏰10am-8pm; 🍴) Devour generously portioned Mexican-American takeout – potato burritos, fish taco salads, vegetarian *sopes* (fried and filled corn-dough rounds) and more – from this modest drive-in. The plastic picnic tables outdoors afford views of the Mission's walls. Cash only.

El Campeon MEXICAN $
(31921 Camino Capistrano; ⏰6:30am-9pm; 🍴) If you want real-deal Mexican food, detour south of the Mission to this butcher shop and *panadería* (bakery) that piles its grilled-meat tacos, tostadas and burritos into freshly made tortillas. *Aguas frescas* (fruit drinks) come in fruity flavors like watermelon, strawberry and grapefruit.

Coach House NIGHTCLUB
(☎949-496-8930; www.thecoachhouse.com; 33157 Camino Capistrano) Long-running live-music venue features a roster of local and national rock, indie, alternative and retro bands; expect a cover charge of $15 to $40, depending on who's playing. Recent performers include Dada, Lisa Loeb and the Sierra Leone Refugee All-Stars.

Sample local fruits, veggies and specialty foods at downtown's weekly **farmers market** (⏰3-6pm Wed, to 7pm Apr-Oct).

❶ Getting There & Away

BUS From Laguna Beach, ride **OCTA** (☎714-560-6282; www.octa.net) bus 1 south to Dana Point. At the intersection of PCH and Del Obispo St, catch bus 91 northbound toward Mission Viejo, which drops you near the Mission. Buses run every 30 to 60 minutes. The trips takes about an hour. You'll have to pay the one-way fare ($1.50, exact change) twice.

CAR & MOTORCYCLE Drivers should take I-5 exit 82 (Ortega Hwy), then head west about 0.25 miles.

TRAIN The **Amtrak** (☎800-872-7245; www.amtrak.com; 26701 Verdugo St) depot is one block south and west of the Mission. You could arrive by train from LA ($17, 1½ hours) or San Diego ($18, 80 minutes) in time for lunch, visit the mission and be back in the city for dinner. A few daily **Metrolink** (☎800-371-5465; www.metrolinktrains.com) commuter trains link San Juan Capistrano to Orange ($8, 45 minutes), with limited connections to Anaheim.

Dana Point

POP 37,326

Dana Point was once called 'the only romantic spot on the coast.' Too bad that quote dates from seafarer Richard Dana's voyage here in the 1830s. For the last few decades, Dana Point has never quite mustered the same recognition as its more charismatic neighbors to the north. But changes are afoot. Stay tuned, and come check out these 7 miles of scenic coastal bluffs before word gets out.

⊙ Sights & Activities

Most attractions cluster in and around artificial Dana Point Harbor, at the foot of Golden Lantern St, just south of PCH off Dana Point Harbor Dr.

Doheny State Beach BEACH
(www.dohenystatebeach.org; 25300 Dana Point Harbor Dr; ⏰6am-10pm; 🐾) Adjacent to the southern border of Dana Point Harbor, this mile-long beach is great for swimmers, surfers, surf fishers and tidepoolers. You'll also find picnic tables with grills, volleyball courts and a butterfly exhibit at this 62-acre coastal park. All-day parking costs $15. Stop by the parks' **visitors center** (⏰10am-4pm Sat & Sun, hr vary Mon-Fri) to check out the five aquariums, mounted birds and 500-gallon simulated tidepool. Free wi-fi at the snack bar.

Rent bicycles at **Wheel Fun Rentals** (www.wheelfunrentals.com; 25300 Dana Point Harbor Dr; cruiser rental per hr/day $10/28), just south of the picnic area at Doheny State Beach. Off Dana Point Harbor Dr, **Capo Beach Watercraft Rentals** (☎949-661-1690; www.capobeachwatercraft.com; 34512 Embarcadero Pl) and **Dana Point Jet Ski & Kayak Center** (☎949-661-4947; 34671 Puerto Pl) both rent kayaks for harbor paddling. For scuba rentals and dive-boat trips (from

$89), try **Beach Cities Scuba** (☑949-443-3858; www.beachcitiesscuba.com; 34283 Pacific Coast Hwy).

Ocean Institute   NATURE CENTER
(☑949-496-2274; www.ocean-institute.org; 24200 Dana Point Harbor Dr; adult/3-12yr $6.50/4.50; ◷usually 10am-3pm Sat & Sun; ▣) This child-friendly educational center encompasses four separate ocean-centric 'adventures.' On Sundays, admission includes the opportunity to discover what life was like aboard an early 19th-century tall ship, the brig **Pilgrim**. Guided tours of this full-size replica of the ship sailed by Richard Dana during his journey around Cape Horn to California are offered hourly.

The **Ocean Education Center** is reserved for school groups on weekdays, but on weekends families are welcome to enjoy the interactive marine-focused exhibits. You can also board the **R/V Sea Explorer** (adult/4-12yr from $35/22), a 70ft-long floating lab, for a science-focused snorkeling cruise or blue whale safari, or join a 'pyrate' adventure or gray-whale-watching cruise on the **Spirit of Dana Point** (adult/4-12yr $40/23), a replica of an American Revolution–era tall ship. Make reservations.

Salt Creek Beach   BEACH
(www.ocparks.com/saltcreekbeach; 33333 S Pacific Coast Hwy, off Ritz Carlton Dr; ◷5am-midnight) Just south of the Laguna Beach boundary, this 18-acre county-run park is popular with surfers, sunbathers, bodysurfers and tidepoolers. Families make the most of the park's picnic tables, grills, restrooms and showers – all sprawling beneath the elegant bluff-top Ritz Carlton resort. Open in summer, a beach concession stand rents boogie boards, beach chairs and umbrellas. Pay-and-display parking costs $1 per hour. Call ahead to check the center's opening times, which are subject to change.

TOP FIVE OC SURF SPOTS

» Huntington Pier (p238), Huntington Beach

» Newport Pier (p246), Newport Beach

» Trestles (p264), San Clemente

» T-Street (p264), San Clemente

» Doheny State Beach (p262), Dana Point

⊙ Tours

In Mariner's Village off Dana Point Harbor Dr, Dana Wharf is the starting point for most boat tours and trips to Catalina Island. For more kid-friendly whale-watching tours and coastal cruises, book ahead with the **Ocean Institute**.

Capt Dave's Dolphin & Whale Safari
                              BOAT TOURS
(☑949-488-2828; www.dolphinsafari.com; 34451 Ensenada Pl; adult/3-12yr from $55/35) Year-round dolphin- and whale-watching trips on a catamaran equipped with underwater viewing windows, plasma TV screens and stereophonic headphones that let you listen in on the pods.

Dana Wharf Sportfishing   BOAT TOURS
(☑949-496-5794, tickets 800-979-3370; www.danawharf.com; 34675 Golden Lantern St; sportfishing trips adult/3-12yr from $39/25, whale-watching tours from $25/15) Half-day sportfishing trips are best for beginners. Whale-watching tours for families operate both winter and summer.

✦✦ Festivals & Events

Festival of Whales (www.dpfestivalofwhales.com) A parade, street fair, nature walks and talks, canoe races, surfing clinics, art exhibitions, live music, and surf 'woody' wagon and hot-rod show make up the merriment.

Doheny Blues Festival (www.omegaevents.com/dohenyblues) Blues legends such as Taj Mahal and Otis Taylor perform alongside up-and-comers over a weekend of funky live music performances and family fun at Doheny State Beach, usually in mid-May.

Tall Ships Festival (www.tallshipsfestival.com) In mid-September, the Ocean Institute hosts the West Coast's largest gathering of tall ships, with living-history encampments, scrimshaw carving demonstrations and lots more family-friendly marine-themed activities.

🛏 Sleeping & Eating

Regularly voted the county's best campground, **Doheny State Beach** (☑800-444-7275; www.reserveamerica.com; 25300 Dana Point Harbor Dr; inland/beachfront campsites $35/60) offers picnic tables, fire rings, restrooms and showers, but little shade.

Mostly chain midrange motels and luxury resorts are what you'll find along PCH.

The latter include the oceanfront Ritz-Carlton Laguna Niguel (☎949-240-2000; www.ritzcarlton.com; 1 Ritz-Carlton Dr; r from $420; @🛈🕾🏊), well-positioned for catching sunsets at Salt Creek Beach. For budget motels, head inland along I-405 (San Diego Fwy) back toward Irvine.

Those hankering for straight-off-the-boat seafood can fill their bellies at pierside seafood restaurants around Dana Point Harbor. Take a wander and see what looks fresh and what tickles your fancy. At Dana Wharf, Turk's (34683 Golden Lantern St; mains $5-16; ⊙7am-2am) dive bar is so dark it feels like you're drinking while jailed in the brig of a ship, but never mind. There's plenty of good pub grub (including burgers and fish-and-chips), Bloody Marys and beers, a mellow crowd and a groovy jukebox.

ℹ Information

Visitors Center (www.danapoint.org; ⊙9am-4pm Fri-Sun late May-early Sep) Stop at this tiny booth at the corner of Golden Lantern St and Dana Point Harbor Dr for tourist brochures and maps. Gung-ho volunteers sure love their city.

ℹ Getting There & Around

From the harbor, **Catalina Express** (☎800-481-3470; www.catalinaexpress.com; 34675 Golden Lantern St; round-trip adult/2-11yr/senior $69/53/62) makes daily round-trips to Catalina Island (p211), taking 90 minutes each way.

OCTA (☎714-560-6282; www.octa.net) bus 1 connects Dana Point with the OC's other beach towns every 30 to 60 minutes. The one-way fare is $1.50 (exact change).

Four-hour public parking at the harbor is free, or pay $5 per day (overnight $10).

San Clemente

POP 61,610

Just before reaching San Diego County, PCH slows down and rolls past the laid-back surf town of San Clemente. Home to surfing legends, top-notch surfboard companies and *Surfing* magazine, this unpretentious enclave may be one of the last spots in the OC where you can authentically live the surf lifestyle. Right on, brah.

A quick detour inland, the **Surfing Heritage Foundation** (☎949-388-0313; www.surfingheritage.com; 101 Calle Iglesia; donations welcome; ⊙1-5pm Mon-Fri) tells the history of the sport by exhibiting surfboards ridden by the greats, from Duke Kahanomoku to Kelly Slater. Call for directions.

Otherwise, turn south off PCH and follow **Avenida del Mar** as it winds south through San Clemente's retro downtown district, where antiques and vintage shops, eclectic boutiques, cafes, restaurants and bars line the main drag. Keep curving downhill toward the ocean until you hit **San Clemente City Beach**, stretching beside the historic 1296ft-long **San Clemente Pier** (611 Avenida Victoria; ⊙4am-midnight), where Prohibition-era bootleggers once brought liquor ashore. Surfers go north of the pier, while swimmers and bodysurfers take the south side. Further south along the coast, at the foot of Trafalgar Street, **T-Street** is another popular surf break.

🛏 Sleeping & Eating

If you can't help but linger overnight, the breezy B&B rooms at **Casa Tropicana** (☎949-492-1234, 800-492-1245; www.casatropicana.com; 610 Avenida Victoria; r $285-475; @🛈) all have contemporary beachy design, private baths and ocean-view decks. Also nearby the pier, **La Galette Creperie** (www.

DON'T MISS

TRESTLES

Surfers won't want to miss world-renowned **Trestles**, just southeast of San Clemente. It's famous for its natural surf break that consistently churns out perfect waves, even in summer. Surfers and environmentalists recently joined hands to successfully fight off the extension of a nearby toll road that would have negatively affected the waves – visit www.surfrider.org/savetrestles to learn more.

Trestles lies inside protected **San Onofre State Beach** (www.parks.ca.gov), which has rugged bluff-top walking trails, swimming beaches and a developed inland **campground** (☎800-444-7275; www.reserveamerica.com; campsites $35-60) with flush toilets, indoor hot showers, picnic tables and fire pits. To get here, exit I-5 at Los Christianos Rd. All-day beach parking costs $15.

lagalettecreperie.com; 612 Avenida Victoria; mains $6-9; ⊙7am-3pm) is a brunch spot for sweet and savory crepes – try the molten chocolate or chicken with maple barbecue sauce.

Surfers grab their breakfast burritos and eggy seaside scramblers inland at **Pipes Cafe** (www.pipoccafe.com; 2017 S El Camino Real; mains $6-9; ⊙7am-3pm), which also has a coffee bar. You'll find more wet suit–clad crowds at the tiki-style **Bagel Shack** (www.thebagelshack.com; 777 S El Camino Real; items $1-6; ⊙5:30am-2:30pm), which mixes fruit smoothies too. It's directly uphill from T-Street. Also just off the I-5 (San Diego Fwy), where chain motels and hotels cluster, **Riders Club Cafe** (www.ridersclubcafe.com; 1701 N El Camino Real; mains $5-10; ⊙11am-9pm Tue-Thu & Sun, to 10pm Fri & Sat) grills juicy, top-quality burgers and has microbrewed beers on tap. Their eco-culinary motto: 'Slow Fast Food.'

❶ Getting There & Around

OCTA (☑714-560-6282; www.octa.net) bus 1 heads south from Dana Point every 30 to 60 minutes. At San Clemente's **Metrolink station** (☑800-371-5465; www.metrolinktrains.com), transfer to OCTA bus 191, which runs hourly to San Clemente Pier. You'll need to pay the one-way fare ($1.50, exact change) twice.

Two daily **Amtrak** (☑800-872-7245; www.amtrak.com) trains between San Diego ($17, 75 minutes) and LA ($18, 90 minutes), via San Juan Capistrano and Anaheim, stop at San Clemente Pier.

San Clemente is about 6 miles southeast of Dana Point via PCH. Pay-and-display parking at the pier costs $1 per hour.

San Diego

Best Places to Eat

» Cucina Urbana (p293)

» Café Chloe (p291)

» Urban Solace (p293)

» Old Town Mexican Cafe (p293)

» Las Olas (p323)

Best Places to Stay

» Hotel del Coronado (p307)

» US Grant Hotel (p277)

» Hotel Solamar (p287)

» Hotel Indigo (p287)

» Lodge at Torrey Pines (p317)

Why Go?

New York has its cabbie, Chicago its bluesman and Seattle its coffee-drinking boho. San Diego, meanwhile, has the valet guy in a polo shirt, khaki shorts and crisp new sneakers. With his perfectly tousled hair, great tan and gentle enthusiasm, he looks like he's on a perennial spring break, and when he wishes you welcome, he really means it.

This may sound pejorative, but our intention is the opposite. San Diego calls itself 'America's Finest City' and its breezy confidence and sunny countenance filter down even to folks you encounter every day on the street. It's the nation's eighth-largest city, yet we're hard-pressed to think of a place of any size that's more laid-back.

What's not to love? San Diego bursts with world-famous attractions for visitors, including the zoo, SeaWorld, Legoland and the museums of Balboa Park, plus a bubbling downtown and beaches ranging from ritzy to raucous, and America's most perfect weather.

When to Go

San Diego

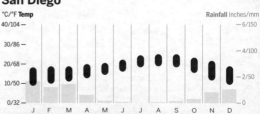

June–August	September–October, March–May	November–February
High season. Temperatures and hotel rates are highest.	Shoulder seasons; moderate rates.	Low season while most of America escapes the cold.

History

Evidence of human habitation in the region goes back to at least 18,000 BC, in the form of middens (ancient refuse heaps). When Spanish explorer Juan Rodríguez Cabrillo became the first European to sail into San Diego Bay in 1542, the region was divided peaceably between the native Kumeyaay and Luiseño/Juaneño peoples. Their way of life continued undisturbed until Catholic missionary Father Junípero Serra and Gaspar de Portolá arrived in 1769. These newcomers founded the first permanent European settlement in California – a mission and fort on the hill now known as the Presidio.

When the United States took California from Mexico following the Mexican-American War of the 1840s, San Diego was little more than a ramshackle village. But San Francisco property speculator William Heath Davis saw a fortune to be made. In the 1850s he bought 160 acres of bay-front property and erected homes, a wharf and warehouses. 'Davis' Folly' eventually went bust, but just a decade later, another San Francisco speculator, Alonzo E Horton, acquired 960 acres of waterfront land and promoted it as 'New Town.' This time the idea stuck.

Gold was discovered in the hills east of San Diego in 1869, and the ensuing rush resulted in the construction of the railroad in 1884. It also led to a classic Wild West culture, with saloons, gambling houses and brothels behind the respectable Victorian facades of the present-day Gaslamp Quarter. But when gold played out, the economy took a nosedive and the city's population plummeted by as much as 50%.

Spurred by San Francisco's international exhibition of 1914, San Diego's staged the Panama-California Exposition (1915–16), aiming to attract investment to the city with its deepwater port, railroad hub and perfect climate. Boosters built exhibition halls in the romantic Spanish Colonial style that still defines much of the city today.

However it was the 1941 bombing of Pearl Harbor that permanently made San Diego. Top brass quickly chose San Diego, with its excellent, protected port, as home of the US Pacific Fleet. The military literally reshaped the city, dredging the harbor, building landfill islands and constructing vast tracts of instant housing (see also p418).

The opening of a University of California campus in the 1960s heralded a new era as students and faculty slowly drove a liberal wedge into the city's homogenous, flag-and-family culture. The university, especially strong in the sciences, has also become a biotech incubator. The 2010 census is showing for the first time that the non-white population has grown to parity with the county's white population.

Coastal communities, including Coronado, Ocean, Mission and Pacific Beaches, La Jolla and North County are covered in separate sections later in this chapter. San Diego is a fantastic destination for families – see p52 for ideas.

⊙ Sights

SAN DIEGO ZOO & BALBOA PARK

San Diego's Zoo is a highlight of any trip to California and should be a high priority for first-time visitors. The Zoo occupies some prime real estate in Balboa Park, which itself is packed with museums and gardens. To visit all the sights would take days, but you can refine your plans at the Balboa Park Visitors Center (Map p274; www.balboapark.org; 1549 El Prado; ◷9:30am-4:30pm), in the House of Hospitality. Pick up a park map (suggested donation $1) and the latest opening schedule (the ones printed here are guidelines). If you plan to visit a lot of museums, you'll save money with admission passes including the **Passport to Balboa Park** (good for one-time entry to 13 museums within one week, adult/child $45/24), a **Stay for the Day** pass (five museums for $35) and the **Combo Pass** (Passport plus zoo admission adult/child $75/39). Free tours depart the Visitors Center to uncover the park's architectural heritage (9:30am on the first Wednesday of the month) and nature and history, led by rangers (1pm Tuesday and Sunday).

Balboa Park is easily reached from Downtown on bus 7, 7A or 7B along Park Blvd. By car, Park Blvd provides easy access to free parking. El Prado is an extension of Laurel St, which crosses Cabrillo Bridge with the Cabrillo Fwy (CA163) 120ft below. Make a point of driving this stretch of freeway: the steep roadsides, lush with hanging greenery, look like a rain-forest gorge.

The free Balboa Park Tram bus makes a continuous loop; however, it's easiest and most enjoyable to walk.

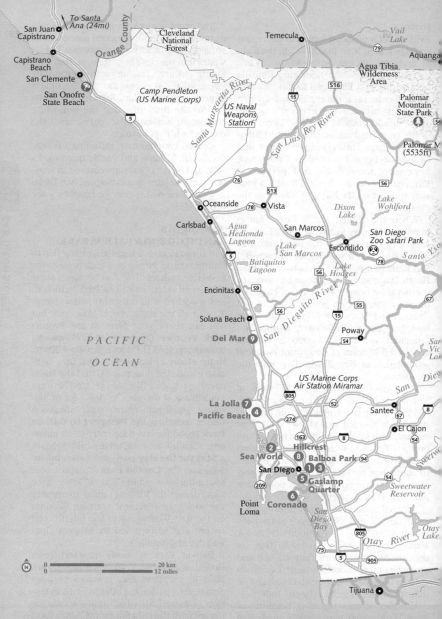

San Diego Highlights

① Cooing at koalas and pandering to pandas at the **San Diego Zoo** (p270)

② Cheering for Shamu at **SeaWorld** (p303)

③ Museum-hopping in **Balboa Park** (p276)

④ Skating seaside in **Pacific Beach** (p303)

⑤ Swilling margaritas in **Old Town** (p296) and pub-crawling downtown's **Gaslamp Quarter** (p295)

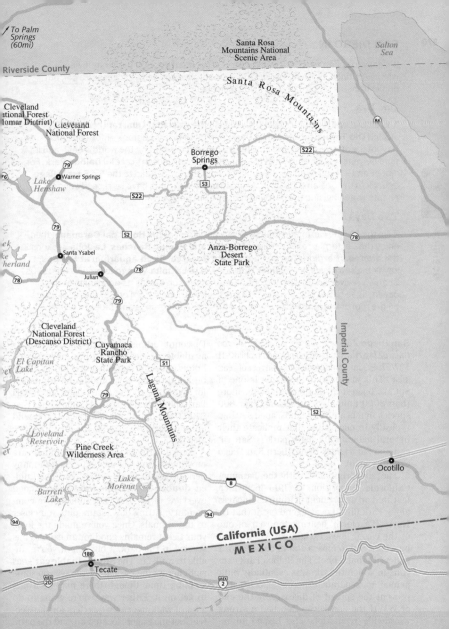

6 Marveling at the historic **Hotel del Coronado** (p301)

7 Hang gliding, kayaking or giving your credit card a workout in **La Jolla** (p312)

8 Sampling fish tacos or the next great taste in **Hillcrest and North Park** (p293)

9 Mingling with the hoi polloi at **Del Mar Racetrack** (p321)

SAN DIEGO IN...

It's easy to spend most of a week in San Diego, but if your time is limited, here's a whirlwind itinerary. Things will go more smoothly if you've got access to a car, but public transportation can work if you plan ahead.

One Day

Rub elbows with the locals over breakfast in the **Gaslamp Quarter** then ramble around **Old Town State Historic Park** for a bit of history before a Mexican lunch. Devote the afternoon to the **San Diego Zoo**, which is among the world's best, and if time permits visit one or two of the museums or gardens in graceful **Balboa Park**. For dinner and – if you're up for it – a night out on the town, head to the hip **East Village** or back to the Gaslamp Quarter, where many restaurants have terrace seating for people-watching, and the partying ranges from posh to raucous.

Two Days

Take the ferry to Coronado for a sea-view breakfast at the **Hotel del Coronado**, then enjoy the California beach scene at **Mission and Pacific Beaches**. **La Jolla** beckons this afternoon: explore **Torrey Pines State Reserve**, **Birch Aquarium at Scripps**, kayak the **sea caves**, try a **glider ride** or head to **La Jolla Village** to browse the 1920s Spanish-revival landmarks and boutiques. As the sun begins its descent over the ocean, head to **Del Mar**, where you can cheer or snuggle from one of the restaurants on the roof of **Del Mar Plaza** as the sky turns brilliant orange and fades to black.

San Diego Zoo   ZOO
(Map p274; www.sandiegozoo.org; adult/child 3-11 $37/27; ☺9am-8pm summer, to 4pm rest of year; P⛽) This justifiably famous zoo is one of SoCal's biggest attractions, showing more than 3000 animals representing over 800 species in a beautifully landscaped setting, typically in enclosures that replicate their natural habitats. Its sister park is San Diego Zoo Safari Park in northern San Diego County (p326).

The zoo originated with the Panama-California Exposition of 1915–16, which featured an assortment of animals in cages along Park Blvd. Local legend has it that Dr Harry Wegeforth, hearing the roar of one of the caged lions, exclaimed, 'Wouldn't it be wonderful to have a zoo in San Diego? I believe I'll build one!' The Balboa Park canyons in which the zoo was eventually built helped to separate different species and prevent the spread of disease. By the end of WWII the San Diego Zoo had a strong worldwide reputation, and helped to rebuild collections of European zoos that had been devastated by the war.

The zoo is located in the northern part of Balboa Park. The (free) parking lot and the zoo fill up on weekends. Bus 7 will get you there from Downtown. To leave the zoo and return the same day, get a hand stamp from the information booth near the entrance.

Discount admission coupons are widely available in local magazines, newspapers, hotels and information-center kiosks. Combination tickets cover unlimited admission for five days to the San Diego Zoo Safari Park (p326) and SeaWorld (p303). They cost $70/50 per adult/child for the zoo and wild animal park, or $121/99 for all three. See also p455.

Arrive early, as many of the animals are most active in the morning – though many perk up again in the afternoon. The guided **double-decker bus tour** gives a good overview of the zoo with informative commentary: sitting downstairs puts you closer to the animals. Once you've made the loop, your ticket remains good for an express bus service in the park, a big help if you're unable to walk far. The **Skyfari cable car** goes right across the park and can save you some walking time, though there may be a line to get on it. Either way, you're going to do a lot of walking: carry quarters for the electric foot-massagers located around the park. Inquire about facilities for disabled visitors.

Pick up a map at the entrance to the zoo to find your own favorite exhibits. The **koalas** are so popular that Australians may be surprised to find them a sort of unofficial symbol of San Diego, and the **giant pandas** run a close second. The **Komodo dragon**, an Indonesian lizard that can grow up to

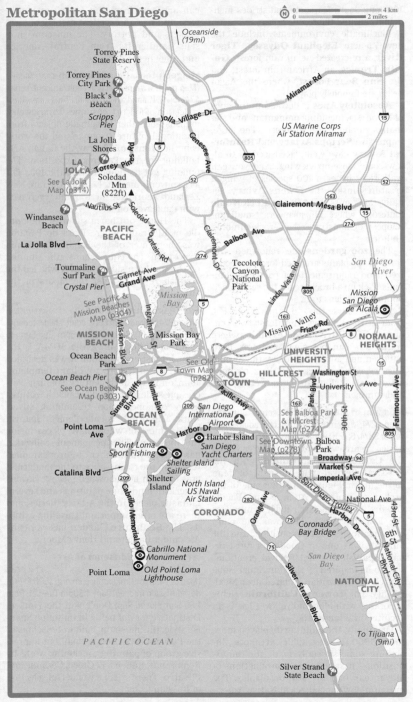

10ft long, looks fearsome and strides menacingly around the reptile house.

Bioclimatic environments include the new 7.5-acre **Elephant Odyssey**; **Tiger River**, a re-created Asian rain forest; **Gorilla Tropics**, an African rain forest; and the **Sun Bear Forest**, where the Asian bears are famously playful.

Absolutely Apes is devoted to the apes of Indonesia, including orangutans and siamangs climbing in lush forests. The large, impressive **Scripps Aviary** and **Rainforest Aviary** have well-placed feeders to allow some close-up viewing. And you can walk right beneath 100 species of winged creatures inside the **Owens Aviary**. Finally, don't miss the **African Rock Kopje** (outcrop), where klipspringers (small antelopes) demonstrate their rock-climbing abilities.

The **zoo gardens** are renowned and some of the plants are used for the specialized food requirements of particular animals. Pick up a brochure for the self-guided botanical gardens tour.

And of course the zoo is made for kids, from **animal shows** in at least two venues, to a **children's zoo exhibit** (where youngsters can pet small critters). Both children and adults will enjoy the animal nursery, where you can see the zoo's newest arrivals. Babies are born every spring and summer.

Museum of Man ANTHROPOLOGICAL MUSEUM
(Map p274; www.museumofman.org; adult/child/senior $8/4/6; ☉10am-4:30pm) El Prado passes under an archway and into an area called the **California Quadrangle**, with the Classical Revival-style Museum of Man to the north. Figures on either side of the arch represent the Atlantic and Pacific Oceans, while the arch itself symbolizes the Panama Canal. This was the main entrance for the 1915 exposition, and the building was one of Goodhue's most ornate Spanish Colonial Revival creations, said to be inspired by the churrigueresque church of Tepotzotlán situated near Mexico City. The **Tower of California**, richly decorated with blue and yellow tiles, is an architectural landmark.

Originally, the building displayed more than 5000 ethnographic artifacts, including some specially made for the exposition – cast concrete reproductions of Mayan carvings are still on display. The museum now specializes in Native American artifacts from the American Southwest and has an excellent display of local baskets and pottery. The museum shop sells handicrafts from Central America and elsewhere.

Mingei International Museum CRAFT MUSEUM
(Map p274; www.mingei.org; adult/student/senior $7/4/5; ☉10am-4pm Tue-Sun) This excellent collection of folk art, costumes, toys, jewelry, utensils and other handmade objects from traditional cultures from around the world is in the **House of Charm**, the Indian Arts building for the Panama Exposition. The building got its name during the 1935 fair as a souvenir market. Look for the rare New Zealand kauri tree (a fragrant evergreen with flat leaves) outside.

The House of Charm sits near the middle of El Prado, where Plaza de Panama was the center of the Panama-California Exposition. The equestrian statue sitauted on the southern side is **El Cid**, who led the Spanish revolt against the Moors in the 11th century.

San Diego Museum of Art ART MUSEUM
(Map p274; www.sdmart.org; adult/child/student/senior $12/4.50/8/9; ☉10am-5pm Tue-Sun, to 9pm Thu) Built in 1924, the SDMA is the city's largest art museum. It was designed by San Diego architect William Templeton Johnson in the 16th-century Spanish plateresque style, so named because it features heavy ornamentation resembling silverwork. The ornate facade depicts Spanish artists, most of whom have pieces inside the museum. The permanent collection has works by a number of European masters from the renaissance to the modernist eras (though no renowned pieces), various American landscape paintings and several fantastic pieces in the Asian galleries, and there are often important traveling exhibits. The **Sculpture Garden** has works by Alexander Calder and Henry Moore.

TOP CHOICE **Timken Museum of Art**
ART MUSEUM
(Map p274; www.timkenmuseum.org; 1500 El Prado; admission free; ☉10am-4:30pm Tue-Sat, from 1:30 Sun, closed Sep) Don't skip the Timken. Distinctive for *not* being in imitation Spanish style, this museum, built in 1965, houses the Putnam collection, a small but impressive group of paintings, including works by Rembrandt, Rubens, El Greco, Cézanne and Pissaro. There's also a wonderful selection of Russian icons.

Botanical Building `FREE`
CONSERVATORY

(Map p274; admission free; ☉Fri-Wed)
The Botanical Building looks lovely from
El Prado, where you can see it reflected in
the large lily pond that was used for hy-
drotherapy in WWII when the navy took
over the park. The building's central dome
and two wings are covered with redwood
lathes, which let filtered sunlight into the
collection of tropical plants and ferns. The
planting changes every season; in December there's a particularly beautiful poinsettia display.

Casa de Balboa
MUSEUMS

(Map p274) Dating from the 1915 exhibition,
this building houses three museums.

Museum of Photographic Arts
(Map p274; www.mopa.org; adult/student/senior/
child $8/5/6/free; ☉10am-5pm, to 9pm Thu,
closed Mon) Has some 7000 photos in its
permanent collection, tracing the history
of photography, and special exhibits from
crowd-pleasing landscapes by Ansel Adams
to avant-garde cell-phone photography.

San Diego History Center
(Map p274; www.sandiegohistory.org; adult/child/
student & senior $5/2/4; ☉10am-5pm Tue-Sun)
The San Diego Historical Society operates
this center, covering the American period
of San Diego from about 1848.

Model Railroad Museum
(Map p274; www.sdmrm.org; adult/student/
senior/child under 15 $7/3/6/free with adult;
☉11am-4pm Tue-Fri, 11am-5pm Sat & Sun; ♿)
Your (inner) four-year-old boy will love this
railroad museum, one of the largest in the
world. It has some 40,000 sq ft of amazingly landscaped working models of actual
Southern California railroads, both historical and contemporary.

Reuben H Fleet Space Theater & Science Center
SCIENCE MUSEUM

(Map p274; www.rhfleet.org; adult/child & senior
$14.50/11.75; ☉from 10am, closing times vary;
♿) One of Balboa Park's most publicized
venues, this hands-on science museum
features interactive displays (though with
less flash and dazzle than at others you
may have visited) and a toddler room.
Look out for opportunities to build gigantic structures with Keva planks and visit
the **Gallery of Illusions and Percep-
tions**. The biggest drawcard is the huge-
screen **IMAX theater** (one film included
in admission, additional films $5), which

screens several different films each day.
The hemispherical, wraparound screen
and 152-speaker state-of-the-art sound system create sensations ranging from pretty
cool to mind-blowing.

Natural History Museum
SCIENCE MUSEUM

(Map p274; www.sdnhm.org; adult/child/student/
senior $17/11/12/16; ☉10am-5pm; ♿) The orig-
inal 1933 building by William Templeton
Johnson has been renovated into a museum
with beautiful spaces and a giant-screen
cinema. Feature movies change but always
focus on the natural world; kids love them.
The museum houses 7.5 million specimens,
including rocks, fossils and taxidermied
animals, as well as an impressive dinosaur
skeleton and a California fault-line exhibit.
Children's programs are held most weekends. The museum also arranges field trips
and nature walks in Balboa Park and further afield.

Spanish Village Art Center `FREE`
ARTIST COLONY

(Map p274; admission free; ☉11am-4pm) Behind
the Natural History Museum is a grassy
square with a magnificent Moreton Bay
fig tree (sorry, climbing is prohibited). Opposite the square stand there's an enclave
of small tiled cottages (billed by park au-
thorities as 'an authentic reproduction of
an ancient village in Spain') that are rented
out as artists' studios, where you can watch
potters, jewelers, glass blowers, painters
and sculptors churn out their crafts. North
of the Spanish Village there's a 1910 **carousel** (admission $2; ☉11am-5pm daily late
Jun–early Sep, to 4:30pm Sat & Sun rest of year;
♿) with most of the original animals, and
a **miniature railroad** (admission $2; ☉11am-
6:30pm daily mid-Jun-early Sep, to 4:30pm Sat
& Sun rest of year; ♿) offering three-minute
rides.

Spreckels Organ Pavilion `TOP CHOICE`
MUSIC

(Map p274) Going south from Plaza de
Panama, you can't miss the circle of seating
and the curved colonnade in front of the
band shell housing the organ said to be the
world's largest outdoor musical instrument.
Donated by the Spreckels family of sugar
fortune and fame, the pipe organ came with
the stipulation that San Diego must always
have an official organist. Make a point of
attending the free **concerts** (www.sosorgan.
com), held throughout the year from 2pm
to 3pm Sunday and 7:30pm Monday from
mid-June to August.

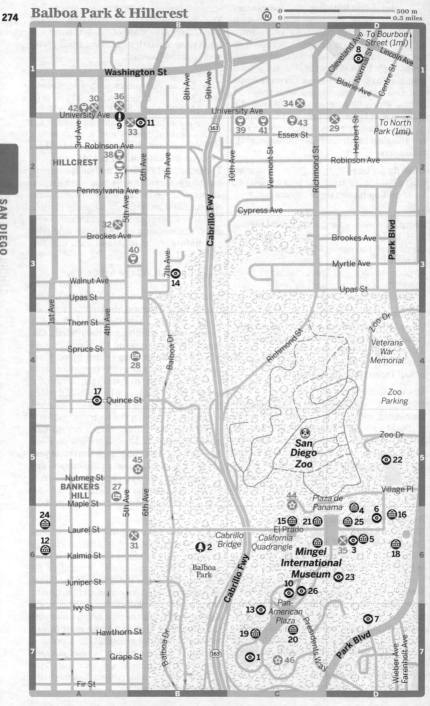

Pan-American Plaza VARIOUS
(Map p274) The plaza is now simply a large parking lot southwest of the Spreckels Organ. As you approach it from the organ, the **UN Building** is situated on the right-hand side. Its **gift shop** (Map p274; ⊙10am-4:30pm) has good stationery, jewelry and candy, and donates profits to worldwide children's charities.

FREE **House of Pacific Relations** MUSEUM
(Map p274; www.sdhpr.org; admission free; ⊙noon-4pm Sun) Near the UN, this place actually comprises 15 cottages from the 1915 exposition, inside which you will find furnishings and displays from various countries, with about as many built since. When the cottages are open to the public, they often have crafts and food for sale.

Marie Hitchcock Puppet Theater PUPPETS
(Map p274; www.balboaparkpuppets.com; adult/child/senior $5/3/4; ☷) This theater in the Palisades Building puts on terrific hand- and rod-puppet shows (11am, 1pm and 2:30pm Wednesday to Sunday in summer, shorter hours in the rest of the year), and also has puppet-making workshops.

San Diego Automotive Museum
AUTO MUSEUM
(Map p274; www.sdautomuseum.org; 2080 Pan American Plaza; adult/child/student/senior $8/4/5/6; ⊙10am-5pm) This museum has a collection of more than 60 cars and motorcycles, perfectly restored and well displayed, with classics including a 1937 Cord and a collection of motorcycles manufactured by Indians. Special exhibits change quarterly.

Early plans for San Diego included a 1400-acre City Park at the northeastern corner of what was to become downtown, in what was all bare hilltops, chaparral and deep arroyos. Enter Kate O Sessions, a UC Berkeley botany graduate who in 1892 started a nursery on the site to landscape fashionable gardens for the city's emerging elite. The city granted her 30 acres of land in return for planting 100 trees a year in the park and donating 300 more for placement throughout the city. By the early 20th century, Balboa Park (named for the Spanish conquistador believed to be the first European to sight the Pacific Ocean) had become a well-loved part of San Diego.

In 1915–16, Balboa Park hosted much of the Panama-California Exposition. New Yorkers Bertram Goodhue and Carlton Winslow designed the expo's pavilions in a romantic, Spanish Colonial style with beaux-art and baroque flourishes. The pavilions were meant to be temporary – constructed largely of stucco, chicken wire, plaster, hemp and horsehair – but they proved so popular that many were later replaced with durable concrete structures in the same style. These buildings now house the museums along El Prado, the main pedestrian thoroughfare in the park.

Another expo, the 1935 Pacific-California Exposition, brought new buildings southwest of El Prado around the Pan-American Plaza. The Spanish Colonial architectural theme was expanded to include the whole New World, from indigenous styles (some of the buildings had Pueblo Indian and Mayan influences) through to the 20th century.

Air & Space Museum   SCIENCE MUSEUM
(Map p274; www.aerospacemuseum.org; adult/child/student & senior $16.50/6/13.50; ◎10am-5:30pm Jun-Aug, to 4:30pm Sep-May; ⓘ) The round building at the southern end of the plaza houses an excellent museum with an extensive display of aircrafts – originals, replicas, models and Charles Lindbergh memorabilia.

Starlight Bowl   PERFORMANCE VENUE
(Map p274; www.starlighttheatre.org) A summer season of musicals and light opera is presented at this amphitheater.

San Diego Hall of Champions Sports Museum   SPORTS MUSEUM
(Map p274; www.sdhoc.com; adult/senior & student/child $8/6/4; ◎10am-4:30pm) The Federal Building was built for the 1935 exposition and now holds this hall of fame for San Diego sports figures. Permanent and temporary exhibits cover themes as wide-ranging as Ted Williams, skateboarder Tony Hawk and the World Series of Poker. There's also a media center, in which kids can call the commentary on a game.

Centro Cultural de la Raza
   MEXICAN & INDIGENOUS ART
(Map p274; www.centroraza.com; suggested donation $5; ◎noon-4pm Tue-Fri, 10am-4pm Sat & Sun) The center hosts powerful exhibitions of Mexican and Native American art, including temporary exhibits of contemporary in-

digenous artwork. The round, steel building, which is actually a converted water tank, sits way out on the edge of the main museum area; easiest access is from Park Blvd.

Marston House   ARCHITECTURAL SIGNIFICANCE
(Map p274; 3525 Seventh Ave; adult/child/senior $8/3/4; ◎10am-5pm Thu-Mon by 45min tour) In the far northwestern corner of Balboa Park is the former home of George Marston, philanthropist and founder of the San Diego Historical Society. Built in 1904, Marston House was designed by noted San Diego architects William Hebbard and Irving Gill, and is a fine example of the American Arts and Crafts style with furnishings and decorative objects.

Balboa Park Gardens   GARDENS
(Map p274) Balboa Park includes a number of gardens, reflecting different horticultural styles and environments, including **Alcazar Garden**, a formal, Spanish-style garden; **Palm Canyon**, with more than 50 species of palms; **Japanese Friendship Garden** (www.niwa.org; adult/child/senior $4/2/2.50; ◎10am-5pm Mon-Fri, to 4pm Sat & Sun late May-early Sep, 10am-4pm Tue-Sun early Sep-late May); **Australian Garden**; **Rose Garden**; and **Desert Garden** (best in spring). **Florida Canyon** gives an idea of the San Diego landscape before Spanish settlement. Free weekly **Offshoot tours** (www.balboapark.org/info/tours.php; ◎10am Sat Jan-Thanksgiving) depart the Balboa Park visitors center and cover a ro-

tating selection of themes including history and botany.

Casa del Prado   ARCHITECTURAL SIGNIFICANCE
(Map p274) This is one of the most handsome buildings along El Prado. Rebuilt after an earthquake, it now stages theater and dance performances.

DOWNTOWN SAN DIEGO
Downtown can be divided into several neighborhoods. The Gaslamp Quarter is at the center of it all, while a couple of museums are interspersed among the high-rises of the Financial District, near Broadway. East of Downtown is the East Village, an up-and-coming enclave for local hipsters with worldly restaurants and fun nightspots.

When Alonzo Horton established New Town San Diego in 1867, 5th Ave was its main street, lined with saloons, gambling joints, bordellos and opium dens; it became notoriously known as the Stingaree. By the 1960s it had declined to a skid row of flophouses and bars. In the early 1980s, when developers started thinking about demolition, protests from preservationists saved the area.

Good thing – restored 1870s to 1920s buildings now house restaurants, bars, galleries and theaters amid wrought-iron, 19th-century-style street lamps, trees and brick sidewalks. The 16-block area south of Broadway between 4th and 6th Aves is designated a National Historic District, and development is strictly controlled. There's still a bit of sleaze though, with a few 'adult entertainment' shops, but we'll say they lend texture.

Museum of Contemporary Art San Diego   MUSEUM
(Map p278; www.mcasd.org; 1001 & 1100 Kettner Blvd; adult/under 25yr/senior $10/free/$5; ◎11am-6pm Sat-Tue, to 9pm Thu & Fri, guided tours 6pm Thu, 2pm Sat & Sun) Adjacent to and across from a San Diego Trolley stop, this museum has brought innovative artwork to San Diegans since the 1960s in the La Jolla branch (p313); check local listings for exhibits. Across from the main building, a slickly renovated section of San Diego's train station houses permanent works by Jenny Holzer and Richard Serra. Tickets are valid for seven days in all locations.

While here, stop at San Diego's **Santa Fe Depot** (aka Union Station), which looks a lot like a piece from a model railway, with Spanish-style tile work and a historic Santa Fe Railway sign on top. It was built in conjunction with the 1915 exposition in the hopes that the Santa Fe Railway would make San Diego its terminus, although that designation eventually went to Los Angeles.

TOP CHOICE New Children's Museum   MUSEUM
(Map p278; www.thinkplaycreate.org; 200 West Island Ave; adult/child/senior $10/10/5; ⊞) This interactive children's museum is new both chronologically (opened 2008) and conceptually. Installations are designed by artists, so tykes can learn principles of movement and physics while simultaneously being exposed to art and working out the ants in their pants. Exhibits change every 18 months or so, but we recently saw a climbing wall covered with graffiti art, a pillowfight in a room with mattress-like walls, and human-powered 'legway' scooters.

FREE San Diego Chinese Historical Museum   MUSEUM
(Map p278; 404 3rd Ave; admission free; ◎10:30am-4pm Tue-Sun) The historic heart of San Diego's Chinese community is 3rd Ave. Immigrants were once taught English and religion in the Chinese Mission Building, built in the 1920s and designed by Louis J Gill (minimalist San Diego architect Irving Gill's nephew). The small, white stucco structure has red tiles decorating the roofline, hardwood floors, and an inviting backyard. Displays include Chinese-American artifacts and local art objects.

Petco Park   SPORT STADIUM
(Map p278; www.padres.com; 100 Park Blvd) Just a quick stroll southeast of the Gaslamp is Downtown's newest landmark, the baseball stadium of the San Diego Padres. It's one of the most beautiful in baseball. If you can't attend a game (see p298), take an 80-minute behind-the-scenes tour (adult/child/senior $11/7/8) which might include bullpen, press box and luxury suite. They run at 10:30am, 12:30pm and 2:30pm June to August, and less frequently in April, May and September.

US Grant Hotel   HISTORIC HOTEL
(Map p278; ☎619-232-3121; 326 Broadway) No hotel in town can compare to the Hotel del Coronado (p301) for history, but US Grant, built in 1910, comes close. It's on the National Register of Historic Places for a past including celebrity guests, magnificent ballrooms, a one-time Turkish bath and a speakeasy. It had a big-bucks makeover in

SAN DIEGO

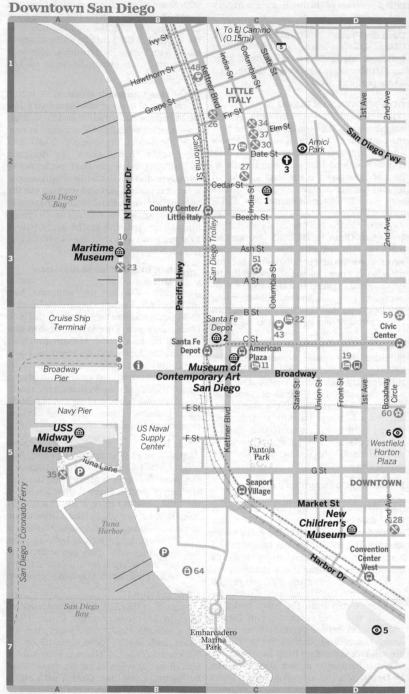

2006; visitors can take a free tour with advance reservation by calling the concierge desk. See also p307 for sleeping options here.

William Heath Davis House
MUSEUM

(Map p278; www.gaslampquarter.org; 410 Island Ave at 4th Ave; adult/senior & student $5/4; ☺10am-6pm Tue-Sat, 9am-3pm Sun) This is one of nine prefabricated houses that Davis brought from Maine in 1850. It contains a small museum with 19th-century furnishings. From here, the Gaslamp Quarter Historical Foundation leads a weekly, two-hour **walking tour** (adult/senior & student $10/8; ☺11am Sat) and includes admission to the house. The tour's subject matter and stop-and-go walking probably won't appeal to most children.

Westfield Horton Plaza
ARCHITECTURAL SIGNIFICANCE

(Map p278; www.westfield.com/hortonplaza; ☺10am-9pm Mon-Fri, to 8pm Sat, 11am-7pm Sun; ℗) At the edge of the Gaslamp is a five-story, seven-block shopping mall that was credited with bringing visitors back to Downtown. It's not very inviting from the outside; critics say it turns its back on Downtown (though when it was built in 1985 there wasn't much to welcome visitors). Inside, however, Los Angeles–based urban architect Jon Jerde – who also designed Universal CityWalk (p184) – created fanciful, colorful, toy-town arches and postmodernist balconies making it feel slightly like an MC Escher drawing. Parking is free for three hours with validation.

EMBARCADERO & THE WATERFRONT
South and west of the Gaslamp Quarter, San Diego's well-manicured waterfront promenades stretch along Harbor Dr, and are perfect for strolling or jogging (or watching members of the US Navy doing same).

Maritime Museum
MUSEUM

(Map p278; www.sdmaritime.com; 1492 N Harbor Dr; adult/child/senior $14/8/11; ☺9am-8pm, to 9pm late May-early Sep; ⓘ) This museum is easy to find: look for the 100ft-high masts of the iron-hulled square-rigger *Star of India*. Built on the Isle of Man and launched in 1863, the tall ship plied the England–India trade route, carried immigrants to New Zealand, became a trading ship based in Hawaii and, finally, worked the Alaskan salmon fisheries before winding up here.

Downtown San Diego

SAN DIEGO

It's a handsome vessel, but don't expect anything romantic or glamorous on board.

Also moored here: the *California,* California's official tall ship, and the *America* of America's Cup fame. These go out on excursions from a few hours to overnight, from $20 per person for the shorter cruises. The 1914 *Pilot,* which took harbor pilots to their merchant ships, has narrated rides that last 45 minutes and cost $3.

USS Midway Museum
MUSEUM

(Map p278; ☑619-544-9600; www.midway.org; Navy Pier; adult/child/senior/student $18/10/15/15; ☺10am-5pm; P🚻) The giant aircraft carrier USS *Midway* was one of the navy's flagships from 1945 to 1991, last playing a combat role in the first Gulf War. On the flight deck of the hulking vessel, walk right up to some 25 restored aircraft including an F-14 Tomcat and F-4 Phantom jet fighter. Admission includes an audio tour, along the narrow confines of the upper decks to the bridge, admiral's war room, brig and 'pri-fly' (primary flight control; the carrier's equivalent of a control tower). If lines are long, docents are there to illuminate and enliven. There are also three flight simulators (phone for rates and reservations). Some inside areas get stuffy on warm summer days: come early to avoid midday heat and crowds. Allow for two to four hours on board. Parking costs from $5/10 for one/10 hours.

San Diego Convention Center
ARCHITECTURAL SIGNIFICANCE

(Map p278; www.sdccc.org; Harbor Dr) Wrapping southeast along the **Embarcadero Marina Park** – where there's a public fishing pier and an open-air amphitheater with free summer concerts – you'll see the 'sails' of this structure, designed by Canadian avant-garde architect Arthur Erickson and opened in 1989, stretching for half a mile. It books out five years in advance with close to a million visitors annually. Two hours free parking with validation.

OLD TOWN

Under the Mexican government, which took power in 1821, any settlement with a population of 500 or more was entitled to become a 'pueblo,' and the area below the Presidio became the first official civilian Mexican settlement in California – the Pueblo de San Diego. A plaza was laid out around Casa Estudillo, home of the pueblo's commandant, and within 10 years it was surrounded by about 40 huts and several houses. This square mile of land (roughly 10 times what remains today) was also the center of American San Diego until the fire of 1872, after which the city's main body moved to the new Horton subdivision (now Downtown).

John Spreckels built a trolley line from Horton's New Town to Old Town in the 1920s and, to attract passengers, began restoring the old district. In 1968 the area was named Old Town State Historic Park, archaeological work began, and the few surviving original buildings were restored. Other structures were rebuilt, and the area is now a pedestrian district of shade trees, a large open plaza, and shops and restaurants.

Old Town Transit Center is an important transit hub for the *Coaster* commuter train, the San Diego Trolley and buses. Old Town Trolley tours stop southeast of the plaza on Twiggs St. There is free parking in lots and on streets around Old Town.

FREE Old Town State Historic Park
HISTORIC VILLAGE

(Map p282; ☑619-220-5422; www.parks.ca.gov; Wallace St; admission free; ☺10am-5pm) This park has an excellent American-period museum in the Robinson-Rose House at the southern end of the plaza. You'll also find good history books for sale, a diorama depicting the original pueblo and the park's **visitors center**. If you're particularly interested in history, pick up a copy of the *Old Town San Diego State Historic Park Tour Guide & Brief History* ($3), or take a guided tour (free) from the visitors center at 11am and 2pm daily. You can also pick up a self-guided tour map.

Across from the center the restored **Casa de Estudillo** is filled with authentic period furniture. Other buildings around the plaza include a blacksmith shop, print shop and a candle-dipping shop – call the visitors center for hours.

The **Bazaar del Mundo**, just off the plaza's northwestern corner, is a colorful collection of import shops and restaurants – great for Mexican souvenirs without the trip to Tijuana. Along San Diego Ave, on the southern side of the plaza, small, historical-looking buildings (only one is authentic) house more souvenir and gift shops.

Whaley House
MUSEUM

(Map p282; www.whaleyhouse.org; 2476 San Diego Ave; adult/child $6/4; ☺10am-10pm daily Jun-Aug, to 5pm Mon & Tue, to 10pm Thu-Sun Sep-May; 🚻) Two blocks from the Old Town perimeter sits the city's oldest brick building, officially certified as haunted by the US Department of Commerce. Check out the collection of period furniture and clothing from when the house served as a courthouse, theater and private residence.

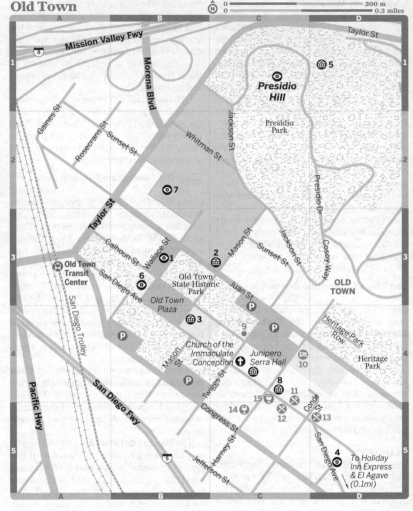

El Campo Santo
CEMETERY

(Map p282) Continuing east, after San Diego Ave forks right at Conde St, you'll find this cemetery which dates from 1849 (restored 1933). It is the resting place of some 20 souls, a simple dirt yard with the biographies of the deceased on signage above the graves.

Casa de Carillo
ARCHITECTURAL SIGNIFICANCE

(Map p282; cnr Juan St & Wallace St) Just north of Old Town, this house dates from about 1820 and is said to be the oldest house in San Diego. It is now the pro shop for the public 18-hole **Presidio Hills Golf Course** (www.presidiohillsgolf.com; greens fee $10).

Presidio Hill
HISTORIC SITE

(Map p282) In 1769 Padre Junípero Serra and Gaspar de Portolá established the first Spanish settlement in California overlooking the valley of the San Diego River. You can walk up from Old Town along Mason St for excellent views of San Diego Bay and Mission Valley. Atop the hill, **Presidio Park** has several walking trails and shaded benches. A large cross, made with tiles from the original mission, commemorates Padre Serra. American forces occupied the hill in 1846, during the Mexican-American War, and named it Fort Stockton, for American

Old Town

commander Robert Stockton. A flagpole, a cannon, some plaques and earth walls now form the **Fort Stockton Memorial**. The nearby **El Charro Statue**, a bicentennial gift to the city from Mexico, depicts a Mexican cowboy on horseback. Nothing remains of the original Presidio structures.

Junípero Serra Museum MUSEUM
(Map p282; www.sandiegohistory.org; 2727 Presidio Dr; adult/child/student & senior $5/2/4; ☺10am-5pm Sat & Sun) Located in one of the most important historical buildings in the city, this small but interesting collection of artifacts and pictures is from the Mission and rancho periods, and it gives a good sense of the earliest days of European settlement up to 1929 when the museum was founded.

LITTLE ITALY
Bounded by Hawthorn and Ash Sts on the north and south, and Front St and the waterfront on the east and west, San Diego's Little Italy was settled in the mid-19th century by Italian immigrants, mostly fishermen and their families, who created a cohesive and thriving community. They enjoyed a booming fish industry and whiskey trade (which some claim was backed by local Mafia).

When the I-5 was completed in 1962, the heart (and, many say, soul) of the area was destroyed; entire blocks were demolished, and increased traffic turned once-quiet streets into busy thoroughfares. Over the last few years, however, exciting contemporary architecture has made Little Italy one of the hippest places to live, eat and gallery-hop downtown, especially along India St.

Our Lady of the Rosary Catholic Church
CHURCH
(Map p278; cnr State & Date Sts) Built in 1925, this is still a hub for Little Italy activity. Its rich ceiling murals, painted by an Italian who was flown over to do the work, are among San Diego's best pieces of religious art. Across the street in **Amici Park**, locals play bocce, an Italian form of outdoor bowling.

Firehouse Museum MUSEUM
(Map p278; 1572 Columbia St at Cedar St; admission $2; ☺10am-2pm Thu & Fri, to 4pm Sat & Sun) This museum preserves a historic collection of fire-fighting equipment and has exhibits depicting some of San Diego's 'hottest' moments.

MISSION VALLEY
This best known historical sight here is the restored Mission San Diego de Alcalá, but more visitors come for the shopping centers (p298) and hotels (p290).

The San Diego River, originally the most reliable freshwater source for crops and livestock of the early mission, ran through the valley. However, sometimes it would dry up and other times it would flood, until dams were completed upstream in the 1950s. Nowadays the unlovely I-8 now runs its length, but the San Diego Trolley gets here from Downtown, cutting through a scenic corridor of riparian land (and golf courses) not seen from the freeway.

TOP CHOICE **Mission San Diego de Alcalá**
HISTORIC SITE
(Map p278; www.missionsandiego.com; 10818 San Diego Mission Rd at Friars Rd; adult/child/senior $3/1/2; ☺9am-4:45pm) Although the site of the first California mission was on Presidio Hill (p282), in 1774 Padre Junípero Serra moved it about 7 miles upriver to this location, closer to water and more arable land. In 1784 the missionaries built a solid adobe

and timber church, which was destroyed by an earthquake in 1803. The church was promptly rebuilt, and at least some of it still stands on a slope overlooking Mission Valley. With the end of the mission system in the 1830s, the buildings were turned over to the Mexican government and fell into disrepair. Some accounts say that they were reduced to a facade and a few crumbling walls by the 1920s.

Extensive restoration began in 1931, with financial support from local citizens and the Hearst Foundation, a philanthropic organization funded by one of California's most influential families. The pretty white church and buildings you see now are the fruits of that work.

The Visitors center inside the mission has friendly and informative staff. The mission sits north of I-8, off the Mission Gorge Rd exit; from the Mission trolley stop, walk two blocks north and turn right onto San Diego Mission Rd.

UPTOWN: BANKERS HILL, HILLCREST & NORTH PARK

Uptown is roughly a triangle north of Downtown, east of Old Town and south of Mission Valley. There aren't any big-ticket sights here, but this string of neighborhoods is a good place to see some Victorian and art deco architecture and observe day-to-day life. Hillcrest, particularly, is one of San Diego's most diverse and desirable neighborhoods.

In the late 19th century it was fashionable to live in the hills north of Downtown, since only those who owned a horse-drawn carriage could afford it. Called **Bankers Hill** after some of the wealthy residents – or Pill Hill because of the many doctors there – the upscale heights had unobstructed views of the bay and Point Loma before I-5 was built.

Among the Victorian mansions, the 1889 Long-Waterman House (Map p274; 2408 1st Ave) is easily recognized by its towers, gables, bay windows and verandah; it was once the home of former California governor Robert Waterman. Also notable is the Timken House (Map p274), one block north. The 375ft **Spruce St Footbridge** hangs over a deep canyon between Front and Brant Sts. The Quince St Bridge (Map p274), between 3rd and 4th Aves, is a wood-trestle bridge built in 1905 and refurbished in 1988 after community activists protested its slated demolition. In **Mission Hills**,

a 1970s shingled complex at the corner of Washington and India Sts houses mostly eateries.

The heart of Uptown is **Hillcrest**, the first suburban real-estate development in San Diego. Driving around, you'll see the work of many of San Diego's best-known early-20th-century architects, including Irving Gill and William Templeton Johnson, alongside Mediterranean, Spanish Mission and Arts and Crafts styles. But Hillcrest's chief attraction is its lively street life, due largely to its status as the center of San Diego's gay and lesbian community.

Begin at the Hillcrest Gateway (Map p274), an illuminated electric sign that arches over University Ave at 5th Ave. East on University Ave at No 535, look for the 1928 Kahn Building (Map p274), an original commercial building with architectural elements that border on kitsch. South of University Ave along 5th Ave, there's a variety of new and used bookstores. Hillcrest's farmers market (Map p274; 5th Ave, cnr Normal & Lincoln Sts; ⊘9am-1pm Sun) is considered the best in town, great for watching fresh faces acquiring fresh produce.

East of Hillcrest is the bohemian neighborhood of **North Park**, centered on 30th and University Aves. Around the Birch North Park Theater, home of the Lyric Opera San Diego (p297), is a growing center of art in small galleries and frame shops around Ray St, plus an inordinate number of hair salons and a low-key gourmet scene. Follow Park Ave north into University Heights, where there's a cluster of bars.

☞ Tours

Look for discounts in tourist literature or online.

Old Town Trolley Tours   HOP-ON/HOP-OFF (www.trolleytours.com; adult/child $34/17; ⊘9am-7pm; ⊕) Not to be confused with the municipal San Diego Trolley (p300), this outfit operates hop-on-hop-off, open-air buses decorated like old-style streetcars, looping around the main attractions of Downtown and Coronado in about two hours, every 30 minutes or so. The official trolley stand is in Old Town, but you can start or stop at any trolley-tour stop (well marked with orange).

Seal Tour   AMPHIBIOUS (adult/child $34/19, ⊘hourly 10:30am-6pm; ⊕), The Old Town Trolley Tours folk operate a 90-minute tour that departs from Seaport

Times are tough in Tijuana, as with many Mexican border towns. For years, 'TJ' was a cheap, convivial borderland escape for hard-partying San Diegans, Angelenos, sailors and college kids. But a double-whammy of drug-related violence and the global recession has turned once-bustling tourist areas into ghost towns. (For more border-crossing information and travel warnings, see p463.)

If you do go, the San Diego Trolley (p300) runs from downtown to San Ysidro. Cross the border on foot, and pick up a map at the border station for the approximately 20-minute walk; follow signs reading 'Centro Downtown.' If traveling by taxi from the Mexican side of the border, take a white and green one (these have meters). Driving into Mexico is not recommended: directions can be difficult, there are reports of smash-and-grab theft, separate Mexican auto insurance is required (purchase at shops on the US side of the border crossing for $15 to $25 per day depending on value of vehicle and length of stay in Mexico) and the waits to cross back into the US can seem eternal. Many drivers get around this by parking on the US side of the border and walking across. Take I-5 south and look for signs for the last US exit. Once there, park at one of the many lots in the area; average cost is around $8 per 24 hours.

Avenida Revolución ('La Revo') is the main tourist drag. Other sightseeing highlights include **Museo de las Californias** (cnr Paseo de los Heroes & Av Independencia; adult/child $2/1.50, Sun free; ⏱10am-7pm Tue-Sun), inside Centro Cultural Tijuana (CECUT), for an excellent history of Baja California from prehistory to the present; there's signage in English. **Catedral de Nuestra Señora de Guadalupe** (Cathedral of our Lady of Guadalupe; cnr Av Niños Héroes & Calle 2a) is Tijuana's oldest church. **Mercado El Popo** (cnr Calle 2a & Av Constitución) is a colorful market selling needs from tamarind pods to religious iconography.

For a meal, try **La Especial** (☎011-52-664-685-6654; Av Revolución 718; breakfast $5-12, mains $6-12; ⏱9am-10pm Sun-Thu, to 11:30pm Fri & Sat), a woodsy dining room in a shopping arcade below Hotel Lafayette, serving classics like carne asada. The venerable though shopworn **Hotel Caesar** (☎011-52-664-685-1606; Av Revolución 827; Caesar salad $6; ⏱9am-midnight) is the birthplace of the Caesar salad.

See p458 for passport and customs information.

Village or the Maritime Museum and ventures in and around San Diego Bay in an amphibious vehicle.

Taste of San Diego　　　　FOOD
(www.atasteof-sandiego.com; adult $75-99) This new tour company introduces visitors to the city's gastronomic treasures from Downtown to diners and dives, with enthusiastic native San Diegan guides. Come hungry.

San Diego Scenic Tours　　　BUS
(www.sandiegoscenictours.com; adult $34-66, child 3-11yr $17-33) Half- and full-day bus tours around San Diego and Tijuana, some of which build in time to shop and dine. You can combine some tours with a harbor cruise.

Gray Line　　　　　　　　BUS
(www.sandiegograyline.com; adult $30-72, child 3-11yr $17-43) A large outfit offering bus tours around the city and to Mexico, in addition to more expensive excursions to attractions throughout SoCal: Wild Animal Park, SeaWorld, Legoland, Disneyland and Universal Studios Hollywood.

San Diego Harbor Excursion　　HARBOR
(www.sdhe.com; adult $10-50, child $15-40; 🚢) Harbor, nature and seasonal whale-watching cruises from the Embarcadero, from one to several hours long.

Hornblower Cruises　　　　HARBOR
(www.hornblower.com; adult/child from $20/10; 🚢) In addition to sightseeing cruises, Hornblower specializes in catered cruises with drinks, dinner or brunch (catered cruises: $54 to $90, food only).

✹✹ Festivals & Events
March

Ocean Beach Kite Festival　　OUTDOORS
The first Saturday in March brings kite making, decorating and flying, as well as competitions.

SAN DIEGO COUNTY DRIVING TOUR

What to See

This route traces San Diego's evolution from its European 'discovery' to the Mission Era. Start at the **Cabrillo National Monument** (p302), where Portuguese explorer Juan Rodríguez Cabrillo first laid eyes on San Diego. The **visitors center** describes Cabrillo's 1542 voyage up the California coast.

Next stop at **Fort Rosecrans National Cemetery**, which, while not connected to the city's earliest history is significant nonetheless. Some 99,000 war dead are memorialized here, including those whose remains have not been recovered. The hilltop views alone are quite a tribute, with the ocean on one side and the harbor on the other.

In 1769, a band of missionaries led by the Franciscan friar Junípero Serra founded the first of the 21 California missions, and a small *pueblo* (village) grew around it. Now that village is known as Old Town, and the **Old Town State Historic Park** (p281) is an excellent place to browse for an hour or two. Walk or drive Mason St up to **Presidio Hill** to get the views the old padres had. **San Diego Ave**, east of the historic park, is packed with restaurants for a snack, meal or margarita.

The Presidio site turned out to be less than ideal, and in 1774 the mission was moved about seven miles upriver. Here the **Mission Basilica San Diego de Alcalá** (p283) is a modest rectangle embracing a tranquil garden, far from the city's bustle.

The Route

From the gate of the Cabrillo National Monument, Fort Rosecrans National Cemetery is about 0.8 miles on Cabrillo Monument Dr. Continuing on, Cabrillo Monument Dr changes names to Catalina Blvd. Bear right when you reach Chatsworth Blvd, follow it 2.2 miles through this mostly residential neighborhood, and turn left on Rosecrans St. Bear right on Rosecrans St where the road forks, and after the freeway overpass and Old Town Transit Center, turn right onto Congress Ave, where there are several free parking lots for Old Town. From Old Town, return to the Transit Center and turn right on Taylor St, which merges onto I-8 East. After 4.5 miles, exit Fairmount Ave, turn left and it changes names to Mission Gorge Rd; at the car dealerships, turn left onto San Diego Mission Rd, and the mission is about 0.4 miles ahead on your right.

Time & Mileage

It's about 16 miles one way (about 30 minutes driving time), but you'll want to allow at least a half-day with stops.

March/April

San Diego Crew Classic   SPORTING EVENT
(www.crewclassic.org) The national college rowing regatta takes places in late March/early April at Crown Point Shores Park in Mission Bay.

June

Rock 'n' Roll Marathon   SPORTING EVENT
(www.rnrmarathon.com) Live bands perform at each mile mark of this 26.2-mile race, with a big concert at the finish line. Early June.

San Diego County Fair   COUNTY FAIR
(www.sdfair.com) Mid-June to July 4; well over a million people watch headline acts and enjoy hundreds of carnival rides and shows at the Del Mar Fairgrounds.

July

Opening Day at Del Mar Racetrack   SPORTING EVENT
(www.dmtc.com) Outrageous hats, cocktails and general merriment kicks off the horseracing season, 'where the turf meets the surf'; July 21. Racing through early September.

US Open Sandcastle Competition   OUTDOOR
(www.usopensandcastle.com) You won't believe what can be made out of sand at the amazing sandcastle-building competition

held mid- or late July in Imperial Beach, south of Coronado.

San Diego LGBT Pride   COMMUNITY FESTIVAL
(www.sdpride.org) The city's gay community celebrates in Hillcrest and Balboa Park at the month's end, with parades, parties, performances, art shows and more.

Comic-Con International   CONVENTION
(www.comic-con.org) America's largest event for collectors of comic, pop culture and movie memorabilia, at the San Diego Convention Center. Late July.

August

Old Globe Festival   ARTS
(www.oldglobe.org) Renowned performance festival at this theater (p298) in Balboa Park, with Shakespearean and lesser-known plays.

September

Bayfair   SPORTING EVENT
(www.thunderboats.net) Some of the world's fastest speedboats compete on Mission Bay in mid-September.

San Diego Film Festival   ARTS
(www.sdff.org) The silver screen takes center stage in the Gaslamp Quarter, with screenings, panel discussions, parties and a good chance of star sightings. Late September to early October.

Fleet Week   MILITARY
(www.fleetweeksandiego.org) Actually more like 'Fleet Month.' The US military shows its pride in events including a sea and air parade, special tours of ships, and the Miramar Air Show, the world's largest. Late September to late October.

October

Little Italy Festa   COMMUNITY FESTIVAL
(www.littleitalysd.com) Come for the tastes and aromas of old Italia, and stay for Gesso Italiano, chalk-art drawn directly onto the streets. Mid-month.

December

December Nights   HOLIDAY FESTIVAL
(www.balboapark.org) This festival in Balboa Park includes crafts, carols and a candle-light parade.

Harbor Parade of Lights   HOLIDAY FESTIVAL
(www.sdparadeoflights.org) Dozens of decorated, illuminated boats float in procession on the harbor on two Sunday evenings in December.

Las Posadas and Luminaries   HOLIDAY FESTIVAL
(www.fiestadereyes.org) This traditional Latin Christmas celebration in Old Town re-enacts Mary and Joseph seeking shelter.

🛏 Sleeping

This chapter lists high-season (summer) rates for single-or double-occupancy rooms. Prices drop significantly between September and June. Whatever time of year, ask about specials, suites and package deals.

The San Diego Convention & Visitor Bureau runs a **room-reservation line** (☏800-350-6205; www.sandiego.org).

DOWNTOWN SAN DIEGO
Downtown is San Diego's most convenient place to stay, for its wealth of restaurants and hotels and easy access to transit.

US Grant Hotel   LUXURY $$$
(Map p278; ☏619-232-3121, 800-237-5029; www.starwood.com; 326 Broadway; r from $249; P@🛜) This 1910 hotel was built as the fancy city counterpart to the Hotel del Coronado and hosted everyone from Albert Einstein to Harry Truman. Today's quietly flashy lobby combines chocolate-brown and ocean-blue accents, and rooms boast original artwork on the headboards. It's owned by members of the Sycuan tribe of Native Americans. Parking costs $32. See also p277.

Hotel Indigo   GREEN, CONTEMPORARY $$
(Map p278; ☏619-727-4000, 877-846-3446; www.hotelindigo.com/sandiego; 509 9th Ave; r from $200; P@🛜🐾) San Diego's first hotel to be certified green (opened 2009), the Indigo proves that enviro can still be comfy, what with green roofs, sustainable construction, windows that open (there's a concept!) and cheery design motifs inspired by local waters and California poppies. Bonus: when the Padres are playing, you can watch the game from some rooms or the roof deck. Parking is $32.

Hotel Solamar   BOUTIQUE, CONTEMPORARY $$
(Map p278; ☏619-531-8740, 877-230-0300; www.hotelsolamar.com; 435 6th Ave; r $169-299; P@🛜🏊) A great compromise in the Gaslamp: hip style that needn't break the bank. Lounge beats provide the soundtrack to your view of skyscrapers from the pool deck with bar. There's a fitness center and yoga kit and a nightly complimentary wine hour. Parking costs $35.

GAY & LESBIAN SAN DIEGO

Historians trace the roots of San Diego's thriving gay community to WWII. Amid the enforced intimacy of military life, gay men from around the US were suddenly able to create strong if clandestine social networks. Post-war, many of these new friends stayed.

In the late 1960s, a newly politicized gay community made its unofficial headquarters in Hillcrest, which still has the highest concentration of LGBT bars, restaurants, cafes and bookstores. The scene is generally more casual and friendly than in San Francisco or LA. The following should give you a good start, or pick up the free, widely available, *Gay and Lesbian Times*. See also Hillcrest restaurant listings (p293).

Obelisk BOOKSTORE
(1029 University Ave, Hillcrest; ⏲10am-9pm Mon-Thu, to 10pm Fri & Sat, 11am-9pm Sun) LA no longer has a legit gay bookstore, but San Diego's Obelisk is still going strong.

Babycakes COFFEEHOUSE
(Map p274; 3766 5th Ave, Hillcrest; ⏲9am-11pm Sun-Thu, to midnight Fri & Sat; 📶) Hillcrest location, tropical garden, cupcakes and wireless. What more could you ask?

Bourbon Street BAR
(www.bourbonstreetsd.com; 4612 Park Blvd, University Heights) Away from Hillcrest's central strip, this gay bar's layout of rooms and courtyards, bar and dancefloor, makes for easy mingling during bingo nights, guest DJ appearances and martini happy hours.

Top of the Park CLUB NIGHT
(Map p274; 525 Spruce St, Hillcrest; ⏲Friday evening) Start your weekend off big with after-work cocktails surrounded by a veritable gaggle of gays in the penthouse restaurant of the Park Manor Suites (p290).

Se San Diego CONTEMPORARY $$$
(Map p278; ☎619-515-3000; www.sesandiego.com; 1047 5th Ave; r from $249; P@📶≋) This new hotel brings Hollywood glam to San Diego. The 9000lb bronze front door pivots to reveal Nepalese carpets and walls covered in silver leaf, and the texture fest continues with crystal beads, stingray skin and woven leather. There's doting service, a chic restaurant, lovely spa and, should you need it, a music studio. Parking is $36.

W Hotel CONTEMPORARY, SCENE $$
(Map p278; ☎619-231-8220, 888-625-5144; www.whotels.com; 421 West B St; r from $230; P@📶≋) Sexy and stylin', the W fills the otherwise quiet gap between Downtown and Little Italy. The Living Room lobby lounge is aggressively decked out in surf colors (designed by *Queer Eye for the Straight Guy's* Thom Filicia), and there's a spa and roof-top 'beach bar' with heated sand and DJs. Parking costs $28.

TOP CHOICE **La Pensione Hotel** BOUTIQUE $$
(Map p278; ☎619-236-8000, 800-232-4683; www.lapensionehotel.com; 606 W Date St; r $90-160; P@📶) Around a frescoed courtyard at the corner of busy India St in Little Italy, the recently renovated La Pensione has rooms with queen-size beds and private bathrooms, and is within walking distance to most Downtown attractions. There's an attractive cafe downstairs. Parking is $10.

Sofia Hotel HERITAGE $$
(Map p278; ☎619-234-9200, 800-826-0009; www.thesofiahotel.com; 150 W Broadway; r from $159; P@📶🐾)Across from Westfield Horton Plaza, the historic Sofia has 212 rooms so fashionable you'd never guess it's right down the block from the Greyhound station. There are also in-room spa services, concierge, complimentary guided walks around the Gaslamp Quarter (Saturday and Sunday) and a fitness and yoga studio. Parking costs $30.

Courtyard by Marriott San Diego Downtown HERITAGE $$
(Map p278; ☎619-446-3000; www.marriott.com/sancd; 530 Broadway; r $129-229; P@📶👪) Yeah, we know. But this Courtyard is cool because it's in a 1928 bank tower. Spacious rooms occupy the former offices, connected by hallways of vintage marble. Some rooms have views to the harbor and Coronado Bay Bridge. Plus, it's got an active green program, including retrofitting equipment with low-wattage bulbs, digital thermostats and motion sensors. Parking is $30.

The Hole
BAR

(2820 Lytton St, Point Loma) This gay dive is surrounded by auto repair shops, all the better for camo. Head down to the patio to find manly men enjoying Sunday beer busts, wet-underwear contests and more.

Urban Mo's
BAR/RESTAURANT

(Map p274; 308 University Ave, Hillcrest) Equal parts bar and restaurant, Urban Mo's isn't particularly well known for great food, service or prices, but it's popular nonetheless for its thumping club beats, casual vibe, dancefloor and happy hours.

Rich's
DANCE CLUB

(Map p274; 1051 University Ave, Hillcrest; ⏰Tue-Sun) DJs shower the crowd with Latin, techno, pop and house at one of San Diego's biggest gay dance clubs, situated in Hillcrest.

Brass Rail
BAR

(Map p274; 3796 5th Ave, Hillcrest) The city's oldest gay bar has a different music style nightly, from Latin to African to Top 40. It also gets its share of straight folk and has lots of games to play, including pinball, pool and darts.

Flicks
BAR

(Map p274; 1017 University Ave, Hillcrest) Video bar dominated by big screens, plus trivia, karaoke and more. Fun place to hang out and nurse a drink, sort of like Starbucks with booze.

500 West Hotel & Hostel
BUDGET, HOSTEL $

(Map p278; ☎619-234-5252, 866-500-7533; www.500westhotel.com; 500 W Broadway; dm/s/d/tw without bathroom $25/59/69/79; @🛜) Rooms are shoebox-sized and bathrooms are down the hallway in this 1920s YMCA building (renovated in 2004), but hipsters on a budget love the bright decor, tiny flat-screen TVs, communal kitchen (or diner-style restaurant), gym at the Y ($5) and easy access to trolleys and long-distance buses. No air-con.

Horton Grand Hotel
HERITAGE $$

(Map p278; ☎619-544-1886, 800-542-1886; www.hortongrand.com; 311 Island Ave; r from $179; 🅿@🛜) Some rooms in this 1886 brick hotel in the Gaslamp have wrought-iron balconies on the street, but the rooms facing the inner courtyard are the quietest. All are individually decorated in Victoriana and have gas fireplaces. Parking costs $25.

HI San Diego Downtown Hostel
HOSTEL $

(Map p278; ☎619-525-1531, 888-464-4872; www.sandiegohostels.org; 521 Market St; dm/d/tr incl breakfast $38/61/94; @🛜) Centrally located in the Gaslamp Quarter, this HI facility is handy to public transportation and night-life and has a wide range of rooms including some with private bath. It has 24-hour access.

USA Hostels San Diego
HOSTEL $

(Map p278; ☎619-232-3100, 800-438-8622; www.usahostels.com; 726 5th Ave; dm/d incl breakfast $35/85; @🛜) Housed in a former Victorian-era hotel, this convivial Gaslamp hostel has cheerful rooms, a full kitchen, a communal lounge for chilling and in-house parties and beach barbecues. Rates include linens, lockers and pancakes for breakfast. No air-con.

OLD TOWN

Best Western Hacienda Hotel
HOTEL $$

(Map p282; ☎619-298-4707, 800-888-1991; www.haciendahotel-oldtown.com; 4041 Harney St; r $159-189; 🅿@🛜♿🛜) On four well-landscaped acres on the hillside above Old Town's restaurant row, the Hacienda has

CAR FREE

Base yourself in Old Town, and you may not need a car. Many lodgings offer free airport shuttles, and there are convenient transit links on the other side of the state park.

MISSION VALLEY HOTELS

Downtown rates got you down? Beach booked? A couple dozen mostly chain hotels and motels along I-8 in Mission Valley offer in quantity and price what their neighborhood lacks in charm – they're popular for conventions, family vacations and shopping excursions. Outside of the summer peak, weekday rates are occasionally as low as $80. Here are some choices.

Handley Hotel (☎619-298-0511, 800-843-4343; www.handlery.com; 950 Hotel Circle N; r $139-179; P@🖥🐾🏊) The Handlery has attractive furnishings (wooden armoires and writing desks) and a complimentary shuttle to area attractions. Parking costs $12.

Crowne Plaza San Diego (☎619-297-1101; www.cp-sandiego.com; 2270 Hotel Circle N; r from $129; P@🖥🐾🏊) Leafy convention-class hotel with a Polynesian theme (koi ponds and waterfalls) and rooms with super-comfy mattresses. Parking costs $12.

Town & Country Hotel (☎619-291-7131, 800-772-8527; www.towncountry.com; 500 Hotel Circle N; r from $195; P@🖥🐾🏊) This property is so big that golf carts shuttle around four swimming pools, rose bushes, palms and a 10-story tower. There's a trolley stop and bridge to Fashion Valley shopping center. Parking costs $14.

199 rooms over eight buildings, neatly and conservatively decorated, some with pull-out sofas. Add in a workout room and Jacuzzi. Parking costs $12.

Holiday Inn Express   HOTEL **$$**
(☎619-299-7400, 800-465-4329; www.hiexpress.com/ex-oldtown; 3900 Old Town Ave; r $130-160; P@🖥🐾🏊) Hacienda-style building at the edge of Old Town. Rooms are clean, spacious and up to date with hardwood mission-style furniture and extras such as microwaves and refrigerators. Good value. Parking is $12.

HILLCREST & BANKERS HILL

TOP CHOICE **Britt Scripps Inn**   B&B **$$**
(Map p274; ☎619-230-1991, 888-881-1991; www.brittscripps.com; 406 Maple St; r incl breakfast from $200; P🖥) This nine-room Victorian belle just off Balboa Park offers a rare alchemy of high-tech and tradition. Vintage fixtures and furnishings and a grand stained-glass window seamlessly pair with flat-screen TVs and high-speed internet. Rates (which can rise steeply in peak season) include a gourmet breakfast and evening wine-and-cheese reception in the cozy parlor.

Park Manor Suites   HOTEL, GAY-FRIENDLY **$$**
(Map p274; ☎619-291-0999, 800-874-2649; www.parkmanorsuites.com; 525 Spruce St; r incl breakfast $129-229; P🖥) This 74-room gay-friendly place, facing Balboa Park and a reasonable walk to central Hillcrest, used to be an apartment building, meaning mostly large rooms with kitchens, vast closets and early American decor. Breakfast is served on the top floor, with sweeping Downtown-to-ocean views. On Friday nights, the penthouse becomes a gay party scene (p289).

KOA   CAMPING **$**
(☎619-427-3601, 800-562-9877; www.sandiegokoa.com; 111 N 2nd Ave, Chula Vista; tent sites $40-61, RV sites $48-89, cabins $59-109; P@🖥🐾🏊🐕) There are two campgrounds within reach of Downtown; this one is about 8 miles south with good camping facilities for families like a pool and bike rental, plus a Jacuzzi for mom and dad and off-leash dog park for Fido.

Campland on the Bay   CAMPING **$**
(☎858-581-4260, 800-422-9386; www.campland.com; 2211 Pacific Beach Dr, Mission Bay; RV & campsites $46-126, beachfront from $166; P🖥🐾🏊) In the opposite direction to KOA, this place has more than 40 acres fronting Mission Bay. Amenities include a restaurant, two pools, boat rentals and full RV hookups. The cost of the site can vary depending on their proximity to the water; reservations are recommended. Off-season discounts.

✕ Eating

Despite its border location, San Diego's food scene doesn't have the ethnic breadth of LA's, but there's a growing locavore and gourmet scene, especially in North Park, and some of the less expensive options are fun and satisfying. Reservations are recommended, especially on weekends.

GASLAMP QUARTER

There are some 100 restaurants in the Gaslamp, many of them very good. Some have bar scenes too. See also Karl Strauss Brewery & Grill (p295).

Oceanaire
SEAFOOD $$$

(Map p278; ☑619-858-2277; 400 J St; mains $19-46; ☺dinner) The look is art deco ocean liner, and the service is just as elegant, with an oyster bar and creations like Maryland blue-crab cakes and horseradish-crusted Alaskan halibut. If you don't feel like a total splurge, the prix fixe menu (5pm to 7pm) is $30 for three courses.

TOP CHOICE Gaslamp Strip Club
STEAK $$

(Map p278; ☑619-231-3140; 340 5th Ave; mains $14-24; ☺5pm-10pm Sun-Thu, to midnight Fri & Sat) Pull your own bottle from the wine vault, then char your own favorite cut of steak, chicken or fish on the open grills in the retro-Vegas dining room at Downtown's best bargain for steak. No bottle costs more than $36, no steak more than $24. Fab, creative martinis and 'pin-up' art by Alberto Vargas. Tons of fun. No one under 21 allowed.

Café 222
BREAKFAST, BRUNCH $

(Map p278; ☑619-236-9902; 222 Island Ave; mains $7-12; ☺7am-1:45pm; ☻) Downtown's favorite breakfast place serves renowned pumpkin waffles, buttermilk, orange-pecan or granola pancakes, and eggs in scrambles or benedicts. They also sell lunchtime sandwiches and salads, but we always go for breakfast (available until closing).

Croce's Restaurant & Jazz Bar
CONTEMPORARY AMERICAN, JAZZ CLUB $$$

(Map p278; ☑619-233-4355; 802 5th Ave; mains breakfast & lunch $7-16, dinner $24-35; ☺breakfast & lunch Sat & Sun, dinner daily) Empty tables are a rare sight at this sizzling restaurant, a pioneer of the Gaslamp and Ingrid Croce's tribute to her late husband, singer Jim Croce. Both the contemporary American cooking and the musicians who perform nightly hit the right notes. There's also an acclaimed wine list.

Red Pearl Kitchen
ASIAN FUSION $$

(Map p278; ☑619-231-1100; 440 J St; mains $12-24; ☺5:30pm-2am) Orange County's restaurateurs of record, Tim and Liza Goodell, are behind this slick and chic pan-Asian tapas bar, from dim sum to dessert: lump crab *shu mai* dumplings, miso-glazed salmon, shaking Kobe beef with papaya and mint...

Cheese Shop
DINER, HISTORIC $$

(Map p278; ☑619-232-2303; 627 4th Ave; mains breakfast $4-10, lunch $8-19, dinner $8-15; ☺breakfast, lunch & dinner; ☻) Less actual cheese shop than old-fashioned luncheonette, with long wooden counter, cozy booths and brick walls. Breakfasts are classics (have the corned-beef hash and you won't eat until dinner), or try the overstuffed sandwiches or house-roasted pork loin at lunch. They had just started dinner service as of this writing.

Bandar
MIDDLE-EASTERN $$

(Map p278; ☑619-238-0101; 825 4th Ave; mains lunch $12-20, dinner $19-29) Exotic spices and fragrant cooking make this white-tablecloth Persian–Middle Eastern a favorite for giant kebabs and salads that zing with flavor. Come hungry: portions are huge.

Dick's Last Resort
PUB, PARTY $$

(Map p278; ☑619-231-9100; 345 4th Ave; mains lunch $8-20, dinner $12-27; ☺11am-1:30am) At Dick's, a legendary indoor-outdoor place with a riotously fun atmosphere, you can carry on in full voice while guzzling beer and chowing down on burgers, pork ribs, fried chicken and fish, while the staff makes you a giant hat out of table paper. None of the other revelers will care a whit.

EAST VILLAGE

Ask San Diego gourmets about the best new restaurants in town, and surely one of the following will come up in this newly gentrifying neighborhood.

Café Chloe
FRENCH $$

(Map p278; ☑619-232-3242; 721 9th Ave; mains breakfast $7-12, lunch $11.50-13, dinner $15-23; ☺7:30am-10pm Mon-Fri, 8:30am-10:30pm Sat, 8:30am-9:30pm Sun) This delightful corner French bistro has a simple style and gets the standards perfect, and everything else as well. Mac 'n' cheese transforms into macaroni, pancetta and French blue gratin, and the steak frites is served with herb butter and salad. Wonderful egg dishes for weekend brunch.

TOP FIVE CHEAP EATS

Basic

PIZZA $

(Map p278; ☑619-531-8869; www.barbasic.com; 410 10th Ave; small/large pizzas from $9/14; ⊙11:30am-2am) East Village hipsters feast on fragrant New Haven–style, thin-crust, brick-oven-baked pizzas under Basic's high-ceilinged roof (it's in a former warehouse). Small pizzas are pretty large but also pretty light. Some nights are theme nights – art, DJs and more – it can get pretty loud. The only other menu item: basic salad ($8), which is anything but, with sliced pears, candied walnuts, etc.

Proper

GASTRO-PUB $$

(Map p278; ☑619-255-7520; 795 J St; small dishes $7-19; ⊙4-10pm Mon-Thu, 11am-10pm Fri, 10am-10pm Sat & Sun; ▦) Why suffer through burgers and beer when this new gastropub serves gourmet pub grub (Guinness short ribs, mussels and chips). There's also a cheap kids' menu. It's next to Wine Steals by Petco Park.

Valentine's

MEXICAN $

(Map p278; ☑619-234-8256; 844 Market St; mains $3.50-7; ⊙7:30am-midnight Mon-Thu, to 3am Fri, 8:30am-3am Sat, 8:30am-midnight Sun) There's nothing urbane about this home-style Mexican joint, but it's a local institution. Apart from the usual tacos and burritos, the *carne asada* fries (French fries topped like nachos with grilled beef, sour cream, guacamole and such) are messy, coronary-inducing and oh so *bueno*. Late weekend hours mean it's great after a rager.

LITTLE ITALY

Little Italy is – surprise! – happy hunting ground for cafes and trattorias, on India St and around Date St. Here are just some suggestions; you'll find plenty more with a little exploring.

Bencotto

UPSCALE ITALIAN $$

(Map p278; ☑619-450-4786; 750 W Fir St; mains $12-19; ⊙11:30am-9:30pm Sun-Thu, to 10:30pm Fri & Sat) This newcomer opened in 2009 and instantly became one of the city's hottest restaurants. It's the embodiment of the new Little Italy – contemporary, angular, multistory, architect-designed, arty and green – and the food is great too, from fresh-sliced prosciutto to freshly made pasta *a modo tuo* (your way). Lunches from $8.

Café Zucchero

UPSCALE ITALIAN $$

(Map p278; ☑619-531-1731; 1731 India St; mains lunch $8-17, dinner $13-20; ⊙breakfast, lunch & dinner) Old-school Little Italy spot, the kind with a brass rail and marble floor for a bang-up Italian dinner. There's a pizza menu like a phone book, pastas and meat and seafood dishes, but save room (or make a special stop) for pastries by the dozen or a freezer-case's worth of *gelati*.

Filippi's Pizza Grotto

PIZZA, DELI $$

(Map p278; ☑619-232-5094; 1747 India St; dishes $5-20; ⊙9am-10pm Sun & Mon, to 10:30pm Tue-Thu, to 11:30pm Fri & Sat; ▦) There are often lines out the door for Filippi's old-school Italian cooking (pizza, spaghetti and ravioli) served on red-and-white-checked tablecloths in the dining room festooned with murals of *la bella Italia*. The front of the shop is an excellent Italian deli.

Burger Lounge

BURGERS $

(Map p278; ☑619-237-7878; 1608 India St; burgers $8; ⊙10:30am-10pm Sun-Thu, to midnight Fri & Sat; ▦) This swingin' corner place serves chic comfort food. There's just a simple menu, but what they do with it! Plump burgers (beef, turkey or veggie), crisp fries, great salads and for dessert: cupcakes!

Mimmo's Italian Village

ITALIAN $

(Map p278; ☑619-239-3710; 1743 India St; meals under $10; ⊙8am-4pm Mon-Sat; ▦) In a tall-ceilinged space decorated like (wait for it) an Italian village complete with mini Ponte Vecchio, Mimmo's deli serves salads, hot and cold sandwiches, and lunch specials, such as lasagna and eggplant parmigiana.

EMBARCADERO & THE WATERFRONT

Anthony's Fish Grotto & Fishette

SEAFOOD $

(Map p278; 1360 N Harbor Dr; ▦) Fishette (☑619-232-2175; mains $7.50-12; ⊙10am-9pm Mon-Fri, 8am-9pm Sat & Sun); Grotto (☑619-232-5105; mains lunch $8-15, dinner $12-25; ⊙11am-9:30pm Sun-Thu, 11am-10pm Sat & Sun) Next to the Maritime Museum, this pair of restaurants serves seafood and chowders with views of the tall ships on the harbor. The sit-down Grotto has an old-style nautical theme (ahoy, mateys!), while the counter at the Fishette serves a more limited menu (think fish and chips or sandwiches) that you eat out on the deck.

Fish Market

SEAFOOD $$$

(Map p278; ☑619-232-3474; 750 N Harbor Dr; mains lunch $10-28, dinner $13-35; ⊙11am-10pm) For a daily market menu of sushi to smoked fish, chowder to the raw bar, steamers to cioppino and grilled fish, all with a harbor view in a snappy dining room, walk to Tuna

Harbor, opposite the port side of the USS *Midway*. Snag a window table if you can.

BALBOA PARK

Prado   CALIFORNIAN $$$
(Map p274; ☑619-557-9441; 1549 El Prado; mains lunch $13-20, dinner $20-36; ☺11:30am-3pm Mon-Fri, 11am-3pm Sat & Sun, dinner from 5pm Tue-Sun) In one of San Diego's most beautiful dining rooms, feast on Cal-eclectic cooking by one of San Diego's most renowned chefs: bakery sandwiches, chicken and *orecchiette* pasta, and pork prime rib. Go for a civilized lunch on the verandah or for afternoon cocktails and appetizers in the bar.

OLD TOWN
At the Mexican eateries all along San Diego Ave, hard-working ladies churn out an estimated 210,000 fresh tortillas per month and most have great bar scenes too. Choose your setting: party, local or sublime.

Old Town Mexican Cafe   MEXICAN $$
(Map p282; ☑619-297-4330; 2489 San Diego Ave; mains $3-19; ☺7am-midnight; 🍴) Watch the staff turn out tortillas in the window while you wait to be seated at this local legend. Then enjoy *machacas* (shredded pork with onions and peppers) *carnitas* (grilled pork) and *posole* (hominy stew). For breakfast: *chilaquiles* (tortilla chips salsa or *mole*, broiled or grilled with cheese). If the carpet has seen better days, that only lends authenticity.

El Agave   UPSCALE MEXICAN $$$
(Map p282; ☑619-220-0692; 2304 San Diego Ave; mains lunch $10-18, dinner $18-27; ☺11am-10pm) Candlelight flickers on the bottles adorning the walls of this romantic 2nd-floor, white-tablecloth, high-end place catering to cognoscenti. The *mole* is superb, and there are a whopping 1500 different tequilas to choose from.

Zócalo   NUEVO LATINO $$
(Map p282; ☑619-298-9840; 2444 San Diego Ave; mains lunch $9-17, dinner $12-24; ☺11am-9:30 Mon-Sat, 10:30am-9pm Sun) Nuevo Latino cuisine in an upscale setting: think tamarind chipotle salmon or a *medianoche* sandwich of pork, ham pickles and Swiss cheese. There's a great happy hour (time varies) with deals on fish tacos, artichoke fritters and more.

Fred's   MEXICAN, PARTY $$
(Map p282; ☑619-858-8226; 2470 San Diego Ave; mains $9-14; ☺11am-11pm Sun, Mon, Wed & Thu, to midnight Tue, Fri & Sat) Every night party people on a budget crowd into raucous Fred's, especially on bargain 'Taco-licious Tuesday.' The straight-down-the-middle enchiladas, burritos and tacos won't set standards, but it's hard not to love the colorful interior and rangy patio.

BANKERS HILL, HILLCREST & NORTH PARK
See also Gay & Lesbian San Diego (p289) for bar-restaurants in Hillcrest. Also note the Hillcrest location of Porkyland (p318).

⬛TOP CHOICE Cucina Urbana   CALIFORNIA-ITALIAN $$
(Map p274; ☑619-239-2222; 505 Laurel St; mains lunch $10-17, dinner $12-20; ☺11:30am-2pm Tue-Fri, 5-9pm Sun & Mon, 5pm-10pm Tue-Thu, 5pm-midnight Fri & Sat) In this new corner place with a modern rustic ambience, business gets done, celebrations get celebrated and friends hug and kiss – over refined yet affordable Cal Ital cooking. Look for short rib pappardelle, pizzas like foraged mushroom with taleggio cheese and braised leeks, and smart cocktails and local 'brewskies'. For dinner, book well in advance.

⬛TOP CHOICE Urban Solace   CALIFORNIAN $$
(☑619-295-6464; 3823 30th St, North Park; mains lunch $8-16, dinner $9-18; ☺11:30am-10pm Mon-Thu, to 11pm Fri, 5-11pm Sat, 5-9pm Sun) North Park's young hip gourmets revel in creative comfort food here: meatloaf of ground lamb, fig, pine nuts and feta, mac 'n' cheese with duck confit, chicken and dumplings. The setting's surprisingly chill for such great eats; maybe it's the cocktails like mojitos made with bourbon.

Linkery   SAUSAGES $$
(☑619-255-8778; 3794 30th St, North Park; mains $9-24; ☺5.30-11:30pm daily, lunch Fri-Sun) A daily menu of artisan sausages and hand-cured meats from sustainably raised animals is the thing here – on a roll, in tacos, on a board with cheese or in *choucroute* (French stew), for example. Vegetarians: don't worry; you're covered too, and there's a great beer and wine list.

Hash House a Go Go   BAKERY/CAFE $$
(Map p274; ☑619-298-4646; 3628 5th Ave; breakfast mains $8-16; ☺7:30am-2pm Tue-Fri, to 2:30pm Sat-Mon, dinner Tue-Sun) This buzzing bungalow makes biscuits and gravy straight outta Carolina, towering benedicts, large-as-your-head pancakes and – wait for it – hash seven different ways. Come hungry. Eat your whole breakfast, and you may not need dinner.

DON'T MISS

SOUTH PARK'S KITCHEN

Heart and soul of the funky South Park neighborhood (south of North Park and east of Balboa Park) is **Big Kitchen** (☑619-234-5789; 3003 Grape St, South Park; mains $5-13.50; ⊘8am-2pm; ♿). All are welcome (though credit cards are not) at this friendly enclave of food, art, music and civic bonhomie. Omelets and challah French toast are stupendous, and breakfast combos are named for regulars including Whoopi Goldberg, who used to wait tables here.

Bread & Cie   BAKERY, CAFE **$**
(Map p274; ☑619-683-9322; 350 University Ave; pastries $2-4, sandwiches $5-8; ⊘7am-7pm Mon-Fri, to 6pm Sat, 8am-6pm Sun; ♿) Aside from crafting some of San Diego's best breads (including anise and fig, kalamata black olive and three-raisin), this wide-open bakery-deli makes fabulous sandwiches with fillings such as curried-chicken salad and Black Forest ham. Boxed lunches cost $10. Great pastries, too.

Saigon on Fifth   VIETNAMESE **$$**
(Map p274; ☑619-220-8828; 3900 5th Ave; mains $7-16; ⊘11am-midnight; ℗) This Vietnamese place tries hard and succeeds, with dishes like fresh spring rolls, fish of Hue (with garlic, ginger and lemongrass) and rockin' 'spicy noodles.' Staff dress nicely and the room is elegant but not overbearing.

Khyber Pass   AFGHAN **$$**
(Map p274; ☑619-294-7579; 523 University Ave; mains $13-21; ⊘11:30am-10pm) Afghan tapestries and moody photos set the atmosphere in this tall-ceilinged space, with adventuresome Afghan cooking. If you've never had it, it's kind of like Indian meets Middle Eastern: yogurt curries, kabobs, stews and more. A few high-end dishes (eg rack of lamb kabob) are up to $30.

Baja Betty's   MEXICAN **$$**
(Map p274; ☑619-269-8510; 1421 University Ave; mains $10-15; ⊘11am-midnight Mon-Fri, 10am-1am Sat, 10am-midnight Sun) Gay-owned and straight-friendly, this restaurant-bar is always a party with a just-back-from-Margaritaville vibe (and dozens of tequilas to take you back there) alongside dishes like Mexi Queen queso dip, You Go Grill swordfish tacos and Fire in the Hole fajitas.

Ono Sushi   JAPANESE, CONTEMPORARY **$$**
(Map p274; ☑619-298-0616; 1236 University Ave; mains $9-18; ⊘from 5pm Mon-Fri, noon Sat & Sun) Oh yes. Ono bucks tradition with its specialty rolls (the PD roll has spicy crab, sprouts and seared albacore) and Pacific rim–style appetizers and mains like macadamia-crusted chicken breast. Expect a wait at peak times, and enjoy cocktails after the kitchen closes.

San Diego Chicken Pie Shop   MEAT PIES **$**
(☑619-295-0156; 2633 El Cajon Blvd, North Park; pies from $2.60, mains $5-14; ⊘10am-8pm Mon-Fri, 8am-8pm Sat & Sun) It's out of the way and looks like it hasn't been redecorated since the Carter administration, but local foodies love the namesake chicken pies, which don't muck up the chicken and creamy gravy with vegetables. Other mains include bacon and eggs for breakfast, and fish and steaks the rest of the day.

MISSION HILLS

North from Little Italy on India St, where it meets Washington St, there's a block of well-known eateries.

Saffron   THAI **$**
(☑619-574-0177; 3731 India St; mains $5-9.50; ⊘10:30am-9pm Mon-Thu & Sat, to 10pm Fri, 11am-9pm Sun) This much admired place is actually two shops – Saffron Thai Grilled Chicken and **Noodles & Saté** (☑619-574-7737; 3737 India St; mains $5-9; ⊘lunch & dinner) a few doors down, but you can get both at either shop and enjoy it in the noodle shop. Chicken is cooked over a charcoal-grill and comes with a choice of sauces, salad, jasmine rice and a menu of finger foods. Culinary fans over the years have included Julia Child and Martha Stewart.

Wine Vault & Bistro   CALIFORNIAN **$$**
(☑619-295-3939; www.winevaultbistro.com; 3731-A India St; prix-fixe dinner from $20) Perched atop staircases, this spare yet homey white space with white chairs might recall Nantucket or Napa, and that's appropriate given that meals are meant to pair with wine. Menus and hours change virtually nightly, so check the calendar on the website for details and reservations.

Shakespeare Pub & Grille BRITISH PUB $$

(📞619-299-0230; 3701 India St; dishes $5-15; ⏰10am-midnight Sun-Thu, to 1am Fri & Sat) One of San Diego's most authentic English ale houses, Shakespeare is the place for darts, soccer by satellite, beer on tap and pub grub, including fish and chips, and bangers and mash. It also has a great sundeck. On weekends, load up with a British breakfast: bacon, mushrooms, black and white pudding and more, served from 8am to noon.

El Indio MEXICAN $

(📞619-299-0333; 3695 India St; dishes $3-9; ⏰8am-9pm; 🅿️👶) Counter-service shop famous since 1940 for its taquitos, tamales and excellent breakfast burritos. Eat in a rudimentary dining room or at picnic tables under metal umbrellas across the street.

 Drinking
=======

San Diego may not have the swinging night scene of LA, but being in the Gaslamp Quarter it's hard to tell.

GASLAMP QUARTER

The Gaslamp has the city's highest concentration of bars and nightclubs. Many establishments do double (even triple) duty as restaurants, bars and clubs.

Vin de Syrah LOUNGE

(Map p278; www.vindesyrah.com; 901 5th Ave) Head down the stairs beneath the Melting Pot restaurant – or is it down the rabbit hole – into this basement bar that's like an alternative universe. Leaves dangle from the walls, and butterflies soar overhead beneath toadstools-shaped umbrellas. Reserve a booth, if you can.

Dublin Square IRISH PUB

(Map p278; www.dublinsquareirishpub.com; 544 4th Ave) Guinness? Check. Corned beef? Check. But what sets this rambling pub apart is its selection of nightly music. Try to go when the band Fooks is playing – check website for schedule. Meals are served from 11:30am to 10:30pm daily, and from 8am Saturday and Sunday.

Quality Social UPSCALE DIVE

(Map p278; www.qualitysocial.com; 789 6th Ave) It sounds like an oxymoron: an upscale dive bar. This concrete box has big windows out to the street, loud music and lots of beers, but you can snack on charcuterie and artisanal cheeses. Look also for $6 shots and cocktails like 'Not Your Grandma's Gin & Tonic.' Check the website for special events.

SURF & SUDS

'The beer that made San Diego famous' may not quite roll off the tongue, but never mind: America's Finest City is home to some of America's finest brew pubs. The **San Diego Brewers Guild** (www.sandiegobrewersguild.org) counts some 40 member establishments. Hop over to the guild's website (get it?) or pick up one of their pamphlets around town. Here are some pubs to get you started.

Karl Strauss Brewery & Grill (www.karlstrauss.com) Downtown (Map p278; 1157 Columbia St); La Jolla (Map p314; cnr Wall St & Herschel Ave; mains $9-29) San Diego meets Bavaria at this longtime favorite, where wait staff will instruct you in which beers pair with your food choices. Go on Thursday 'cask nights.'

Coronado Brewing Co (www.coronadobrewingcompany.com; 170 Orange Ave, Coronado; ⏰from 11am) Delicious Coronado Golden house brew goes well with pizzas, pastas, sandwiches and fries; near the ferry terminal.

Pacific Beach Ale House (Map p304; www.pbalehouse.com; 721 Grand Ave, Pacific Beach; mains $9-25; ⏰11am-2am) Contempo-cool setting and a huge menu including lobster mac 'n' cheese, steamed clams and bistro meatloaf.

Pizza Port (www.pizzaport.com; 571 Carlsbad Village Dr, Carlsbad; pizzas $8-23; ⏰11am-11pm) Rockin' and raucous barn of a space with surf art and 'anti-wimpy' pizzas to go with the signature 'sharkbite red' brew.

To leave the driving to someone else, **Brewery Tours of San Diego** (📞619-961-7999; www.brewerytoursofsandiego.com; tour per person incl lunch $85) offers bus tours to three different breweries for a variety of tastes.

DIVINE WINE

Part wine shop, part gourmet cheese and charcuterie bar, the explosively popular **Wine Steals** (www.winestealssd.com; cheese & charcuterie boards $12-25, wraps & pizzas from $6.50; ⊘11am-11pm Sun, 4-11pm Mon-Wed, 11am-midnight Thu-Sat) East Village (Map p278; 793 J St, Downtown); Hillcrest (Map p274; 1243 University Ave) sells just that: inexpensive wines by the bottle (to drink in or take home), as well as 'barrel' wines by the glass and upscale pub grub.

Onyx Room & Thin LOUNGE, DANCE CLUB
(Map p278; 852 5th Ave) The candlelit Onyx is a downstairs jazz lounge with a dance floor; Thin is an ultracool, industrial-look upstairs bar, great for cocktails and conversation. Wear nice shoes.

Star Bar NEIGHBORHOOD
(Map p278; 423 E St) When you've had it with gentrified style and you're looking for a historic dive, head to this old-school bar decorated year-round with Christmas lights for the cheapest drinks in the Gaslamp.

FINANCIAL DISTRICT & LITTLE ITALY

El Camino MEXICAN-STYLE LOUNGE
(Map p278; 2400 India St) We're not sure what it means that this buzzy watering hole has a Dia de los Muertos (Mexican Day of the Dead holiday) theme in the flight path of San Diego Airport – watch planes land from the outdoor patio – but whatever, dude. The clientele is cool, design mod, the drinks strong and there are *fabuloso* Mexican vittles.

W Hotel FASHIONABLE, BEACH BAR
(Map p278; 421 West B St) The silicone set twirls around in Louis Vuitton on the catwalk of the W Hotel on Thursday, Friday and Saturday nights, but the best night to go here is Thursday, when there's usually not a long line to get inside to stand around on the sandy 'beach bar.' on a roof deck.

Waterfront NEIGHBORHOOD
(Map p278; 2044 Kettner Blvd) San Diego's first liquor license was granted to this place in the 1930s (it was on the waterfront until the harbor was filled and the airport built). A room full of historic bric-a-brac, big windows looking onto the street and the spirits of those who went before make this a wonderful place to spend the afternoon or evening.

EAST VILLAGE

While out-of-towners frolic happily in the Gaslamp Quarter, locals instead head east to these more insider-y bars.

East Village Tavern & Bowl BOWLING CLUB
(Map p278; 930 Market St, East Village; ⊘11:30am-1am, from 10am Sat & Sun) This large sports bar a few blocks from Petco Park has six bowling lanes (thankfully, behind a wall for effective soundproofing). Pub menu (dishes $6-11; pulled pork sliders, applewood BLT) is served all day.

Noble Experiment SPEAKEASY
(⌕text 619-888-4713) This place is literally a find. Open a secret door and enter a contemporary speakeasy with miniature gold skulls on the walls, classical paintings on the ceilings and some 400 cocktails on the list (from $12). The hard part: getting in. Text for a reservation, and they'll tell you if your requested time is available and how to find it.

BANKERS HILL & OLD TOWN

For Hillcrest listings, see Gay & Lesbian San Diego (p289) and Wine Steals (p296). Most Old Town restaurants (p293) are also known for their bar scenes.

Nunu's Cocktail Lounge
HIPSTER, NEIGHBORHOOD
(Map p274; 3537 5th Ave) Dark and divey, this hipster haven started pouring when JFK was president and still looks the part with its curvy booths, big bar and lovably kitsch decor. Smoking patio.

Harney Sushi HIPSTER
(Map p282; 3964 Harney St) Yes, it's a sushi bar (dishes $4 to $15), but the *bar* bar takes over late at night as a rotation of DJs spins music from reggae to house to techno for a hip, younger crowd.

Old Town Saloon NEIGHBORHOOD
(Map p282; 2495 San Diego Ave) This one's for the locals, so be cool. Swill a Bud Light, and play pool at one of four tables.

☆ Entertainment

Check out the *San Diego Reader* or the San Diego *Union-Tribune* for the latest movies, theater, galleries and music gigs around town. **Arts Tix** (Map p278; ☑619-497-5000; www.sdartstix.com; cnr 3rd Ave & Broadway; ⊙noon-6pm Tue-Thu, 11am-6pm Fri & Sat, noon-5pm Sun), in a kiosk outside Westfield Horton Plaza, has half-price tickets for same-day evening or next-day matinee performances and offers discounted tickets to other events. **Ticketmaster** (☑619-220-8497; www.ticketmaster.com) and **House of Blues** (www.hob.com) sell tickets to other gigs around the city.

Nightclubs & Live Music

Anthology   JAZZ
(Map p278; www.anthologysd.com; 1337 India St; cover to $60) Opened in 2007 just south of Little Italy, Anthology presents live jazz in a swank supper-club setting. It books both up-and-comers and big-name performers including Everclear and *American Idol*'s Kris Allen.

Casbah   ROCK
(www.casbahmusic.com; 2501 Kettner Blvd) Bands from Smashing Pumpkins to Death Cab for Cutie all rocked the Casbah on their way up the charts and it's still a good place to catch tomorrow's headliners.

4th & B   CLUB
(Map p278; www.4thandB.com; 345 B St) This midsized venue has music lovers head-bobbing with performances from an eclectic mix of talent and club nights, from un-signed hopefuls to Psychedelic Furs, Snoop Dogg and the Last Comic Standing tour. Rest your feet – and eardrums – in the lounge. There's often a cover charge.

On Broadway   DANCE CLUB
(Map p278; www.obec.tv; 615 Broadway; cover $20; ⊙Fri & Sat) Sprawling double-decker dance spot where DJs mix it up on – count them – five dancefloors. Dress to impress, or forget about making it past the velvet-rope goons.

Shout House   PIANO BAR
(Map p278; 655 4th Ave; cover to $10) Good, clean fun at this cavernous Gaslamp bar with dueling pianos. Talented players have an amazing repertoire: standards, rock and more. We once heard Justin Timberlake's 'Dick in a Box' (OK, maybe it's not so clean). The crowd ranges from college-age to conventioneers.

Stingaree   DANCE CLUB
(Map p278; www.stingsandiego.com; 454 6th Ave) Vegas-style decor provides the backdrop for San Diego's most-likely-to-spot-a-celebrity club. It's the place where San Diego professional athletes are most likely to tie one on before doing something TMZ-worthy. Table service for your drinks and cabanas on the roof. Cover charges vary and can be expensive.

Also recommended:

Café Sevilla   LATIN/SPANISH
(Map p278; 555 4th Ave) Tango, flamenco and tapas.

Croce's Restaurant & Jazz Bar
                                    JAZZ, BLUES, R&B
(Map p278; 802 5th Ave) Jim Croce's legacy lives on here; see also p291.

House of Blues   BLUES, R&B
(Map p278; www.hob.com; 1055 5th Ave) You know what this is.

Classical Music & Opera

San Diego Symphony   CLASSICAL
(Map p278; www.sandiegosymphony.com; 750 B St) This accomplished orchestra presents classical and family concerts in **Copley Symphony Hall**. Look for Summer Pops concerts at Embarcadero Marina Park South.

Orchestra Nova   CLASSICAL
(formerly San Diego Chamber Orchestra; ☑858-350-0290, 760-753-6402; www.sdco.org; tickets $20-35) High-caliber performances of small orchestral works are the hallmarks of this orchestra, whose season runs from October to May. Venues include **St Paul's Cathedral** (Map p274; 2728 6th Ave), on the western edge of Balboa Park, and the La Jolla branch of the Museum of Contemporary Art (p313).

San Diego Opera   OPERA
(Map p278; www.sdopera.com; Civic Theatre, 1100 3rd Ave at B St) This is ranked among America's top 10 opera companies, under the direction of Maestro Karen Keltner.

Lyric Opera San Diego   LIGHT OPERA
(www.lyricoperasandiego.org) For light opera, musical theater, movies and musical extravaganzas, this reasonably priced company stages shows at the **Birch North Park Theater** (2891 University Ave) in North Park.

Cinemas

Current movies fill multiplexes at big malls and in Hillcrest. Check local papers or visit www.moviefone.com.

Cinema Under the Stars   OUTDOOR CINEMA
(www.topspresents.com; 4040 Goldfinch St; tickets $13.50) This unique venue screens mostly classic American films on a heated patio in Mission Hills, a few nights a week from March to November.

Theater

Theater thrives in San Diego and is one of the city's greatest cultural attractions. Book tickets at the box office or with one of the agencies listed in the introduction to this section.

Old Globe Theaters   SHAKESPEARE
(Map p274; www.theoldglobe.org) Worth special mention are Balboa Park's Old Globe Theaters, where visitors to the 1935–36 Pacific-California Exposition enjoyed 40-minute renditions of Shakespeare's greatest hits, and which later became home to a popular summer Shakespeare festival. After being destroyed by arson in the 1970s, it was rebuilt in the style of the original 17th-century Old Globe in England. Between the three stages here – Old Globe, Cassius Carter Stage and the outdoor Lowell Davies Festival Theater – there are performances most days, including non-Shakespearean works.

Other venues:

Horton Grand Theatre   THEATER
(Map p278; ☎619-234-9583; 444 4th Ave)

Lamb's Players Theater   THEATER
(www.lambsplayers.org; 1142 Orange Ave, Coronado)

National Comedy Theatre   COMEDY
(www.nationalcomedy.com; 3717 India St, Mission Hills)

San Diego Junior Theatre   CHILDREN'S THEATER
(Map p274; www.juniortheatre.com; Casa del Prado, Balboa Park)

San Diego Repertory Theatre   THEATER
(Map p278; www.sdrep.com; Lyceum Theater, 79 Horton Plaza)

La Jolla Playhouse   THEATER
(☎858-550-1010; www.lajollaplayhouse.com; UCSD) See p318.

Spectator Sports

Petco Park   BASEBALL
(Map p278; www.padres.com; 100 Park Blvd; tickets $10-61; ☺season Apr-early Oct) The San Diego Padres Major League Baseball team plays in this handsome stadium right in the East Village. Tickets are usually avail-

able at the gate unless it's crucial to the standings or the LA Dodgers are in town. See p277 for information about touring the stadium.

Qualcomm Stadium   FOOTBALL
(www.chargers.com; 9449 Friars Rd; tickets from $54; ☺season Aug-Jan) The San Diego Chargers, SoCal's only National Football League team, play at this stadium in Mission Valley (there's a trolley stop right in front).

🛍 Shopping

Souvenir hunters will find stuffed Shamus at SeaWorld, realistic-looking rubber snakes at the zoo, or reprinted historical photos at the Museum of San Diego History. The Spanish Village Art Center in Balboa Park (p273) is a good place to find paintings (mostly watercolors) of local scenes.

Given that adventure-sports gods Tony Hawk and Shawn White are San Diegans, surf and skate clothing are natural purchases here. There's a strip of stores including Quicksilver, Oakley, Puma and Skatewear in the Gaslamp Quarter, on 5th Ave between J St and Island Ave.

Seaport Village   SHOPPING DISTRICT
(Map p278; www.seaportvillage.com; ☺10am-10pm; P ♿) Neither seaport nor village, this 14-acre collection of novelty shops and restaurants has a faux–New England theme. It's touristy and twee but good for souvenir shopping and casual eats.

Adams Avenue   ANTIQUES
(www.adamsaveonline.com) This is San Diego's main 'antique row,' and cuts across some of San Diego's less-visited neighborhoods. You'll find the greatest concentration of shops around Normal Heights between the I-805 and I-15. The area has dozens of shops selling furniture, art and antiques from around the world. For other antique shopping, check Newport Ave in the Ocean Beach neighborhood (p302).

Kobey's Swap Meet   FLEA MARKET
(www.kobeyswap.com; 3500 Sports Arena Blvd; admission Fri 50¢, Sat & Sun $1; ☺7am-3pm Fri-Sun; P) The depth and breadth is awesome at the weekly flea market in the parking lot of the San Diego Sports Arena, and often the bargains are too. Look for all sorts of new and used items including sunglasses, clothing, jewelry, produce, flowers and plants, tools and furniture.

Le Travel Store BOOKSHOP
(Map p278; 745 4th Ave) Every shopping mall in San Diego has at least one bookshop, usually of the large, chain variety. This one has an excellent selection of maps, travel guides and accessories, and helpful staff.

Among malls for general shopping plus movies and restaurants, Westfield Horton Plaza Center (p279) is the most central. The San Diego Trolley Green Line takes you to the three large malls in Mission Valley:

Fashion Valley MALL
(www.simon.com; 7007 Friars Rd; ☉10am-9pm Mon-Sat, 11am-7pm Sun) Premier shops here include Tiffany & Co, Burberry, James Perse and Restoration Hardware, and department stores Neiman Marcus, Saks Fifth Avenue, Macy's and Nordstrom.

Westfield Mission Valley MALL
(www.westfield.com/missionvalley; 1640 Camino del Rio N; ☉10am-9pm Mon-Sat, 11am-6pm Sun) This mall is more casual with shops like Target, Hot Topic and Loehmann's.

Hazard Center MALL
(www.hazardcenter.com; 7510-7610 Hazard Center Dr) The smallest of the three Mission Valley malls.

ℹ Information

Internet Access

All public libraries provide free internet access; no library card is required. You can make reservations one day in advance by calling the main library. You can also pay to log on at **FedEx Office stores** (www.fedex.com) or try coffeehouses.

Libraries

Main library (www.sannet.gov/public-library; 820 E St; ☉noon-8pm Mon & Wed, 9:30am-5:30pm Tue & Thu & Fri, 1-5pm Sun; 🛜) About two blocks east of the Gaslamp Quarter. Phone or check the website for smaller branch libraries, and remember: each city has its own library system.

Media

KPBS 89.5 FM (www.kpbs.org) National Public Radio station.

San Diego Magazine (www.sandiegomagazine.com) Glossy monthly.

San Diego Union-Tribune (www.signonsandiego.com) The city's major daily.

FREE LISTINGS MAGAZINES These tabloid-sized magazines cover the active music, art and theater scenes. Find them in shops and cafes:

Citybeat (www.sdcitybeat.com)

San Diego Reader (www.sdreader.com)

Medical Services

Scripps Mercy Hospital (☎619-294-8111; www.scripps.org; 4077 5th Ave, Hillcrest; ☉emergency room 24hr)

Rite-Aid pharmacies (☎800-748-3243, www.riteaid.com) Call for the branch nearest you.

Money

You'll find ATMs throughout San Diego.

Travelex (177 Horton Plaza; ☉10am-7pm Mon-Fri, to 6pm Sat, 11am-4pm Sun) For foreign-currency exchange.

Post

For post-office locations, call ☎800-275-8777 or log on to www.usps.com.

Downtown Post Office (815 E St; ☉9am-5pm Mon-Fri)

Tourist Information

International Visitors Information Center (☎619-236-1212; 1040-1/3 W Broadway at Harbor Dr; ☉9am-5pm) At the city's official visitors center, located along the Embarcadero across from Broadway Pier, helpful staff offer very detailed neighborhood maps, sell discounted tickets to attractions and maintain a hotel reservation hotline.

Websites

Lonely Planet (www.lonelyplanet.com/usa/san-diego) Planning advice, author recommendations, traveler reviews and insider tips.

San Diego Convention & Visitors Bureau (www.sandiego.org) Search hotels, sights, dining, rental cars and more, and make reservations.

Sandiego.com (www.sandiego.com) Comprehensive ad-based portal to all things San Diegan, from fun stuff to serious news.

ℹ Getting There & Away

Air

Because of the limited length of runways, most flights to **San Diego International Airport-Lindbergh Field** (SAN; ☎619-400-2404; www.san.org) are domestic. The airfield sits just 3 miles west of Downtown; plane-spotters will thrill watching jets come in over Balboa Park for landing. Coming from overseas, you'll likely change flights – and clear US customs – at one of the major US gateway airports, such as LA, San Francisco, Chicago, New York or Miami.

The standard one-way fare between LA and San Diego is about $100 and takes about 35 minutes; unless you're connecting through LA, you're usually better off driving.

To/from other US cities, flights to San Diego are generally up to about $120 more expensive than those to LA. All major US airlines serve San Diego, plus Aeromexico, Air Canada and the Canadian carrier WestJet.

Bus

Greyhound (☑800-231-2222; www.greyhound.com; 120 W Broadway) serves San Diego from cities across North America. Inquire about discounts and special fares.

Buses depart frequently for LA; the standard one-way/round-trip fare is $18/29 and the trip takes 2½ to four hours. There are several daily departures to Anaheim ($18/29, about 2¼ hours).

Buses to San Francisco (from $74/146, 12 hours, about eight daily) require a transfer in Los Angeles; round-trip airfares often costs about the same. Most buses to Las Vegas (one-way/round-trip $51/92, eight to nine hours, about nine daily) require a transfer in LA or San Bernardino.

Car & Motorcycle

Allow two hours from LA in non-peak traffic.

Train

Amtrak (☑800-872-7245; www.amtrak.com) runs the *Pacific Surfliner* several times daily to Anaheim ($23, two hours), Los Angeles ($33, 2¾ hours) and Santa Barbara ($34, 6½ hours) from the historic **Union Station** (Santa Fe Depot; 1055 Kettner Blvd).

Getting Around

While most people get around by car, it's possible to have an entire San Diego vacation using municipal buses and trolleys run by the **Metropolitan Transit System** (MTS; ☑619-233-3004; www.transit.511sd.com) and your own two feet. Most buses/trolleys cost $2.25/2.50 per ride. Transfers are not available, so purchase a day pass if you're going to be taking more than two rides in a day. The **Transit Store** (☑619-234-1060; www.transit.511sd.com; 102 Broadway; ☺9am-5pm Mon-Fri) is one-stop shopping for route maps, tickets and one-/two-/three-/four-day passes ($5/9/12/15). Same-day passes are also available from bus drivers. At trolley stations, purchase tickets from vending machines.

For information on reaching San Diego's north coast by train see p319.

To/From the Airport

Bus 992 (the Flyer, $2.25) operates at 10- to 15-minute intervals between the airport and Downtown, with stops along Broadway. Airport shuttle services (from about $13 to Downtown, more to other destinations) include the **Super Shuttle** (☑800-974-8885; www.supershuttle.com) but these travel at their own pace and may drop off several others before your stop; call to reserve a day or two ahead. Taxis between Downtown and the airport typically cost between $10 and $16.

Bus

MTS (www.sdmts.com) covers most of the metropolitan area, North County, La Jolla and the beaches. It's most convenient if you're based Downtown and not staying out late.

For route and fare information, call ☑619-233-3004 or 800-266-6883; operators are available 5:30am to 8:30pm Monday to Friday, and 8am to 5pm Saturday and Sunday (note that the 800 number works only within San Diego). For 24-hour automated information, call ☑619-685-4900.

Fares cost $2.25 for most trips, including a transfer good for up to two hours; express routes and trolleys cost $2.50. Exact fare is required on all buses.

Useful routes to/from Downtown:

No 3 Balboa Park, Hillcrest, UCSD Medical Center

No 7, 7A, 7B Balboa Park, Zoo, Hillcrest, North Park

No 8/9 Old Town to Pacific Beach, SeaWorld

No 30 Old Town, Pacific Beach, La Jolla, University Towne Centre

No 35 Old Town to Ocean Beach

No 901 Coronado

Car

All the big-name car-rental companies (see p466) have desks at the airport, and lesser-known ones may be cheaper. Shop around – prices vary widely, even from day to day within the same company. The airport has free direct phones to a number of car-rental companies. Rental rates tend to be comparable to LA ($40 to $80 per day). Smaller agencies include **West Coast Rent a Car** (☑619-544-0606; 834 W Grape St), in Little Italy.

Taxi

Taxi fares vary, but plan on about $2.40 to start, plus $2.60 for each additional mile. Established companies include the following:

Orange Cab (☑619-223-5555; www.orangecabsandiego.com)

Yellow Cab (☑619-444-4444; www.driveu.com)

Trolley

Municipal trolleys (not to be confused with Old Town Trolley tourist buses) operate on three main lines. From the transit center across from the Santa Fe Depot, **Blue Line** trolleys go south to San Ysidro (Mexico border) and north to Old Town Transit Center. The **Green Line** runs from Old Town east through Mission Valley. The **Orange Line** connects the Convention Center and Seaport Village with Downtown, but otherwise it's less useful for visitors. Trolleys run between about 4:15am and 1am daily at 15-minute in-

FREE RIDE

On Saturdays and Sundays, up to two children can ride the trolley for free with each fare-paying adult.

torvals during the day, and every 30 minutes in the evening. The Blue Line continues a limited all-night service on Saturday. Fares are $2.50 per ride, valid for two hours from the time of purchase at vending machines on the station platforms.

Water Taxi

San Diego Harbor Excursion (☎619-235-8294; per person $7; ⊙9am-9pm Sun-Thu, to 11pm Fri & Sat) operates a water taxi, serving mostly Downtown and Coronado.

Coronado & the Beaches

Whoosh – here comes a skateboarder. And there goes a wet-suited surfer toting his board to the break, while a Chanel-clad lady lifts a coffee cup off a porcelain saucer. San Diego's coastal communities offer all that and more.

The city of Coronado, with its landmark 1888 Hotel del Coronado and one of America's top-rated beaches, sits across San Diego Bay from Downtown, accessible via a long bridge or a short ferry ride. At the entrance to the bay, Point Loma has sweeping views across sea and city from the Cabrillo National Monument. Mission Bay, northwest of Downtown, has lagoons, parks and recreation from waterskiing to camping and the world-famous SeaWorld. The nearby coast – Ocean, Mission and Pacific Beaches – epitomizes the SoCal beach scene. See also La Jolla (p312) and San Diego's North Coast (p319).

We've organized this section beginning with Coronado and heading north.

⊙ Sights

CORONADO

Across the bay from Downtown San Diego, Coronado is a civilized escape from the jumble of the city and the chaos of the beaches. After crossing the bay by ferry or via the elegantly curved 2.12-mile-long Coronado Bay Bridge (1969), follow the tree-lined, manicured median strip of Orange Ave a mile or so toward the commercial center, Coronado Village. Then park your car; you won't need it again until you leave.

The story of Coronado is in many ways the story of the Hotel del Coronado, opened in 1888 by John D Spreckels, the millionaire who bankrolled the first rail line to San Diego, took over Coronado and turned the island into one of the West Coast's most fashionable getaways.

For information on ferries, water taxis and bike rentals, see p312. Alternatively, bus 901 from Downtown San Diego runs along Orange Ave to the Hotel del Coronado. The Old Town Trolley tour (p284) stops in front of Mc P's Irish Pub.

Hotel del Coronado   HISTORIC HOTEL
(☎619-435-6611, 800-582-2595; www.hoteldel. com; 1500 Orange Ave; ⊞) Few hotels in the world are as easily recognized or as much loved as the 'Hotel del.' The world's largest resort when it was built, the all-timber, whitewashed main building offers conical towers, cupolas, turrets, balconies, dormer windows and cavernous public spaces typical of their designers, railroad-depot architects James and Merritt Reed. Acres of polished wood give the interior a warm, old-fashioned feel that conjures daydreams of Panama hats and linen suits.

Guests have included 10 US presidents and world royalty – pictures and mementos are displayed in the hotel's history gallery. There's speculation that Edward (then Prince of Wales) first met Mrs Simpson (then Mrs Spencer) when he visited in 1920, though the two did not become an item until years later. The hotel achieved its widest exposure when it was featured in the 1959 movie *Some Like It Hot,* which earned it a lasting association with Marilyn Monroe. There's an interesting resident ghost story, too, about a jilted woman who haunts the hotel; some claim she silently appears in hallways and on the TV screen in the room where she had her heart broken. See p307 for details on staying here, and p309 for the 1500 restaurant.

For a taste of the Del without a stay, enjoy breakfast or lunch at the beach-view **Sheerwater** restaurant or splurge on Sunday brunch under the grand dome of the spectacular **Crown Room** (adult/child $74.50/$23, ⊙9:30am-2pm Sun), designed by L Frank Baum, who wrote *The Wonderful Wizard of Oz.*

Coronado Municipal Beach   BEACH
Just beyond the 'Hotel Del,' this beach has been ranked in America's top 10 by the Travel Channel. Four-and-a-half miles

south of Coronado Village is the white-sand **Silver Strand State Beach** (www.parks.ca.gov; P⛱). Both have warm, calm water, perfect for swimming and good for families. Silver Strand (parking up to $8), a long, narrow sand spit, continues south to **Imperial Beach** and connects Coronado to the mainland, though people still call it 'Coronado Island.'

Visitors Center   ART & TOURS
(☏619-437-8788, 866-599-7242; www.coronadovisitorcenter.com; 1100 Orange Ave; ⊙9am-5pm Mon-Fri, 10am-5pm Sat & Sun) Coronado's Visitors centerdoubles as the **Coronado Museum of History and Art** (suggested donation $4) and offers 90-minute historical **walking tours** (tour $15; ⊙11am Tue, Thu & Sat).

POINT LOMA
On maps Point Loma looks like an elephant's trunk guarding the entrance to San Diego Bay.

The highlight here is the Cabrillo National Monument, but back at sea level and several miles away, San Diego's first fishing boats were based at Point Loma, and in the 19th century whalers dragged carcasses here to extract the whale oil. Chinese fishermen settled on the harbor side of the point in the 1860s, but were forced off in 1888 when the US Congress passed the Scott Act, prohibiting anyone without citizenship papers from entering the area. Portuguese fishing families arrived approximately 50 years later and established a permanent community around the same time that Italian immigrants settled in present-day Little Italy. Point Loma's **Portuguese Hall** remains a hub of activity for locals.

Charles Lindbergh tested his *Spirit of St Louis* airplane in 1927 on the tidal flats of **Loma Portal**, where Point Loma joins the mainland (at the elephant's neck). The following year a functioning airport was established at his airstrip; it was named Lindbergh Field, now San Diego International Airport.

Cabrillo National Monument   HISTORIC SITE
(www.nps.gov/cabr; per car/person $5/3; ⊙9am-5pm) At the very tip, atop a hill, this is San Diego's finest locale for history and views. It's also the best place in town to see the gray-whale migration (January to March) from land. After a few minutes here you may forget you're in a major metropolitan area.

The monument's **visitors center** has an excellent, old-school presentation on Portuguese explorer Juan Rodríguez Cabrillo's 1542 voyage up the California coast, plus good exhibits on the native inhabitants and the area's natural history. The 1854 **Old Point Loma Lighthouse**, atop the point, is furnished with typical pieces from the late 19th century, including lamps and picture frames hand-covered with hundreds of shells – testimony to the long, lonely nights endured by lighthouse keepers. On the ocean side, drive down to the **tide pools** (⊙9am-4:30pm) to look for anemones, starfish, crabs, limpets and dead man's fingers (thin, tubular seaweed), best seen in low tide in winter. You could walk it, but it's a steep mile down (and back up).

See also the driving tour (p286) that begins here. If you're not driving, the monument can be reached by bus 84 from Old Town Transit Center.

OCEAN BEACH
San Diego's most bohemian seaside community is a place of seriously scruffy haircuts, facial hair and body art. You can get tattooed, shop for antiques and walk into a restaurant barefoot and shirtless without anyone batting an eye. Newport Ave, the main drag, runs perpendicular to the beach through a compact business district of bars, surf shops, music stores, used-clothing stores and antiques consignment stores.

Ocean Beach Pier   PIER
(Map p303) This half-mile-long peir has all the architectural allure of a freeway ramp, but at its end you'll have a great perspective on the coast. There's also a **bait and tackle shop** (Map p303; ⊙7am-9pm Mon-Fri, 7am-10pm Sat & Sun) where you can rent fishing poles ($17 per day) to fish off the pier.

Ocean Beach Coast   BEACHES
Just north of the pier, near the end of Newport Ave, is the beach scene's epicenter, with volleyball courts and sunset barbecues. Further north on **Dog Beach** (Map p303) pups chase birds around the marshy area where the San Diego River meets the sea. Head a few blocks south of the pier to **Sunset Cliffs Park**, where surfing and sunsets are the main attractions.

There are good surf breaks at the cliffs and, to the south, off Point Loma. Under the pier, skillful surfers slalom the pilings, but the rips and currents can be deadly unless you know what you're doing.

Ocean Beach Farmers Market MARKET
(Map p303; 4900 Block of Newport Ave; ⏱4-7pm Wed Oct-May, 4-8pm Wed Jun-Sep) If you're here on Wednesday afternoon, stop by the farmers market to see street performers and sample fresh food.

MISSION BEACH & PACIFIC BEACH

This is the SoCal of the movies: buffed surfers and bronzed bohemians pack the 3-mile-long stretch of beach from South Mission Jetty to Pacific Beach Point, to cheer the setting sun at these perfect sand beaches. While there's lots to do here, perhaps the best use of an afternoon is to walk along the boardwalk, spread a blanket or kick back over cocktails and take in the scenery.

TOP CHOICE **SeaWorld** AMUSEMENT PARK
(www.seaworldsandiego.com; 500 Sea-World Dr; adult/child 3-9yr $69/59; P🚼) One of the west's most popular theme parks, Sea-World opened here in 1964, and killer whale Shamu has become an unofficial symbol of the city. It's easy to spend a day here, shuttling among shows, rides and exhibits – pick up a map at the entry and plan your day around scheduled events.

SeaWorld's highlights are live shows featuring trained dolphins, sea lions and killer whales. **Believe** is the most visually spectacular, a 30-minute show starring Shamu and killer whale *compadres* gliding, leaping, diving and flipping through the water while interacting with each other, their trainers and the audience. Avoid marked 'soak zones' near the pools or you *will* get wet (though of course that may be just what you want). Some of the showmanship may be a bit, well, *awww*, but the creatures inspire pure *awe* – we'll admit we got a little choked up when 12-year-old Caleb from Indiana got to hold Shamu's flipper.

There are numerous other installations where you can see and learn about underwater creatures, as well as petting pools where you can touch the slippery surface of a dolphin or manta ray. In **Penguin Encounter**, several penguin species share a habitat that faithfully simulates Antarctic living conditions. The temperature behind the glass-enclosed space is a constant 25°F, but light conditions change according to South Pole seasons. So, if you're visiting in July (winter in Antarctica), expect to catch them waddling and swimming in near-darkness in the middle of the day. You'll

Ocean Beach

⊙ Sights
1 Dog Beach	A1
2 Ocean Beach Farmers Market	B3
3 Ocean Beach Pier	A2

⊙ Sleeping
4 Ocean Beach International Hostel	B3

⊗ Eating
5 Hodad's	A2
6 Ortega's Cocina	B3

⊙⊙ Drinking
7 Jungle Java	A2
8 Nick's at the Pier	A2
9 Winston's	B2

⊙ Shopping
10 Cow	A2
11 Galactic	B3
12 Mallory's	B3
13 Newport Avenue Antique Center	B3
14 South Coast Longboards	A2

see dozens of sharks as you walk through a 57ft acrylic tube at **Shark Encounter**. Species include blacktip and whitetip, reef and sand tiger sharks, some of them impressively large.

Several amusement-park-style rides include **Journey to Atlantis**, a combination flume ride and roller coaster; and **Wild Arctic**, a simulated helicopter flight followed by a walk past beluga whales and polar bears. Expect long waits for rides, shows and exhibits during peak seasons.

The park is shamefully commercial – you'll be subjected to deafeningly loud advertisements (many designed to appeal to small eyes and ears) as you wait in lines, there's a corporate logo on everything in sight, and gift shops are unavoidable. Still, SeaWorld manages to do its share for animal conservation, rescue, rehabilitation, breeding and research.

At full price it's a rather expensive day out, especially if you're with kids to whom you can't say no; even the tiniest stuffed Shamu costs $9 and it's almost $4 for a churro. Plus, the park prohibits coolers and picnic lunches (keep a cooler in the car and picnic outside the gates – be sure to get a hand-stamp for re-entry).

That said, good deals are often available for multiple days at SeaWorld or combination tickets with other parks including San Diego Zoo and Wild Animal Park, Universal Studios Hollywood and/or Disneyland. Inquire at tourist offices and hotels.

Opening hours vary – check the website for details. By car, take SeaWorld Dr off I-5 less than a mile north of where it intersects with I-8. Parking costs $12. Check with the Metropolitan Transit System (p300) for public transit. Some hotels offer shuttles.

Mission & Pacific Beaches   BEACHES

The beach scene is concentrated in a narrow strip of land between the ocean and Mission Bay. San Diego's best people-watching is on the **Ocean Front Walk**, the boardwalk that connects the two beaches. It's crowded with joggers, inline skaters and cyclists anytime of the year. On warm summer weekends, oiled bodies, packed like sardines, cover the beach from end to end. A block off the beach, Mission Blvd (the main north–south road), is lined with surf, smoke and swimwear shops. At peak times it can get so crowded that the police simply close it down, and parking around noon is just not gonna happen.

Cheap Rentals (Map p304; 📞858-488-9070, 800-941-7761; 3689 Mission Blvd, Pacific Beach; ⊘9am-7pm summer, to 5pm rest of year) rents bikes and skates ($5/12 per hour/day), plus surfboards ($15 per day) and wetsuits ($10 per day). It also takes reservations for rentals.

In Pacific Beach, to the north, activity extends inland, particularly along Garnet (say gar-*net*) Ave, lined with bars, restaurants and used-clothing stores, mostly targeted at a 20-something crowd. At the ocean end of Garnet Ave, **Crystal Pier** is a mellow place to fish or gaze out to sea.

FREE **Belmont Park**   AMUSEMENT PARK
(www.belmontpark.com; park free, rides $1 6, unlimited rides adult/child $23/16; ⊘from 11am; 🚸) This old-style family amusement park at the southern end of Mission Beach has been here since 1925, and when it was threatened with demolition in the mid-1990s, community action saved it. Now there's a large indoor pool, known as the **Plunge**, and the **Giant Dipper**, a classic wooden roller coaster that'll shake the teeth right outta your mouth, plus bumper cars, a tilt-a-whirl, carousel and other classics. More modern attractions include wave machines like **Flowrider** (admission free, wave-riding per hr $30), for simulated surfing. Even if it sits on dry land, it's pretty much to San Diego what the Santa Monica Pier amusement park is to LA.

Mission Bay   OUTDOOR ACTIVITIES
In the 18th century, the mouth of the San Diego River formed a shallow bay when the river flowed and a marshy swamp when it didn't – the Spanish called it False Bay. After WWII an extraordinary combination of civic vision and coastal engineering turned the swamp into a 7-sq-mile playground, with 27 miles of shoreline and 90 acres of public parks on islands, coves and peninsulas. A quarter of that land has been leased to hotels, boat yards and other businesses.

Kite flying is popular in Mission Bay Park, beach volleyball is big on Fiesta Island, and there's delightful cycling and inline skating on the miles of smooth bike paths. Sailing, windsurfing and kayaking dominate the waters in northwest Mission Bay, while waterskiers zip around Fiesta Island. For equipment rentals, see p305.

🏃 Activities

Bahia Belle   CRUISES
(www.sternwheelers.com; 998 West Mission Bay Dr; adult/child $10/3) For a lovely time without adrenaline overload, board this floating bar disguised as a stern-wheeler paddle-boat. It offers 30-minute cruises between two resort hotels, the Catamaran and the Bahia, on Friday and Saturday evenings January to May and September to November; Wednesday to Saturday in June; and daily in July and August. Cruises start at 6:30pm; call for exact departure times.

Surfing
A good number of San Diegans moved here for the surfing, and boy is it good. Even beginners will understand why it's so popular.

Fall brings strong swells and offshore Santa Ana winds. In summer swells come from the south and southwest, and in winter from the west and northwest. Spring brings more frequent onshore winds, but the surfing can still be good. For the latest beach, weather and surf reports, call 📞619-221-8824.

Beginners should head to Mission or Pacific Beaches, where the waves are gentle. North of Crystal Pier, Tourmaline Surf Beach is an especially good place to take your first strokes.

Pacific Beach Surf Shop   SURF SCHOOL
(Map p304; www.pacificbeachsurfschool.com; suite 161, 4150 Mission Blvd, Pacific Beach; lesson per person for 1/2 people $80/75, 3-5 people $70) This shop provides instruction through its Pacific Beach Surf School. It has friendly service, and also rents wetsuits and both soft (foam) and hard (fiberglass) boards. Call ahead for lessons. Rental rates vary depending on the quality of the equipment, but generally soft boards cost from $15/20 per half-/full day; wet suits cost $5. See also Cheap Rentals in Mission Beach.

Bob's Mission Surf   SURF EQUIPMENT
(Map p304; www.missionsurf.com; 4320 Mission Blvd, Pacific Beach) Rents equipment for similar rates to Pacific Beach Surf Shop.

TOP BEACHES IN SAN DIEGO

Determining San Diego's best beaches is like comparing jewels at Tiffany. **Coronado Municipal Beach** is rated tops overall by the Travel Channel; others depend on what you're looking for.

Bodysurfing: Pacific Beach and La Jolla Shores. Experienced bodysurfers can head to La Jolla for the big swells of Boomer Beach near La Jolla Cove, or the *whomp* (forceful tubes that break directly onshore) at Windansea or the beach at the end of Sea Lane.

Family friendly: Shell Beach (La Jolla), 15th St Beach (Del Mar), Moonlight Beach (Encinitas).

Nude beach: Black's Beach

Surf breaks, from south to north: Imperial Beach (best in winter); Point Loma (reef breaks, less accessible but less crowded; best during winter); Sunset Cliffs (Ocean Beach); Pacific Beach; in La Jolla: Big Rock (California's Pipeline), Windansea (hot reef break, best at medium to low tide), La Jolla Shores (beach break, best in winter) and Black's Beach (a fast, powerful wave); Cardiff State Beach; San Elijo State Beach (Cardiff); Swami's (Encinitas); Carlsbad State Beach and Oceanside.

Teen scene: Mission Beach, Pacific Beach.

Diving & Snorkeling

Off the coast of San Diego County, divers will find kelp beds, shipwrecks (including the *Yukon,* a WWII destroyer sunk off Mission Beach in 2000) and canyons deep enough to host bat rays, octopuses and squid. For current conditions, call ☏619-221-8824.

Fishing

The most popular public fishing piers are Imperial Beach Pier, Embarcadero Fishing Pier, Shelter Island Fishing Pier, Ocean Beach Pier and Crystal Pier at Pacific Beach. Generally the best pier fishing is from April to October, and no license is required. For offshore fishing, catches can include barracuda, bass and yellowtail and, in summer, albacore. A state fishing license is required for people over 16 for offshore fishing – one day/two day/calendar year costs $13.40/20.75/42.25, available from operators that run daily fishing trips (from about $42/32 per adult/child for a near-shore, half-day trip), including these around Mission Bay and Point Loma:

H&M Landing FISHING CHARTER
(☏619-222-1144; www.hmlanding.com; 2803 Emerson St, Point Loma)

Point Loma Sport Fishing FISHING CHARTER
(☏619-223-1627; www.pointlomasportfishing. com; 1403 Scott St, Point Loma)

Seaforth Sportfishing FISHING CHARTER
(☏619-224-3383; www.seaforthlanding.com; 1717 Quivira Rd, Mission Bay)

Boating

You can rent powerboats (from $105 per hour), sailboats (from $25 per hour), and kayaks (from $13 per hour) and canoes on Mission Bay.

Mission Bay Sportcenter BOAT RENTAL
(Map p304; ☏858-488-1004; www.missionbay sportcenter.com; 1010 Santa Clara Pl)

Resort Watersports BOAT RENTAL
(Map p304; ☏858-488-2582; www.resortwater sports.com) Located at the Bahia and Catamaran resort hotels.

KAYAKING

Ocean kayaking is a good way to see sea life, and explore cliffs and caves inaccessible from land.

Family Kayak KAYAK RENTAL
(☏619-282-3520; www.familykayak.com; ⛟) Guided tours (adult/child from $42/17) and lessons. Inquire about longer tours.

SAILING

Experienced sailors are available to charter boats ranging from catamarans to yachts. Prices start at about $110 for four hours and rise steeply. Charter operators around Shelter and Harbor Islands (on the west side of San Diego Bay near the airport) include the following:

Harbor Sailboats BOAT CHARTER
(☏619-291-9568, 800-854-6625; www.harbor sailboats.com; suite 104, 2040 Harbor Island Dr)

Harbor Yacht Clubs
BOAT CHARTER
(☎800-553-7245; www.harboryc.com; 1880 Harbor Island Dr)

Shelter Island Sailing
BOAT CHARTER
(☎619-222-0351; www.shelterislandsailing.com; 2240 Shelter Island Dr)

Whale-Watching

Gray whales pass San Diego from mid-December to late February on their way south to Baja California, and again in mid-March on their way back up to Alaskan waters. Their 12,000-mile round-trip journey is the longest migration of any mammal on earth.

Cabrillo National Monument (p302) is the best place to see the whales from land, where you'll also find exhibits, whale-related ranger programs and a shelter from which to watch the whales breach (bring binoculars).

Half-day whale-watching boat trips are offered by all of the companies that run daily fishing trips. The trips generally cost $20/15 per adult/child for a three-hour excursion, and the companies will even give you a free pass to return again if you don't spot any whales. Look for coupons and special offers at tourist kiosks around town, and online.

🛏 Sleeping
CORONADO

A stay in Coronado Village (around the Hotel del Coronado) puts you close to the beach, shops and restaurants. The northern end is an easy walk to the ferry. The lower the building number, the closer to the ferry.

Hotel del Coronado
HISTORIC, LUXURY $$$
(☎619-435-6611, 800-468-3533; www.hoteldel.com; 1500 Orange Ave; r from $380; P@🛜🏊♿) San Diego's iconic hotel provides the essential Coronado experience: over a century of history, tennis courts, a pool, full-service spa, shops, restaurants, manicured grounds and a white-sand beach. Even the basic rooms have luxurious marbled bathrooms. Note: half the accommodations are not in the main Victorian-era hotel but in an adjacent seven-story building constructed in the 1970s. For a sense of place, book a room in the original hotel. Parking is $25. See also p301 and p309.

Crown City Inn
MOTEL $$
(☎619-435-3116, 800-422-1173; www.crowncityinn.com; 520 Orange Ave; r $119-200; P@🛜♿🐾) This two-story motel with exterior corridors encircles a small parking area with a little pool, with loaner bikes for easy getaways. If its floral-accented rooms were nearer the beach, they would start at $200 per night. The bistro onsite is a local fave.

El Cordova Hotel
HISTORIC $$
(☎619-435-4131, 800-229-2032, www.elcordovahotel.com; 1351 Orange Ave; r from $199; P🛜@🏊♿) This exceedingly cozy Mediterranean-style former mansion from 1902 has rooms and suites around an outdoor courtyard of shops, restaurants, pool, hot tub and barbecue grills. Rooms are charming in an antiquey sort of way, though nothing fancy. Parking costs $6.

Coronado Village Inn
HISTORIC $
(☎619-435-9318; www.coronadovillageinn.com; 1017 Park Pl; s/d from $85/95; 🛜) The top budget choice in pricey downtown Coronado is this tidy, Spanish-style, 15-room hotel that has a sense of history (1928). It's two blocks from the beach, half a block to shops and restaurants, but has no air-conditioning or oversized bathrooms.

Coronado Inn
MOTEL $$
(☎619-435-4121, 800-598-6624; www.coronadoinn.com; 266 Orange Ave; r incl breakfast from $149, with kitchen from $199; P@🛜🏊♿🐾🐕) The friendly owner keeps this handsome motel near the ferry in tip-top shape, amid palms, little wooden gazebos, nautical-blue deck chairs around the pool, and afternoon snacks.

Glorietta Bay Inn
HISTORIC $$
(☎619-435-3101, 800-283-9383; www.gloriettabayinn.com; 1630 Glorietta Blvd; r incl breakfast from $205; P@🛜🏊♿) Overshadowed by the neighboring Hotel Del, the Glorietta is built in and around the 1908 Spreckels Mansion – (11 rooms in the mansion, 89 in boxier two-story buildings). Rooms have handsome furnishings and extras such as triple-sheeted beds and high-end bath products. Mansion rooms are more expensive and have extra amenities including 600-thread-count sheets. Stop in and see the gorgeous music room, even if you're not staying here. Parking is $10.

Loews Coronado Bay Resort
RESORT $$$
(☎619-424-4000, 800-235-6397; www.loewshotels.com; 4000 Coronado Bay Rd; r $229-299; P@🛜♿) Way down Silver Strand (there's a complimentary shuttle to Coronado Village), the 439-room Loews is practically

surrounded by water, plus three outdoor pools and its own private marina with boat rentals. Rooms are sea-hued with dark woods and rattans, the lobby is all brass rails, and there are plenty of kids' programs. Parking is $22. See also the Mistral restaurant, p309.

POINT LOMA AREA

Although it's a bit out of the way, Point Loma boasts some fun accommodations. Head to Shelter Island for tiki-style hotels.

Pearl Hotel   BOUTIQUE-MID-CENTURY **$$**
(619-226-6100; www.thepearlsd.com; 1410 Rosecrans Ave; r $99-169;) The midcentury modern Pearl feels more Palm Springs than San Diego. The 23 rooms in its 1959 shell have soothing blue hues, trippy surf motifs and betas in fishbowls. There's a lively pool scene (including 'dive-in' movies on Wednesday nights), or play Jenga or Parcheesi in the lobby. Light sleepers: request a room away from busy street traffic. Parking is $10.

Humphrey's Half Moon Inn & Suites   POLYNESIAN **$$**
(619-224-3411, 800-345-9995; www.halfmooninn.com; 2303 Shelter Island Dr; r $150-229, ste $190-269;) Fans of boating, jazz and Polynesian style will feel at home in this harborside resort. Its 182 rooms and suites are clustered amid koi ponds and padding mallards, in buildings like Hawaiian *lanais*. Some have balconies. There's a good jazz club on site. Parking is $10.

Best Western Island Palms Hotel   POLYNESIAN **$$$**
(619-222-0561; www.islandpalms.com; 2051 Shelter Island Dr; r from $219;) Namesake palms adorn the lobby and grounds around the archipelago of little Polynesian-style buildings housing the resort's 174 rooms. It has comfortable, well-maintained upper-end-chain-motel-style rooms, plus free bike rentals.

HI San Diego Point Loma Hostel   HOSTEL **$**
(619-223-4778, 800-909-4776, ext 157; www.sandiegohostels.org; 3790 Udall St; dm incl breakfast $17-28;) It's a 20-minute walk from the heart of Ocean Beach to this hostel, in a largely residential area, and close to a market and library. There are free excursions around town and to Tijuana, movie nights and barbecues. Bus 923 runs along nearby Voltaire St. No lock-out times. No air-con.

OCEAN BEACH

Ocean Beach (OB) is under the outbound flight path of San Diego airport, which won't be a problem if you rise at 6am. Light or late sleepers should stay elsewhere or bring earplugs.

TOP CHOICE **Inn at Sunset Cliffs**   BOUTIQUE HOTEL **$$**
(619-222-7901, 866-786-2543; www.innatsunsetcliffs.com; 1370 Sunset Cliffs Blvd; r from $149;) At the south end of Ocean Beach, wake up to the sound of surf crashing onto the rocky shore. This low-key 1965 charmer wraps around a flower-bedecked courtyard with small heated pool. Its 24 breezy rooms are compact, but most have attractive stone and tile bathrooms, and some suites have full kitchens. Even if the ocean air occasionally takes its toll on exterior surfaces, it's hard not to love this place.

Ocean Beach International Hostel   HOSTEL **$**
(Map p303; 619-223-7873, 800-339-7263; www.californiahostel.com; 4961 Newport Ave; dm incl breakfast $25;) The cheapest option is only a couple of blocks from the ocean; it's a friendly, fun place that's reserved for international travelers and educators, with barbecues, bonfires and more. Free transfer from airport, bus or train station on arrival. No air-con.

PACIFIC BEACH

Tower23 Hotel   BOUTIQUE HOTEL **$$$**
(Map p304; 866-869-3723; www.t23hotel.com; 723 Felspar St; r from $309;) If you like your beach stay with contemporary cool style, this is the place for you. This once-blah property has been transformed into a modernist show place, with minimalist decor, lots of teals and mint blues and a sense of humor. There's no pool, but dude, you're right on the beach. See also Jordan restaurant (p310). Parking is $20.

TOP CHOICE **Crystal Pier Hotel**   COTTAGES **$$$**
(Map p304; 858-483-6983, 800-748-5894; www.crystalpier.com; 4500 Ocean Blvd; cottages $300-500;) Charming, wonderful and unlike anyplace else in San Diego, Crystal Pier has cottages built right on the pier above the water. All 29 cottages have full ocean views and kitchens; most date from 1936. Newer, larger cottages sleep up to six. Book eight to 11 months in advance for summer reservations. Minimum-stay requirements vary by season. No air-con.

Catamaran Resort Hotel
RESORT, POLYNESIAN **$$**

(Map p304; ☑858-488-1081, 800-422-8386; www.catamaranresort.com; 3999 Mission Blvd; r from $159; P@🛜🏊♿🐾) Tropical landscaping and tiki decor fill this bayside resort (there's a luau on some summer evenings!). A plethora of activities make it a perfect place for families (sailing, kayaking, tennis, biking, skating, spa-ing, etc), or board the *Bahia Belle* (p305) from here. Rooms are in low-rise buildings or in a 14-story tower; some have views and full kitchens. The staff is warm and helpful. Parking costs $13.

Banana Bungalow
HOSTEL **$**

(Map p304; ☑858-273-3060; www.bananabungalow.com; 707 Reed Ave; dm incl breakfast $25, d incl breakfast $105; 🛜) Right on Pacific Beach, the Bungalow has a top location, a beach-party atmosphere and is reasonably clean, but it's very basic and gets crowded. Shared rooms are mixed-gender. The communal patio fronts right on the boardwalk; it's a great place for people-watching and beer drinking. No air-con.

Beach Cottages
HISTORIC **$$**

(Map p304; ☑858-483-7440; www.beachcottages.com; 4255 Ocean Blvd; r from $140 cottages from $305; P@🛜♿) Family owned and operated, Beach Cottages has everything from plain motel rooms to cozy 1940s cottages, just across the bike path from the sand. Sure, they're nothing fancy, but there's a loveable throwback feel to the clapboard construction, ping-pong, shuffleboard and rattan furniture. It can be a real bargain if you're traveling in a group. No air-con.

MISSION BAY

Just south of Mission Beach, Mission Bay has waterfront lodging at lower prices than on the ocean. See also Campland on the Bay (p290).

Paradise Point Resort
RESORT **$$$**

(☑858-274-4630, 800-344-2626; www.paradisepoint.com; 1404 Vacation Rd; r from $149-359; P@🛜🏊♿🐾) The grounds are so lush and dotted with so many palms that you'll feel like you're in Hawaii at this upper-end resort, whose 462 rooms are in small ground-floor bungalows. Features for kids include a putting green and summer movies in one of the five swimming pools. Full-service spa. Parking costs $25.

 Eating

CORONADO

See also Coronado Brewing Co, p295.

1500 Ocean
CALIFORNIAN **$$$**

(☑619-435-6611; Hotel del Coronado, 1500 Orange Ave; mains $28-44; ⊗5:30-10pm Tue-Sun) It's hard to beat the romance of supping at the Hotel del Coronado, especially at a table overlooking the sea from the verandah of its 1st-class dining room, where silver service and coastal cuisine with local ingredients set the perfect tone for popping the question or fêting an important anniversary. See also p301.

Primavera
ITALIAN **$$$**

(☑619-435-0454; 932 Orange Ave; mains $19-39; ⊗5-10pm) A subdued, romantic setting for subdued, romantic Italian fare presented by black-tied waiters. It's known for steaks, seafood dishes like shrimp in mushroom and champagne sauce over pasta, and a veal chop so big two can share it, plus an excellent wine list. Prices are high, but you get what you pay for.

Mistral
FRENCH, CONTEMPORARY **$$$**

(☑619-424-4000; Loews Coronado Bay Resort, 4000 Coronado Bay Rd; mains $19-32; ⊗5:30-9:30pm Tue-Sat) The many-windowed grand dining room at the Loews resort is for romantic, white-tablecloth farm-to-kitchen Euro-Cal dining with views. Lobster risotto and steamed Alaskan halibut with lemon verbena and black mussels are to die for.

Cafe 1134
CAFE, ECLECTIC **$**

(☑619-437-1134; 1134 Orange Ave; mains $5-10; ⊗6am-9pm) This local classic is bright and airy with tall ceilings and stained-glass accents, serving scrambles, muffins and strong coffee at breakfast; at lunch and dinner there are soups, quiches and salads.

Boney's Bayside Market
MARKET

(155 Orange Ave; sandwiches $4-7; ⊗8:30am-9pm) For picnics, stop by this market near the ferry for fantastic (mostly) healthy sandwiches and an extensive assortment of salads.

POINT LOMA AREA

See also the great restaurant at the Pearl Hotel (p308).

Bali Hai
POLYNESIAN **$$**

(☑619-222-1181; 2230 Shelter Island Dr; mains lunch $14-17, dinner $16-24; ⊗11:30am-3pm Mon-Sat, 4-9pm Sun, 5-9pm Mon-Thu, 5-10pm Fri & Sat; P) Thanks to a 2010 renovation, a new generation can enjoy the tiki aesthetic and Hawaiian-themed meals like chicken of the gods (with tangy orange and cream sauces) at this long-time special occasion restaurant. The best part: views through its circular wall of windows, clear across San Diego Bay.

Point Loma Seafoods
TOP CHOICE

SEAFOOD, COUNTER SERVICE **$$**

(☎619-223-1109; 2805 Emerson St; mains $8-14; ☺9am-6:30pm Mon-Sat, 11am-6:30pm Sun) Order at the counter at this fish-market-cum-deli and grab a seat at a picnic table for off-the-boat-fresh seafood and some icy cold beer. Located in the Shelter Island Marina, it's a San Diego institution. Great sushi, too.

Corvette Diner
DINER **$**

(☎619-542-1476; 2965 Historic Decatur Rd; mains $8-11.50; ☺11:30am-9pm Sun-Thu, to 11pm Fri & Sat; 🖈) Your kids will be your BFFs for bringing them to this over-the-top '50s-themed diner. DJs spins rock-and-roll classics, waiters dance in the aisles, and kids wear drinking straws in their hair. It's a bit out of the way, in the newly redone former military base Liberty Station; enter off Lytton St. (Oh, and the food is good, too. Try the meatloaf.)

Brigantine
SEAFOOD **$$**

(mains lunch $9-15, dinner $14-32; ☺11:30am-10:30pm Mon-Thu, to 11pm Fri & Sat, 4-10:30pm Sun) Shelter Island ☎619-224-2871; 2725 Shelter Island Dr); Coronado (☎619-435-4166; 1333 Orange Ave); Del Mar (☎858-481-1166; 3263 Camino del Mar) At this respected local seafood chain, lunch is heavy on sandwiches (and famous fish tacos), while dinners are fancier with dishes like marinated swordfish. At the Shelter Island Dr branch you can sit on the balcony and you can peek through palm fronds to the harbor. Awesome happy hours.

OCEAN BEACH

Hodad's
BURGERS **$**

(Map p303; ☎619-224-4623; 5010 Newport Ave; burgers $4-9; ☺11am-9pm Sun-Thu, to 10pm Fri & Sat; 🖈) OB's legendary burger joint serves great shakes, massive baskets of onion rings and succulent hamburgers wrapped in paper. The walls are covered in license plates, grunge/surf-rock plays (loud!) and your bearded, tattooed server might sidle in to your booth to take your order. No shirt, no shoes, no problem.

Ortega's Cocina
CAFE **$**

(Map p303; ☎619-222-4205; 4888 Newport Ave; mains $4-15; ☺8am-10pm Mon-Sat, 8am-9pm Sun) Tiny, family-run Ortega's is so popular that people often queue for a spot at the counter. Seafood, *moles, tortas* (sandwiches) and handmade tamales are the specialties, but all its dishes are soulful and classic.

OB People's Market
VEGETARIAN **$**

(☎619-224-1387; 4765 Voltaire St; ☺8am-9pm; 🖈) For vegetarian groceries, check out this organic cooperative with bulk foods, fresh soups, and excellent pre-made sandwiches, salads and wraps, most under $5. No meat.

PACIFIC BEACH

World Famous
CALIFORNIA, SEAFOOD **$$$**

(Map p304; ☎858-272-3100; 711 Pacific Beach Dr; mains breakfast & lunch $7-13, dinner $10-27; ☺7am-11pm) Watch the surf while enjoying 'California coastal cuisine,' an ever-changing all-day menu of inventive dishes from the sea (lobster Benedict for breakfast or lunch; banana rum mahi-mahi), plus steaks, salads and lunchtime sandwiches and burgers and occasional specials like fish or lobster taco night. There's a great bar too.

Jordan
CALIFORNIA, ECLECTIC **$$$**

(JRDN; Map p304; ☎858-270-5736; Tower23 Hotel, 723 Felspar St; mains breakfast & lunch $9-14, dinner $26-46; ☺breakfast, lunch & dinner) A big heaping dose of chic amid PB's congenital laid-back feel. There's both an ocean view and a futuristic interior (and most excellent bar scene). Sustainably farmed meats and seafood join local veggies to create festivals on the plate. Try the lobster BLT, or 'build your own' steak with green onion 'creamers' (aka mashed potatoes).

Kono's
CASUAL **$**

(Map p304; ☎858-483-1669; 704 Garnet Ave; dishes from $5; ☺7am-3pm Mon-Fri, 7am-4pm Sat & Sun) This place makes $5 breakfast burritos that you eat out of a basket in view of Crystal Pier (patio seating available). It's always crowded but well worth the wait.

Green Flash
CAFE **$$**

(Map p304; ☎619-270-7715; 701 Thomas Ave; mains breakfast & lunch $5-15, dinner $9-30; ☺8am-10pm) A terrific casual breakfast or lunch spot for eggs, meaty burgers, big salads and triple-decker clubs, the Flash also has a weekday sunset special meals ($11; 4:30pm to 6pm Sunday to Thursday), with happy hour until 7pm Monday through Friday. Score a table outside on the patio.

 Drinking & Entertainment

PB's nightlife caters to mostly 20-somethings on a bender. If you've been there/done that, you might prefer one of the quieter coffee houses or restaurant bars, or head to the options in Ocean Beach or Coronado. Drivers: watch for PB pedestrians who have overindulged. See also Pacific Beach Ale House (p295).

710 Beach Club   LIVE MUSIC
(Map p304; www.710beachclub.com; 710 Garnet Ave, Pacific Beach) PB's main venue for live music books a solid lineup of rock, karaoke and comedy.

Moondoggies   INDOOR-OUTDOOR
(Map p304; 832 Garnet Ave, Pacific Beach) Moondoggies has a large patio, big-screen TVs, pool tables, cheap eats day and night, and an extensive tap selection including flavored microbrews.

Bub's Dive   DIVE BAR
(Map p304; 1030 Garnet Ave, Pacific Beach) The frat party continues over tater tots and wings, at this rowdy spot where you might find yourself belting out 'build me up…Buttercup…' with a passel of new buds.

Society Billiard Cafe   BILLIARDS
(Map p304; 1051 Garnet Ave, Pacific Beach; ☺noon-2pm) Why settle for a beat-up pool table in the back of a dark bar when you can visit San Diego's plushest pool hall? The billiard room has about a dozen full-sized tables, snacks and a bar.

Winston's   LIVE MUSIC
(Map p303; www.winstonsob.com; 1921 Bacon St, Ocean Beach) Bands play most nights, and each night has a different happening: open mic, karaoke, comedy, cover bands for the Grateful Dead and Red Hot Chili Peppers, local artists, game day etc.

Nick's at the Pier   SPORTS BAR
(Map p303; 5083 Santa Monica Ave, Ocean Beach) Beachfront Nick's could get by on its looks alone, with a circular, ocean-view dining room (serving great seafood entrees – kitchen open until 1am), but there's also a rousing sports bar known for mojitos.

Coaster Saloon   NEIGHBORHOOD BAR
(744 Ventura Pl, Mission Beach) Old-fashioned neighborhood dive bar with front-row views of the Belmont Park roller coaster. It draws an unpretentious crowd for events like Wii-bowling. Good margaritas too.

Café 976   COFFEE HOUSE
(Map p304; 976 Felspar St, Pacific Beach; ☺7am-11pm) Not everyone in PB spends the days surfing; some drink coffee and read books at this delightful side-street cafe in a converted old wooden house ensconced in rose bushes and flowering trees.

Jungle Java   COFFEE HOUSE
(Map p303; 5047 Newport Ave, Ocean Beach; ☺7am-6pm Mon, Tue & Thu, to 8pm Wed & Fri-Sun) Funky-dunky, canopy-covered cafe and plant shop, also crammed with crafts and art treasures.

Mc P's Irish Pub   PUB
(www.mcpspub.com; 1107 Orange Ave, Coronado) Dyed-in-the-wool Irish pub that's been there for a generation. Pints o' Guinness complement down-home Irish fare – corned beef, stew, meatloaf – as you listen to nightly live music from rock to Irish folk. Indoor and patio seating.

 Shopping

Most of coastal San Diego's shopping is limited to surf shops and bikini boutiques. A notable exception: Newport Ave in Ocean Beach, where a dozen antiques consignment shops line the main drag. **Newport Avenue Antique Center** (Map p303; 4864 Newport Ave) and **Mallory's** (Map p303; 4916 Newport Ave) are good places to start. **Cow** (Map p303; 5029 Newport Ave) gives the same treatment to music, and **Galactic** (Map p303; 4981 Newport Ave) to comics and video. Thrift shoppers should head to Garnet Ave in Pacific Beach for vintage and recycled drag. Most stores buy, sell and trade.

Pangaea Outpost   FASHION
(Map p304; 909 Garnet Ave, Pacific Beach) Like a mini-world unto themselves, the 70-plus merchants here offer a supremely eclectic selection of clothing, jewelry, wraps, handbags and semi-precious stones (just for starters!) from all around the world.

South Coast Wahines   SURFWEAR
(Map p304; 4500 Ocean Blvd, Pacific Beach) At the foot of Garnet Ave at Crystal Pier in Pacific Beach, this store carries spiffy surf apparel for women.

Pilar's Beachwear   SWIMWEAR
(3745 Mission Blvd, Mission Beach) For swimwear, women should head to this shop, which has all the latest styles in all sizes.

Gone Bananas SWIMWEAR
(Map p304; 3785 Mission Blvd, Mission Beach) More swimwear up the street from Pilar's.

South Coast Longboards SURF SHOP
(Map p303; 5023 Newport Ave, Ocean Beach) Apathetic surfer dudes staff the counter at this beach-apparel and surf-gear shop that carries a good selection of Quiksilver, Hurley, Billabong and O'Neill for men and women. Oh yes, you can buy a surfboard here too.

Buffalo Exchange FASHION
(Map p304; 1007 Garnet Ave, Pacific Beach) If you need something to wear to dinner, this store carries a good selection of contemporary and vintage fashions, including designer labels.

🛈 Information

Coronado Post Office (☎877-275-8777; www. usps.com; 1320 Ynez Pl; ⊗8:30am-5pm Mon-Fri, 9am-noon Sat). Check the website or phone for other branches.

Coronado Public Library (☎619-522-7390; www.coronado.ca.us/library; 640 Orange Ave; ⊗10am-9pm Mon-Thu, to 6pm Fri & Sat, 1-5pm Sun; @ 🕾) Occupies a museum-like building and offers children's programs and internet access. For library branches elsewhere, visit www.sannet.gov/public-library.

Coronado Visitors Center (☎619-437-8788, 866-599-7242; www.coronadovisitorcenter. com; 1100 Orange Ave; ⊗9am-5pm Mon-Fri, 10am-5pm Sat & Sun) San Diego Convention & Visitors Bureau's visitors centers serve other beach communities.

🛈 Getting There & Around

For details on getting to and from the San Diego metropolitan area, as well as getting to and from the airport, riding MTS buses, and traveling by train, taxi and rental car, see p300.

Bicycle

Mostly flat Pacific Beach, Mission Beach, Mission Bay and Coronado are all great places to ride a bike. Visit **icommute** (www.icommutesd. com) and follow the bike links for maps and information about biking in the region. Public buses are equipped with bike racks.

The following outfits all rent bicycles, from mountain and road bikes to kids' bikes and cruisers. In general, expect to pay about $7 per hour, $10 to $20 per half-day (four hours) and $20 to $25 per day.

Bikes & Beyond (☎619-435-7180; Coronado Ferry Landing) At the foot of B Ave.

Cheap Rentals (☎858-488-9070, 800-941-7761; www.cheap-rentals.com; 3689 Mission Blvd, Mission Beach)

Holland's Bicycles (☎619-435-3153; www. hollandsbicycles.com; 977 Orange Ave, Coronado)

Boat

San Diego Harbor Excursion operates the hourly **Coronado Ferry** (☎619-234-4111; www.sdhe. com; one way/round-trip $3.75/7.50; ⊗departures 9am-9pm Mon-Fri, to 10pm Sat & Sun) shuttling between the **Broadway Pier** (1050 N Harbor Dr) on the Embarcadero to the ferry landing at the foot of B Ave, two blocks south of Orange Ave. See also p301.

La Jolla

Immaculately landscaped parks, white-sand coves, upscale boutiques and cliffs above deep, clear blue waters make it easy to understand why 'La Jolla' translates from Spanish as 'the jewel' – say la-*hoy*-yah, if you please. The name may actually date from Native Americans who inhabited the area from 10,000 years ago to the mid-19th century, who called the place 'mut la hoya, la hoya' – the place of many caves. Whether your interest is jewels or caves, you'll feel at home in this lovely enclave. It also has some of the county's best restaurants.

Today's La Jolla has its roots in 1897, when newspaper heiress Ellen Browning Scripps moved here, acquiring much of the land along Prospect St, which she subsequently donated to community uses. She hired Irving Gill to design local institutions, such as the Bishop's School and the **La Jolla Woman's Club** (715 Silverado St), setting the unadorned Mediterranean architectural tone of arches, colonnades, palm trees, red-tile roofs and pale stucco.

The surrounding area is home to the University of California San Diego (UCSD), several renowned research institutes and a new-money residential area called the Golden Triangle, bounded by I-5, I-805 and Hwy 52.

⊙ Sights

DOWNTOWN LA JOLLA

La Jolla Village sits atop cliffs with the ocean on three sides. The main crossroads, Girard Ave and Prospect St, are the x and y axes of some of San Diego's best restaurants and certainly its best boutique shopping. For a bit of old La Jolla, head southwest from Girard Ave along Prospect St. Number 780 Prospect St was originally Ellen Browning Scripps' guest cottage, now part of the La Jolla Historical Society.

La Jolla Historical Society MUSEUM
(780 Prospect; ☉noon-4pm Thu & Fri) Around the corner from Browning Scripps' cottage, this place has vintage photos and beach memorabilia (think old bathing costumes and lifeguard buoys). Further southwest on Prospect St there's **St James Episcopal Church**, the **La Jolla Recreation Center** and the **Bishop's School** (cnr Prospect St & La Jolla Blvd), all built in the early 20th century.

Museum of Contemporary Art San Diego MUSEUM
(www.mcasd.org; 700 Prospect St; adult/senior/under 25yr $10/5/free; ☉11am-5pm Fri-Tue, to 7pm Thu) La Jolla's branch of this museum gets changing, world-class exhibitions. Originally designed by Irving Gill in 1916 as the home of Ellen Browning Scripps, the building was renovated by Philadelphia's postmodern architect Robert Venturi and has an Andy Goldsworthy sculpture out the front; tickets are good for one week at all three of the museum's locations.

Athenaeum LIBRARY
(☑858-454-5872; 1008 Wall St; ☉10am-5:30pm Tue-Sat, to 8:30pm Wed) Housed in a graceful Spanish renaissance structure, this space is devoted exclusively to art and music. Its reading room is a lovely place to relax and read, and it hosts a series of concerts from chamber music to jazz.

THE COAST
A wonderful walking path skirts the shoreline for half a mile. At the west it begins at **Children's Pool**, where a jetty protects the beach from big waves. Originally intended to give La Jolla's youth a safe place to frolic, this beach is now given over to sea lions, which you can view up close as they lounge on the shore (see boxed text p316).

Atop Point La Jolla, at the path's eastern end, **Ellen Browning Scripps Park** is a tidy expanse of green lawns and palm trees, with **La Jolla Cove** to the north. The cove's gem of a beach provides access to some of the best snorkeling around; it's also popular with rough-water swimmers.

Look for the white buoys offshore from Point La Jolla to Scripps Pier (visible to the north) that mark the **San Diego-La Jolla Underwater Park Ecological Reserve**, a protected zone with a variety of marine life, kelp forests, reefs and canyons (see p316).

See p316 for info about surfing this area.

Cave Store CAVES
(1325 Cave St; adult/child $4/3; ☉10am-5pm) Waves have carved a series of caves into the sandstone cliffs east of La Jolla Cove. The largest is called Sunny Jim Cave, which you can access via this store. Taller visitors, watch your head as you descend the 145 steps.

LA JOLLA SHORES
Called simply 'the Shores,' the area northeast of La Jolla Cove is where La Jolla's cliffs meet the wide, sandy beaches north to Del Mar (p319). Primarily residential, the Shores is home to the members-only La Jolla Beach and Tennis Club (its orange-tile roof is visible from La Jolla Cove) and Kellogg City Park, whose beachside playground is good for families. Take La Jolla Shores Dr north from Torrey Pines Rd, and turn west onto Ave de la Playa. The waves here are gentle enough for beginner surfers, and kayakers can launch from the shore without much problem.

Birch Aquarium at Scripps AQUARIUM
(www.aquarium.ucsd.edu; 2300 Expedition Way; adult/child/student & senior $12/8.50/9; ☉9am-5pm; P) Marine scientists were working at the Birch Aquarium at Scripps Institution of Oceanography (SIO) as early as 1910 and, helped by donations from the ever-generous Scripps family, the institute has grown to be one of the world's largest marine research institutions. It is now a part of UCSD, and its pier is a landmark. Off N Torrey Pines Rd, the aquarium has brilliant displays. The **Hall of Fishes** has more than 30 fish tanks, simulating marine environments from the Pacific Northwest to tropical seas. If you're interested in studying oceanography or seeing the campus, pick up the self-guided campus-tour brochure. The SIO is not to be confused with the **Scripps Research Institute** (10550 Torrey Pines Rd), a private, nonprofit biomedical research organization.

Salk Institute ARCHITECTURAL SIGNIFICANCE
(www.salk.edu; 10010 N Torrey Pines Rd; ☉tours by reservation noon Mon-Fri; P) In 1960 Jonas Salk, the polio-prevention pioneer, founded the Salk Institute for biological and biomedical research. San Diego County donated 27 acres of land, the March of Dimes provided financial support and renowned architect Louis Kahn designed the building, completed in 1965. It is regarded as a modern masterpiece, with its classically proportioned

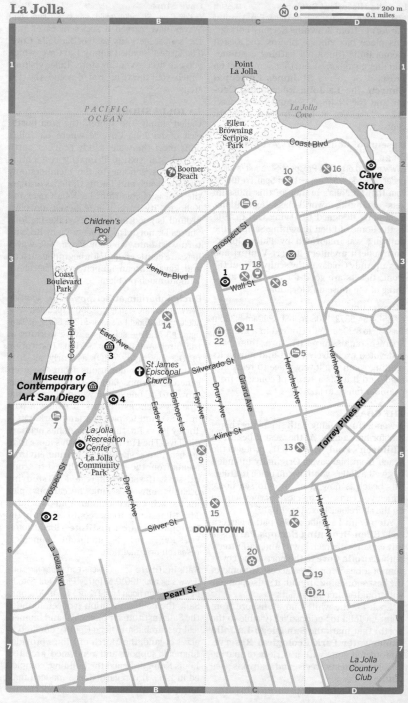

SAN DIEGO

N

0 — 200 m
0 — 0.1 miles

PACIFIC OCEAN

Point La Jolla

La Jolla Cove

Ellen Browning Scripps Park

Coast Blvd

Boomer Beach

10

16

Cave Store

6

Children's Pool

Prospect St

Coast Boulevard Park

Jenner Blvd

1

17 18

Wall St

8

Eads Ave

3

14

11

22

St James Episcopal Church

Silverado St

Herschel Ave

5

Ivanhoe Ave

Coast Blvd

Museum of Contemporary Art San Diego

4

Eads Ave

Bishops La

Fay Ave

Drury Ave

Girard Ave

Torrey Pines Rd

7

La Jolla Recreation Center

La Jolla Community Park

Kline St

13

9

Draper Ave

Prospect St

15

DOWNTOWN

12

Herschel Ave

2

Silver St

20

19

La Jolla Blvd

21

Pearl St

La Jolla Country Club

travertine marble plaza and cubist, mirror-glass laboratory blocks framing a perfect view of the Pacific, and the fountain in the courtyard symbolizing the River of Life. The Salk Institute attracts the best scientists to work in a research-only environment. The original buildings were expanded with new laboratories designed by Jack McAllister, a follower of Kahn's work.

Torrey Pines State Reserve NATURE PRESERVE
(www.torreypine.org; 12600 N Torrey Pines Rd; ⊙8am-dusk; ℗) Between N Torrey Pines Rd and the ocean, and from the Torrey Pines Gliderport to Del Mar, this reserve preserves the last mainland stands of the Torrey pine *(Pinus torreyana),* a species adapted to sparse rainfall and sandy, stony soils. Steep sandstone gullies have eroded into wonderfully textured surfaces, and the views over the ocean and north are superb.

The main access road, Torrey Pines Scenic Dr, off N Torrey Pines Rd (bues 41 and 301) at the reserve's northern end, leads to a simple adobe. It was built as a lodge in 1922 by – who else? – Ellen Browning Scripps, and now serves as a **visitors center** with good displays on the local flora and fauna. Rangers lead **nature walks** from here at 10am and 2pm on weekends and holidays. Several walking trails wind through the reserve and down to the beach.

Torrey Pines State Reserve and La Jolla Cove are also good spots for whale watching. Parking costs $10.

University of California, San Diego
UNIVERSITY
(www.ucsd.edu) UCSD was established in 1960, and now has more than 18,000 students and an excellent academic reputation, particularly for mathematics and science programs. It lies on rolling coastal hills in a parklike setting, surrounded by tall, fragrant eucalyptus trees. Its most distinctive structure is the **Geisel Library**, an upside-down pyramid of glass and concrete, whose namesake, children's author Theodor Geisel, is better known as Dr Seuss, creator of the *Cat in the Hat.* He and his wife contributed substantially to the library, which exhibits a collection of his drawings and books on the ground floor.

From the eastern side of the library's second level, an allegorical snake created by artist Alexis Smith winds down a native California plant garden past an enormous marble copy of John Milton's *Paradise Lost.* The piece is part of the **Stuart Collection** of outdoor sculptures spread around campus. Other works include Niki de Saint Phalle's *Sun God,* Bruce Nauman's *Vices & Virtues* (which spells out seven of each in huge neon letters), Robert Irwin's very blue *Fence* and a forest of talking trees. Download a map of the art at www.stuartcollection.ucsd.edu. The **UCSD bookstore** (Price Center) has excellent stock and helpful staff. See also the La Jolla Playhouse (p318).

✦ Activities

La Jolla Beaches
BEACHES

Some of the county's best beaches are north of the Shores in **Torrey Pines City Park**, which covers the coastline from the Salk Institute up to the Torrey Pines State Reserve. At extreme low tides (about twice per year), you can walk from the Shores north to Del Mar along the beach. Hang-gliders and paragliders launch into the sea breezes rising over the cliffs at **Torrey Pines Gliderport**, at the end of Torrey Pines Scenic Dr. It's a beautiful sight – tandem flights are available if you can't resist trying it (p316). Down below, **Black's Beach** is one of America's most storied clothing-optional venues – though bathing suits are technically required, most folks here don't seem to know that; there's a gay section at the far (north) end.

San Diego-La Jolla Underwater Park Ecological Reserve
DIVING

Some of California's best and most accessible (no boat needed) diving is in this reserve, accessible from La Jolla Cove. With an average depth of 20ft, the 6000 acres of look-but-don't-touch underwater real estate is great for snorkeling, too. Ever-present are the spectacular, bright orange Garibaldi fish – California's official state fish and a protected species (there's a $500 fine for poaching one). Further out you'll see forests of giant California kelp (which can increase its length by up to 3ft per day) and the 100ft-deep La Jolla Canyon.

A number of commercial outfits conduct scuba-diving courses, sell or rent equipment, fill tanks, and conduct boat trips to nearby wrecks and islands. The Cave Store (p313) rents snorkel and fin sets ($20) or, by the water, **OEX** (☎858-454-6195; www.oexpress.com; 2158 Avenida de la Playa, full set $30) is a full-service PADI dive shop in La Jolla Shores that provides rentals and instruction. Scuba gear rentals/dive tours/kayak rentals start at $60/110/28.

Windansea Beach
SURFING

Experienced surfers can head to this beach, 2 miles south of downtown (take La Jolla Blvd south and turn west on Nautilus St); the surf's consistent peak (a powerful reef break that's not for beginners) works best at medium to low tide. However, some of the locals can be unfriendly toward outsiders.

SEALS VS SWIMMERS

La Jolla's Children's Pool was created in the early 1930s when the state deeded the area to the city as a public park and children's pool. Then came the seals, drawing tourists but gradually nudging out swimmers completely by 1997. Animal rights groups and swimmers duked it out in court to protect the cove as a rookery while swimmers and divers wanted the seals – whose presence raises bacterial levels in the waters to unsafe levels – removed. State and federal courts have consistently ruled that the seals must go, but Mother Nature may be the final authority. For now the seals remain, surrounded by a simple rope barrier to keep humans at bay.

Big Rock
SURFING

You'll find a more pleasant welcome immediately south of Windansea Beach, at the foot of Palomar Ave. Big Rock is California's version of Hawaii's Pipeline, which has steep, hollow, gnarly tubes. The name comes from the large chunk of reef protruding just offshore – a great spot for **tide-pooling** at low tide. La Jolla Shores and Black's Beach are also popular surfing spots.

Surf Diva
SURF SCHOOL

(☎858-454-8273; www.surfdiva.com; 2160 Avenida de la Playa) The wonderful women here offer surf classes from $60.

Torrey Pines Gliderport
HANG GLIDING

(☎858-452-9858; www.flytorrey.com; 2800 Torrey Pines Scenic Dr; 20min paragliding $150, hang gliding tandem flight per person $200) Conditions permitting, glider riders hang at this world-famous gliding location. It's also one of the best gliding schools in the country. Experienced pilots can join in if they have a USHGA Hang 4 (paragliders need a P3 rating) and take out an associate membership of the Torrey Pines Hang Glider Association.

🛏 Sleeping

Lodging in central La Jolla ain't cheap, but lower-priced chains are a quick drive outside the village. We've given high-season (summer, June to August) rack rates here. Inquire about specials and packages, and lower rates at other times of year.

Lodge at Torrey Pines CRAFTSMAN, GOLF $$$
(☎858-453-4420, 800-995-4507; www.lodge
torreypines.com; 11480 N Torrey Pines Rd; r from
$350; P@≊) Inspired by the architecture
of Greene & Greene, the turn-of-the-20th-
century Arts and Crafts masters who de-
signed the Gamble House in Pasadena, the
Lodge is built in Craftsman style down to
the lap joints in the cherry-wood wainscot-
ing and the column footings of random-
set stone. Discreetly luxurious rooms
have Mission oak-and-leather furniture à
la Stickley, Tiffany-style lamps, plein-air
paintings and basket-weave bathroom-
floor tiling in marble. There's a stellar full-
service spa and even a croquet lawn. Park-
ing costs $22.

La Valencia HISTORIC $$$
TOP CHOICE (Map p314; ☎858-454-0771, 800-451-
0772; www.lavalencia.com; 1132 Prospect St; r
from $295; P☎@≊) Publicity stills of
Lon Cheney, Lillian Gish and Greta Garbo
line the hallways of this 1926 landmark:
pink-walled, Mediterranean-style and designed by William Templeton Johnson.
Among its 116 rooms, the ones in the main
building are rather compact (befitting the
era), but villas are spacious and in any case
the property wins for Old Hollywood romance. Even if you don't stay, consider lift-
ing a toast – and a pinkie – to the sunset
from its Spanish revival lounge, la Sala.
Parking is $25.

La Jolla Village Lodge MID-CENTURY MOTEL $$
(Map p314; ☎858-551-2001, 877-551-2001; www.
lajollavillagelodge.com; 1141 Silverado St; r incl
breakfast $100-200; P☎≊) At the edge of
downtown La Jolla, this 30-room 1950s-
era motel was recently restored in period
style with custom-built tables and chairs,
teak headboards and new mattresses. Flat-
screen TVs (in some rooms) are a conces-
sion to the 21st century. A roof deck gives
long-distance views.

Scripps Inn WATERSIDE, B&B $$
(Map p314; ☎858-454-3391, 866-860-6318;
555 Coast Blvd; r & ste incl breakfast from $185;
P☎) Tucked just behind the Museum of
Contemporary Art, across from the water,
this cozy inn feels like a well-loved beach
cottage, bedecked with climbing vines.
Its airy, rather spacious rooms combine
blond-wood and sandpiper motifs, and
most have sleep-sofas. The 14 units fill up
quickly – book early. No air-con. Parking
is $10.

Estancia La Jolla Hotel & Spa
LUXURY RESORT $$$
(☎858-550-1000, 877-437-8262; www.estanciala
jolla.com; 9700 N Torrey Pines Rd; r $199-349;
P@☎≊) Outside the town center, this
rambling rancho-style resort with its path-
ways, patios and lush gardens is down-to-
earth, romantic and cushy all at once. Un-
wind by the huge pool, during an expert
massage at the spa, or while sipping killer
margaritas by the outdoor fireplace. Rooms
feature custom furniture, luxurious linens
and big bathrooms. Two restaurants. Park-
ing costs $25.

✖ Eating

George's at the Cove CALIFORNIAN $$$
(Map p314; ☎858-454-4244; www.georgesatthe
cove.com; 1250 Prospect St; mains $11-48;
⊙11am-11pm) If you've got to the urge to
splurge, the Euro-Cal cooking is as dramatic as the oceanfront location thanks
to the bottomless imagination of chef Trey
Foshée. George's has graced just about every list of top restaurants in California, and
indeed the USA. Three venues allow you to
enjoy it at different price points: Ocean Terrace, George's Bar and George's California
Modern.

Whisknladle CALIFORNIAN $$$
(Map p314; ☎858-551-7575; 1044 Wall St; dishes
$9-32; ⊙lunch & dinner) This newcomer has
earned oodles of kudos for its 'slow food'
preparations of local, farm-fresh ingredi-
ents, served on a breezy covered patio and
meant for sharing. The menu changes daily,
but it's always clever. So are the cocktails
(the London's Burning mixes gin and jala-
peño water).

Trattoria Acqua ITALIAN $$$
(Map p314; ☎858-454-0709; 1298 Prospect St;
mains lunch $9-25, dinner $15-28; ⊙11:30am-
2:30pm & 5-9pm Mon-Thu, 11:30am-2:30pm &
5-10pm Fri, 5-10pm Sat, 5-9:30pm Sun) Ahh-
lovely by day, ooh-dreamy by night, and set
into the hillside like an ocean-view treehouse. There's scrumptious northern Italian cuisine with Cal-coastal touches: salad
of crab, avocado, tomato and mango; ravioli
filled with butternut squash; crushed Ama-
retto cookies and lobster pot pie.

Marine Room AMERICAN-CONTEMPORARY $$$
(☎858-459-7222; 2000 Spindrift Dr; mains $26-
46; ⊙6-10pm) It's yet another only-in-La Jol-
la experience. When money is no object and
you want high-drama cooking and views,

book a sunset table at this fancy dining room outside the town center. You'll feast on highly stylized contemporary-fusion meats and seafood, while waves splash against the window at high tide. Lounge menu too (4pm to 6pm Sunday to Friday).

Roppongi
ASIAN-FUSION $$$
(Map p314; ☑858-551-5252; 875 Prospect St; tapas $10-25, mains $18-32; ☺11:30am-9:30pm) Tapas-style Asian-fusion really shines at this gorgeous eatery with clever lighting that makes everyone look good. The Polynesian crab stack, piled high and tossed at table, is a killer choice, and the ahi (yellowfin) tuna with watermelon a surprising flavor bomb. Great wines and sakes, too.

TOP CHOICE Porkyland
MEXICAN $
La Jolla (Map p314; ☑858-459-1708; 1030 Torrey Pines Rd; dishes $3-8; ☺9am-8pm); Hillcrest (☑619-233-5139; 646 University Ave; ☺10am-9pm Mon-Thu, 10am-10pm Fri & Sat, 11am-7pm Sun) The branch of this tiny Mexican joint on the edge of central La Jolla has no atmosphere, but the burritos and fish tacos have a devoted following. The verde carnitas burrito ($6) will make your taste buds roar (in a good way) and still leave you money for beer.

Tapénade
FRENCH-CONTEMPORARY $$$
(Map p314; ☑858-551-7500; 7612 Fay Ave; mains lunch $14-19, dinner $24-36; ☺11:30am-2:30pm Tue-Fri, 5:30-9:30pm Sun-Thu, 5:30-10pm Sat & Sun) Foodies thrill for the brilliant, sunny flavors of Tapénade, San Diego's finest for Provençal French (think ratatouille and wine reductions, not potatoes and cream-based sauces). Consistently voted one of San Diego's top restaurants, Tapénade dazzles classics like coq au vin to outré lobster with Tahitian vanilla. Gourmets on a budget should try the two-course Riviera lunch for $22 or the three-course sunset dinner for $30 (served 5:30pm to 6:30pm Sunday to Thursday).

The Cottage
AMERICAN-CONTEMPORARY $$
(Map p314; ☑858-454-8409; 7702 Fay Ave; mains breakfast $9-12, lunch $10-19, dinner $11-26; ☺7:30am-9pm) Shhh! Don't tell anybody that the stuffed French toast, eggs La Jolla (with Canadian bacon, mushrooms, spinach and garlic and balsamic vinegar), fish tacos and granola-crusted mahi mahi make this place a local favorite. It's crowded enough as it is, especially on weekends for brunch. Expect a wait if you arrive much after 8:30am.

Girard Gourmet
BAKERY, DELICATESSEN $
(Map p314; ☑858-454-3321; 7837 Girard Ave; dishes $5-9; ☺7am-9pm Mon-Sat, to 7pm Sun) There's everything from chicken salad to chocolate cake at this Belgian delicatessen, which makes its own pastries and serves pre-plated hot foods and sandwiches you select from the glass case. La Jolla's best bargain. Bonus: cookies shaped like surfboards or spaniels.

Harry's Coffee Shop
COFFEE SHOP $
(Map p314; ☑858-454-7381; 7545 Girard Ave; dishes $4-11; ☺6am-3pm; ☑) This classic 1960 coffee shop has a posse of regulars from blue-haired socialites to sports celebs. The food is standard-issue American – pancakes, tuna melts, iceberg-lettuce salads – but it's the aura of the place that makes it special.

Also look for an outpost of **Burger Lounge** (☑858-456-0196; 1101 Wall St) here; see p292.

🍷 Drinking & Entertainment

La Jolla has a cluster of bars clustered around Prospect St and Girard Ave. See also La Sala, in La Valencia Hotel (p317), and Karl Strauss Brewery (p295).

Pannikin
CAFE
(Map p314; ☺6am-7pm Mon-Fri, 6:30am-7pm Sat & Sun; ☑) A few blocks from the water, this beach-shack of a cafe with a generous balcony is popular for its Italian espresso and Mexican chocolate, and occasional live music. Like all the Pannikins, it's a North County institution.

Comedy Store
COMEDY CLUB
(Map p314; ☑858-454-9176; www.comedystore lajolla.com; 916 Pearl St) One of the area's most established comedy venues, the Comedy Store also serves meals, drinks and barrels of laughs. Expect a cover charge ($15 to $20 on weekends with a two-drink minimum), and some of tomorrow's big names.

La Jolla Symphony & Chorus
CLASSICAL MUSIC
(☑619-534-4637; www.lajollasymphony.com) Come here for quality concerts at UCSD's Mandeville Auditorium running from October to June.

La Jolla Playhouse
THEATER
(☑858-550-1010; www.lajollaplayhouse.com) Inside the Mandell Weiss Center for the Performing Arts, this theater has sent dozens of productions to Broadway, from 1984's *Big River* to the 2010 Tony winner *Memphis*.

Shopping

La Jolla's skirt-and-sweater crowd pays retail for cashmere sweaters and expensive tchotchkes downtown: paintings, sculpture and decorative items, and small boutiques fill the gaps between Talbot's, Banana Republic, Ralph Lauren, Jos A Bank and Armani Exchange.

Westfield University Towne Centre MALL
(UTC; 4545 La Jolla Village Dr) Mall shoppers: make a beeline for this large mall out of downtown La Jolla and east of I-5; anchor stores include Nordstrom, Macy's and Sears, and for non-shoppers there are movies and an indoor ice skating rink, Icetown (☑858-452-9110; www.icetown.com); call for opening hours. It's also the transit hub for La Jolla.

These bookstores have good selections and host readings and author events:

DG Wills BOOKSHOP
(Map p314; 7461 Girard Ave)

Warwick's BOOKSHOP
(Map p314; 7812 Girard Ave)

❶ Information

La Jolla Visitors center(☑619-236-1212; www.sandiego.org; 7966 Herschel St; ☉9am-5pm Mon-Sat, 10am-5pm Sun) This outpost of the San Diego Convention & Visitors Bureau also promotes La Jolla.

Travelex (University Towne Centre; ☉10am-7pm Mon-Fri, to 6pm Sat, 11am-4pm Sun) Foreign-currency exchange at inland shopping mall.

❶ Getting There & Away

Via I-5 from Downtown San Diego, take the La Jolla Pkwy exit, and head west toward Torrey Pines Rd, from where it's a right turn to Prospect St. By public transit, take bus 30 from the Old Town Transit Center to Westfield UTC Shopping Center, with stops in La Jolla.

SAN DIEGO NORTH COUNTY COAST

Like pearls on a strand, a handful of small beach towns extends northward from La Jolla. 'North County', as locals call it, begins with pretty Del Mar and continues through low-key Solana Beach, Encinitas and Carlsbad (home of Legoland), before hitting Oceanside, largely a bedroom community for Camp Pendleton Marine Base.

North County's coast evokes the San Diego of 40 years ago, even if inland development, especially east of I-5, has created giant bedroom communities for San Diego and Orange Counties. The beaches are terrific, and the small seaside towns are great for a number of days of soaking up the laid-back SoCal scene, working on your tan and catching up on your reading while watching the California sun glisten on the Pacific.

All that, and only about a half-hour's drive from Downtown San Diego. Will wonders never cease?

❶ Getting There & Away

N Torrey Pines Rd from La Jolla is the most scenic approach from the south. Heading north along the coast, S21 changes its name from Camino del Mar to Coast Hwy 101 to Old Hwy 101. If you're in a hurry or headed out of town, the faster I-5 parallels it to the east. Traffic can snarl everywhere during rush hour and race or fair season when heading toward Del Mar Racetrack.

Bus 101 departs from University Towne Centre and follows the coastal road to Oceanside, while bus 310 operates express service up I-5; for information call the **North County Transit District** (NCTD; ☑760-966-6500; www. gonctd.com). NCTD also operates the **Coaster commuter train** (www.gonctd.com; tickets $5-6.50), which originates in San Diego and makes stops in Solana Beach, Encinitas, Carlsbad and Oceanside. There are 11 daily trains in each direction from Monday to Friday. On Saturday, there are six trains only, and there is no Sunday service.

All NCTD buses and trains have bike racks. Greyhound buses stop at Oceanside and San Diego, but nowhere in between.

Del Mar

POP 4550

The ritziest of North County's seaside suburbs, with a Tudor aesthetic that somehow doesn't feel out of place, Del Mar boasts good (if pricey) restaurants, unique galleries, high-end boutiques and, north of town, the west coast's most renowned horse-racing track, which is also the site of the annual county fair. Downtown Del Mar (sometimes called 'the village') extends for about a mile along Camino del Mar. At its hub, where 15th St crosses Camino del Mar, the tastefully designed Del Mar Plaza shopping center has restaurants, boutiques and upper-level terraces that look out to sea.

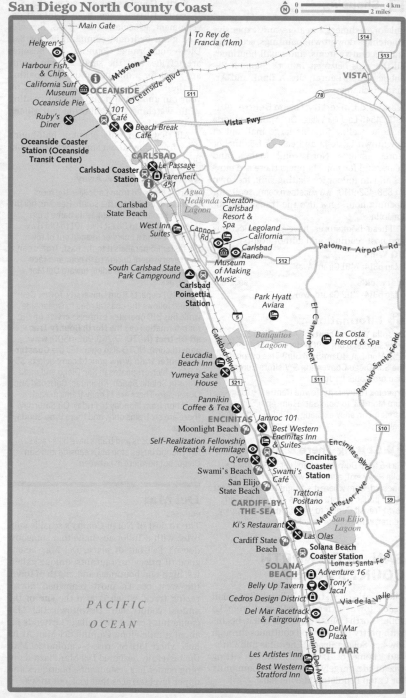

0 4 km
0 2 miles

Helgren's

Main Gate

To Rey de
Francia (1km)

Harbour Fish
& Chips
California Surf
Museum
OCEANSIDE
Oceanside Pier

VISTA

S14

S13

Mission Ave

Oceanside Blvd

S11

Ruby's
Diner

101
Café

Beach Break
Café

Vista Fwy

**Oceanside Coaster
Station (Oceanside
Transit Center)**

CARLSBAD

Le Passage
Farenheit
451

**Carlsbad Coaster
Station**

Agua
Hedionda
Lagoon

Carlsbad
State Beach

Sheraton
Carlsbad
Resort &
Spa

Legoland
California

West Inn
Suites

Cannon
Rd

Carlsbad
Ranch

Palomar Airport Rd

South Carlsbad State
Park Campground

Museum
of Making
Music

S12

**Carlsbad
Poinsettia
Station**

Park Hyatt
Aviara

Batiquitos
Lagoon

La Costa
Resort & Spa

Rancho Santa Fe Rd

Leucadia
Beach Inn

Yumeya Sake
House

S21

S11

El Camino Real

Pannikin
Coffee & Tea

ENCINITAS

Jamroc 101

Moonlight Beach

S10

Self-Realization Fellowship
Retreat & Hermitage

Best Western
Encinitas Inn
& Suites

Q'ero

**Encinitas
Coaster
Station**

Encinitas Blvd

Swami's Beach

Swami's
Café

San Elijo
State Beach

Trattoria
Positano

**CARDIFF-BY-
THE-SEA**

San Elijo
Lagoon

Manchester Ave

S9

Ki's Restaurant

Las Olas

Cardiff State
Beach

**Solana Beach
Coaster Station**

Lomas Santa Fe Dr

**SOLANA
BEACH**

Adventure 16

Belly Up Tavern

Tony's
Jacal

Cedros Design District

Via de la Valle

Del Mar Racetrack
& Fairgrounds

Camino Del Mar

Del Mar
Plaza

**PACIFIC
OCEAN**

Les Artistes Inn

DEL MAR

Best Western
Stratford Inn

⊙ Sights & Activities

Del Mar Racetrack & Fairgrounds
RACETRACK
(www.delmarracing.com; admission from $6; ⊘mid-Jul–early Sep) Del Mar's biggest draw was founded in 1937 by a prestigious group including Bing Crosby and Jimmy Durante. It's worth trying to brave the crowds on opening day, if nothing else to see the amazing spectacle of ladies wearing over-the-top hats. Driving here on opening day... just don't. The rest of the season, you'll have to be satisfied with the mere visual perfection of the track's lush gardens and pink, Mediterranean-style architecture.

Seagrove Park
PARK
At the beach end of 15th St, this park abuts the beach and overlooks the ocean. This little stretch of well-groomed beachfront lawn is a community hub and perfect for a picnic.

California Dreamin'
BALLOONING
(☎800-373-3359; www.californiadreamin.com; per person from $288) Brightly colored hot-air balloons are a trademark of the skies above Del Mar, on the northern fringe of the metropolitan area. For flights, contact California Dreamin', which also serves Temecula.

⊨ Sleeping

In summer, especially around opening day at Del Mar Racetrack, rooms in Del Mar fill up and rates soar. Discounts may be available midweek. The following choices are in the town center; there are less expensive chain properties out of town, near the 5 Fwy.

L'Auberge Del Mar Resort & Spa LUXURY $$$
(☎858-259-1515, 800-553-1336; www.lauberge delmar.com; 1540 Camino Del Mar; r $350-540; P@🛜🌊🐕) Rebuilt in the 1990s on the grounds of the historic Hotel del Mar, where 1920s Hollywood celebrities once frolicked, L'Auberge continues a tradition of European-style elegance with luxurious linens, a spa and lovely grounds. It feels so intimate and the service is so individual, you'd never know there are 120 rooms. Parking is $25.

Les Artistes Inn
BOUTIQUE $$
(☎858-755-4646; www.lesartistesinn.com; 944 Camino Del Mar; r $165-250; P@🛜🌊) Behind the eclectic Craftsman-style façade of this inn set back from Camino del Mar, each of the 12 spacious rooms is meticulously furnished in the style of an artist or art movement: Botero through O'Keefe to van Gogh, even Zen.

Best Western Stratford Inn HOTEL $$
(☎858-755-1501, 800-446-7229; www.pacifica host.com; 710 Camino Del Mar; r incl breakfast $149-244; P@🛜🌊🐕🍸) The sprawling Stratford has large, recently renovated rooms, lots of wood in its construction, a spa for foot and body treatments, laundry facilities, two pools and new fitness and business centers. Some units have kitchenettes and distant ocean views.

Clarion Del Mar Inn MOTEL $$
(☎858-755-9765, 800-451-4515; www.delmarinn. com; 720 Camino Del Mar; r incl breakfast $119-229; P@🛜🌊🐕) This well-kept, 81-room hotel tries hard to please with very helpful staff, pool and large-ish rooms (many with balconies and kitchens or bathroom vanities with granite countertops), all furnished with Victorian-style furniture.

✕ Eating

En Fuego
MEXICAN $$
(☎858-792-6551; 1342 Camino Del Mar; mains $11-18; ⊘from 11:30am Mon-Fri, 10:30am Sat & Sun) On the site of Del Mar's first restaurant, this multilevel Nuevo Mexicano spot is both restaurant and bar. Specialties on the forward-thinking menu include borracho shrimp (sautéed in tequila) and honey habanero chicken (in a sweet spicy glaze), with lots of indoor-outdoor space to enjoy them.

Jake's Del Mar SEAFOOD, WATERSIDE $$$
(☎858-755-2002; 1660 Coast Blvd; mains lunch $9-14, dinner $18-32; ⊘lunch Tue-Sun, dinner daily) Head to Jake's for beachside drinks and half-price appetizers from 4pm to 6pm weekdays and 2:30pm to 4:30pm on Saturday. The view's great, the atmosphere chic and the food imaginative, like heart of palm salad, poke rolls and lemongrass beef tenderloin.

Zel's AMERICAN CONTEMPORARY $$
(☎858-755-0076; 1247 Camino Del Mar; mains lunch $9-12, dinner $9-18; ⊘5-10pm Tue-Thu, 5-11pm Fri, 8:30am-2pm & 5-11pm Sat, 8:30am-2pm Sun) Zel was a longstanding local merchant, and his grandson continues the family tradition of welcoming locals and visitors, over excellent flatbread pizzas (like chicken confit with asparagus, truffle oil, arugula and avocado), burgers from the local Brandt farm and lots of local beers.

Americana AMERICAN CONTEMPORARY **$$**
(☎858-794-6838; 1454 Camino del Mar; mains breakfast & lunch $7-14, dinner $14-23; ⊙7am-3pm Sun-Mon, to 10pm Tue-Sat) This quietly chichi and much-loved local landmark serves a diverse lineup of regional American cuisine, including some dishes you may not have thought of: cheese grits to chicken Reubens, sesame salmon on succotash to seared duck breast with Israeli couscous, all amid checkerboard linoleum floors, giant windows and homey wainscoting.

Head to **Del Mar Plaza** (1555 Camino Del Mar) to pick up groceries and sandwiches for the beach at **Harvest Ranch Market** (⊙9am-8pm). Or check out the rooftop patio and its upscale restaurants for North County's best vantage points, especially at sunset – **Il Fornaio** (☎858-755-8876; mains lunch $11-19, dinner $13-27; ⊙11:30am-10pm Sun-Thu, to 11pm Fri & Sat) for pizzas, pastas, salads and steak; the futuristic **Pacifica Del Mar** (☎858-792-0476; mains lunch $11-18, dinner $19-35) with fresh seafood and inventive preparations (arrive by 6pm for two-course prix-fixe menu, $22); and **Rendezvous** (☎858-755-2669; mains lunch $8-12, dinner $12-17; ⊙11:30am-3pm daily, plus 4-9:30pm Sun-Thu, 4-10pm Fri & Sat), which despite the French name serves popular Chinese and Asian fusion dishes including pricey filet mignon ($28).

Solana Beach
POP 13,050

Solana Beach is the next town north from Del Mar – it's not as posh, but it has good beaches and the **Cedros Design District** (Cedros Ave), four contemporary blocks where interior designers from all over the region come for inspiration and merchandise from buttons to bathrooms, paint to photographs and even garden supplies. The cavernous **Solo** (309 S Cedros Ave) is a good place to start, with design books, trinkets, furniture and accessories, and a design office in the back. Other offerings include antiques shops, handcrafted-clothing boutiques, and camping and travel gear at **Adventure 16** (143 S Cedros Ave, Suite M).

The **Belly Up Tavern** (www.bellyup.com; 143 S Cedros Ave; cover $5-40) is a converted warehouse and bar that consistently books good bands from jazz to funk, and big names like Ludacris to tribute bands. Its **Wild Note Café** (☎858-259-7310; 143 S Cedros Ave; mains lunch $9-13, dinner $13-22; ⊙11am-3pm Mon, to 9pm Tue-Thu, to 10pm Fri & Sat) serves upscale pub food and fancier fare such as Dijon-herb crusted salmon and brie burgers.

Across the street, order at the counter and sit outside at the all-veg **Zinc Café** (☎858-793-5436; 132 S Cedros Ave; mains $6-11; ⊙7am-5pm; 🍴), which serves breakfasts, salads, vegetarian chili and pizza good enough to satisfy all but the most hardcore carnivores.

A short drive from the town center, **Tony's Jacal** (☎858-755-2274; 621 Valley Ave; mains $7-16; ⊙11am-2pm Mon-Sat, plus 5-9:30pm Mon-Sat, 3-9:30pm Sun), in business since 1946 (current building from the '60s), has rough-hewn wood beams, dark wood paneling, icy-delicious margaritas and some of North County's best traditional Mexican. Make reservations for dinner. (Valley Ave goes north of Via de la Valle, just west of I-5.)

Cardiff-by-the-Sea
POP 10,000

Cardiff is a beach town good for surfing and popular with a laid-back crowd. There is a town center, with the perfunctory supermarkets and everyday shops along San Elijo Ave, about 0.25 miles from the ocean and across the railroad tracks, but the real action is the miles of restaurants and surf shops along Hwy 101. With largely unobstructed views, it's may be North County's best place to go for surfers and surf-watchers.

FREE **San Elijo Lagoon** NATURE RESERVE
(www.sanelijo.org; 2710 Manchester Ave; admission free; ⊙9am-5pm; 🅿) The other main draw is this 1000-acre ecological preserve popular with bird-watchers for its herons, coots, terns, ducks, egrets and more than 250 other species. A 7-mile network of trails leads through the area.

Cardiff State Beach BEACH
(www.parks.ca.gov; ⊙7am-sunset; 🅿) Just south of Cardiff-by-the-Sea, the surf break on the reef here is mostly popular with long boarders, but it gets very good at low tide with a big north swell. Parking costs $10.

San Elijo State Beach BEACH
A little further north of Cardiff State Beach, San Elijo State Beach has good winter waves and $15 parking.

🛏 Sleeping & Eating

San Elijo State Beach Campground
CAMPGROUND **$**

(📞760-753-5091, reservations 800-444-7275; tent/RV sites in summer from $35/55) Overlooks the surf at the end of Birmingham Dr.

Las Olas
MEXICAN **$$**

(mains $8.50-16.50, ⏲11am-9pm Mon-Thu, to 9:30pm Fri, 10am-9:30pm Sat, 10am-9pm Sun; P 🎁); Cardiff-by-the-Sea (📞760-942-1860; 2655 S Hwy 101); Carlsbad (📞760-434-5850; 2939 Carlsbad Blvd) For fish tacos with a sea view, Las Olas is so popular it has its own traffic light, right across the street from the beach. Lobster is served Puerto Nuevo–style, named for the legendary lobster village on the Baja peninsula. House cocktails include pineapple and chili margaritas and drinks made with RIP (rum infused with pineapple). There's another location in Carlsbad, though it doesn't face the ocean.

Trattoria Positano
ITALIAN **$$$**

(📞760-632-0111; 2171 San Elijo Ave; mains $15-31; ⏲lunch Mon-Sat, dinner daily) This streetside storefront looks rather plain from the outside, but inside this shop run by three sisters is awash with warm tones and white-tablecloth service. The garlicky tomato sauce for your bread is addictive, as is pasta with crabmeat and asparagus.

Ki's Restaurant
CALIFORNIAN **$$**

(📞760-436-5236; 2591 S Coast Hwy 101; mains breakfast $5-9, lunch $7-14, dinner $13-25; ⏲8am-9pm; P) Across from the beach, Ki's is actually two restaurants as well as a great indie cafe and a hub of local activity. At the juice bar on the first floor are awesome smoothies, healthy burgers, salads, tacos and butternut squash and corn enchiladas. Upstairs there's a great ocean view from the sit-down restaurant where from 4pm daily fancier dishes like macadamia-coated mahimahi with Thai peanut sauce are served. Monday nights, look for 1920s-style jazz, often performed by Ki herself.

Encinitas

POP 63,900

Peaceful Encinitas has a decidedly down-to-earth vibe and a laid-back beach town main street, perfect for a relaxing day trip or weekend escape. North of central Encinitas, yet still part of the city, is **Leucadia**, a leafy stretch of N Hwy 101 with a hippie vibe of used clothing stores and taco shops.

👁 Sights

Self-Realization Fellowship Retreat & Hermitage
RETREAT

(215 K St; ⏲9am-5pm Tue-Sat, 11am-5pm Sun) Yogi Paramahansa Yogananda founded his center here in 1937, and the town has been a magnet for holistic healers and natural-lifestyle seekers ever since. The gold lotus domes of the hermitage – conspicuous on South Coast Hwy 101 – mark the southern end of Encinitas and the turn-out for **Swami's Beach**, a powerful reef break surfed by territorial locals. The fellowship's compact but lovely **Meditation Garden** has wonderful ocean vistas, a stream and koi pond. If you're interested in more detailed exploration of meditation and the religion's principles, visit www.yogananda-srf.org.

San Diego Botanic Garden
GARDEN

(www.sdbgarden.com; 230 Quail Gardens Drive; adult/child/senior $12/6/8; ⏲9am-5pm; P 🎁) This 30-acre garden has a large collection of California native plants and flora of different regions of the world, including Australia and Central America. There are special activities in the children's garden (10am Tuesday to Thursday); check the website for a schedule. From I-5, go east on Encinitas Blvd to turn left on Quail Gardens Dr.

Lux Art Institute
ART CENTER

(www.luxartinstitute.org; 1550 S El Camino Real; 2-visit admission $10; ⏲1-5pm Thu & Fri, 11am-5pm Sat; P) A few miles east of central Encinitas, this new institute lets spectators be present at the creation of art. A changing lineup of artists in residence take turns crafting major pieces, from concept to construction, while spectators watch in the 'green' studio building. Creative types will want to make a beeline. From Encinitas, take Encinitas Blvd east and turn right onto S El Camino Real, for about 1.3 miles.

🛏 Sleeping & Eating

CENTRAL ENCINITAS

Best Western Encinitas Inn & Suites
MOTEL **$$**

(📞760-942-7455, 866-326-4648; www.bwencinitas.com; 85 Encinitas Blvd; r incl breakfast from $169; P @ 🛜 🐾 🎁 🌊) Atop a hill between the Freeway, shopping center and Coast Hwy is this hexagonal hotel, a few minutes on foot from the sand. It has all modern conveniences and recently renovated bedding and carpets. Some rooms have ocean or park views.

TOP CHOICE Trattoria I Trulli ITALIAN $$

(☎760-943-6800; 830 S Coast Hwy 101; mains lunch $12-20, dinner $13-23; ⊙11:30am-2:30pm daily, plus 5-10pm Sun-Thu, to 10:30pm Fri & Sat) Country-style seating indoors and great people watching on the sidewalk. Just one taste of the homemade gnocchi, ravioli or lasagna, salmon in brandy mustard sauce or *pollo uno zero uno* (101; chicken stuffed with cheese, spinach and artichokes in mushroom sauce) and you'll know why this mom-and-pop Italian trattoria is always packed. Reservations are recommended.

Q'ero PERUVIAN $$

(☎760-753-9050; 540 S Coast Hwy 101; mains lunch $7-15, dinner $19-26; ⊙11am-3pm & 5-9pm Mon-Thu, 11am-3pm & 5-10pm Fri, 11:30am-11pm Sat) The flavors of Peru tempt from this tiny but atmospheric storefront. Try small plates like *ceviche* or *papa rellena* (potato inside ground beef), or mains like *lomo saltado* of Kobe beef or *aji gallina* (chicken in toasted walnut and chili sauce). Reservations recommended at dinner.

El Callejon MEXICAN $$

(☎760-634-2793; 345 S Coast Hwy 101; mains $5-23; ⊙11am-10pm; 🍴🍷) A raucous, fun, local favorite, this indoor-outdoor cantina is at the north end of the town center. The menu is as long as the phone book of a small village, and would take you over two years of trying a different tequila every day to go through their tequila list.

Swami's Café CAFE $

(☎760-944-0612; 1163 S Coast Hwy 101; mains $5-9; ⊙7am-sunset; 🍷) For breakfast burritos, multigrain pancakes, stir-frys, salads, smoothies and three-egg *ohm*-lettes (sorry, we couldn't resist), you can't beat Swami's. Vegetarians will be satisfied too. Most of the seating is out on an umbrella-covered patio.

NORTH ENCINITAS/LEUCADIA

Leucadia Beach Inn MOTEL $

(☎760-943-7461; www.leucadiabeachinn.org; 1322 N Coast Hwy; r $85-145; 🅿🍷) All sparkling-clean rooms in this charming 1920s courtyard motel have tile floors and bright paint jobs, and many have full kitchenettes. The beach is a few blocks' walk. No phones or internet access from rooms. It's across Hwy 101 from the train tracks, so light sleepers should take earplugs or look elsewhere.

TOP CHOICE Yumeya Sake House JAPANESE $$

(☎760-633-4288; 1246 N Coast Hwy 101; dishes $2-10; ⊙from 5:30pm Tue-Sat) This simple roadside *izakaya* (Japanese pub) has loyal fans thanks to its large assortment of favorites: tempura, *kushi-katsu* (fried meats on skewers), udon noodles and small plates like black cod with miso and bay scallops with *shimeji* mushrooms. Plus, there's a great sake selection, Japanese beers and *shochu* (Japanese distilled spirit), all with a cheery reggae soundtrack.

Pannikin Coffee & Tea CAFE $

(☎760-436-0033; 510 N Coast Hwy 101; mains $4-8; ⊙6am-6pm) In a sunny yellow wooden building that used to be the Encinitas train station (transported from its original site), Pannikin is an adorable sprawl of nooks, crannies and balconies. Muffins and coffees are wonderful, natch, and bagel and lox with steamed scrambled eggs is very attractive indeed.

Jamroc 101 JAMAICAN $$

(☎760-436-3162; 101 N Coast Hwy 101; mains $8-16; ⊙11:30am-8:30pm Sun-Thu, to 10pm Fri & Sat) It's little more than a roadside stand just north of central Encinitas, but what a roadside stand! An island paint job and the obligatory reggae soundtrack make it as bright and sunny inside as out, all the better to enjoy jerk chicken and crispy fried plantains.

Drinking

Daley Double BAR

(546 S Coast Hwy 101) Once Encinitas' most notorious dive bar, it's now Encinitas' hippest dive bar. Fantastic Old West saloon-style murals make a great backdrop for good old-fashioned sipping and flirting. Expect a line out the door on weekends.

Entertainment

La Paloma Theater

(471 S Coast Hwy 101) Built in 1928, this landmark – and central Encinitas' main attraction – shows arthouse movies nightly and stages occasional concerts.

Carlsbad

POP 78,500

Most visitors come to Carlsbad for Legoland and head right back out, and that's too bad because they've missed the charming, intimate Carlsbad Village with shopping, dining and beaching nearby. It's bordered by I-5 and Carlsbad Blvd, which run north–south and are connected by Carlsbad Village Dr running east–west.

Carlsbad came into being with the railroad in the 1880s. John Frazier, an early homesteader, sank a well and found water that had a high mineral content, supposedly identical to that of spa water in Karlsbad, Bohemia (now the Czech Republic). He built a grand spa hotel, which prospered until the 1930s. That Queen Anne–style building is now the restaurant and bar **Ocean House** (760-729-4131; 2978 Carlsbad Blvd), though there are better dining choices in town.

If you've come looking for Carlsbad Caverns, you're outta luck. Those are in New Mexico.

Sights & Activities

TOP CHOICE **Legoland California** THEME PARK (www.lego.com/legoland/california; 1 Legoland Dr; adult/child & senior $67/57; 10am-5pm;) A fantasy environment built largely of those little colored plastic blocks from Denmark. Many rides and attractions arc targeted to elementary schoolers: a junior 'driving school', a jungle cruise lined with Lego animals, wacky 'sky cruiser' pedal cars on a track, and fairytale, princess, pirate, adventurer and dino-themed escapades. If you have budding scientists (age 10 and over) with you, sign them up on arrival at the park for an appointment for **Mindstorms**, where they can make computerized Lego robots. There are also lots of low-thrill activities like face painting.

Age aside, the whole family will probably get a kick out of **Miniland**, recreating the skylines of New York, Washington, DC, San Francisco and Las Vegas entirely of Lego blocks, alongside many world monuments. New York's 25ft Freedom Tower (to replace the World Trade Center) was built according to the real winning design, years before the actual building will be complete.

Compared with some of the bigger, flashier theme parks such as Disneyland and SeaWorld, Legoland is rather low-key and far less commercial – though there are plenty of opportunities to buy Lego. At least it sparks creativity.

One could easily spend an entire day at Legoland (not least because of long lines to get into some of the more popular attractions); a second day of admission to Lego-

land costs $15. To spend even more time there are the adjacent **Sea Life Aquarium** (in which real sea creatures swim among Lego creations) and **Legoland Water Park**. The most expensive 'Resort Hopper' combination ticket (adult/child & senior $87/77) gives a discount off the regular prices for all three attractions, or you can mix and match at different price points. Check the website and tourist kiosks for other discount opportunities. The website also has further details on extended hours in July and August, and closures from September to May; opening hours can vary hugely during these months. Parking is $12.

From I-5, take the Legoland/Cannon Rd exit and follow the signage. By public transit, take the *Coaster* commuter train (p319) to Carlsbad Village Station; from here bus 321 operated by **North County Transit District** (www.gonctd.com; ticket $2, 20 mins; 7:55am, 8:55am & 9:55am Mon-Fri) stops at the park.

Carlsbad Coast BEACHES
Carlsbad's long, sandy beaches are great for walking and searching for seashells. Good access is from Carlsbad Blvd, two blocks south of Carlsbad Village Dr, where there's a boardwalk, rest rooms and free parking.

Carlsbad Ranch FLOWER FIELDS
(www.theflowerfields.com; adult/child $10/5; 9am-6pm early Mar–mid-May) The 50-acre flower fields of Carlsbad Ranch are ablaze in a sea of the carmine, saffron and snow-white blossoms of ranunculuses. Take the Palomar Airport Rd exit off of I-5, head the short block east and turn right to the flower fields. Outside of the official season, there are some rose gardens on the site which, depending on the condition of the blooms, may be accessed via the Armstrong Garden Center next door.

Batiquitos Lagoon NATURE RESERVE
One of the last remaining tidal wetlands in California, Batiquitos Lagoon separates Carlsbad from Encinitas. A self-guided tour lets you explore area plants, including the prickly pear cactus, coastal sage scrub and eucalyptus trees, as well as lagoon birds such as the great heron and the snowy egret. One of the artificial islands in the lagoon is a nesting site for the California least tern and the western snowy plover, both endangered species. You can hike the reserve anytime, but stop by the **Nature Center** (www.batiquitosfoundation.org; 9am-noon Mon-Fri, to 3pm Sat & Sun) if it's open.

SAN DIEGO ZOO SAFARI PARK

Since the early 1960s, the San Diego Zoological Society has been developing this 1800-acre, open-range zoo (www.sandiegozoo.org; 15500 San Pasqual Valley Rd, Escondido; adult/3-11yr $37/27; ⏰9am-8pm summer, to 4pm rest of year; P🚼) where herds of giraffes, zebras, rhinos and other animals roam the open valley floor. For an instant safari feel, board the **Journey to Africa** tram ride, which tours you around the second-largest continent in under half an hour.

Elsewhere, animals are in enclosures so naturalistic it's as if the humans are guests, and there's a petting krall and animal shows; pick up a map and schedule. Special programs, like a 'photo caravan', zip-lining, a chance to observe a cheetah whizz by while chasing a mechanical rabbit, and even sleepovers (yowza!) are available for additional payment and with a reservation.

The park's just north of Hwy 78, 5 miles east of I-15 from the Via Rancho Parkway exit. Parking is $9. Plan on 45 minutes transit by car from San Diego, except in rush hour when that figure can double. For bus information contact **North San Diego County Transit District** (☎619-233-3004, from North County 800-266-6883; www.gonctd.com).

See p270 for combination tickets including other regional attractions.

Other Attractions

Carlsbad has a number of attractions outside the village and Legoland areas. You pretty much need a car to reach them, and it's best to phone for directions since they can be hard to find.

Chopra Center　　　　MIND-BODY CENTER
(www.chopra.com) Slow down with alternative-health guru Deepak Chopra, who leads seminars on mind-body medicine, complemented by specialized spa treatments, at this center at La Costa Resort & Spa (p326).

Museum of Making Music　　　MUSEUM
(www.museumofmakingmusic.com; 5790 Armada Dr; adult/child & senior $7/5; ⏰10am-5pm Tue-Sun) Historical exhibits and listening stations of 450 instruments from the 1890s to the present.

K1 Speed　　　　INDOOR KARTING
(www.k1speed.com; 14-lap race $20; ⏰11am-7pm Sun, to 9pm Mon, to 10pm Tue-Thu, to 11pm Fri, 10am-11pm Sat) To pick up the pace, this place fills your need for speed with indoor karting (electric drag racing). They supply all the necessary equipment including helmet and 'head socks'; first-timers must purchase a special license, $5 extra. It's in an office park east of I-5; inquire about midweek discounts.

Crossings at Carlsbad　　　　GOLF
(www.thecrossingsatcarlsbad.com; 5800 the Crossings Dr) Carlsbad is an important center for golf; some major equipment manufacturers are based here including Titleist and Taylor Made. The Crossings at Carlsbad is a new 6850-yard municipal course, and the Park Hyatt Aviara and La Costa resorts both have landmark golf courses.

🛏 Sleeping

La Costa Resort & Spa　　LUXURY, GOLF, SPA **$$$**
(☎760-438-9111, 800-729-4772; www.lacosta.com; Costa Del Mar Rd; r from $300; P@🛜🏊🚼) A splurge-worthy luxury resort, La Costa offers a sprawling, whitewashed 800-room campus overlooking Batiquitos Lagoon. It's got two PGA golf courses, excellent children's programs including pools with multiple slides, nursery and educational programming, venues for grownups including the stunning spa and Chopra Center, lovely restaurants and a touch of Hollywood history. Check out their discounted packages.

West Inn & Suites　　　　HOTEL **$$$**
(☎760-208-4929, 866-375-4705; 4970 Av Encinas; r incl breakfast from $229; P@🛜🏊🚼🐾) About halfway between Legoland and Carlsbad Village, this independently run, 86-room inn caters in equal parts to business folk (note the computer and fitness centers) and vacationing families (note the sparkling pool and shuttle service to the beach and Legoland). You'd think you'd be paying a lot more as you enjoy your king-size bed, fresh orchids, Aveda bath products and 30in flat-screen TV.

Sheraton Carlsbad Resort & Spa HOTEL $$
(☎760-827-2400, 800-444-3515; www.sheraton carlsbad.com; 5480 Grand Pacific Dr; r from $189; 🅿@🛜🌊🏊🐾) Walk to Legoland from this 250-room hotel, a crisp, family-friendly neo-Craftsman facility opened in 2009. While kids play ping pong and foosball and splash in the giant pool, harried moms and dads can take turns in the hotel's spa. Parking is $12, but there's a free shuttle into Carlsbad Village and other nearby locations.

Park Hyatt Aviara Resort LUXURY, GOLF $$$
(☎760-603-6800; 877-599-5603; www.park aviara.hyatt.com; 7100 Four Seasons Point; r from $375; 🅿@🛜🌊🐾) From the marble bathrooms in sumptuous suites to the attendant bringing round water in the fitness center and the Camp Hyatt kids program, this tippy-top resort offers superb service and top-flight amenities, golf, tennis and more. The Argyle steakhouse is worth a trip by itself. Aviara looks out over Batiquitos Lagoon and offers discounted packages. Parking costs $30.

South Carlsbad State Park Campground CAMPGROUND $
(☎760-438-3143, reservations 800-444-7275; www.reserveamerica.com; RV/campsites $50/35; 🅿) Three miles south of town, this campground has over 200 tent and RV sites.

✕ Eating
State St just north of Carlsbad Village Dr is Carlsbad's most charming stretch, with a number of restaurants worth browsing.

Vigilucci's Cucina Italiana ITALIAN $$
(☎760-434-2500; 2943 State St; mains lunch $8-18, dinner $11-29; 🕙11am-10pm) There's white-tablecloth service and a lovely sidewalk terrace at this State St institution. For lunch try pastas or panini (the one with parma ham and portobello mushrooms is a fave), while dinner might be pappardelle with four kinds of mushrooms or linguine alla Luciana (with baby calamari, garlic and tomato sauce).

Le Passage FRENCH $$$
(☎760-729-7097; 2961 State St; mains lunch $8-16, dinner $16-30; 🕙11am-3pm Tue-Fri, noon-3pm Sat, dinner from 5pm Tue-Sat) Escape from the beach fray at this country French bistro. There's a *rustique* interior and cozy back patio on which to enjoy lavender-roasted chicken or steak au poivre with pomme frites.

French Pastry Cafe BAKERY, CAFE $
(☎760-729-2241; 1005 Carlsbad Village Dr; mains $6; 🕙7am-6pm) Its location may be in a drab-looking shopping center just off I-5, but it's the real deal for croissants and brioches baked daily and kick-start espresso, plus omelettes, salads and sandwiches until 2:30pm. Drop in on your way to Legoland.

For a luxury experience, also check out the restaurants at La Costa Resort & Spa and Park Hyatt Aviara. At the other end of the scale are the brew pub **Pizza Port** (p295), and the local branch of **Las Olas** (p323).

🔒 Shopping
Carlsbad Premium Outlets OUTLET SHOPPING
(www.premiumoutlets.com; Paseo del Norte; 🕙10am-8pm) Big-name retailers, such as Calvin Klein and Coach, have off-price boutiques among the 90 shops here. Take I-5 to Palomar Airport Rd; go east to Paseo del Norte and turn north.

Farenheit 451 BOOKSHOP
(325 Carlsbad Village Dr) Back in town, this is an honest-to-goodness old style bookshop, selling mainly used books, including rare and first editions in plastic sleeves. They even have a no-cell-phone policy; bless their hearts.

ℹ Information
Carlsbad Visitors center (☎760-434-6093;
www.visitcarlsbad.com; 400 Carlsbad Village Dr) Housed in the original 1887 Santa Fe train depot.

Oceanside
POP 175,000

The largest North County town, Oceanside is home to many who work at giant Camp Pendleton Marine Base just to the north. The huge military presence mixes with an attractive natural setting, surf shops and head shops in its downtown, giving way to a condo-lined oceanfront. Perhaps due to its more transient populace, Oceanside feels more functional than its coastal neighbors.

⦿ Sights & Activities
Oceanside Pier PIER
This wooden pier extends more than 1900ft out to sea. Bait-and-tackle shops rent poles to the many anglers who line its wooden fences (hour/day $5/15). Two major surf competitions – the West Coast Pro-Am and

the National Scholastic Surf Association (NSSA) – take place near the pier each June.

California Surf Museum
MUSEUM
(www.surfmuseum.org; 312 Pier View Way; adult/student/child $3/1/free, Thu free; ⏲10am-4pm Fri-Wed, to 8pm Thu) See a history of surf contests at this wonderful museum relocated into tubular new digs in 2009. Exhibits change annually along different themes (eg women of surfing) and include a timeline of surfing history, surf-themed art, and a radical collection of boards.

Museum of Art
MUSEUM
(www.oma-online.org; 312 Pier View Way; adult/senior/student $8/5/3; ⏲10am-4pm Tue-Sat, 1-4pm Sun) This museum also underwent a recent revamp and it now stands at an impressive 16,000 sq ft. There are about 10 rotating exhibits a year, with an emphasis on SoCal artists (especially from the San Diego region) and local cultures.

Mission San Luis Rey de Francia
MISSION
(1798; www.sanluisrey.org; 4050 Mission Ave, Hwy 76; adult/child/senior $5/4/6; ⏲10am-4pm) About 4.5 miles inland from central Oceanside, this was the largest California mission and the most successful in recruiting Native American converts. At one point some 3000 neophytes lived and worked here. After the Mexican government secularized the missions, San Luis fell into ruin; the adobe walls of the church, from 1811, are the only original parts left. Inside are displays on work and life in the mission, with some original religious art and artifacts. The mission is 4.5 miles inland.

Historic buildings
HISTORY
Little remains from the 1880s, when the new Santa Fe coastal railway came through Oceanside, but a few buildings designed by Irving Gill and Julia Morgan still stand. The Welcome Center has a pamphlet describing a self-guided history walk.

Helgren's
BOAT CHARTERS
(www.helgrensportfishing.com; 315 Harbor Dr S; P) At the northern end of the waterfront, the extensive Oceanside Harbor provides slips for hundreds of boats. This outfit leads a variety of charter trips for sportfishing (from $48 per half-day) and whale-watching (adult/child $25/15).

Asylum Surf
SURF HIRE
(www.asylumboardshop.com; 310 Mission Ave; surfboards 2hr/full day $10/20, wet suits $5/10) Surfers can rent equipment here.

Surfcamps USA
SURF CAMPS
(www.surfcampsusa.com; ♿) Surfers can rent equipment and purchase gear and surf clothing at this central shop.

🛏 Sleeping & Eating

Wyndham Oceanside Pier Resort
RESORT HOTEL $$$
(☎800-989-1848; www.wyndham.com; 333 N Meyers St; r $199-319; P@🛜🏊♿) This beach- and pierside time-share rents out rooms when available. They're mostly two-bedroom suites sleeping up to six people with full kitchen and laundry facilities, plus water-view pool deck, fitness center and activities for the kids.

101 Café
DINER $
(☎760-722-5220; 631 S Coast Hwy; most mains $6-10; ⏲7am-midnight; P♿) This tiny 1928 streamline moderne diner serves the classics: omelets, burgers etc. If you're lucky, you'll catch the owner and can quiz him about local history.

333 Pacific
SEAFOOD, STEAK $$$
(☎760-433-3333; 333 N Pacific St; mains lunch $13-20; dinner $21-43; ⏲lunch Tue-Sun, dinner nightly) Stare right at the pier from this new spot downstairs at the Wyndham, but also take time to admire the slick decor inside. Lunch is a better deal (with arguably more adventurous fare – kobe or ahi sliders, chimichurri fish tacos, crab-shrimp cheddar melt) than the fine steaks and seafood for dinner.

Harbor Fish & Chips
SEAFOOD $
(☎760-722-4977; 276 Harbor Dr S; mains $6-14; ⏲11am-9pm Sun-Thu, to 10pm Fri & Sat; P♿) Nuthin' fancy about this harborside chippie from the '60s, but when the fish is fried to a deep crackle and you eat it at a picnic table while classic pop tunes play on the radio, you still feel pretty good. There's a large local following and taxidermied catches on the walls.

Beach Break Café
CASUAL $
(☎760-439-6355; 1902 S Coast Hwy; mains $6-10; ⏲7am-2pm; P♿) Fuel up before surfing on omelets, scrambles and pancakes, or afterwards on sandwiches, tacos and salads at this surfers' diner on the east side of the road in a small shopping center.

Ruby's Diner
DINER $
(☎760-433-7829; 1 Oceanside Pier; mains $8-14; ⏲7am-9pm Sun-Thu, to 10pm Fri & Sat; ♿) This mid-priced '50s-style diner has good burg-

ers and milkshakes, big breakfasts and a full bar. Yes, it's a chain, but it's right at the end of the pier.

Kealani's HAWAIIAN **$**
(☎760-722-5642; 207 N Coast Hwy; mains $4-8; ⊙11am-8pm Mon, Tue & Thu-Sat, to 6pm Wed; ⛟) Traditional Hawaiian plate lunches, such as kalua pig, teriyaki chicken and grilled mahimahi are the thing in this cheery storefront with booths like little grass shacks.

ⓘ Information

California Welcome Center (☎760-721-1101, 800-350-7873; www.oceansidechamber.com, www.californiawelcomecenter.org; 928 N Coast Hwy; ⊙9am-5pm) Stop in at this center with helpful staff to get coupons for local attractions, as well as maps and information for the San Diego area and the entire state.

ⓘ Getting There & Away

Oceanside Transit Center (235 S Tremont St) Amtrak, Greyhound, the *Coaster* and MTS buses all stop here.

NORTH OF SAN DIEGO COUNTRY

Temecula

Temecula has become a popular short-break destination for its Old West Americana main street, nearly two dozen wineries, and California's largest casino, Pechanga.

Temecula means 'Place of the Sun' in the language of the native Luiseño people, who were present when Fr Fermin Lasuen became the first Spanish missionary to visit in 1797. In the 1820s the area became a ranching outpost for the Mission San Luis Rey, in present-day Oceanside. Later, Temecula became a stop on the Butterfield stagecoach line (1858–61) and the California Southern railroad.

But it's Temecula's late-20th-century growth that's been most astonishing, from 2700 people in 1970 – the city didn't get its first traffic light until 1984 – to some 91,000 residents today. Between Old Town and the wineries is a buffer zone of off-putting suburban sprawl. Ignore that and you'll do fine.

Temecula is in the southeast corner of Riverside County, near San Diego and Orange Counties. The five-block Old Town

Front St, heart of Old Town Temecula, is a minute's drive from the I-15 Freeway. From here, Rancho California Rd is the main route into wine country.

⊙ Sights & Activities

Front St HISTORIC DISTRICT
Old Town Front St's turn of-the-last-century storefronts make for an attractive stroll – pick up the *Historic Old Town Temecula* leaflet with building descriptions. En route, sample local products at shops like **Temecula Olive Oil Company** (www.temeculaoliveoil.com; 28653 Old Town Front St) and **Temecula House of Jerky** (28665 Old Town Front St). The latter offers ostrich, buffalo, venison and more traditional beasties. Hundreds of **antique dealers** populate the neighborhood, most agglomerated into large antique halls.

Wine Country
Wine tasting is big in the rolling hills east of Old Town, about 10 minutes' drive away. The newness of the wineries and the preponderance of large gift shops make them less quaint than elsewhere in California, but you can find award-winning and creative wines.

Wilson Creek WINERY
(www.wilsoncreekwinery.com; 35960 Rancho California Rd; tasting $12; ⊙10am-5pm) This place makes almond champagne (infused with almond oil in the fermentation process) and a chocolate-infused port.

Longshadow Ranch WINERY
(www.longshadowranchwinery.com; 39847 Calle Contento; tasting $10; ⊙noon-5pm Mon-Fri, 10am-5pm Sat & Sun; ⛟) A nice stop if you've got children in tow; the kids can look at Clydesdales and goats while mommy and daddy sip.

Leonesse Cellars WINERY
(www.leonessecellars.com; 38311 De Portola Rd; tasting $12; ⊙11am-5pm) Further afield, this place offers award-winning viognier and melange des reves, plus sweeping views from its sort-of-Teutonic tower.

Grapeline Temecula TRANSPORTATION
(☎888-894-6379; www.gogrape.com) To leave the driving to someone else, this outfit offers day-long wine shuttles among the vineyards by minivan with pickup at many of the area's lodgings. Rates start at $52 per person; tastings (discount coupons available) and lunch are extra.

California Dreamin' BALLOONING
(☎800-373-3359; www.californiadreamin.com; per person from $133) To see the region from the air, contact this outfit which operates hot-air balloon rides.

🛏 Sleeping

Palomar Inn Hotel HISTORIC $
(☎951-676-6503; www.palomarinntemecula. com; 28522 Old Town Front St; r weekday/weekend from $46/70; P🖥) This 1927 10-room hostelry is Old Town's cheapest, and it feels like a rooming house in the Old West. Eight of the rooms have shared bathroom. Still, the price is right and the location is primo, upstairs from Temecula House of Wine.

Loma Vista B&B B&B $$
(☎951-676-7047, 877-676-7047; www.loma vistabb.com; 33350 La Serena Way; r incl breakfast $130-220; P) Welcoming hilltop B&B with 10 rooms (four with vineyard-view balconies) and a hot tub. Rooms are individually furnished from country to art deco styles. Known for delicious full breakfasts.

South Coast Winery RESORT $$$
(☎951-587-9463; www.wineresort.com; 34843 Rancho California Rd; r from $209; P🖥🖥) A very Temecula way to stay – 76 villa rooms dot the edge of the vineyards, around a spa and a well-maintained fitness facility. Your room key comes with a wine glossary and rates include a bottle of wine and tastings. Parking is $15.

🍴 Eating & Drinking

Vineyard Rose CALIFORNIAN, WINE MENU $$$
(☎951-587-9463; 34843 Rancho California Rd; lunch mains $10-20, dinner mains $17-40; ⊙7am-10:45am & 11:30am-3pm Mon-Fri, 7am-3:30pm Sat & Sun, plus 5:30-9pm Sun-Thu, to 10pm Fri & Sat; P) South Coast Winery's gracious main restaurant has a Craftsman-style barn feel and vineyard views from the balcony. Salads and pizzas are popular at lunch, or lobster ravioli and rib-eye at dinner. At breakfast, the bananas Foster pancake with vanilla-bean sauce may make your head spin.

Swing Inn Cafe DINER $
(☎951-676-2321; 28676 Old Town Front St; mains $5-14; ⊙5am-9pm; 🖥) A proud local institution since 1927, with red leatherette seating and windows to watch the world go by. The Swing Inn serves three square meals, but everyone goes for breakfast (to $10.50) – luckily it's served all day. The biscuits and gravy are renowned.

Mad Madeline's Grill HAMBURGER, BARBECUE $
(☎951-669-3776; 28495 Old Town Front St; mains $8-13; ⊙11am-5pm Mon-Thu, to 9pm Fri & Sat, to 7pm Sun; P🖥) Award-winning burgers (served about 20 ways) are the thing in this cheerful red-and-white wooden roadhouse in the center of Old Town, plus onion rings worth breaking your diet for. On Fridays nights, look for smoked baby-back ribs too.

Bank of Mexican Food MEXICAN $
(☎951-676-6160; 28645 Old Town Front St; mains $7-13; ⊙11am-9pm Mon-Thu, to midnight Fri, 8am-10am Sat & Sun; 🖥) In this handsome former bank (c 1913), try mahi tacos, huevos rancheros or anything with the righteous Mexican rice. A new patio bar stays open until late.

☆ Entertainment

Many wineries offer entertainment, from guitar soloists to chamber concerts. Check at the visitors center or www.temeculacvb. com for upcoming events.

Pechanga Resort & Casino CASINO
(www.pechanga.com; 45000 Pechanga Pkwy) This Native American–owned casino-hotel books stand-up acts in its comedy club, and the 1200-seat Pechanga Theater hosts the likes of the Beach Boys and Kathy Griffin.

ℹ Information

Visitors center (☎951-491-6085, 888-363-2852; www.temeculacvb.com; 26798 Ynez Ct; ⊙9am-5pm Mon-Fri) Temecula Valley Convention & Visitors Bureau operates this cheery center.

ℹ Getting There & Away

Temecula is just off the I-15 freeway, which begins in San Diego. Either of the Rancho California Rd or Rte 79 exits will take you to Old Town Front St. Allow 45 minutes from San Diego, 55 from Anaheim, 75 from Palm Springs or 80 from LA.

Greyhound stop (☎951-676-9768; 28464 Old Town Front St) Sells tickets for twice-daily buses heading to San Diego (from $20.50).

Palm Springs & the Deserts

Includes »

Best Places to Eat

» Trio (p344)
» Palm Korea (p347)
» Crossroads Café (p356)
» Wang's in the Desert (p345)
» Sage (p366)

Best Places to Stay

» Orbit In (p343)
» Ace Hotel & Swim Club (p342)
» Parker Palm Springs (p342)
» El Morocco Inn & Spa (p343)
» La Quinta Resort & Club (p344)

Why Go?

The desert is a land of contradictions: vast yet intimate, remote yet sophisticated, searing yet restorative. At first glance it may appear barren and boring, but look closer and you'll notice harrowing beauty: weathered peaks, subliminally erotic sand dunes, purple-tinged mountains, groves of cacti, tiny wildflowers pushing up from caramel-colored soil for their brief lives, and uncountable stars.

Palm Springs and the Coachella Valley, which stretches to the southeast, are the desert's chief draw for poolside lounging, golf, tennis and the 'it' factor. Nearby, Joshua Tree National Park is a favorite of hikers and rock climbers. Beyond the nearly 2-mile-high San Jacinto Mountains, gigantic Anza-Borrego Desert State Park thrills with wide-open spaces and desolate hills. Julian, to its southwest toward San Diego, was the base of Southern California's gold rush.

Spend some time here, and you too may understand why so many find this land so magical, chic and irresistible.

When to Go
Palm Springs

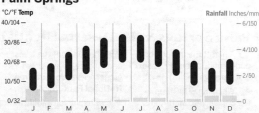

| Dec-Apr Moderate temperatures lure in 'snowbirds' and LA weekend trippers. | May–mid-Jun, mid-Sep–Nov Crowds thin out as temperatures arc during shoulder season. | Jun-Sep Some inns and restaurants close in summer's heat; many of the rest offer great deals. |

PALM SPRINGS & COACHELLA VALLEY

POP 47, 806

The Rat Pack is back, baby, or at least its hangout is. In the 1950s and '60s, Palm Springs, some 100 miles east of LA, was the swinging getaway of Sinatra, Elvis, Liberace and dozens of other stars, partying the night away in futuristic homes built just for them. Once the Rat Pack packed it in, the 300-sq-mile Coachella (co-*chell*-a) Valley gave over to retirees in golf clothing and grew, well, *not* hip. That was until the mid-

PALM SPRINGS & THE DESERTS PALM SPRINGS & COACHELLA VALLEY

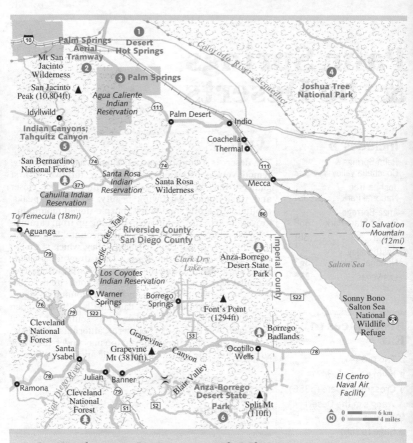

Palm Springs & the Deserts Highlights

❶ A nighttime mineral bath under infinite stars in **Desert Hot Springs** (p343)

❷ Whisking 6000ft up the San Jacinto Mountains aboard the **Palm Springs Aerial Tramway** (p335)

❸ Marveling at Palm Springs Modernist masterpieces (p338)

❹ Checking out the trees and zipping up and down giant rocks at **Joshua Tree National Park** (p351)

❺ Watching for wildlife in **Indian Canyons** (p339) or **Tahquitz Canyon** (p339)

❻ Gazing at the vast expanse of desert that unfurls below you from

Font's Point at **Anza-Borrego Desert State Park** (p358)

❼ Testing your depth perception with a mandatory photo shoot at the salt flats in **Badwater** (p363).

❽ Partying with Elvis, Cirque Du Soleil style, at the **Aria** (p365), one of several captivating Cirque shows in Las Vegas.

1990s, when a new generation latched onto the city's retro-chic charms: kidney-shaped pools, steel-and-glass bungalows, boutique hotels with vintage decor, and piano bars serving perfect martinis. In today's Palm Springs, retirees mix amiably with hipsters and a significant gay and lesbian contingent.

Around Palm Springs, hike palm-studded canyons or ski through silky snow (or both in the same day), play golf, shop at massive malls or high-toned boutiques, explore museums, sample a date milkshake, tour a windmill or straddle a fault line.

'Down Valley,' as the Coachella Valley southeast of Palm Springs is called, boasts world-class golf resorts, ritzy shopping and expensive retirement homes in the cities of Rancho Mirage, Palm Desert, Indian Wells and La Quinta. Indio, America's date capital, sits at the valley's southern end. North of town, Desert Hot Springs is emerging from a slump as a down-and-outpost thanks to tiny, design-y hotels atop those namesake springs.

The region is part of what locals call the Inland Empire, comprising Riverside County to the south and San Bernardino County to the north. The latter is the nation's largest county, at 20,105 sq miles (52,073 sq km).

History

For more than a thousand years, Cahuilla (ka-*wee*-ya) tribespeople occupied the canyons on the southwest edge of the Coachella Valley, where permanent streams flowed from the San Jacinto Mountains. Early Spanish explorers called the hot springs where the city of Palm Springs now stands Agua Caliente (hot water), a term later used to refer to the local band of Cahuillas.

In 1876 the federal government divided the valley into a checkerboard pattern. The Southern Pacific Railroad received odd-numbered sections and the even-numbered sections were given to the Agua Caliente as their reservation. But boundaries were not established until the 1940s and by then much of the Native American land had been built on. (Tribes today are quite wealthy, though, thanks largely to gaming casinos.)

Indio began as a railway-construction camp and its artesian water was tapped to irrigate crops. Date palms were imported in 1890 and have become a major crop in the valley, along with citrus fruits and table grapes.

In the 1920s Palm Springs became a winter playground for Hollywood celebrities, and so it stayed until the 1960s. But inexpensive real estate in Down Valley towns such as Palm Desert and Rancho Mirage drew golf-club-swinging retirees, and air travel meant that stars could go elsewhere. By the 1980s a Palm Springs vacation was an afterthought.

The key to its renaissance has been architecture. In recent decades, the world has rediscovered the retro-chic mid-century modern style innovated in Palm Springs (see p338), new construction has taken place, and visitors of all stripes have flocked back.

◉ Sights
PALM SPRINGS
Palm Springs Art Museum   MUSEUM
(Map p336; www.psmuseum.org; 101 N Museum Dr; adult/student/senior/child $12.50/5/10.50/ free, 4-8pm Thu free; ⊙10am-5pm Tue, Wed & Fri-Sun, noon-8pm Thu) This museum has a worthy modern-art collection (including an impressive piece by Seattle glass-artist Dale Chihuly), desert and contemporary American paintings and pre-Columbian and Native American art. Temporary exhibits – including painting, glass, photography and design – include some big names like Richard Avedon, John Baldessari and Palm Springs' own Donald Wexler. The 433-seat Annenberg Theater presents frequent musical performances, films and lectures.

Palm Springs Air Museum   MILITARY MUSEUM
(www.air-museum.org; 745 N Gene Autry Trail; adult/child/senior & student 13-17yr/$12/5/10, senior Sat $12; ⊙10am-5pm) Adjacent to the Palm Springs International Airport, the Air Museum has an exceptional collection of WWII aircraft, photos and flight memorabilia, as well as a large theater where documentaries are shown regularly for no additional charge.

Moorten Botanical Gardens   GARDEN
(Map p336; ☑760-327-6555; www.moorten garden.com; 1701 S Palm Canyon Dr; adult/child $4/2; ⊙9am-4pm Mon, Tue & Thu-Sat, 10am-4pm Sun, call ahead for summer closures) Tahquitz too taxing? The Living Desert too far? This plant collection packs some 3000 specimens of cacti, succulents and other desert flora into a small lot south of town. Founded in 1938, the garden became the life's passion of Slim Moorten, one of the original Keystone Cops, and his wife Patricia; today their son Clark is an expert on low-water vegetation.

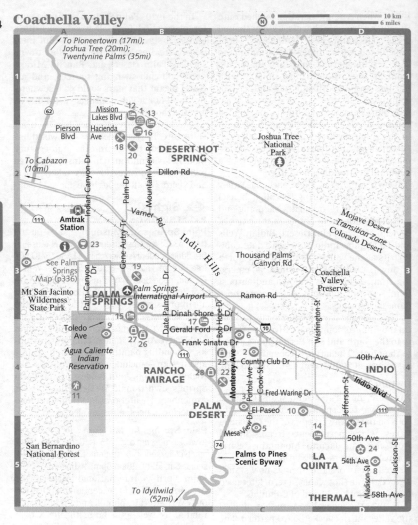

PALM SPRINGS & THE DESERTS PALM SPRINGS & COACHELLA VALLEY

Knott's Soak City USA WATER PARK
(Map p334; ☎760-327-0499; www.knotts.com;
1500 S Gene Autry Trail; adult/child $31/20;
⊗hours vary, check website or phone; ℗) On a
hot day the kids will go nuts for this water
park, with activities including Pacific Spin
'river rafting,' slides, tube rides and wave
pools. Parking is $10.

Village Green Heritage Center HISTORY
(Map p336; 221 S Palm Canyon Dr) This grassy
little square in the heart of downtown has
some 'heritage' attractions, though most
people use it as a place to sit and eat ice
cream and fudge, which you can buy at the

nearby sweets store. The true historic sites
surrounding the square include the **Agua
Caliente Cultural Museum** (Map p336; www.
accmuseum.org; admission free; ⊗10am-5pm
Wed-Sat, noon-5pm Sun), which has pictures
of and artifacts from the tribe's history;
Ruddy's General Store (Map p336; admission
$1), a reproduction of a 1930s general store;
and the 1884 **McCallum Adobe** (Map p336;
admission $1), said to be the oldest building
in Palm Springs. Admission hours vary; for
more information, call the **Palm Springs
Historical Society** (☎760-323-8297; www.
palmspringshistoricalsociety.org).

AROUND PALM SPRINGS

Living Desert   ZOO

(Map p334; ☑760-346-5694; www.livingdesert
.org; 47900 Portola Ave, Palm Desert; adult/
child Oct-May $12.50/7.50, Jun-Sep $12.75/7.75;
⊙9am-5pm Oct-May, 8am-1:30pm Jun-Sep) This
excellent desert-species zoo and botanical
gardens presents a wide variety of desert
plants and animals from North America
(including bighorn sheep, mountain lions
and birds of prey) and Africa (gazelles, oryx
and more) plus exhibits on desert geology
and Native American culture. Some exhibits, including the Fanciful Flyers display of
butterflies and hummingbirds, open only
in high season (October to April). Plan for
1½ to 3½ hours to explore the Living Desert, and check the website for additional
nighttime and seasonal activities.

Cabot's Pueblo Museum   MUSEUM

(Mapp334;☑760-329-7610;www.cabotsmuseum.
org; 67-616 E Desert View Ave, Desert Hot Springs;
adult/child $10/8; ⊙9am-4pm Oct-Apr, to 1pm
May-Sep, closed Mon all year) Inside a rambling
1913 adobe house built by Cabot Yerxa, a
wealthy East Coaster of the legendary Boston Cabot clan who traded high society for
the solitude of the desert, this quirky museum displays Native American basketry
and pottery, as well as a photo collection

from Cabot's turn-of-the-century travels to
Alaska. It's also a great story told at an idiosyncratic venue. Although the grounds are
open for free, admission to the house is by
45-minute tour only.

🏃 Activities

TOP CHOICE Palm Springs Aerial Tramway

HIKING, SNOW ACTIVITIES

(Map p334; ☑888-515-8726, 760-325-1391; www.
pstramway.com; 1 Tram Way; round-trip adult/
child/senior $23.25/16.25/21.15, after 3pm adult/
child $20.25/13.25; ⊙10am-9:45pm Mon-Fri, 8am-
9:45pm Sat & Sun) A highlight of Palm Springs,
this cable car rotates ever so slightly as it
climbs nearly 6000 vertical feet, from the
desert floor up the San Jacinto Mountains,
in about 10 minutes. You ascend through
visibly different vegetation zones, from the
Valley Station (2643ft) to the Mountain
Station (8516ft). It's 30°F to 40°F cooler as
you step out into pine forest at the top, so
bring some warm clothing – the trip up is
said to be the equivalent (in temperature)
of driving from Mexico to Canada.

The Mountain Station at the top of the
tramway has an observation area and a
theater showing documentaries on the
tramway and the park, plus a lounge and
restaurants.

Palm Springs

0 — 800 m
0 — 0.4 miles

4 Toucans (0.25mi)

21

W Vista Chino

E Camino Monte Vista **3**

N Palm Canyon Dr

N Av Caballeros

N Sunrise Way

Tachevah Dr

51

N Indian Canyon Dr

9

Tamarisk Rd

35
50
34
26 **25** Granvia Valmonte
1 **47**
40 **16**

Alejo Rd

38
49

45

Amado Rd

Skyline Trail

Palm Springs Art Museum

N Museum Dr

Andreas Rd
6

Palm Springs City Hall(0.6mi)

Tahquitz Canyon Way

32

13 **15** **30** **36** **29** **44**
20 **48** **39**
Arenas Rd
S Tahquitz Dr
S Patencio Rd
46 **28** **24**
43
7 **37**
W Baristo Rd

S Cahuilla Rd
S Indian Canyon Dr
Calle Encilia
S Av Caballeros

Baristo Rd

33

17
23 **42**
2

Belardo Rd

Ramon Rd

S Palm Canyon Dr

18
Grenfall Rd
19

S Sunrise Way

Sunny Dunes Dr

22

San Lorenzo Rd

Mesquite Ave

8

27

5
14 **11**

Jensen's Finest Foods (0.25mi)

E Palm Canyon Dr

12 **10** **41**

31

S Palm Canyon Dr

PALM SPRINGS & COACHELLA VALLEY ACTIVITIES

Take time (a day or two if you're a back-country enthusiast) at the top to enjoy the **Mt San Jacinto Wilderness State Park.** There are 54 miles of trails, including a nontechnical route up to the San Jacinto peak (10,834ft), for hiking in summer, and snowshoeing and cross-country skiing in winter. There are also several basic camp-grounds ($5 per person). Anyone heading into the backcountry (even for a few hours) must register for a wilderness permit at the ranger station just outside the Moun-tain Station; for information and advance permits, contact the **state park rangers**

(☎951-659-2607). Pick up maps, books and gifts at the State Park Visitor Informa-tion Center at the Mountain Station. At the nearby Adventure Center you can rent snowshoes ($18 per day), boots ($8 per day) and cross-country skis ($21 per day). Staff members are knowledgeable about snow conditions and backcountry routes.

A **Ride 'n' Dine combination ticket** (adult/child $36/23.50) includes a simple din-ner (think roast beef or turkey plus sides) at the **Pines Cafe** in the Mountain Station, from 3pm. The restaurant, **Peaks** (☎760-325-4537; mains lunch $9-13, dinner $17-34;

PALM SPRINGS MODERN

Palm Springs has always been a party town. When snowbirds from Minneapolis, Pittsburgh or LA wanted a vacation home, they wanted it flashy. A generation of architects – William F Cody, Albert Frey, Richard Neutra, Donald Wexler, E Stewart Williams, the Alexander brothers and others – used the city as their testing ground for their innovative, exuberant forms and techniques that are now commonplace: long overhangs and flying roofs to protect from the sun, rail-thin supports, clerestory windows and easy transitions between indoors and out.

Sinatra, Elvis, Liberace and their contemporaries strove to outdo each other with their homes, while enjoying long games of tennis on warm mornings before relaxing over cocktails by the pool. At one point in the 1950s, every real-estate ad in the Yellow Pages featured an illustration of a modernist building.

Starting after WWII and continuing through the 1960s, golf took over from tennis in prominence, and with little remaining real estate in Palm Springs, new construction moved Down Valley. The result: Palm Springs real estate withered.

But in the mid-1990s fashion photographers began to rediscover these architectural treasures, which led to a second boom, this time in restoration. If you're not here during Modernism Week (p341), take a guided or self-guided tour (p340) for an in-depth look, or here are some easily visible public buildings to get you started:

Tramway Gas Station – now Palm Springs' visitors center (p350)

Del Marcos Hotel (p343)

Kaufmann House (Map p336; 470 W Vista Chino)

Chase Bank (Map p336; 499 S Palm Canyon Dr)

Palm Springs City Hall (off Map p336; 2300 E Tahquitz Canyon Way)

⊙lunch & dinner), features a more upscale meat-and-seafood menu, local produce and brilliant views. Reservations are recommended. If you choose to dine up here, be sure to allow time for a leisurely look around at the top.

Allow at least three hours to park, ride the tram and take a leisurely stroll once at the top. It's also possible to hike to the mountain via the **Skyline Trail** (Map p336), which starts close to the Palm Springs Art Museum. This extremely challenging hike is recommended only for the very fit who have a whole day to spend; depart no later than 7am. The reward, besides some stellar views and multiple climatic zones, is a discounted ride back down (adult/child $12/8).

Cycling

Palm Springs and the valley have an excellent network of bike paths that are great for getting around. If your hotel doesn't have loaner bikes, rent bikes for city use at **Bike Palm Springs** (Map p336; ☑760-832-8912; www.bikepsrentals.com; 625 N Palm Canyon Dr, Palm Springs; half-day/full day/week from $15/25/100). **Fun Seekers** (Map p334; ☑760-340-3861; www.4funseekers.com; 73865 Hwy 111, Palm Desert; hr/day/week from $8/30/75) rents and sells bikes for city and mountain use, plus mopeds and even Segways, and will deliver and pick up equipment (for a fee). Rates at both shops depend on type of bike.

Golf

The Coachella Valley boasts more than 100 public, semiprivate, private and resort golf courses. Top resorts include **Marriott's Shadow Ridge** (Map p334; ☑760-674-2700; www.golfshadowridge.com) and **Desert Willow** (Map p334; ☑760-346-7060; www.desertwillow.com), both in Palm Desert, and **SilverRock** (Map p334; ☑888-600-7272; www.silverrock.com) and **La Quinta** (Map p334; ☑760-564-4111; www.laquintaresort.com/golf), both in La Quinta. Greens fees run from $25 to $250 or more, depending on the course, season and day of the week; inquire directly or through your hotel. Alternatively, **Stand-by Golf** (☑760-321-2665; www.standbygolf.com) can book tee times at a discount for play at some 40 courses.

Golf spectators can check with tourist offices for information on upcoming large-purse big-name tournaments including the Bob Hope Classic.

Hiking

The best way to appreciate the subtlety of the desert is on foot, as long as you protect yourself from the heat (see p355).

TOP CHOICE **Tahquitz Canyon** HIKING
(Mapp336; ☑760-416-7044; www.tahquitz canyon.com; 500 W Mesquite Ave; adult/child $12.50/6; ⊙7:30am-5pm daily Oct-Jun, Fri-Sun Jul-Sep) Opened in 1999 after having been closed for 30 years, Tahquitz Canyon is a historic and sacred centerpiece for the Agua Caliente people. It was traditionally home to Agua Caliente ancestors, but was taken over by teenage squatters in the 1960s. Eventually the canyon became a point of contention between the Agua Caliente, local law-enforcement agencies and squatters who claimed the right to live in its alcoves and caves. A clean-up rid the canyon of inhabitants, but it took years to haul trash, erase graffiti and get the area back to its natural state. Rangers lead informative 2-mile, 2½-hour hikes at 8am, 10am, noon and 2pm daily (limited tours in summer); call for reservations. Self-guided hiking is also available. The visitors center at the canyon entrance shows a video about the legend of Tahquitz, a shaman of the Cahuilla people. There are also exhibits about the canyon and a great view over the valley.

Indian Canyons HIKING
(Map p334; www.indian-canyons.com; adult/child $8/4; ⊙8am-5pm daily Oct-Jun, Fri-Sun Jul-Sep) Streams flowing from the San Jacinto Mountains sustain a rich variety of plants in the canyons around Palm Springs. The canyons were home to Native American communities for hundreds of years and are now part of the Agua Caliente Indian Reservation. It's a delight to hike through these canyon oases, shaded by fan palms and surrounded by towering cliffs. From downtown, head south on Palm Canyon Dr (continue straight when the main road turns east) for about 2 miles to the reservation entrance. From here, it's 3 miles up to the Trading Post, which sells hats, maps, water and knickknacks. Trail posts at the entrance to each canyon can provide you with maps and hiking info, or inquire about 1.5-hour ranger-led hikes. Closest to the entrance gate of the reservation is **Andreas Canyon**, where there's a pleasant picnic area. Nearby are imposing rock formations where you

---

EARTH, WIND & WATER

Spend a day splashing in the pool, golfing on a lush green fairway or shopping in air-conditioned comfort, and you might wonder...where exactly does the Coachella Valley get all these resources? Renewable energy is big business out here and getting bigger.

More than 2000 wind turbines, some more than 300ft (91m) tall, line the San Gorgonio Pass on the drive into Palm Springs from LA. The tourist board says that it's one of the windiest places in the world, and according to the American Wind Energy Association, these turbine collectively generate over 500 megawatts annually for California's power grid, enough to power some 375,000 homes. As of 2009, the US government's Energy Information Administration reported that California produced about 2.67 percent of its power needs from wind, about 50% more than the national average.

The big news these days, though, is giant solar arrays involving hundreds of thousands of mirrors strategically placed on the desert floor. As of late 2010, regulators had approved six of these plants in SoCal, including a 7000-acre, one-gigawatt plant in Blythe, Riverside County, and the 3600-acre Ivanpah plant near the California–Nevada border (visible from I-15 toward Las Vegas). Southeast of the Coachella Valley, the area around the Salton Sea and south toward the Mexican border, is a hotbed, so to speak, of geothermal energy.

Most of the valley's water, meanwhile, comes from a giant aquifer below ground (there's a reason it's called Palm Springs). Real-estate developers and golf-course operators say that the water they pump drains right back into the aquifer, ensuring a supply for years to come: partially true. Much of the water evaporates, and some of the water that does reach the aquifer picks up salts as it percolates through the ground. So much water is being taken out of the ground that the Coachella Valley is sinking about an inch per year. Locals have realized that they can't turn the desert into a rainforest, and water conservation is always on people's minds. Still, don't expect to see the profitable golf courses turn to sand anytime soon.

DINO-MIGHT

You may do two double takes in Cabazon, a 17-mile drive west of Palm Springs: the first when you see a giant T-Rex and Apatosaurus north of the I-10 freeway and the second when you see how they're being pitched. Claude K Bell, a sculptor for Knott's Berry Farm in Orange County, spent 1964 to 1975 creating these concrete behemoths (55ft and 45ft tall, respectively). They've since been joined by a park of dozens of smaller robotic dinos and other attractions for kids like 'panning' for 'gems.' The **World's Biggest Dinosaurs** (☎951-922-0076; www.worldsbiggestdinosaurs.com; 50770 Seminole Dr, Cabazon; adult/child $7/6; ☺10am-6pm, T-Rex hr vary) remained a temple of tourist kitsch until 2005, when they were purchased by a group of creation scientists, who contend that God created the original dinosaurs in one day, along with the other animals. In the gift shop in the Bronto belly, alongside the sort of dino-swag you might find at other science museums, you can read about alleged hoaxes and fallacies of Darwinism and the theory of evolution, alongside biblical quotes which management says prove that dinosaurs and humans existed at the same time.

can find Native American mortar holes, used for grinding seeds, and some rock art. The trail up the canyon is an easy walk. A 20-minute walk south from Andreas Canyon is **Murray Canyon**. It has good birdwatching, and bighorn sheep might be seen on the slopes above the canyon. Following the winding access road to the end brings you to the 15-mile-long **Palm Canyon**, the most extensive of the canyons, with good trails and a store selling snacks and souvenirs. In the morning look for animal tracks in the sandy patches.

Desert Safari　　　　　　　　HIKING
(☎760-861-6292; www.palmspringshiking.com) Has been offering educational guided hiking trips locally and in Joshua Tree National Park for over two decades. It operates fewer trips during summer.

Horseback Riding

Smoke Tree Stables　　　HORSEBACK RIDING
(Map p334; ☎760-327-1372; www.smoketree stables.com; 2500 Toledo Ave; 1/2hr guided rides from $50/90; ☺8am-5pm mid-Sep–mid-Jun, 8am-noon mid-Jun–mid-Sep, summer closures vary) Arranges trail rides, from one-hour group outings to all-day treks with experienced guides. Private guides can also be arranged.

🐾 Tours
Guided Tours

TOP CHOICE **Palm Springs Modern Tours**
　　　　　　　　　　　　　ARCHITECTURE
(☎760-318-6118; psmoderntours@aol.com; tours $75) Three-hour van tours provide detailed descriptions of architecture from

the 1920s to the '70s, with special attention to the '50s and '60s, by the encyclopedic, engaging and enthusiastic Robert Imber. Reservation only.

Celebrity Tours　　　CELEBRITY HOMES
(Map p334; ☎760-770-2700; www.thecelebrity tour.com; 67555 E Palm Canyon Dr, Cathedral City; tours adult/child/senior $44/19/40) Offers 2½ hours of gossip and glamour in a reservation-only bus tour of homes of bygone Hollywood stars, from Liberace to Lucy. You can do it yourself with a map from the visitors center, but you'll miss the insider commentary.

Desert Adventures　　　　OUTDOOR
(☎888-440-5337, 760-340-2345; www.red jeep.com; tours per person from $100) Runs excellent guided jeep tours, including the Joshua Tree National Park, twilight adventures and the shake-rattle-and-roll country of the San Andreas Fault. Driverguides are full of information on the natural environment and Native American lore.

Elite Land Tours　　　　　OUTDOOR
(☎760-318-1200, 800-514-4866; www.eliteland tours.com; most tours $39-119) This outfit offers a huge range of respected tours throughout the region, including the windmills, Joshua Tree National Park, forays into the desert, Pioneertown, and even to Hollywood, San Diego and Santa Barbara, all in vehicles from Hummers to jet fighters ($8500!). Prices vary by tour and number of guests.

Palm Springs Windmill Tours　　OUTDOOR
(☎760-320-1365; www.thebestofthebesttours. com; 90min tours adult/child/senior $30/10/27;

⊙9am, 11am & 2pm, call for summer hr) Learn all about the groves of whirring turbines that are the gateway into town, by van or minibus. Reservations required.

Self-Guided Tours

The visitors center has brochures for self-guided tours, including public art and historic sites (free), modernism ($5) and stars' homes ($5), though you'll miss out on banter and commentary.

★☆ Festivals & Events

In addition to these annual events, Downtown Palm Springs turns into the **Village-Fest street fair** (⊙6-10pm Thu Oct-May, 7-10pm Thu Jun-Sep) every Thursday night. Palm Canyon Dr between Amado and Baristo Rds bursts with local farmers selling produce, artists selling their work and tents for on-the-spot massage.

Palm Springs International Film Festival   FILM
(www.psfilmfest.org) Early January brings the city's film festival with over 200

flicks from more than 60 countries. There's also a short film festival held in late June.

Modernism Week   ARCHITECTURE
(www.modernismweek.com) Ten days in mid-February, comprising several dozen events including a modernism art show, lectures, screenings and architecture tours. Book well ahead.

BNP Paribas Open   SPORTING EVENT
(www.bnpparibasopen.com) Many of the world's top tennis players gather at the Indian Wells Tennis Garden in mid-March, attracting spectators from around the world as well.

Dinah Shore Weekend   LESBIAN
(www.dinahshoreweekend.com) Billed as the largest lesbian event in the world, the Dinah Weekend is actually several days of lesbian comedy, pool parties, mixers, dances and more on the occasion of the Kraft Nabisco (formerly Dinah Shore) LPGA Golf Tournament. Late March to early April.

SPA MOI

This big-sky country is also big-spa country. A few favorites, simple to sumptuous, are listed here. Make reservations, or ask in your hotel about in-room services.

Well
(Map p334; ☑760-837-2336, 866-843-9355; 40-500 Indian Wells Lane, Indian Wells) The multi-award-winning spa at the Miramonte Resort offers couples' massage, body-painting parties, wine baths and watsu massage.

Palm Springs Yacht Club
(Map p334; ☑760-321-4606; www.palmspringsyachtclub.com; 4200 E Palm Canyon Dr) Ritzy, glitzy and fabulous, the spa at the Parker Palm Springs is a fave of society ladies and the occasional celeb seeking massages and a facial.

Spa La Quinta
(Map p334; ☑760-777-4800; www.laquintaresort.com; 49-499 Eisenhower Dr, La Quinta) Relax in the posh and palmy garden before your massage or facial; special treatments available for golfers and tennis players.

Estrella
(Map p336; ☑760-320-4117; www.viceroypalmsprings.com; 415 S Belardo Rd) Swanky full-service spa at the Viceroy, with salt scrubs, wraps, facials, botanical baths, a high-end salon and outdoor activities like hikes.

East Canyon Hotel & Spa
(Map p336; ☑760-320-1928; www.eastcanyonps.com; 288 E Camino Monte Vista) Palm Springs' only exclusively gay spa has facials, wraps (try the aloe wrap), massages and more.

Spa Resort Casino
(Map p336; ☑760-325-1461; www.sparesortcasino.com; 100 N Indian Canyon Dr) The valley's original hot springs are at this Native American casino hotel. For $40 you can buy the 'taking of the waters' course through multiple baths, steam rooms and saunas.

White Party   GAY
(www.jeffreysanker.com) On Easter weekend, this four-day-long party is one of the biggest gay dance events in the US.

Coachella Music & Arts Festival   MUSIC
(www.coachella.com; 3-day pass $269) In late April or early May, 25 miles east of Palm Springs, Indio's **Empire Polo Club** (Map p334) hosts one of the hottest music festivals of its kind. Performers over the past few years have ranged from hip indie no-names to Jay-Z, Gorillaz and somebody called Madonna.

Stagecoach Festival   MUSIC
(www.stagecoachfestival.com) The weekend after Coachella, and in the same venue, appear new artists and a who's who of country: Keith Urban, Brooks and Dunn, Merle Haggard and more.

Golf Cart Parade   COMMUNITY
(www.golfcartparade.com) Each October dozens of elaborately decorated golf carts from around the region take to El Paseo in Palm Desert, reputed to be the world's only parade of its kind. And those folks in Pasadena thought their Rose Bowl Parade was so special.

Palm Springs Pride   GAY & LESBIAN
(www.pspride.org) The region's gay-pride festival takes place in early November, with a parade, dozens of entertainers including DJs, and dance and cultural events.

🛏 Sleeping

One of the best things about the Coachella Valley is its variety of quality accommodations, with stylish options in all price categories and for all tastes from hipster to golfster. High-season rack rates are quoted here; inquire about significantly discounted rates in the off-season or weekdays year-round. Many small inns include continental breakfast, though some breakfasts are better than others. Campers can head to Joshua Tree National Park or Mount San Jacinto Wilderness State Park.

PALM SPRINGS

After hours, pick up a printout at the visitors center of available rooms and rates. Pets are welcome at most Palm Springs lodgings, but you must make a reservation and pay an additional fee, $100 and up at some of the fancier places. Where pet fees are $25 or less, we've included the pet-friendly icon.

TOP
CHOICE **Parker Palm Springs**
                 RESORT, FASHIONABLE $$$
(Map p334; ☎760-770-5000, 888-450-9488; www.theparkerpalmsprings.com; 4200 E Palm Canyon Dr; r from $300; P@🛋🖥) Featured in the Bravo TV series *Welcome to the Parker,* this posh full-service resort boasts whimsical decor by designer-du-jour Jonathan Adler. Norma's and Mr Parker's restaurants are to die for and the grounds boast hammocks, a sceney pool, lawn bowling and the Palm Springs Yacht Club spa.

Riviera Resort & Spa
           MID-CENTURY, FASHIONABLE $$$
(Map p336; ☎760-327-8311, 866-588-8311; www.psriviera.com; 1600 N Indian Canyon Dr; r from $249; P@🛋🖥) Marilyn, Deano and Frank stayed here, and *Palm Springs Weekend* was filmed on the 24 acres of this late-'50s modernist gem, yet it sat unloved for years until a 2008 renovation. Now the six buildings that house its 406 rooms make a spoke pattern around the amoeba-shaped pool with fire pits for congregating. The Circa 59 restaurant is pricey but fine. The Sidebar somehow manages to be simultaneously posh and low-key.

Ace Hotel & Swim Club
                    MID-CENTURY, HIPSTER $$
(Map p336; ☎760-325-9900, 877-223-5050; www.acehotel.com/palmsprings; 701 E Palm Canyon Dr; r from $159; P@🛋🖥🐾) The newly refurbished Ace proves that even a one-time Howard Johnson's can be cool. Rooms are a happy humble-jumble of natural fibers, magazine photos clipped to the headboards and mismatched furniture, all around an irregular-shaped pool where tattooed hipsters (some with kids) frolic and go for steams and saunas. The King's Highway restaurant and Amigo Room bar serve a similar demographic. Steep off-season discounts.

Colony Palms Hotel   SPANISH COLONIAL $$
(Map p336; ☎760-969-1800, 800-577-2187; www.colonypalmshotel.com; 572 N Indian Canyon Dr; r from $140; P@🛋🖥) In a 1930s building originally a speakeasy and brothel owned by Detroit mobsters, the Colony Palms underwent a $17-million renovation in 2008 and never looked back. Lush Uzbek and Turkish fabrics and tapestries line the walls and furniture, and hand-painted tile 'carpets' grace the bathroom floors of its 56 rooms. They're all around a pool and courtyard filled with flowering trees, citrus and

star jasmine. The Purple Palm restaurant is a must for Sunday jazz brunch. Resort fee ($23) covers parking, internet and more.

Viceroy
HOTEL, DESIGN $$

(Map p336; ✆760-320-4117, 800-237-3687; www.viceroypalmsprings.com; 415 S Belardo Rd; r from $199; ⚘☎) Wear a Pucci dress and blend right in at this 1960s-chic miniresort done up in black, white and lemon yellow by *Top Design*'s Kelly Wearstler. There's also a full-service spa, as well as a fab but pricey restaurant for a white-linen luncheon or swanky supper.

Del Marcos Hotel
MID-CENTURY $$

(Map p336; ✆760-325-6902, 800-676-1214; www.delmarcoshotel.com; 225 W Baristo Rd; r incl breakfast $119-219; ℗@⚘☎❄) After suffering years of bad remodels, this 1947 gem finally looks like it should. Groovy tunes in the lobby usher you to a saltwater pool and ineffably chic rooms named for local architectural luminaries. Breakfast is simple, but if you want more you're one block from eateries on Palm Canyon Dr.

TOP CHOICE Orbit In
MID-CENTURY $$

(Map p336; ✆760-323-3585, 877-996-7248; www.orbitin.com; 562 W Arenas Rd; r incl breakfast $140-259; ℗@⚘☎) It's back to the 1950s at Palm Springs' retro property of record, with high-end original mid-century furniture (think Eames, Noguchi and more) around a quiet pool. If the original Orbit In is full, you might opt for its sister property, the Hideway, just down the block and done by the same architect and designer.

Chase Hotel at Palm Springs
MID-CENTURY MOTEL $$

(Map p336; ✆760-320-8866, 877-532-4273; www.chasehotelpalmsprings.com; 200 W Arenas Rd; r incl breakfast $109-139; ℗@⚘☎❄) A classic mid-century motel complex with large open spaces, the Chase has 26 immaculately kept oversized rooms decorated with contemporary furnishings. It's great value. Friendly service.

Casa Cody
HISTORIC $$

(Map p336; ✆760-320-9346, 800-231-2639; www.casacody.com; 175 S Cahuilla Rd; r incl breakfast $99-189, ste $199-389; ℗⚘☎❄) Tucked behind billowing bougainvillea, this century-old adobe inn with individual Spanish-style bungalows once hosted Charlie Chaplin. Units have desert-themed decor, including some with full kitchens, wood-burning fireplaces and private patios.

Caliente Tropics Resort
MID-CENTURY MOTEL $$

(Map p336; ✆760-327-1391, 866-277-0999; www.calientetropics.com; 411 E Palm Canyon Dr; r $125-240; ℗⚘☎❄) Impeccably kept 90-room tiki-style motor lodge where Elvis Presley and Nancy Sinatra once splashed poolside. Children and pets are welcome (make reservations for pets).

Alpine Gardens Hotel
MOTEL, HISTORIC $

(Map p336; ✆760-323-2231, 888-299-7455; www.alpinegardens.com; 1586 E Palm Canyon Dr; r $75-145; ℗@⚘☎) All 10 rooms at this beautifully landscaped, impeccably kept motel (c 1954), have redwood beams in the ceilings, refrigerators and slightly kitsch but extra charming furnishings. Some rooms have full kitchens. Top in its class.

7 Springs
BOUTIQUE $

(Map p336; ✆760-320-9110, 800-381-0684; www.7springs.info; 950 N Indian Canyon Dr; r from $80; ℗⚘☎❄) Bargain-priced contempo cool. This former apartment complex has 48 rooms, all laid out differently but decorated with geometric carpeting and marble floors. Shared facilities include pool, Jacuzzis and barbecue grills.

AROUND PALM SPRINGS

Desert Hot Springs is known for small, Palm Springs–style inns with the advantage of being at the hot-spring source. The classic Down Valley stays are resorts as big as some college campuses, catering to golfers and spa-goers, where rack rates are pricey, but there are often discounts and package deals.

DESERT HOT SPRINGS

TOP CHOICE El Morocco Inn & Spa
BOUTIQUE $$$

(Map p334; ✆760-288-2527; www.elmoroccoinn.com; 66810 4th St; r $179-229 incl continental breakfast; ℗⚘☎) If minimalist modernism leaves you cold, El Morocco bursts with color and intrigue worthy of Bogey and Bergman, in 10 rooms, with a pool deck, a library and a pool bar where Morocco-tinis are served nightly at the complimentary happy hour. The enthusiastic owner is a font of local info.

Sagewater Spa
BOUTIQUE, MID-CENTURY $$$

(Map p334; ✆760-220-1554; www.sagewaterspa.com; 12689 Elisio Rd; r $195-250; ℗⚘☎) It's minimalist to the max at this seven-room, adults-only inn with two spa pools (warm and warmer), on a hillside with views across the valley. Rooms have concrete floors and a white-on-white color scheme inflected with

DRIVING TOUR: PALMS TO PINES SCENIC BYWAY

What to See

This day trip from Palm Springs ascends to piney forests and descends back to the desert floor in a mere couple hours. As you ascend from the desert floor, the landscape quickly changes to Ponderosa-forested mountains. Look for bald eagles above and bobcats below, and when you're done take a break for cheap shopping!

The Route

From Palm Springs, take Hwy 111 southeast to Palm Desert, and turn right onto Palms to Pines Scenic Byway (CA74), across from Monterey Ave. At Mountain Center, connect with Rte 243 north, also called the Banning-Idyllwild Panoramic Hwy. It's about 28 winding miles to Banning, where you can connect back to I-10 east toward Palm Springs.

Time & Mileage

It's about 68 miles one way between Palm Desert and Banning. With time for twists, turns, oohs and aahs, allow about 1¾ hours' drive time, plus whatever it takes to get to and from Palm Springs.

the occasional – wait for it – sage accent. Homemade coffee cake.

Hope Springs Resort   BOUTIQUE **$$**
(Map p334; ☑760-329-4003; www.hopesprings resort.com; 68075 Club Circle Dr; r from $140-185; ▣ ☲) This modernist mecca put Desert Hot Springs on the map for stylish stays, and it continues to dazzle with 10 rooms featuring impeccable period furniture, palm- and cactus-filled public spaces, fantastic views and natural hot springs flowing through three pools. The sign out front reads 'Cactus Springs'.

DOWN VALLEY

TOP CHOICE **La Quinta Resort & Club**   RESORT **$$$**
(Map p334; ☑760-564-4111, 800-598-3828; www.laquintaresort.com; 49499 Eisenhower Dr, La Quinta; r from $359; ▣@⬒☲⬛) Opened in 1926, the sprawling La Quinta has a Spanish Colonial–style lobby, cushy ultraprivate bungalows (many with private outdoor Jacuzzi), spectacular grounds, plush and lush spa, 41 pools and 90 holes of golf. Among its myriad dining choices, the beamed hacienda-style **Morgan's** is the fanciest. Its contemporary California menu boasts offerings such as gem Bibb lettuce and Bosc pear salad with smoked bacon and Maytag blue cheese, or wild coho salmon with sweet pepper and corn polenta.

Westin Mission Hills   RESORT **$$$**
(Map p334; 760-328-5955, 800-937-8461; 71333 Dinah Shore Dr, Rancho Mirage; r from $249; ▣@⬒⬛⬛) This Down Valley golf resort offers two courses, numerous pools, tennis courts, an enormous spa, and desert tones in its 512 spacious guest rooms (all with Westin's 'heavenly beds' and private balcony).

✕ Eating

As a relatively small city, Palm Springs doesn't have the breadth of cuisine offerings of LA, but there are certainly enough quality options to keep foodies happy on short trips.

PALM SPRINGS

TOP CHOICE **Trio**   AMERICAN-CONTEMPORARY **$$**
(Map p336; ☑760-864-8746; www.trio palmsprings.com; 707 N Palm Canyon Dr; mains $12-22; ☺dinner) The winning formula in this '60s modern space: contemporary American comfort food (think fried artichoke hearts and Yankee pot roast), splashy artwork, picture windows and sculptural lighting fixtures. Desserts, like the Trio nut torte, are all baked in-house.

Copley's on Palm Canyon   AMERICAN **$$$**
(Map p336; ☑760-327-1196; 445 N Palm Canyon Dr; mains $25-35; ☺10am-2pm Sunday Jan–mid-May, dinner Tue-Sun mid-May–Dec, closed late Jul-late Aug) On the former Cary Grant estate, Andrew Manion Copley gets seriously inventive: think prosciutto-wrapped duck breast and 'Oh My Lobster Pot Pie.' Bring your sweetie and your credit card.

Johannes CONTINENTAL $$$
(Map p336; ☑760-778-0017; 196 S Indian Canyon Dr; mains $22-26; ☺dinner Tue-Sun) The chef-owner's Austrian roots shine through the contemporary Euro-Cal cuisine at this sedately decorated storefront. Diners rave over imaginative cooking without a lot of fuss: pan-seared ahi in apricot sauce to Wiener schnitzel with cranberries.

Spencer's AMERICAN-CONTEMPORARY $$$
(Map p336; ☑760-327-3446; 701 W Baristo Rd; mains lunch $10-23, dinner $19-40; ☺lunch Mon-Fri, dinner nightly, brunch 9am-2:30pm Sat & Sun; ☑) Dramatically built into lush gardens by the mountainside and offering big-city clean lines and sophistication (look for the piano player), Spencer's serves swanky cuisine like breakfast cocktails, lobster club sandwich, excellent burgers and steaks, and chicken with tarragon reduction. Wear your white shoes.

Matchbox PIZZA $$
(Map p336; ☑760-778-6000; 155 S Palm Canyon Dr; mains $10-26, pizzas small/large from $13/19; ☺dinner, closing times vary) Posh pizzas like chicken pesto, salads including spinach with roast tomatoes and candied walnuts, and a big bar scene with 'manly' and 'girlie' martinis and about a dozen unusual draft beers make this new place a hit. Feel posh yourself on the balcony overlooking the courtyard across from the Plaza.

TOP CHOICE **Cheeky's** AMERICAN-CONTEMPORARY $$
(Map p336; ☑760-327-7595; www.cheekysps.com; 622 N Palm Canyon Dr; mains $7-13; ☺8am-2pm Wed-Mon) A much-loved newcomer, Cheeky's has spare decor that shows off the imaginative breakfasts and lunches. The organic menu changes weekly (check website), but if we mention Eureka lemon-curd buttermilk waffles or rosemary-roasted leg of lamb in pita with tabbouleh, tahini and lettuce, do you get the idea?

King's Highway AMERICAN, CONTEMPORARY $$
(Map p336; ☑760-325-9900; 701 E Palm Canyon Dr; mains breakfast $7-11, lunch & dinner $9-30; ☺7am-10pm Sun-Thu, 7am-11pm Fri & Sat; ☑) The restaurant at the Ace Hotel is like a diner for hipsters, with terrazzo floor, big open windows and a long counter. Organic, locally raised offerings span the cowboy steak and frites to tasty vegetarian dishes like the black-bean burger.

Wang's in the Desert ASIAN FUSION $$
(Map p336; ☑760-325-9264; 424 S Indian Canyon Dr; mains $9-17; ☺5-9:30pm Sun-Thu, 5-10:30pm Fri & Sat, closed 3 weeks in Aug; ☑) The menu may sound like standard-issue upscale Chinese (chicken lettuce wraps, Mongolian beef), but the atmosphere is anything but. Swank and mood-lit with indoor koi pond and giant cocktails, Wang's is the darling of the in-crowd and *the* late Sunday-afternoon gay-gathering place for cocktails (call for early happy-hour times). Kiss, kiss.

Escena Grill GOLF RESORT $$
(Map p334; ☑760-778-2737; 1100 Clubhouse View; mains breakfast $5-13, lunch $7-13, dinner $15-23; ☺6am-3pm Sun-Wed, 6am-9pm, Thu-Sat) Even if you're not a golf-club kind of person, you may well love this spot, and not just for its 21st-century interpretation of a mid-century modern dining room and patio with stunning course and mountain views. Deep-cooked potato chips go *kaah-runch,* and you can follow them up with the Mulligan Cobb salad or Baja fish tacos. A bit out of town but worth the trip.

THAT ONE, I NEVER GO TO!

Requirements to be a certified Old Hollywood hangout: retired stars, lots of sun, a pool, palm trees and a Jewish deli. Palm Springs has not one but two of the last, each with its passionate fans. As impartial journalists we see merits in both, so we're not going to say that one makes you *kvell,* while the other one...*feh!* **Sherman's** (Map p336; ☑760-329-1199; 401 E Tahquitz Canyon Way; mains $7-17; ☺7am-9pm; ☑☀) has been in business since 1995 in a strip-mall storefront with long terrace. It serves early-bird dinners and is festooned with headshots of aficionados no less than Don Rickles and Milton Berle. Newer **Manhattan in the Desert** (☑760-322-3354; 2665 E Palm Canyon Dr; mains $6-19; ☺7am-9pm Sun-Thu, to 10pm Fri & Sat; ☑☀) has a more impressive deli counter, more polished surroundings and simply massive slices of cake, mirroring the enormity of its sandwiches. There are also not-so-traditional build-your-own pizzas.

GAY & LESBIAN PALM SPRINGS

Palm Springs is one of America's great gay destinations, a sort of Provincetown in the desert. Large annual events include the White Party, Dinah Weekend and Palm Springs Pride, but just about any weekend of the year you're likely to find gay and lesbian Angelenos relaxing in their second homes or lounging at resorts, or mingling at night with a large local contingent.

Lodging

Gay lodging in Palm Springs, approximately 40 resorts in all, ranges from sleazy to sumptuous. Since they're small properties, many are conducive to finding companions for dinner, drinks, daytime activities or...other stuff. Some of the better ones are listed here.

Men's resorts tend to be concentrated in the Warm Sands neighborhood, just southeast of downtown Palm Springs, or on San Lorenzo Rd, about a mile away. Lesbian resorts (fewer in number) are throughout town. Most men's resorts are clothing-optional.

Inndulge
BOUTIQUE, MID-CENTURY **$$**

(Map p336; ☎760-327-1408, 800-833-5675; www.inndulge.com; 601 Grenfall Rd; r incl breakfast from $149; P@🛜🏊) This midrange men's option gets plenty of repeat customers for its 1950s shell, variety of rooms and suites with mission furniture, fridges (some rooms also have kitchens), gay-themed photo posters, pool and hot tub that encourage mingling, and summer specials.

Santiago
BOUTIQUE **$$**

(Map p336; ☎760-322-1300, 800-710-7729; www.santiagoresort.com; 650 San Lorenzo Rd; r incl breakfast from $179; P🛜🏊) Smartly remodeled in 2006, this 24-room men's resort in a two-story courtyard-style building features muted colors, frosted-glass showers, CD clock radios and original erotic artwork. There are excellent mountain views from the huge pool, and a hammock out back.

Hacienda at Warm Sands
BOUTIQUE, LUXURY **$$$**

(Map p336; ☎760-327-8111, 800-359-2007; www.thehacienda.com; 586 Warm Sands Dr; r incl breakfast & lunch $150-399; P@🛜🏊) The Hacienda raises the bar for service and luxury in gay lodging. Choose from nine different pillow types in its 10 generously proportioned rooms. The genial innkeepers are never intrusive, always available. Flawless landscaping.

Casitas Laquita
BOUTIQUE **$$**

(Map p336; ☎760-416-9999, 877-203-3410; www.casitaslaquita.com; 450 E Palm Canyon Dr; r $145-155, ste incl breakfast from $195; P🛜🏊) All the rooms are individually decorated

---

El Mirasol
MEXICAN **$$**

(Map p336; ☎760-323-0721; 140 E Palm Canyon Dr; mains $7-19; ⊙11am-10pm) There are showier Mexican places in town, but everyone ends up back at El Mirasol, with its informal decor, copious margaritas and snappy dishes from guacamole to tacos to chicken mole and enchiladas in verde sauce. Indoor and outdoor seating available.

Thai Smile
THAI **$$**

(Map p336; ☎760-320-5503; www.thaismile palmsprings.com; 651 N Palm Canyon Dr; mains lunch $8-9, dinner $9-20; ⊙11:30am-9:30pm; P) Respected, casual eatery serving standards (pad Thai, curries) and unusual dishes (grilled eggplant salad or a large seafood menu including spicy devil scallops). There

is a second branch in **Palm Desert** (Map p334; ☎760-341-6565; 42-467 Bob Hope Dr; ⊙11:30am-9:30pm; P).

Fisherman's Market & Grill
SEAFOOD **$$**

(Map p336; ☎760-327-1766; 235 S Indian Canyon Dr; mains lunch $8-16, dinner $9-24; ⊙11am-9pm Mon-Sat, noon-9pm Sun; 🦽) Just what it says: this place is both market and restaurant, where you order from the refrigerator case and your choice is prepared fresh for you. Quite a surprise 100 miles from the ocean, and a perennial fave. The fish-and-chips is a classic, as are combos with coleslaw and fries or rice.

Tyler's Burgers
HAMBURGER STAND **$**

(Map p336; ☎760-325-2990; 149 S Indian Canyon Dr; dishes $4-7; ⊙11am-4pm Mon-Sat, closed mid-

and have kitchens at this recently remodeled historic (1932) Spanish-style compound for lesbians, which has a great pool and manicured grounds. If you can swing it, book the romantic cottage with its private backyard, hot tub and barbecue.

Eating

Every restaurant in central Palm Springs has a significant gay clientele. Some of the more popular gay hangouts include Trio and Wang's in the Desert, and bars Azul and Tropicale also have extensive food menus. **Bongo Johnny's** (Map p336; ✆760-866-1905; 214 E Arenas Rd; lunch mains $9-14, dinner mains to $19; ⏰8am-10:45pm Sun-Thu, to 11:45pm Fri & Sat) is a cheap and cheerful bar and grill for burgers, sandwiches and salads. The designy coffeehouse Koffi serves lighter fare.

Nightlife

Arenas Rd east of Indian Canyon Dr is gay-nightlife central. Park 'n' party. The following are a good start:

Toucans   VIDEO & DANCE BAR, TIKI
(2100 N Palm Canyon Dr) A couple miles from Arenas, this locals' hangout has something for everyone: gay, lesbian, tropical froufrou, trivia network, smoking patio and dancefloor. Packed on weekends. Frequent drink specials.

Hunter's   DANCE BAR
(Map p336; 302 E Arenas Rd) Mostly male clientele, lots of TV screens, a fun dance scene and two pool tables.

Streetbar   DANCE, KARAOKE
(Map p336; 244 E Arenas Rd) Congenial mix of locals, visitors and occasional drag performers. Streetside patio for watching the crowd go by.

Spurline   VIDEO BAR
(Map p336; 200 S Indian Canyon Dr) Visit this smaller video bar on a night when there are show tunes from Broadway and Hollywood, and the scene gets fun and silly, à la Chicago's Sidetrack.

Azul   BAR-RESTAURANT
(Map p336; 369 N Palm Canyon Dr; dishes $6-16) Gay and straight comfortably mingle as this tapas restaurant develops a fun bar scene in the early-evening happy hour, especially on a large patio with booths like covered porch swings.

Jul–Aug & some Mondays in warmer months) The city's favorite burger stand has a magazine rack stocked with the *Robb Report* and financial magazines. It's at La Plaza, a historic drive-thru shopping street in the town center. Expect a wait.

Native Foods   VEGETARIAN $
(Map p336; ✆760-416-0070; www.nativefoods.com; 1775 E Palm Canyon Dr; mains $8-11; ⏰11:30am-9:30pm Mon-Sat, closed Jul–mid-Aug; P🐾🖙✎🍴) Vegan food so good it's seitan-ic (...seitan being a wheat-gluten-based dish). Soy and wheat proteins stand in for beef and chicken in tacos, burgers and bowls. It's tucked away in a rather pleasant outdoor mall, with giant masks on the wall.

Jensen's Finest Foods   SUPERMARKET, DELI $
(✆760-325-8282; 2465 E Palm Canyon Dr; sandwiches $7; ⏰7am-9pm) Local supermarket with fabulous specialty sandwiches for that desert hike, attractive salads and prepared foods, and homemade baked goods such as Mexican wedding cookies and apple fritters.

AROUND PALM SPRINGS
See also Morgan's at La Quinta Resort.

Palm Korea   KOREAN $$
(Map p334; ✆760-329-2277; 13440 Palm Dr; mains $9-20; ⏰11am-9pm) A delicious legacy of the influx of ethnic Koreans to Desert Hot Springs for the curative waters, this humble little shop punches above its

THE PERFECT DATE

Come to the Coachella Valley and find the date of your dreams – the kind that grows on trees, that is. Some 90% of US date production happens here, with dozens of permutations of shape, size, juiciness, packaging and species, with exotic names like halawy, deglet, blonde and honey.

Dates grow around Indio, at the southeast end of the valley, atop some 4300 acres of date palms with ancestries that trace back to the Middle East and North Africa; they began to be imported about a century ago. The region's most famous variety, the medjool, arrived in the 1920s from Morocco. Some varieties will keep for years without refrigeration.

The shops at date orchards let you sample different varieties for free, an act of shameless but delicious self-promotion. Another signature taste of the valley is the date shake: crushed dates mixed into a vanilla milkshake (about $4). Be careful – they're richer than they look! At **Shields Date Gardens** (Map p334; ☑760-347-0996; www.shieldsdates.com; 80-225 Hwy 111, Indio; ☺9am-5pm) you can watch the film *Romance & Sex Life of the Date*, really more of a history of dates and date-growing in the Coachella Valley. **Oasis Date Gardens** (☑800-827-8017; www.oasisdategardens. com; 59-111 Hwy 111, Thermal; ☺9am-4pm) is on the way to the Salton Sea. Or for a quick grab-n-go on your way to or from LA, **Hadley Fruit Orchards** (☑888-854-5655; www. hadleyfruitorchards.com; 48980 Seminole Dr, Cabazon; ☺9am-7pm Mon-Thu, 8am-8pm Fri-Sun) claims to have invented trail mix.

weight, garnering attention from both national media and ardent foodie fans. Succulent barbecue dishes such as *bulgogi* (thin sliced beef) and *kalbi* (beef ribs) can be grilled at the table or in the kitchen, or enjoy spicy tofu stew or *bibimbap* (rice, vegetables and other ingredients).

Capri ITALIAN, STEAK HOUSE $$$
(Map p334; ☑760-329-6833; 12260 Palm Dr; mains $13-26; ☺11am-2pm Tue-Fri, 5-9pm Tue-Thu & Sun, 5-10pm Fri & Sat) The aroma of garlic hangs in the air at this family-run, old-school East Coast–style Italian joint, serving trusty standbys like pasta with meatballs and chicken or veal marsala. It does double duty as DHS's steak house of record, with fillets and sirloins dry-aged in-house.

🍸 Drinking

In addition to stand-alone bars, many restaurants and hotels have swinging bar scenes. Check out Wang's, Azul, Matchbox and the bars at the Parker, Riviera and Ace hotels.

Tropicale LOUNGE-BAR
(Map p336; ☑760-866-1952; 330 E Amado Rd) There's a Miami-nice feel at this aqua bar and restaurant, all the better to quaff mojitos like basil lemongrass or cucumber watermelon, and fun tiki-style drinkies. There's a patio out back for nice weather.

Citron FASHIONABLE HOTEL BAR
(Map p336; www.viceroypalmsprings.com; 415 S Belardo Rd; P) Opinions waver about the food at the restaurant at the Viceroy, but everyone agrees that the bar scene is supercool.

Village Pub NEIGHBORHOOD BAR
(Map p336; 266 S Palm Canyon Dr; ☎) A casual local dive perfect for kicking back with your buds over some live music, darts and beer on tap.

Koffi COFFEE BAR
(Map p336; 1700 S Camino Real; ☺5:30am-8pm; ☎) This appropriately cool, minimalist cafe serves strong organic coffee. The **N Palm Canyon location** (Map p336; 515 N Palm Canyon Dr) has a big gay following.

☆ Entertainment

Palm Springs Follies REVUE
(Map p336; www.psfollies.com; 128 S Palm Canyon Dr; tickets $50-140; ☺evening shows & matinees Nov-May) The historic Plaza Theater, dating from 1936, hosts this Ziegfeld Follies–style revue that includes music, dancing, showgirls and comedy. The twist? Many of the performers are as old as the theater – all are over 50, some are into their 80s. But this is no amateur hour; in their heyday many of these old-timers hoofed it alongside Hollywood and Broadway's biggest, who occasionally guest-star. The cast from

the past delivers high-energy shows with flash, splash, inspiration and patriotism.

Melvyn's
PIANO & JAZZ BAR

(Map p336; 200 W Ramon Rd) The likes of Sinatra and McQueen were among the early customers at this swanky watering hole at the Ingleside Inn, and it still retains that feel. Nowadays a Benz, Beemer and Bentley crowd listens to music from piano and vocals to jazz combos while quaffing martinis at the burnished bar. Sunday-afternoon jazz is a long-standing tradition.

Spa Resort Casino
CASINO

(Map p336; www.sparesortcasino.com; 401 E Amado Rd; ◷24hr) Legal gambling is possible just a few blocks from Palm Canyon Dr, at the casino operated by Palm Springs' own Agua Caliente Band of Cahuilla Indians. It feels like Vegas-lite.

Morongo Casino
CASINO

(www.morongocasinoresort.com; 49500 Seminole Dr, Cabazon; ◷24hr) In addition to gambling, the casino operated by the Morongo Band of Mission Indians showcases some big-name talent including Enrique Iglesias, Bill Maher and Melissa Etheridge. It's about 20 minutes' drive west of Palm Springs, easily visible from I-10.

Shanghai Red's
BLUES

(Map p336; 200 W Ramon Rd) Behind Fisherman's Market is this venue for blues in an informal courtyard setting, on Friday and Saturday nights. Bonus: peel 'n' eat shrimp.

Palm Canyon Theatre
BROADWAY SHOWS

(Map p336; www.palmcanyontheatre.org; 538 N Palm Canyon Dr; tickets $26-32) This theater stages professional productions of stageplays and musicals from mid-September to mid-May.

🔒 Shopping

In the Uptown neighborhood of Palm Springs, Palm Canyon Dr is HQ for mid-century modernist furniture and accessories, with discerning dealers who know their Bertoia from their Brancusi. Continuing into central Palm Springs, Palm Canyon Dr is more geared toward gift and T-shirt shops and galleries aimed at tourists. For major mall shopping, head Down Valley, where the pickings run from everyday to deluxe.

Trina Turk
WOMEN'S CLOTHING

(Map p336; 891 N Palm Canyon Dr) Find shagadelic resort-chic drag at Palm Springs' best – some say only – clothing boutique. If you're a lover of hip clothes, don't miss this place.

Modern Way
FURNITURE

(Map p336; 745 N Palm Canyon Dr) The largest, oldest and most stylin' consignment shop for collectors of modern furniture. The visitors center maintains a list of this and lots more.

Estate Sale Company
RESALE

(Map p334; 4185 E Palm Canyon Dr) Several galleries and outdoor spaces read like a history of furniture from the second half of the 20th century. Some of it might just as easily be found at a yard sale, but alongside are some real gems.

El Paseo
SHOPPING MALL

(Map p334; www.elpaseo.com) For serious shopping at midrange and high-end retailers, head to El Paseo, the main shopping street in Palm Desert, dubbed the Rodeo Dr of the desert. To get there, head 14 miles southeast of Palm Springs via Hwy 111. El Paseo runs parallel to Hwy 111, one block south of the highway.

GO, DADDY-O!

The high percentage of well-heeled retirees living in the Coachella Valley, and their propensity to pass on to the next world, means there's a constant replenishment of retro threads at local secondhand stores. Today's hipsters can buy the real deal, as cool as when they were first worn a generation or two ago. **Resale Therapy** (Map p334; www.shopresaletherapy.com; 4109 E Palm Canyon Dr, Palm Springs; ◷10am-5pm Mon-Sat, 11am-4pm Sun) is 5000 sq ft of consignment couture and name brands for men and women. **Angel View** (Map p336; ☏760-323-8771, 760-320-1733; 462 N Indian Canyon Dr) is the thrift-store chain of record (benefiting the Crippled Children's Foundation) and has a fancier boutique next door, while at the Eisenhower Medical Center, **Collector's Corner** (Map p334; 71280 Hwy 111, Rancho Mirage) draws enthusiastic bargain hunters from across the valley.

DON'T MISS

OUTLET MALLS

Near Palm Springs, the adjacent malls **Desert Hills Premium Outlets** (www.premium outlets.com; 48400 Seminole Dr, Cabazon) and **Cabazon Outlets** (www.cabazonoutlets. com; 48750 Seminole Dr, Cabazon) will appeal to discount shoppers. Stop on your way to or from LA for stores selling everything from Gap to Gucci, housewares to sunglasses. Some purchases are major bargains while others are mere great deals. For big purchases, scope out prices at home beforehand. The malls are just off I-10 in Cabazon, about 20 minutes northwest of central Palm Springs.

River at Rancho Mirage   SHOPPING MALL
(Map p334; 71-800 Hwy 111 at Bob Hope Dr, Rancho Mirage) Among the shopping centers en route to El Paseo, the River has about 20 upscale stores, restaurants and a big movie complex.

ℹ Information

Internet Access
Wi-fi is also available at coffeehouses.

Palm Springs Public Library (☎760-322-7323; www.palmspringslibrary.org; 300 Sunrise Way; ⏰10am-7pm Tue, to 5pm Wed-Sat) Internet access from installed computers and free wi-fi with your own computer.

Media
Desert Sun (www.mydesert.com) Palm Springs' daily newspaper concentrates on local news.

KWXY 1340AM, 98.5FM Campy cocktail music from the '40s through the Rat Pack and '70s, to match Palm Springs' mid-century architecture.

Los Angeles Times (www.losangelestimes. com) The West Coast's most important newspaper gets delivered to Palm Springs daily.

Press-Enterprise (www.pe.com) Daily newspaper published out of Riverside, the county seat.

Medical Services
Desert Regional Medical Center (☎760-323-6511; www.desertmedctr.com; 1150 N Indian Canyon Dr) Has 24-hour emergency care and nonemergency services during normal business hours.

Money
There are banks and ATMs throughout the Coachella Valley. You'll also generally find ATMs in supermarkets.

Anderson Travel (☎760-325-2001; Suite 100, 1801 E Tahquitz Canyon Way; ⏰9am-4:30pm Mon-Fri) Exchanges foreign currency; call ahead if you want to exchange large sums.

Post
Palm Springs Post Office (☎760-322-4111, 800-275-8777; 333 E Amado Rd; ⏰8am-5pm Mon-Fri, 9am-3pm Sat)

Tourist Information
Palm Springs Official Visitors Center (☎760-778-8418, 800-367-7746; www.visit palmsprings.com; 2901 N Palm Canyon Dr; ⏰9am-5pm, seasonal variations possible) North of town, at the turnoff to the Palm Springs Aerial Tramway, this information center occupies what was originally a 1965 Albert Frey–designed gas station. The center distributes the official visitors guide and specialty guides (mobility impaired, gay and lesbian travelers, architecture etc).

ℹ Getting There & Away

Air
Palm Springs International Airport (PSP; ☎760-318-3800; www.palmspringsairport. com; 3400 E Tahquitz Canyon Way) is served year-round by Alaska, American, Delta, Horizon, United and US Airways from gateways including Chicago, Dallas, Denver, Los Angeles, Minneapolis, Phoenix, San Francisco and Seattle. There are additional seasonal services on Air Canada, Continental, Northwest, Sun Country and WestJet. The airport is five minutes' drive to downtown.

Car & Motorcycle
From Los Angeles, I-10 is the main route into and through the Coachella Valley; the journey to Palm Springs takes about two hours.

You can rent a Harley from **Eaglerider** (☎760-779-5001, 877-736-8243; www.eaglerider.com;

STAY COOL

As temperatures soar above 100°F/38°C, one place you might not think to protect yourself from heat is the handle on your car door – these can be especially hot if facing the sun. Some locals keep a towel or potholder handy just for opening the door. For more desert travel tips, see p355.

JW Marriott Hotel, 74855 Country Club Dr, Palm Desert) for around $99/140 per business day/24 hours; motorcycle license required; Vespa scooters and electric bicycles are also available. When motorcycling in the desert, keep yourself adequately hydrated. Hot, dry wind against your body causes rapid dehydration, so avoid riding with your skin exposed for any longer than a few minutes.

Train

Amtrak (☎800-872-7245; www.amtrak.com) serves the unstaffed and kinda creepy North Palm Springs Station, situated on a desolate stretch of desert 4 miles north of downtown Palm Springs, about 0.5 miles south of where Indian Canyon Dr meets I-10; you'll want to have a friend waiting for you when you arrive. *Sunset Limited* trains (one way $36, 2½ hours) connect with LA a few times per week heading in both directions.

❶ Getting Around

To/From the Airport

Unless your hotel provides airport transfers, plan to take a taxi; figure about $12 to downtown hotels.

Shuttle companies serve other valley towns; fares vary by distance. Call for advance reservations.

At Your Service (☎760-343-0666, 888-700-7888; www.limosatyourservice.net) Town car service to Down Valley communities, from $70.

Desert Valley Shuttle (☎760-251-4020, 800-413-3999; www.palmspringsshuttle.com) Van service from about $40.

Car

Unless you're staying in downtown Palm Springs and don't plan to leave, you'll probably want to rent a car for convenience and savings over taxis. Rent one at the airport, where all major agencies have counters.

Public Transportation

SunBus (☎760-343-3451; www.sunline.org; ticket/day pass $1/3) While some gripe about the local bus service's pokiness and reliability, it does serve most of the valley from about 6am to 10pm, and the air-conditioned buses are clean and comfortable. Line 111 follows Hwy 111 between Palm Springs and Palm Desert (one hour) and Indio (about 1½ hours). You can transfer to other lines that loop through the various communities. All buses have wheelchair lifts and a bicycle rack.

Taxi

Call **Yellow Cab** (☎760-775-1477) in advance to reserve. Flag fall is $3.25, and each mile costs $2.65.

Like a scene from a Dr Seuss book, whimsical Joshua trees welcome visitors to this 794,000-acre (321,000-hectare) park at the convergence of the Sonora and Mojave Deserts. Bizarre outcroppings (mostly quartz monzonite) draw rock climbers while flats and oases attract day-hikers, especially in spring when many trees send up a huge, single cream-colored flower. The mystical quality of this stark, boulder-strewn landscape has inspired many artists, most famously the band U2, which named its 1987 album *The Joshua Tree*.

The towns of Joshua Tree (population 4900) and Twentynine Palms (population 30,500) are the best places to base yourself for park access if you're not day-tripping from Palm Springs. Neither town has the panache of Palm Springs, but of the two Joshua Tree has more soul and is favored by artists and writers. Twentynine Palms (named after the original 29 palm trees behind the visitors center) also serves the nearby Marine Corps Air Ground Combat Center (the world's largest marine facility at over 900 sq miles, or twice the footprint of the city of Los Angeles). Don't disparage US troops here, and don't freak out over the occasional kaboom.

◉ Sights

Park (www.nps.gov/jotr; 74485 National Park Dr, Twentynine Palms) admission is $15 per vehicle, payable at any entry gate, good for seven days and including a map/brochure and the seasonal *Joshua Tree Guide*. There are no facilities besides restrooms, so gas up and bring food and plenty of water.

The most whimsically dramatic conglomeration of rocks is known locally as the **Wonderland of Rocks** area, while the biggest trees are near Covington Flats. To see the transition from the low Colorado Desert/Sonoran Desert to the high Mojave, drive along Pinto Basin Rd.

DID YOU KNOW?

The Joshua tree (*Yucca Brevifiola*) was named by Mormon pioneers, whom the tree reminded of the biblical prophet Joshua pointing the way toward the Promised Land.

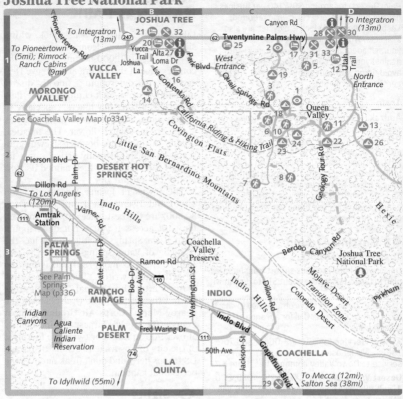

Those who enjoy history and local lore should take the 90-minute walking tour of the **Desert Queen Ranch** (reservations ☏760-367-5555; by tour only adult/child $5/2.50; ☺tours 10am & 1pm daily Oct-May), around 2 miles northeast of Hidden Valley Campground up a dirt road. Russian immigrant William Keys built a homestead on 160 acres here in 1917 and over the following 60 years he set up a full working ranch, school, store and workshop, which still stand pretty much as they did when Keys died in 1969. Reservations strongly suggested – you can also make a reservation at the Oasis Visitors Center.

🏃 Activities

Cycling

Joshua Tree National Park is popular for biking, though roads have no shoulders and bicycles must stay on the roads and trails. Bikes are a great means of transportation in this region: hop on your two-wheel steed to get from your campground to any destination and you'll have gorgeous scenery along the way. See p338 for information about bike hire.

Two favorite bicycle routes are the **Old Dale Rd**, which starts 6.5 miles north of the Cottonwood Visitors Center, and the **Queen Valley** road network, a more gentle set of trails with bike racks along the way to lock up your bikes and go hiking.

Hiking

You should leave the car behind to appreciate Joshua Tree's trippy lunar landscapes. Visitors centers provide maps and advice about the dozen-plus short nature walks (which range from 0.25 miles to 1.3 miles) and six hiking trails that focus on different features of the park (for the kids, pick up a Junior Ranger booklet and ask which trails are most kid-friendly). Trails include **Fortynine Palms Oasis**, **Hidden**

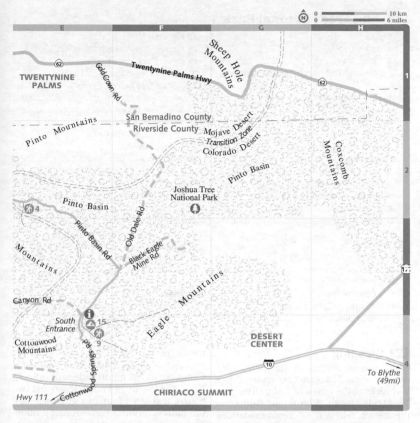

Valley, **Lost Horse Mine**, **Inspiration Point**, **Ryan Mountain**, **Cholla Cactus Garden** and **Lost Palm Oasis**. If you don't have a lot of time, the 0.25-mile **Skull Rock Loop** is an easy walk, as is **Keys View Trail**, which provides views of the entire Coachella Valley.

Overnight backcountry hikers must register (to aid in census-taking, fire safety and rescue efforts) and deposit the stub at one of 12 backcountry boards in parking lots throughout the park. Unregistered vehicles left overnight may be cited or towed.

The well-traveled 16-mile **Boy Scout Trail**, on the western side of the park, starts from either the Indian Cove or Keys West backcountry board.

A 35-mile-long stretch of the **California Riding & Hiking Trail**, administered by California State Parks, passes through Joshua Tree; plan two to three days to hike the trail through the park.

To protect fragile soil crusts (cryptobiotic soil), which allow plant life to grow and keep the desert from blowing away, stay on established trails.

Rock Climbing

From boulders to cracks to multipitch faces, there may be more routes here than anywhere else in the US. The longest climbs are not much more than 100ft or so, but there are many challenging technical routes, and most can be easily top-roped for training. Some of the most popular climbs are in the Hidden Valley area. Check with park staff before setting out.

Shops near the park entrance in Joshua Tree (on Park Dr) have specialized climbing books and route diaries.

For a day of instruction or for a guided climb, contact **Uprising Outdoor Adventure Guides** (☎760-366-3799, 888-254-6266; www.uprising.com; 8hr per person from $120). Also try Fun Seekers in Palm Springs.

Joshua Tree National Park

🛏 Sleeping

There are no lodges in the park, only campgrounds. You can find motels, inns and B&Bs in the towns of Joshua Tree and Twentynine Palms. Twentynine Palms has the bigger selection of accommodations (including national chains; check their websites), but the ones in Joshua Tree have more character and charm.

JOSHUA TREE

Spin & Margie's Desert Hide-a-Way
CABINS $$
(☏760-366-9124; www.deserthideaway.com; 64491 Twentynine Palms Hwy; ste $125-175; ℗🐾📶) Four out of the five boldly colorful, snappy-looking suites have their own kitchens at this delightful and homey inn on three fenced-in acres. Design motifs include corrugated tin, old license plates and cartoon art. Charming, knowledgeable owners ensure a relaxed visit. It's down the dirt Sunkist Rd, about 3 miles east of central Joshua Tree.

Desert Lily
B&B, CABINS $$
(☏760-366-4676, 877-887-7370; www.thedesertlily.com; Joshua Tree Highlands; s/d $140/155, cabins from $165, houses from $235; ℗@📶🐾) Down a dirt road near the western en-trance of the park, this out-of-the-way adobe-style charmer has three B&B guest rooms (breakfast might include eggs Santa Fe or double-stuffed French toast) and two houses that sleep four to eight, including the quirky, original homesteader's cabin. There are sweeping views across the park, and colorful 'desert eclectic' room decor. If all that is still too much stimulation, there are private little 'happy huts' further downhill for a greater escape. There are no phones or TVs in the rooms. Pets are allowed in cabins but not in the main house.

Joshua Tree Retreat Center
CABINS $
(☏760-365-8371; www.jtrcc.org; 59700 Twentynine Palms Hwy; camp sites from $25, r from $50; ℗📶♨) This facility on 420 acres hosts yoga, healing, psychological and spiritual groups, and it also rents rooms to the public in a variety of apartments, cottages and studios. Begun in 1938, many of its buildings are the work of Frank Lloyd Wright and his son Lloyd Wright. A massage studio had just opened, and a pool and sauna were in the works as we went to press. Mostly, though, the reason to come here is to escape to the desert. There's no daily maid service.

Joshua Tree Inn MOTEL $

(☑760-366-1188; www.joshuatreeinn.com; 61259 Twentynine Palms Hwy; r incl breakfast from $85; [P][☎][✿][☼]) Gram Parsons overdosed at this 10-room U-shaped motel (and his fans still flock here to stay in Room 8). Rooms have beamed ceilings and mix-and-match furniture. Vibe: more hippie than hipster.

TWENTYNINE PALMS

29 Palms Inn CABINS $$

(☑760-367-3505; www.29palmsinn.com; 73950 Inn Ave; most rooms & cabins incl breakfast $85-225; [P][@][☎][✿][☼][♻]) Built on and around the 'Oasis of Mara', this charming collection of early-20th-century adobe-and-wood cabins is Twentynine Palms' inn of record. Some cabins have decks and fireplaces, perfect for relaxing on cool desert evenings. The continental breakfast includes scratch muffins. There's also a great restaurant on the premises with vegetables grown on site.

Harmony Motel MOTEL $

(☑760-367-3351; www.harmonymotel.com; 71161 Twentynine Palms Hwy; r $65-90; [P][@][☎][✿][☼][♻]) U2 did the photo shoot for *The Joshua Tree* album here, and that's only one reason it's top pick for its class. The eight-room Harmony is a little designy (corrugated metal fencing around the pool and hot tub) in a variety of styles from desert cool to classic Americana. There are large rooms (several with kitchens), gorgeous views and nooks for reading or meditating. Breakfast is not included, but there's a communal kitchen and library.

JOSHUA TREE NATIONAL PARK

There are nine **campgrounds** (☑877-444-6777; www.recreation.gov; campsites $10-15) in the park. You can rent gear – from tents and bags to stoves and water jugs – from **Joshua Tree Outfitters** (☑760-366-1848; 61707 Twentynine Palms Hwy, Joshua Tree)

Of the campgrounds, only Black Rock Canyon and Cottonwood have shared-use water, flush toilets and dump stations. Water is available at the ranger station near Indian Cove. All other campgrounds have pit toilets, picnic tables and fireplaces. None of the campgrounds have showers.

Black Rock Canyon, **Indian Cove** and the six group sites at **Sheep Pass** may be reserved; check online for dates and details on individual sites. Campsites at **Belle**,

---

DESERT SURVIVAL 101

The desert is an unforgiving place with summertime temperatures up to 120°F (49°C), but if you take precautions you'll have nothing to fear. Here are some tips to help prepare for the worst and expect the best:

» Drink: water. Don't risk being stranded without it. Plan on drinking at least a gallon of water per day, and double that if you're hiking or boozing it up. Your body may be dehydrated before you realize it. If your urine runs darker than pale yellow, it's often a sign that you're getting dehydrated (unless you take a lot of vitamins). Sports drinks high in sodium and potassium are also helpful.

» Eat: salty foods. However, avoid salt tablets unless your physician recommends them. See p456 for more information on heatstroke.

» Wear: loose-fitting, light-colored, long-sleeved clothing. Also wear a hat and use sunscreen and lip balm. Bring warmer clothing for nighttime, especially if you're camping; the desert can be surprisingly chilly after dark.

» Take: compass and map (and know how to use them). Sometimes GPS units malfunction or batteries fail. A small mirror, matches and perhaps even flares can help you signal for help. A tent or groundsheet can provide vital sun protection and increase your visibility. Also useful: flashlight, pocketknife, first-aid kit and extra food and water. Cell phones can be helpful but don't work everywhere.

» Do: be sure your vehicle is in good condition and well gassed up, and don't push it beyond its limits. Never venture alone into remote areas. Always tell someone where you're going and when you'll be back. If you get stuck, stay with your vehicle and wait for rescue; a car is easier to spot than a hiker. If lost while hiking, seek the closest shady spot and stay put. You'll only get dehydrated and exhausted by walking around.

Cottonwood, Hidden Valley, Jumbo Rocks, Ryan and White Tank are available on a first-come, first-served basis. Jumbo Rocks is especially attractive for its sheltered rock alcoves that provide great sunset- and sunrise-viewing platforms. At busy times, during spring and fall, find a site before noon to stake your claim.

Backcountry camping is permitted in most wilderness areas, as long as it's 1 mile from the road and 500ft from any trail; registration is required at one of the 12 back-country boards throughout the park. Fires are strictly forbidden.

✕ Eating

JOSHUA TREE

Crossroads Café   CAFE $
(61715 Twentynine Palms Hwy; mains $6-11; ⊙7am-6:30pm Sun-Thu, to 8pm Fri & Sat; P ⁇ ▦) The much-loved Crossroads serves healthy breakfasts, huge sandwiches, big salads and tasty dinner specials. Earth-goddess atmosphere.

Sam's Pizza   INDIAN, PIZZA $
(☑760-366-9511; 61380 Twentynine Palms Hwy; mains $5-11; ⊙11am-9pm Mon-Sat, 3-8pm Sun; P ⁇) Pizza? Yeah, there's pizza, but *cognoscenti* come here for Indian dishes such as chicken tikka masala and *aloo gobhi*. You can even compromise with curry sauce pizzas. Atmosphere: nonexistant. Solution: takeout.

TWENTYNINE PALMS

Wonder Garden   CAFE $
(☑760-367-2429; 73511 Twentynine Palms Hwy; mains breakfast $3-7, lunch $5-10; ⊙7am-8pm Mon-Fri, 7am-9pm Sat, 11am-8pm Sun; ▦) South-western colors and a weathervane usher you into this cute cafe. Look for turkey and melted brie or Reuben sandwiches, veggie

---

WORTH A TRIP

PIONEERTOWN

From Hwy 62 (Twentynine Palms Hwy) in the town of Yucca Valley, head 5 miles north up Pioneer Town Rd, and you'll drive straight up a hill and into the past. **Pioneertown** (www.pioneertown.com) was built as a movie backdrop in 1946, developed by Roy Rogers, Dale Evans, Gene Autry and other Western stars, and has hardly changed since. The idea was that actors would have homes here, become part of the set and really live the Wild West life they acted out. The main street (Mane St) is lined with buildings that were used in countless Western movies and TV shows, including the *Gene Autry Show*, *Cisco Kid* (film and TV) and *Gunfight at the OK Corral*. You can witness a 'real' all-American **gunfight** (www.pioneertown-posse.org; contributions welcome) in the street here from April to October at 2:30pm on Saturdays. It's a little cheesy but highly kitschy, and kids love it.

Pioneer Bowl (56313 Mane St; ⊙11am-7pm Sat & Sun Apr-Oct) is an old-fashioned bowling alley built for Roy Rogers in 1947. It's still in use, with original equipment and a collection of vintage arcade games – pinball etc. Its saloon sells beer and burgers.

Pappy & Harriet's Pioneertown Palace (☑760-365-5956; www.pappyandharriets. com; mains $7-22; ⊙opens 11am Thu-Sun, 5pm Mon, closing varies with shows) is an Old West honky-tonk bar that defines nightlife in the Joshua Tree area. Expect cowboy hats, cheap beer, and big-as-the-prairie Tex-Mex grub and Santa Maria–style barbecue. Make reservations. Best of all, there's free live music every night it's open. Sometimes it has big names, from Leon Russell to Shelby Lynne, and you'll need tickets.

Around 4.5 miles from Pioneertown are the marvelous **Rimrock Ranch Cabins** (☑760-369-3012; www.rimrockranchcabins.com; 50857 Burns Canyon Rd; cabins $82-128; P ⁇), built in the 1940s as the area's first homestead. They reopened in autumn 2007 after a fire that ravaged outer Pioneertown. The four lovingly decorated cabins each come with a kitchen and a private patio perfect for stargazing. There's also a stand-alone sundeck, an Airstream trailer ($62 per night), and an architecturally acclaimed, newly built mid-century-style home with four beds ($232 per night). Or try the more basic **Pioneertown Motel** (☑760-365-7001; www.pitowninn.com; 5040 Curtis Rd; r $70-100), originally built to board film crews and decorated with Old West knickknacks. Hitch up your horse in its corral ($15).

INTEGRATRON

In the late 1940s former aerospace engineer George van Tassel moved to the desert and began meditating near giant rocks on a desolate stretch some 13 miles north-northwest of Joshua Tree. The story is that visitors from Venus arrived in a flying saucer and told him of a process for cell rejuvenation involving a dome based on principles of sacred geometry. He began work on it in 1953. Van Tassel called the dome at various times a time machine, a rejuvenation machine and an antigravity device. There's no documentation of its actually achieving any of that, but the **Integratron** (760-364-3126; www.integratron.com; 2477 Belfield Boulevard, Landers; depending on number of people, sound baths $10-55; vary, check website) is still worth a visit. The draw today is 30-minute 'sound baths,' in which docents stroke crystal bowls under the acoustically perfect dome; many visitors report an out-of-body experience, so maybe van Tassel realized his goal after all.

wraps and all-important ice cream and smoothies.

Edchada's MEXICAN $
(760-367-2131; 73502 Twentynine Palms Hwy; meals $6-13; 11am-9pm; P) Opinions vary on the food at this standard-issue Mexican eatery, but the margaritas are huge and you won't leave hungry. Look for lunch specials.

Rib Co BARBECUE $$
(760-367-1663; 72183 Twentynine Palms Hwy; mains $9-20; 4-9pm Mon-Thu, noon-10pm Fri & Sat, noon-8pm Sun; P) The fun atmosphere makes this roadside barbecue joint worth a look. Expect sandwiches, burgers, chicken and ribs (some in Jack Daniels glaze), plus salads and sides.

Palm Kabob House MIDDLE EASTERN $
(760-362-8583; 6341 Adobe Rd; mains $5-14; 10am-10pm Sun-Thu, to midnight Fri & Sat) For some troops shipping out to the Arab world, this new spot may be the first taste of the local cuisine: pita sandwiches like shawarma, and the namesake kabobs. Mains come with soup, fries and salads. There are all-American burgers, pastas and chicken for those with a strictly Western palate.

Information

Pick up food and gasoline in the towns of Joshua Tree or Twentynine Palms. In Joshua Tree, **Coyote Corner** (760-366-9683; 6535 Park Blvd; 9am-6pm, longer hr during peak season) sells camping supplies, maps, books and helpful information.

Emergency
For emergency assistance, call 911 from any telephone in the park. You'll find emergency telephones at Hidden Valley Campground and the Indian Cove ranger station. For first aid, contact a ranger.

Internet Resources
National Park Service (www.nps.gov/jotr) The NPS website has extensive information on the park, from activities and accessibility to weather and wildflowers.

Tourist Information
The park has several official **visitors centers** (760-367-5500; www.nps.gov/jotr) and there are several tourist offices.

Black Rock Nature Center (8am-4pm Sat-Thu, noon-8pm Fri, closed Jun-Sep) In the northwest corner of the park.

Cottonwood Visitors Center (8am-4pm) A few miles inside the park's southern entrance.

Joshua Tree Chamber of Commerce (760-366-3723; www.joshuatreechamber.org; 6448 Halley Rd; 9am-5pm Mon-Fri)

Joshua Tree Visitors Center (Park Blvd, Joshua Tree; 8am-5pm)

Oasis Visitors Center (National Monument Dr, Twentynine Palms; 8am-5pm) Stock up on books and maps, and talk to a ranger at park headquarters, just outside the park's northern boundary.

Twentynine Palms Chamber of Commerce (760-367-3445; www.29chamber.com; 73660 Civic Center; 9am-5pm Mon-Fri, 10am-4pm Sat & Sun)

Getting There & Away

The only way to reach Joshua Tree is by car. Rent one in Palm Springs or Los Angeles. From LA the trip takes two to three hours via I-10 and/or Hwy 62; from Palm Springs it takes about an hour, depending on where you enter the park.

IT'S A LONG WAY TO SALVATION MOUNTAIN

Southeast of Joshua Tree, southeast of Indio, southeast even of the Salton Sea (which is about as remote as it gets in SoCal), there's a mountain awash in storybook colors and fantastical patterns even the desert couldn't concoct. Salvation Mountain represents nearly three decades of effort by Leonard Knight (b 1931). He covered this mountain, in the town of Niland, with found objects – tires, hay bales and tree limbs among them – and used donated paints to inscribe messages including 'God is love' and 'Jesus I'm a sinner. Please come upon my body and into my heart.' Whatever your religious persuasion, it's hard not to be moved by the fervor Knight has devoted to this work, and it's become one of the great works of American folk art, declared a national treasure in the US Senate. All these years later, Knight is still building. Salvation Mountain is about 3 miles off Hwy 111, via Main St, which becomes Beal St.

ANZA-BORREGO DESERT STATE PARK

Encompassing some of SoCal's most spectacular and accessible desert scenery, the little-developed Anza-Borrego comprises almost a fifth of San Diego County and extends almost all the way to Mexico, making it the largest desert state park in the USA: over 600,000 acres, about half of the land in the California state-park system.

Human history here goes back 10,000 years, evidenced by the site's Native American pictographs. The park is named for Spanish explorer Juan Bautista de Anza, who arrived in 1774. In 1775 he led some 250 soldiers and colonists through the area, and the *borregos* (Spanish for 'bighorn sheep') they no doubt saw. These are viewable even today, along with jackrabbits, roadrunners, kit fox and mule deer. In the 1850s Borrego Springs became a stop along the Butterfield stagecoach line, which delivered mail between St Louis and San Francisco.

Winter and spring are high season here. In spring, wildflowers bloom in brilliant displays of bright color (pending winter rains), a striking contrast to the subtle earth tones you'll see here all year long. Summers are extremely hot, hotter than in Joshua Tree. The average daily maximum temperature in July is 107°F (42°C), but it's been known to go over 120°F (49°C). If you come here in summer, expect a pretty lonely visit as many places shut down or get just a few visitors, and use extreme caution if engaging in any outdoor activities.

The park's main town, **Borrego Springs** (population 2989, elevation 590ft), is about 40 miles from Palm Springs as the crow flies, but it's about double that if you're driving. The desert's southernmost region is the least visited and – aside from Blair Valley – has few developed trails and facilities.

◉ Sights

NORTHEAST OF BORREGO SPRINGS

Where S22 takes a 90-degree turn to the east, there's a pile of rocks just north of the road. This, the **Peg Leg Smith Monument**, is a monument to Thomas Long 'Peg Leg' Smith: mountain man, fur trapper, Native American fighter, horse thief, liar and Wild West legend. Around 1829 Peg Leg passed through Borrego Springs on his way to LA and supposedly picked up some rocks that were later found to be pure gold. Strangely, he didn't return to the area until the 1850s, when he was unable to find the lode. Nevertheless, he told lots of people about it (often in exchange for a few drinks), and many came to search for the gold and add to the myths.

On the first Saturday of April, the **Peg Leg Smith Liars Contest** is a hilarious event in which amateur liars compete in the Western tradition of telling tall tales. Anyone can enter, so long as the story is about gold and mining in the Southwest, is less than five minutes long and is anything but the truth.

EAST OF BORREGO SPRINGS

A 4-mile dirt road, sometimes passable without a 4WD (check with the visitors center), goes south of S22 to **Font's Point** (1249ft), which offers a spectacular panorama over the Borrego Valley to the west and the Borrego Badlands to the south. Walking the 4 miles to the point is a good way to *really* be amazed when the desert seemingly drops from beneath your feet.

SOUTHEAST OF BORREGO SPRINGS

South of Hwy 78 at Ocotillo Wells there's a **ranger station** (☏760-767-5391). From here, paved Split Mountain Rd takes you past the **Elephant Trees Discovery Trail**, one of the few places to see the unusual 'elephant tree,' named for its resemblance to an elephant's leg. Related to myrrh, the trees have a wonderful fragrance not unlike department stores around the holidays. The trees were thought not to exist in the Colorado Desert until a full-fledged hunt was launched in 1937. Expect to see (and hear) 4WD off-road vehicles around Ocotillo Wells.

About 4 miles south along Split Mountain Rd is a dirt-road turnoff for the primitive Fish Creek campground; it's near **Split Mountain**. The road from here – popular with 4WD enthusiasts – goes through Split Mountain between 600ft-high walls which have been created by earthquakes and erosion. The gorge is about 2 miles long from north to south. At the southern end, steep trails lead up to delicate **wind caves**, carved into the sandstone outcroppings by the wind.

SOUTH OF BORREGO SPRINGS

In the west of the park, around 5 miles southeast of Scissors Crossing (where S2 crosses Hwy 78), is **Blair Valley**, known for its Native American pictographs and *morteros* (hollows in rocks used for grinding seeds). The area also offers nice campgrounds and hiking trails.

A monument at Foot and Walker Pass marks a difficult spot on the Butterfield Overland Stage Route, and in **Box Canyon** you can still see the marks where wagoners had to hack through the rocks to widen the Emigrant Trail. A steep 1-mile climb leads to **Ghost Mountain** and the remains of a house occupied by the family of desert recluse Marshall South.

Activities

Hiking

There is a wide variety of hiking trails on offer.

Borrego Palm Canyon Nature Trail
HIKING

This popular self-guided loop trail goes northwest from the Borrego Palm Canyon Campground (day fee $8 per vehicle). It climbs 350ft in 3 miles past a palm grove and waterfall, a delightful oasis in the dry, rocky countryside.

Hellhole Canyon/Maidenhair Falls Trail
HIKING

This trail starts from the Hellhole Canyon Trailhead, 2 miles west of the visitors center on S22, and climbs past several palm oases to a seasonal waterfall that supports birdlife and a variety of plants.

Pictograph/Smuggler's Canyon Trail
HIKING

In a 3-mile round-trip you can see pictographs and a view of the Vallecito Valley; it starts 3.5 miles from S2 in Blair Valley.

A variety of other short trails have interpretive signs or self-guiding brochures. The 1-mile **Cactus Loop Nature Trail** shows a variety of cacti. Nearby, the 2-mile **Yaqui Well Nature Trail** has many labeled desert plants and passes a natural water hole that attracts a rich variety of birdlife as well as the occasional bighorn sheep in winter. The short **Narrows Earth Trail**, 2 miles east of Tamarisk Grove, highlights the local geology; look for the unusual chuparosa shrubs, which attract hummingbirds.

For last-minute equipment, stop by **Borrego Outfitters** (☏760-767-3502; 519 the Mall).

Mountain Biking

Both primitive roads and paved roads are open to bikes. Popular routes are Grapevine Canyon, Oriflamme Canyon and Canyon Sin Nombre. The visitors center has a free mountain-bike guide in the park magazine. **Carrizo Bikes** (☏760-767-3872; bike hire per 1st hr/additional hr/24hr $10/5/30), in Borrego Springs, rents bikes and also leads guided rides (inquire ahead).

Organized Tours

Anza Borrego Foundation　　　TOURS
(☏760-767-0446; www.theabf.org; 587 Palm Canyon Dr) has an impressive lineup of interpretive programs from stargazing to three-day hikes for the fittest outdoors folk. Phone or check online for upcoming events.

WHERE ARE THE SPRINGS?

Early visitors to the area came across the springs along with the *borregos* (bighorn sheep), lending the town its name. But the springs stopped flowing due to earthquakes. Wait around, though: the next earthquake may yet bring another spring...

🛏 Sleeping

Camping is permitted anywhere in the park as long as you're not within 200yd of any road or water source. Fires must be in metal containers, gathering anything including vegetation (dead or alive) is prohibited; of course, pack out your trash. Information about all campgrounds can be obtained from any ranger station or visitors center in the park, or online at www.parks.ca.gov.

TOP CHOICE Borrego Valley Inn

BOUTIQUE $$$

(☎760-767-0311, 800-333-5810; www.borregovalleyinn.com; 405 Palm Canyon Dr, Borrego Springs; r incl breakfast $200-235; P🖥☎) This small, immaculately kept inn (15 rooms on 9-plus acres), filled with Southwestern artifacts and Native American weavings, is an intimate spa-resort, perfect for adults. One pool is clothing-optional. Rates include a healthy breakfast and all-day soft drinks. Most rooms have kitchenettes.

Palms at Indian Head MID-CENTURY BOUTIQUE $$

(☎760-767-7788, 800-519-2624; www.thepalmsatindianhead.com; 2220 Hoberg Rd, Borrego Springs; r $189-249; P☎) Back in the day, Bing Crosby, Marilyn Monroe and Lon Cheney stayed here, 1 mile north from Palm Canyon Dr and on 240 acres abutting the state park. The 12-room Palms is a real retreat in a 1950s shell with mostly Southwestern-style rooms, no in-room phones or internet. There's a 25yd-long pool and suites have wood-burning fireplaces. No children aged under 13.

Borrego Springs Resort

RESORT $$

(☎760-767-5700, 800-826-7734; www.borregospringsresort.com; 1112 Tilting T Dr, Borrego Springs; r $150-220; P@🖥☎) This 100-room resort was built in 1997, and if it feels like the decor hasn't been upgraded much since, it's still a nice place to stay. The grounds feature desert plants, there are three nine-hole golf courses and rooms in two-story buildings around a swimming pool and jacuzzi. Larger rooms have kitchens, and a new spa was being installed as we went to press.

Palm Canyon Resort

MOTEL $$

(☎760-767-5341, 800-242-0044; www.palmcanyonresort.com; 221 Palm Canyon Dr, Borrego Springs; r $109-189; P🖥☎) A quarter of a mile from the park's visitors center, this cheery 61-unit Old West village–style inn (though built in the 1980s) has comfy motel-style rooms. There are two pools, a restaurant and saloon, a laundry, a store and RV parking.

Hacienda del Sol

CABINS $$

(☎760-767-5442; www.haciendadelsol-borrego.com; 610 Palm Canyon Dr, Borrego Springs; r $75, units with kitchen from $120, cottages from $160; P🖥☎) This 6-acre property has rooms ranging from motel-size to cottages, all pretty spartan and with desert-plant landscaping. It's ideal for groups of mates seeking to socialize around the pool, and has a picnic area with horseshoes and shuffleboard. The larger rooms have a two-night minimum stay.

Borrego Palm Canyon Campground

CAMPING $

(☎800-444-7275; www.reserveamerica.com; tent/RV sites Oct–mid-May $20/29, mid-May–Sep $15/24; P) Has award-winning toilets (rebuilt after a devastating 2003 flash flood), close-together campsites and an amphitheater with lectures on topics like astronomy and local bats.

Tamarisk Grove Campground

CAMPING $

(☎800-444-7275; www.reserveamerica.com; campsites $29; ☺mid-Sep–mid-May; P) Twelve miles south of Borrego Springs, near Hwy 78 and at 1400ft of elevation, this campground is smaller than Borrego Palm Canyon but has more shelter. It also has flush toilets.

Bow Willow Campground

CAMPING $

(campsites $7; P) Has only 16 campsites available, with occasional water, pit toilets, tables and fire pits. No reservations.

There are several other primitive campgrounds in the park which are free and have pit toilets but no water and only minimal facilities.

🍴 Eating

All of the following are in Borrego Springs.

Krazy Coyote Saloon & Grill/Red Ocotillo

AMERICAN $$

(☎760-767-7788; 2220 Hoberg Rd; mains $10-36; ☺7am-9pm, subject to seasonal change; P) The bar and grill at the Palms at Indian Head is two restaurants in one (the Red Ocotillo used to be across town). Now it serves famous martinis and classics like chicken cordon bleu, alongside newer fare like sesame-garlic pork tenderloin. The atmosphere is low-key and the views terrific.

Carmelita's Bar & Grill
MEXICAN $$
(the Mall, 575 Palm Canyon Dr; mains breakfast $5-8, lunch & dinner $10-14; ☺10am-9pm Mon-Fri, 8am-9pm Sat & Sun; [P][🖶]) Enter around the back of the mall for the town's best Mexican. It's casual with serape tablecloths, but there's a full bar and carne asada, steak picado and spicy chipotle chicken breast. Mexican breakfasts include classics like huevos rancheros and breakfast burritos cooked to order.

Carlee's Place
AMERICAN $$
(660 Palm Canyon Dr; mains lunch $7-14, dinner $12-23; ☺kitchen 11am-9pm, bar open later; [P]) Even if the decor feels like it hasn't been updated since the '70s, locals pick Carlee's, near Christmas Circle, for its burgers, pastas, pizzas and steak dinners – the pool table is a big draw too. There's live music on Friday and karaoke on Thursday and Saturday.

Kendall's Cafe
AMERICAN $$
([✆]760-767-3491; the Mall; mains breakfast & lunch $6-13, dinner $9-17; ☺6am-8pm; [P][🖶]) This coffeeshop is a hometown favorite for blueberry pancakes at breakfast and a combination of Mexican (enchiladas, fajitas etc) and straight-down-the-middle American standards the rest of the day.

Center Market
SUPERMARKET $
(590 Palm Canyon Dr; ☺8:30am-6:30pm Mon-Sat, to 5pm Sun; [P]) There's nothing fancy about this humble market, but it covers all the basics. It's in the Center, across from the Mall.

ℹ Information

Permits ($8 per day) are required only for visitors entering campgrounds like Borrego Palm Canyon, Tamarisk Grove and Horse Camp to access trails, camp overnight or go picnicking.

Emergency ([✆]911). Cell phones don't work everywhere in the park; if necessary, climb to the highest peak for service.

Visitors Center ([✆]760-767-4205; www. anzaborrego.statepark.org; 200 Palm Canyon Dr; ☺9am-5pm Oct-May, Sat, Sun & holidays only Jun-Sep) Located 2 miles west of Borrego Springs township. Has award-winning displays and audiovisual presentations. Staff are helpful and informative. The park's excellent newsletter/pamphlet has a trail guide and notes which roads are accessible and by what type of vehicle.

Wildflower Hotline ([✆]760-767-4684) Depending on winter rains, spring wildflowers in Anza-Borrego can be absolutely stunning. Flowers bloom in late February at lower elevations and progress over subsequent months at higher levels. Call for updates.

ℹ Getting There & Away

You'll need a car to get to Anza-Borrego Desert State Park. From San Diego (approximately two hours), I-8 to S2 is easiest because it mostly follows freeway. Alternatively, take the scenic and twisty Hwy 79 from I-8 north through Cuyamaca Rancho State Park and into Julian, then head east on Hwy 78.

From Orange County (via Temecula), take Hwy 79 to S2 and S22; the descent into Borrego Springs is a breathtaking journey. From Palm Springs (1½ hours), take I-10 to Indio, then Hwy 86 south along the Salton Sea. Take a turn west on S22.

AROUND ANZA-BORREGO DESERT STATE PARK

Julian
POP 3000

The mountain hamlet of Julian (elevation 4450ft/1300m), with its three-block main street, is a favorite getaway for city folk for its 1870s streetscape, gold-mining history and famous apple pies. It's actually not in the desert but in the wooded hill country in the center of San Diego County. Whether you come from the deserts or San Diego, by the time you reach it you feel like you've been on a journey.

Prospectors (many Confederate veterans) first arrived here after the Civil War (1861–65), and the discovery of gold in 1869 led to a growth spurt (to a whopping 600); mining continued for over 60 years. Later much of the land was given over to farming, and Julian-farmed apples won prizes at world fairs; today there are about 17,000 trees. Woe to the visitor who does not take home a pie, or at least do some taste-testing at one of the town's many pie shops (slice about $3.50).

Autumn is prime time. Shops and stands sell fresh local apples (inquire locally about child-friendly 'pick-your-own' opportunities). Summer can be hot and slow, with early closures and reduced rates. It gets busy during the Grape Stomp and Apple Days Festivals (early September and early October, respectively). Look for snow in winter.

THE SALTON SEA

Drive along Hwy 111 southeast of Indio and you'll come across a most unexpected sight: California's largest lake in the middle of its largest desert. The Salton Sea has a fascinating past, complicated present and uncertain future.

Geologists say that the Gulf of California once extended about 150 miles north of its present shore to what's now the Coachella Valley, but millions of years' worth of silt flowing through the Colorado River gradually sealed the valley off, leaving a sink behind. By the mid-1800s the sink was the site of salt mines, and geologists realized that the mineral-rich soil would make excellent farmland. Colorado River water was diverted into irrigation canals.

In 1905 the Colorado breached its dikes, and thus the Salton Sea was born; it took 18 months, 1500 workers and half-a-million tons of rock to put the river back on course, but the water remained. Today the sea is about 35 miles long, 15 miles wide and with nearly a third higher salt content than in the gulf.

By midcentury the Salton Sea was stocked with fish including tilapia and corvina, and marketed as the California Riviera, with vacation homes along its shores. The fish, in turn, attracted birds, and the sea remains a prime spot for bird-watching, including migratory and endangered species such as snow geese, mallards, ruddy ducks, white and brown pelicans, bald eagles and peregrine falcons.

These days, however, if you've heard of the Salton Sea at all it's probably due to annual fish die-offs. These, along with the sea's distinctive odor and poor publicity from 1980s environmental studies, have significantly diminished it as a tourist destination (though recent environmental studies have refuted some of the 1980s results). The die-offs are due to phosphorous and nitrogen in runoff from surrounding farmland. The minerals cause algae blooms, and when the algae die they deprive the water – and fish – of oxygen. Even if farming were to stop tomorrow, there are still generations' worth of minerals in the soil, waiting to reach the sink.

One seemingly obvious solution would seem to be to cut off the water to the sea and let it die, but that carries its own dilemma. A dry Salton Sea would leave a dust bowl, with projections of a permanent dust cloud devastating air quality valleywide. The debate rages.

To see the sea for yourself, try the **Salton Sea State Recreation Area** (☎760-393-3052; www.parks.ca.gov; Hwy 111, North Shore), or **Sonny Bono Salton Sea National Wildlife Refuge** (☎760-348-5278; 906 W Sinclair Rd; ☺7am-3:30pm Mon-Fri year-round, 8am-4:30pm Sat & Sun Nov-Mar) is off Hwy 111 between Niland and Calipatria.

◉ Sights & Activities

Eagle and High Peak Mines GOLD-MINE TOURS
(☎760-765-0036; end of C St; adult/child $10/5; ☺from 10am, closing time varies; P ♿) Offers instructive tours of now-defunct gold mines as you go through 1000ft of tunnels and learn to pan for gold.

Julian Pioneer Museum MUSEUM
(2811 Washington St; admission $3; ☺10am-4pm Sat & Sun; additional hr possible) Exhibits mining equipment, period clothing, photos and Native American artifacts.

Doves & Desperadoes RE-ENACTMENTS
Weather permitting, shows take place Sundays at 1pm, 2pm and 3pm on Main St; costumed, comedic re-creations of late 1800s' mining days, minus the bloodshed, cursing and real bullets.

Menghini Winery WINERY
(1150 Julian Orchards Dr; tastings $5; ☺10am-4pm Mon-Fri, to 5pm Sat & Sun) Sitauted about 3 miles north of town, Menghini is one of several wineries in the Julian area; this one offers wine tastings and picnic grounds.

Lake Cuyamaca LAKE
(☎760-765-0515; 15027 Hwy 79; ☺6am-sunset, check times in Dec & Jan) Well stocked with trout, small-mouthed bass and more, and has boats for rent. There's a dog-friendly 3.25-mile walk around the lake.

California Wolf Center WILDLIFE CENTRE
(☎760-765-0030; 18457 Hwy 79; adult/child from $10/6; ☺Sat & Sun by reservation) Offers 1½-hour tours including a slide show and visit with wolf packs.

🛏 Sleeping

Orchard Hill Country Inn   B&B $$$
(☎760-765-1700, 800-716-7242; www.orchard
hill.com; 2502 Washington St; r & cottages incl
breakfast $195-375; P@☎) This romantic,
immaculately maintained B&B features a
Craftsman-style hilltop main lodge and a
dozen cottages on 4 wooded acres. Each
designer-furnished room is different but
might include whirlpool tub, fireplace or
balcony. Full gourmet breakfasts include
homemade jams such as plum, fig or pump-
kin butter.

Observer's Inn   B&B $$
(☎760-765-0088; www.observersinn.com; 3535
Hwy 79; r incl breakfast $160; P☎) About
1.5 miles from central Julian, this secluded
4.5-acre property is perfect for viewing the
night sky through three research-grade
telescopes with the astronomer-owner
($10/20 for guests/nonguests). The inn is
just two rooms in a guesthouse.

Julian Hotel   HISTORIC $$
(☎760-765-0201, 800-734-5854; www.julianhotel.
com; 2032 Main St; r from $135, cottages from $170;
P) In the center of town, this 1897 hos-
telry boasts Victorian furnishings, friendly
owners and a nice complimentary breakfast.
Choose from the main house or cottages.
The original owners were freed slaves.

The **Bed & Breakfast Guild** (☎760-765-
1555; www.julianbnbguild.com; ☺9am-9pm) can
point you to other available rooms.

🍴 Eating & Drinking

Romano's   ITALIAN $$
(☎760-765-1003; 2718 B St; mains $11-20;
☺11:30am-8:30pm Wed-Mon, reduced summer
hr; P) Homestyle Italian cooking in a
gold-country setting, with wood-paneled
walls, Franklin stove, lace curtains and
Johnny Mathis piped in. Hearty main
dishes such as pork chops in creamy garlic sauce and zucchini parmigiana come
with a side of pasta or veggies. Pizzas also
available. Reservations are recommended
at peak times.

Rong Branch   STEAK, BARBECUE $$
(2722 Washington St; most mains $11-18; ☺11am-
9pm Sun-Thu, to 10pm Fri & Sat; P) It's fa-
miliar country cookin' here (think chicken-
fried steak, barbecue, steaks and red beans
and rice) amid country decor. Wash it down
with Julian hard cider. Afterwards, gander
at the kitschy gift shop.

ℹ Information

Central Julian runs along Main St. Inside Town
Hall, the friendly **Chamber of Commerce**
(☎760-765-1857; www.julianca.com; 2129
Main St; ☺10am-4pm) offers info, maps and
brochures.

ℹ Getting There & Away

Julian sits at the junction of routes 78 and 79.
It's about 1¼ hours from San Diego (via I-8 east
to Rte 79 north), North County (via Rte 78) or
Temecula (I-15 south to Rte 78 east). Rte 78
also leads you toward Borrego Springs (40
minutes).

DEATH VALLEY NATIONAL PARK

The name itself evokes all that is harsh
and hellish – a punishing, barren and
lifeless place of Old Testament severity.
Yet closer inspection reveals that nature
is putting on a truly spectacular show in
Death Valley, with water-fluted canyons,
singing sand dunes, palm-shaded oases,
sculpted mountains and plenty of endemic
wildlife. It's truly a land of superlatives,
holding the US records for hottest tem-
perature (134°F/56°C, measured in 1913),
lowest point (Badwater, 282ft below sea
level) and being the largest national park
outside Alaska (4687 sq miles). Peak tour-
ist season is during the spring wildflower
bloom.

◉ Sights & Activities

Start out early in the morning by driving
up to **Zabriskie Point** for spectacular val-
ley views across golden badlands eroded
into waves, pleats and gullies. Escape the
heat by continuing on to **Dante's View** at
5000ft, where you can simultaneously see
the highest (Mt Whitney) and lowest (Bad-
water) points in the contiguous USA. The
drive there takes about 1½ to two hours
round-trip.

Badwater itself, a foreboding landscape
of crinkly salt flats, is a 17-mile drive south
of **Furnace Creek**. Along the way, you'll
want to check out narrow **Golden Canyon**,
easily explored on a 2-mile round-trip walk,
and **Devil's Golf Course**, where salt has
piled up into saw-toothed miniature moun-
tains. A 9-mile detour along **Artists Drive**
is best done in the late afternoon when the
hills erupt in fireworks of color.

WANT MORE?

For further information, head to shop. lonelyplanet.com to purchase a downloadable PDF of The Deserts chapter in Lonely Planet's *California* guide.

Near Stovepipe Wells Village, north of Furnace Creek, you can scramble along the smooth marble walls of **Mosaic Canyon** or roll down powdered sugar at the undulating **Sand Dunes** (magical during a full moon).

Another 36 miles north is the fantastical **Scotty's Castle** (☎760-786-2392; adult/child/senior $11/6/9; ☺9am-5pm), where costumed guides bring to life the strange tale of lovable con-man Death Valley Scotty. About 8 miles west of here, giant **Ubehebe Crater** is the result of a massive volcanic eruption. Hiking to the bottom and back takes about 30 minutes. It's slow going for another 27 miles on a tire-shredding dirt road (high clearance required) to reach the eerie **Racetrack**, where you can ponder the mystery of faint tracks that slow-moving rocks have etched into the dry lakebed.

The most spectacular backcountry adventure, though, is the 27-mile trip along unpaved **Titus Canyon Rd**, which climbs, curves and plunges through the Grapevine Mountains past a ghost town, petroglyphs and dramatic canyon narrows. It's a one-way road accessible only from Hwy 374 near Beatty; the entrance is about 2 miles outside park boundaries.

🛏 Sleeping & Eating

During wildflower season accommodations are often booked solid and campgrounds are full by midmorning, especially on weekends. Campgrounds are first-come, first-served, except for Furnace Creek, which accepts reservations from October to April.

Furnace Creek Resort INN $$$
(☎760-786-2345; www.furnacecreekresort.com; r $330-460; ☺mid-Oct–mid-May; ⊠) Elegant, Mission-style hotel with spring-fed pool and a restaurant that isn't quite as gourmet as advertised.

Texas Spring CAMPING $
(www.death.valley.national-park.com; sites $14; ☺Oct-Apr) Small and best for tents; nice hillside location.

Furnace Creek CAMPING $
(www.death.valley.national-park.com; sites $12-18; ☺year-round) Pleasant grounds, including some shady sites.

Sunset CAMPING $
(www.death.valley.national-park.com; sites $12 ☺Oct-Apr) Huge and RV-oriented.

Stovepipe Wells CAMPING $
(www.death.valley.national-park.com; sites $12; ☺Oct-Apr) Parking-lot style, but close to the sand dunes.

Stovepipe Wells Village LODGE $$
(☎760-786-2387; www.stovepipewells.com; r from $120; @⊠) Long in the tooth, it also has a quirky restaurant that delivers above-par cowboy cooking. Rooms here are good value.

Wrangler Restaurant STEAKHOUSE $$
(breakfast buffet $10, lunch $10-12, mains dinner $19-29; ☺breakfast, lunch & dinner) Furnace Creek Ranch's restaurant serves belly-filling buffet breakfasts and turns into a pricey steakhouse at night.

Forty-Niner Café AMERICAN $$
(www.furnacecreekresort.com; mains $6-19; ☺breakfast, lunch & dinner) Cooks up decent American standards.

19th Hole Bar & Grill AMERICAN $
(www.furnacecreekresort.com; mains $7.75-10.95; ☺lunch Oct-May) Has the juiciest burgers.

ℹ Information

Centrally located Furnace Creek has a general store, restaurants, lodging, post office, gas station, ATM and a **visitors center** (www.nps.gov/deva; ☺8am-5pm) the website of which is an excellent pretrip planning resource. Stovepipe Wells Village, about 24 miles northwest, has a store, gas station, ATM, motel-restaurant and ranger station. Gas and sustenance are also available at Scotty's Castle in the north, and Panamint Springs on the park's western edge. The entrance fee ($20 per vehicle, valid for seven days) must be paid at self-service pay stations located throughout the park. For a free map and newspaper present your receipt at the visitors center.

ℹ Getting There & Away

There is no public transportation to Death Valley. Coming from LA, head north on the I-5 Fwy to CA-14, which turns into US-395 near Inyokern. Turn off onto CA-190 near Olancha and proceed into the park. Gas is expensive inside, so make sure you fill up beforehand.

LAS VEGAS

Vegas is the ultimate escape. A few frenzied sleepless nights here are more intoxicating than a weeklong bender anywhere else. Be as naughty as you want to be, pretend to be someone else entirely, and watch your most devilish fantasies become reality. Sin City stands ready to give you an alibi: what happens in Vegas, stays in Vegas. Who can resist such outrageous temptation? Fuhgeddaboudit. In this city of fake Elvises, everybody gets the chance to live like a king.

◎ Casinos & Sights

There's plenty to do besides gambling at the massive casino-resorts on and off the Strip. From volcanoes to roller coasters, superb restaurants to hot dance clubs, you'll have no trouble being entertained 24/7. Of course there are entire books devoted to Vegas, but here's a peek at the best the city has to offer.

Wynn & Encore CASINO RESORT $$$
(☏702-770-7100, 888-320-9966; www.wynn lasvegas.com; 3131 Las Vegas Blvd; r from $199; P @ ⎙ ⛱) The most expensive hotel-casino built to date exudes an air of secrecy – the entrance is obscured from the Strip by a $130-million man-made mountain. Inside, the copper-toned signature is awash with vibrant floral mosaics, natural light from panoramic windows and alfresco seating. Gawking tourists amble by the Ferrari/Maserati dealership's logo store, haute-couture shops on the Esplanade and sumptuous high-end restaurants. Apparently, all this still wasn't enough for Wynn, who recently built **Encore** (☏770-8000; www.en corelasvegas.com; 3111 Las Vegas Blvd S; r from $219) next door.

Bellagio CASINO RESORT $$$
(☏702-693-7111, 877-987-6667; www.bellagio. com; 3600 Las Vegas Blvd S; r from $209; P @ ⎙ ⛱) Inspired by a lakeside Italian village this pleasure *palazzo* has a gasp-worthy lobby, dancing fountains in a huge lake, world-class restaurants and even a fine-art gallery (adult/child $17/free).

Caesars Palace CASINO RESORT $$$
(☏702-731-7110, 800-634-6001; www.caesars palace.com; 3570 Las Vegas Blvd S; r from $249; P @ ⎙ ⛱) An old-school Greco-Roman fantasyland as over-the-top Vegas as ever with marble reproductions of classical statu-

ary, goddess-costumed waitresses and the swanky Forum Shops.

Venetian CASINO RESORT $$
(☏702-414-4500, 888-283-6423; www.venetian. com; 3355 Las Vegas S; r from 139; P @ ⎙ ⛱) Hand-painted ceiling frescoes, roaming mimes and full-scale reproductions of famous Venice landmarks are found at this romantic if surreal casino where you can take a gondola ride. Rooms are huge, with sunken living rooms and picture windows revealing stunning sunset views over the strip.

Red Rock Casino RESORT SPA $$$
(☏702-797-7777; www.redrocklasvegas.com; 11011 W Charleston Blvd at I-215; r from $240; P @ ⎙ ⛱ ♿) Poised within easy striking distance of the southwestern beauty of Red Rock Canyon, this slick high-concept, high-design casino resort is built for suburbanites. It banks not only on its vast casino, but also on its adventure spa and above-average restaurants.

Aria CASINO RESORT $$
(☏866-359-7757; www.arialasvegas.com; 3730 S Las Vegas Blvd; r from $169; @ ⎙ ⛱) Part of MGM Mirage's massive CityCenter complex and the only casino in the bunch. This resort has a Japanese-inspired spa, heavy-hitter dining rooms and a quirky Cirque du Soleil show, *Viva Elvis*, which has its own official store for die-hard fans of the King.

Mandarin Oriental HOTEL $$$
(☏702-590-8888; www.mandarinoriental.com; 3752 S Las Vegas; r from $255; @ ⎙ ⛱) Also set in the CityCenter maze is this five-star hideaway. Don't let the stuffy doormen deter you, however: anyone is welcome to take the elevators up to the 23rd-floor 'Sky Lobby,' where floor-to-ceiling windows allow glittering Strip views, best enjoyed with a cocktail from Mandarin Bar & Tea Lounge or at Twist by Pierre Gagnaire, a posh French restaurant.

Hard Rock CASINO RESORT $
(☏702-693-5000; www.hardrockhotel.com; 4455 Paradise Rd; r from $69) The world's first rock-and-roll casino sports the most impressive collection of rock-star memorabilia ever assembled under one roof. A newly expanded casino has blackjack tables with Hell's Belles go-go dancers, and there's seasonal swim-up blackjack at the Beach Club, open to the public for **Rehab Pool Parties** on summer Sundays.

Paris Las Vegas CASINO RESORT $$
(702-946-7000, 877-796-2096; www.parislas
vegas.com; 3655 Las Vegas Blvd S; r from $160;
P@ 🛜🏊) This Gallic caricature strives
to capture the essence of the City of Light
with re-created landmarks, including the
impressive ersatz **Eiffel Tower** (adult/child
$10/7, evening admission $15). And with per-
petual blue-sky ceilings, it can feel like
noon at midnight.

✕ Eating

Sage NEW AMERICAN $$$
(877-230-2742; www.arialasvegas.com; Aria,
3730 Las Vegas Blvd S; mains $35-49; ✆dinner
Mon-Sat; ✍) Chef Shawn McClain brings
his Midwestern farm-to-table cuisine to
the Strip. The gorgeous backlit-bar mural
almost steals the scene, but creative twists
on meat-and-potatoes classics and outside-
the-box vegetarian offerings shine. After
dinner, sip an absinthe. Or before. And during. Reservations recommended.

Mon Ami Gabi FRENCH BISTRO $$
(702-944-4224; www.parislasvegas.com; 3655
Las Vegas Blvd S; mains $13-40; ✆lunch & din-
ner; ✍🍴) Grab a sidewalk table below the
Eiffel Tower, order steak-frites or quiche
and watch the world on parade. Squint
and it'll feel just like you're on the Champs
Élysées.

Sinatra ITALIAN $$$
(702-248-3463; www.encorelasvegas.com;
3131 Las Vegas Blvd S; mains $26-52; ✆dinner)
Ol' Blue Eyes would've felt right at home
in these posh casino surrounds. The kitch-
en delivers a mix of heart-warming and
sophisticated Italian-American classics,
from lasagna Bolognese and octopus affog-
ato to osso bucco 'My Way' and spaghetti
and clams with red sauce. Reservations
recommended.

🍷 Drinking & Entertainment

For listings, consult the free *Las Vegas
Weekly* (www.lasvegasweekly.com) and
CityLife (www.lvcitylife.com).

Cirque du Soleil SHOW
(www.cirquedusoleil.com; tickets $94-150; ✆Wed-
Sun) From the aquatic (O) to the surreal
(Mystere), Las Vegas is resplendent in the
spectacular, colorful feats of Cirque du
Soleil's imagination, engineering and ac-
robatic skills. Unless you make like Seth
Rogan in *Knocked Up,* you really can't go
wrong.

WANT MORE?

For in-depth information, reviews and
recommendations at your fingertips,
head to the Apple App Store to purchase Lonely Planet's *Las Vegas City
Guide* iPhone app.

Blush ULTRA LOUNGE
(702-770-3633; www.wynnlasvegas.com; Wynn,
3131 Las Vegas Blvd S; cover $20-30; ✆9pm-4am
Tue-Sat) A long, narrow room beckons with
glowing paper lanterns, gauzy drapery,
candlelit tables, a starlight patio and premium VIP bottle service beside a boutique-
sized onyx dance floor. The cover charge
may be waived before midnight. Two more
no-cover lounges nearby for smoochy
drinks are Wynn's Parasol Up and lakeside
Parasol Down.

Moon NIGHTCLUB
(702-942-6832; www.moon-lasvegas.n9ne
group.com; 53rd fl, Fantasy Tower, Palms, 4321 W
Flamingo Rd; cover $20-40; ✆10pm-4am Tue &
Thu-Sun) A short glass-and-mirror elevator
ride away from the Playboy Club, this futuristic penthouse has a surreal moon roof
that retracts as you find your groove in the
laser-lit fog on the dance floor below. Glass
tiles change color with the mood and beat
of the music. Dress to impress.

Pure NIGHTCLUB
(702-731-7873; www.purethenightclub.com;
Caesars Palace, 3570 Las Vegas Blvd S; cover
$20-40; ✆10pm-4am Tue & Fri-Sun) Gorgeous
females mix the music at this chic modern
club electrified with hues of steely blue,
white and silver. Crowds of fine young
thangs lounge inside a labyrinth, which
leads to a gorgeous Strip-view patio. Strict
dress code.

Joint VENUE
(702-693-5066; www.hardrockhotel.com; Hard
Rock, 4455 Paradise Rd; most tickets $35-175;
✆varies) Concerts at this intimate venue
feel like private shows, even when Coldplay
or the Beastie Boys are in town. Most are
standing-room only, with reservable VIP
balcony seats upstairs.

ℹ Information

Las Vegas Blvd, aka the Strip, is the main north–
south drag and lined with the most famous
hotel-casinos. Downtown Las Vegas is the origi-

nal town center with Fremont St as its main drag. For information, rooms or tickets, contact the **Las Vegas Visitor Information Center** (⏸702-892-0711, 877-847-4858; www.visitlasvegas.com; 3150 Paradise Rd; ⏲8am-5pm), which also offers internet access and free local calls.

ℹ Getting There & Away

McCarran International Airport (LAS; www.mccarran.com) has direct flights from LAX and smaller SoCal airports. **Greyhound** (www.greyhound.com) has inexpensive but slow buses to and from Los Angeles and San Diego.

Las Vegas is 270 miles northeast of LA and is reached in four to five hours by heading east on the I-10, then north on the I-15.

ℹ Getting Around

In town, the **Monorail** (www.lvmonorail.com; $5) stops at some major resort-hotels along the Strip. The **Deuce** (www.thedeucelasvegas.com; $3) is a 24-hour double-decker bus shuttling between the Strip and downtown. The new Ace bus is faster and runs 24 hours between the Strip and downtown, with limited stops.

Santa Barbara

Best Places to Eat

» Root 246 (p397)

» Santa Barbara Shellfish Company (p381)

» Los Olivos Café & Wine Merchant (p396)

» Bouchon (p381)

» Brooks (p403)

Best Places to Stay

» Inn of the Spanish Garden (p378)

» The Biltmore (p378)

» El Capitan Canyon (p379)

» Hadsten House Inn (p397)

» Blue Iguana Inn (p402)

Why Go?

Frankly put, this area is damn pleasant to putter around. Low-slung between lofty mountains and the shimmering Pacific, chic Santa Barbara's red-tiled roofs, white stucco buildings and Mediterranean vibe give credence to its claim of being the 'American Riviera.' It's a surprisingly bewitching place to loll on the beach, eat and drink extraordinarily well, shop a bit and push all your cares off to another day. Nowadays the city's blossoming green movement has brought electric shuttles, urban bike trails, eco-friendly attractions and earth-friendly wine tours. Mother Nature returns the love with hiking, biking, surfing, kayaking, scuba diving and camping opportunities galore, from Channel Islands National Park to arty Ojai, surrounded by hot springs. Meanwhile winemaking is booming in the bucolic Santa Ynez Mountains, where over a hundred wineries vie for your attention. But if all you want to do is relax, no worries – sunny beaches still await.

When to Go

Santa Barbara

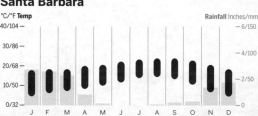

April Balmy temperatures, fewer tourists than in summer. Wildflowers bloom on Channel Islands.

June Summer vacation and beach season begin. Summer Solstice Celebration.

October Sunny blue skies, smaller crowds. Wine country harvest festival.

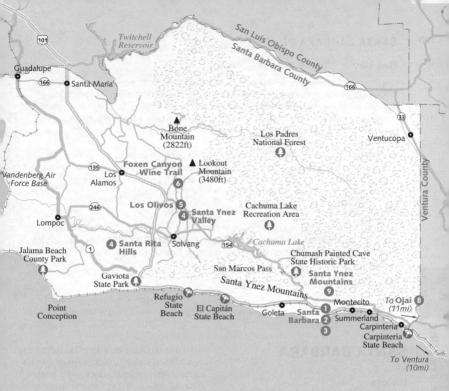

Santa Barbara Highlights

① Strolling **Stearns Wharf** (p371) by the harbor, then lazing on Santa Barbara's cinematic **beaches** (p375)

② Ambling about Spanish-Mexican colonial historic sites, ending up at **Mission Santa Barbara** (p370)

③ Eyeing panoramic views atop the *Vertigo*-esque clock tower of the **Santa Barbara County Courthouse** (p371)

④ Pedaling past vineyards and organic farms in the **Santa Ynez Valley** (p389)

⑤ Boutique shopping and wine tasting in **Los Olivos** (p395)

⑥ Following the rural **Foxen Canyon Wine Trail** (p392) to taste top-rated pinot noir

⑦ Kayaking by sea caves and watching whales in **Channel Islands National Park** (p405)

⑧ Rejuvenating at a day spa in new-agey **Ojai** (p401)

⑨ Hiking past Rattlesnake Canyon's waterfalls in the **Santa Ynez Mountains** (p376)

SANTA BARBARA IN...

One Day

Spend your first morning soaking up rays at **East Beach**, walking out onto **Stearns Wharf** and down by the **harbor**. After lunch visit museums, landmarks and shops downtown, stopping at the **courthouse** for 360-degree views from its clock tower. Finish up at the historic **mission**, then head back to **State Street** after dark.

Two Days

Cycle along the coast, go surfing or sea kayaking, or hike into the Santa Ynez foothills. In the afternoon, savor the indie lifestyle in the **Funk Zone**, with its eclectic shops and Urban Wine Trail. Or detour east to posh **Montecito** for shopping and people-watching and hang loose in **Carpinteria**, a retro beach town.

Three Days

Head up to wine country. Enjoy a do-it-yourself tour via car, motorcycle or bicycle along a scenic wine trail – **Foxen Canyon** and the **Santa Rita Hills** are exceptionally beautiful. Pack a picnic lunch or dine in charming **Los Olivos** or kitschy faux-Danish **Solvang**.

Four Days

On your way back to LA, make time for a detour to arty **Ojai** up in the mountains or a day trip from **Ventura** to **Anacapa Island** in rugged Channel Islands National Park.

SANTA BARBARA

POP 90,900

History

The Chumash people thrived in the area for thousands of years before the arrival of the Spanish, setting up trade routes between the mainland and the Channel Islands, which they reached via redwood canoes known as *tomols*. In 1542 explorer Juan Rodríguez Cabrillo sailed into the channel and claimed it for Spain, then quickly met his doom on a nearby island.

The Chumash had little reason for concern until the permanent return of the Spanish in the late 18th century. Spanish Catholic priests established missions up and down the coast, ostensibly to convert Native Californians to Christianity. But Spanish soldiers often forced the Chumash to construct the missions and presidios (military forts) and provide farm labor. They also rounded up and forced indigenous peoples to leave the Channel Islands. Back on the mainland, the Chumash population shrank dramatically, as many died of European diseases and ill treatment.

Mexican ranchers arrived after winning their independence in 1821. Easterners began migrating en masse with the 1849 gold rush, and by the late 1890s the city of Santa Barbara was an established vacation spot for the wealthy. After a massive earthquake in 1925, laws were passed requiring much of the city to be rebuilt in a faux-Spanish style of white stucco and red-tiled roofs.

⊙ Sights

Mission Santa Barbara   HISTORIC SITE
(☎805-682-4713; www.sbmission.org; 2201 Laguna St; adult/6-15yr/senior $5/1/4; ⊙9am-5pm, last entry 4:30pm; 🅿) Called the 'Queen of the Missions,' Mission Santa Barbara reigns above the city on a hilltop perch about a mile northwest of downtown. It was established on December 4 (the feast day of St Barbara) in 1786, as the 10th California mission. Of California's original 21 Spanish-colonial missions, it's the only one that escaped secularization under Mexican rule. Continuously occupied by Catholic priests since its founding, the mission still functions as a Franciscan friary and an active parish church.

Behind an imposing Doric facade (an architectural homage to an ancient Roman chapel) topped by an unusual twin bell tower, the mission's 1820 stone **church** has striking interior Chumash artwork. Outside is an eerie **cemetery** – look for the skull carvings over the doorway – with

4000 Chumash graves and the elaborate mausoleums of early California settlers. As you walk through the **museum exhibits**, which include Chumash baskets, a missionary's bedroom and time-capsule black-and-white photos, doors will lock behind you, so make sure you're finished before moving on.

El Presidio de Santa Barbara State Historic Park

HISTORIC SITE

(www.sbthp.org; 123 E Cañon Perdido St; adult/senior/under 17yr $5/4/free; ⊙10:30am-4:30pm) Built to defend the mission, this 18th-century former Spanish fort was constructed by Chumash laborers. Its adobe walls are nearly 4ft thick and more than 9ft high. But its mission wasn't solely to protect – the presidio also served as a social and political hub, and as a stopping point for traveling Spanish military.

Today this small urban park harbors some of the city's oldest structures, which seem to be in constant need of propping up and restoring. Be sure to stop by the **chapel**: its interior is radiant with kaleidoscopic color. Admission also includes entry to **Casa de La Guerra**, a grand 19th-century colonial home with Spanish-American heritage exhibits.

FREE Santa Barbara County Courthouse

HISTORIC SITE

(www.santabarbaracourthouse.org; 1100 Anacapa St; ⊙8:30am-4:45pm Mon-Fri, 10am-4:45pm Sat & Sun) Panoramic views from the 85ft clock tower of the courthouse are not to be missed. Built in Spanish-Moorish Revival style in 1929, the courthouse features hand-painted ceilings, wrought-iron chandeliers, and tiles from Tunisia and Spain. Check out the mural room depicting SoCal colonial history on the 2nd floor. You're free to explore on your own, but you'll get a lot more out of a free guided tour offered at 2pm Monday to Saturday, and 10:30am Monday, Tuesday and Friday.

Santa Barbara Historical Museum

MUSEUM

(www.santabarbaramuseum.com; 136 E De La Guerra St; donations appreciated; ⊙10am-5pm Tue-Sat, noon-5pm Sun) Embracing a romantic cloistered Spanish-style adobe courtyard, this peaceful little museum has an endlessly fascinating collection of local memorabilia, ranging from the simply beautiful, such as Chumash woven baskets and colonial-era textiles, to the intriguing, such as an intricately carved coffer that

once belonged to Junípero Serra. Learn about the city's involvement in toppling the last Chinese monarchy, among other interesting footnotes in local history.

Santa Barbara Museum of Art

MUSEUM

(☑805-963-4364; www.sbma.net; 1130 State St; adult/senior & 6-17yr $9/6; Sun by donation; ⊙11am-5pm Tue-Sun) With a collection of over 27,000 works of art, this thoughtfully curated, if petite museum displays modern European and American masters – think Matisse, Hopper and O'Keeffe – along with contemporary photography and classical antiquities. Traipse up to the 2nd floor, where Asian art exhibits include an intricate, colorful Tibetan sand mandala and the iron-chainmail armor of a Japanese warrior. There's also an interactive children's gallery, museum shop and cafe.

Stearns Wharf

HISTORIC SITE

(www.stearnswharf.org; State St at Cabrillo Blvd; P) The southern end of State St gives way to Stearns Wharf, a rough wooden pier lined with souvenir shops, snack stands and seafood shacks. Built in 1872, it's the oldest continuously operating wharf on the West Coast, although the actual structure has been rebuilt more than once after catching fire. During the 1940s it was co-owned by tough-guy actor Jimmy Cagney and his two brothers. If you've got kids, don't miss the **Ty Warner Sea Center** (see boxed text, p378). Parking on the wharf costs $2.50 per hour, with the first 90 minutes free with validation. But trust us, you'd rather walk than drive over the wharf's bumpy wooden slats.

ON THE STREET

Santa Barbara's self-guided 12-block **Red Tile walking tour** is a convenient introduction to downtown's historical highlights. The tour's name comes from the half-moon-shaped red clay tiles covering the roofs of many Spanish Revival–style buildings. You can download a free map of this walking tour, as well as other diverting paths along the waterfront and to the mission, from **Santa Barbara Car Free** (www.santabarbaracarfree.org). For a lazy stroll between wine-tasting rooms, find the city's **Urban Wine Trail** (see p384).

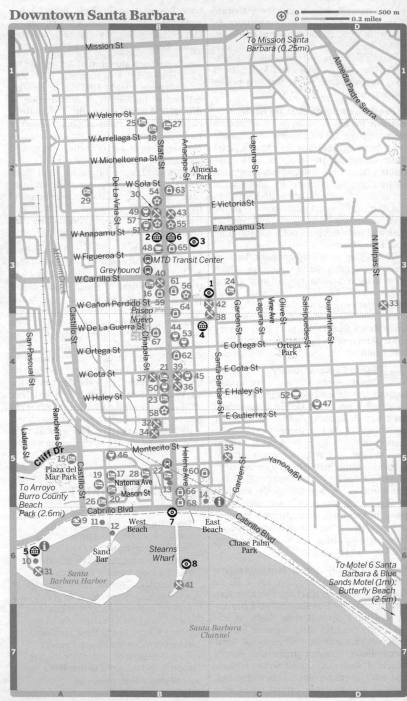

SANTA BARBARA

Mission St

To Mission Santa Barbara (0.25mi)

Almeda Padre Serra

W Valerio St
W Arrellaga St
W Micheltorena St

State St
Anacapa St
Laguna St

Almeda Park

W Sola St
E Victoria St

De La Vina St

W Anapamu St
E Anapamu St

W Figueroa St
MTD Transit Center
Greyhound

W Carrillo St

W Cañon Perdido St
Paseo Nuevo

W De La Guerra St

Castillo St

W Ortega St

Chapala St

W Cota St

W Haley St

Santa Barbara St
Garden St
Vine Ave
Olive St
Laguna St
Salsipuedes St
Quarantina St

E Ortega St
Ortega Park

E Cota St

E Haley St

E Gutierrez St

N Milpas St

San Pascual St
Mission Creek

Ranchería St
Ladera St

Cliff Dr

Plaza del Mar Park

To Arroyo Burro County Beach Park (2.6mi)

Montecito St
Helena Ave
Yanonali St

Natoma Ave
Mason St

Cabrillo Blvd

Garden St

West Beach
East Beach

Cabrillo Blvd

Chase Palm Park

Sand Bar

Stearns Wharf

Santa Barbara Harbor

Santa Barbara Channel

To Motel 6 Santa Barbara & Blue Sands Motel (1mi); Butterfly Beach (2.5m)

Downtown Santa Barbara

Santa Barbara Maritime Museum MUSEUM (www.sbmm.org; 113 Harbor Way; adult/1-5yr/6-17yr & senior $7/2/4, admission free 1st Thu of month; ☺10am-6pm Jun-Aug, to 5pm Sep-May, closed Wed; P⊞) On the harborfront, this modest but jam-packed two-level museum celebrates the town's briny history with memorabilia and hands-on exhibits, including a big-game fishing chair from which you can 'reel in' a trophy marlin. Take a virtual trip through the Santa Barbara Channel and peek through a 45ft-tall US Navy periscope, the latter no longer trained on people's homes. There's 90 minutes of free parking in the nearby lot or take the Lil' Toot water taxi (see p387).

Santa Barbara Botanic Garden　　GARDEN (☑805-682-4726; www.sbbg.org; 1212 Mission Canyon Rd; adult/2-12yr/13-17yr & senior $8/4/6; ☺9am-6pm Mar-Oct, to 5pm Nov-Feb; ℗) After visiting the mission, take a soul-satisfying jaunt through the city's 40-acre botanic garden, devoted to California's native flora. About 5.5 miles of partly wheelchair-accessible trails meander through cacti, redwoods and wildflowers past the old mission dam, originally built by Chumash tribespeople to irrigate the mission's fields. Leashed, well-behaved dogs are welcome. Free guided tours usually depart at 11am on Saturday and Sunday and 2pm daily. If you're driving, head north from the mission to Foothill Blvd (Hwy 192), turn right and then left to continue on Mission Canyon Rd.

FREE **Karpeles Manuscript Library Museum**　　MUSEUM (☑805-962-5322; www.rain.org/~karpeles; 21 W Anapamu St; ☺10am-4pm Wed-Sun) Stuffed with historical written artifacts, this free museum is an embarrassment of riches for history nerds, science geeks and literary and music lovers. One of just eight Kar-

peles manuscript museums nationwide, this one houses an original stone copy of the Declaration of Independence. Rotating exhibits often spotlight literary masterworks, from Shakespeare to Sherlock Holmes.

🏃 Activities

Swimming

Los Baños del Mar　　SWIMMING POOL (☑805-966-6110; 401 Shoreline Dr; adult/senior $6/5; ☺call for public swim schedules) Beyond the top beaches in and around Santa Barbara, you can also swim at this municipal outdoor pool near West Beach that's good for recreational and lap swimming. For kids under eight years old, there's a **wading pool** with a lifeguard; it's open noon to 5pm daily from May through September, weather permitting.

Cycling & Skating

A very scenic paved **beachfront bike path** runs for 3 miles along the waterfront between Andrée Clark Bird Refuge and Leadbetter Beach, past Stearns Wharf and the harbor along Cabrillo Blvd. **Santa Barbara Bicycle Coalition** (www.sbbike.org) offers free downloadable do-it-yourself (DIY) cycling tours of the city, mountains and wine country.

Wheel Fun Rentals　　BICYCLE RENTAL (www.wheelfunrentals.com) Cabrillo Blvd (23 E Cabrillo Blvd; ☺8am-8pm Mar-Oct, to 6pm Nov-Feb); State St (22 State St; ☺8am-8pm daily Apr-Oct, weekends only Nov-Mar) Hourly rentals of beach cruisers ($8), mountain bikes ($9) and two-/four-person surreys ($25/35). Half-/full-day discounts available.

Santa Barbara Bikes-to-Go　　BICYCLE RENTAL (www.sbbikestogo.com) Delivers top-quality road and hybrid mountain bikes to your hotel. Rentals (per day $65 to $95) include helmets and emergency-kit saddle bags. Discounts for multiday rentals; reservations are recommended. Caters for over-18s only.

Boating & Whale-Watching

The following tour companies offer year-round whale-watching boat trips, mostly to see gray whales in winter and spring or humpback and blue whales in summer. You can also wander the harbor, talk to captains and pick a boat based on whom you like best. Just make sure the vessel is Coast

---

TOP FIVE SANTA BARBARA FREEBIES

» Climb to the top of the **courthouse clock tower** (p371).

» Window-shop along **State Street** (p385), ending up at the beach and Stearns Wharf.

» Hike the **Rattlesnake Canyon** trail (boxed text, p377) in the Santa Ynez foothills.

» Browse art and artifacts at the **Santa Barbara Historical Museum** (p371).

» Come for live music, dancing and a parade during **Old Spanish Days Fiesta** (p377).

Santa Barbara's coast faces south, not west – which explains why you can't see the sun set over the ocean from most beaches.

» **East Beach** Santa Barbara's largest and most popular beach is a long, sandy stretch sprawling east of Stearns Wharf, with a dozen volleyball nets for pick-up games, a children's play area and a snack bar. On Sunday afternoons, artists set up booths along the sidewalk, near the recreational bike path.

» **Butterfly Beach** At the far end of East Beach. Armani swimsuits and Gucci sunglasses abound at this narrow but chic swimming beach in front of the Biltmore hotel. Don't be surprised if you spot a celeb! The beach faces west, so you can catch a sunset here.

» **West Beach** Between Stearns Wharf and the harbor are calm waters for kayaking, sailing and stand-up paddle surfing. It's most popular for sunbathing by tourists staying at nearby motels. For swimming, head indoors to Los Baños del Mar.

» **Leadbetter Beach** Farther west of the harbor, this is a fantastic spot for swimming or learning to surf or windsurf. A grassy picnic area atop the cliffs makes it just that much more family-friendly.

» **Arroyo Burro County Beach Park** Near the junction of Cliff Dr and Las Positas Rd, this gem (nicknamed Hendry's) has a parking lot, a picnic area and the family-style Brown Pelican restaurant. It's flat, wide, away from tourists and great for kids, who can go tide-pooling. It's also a popular local surf spot. Look for an off-leash dog area below Douglas Family Preserve.

» **Goleta Beach County Park** (Sandspit Rd, Goleta, www.countyofsb.org/parks; P) In the western suburbs near the University of California Santa Barbara (UCSB) campus, this beach is a locals-only scene. There's a 1500ft-long fishing pier, a bike path and wide, sandy stretches for sunbathing after taking a dip or surfing easy waves. From Hwy 101, take Hwy 217 westbound.

» **Summerland Beach** (p400) Bring your leashed four-legged friends for some windy beachcombing (no swimming). Descend the cliffs from Lookout Park, just across the train tracks south of Hwy 101 (exit 91).

» **Carpinteria State Beach** (p400) About 12 miles east of Santa Barbara off Hwy 101, this mile-long, family-friendly beach has beautifully calm waters great for swimming, wading and tide-pooling, especially for younger kids. Parking $10.

» **El Capitán & Refugio State Beaches** (www.parks.ca.gov; P) These twin beauties are worth the trip over 20 miles west of Santa Barbara via Hwy 101. Popular swimming and sea-kayaking spots, they're connected by a recreational bike path. Parking $10.

Guard–certified. For boat trips to Channel Islands National Park, see p406.

Sea Landing/Condor Express

RENTALS, TOURS

(☎805-963-3564, whale-watching tours 805-882-0088, 888-779-4253; www.sealanding.net, www.condorcruises.com; 301 W Cabrillo Blvd; ⊞) Rent jet skis and jet boats by the harbor, or take a whale-watching excursion aboard the high-speed catamaran *Condor Express*. Most whale-watching trips last 4½ hours and cost $94/50 per adult/child (under 5 free). Whale sightings are guaranteed, so if you miss out the first time, you can take another tour for free.

Santa Barbara Sailing Center

RENTALS, TOURS

(☎805-962-2826, 800-350-9090; www.sbsail.com; 133 Harbor Way; ⊗9am-5pm, to 6pm Apr-Sep) Pay $25 to ride the *Double Dolphin*, a 50ft sailing catamaran, on a two-hour coastal or sunset cruise. Seasonal whale-watching trips cost $30 per adult, $10 for children under 13. If you want to pilot your own craft, rent a paddleboat, rowing scull, motorboat or sailboat.

Sunset Kidd's Sailing Cruises
TOURS

(☎805-962-8222; www.sunsetkidd.com; 125 Harbor Way) Float in an 18-passenger sailboat on a two-hour whale-watching trip ($40); sunset cocktail and full-moon cruises cost the same.

Kayaking

Paddle the calm waters of Santa Barbara's harbor or the coves of the Gaviota coast, or hitch a ride to the Channel Islands for sea caves.

Santa Barbara Adventure Co
RENTALS, TOURS

(☎805-884-9283, 877-885-9283; www.sbad ventureco.com) Leads all kinds of guided kayaking trips, from family-friendly harbor excursions and stargazing floats to Gaviota coastal paddles ($35 to $120). Feeling adventurous? Enquire about surf-kayaking lessons. Single/double kayak rentals cost $25/35 for two hours, $35/45 for six hours.

Paddle Sports
RENTALS, TOURS

(☎805-899-4925, 888-254-2094; www.kayak sb.com; 117b Harbor Way) Guides harbor and coastal kayaking trips ($50 to $115, two-person minimum) and offers instruction for beginners to advanced paddlers. Single/tandem kayak rentals cost $25/40 for two hours, $50/65 all day.

Sea Landing
RENTALS

(☎805-963-3564; www.sealanding.net; 301 W Cabrillo Blvd) Rent single/tandem kayaks for a three-hour flat rate of $15/25 for harbor paddles only.

Surfing

Santa Barbara's south-facing coast and proximity to the windbreaking Channel Islands make it a good spot for plying the waves. Unless you're a novice, conditions are too mellow in summer – come back in winter when ocean swells kick back up. **Leadbetter Point** and **Goleta Beach** are best for beginners. Experts-only **Rincon Point** is near Carpinteria (p401).

Santa Barbara Adventure Co
CLASSES

(☎805-884-9283, 877-885-9283; www.sbad ventureco.com) Learn to surf in four-hour classes (from $100, including lunch).

Surf-n-Wear's Beach House
RENTALS

(☎805-963-1281; www.surfnwear.com; 10 State St) Near Stearns Wharf, rent soft (foam) boards ($10/25/35 per hour/half-/full day) and boogie boards ($4/10/16 per hour/half-/full day).

Paddle Sports
RENTALS

(☎805-899-4925, 888-254-2094; www.kayaksb. com; 117b Harbor Way) Stand-up paddle (SUP) board rentals (two hours $40) and how-to demonstrations ($50, including equipment rental).

Hiking

Gorgeous day hikes await in the foothills of the Santa Ynez Mountains (part of the Los Padres National Forest; see p389). Most trails cut through rugged chaparral and steep canyons – sweat it out and savor jaw-dropping coastal views. Spring and fall are the best seasons for hiking, when temperatures are moderate. Always carry plenty of extra water (for more hiking tips, see p45).

To find even more local trails to explore, visit www.santabarbarahikes.com online. Or visit the **Los Padres National Forest Headquarters** (☎805-968-6640; 6755 Hollister Ave, Goleta; ⊙8:30am-12pm & 1-4:30pm Mon-Fri), west of the airport (from Hwy 101, exit Glen Annie Rd southbound).

Hang Gliding & Paragliding

For soaring ocean views, **Eagle Paragliding** (☎805-968-0980; ww.eagleparagliding.com) and **Fly Above All** (☎805-965-3733; www.flyabove all.com) both offer paragliding lessons (from $200) and tandem flights (from $100). For hang-gliding lessons and tandem flights, book with **Fly Away** (☎805-403-8487; www. flyawayhanggliding.com).

☞ Tours

For more outdoor-oriented tours, including harbor cruises and whale-watching boats, see p374.

Architectural Foundation of Santa Barbara
ART, HISTORY

(☎805-965-6307; www.afsb.org; adult/under 12yr $10/free) Take time out of your weekend morning for a 90-minute guided walking

---

DON'T MISS

MEETING MONARCHS

If you're here in late fall and winter, ask at the Outdoors Santa Barbara Visitors Center (p386) about the best places to see the monarch butterflies roosting in the trees, an extraordinary sight. For a local expert's recommended viewing spots, see the boxed text, p449.

TRAIL NAME	ROUND-TRIP DISTANCE (MI)	DESCRIPTION	TRAILHEAD	DIRECTIONS
Inspiration Point	3.5	Popular with locals walking their dogs and for daily workouts	Tunnel Rd	Turn left off Mission Canyon Dr before reaching the Santa Barbara Botanic Garden
Rattlesnake Canyon	3	Offering shade and waterfalls as you ascend into the canyon; leashed dogs OK	Las Canoas Rd	Turn right off Mission Canyon Dr past the botanic garden
Cold Spring & Montecito Park	up to 9	Woos hikers with small cascades and a spur trail to a summit	Mountain Dr	From Montecito, follow Olive Mill Rd north of Hwy 101 past Sycamore Canyon Rd (Hwy 192), continuing on Hot Springs Rd, then turn left

tour of downtown's art, history and architecture. No reservations required; call or check the website for meet-up times and places.

Land & Sea Tours SIGHTSEEING
(☎805-683-7600; www.out2seesb.com; adult/under 10yr $25/10) If you dig James Bond–style vehicles, take a narrated tour of the city on the *Land Shark,* an amphibious vehicle that drives right into the water. Trips depart from Stearns Wharf; buy tickets on board.

Santa Barbara Adventure Company
OUTDOORS, WINE
(☎805-884-9283, 877-885-9283; www.sbadventureco.com) Maximize your outdoors experience during horseback-riding, mountain-biking and wine-tasting-cycling tours, costing from $35 to $140 per person (two-/four-person minimum).

Santa Barbara Walking Tour ART, HISTORY
(☎805-687-9255, tickets 800-979-3370; www.santabarbarawalkingtours.com; tour $21) Walking tours of downtown's 20th-century public art, from colorful murals and tiled mosaics to hidden fountains and side-street statues. Buy tickets in advance.

🎆 Festivals & Events
Santa Barbara throws a good party. For a current-events calendar, contact the visitors center (p386).

Santa Barbara International Film Festival ARTS & CULTURE
(www.sbfilmfestival.org) Film buffs arrive in droves to watch screenings of the latest in independent US and foreign cinema between mid-January and early February.

Madonnari Italian Street Painting Festival ART & CULTURE
(www.imadonnarifestival.com) Colorful chalk drawings adorn the mission's sidewalks over Memorial Day weekend.

Summer Solstice Celebration PARADE, FAIR
(www.solsticeparade.com) Kicking off the summer in late June, this Mardi Gras–esque State St parade feels more like something out of Burning Man. Live music, food and wine, and arts-and-crafts vendors draw crowds.

French Festival ARTS & CULTURE
(www.santamariafairpark.com) In mid-July, California's biggest Francophile celebration has lots of food and wine, world music and dancing, a mock Eiffel Tower and Statue of Liberty, and even a poodle parade.

Santa Barbara County Fair CARNIVAL, FAIR
(www.santamariafairpark.com; 🖬) In mid-July, this old-fashioned county fair has agriculture booths, rides, and lots of food and wine. The fairgrounds are in Santa Maria, 75 minutes' drive northwest of Santa Barbara via Hwy 101.

SANTA BARBARA FOR CHILDREN

Santa Barbara abounds with family-friendly fun for kids of all ages, from tots to tweens.

» **Arroyo Burro County Beach Park** (see boxed text, p375) A wide, sandy beach, away from the tourists but not too far from downtown.

» **Ty Warner Sea Center** (www.sbnature.org; 211 Stearns Wharf; adult/2-12yr/13-17yr & senior $10/6/7; ☉10am-5pm; ℗♿) From touch tanks full of tide-pool critters and crawl-through aquariums to whale sing-alongs, it's interactive and educational. Tickets include same-day admission to the natural-history museum. Hourly parking $2.50.

» **Santa Barbara Museum of Natural History** (☎805-682-4711; www.sbnature. org; 2559 Puesta del Sol; adult/2-12yr/13-17yr & senior $10/6/7; ☉10am-5pm; ℗♿) Giant skeletons, an insect wall and a pitch-dark planetarium captivate kids' imaginations. Tickets include same-day admission to the Ty Warner Sea Center. It's a short bus ride north of the mission.

» **Santa Barbara Maritime Museum** (p373) Peer through a periscope, reel in a virtual fish, watch underwater films or check out the model ships.

» **Santa Barbara Sailing Center** (p375) Short, one-hour sails around the harbor ($10) let young 'uns see sea lions up close.

» **Lil' Toot water taxi** (p387) Take a joyride along the waterfront on this lil' yellow boat.

Old Spanish Days Fiesta ARTS & CULTURE
(www.oldspanishdays-fiesta.org) The entire city fills up during early August for this long-running – if slightly overblown – festival celebrating Santa Barbara's Spanish and Mexican colonial heritage. Festivities include outdoor markets, food bazaars, live music, flamenco dancing, horseback and rodeo events, and a big ol' parade.

West Beach Festival MUSIC
(www.westbeachfestival.com; ♿) Three days of live rock, reggae and electro beats by the beach, plus special kids' performances, over a late-September weekend; buy tickets in advance.

🛏 Sleeping

Prepare for sticker shock: a bottom-of-the-heap dive motel that typically goes for $65 per night can triple in price during the summer season. Don't show up at the last minute and expect to find any reasonably priced rooms, especially on weekends (when two-night minimums may apply). Rates fluctuate depending on demand, so use the peak-season prices quoted here as a guide only. Because nights are generally cool year-round, most places don't have air-conditioning.

Four Seasons Resort The Biltmore
RESORT HOTEL **$$$**
(☎805-969-2261, 800-819-5053; www.four seasons.com/santabarbara; 1260 Channel Dr; r $595-1095; ℗@🛜🏊♿) Wear white linen and live like Jay Gatsby at the oh-so-cushy 1927 Biltmore, Santa Barbara's iconic Spanish-colonial-style hotel and spa on Butterfly Beach. Every detail is perfect, from bathrooms with custom Mediterranean-style tiles, huge soaking tubs, French-milled soaps and waterfall showers to bedrooms decked out with ultra-high-thread-count sheets and flat-screen plasma TVs. Hideaway garden cottages are idyllic for honeymooners. Air-con standard. Wi-fi in lobby and poolside only.

Inn of the Spanish Garden TOP CHOICE
BOUTIQUE HOTEL **$$$**
(☎805-564-4700, 866-564-4700; www.spanish gardeninn.com; 915 Garden St; r incl breakfast $299-445; ℗🛜🏊) At this Spanish Revival–style inn, casual elegance, top-notch service and an impossibly romantic central courtyard will have you lording about like the don of your own private villa. Beds have luxurious linens, bathrooms have oversize soaking tubs and concierge service is top-notch. Palms surround a small outdoor pool, where a courtyard gets lit with candles after dark so you can enjoy the evening wine bar.

SEI Capitan Canyon
ECO-RESORT **$$$**

(☎805-685-3887, 866-352-2729; www.elcapitan canyon.com; 11560 Calle Real; safari tents $155, cabins $225-350; P🐾🛜🛁🚶) About 20 miles west of Santa Barbara, off Hwy 101 opposite El Capitán State Beach, this 'glamping' resort is for anyone who loves camping, but hates to wake up with dirt under their nails. Die-hard nature lovers shouldn't despair, as un Disneyllke critter sightings keep things real. No cars are allowed up-canyon during peak season, making the woodsy resort feel more peaceful. Safari tents are rustic, with communal bathrooms; creekside cabins are deluxe, some with kitchenettes and soaking tubs. Each cabin or campsite has its own fire pit. Borrow a bicycle to head over to the beach or unwind with a massage.

James House
B&B **$$**

(☎805-569-5853; www.jameshousesanta barbara.com; 1632 Chapala St; r $200 265; P🛜) For a traditional B&B experience, revel in a stately Queen Anne Victorian run by a charmingly hospitable owner. All of the antique-filled rooms are sheer elegance, with none of the shabby-chic look so common at B&Bs. Lofty ceilings, hardwood floors and private bathrooms are par for the course, with some fireplaces and deep soaking tubs. Full sit-down breakfast served.

Canary Hotel
BOUTIQUE HOTEL **$$$**

(☎805-884-0300, 877-468-3515; www.canary santabarbara.com; 31 W Carrillo St; r $325-575; P@🛜) On a busy block downtown, this multistory sleek hotel has a rooftop pool and sunset-watching perch for cocktails. Posh accommodations have four-poster Spanish-framed beds and all mod cons. Beware that 'suites' are just oversized rooms, however. Spa bathroom amenities and in-room yoga DVDs will soothe away stress, but ambient street noise may leave you sleepless. 'Club Canine' extras include organic treats, a Frisbee and dog bed. Pet fee $35. Parking $20.

Brisas del Mar
MOTEL **$$**

(☎805-966-2219, 800-468-1988; www.sbhotels. com; 223 Castillo St; r $185-275; P@🛜🛁) Big kudos for all the freebies (DVDs, continental breakfast, afternoon wine and cheese, evening milk and cookies) and the newer Mediterranean-style front section, although the older motel wing is unlovely. The hotel's respectable sister properties – including the recently renovated Lavender Inn by the Sea

with Southern plantation-style colonnades near the beach – are similarly priced. Aircon standard.

Franciscan Inn
MOTEL **$$**

(☎805-963-8845; www.franciscaninn.com; 109 Bath St; r incl breakfast $155-215; P🛜🛁) Settle into the relaxing, French-country charms of this two-story motel about one block from the beach. Rooms differ in shape and decor, but many have kitchenettes, some have air-con and all evince a pastoral, floral motif – which could prove annoying to curmudgeons and ultimate street fighters. Everyone else embraces the friendly vibe, afternoon cookies and outdoor Jacuzzi. Free continental breakfast.

Harbor House Inn
MOTEL **$$**

(☎805-962-9745, 888-474-6789; www.harbor houseinn.com; 104 Bath St; r $150-305; P@🛜) Down by the harbor, this freshly converted motel offers good-value studios, including two that welcome your four-legged friend with open arms. All of the brightly lit studios have hardwood floors, a beachy design scheme, private bathrooms and small kitchens. Rates include a welcome basket of breakfast goodies, a DVD library and three-speed bikes to borrow. Pet fee $15.

White Jasmine Inn
B&B **$$**

(☎805-966-0589; www.whitejasmineinnsanta barbara.com; 1327 Bath St; r $155-305; P🛜) A 10-minute walk from State St, tucked behind a rose-entwined wooden fence, this cheery inn gathers together an Arts-and-Crafts-style California bungalow and two quaint cottages. Sound-insulated rooms all have private bathrooms and fireplaces, and some are air-conditioned. The art-nouveau suite with a private Jacuzzi patio is a honeymooners' fave. Full breakfast basket delivered daily to your door.

CHEAPER SLEEPS

Santa Barbara's waterfront motels and hotels, especially rooms with ocean views, cost more than traffic-choked places on upper State St, north of downtown. For a cheap room on a summer weekend, you may have to drive south on Hwy 101 toward Carpinteria (12 miles; see p400), Ventura (30 miles, see p403) or Camarillo (44 miles), where chain motels and hotels are typically lower-priced.

CAMPING & CABINS

You won't find a campground anywhere near downtown Santa Barbara, but less than a half-hour drive west via Hwy 101, right on the ocean, are **El Capitán & Refugio State Beaches** (🖂reservations 800-444-7275; www.reserveamerica.com; hike-&-bike tent sites $10, campsites $35-50; Ⓟ). Amenities include flush toilets, hot showers, picnic tables and BBQ grills; parking costs $10. See p375 for beach descriptions and directions. You'll find more family-friendly campgrounds in the **Los Padres National Forest** and at **Cachuma Lake Recreation Area** off Hwy 154 (see boxed text, p389), closer to Santa Barbara's wine country.

Presidio Motel
MOTEL **$$**
(☏805-963-1355; www.thepresidiomotel.com; 1620 State St; r incl breakfast $140-230; Ⓟ🛜) The Presidio is the H&M of motels, a budget option flaunting what it's got with sassy, irresistible style. From mod lounge chairs on the sundeck and artsy photos on the walls to origami dangling from the ceiling, the owners make the most of an older, standard-issue building. Just north of downtown, the Presidio attracts a younger crowd. Air-con standard. Free continental breakfast and loaner bicycles.

Agave Inn
MOTEL **$$**
(☏805-687-6009; www.agaveinnsb.com; 3222 State St; r incl breakfast $120-190; Ⓟ🛜) While it's still just a motel at heart, this boutique-on-a-budget property's 'Mexican pop meets modern' motif livens things up with a color palette out of a Frieda Kahlo painting. Flat-screen TVs, microwaves, minifridges and air-con make it a standout option. Family-sized rooms have kitchenettes and pull-out sofa beds. Guests may borrow cruiser bikes from its sister Presidio Motel. Continental breakfast included.

Marina Beach Motel
MOTEL **$$**
(☏805-963-9311, 877-627-4621; www.marina beachmotel.com; 21 Bath St; r incl breakfast $120-315; reception ⏱7:30am-11pm; Ⓟ@🛜) Family-owned since 1942, this flower-festooned, one-story motor lodge that wraps around a grassy courtyard is worth a stay just for the location. Right by the ocean, tidy remodeled rooms are comfy enough, all with air-con and some with kitchenettes. Complimentary breakfast and beach-cruiser bikes for guests.

Eagle Inn
B&B **$$**
(☏805-965-3586; www.theeagleinn.com; 232 Natoma Ave; d incl breakfast $130-325; Ⓟ@🛜) You can just imagine early-20th-century Santa Barbara socialites strolling under-neath the colorful Spanish, tile-lined archway into this white, two-story inn. This tranquil, family-owned property offers average-sized rooms that may be too flowery for some. For more space and privacy, reserve one of the contemporary cottages out back. Complimentary continental breakfast, DVD library and loaner bikes.

Hotel Santa Barbara
HOTEL **$$**
(☏805-957-9300, 800-549-9869; www.hotel santabarbara.com; 533 State St; r incl breakfast $180-260; Ⓟ@🛜) Old-fashioned yet unpretentious, the 1925 Hotel Santa Barbara has rooms done up with rattan and blond-wood furnishings and sunny Mediterranean colors – Provence meets the beach. Best of all, you can walk everywhere. No air-con means well-worn rooms can be stuffy, not to mention noisy from nonstop partying outside on State St. Continental breakfast included. Parking $7.

Hotel Virginia
HOTEL **$$**
(☏805-805-963-9757, 800-549-1700; www.hotel virginia.com; 17 W Haley St; r $185-250; Ⓟ@🛜) This early-20th-century hotel property downplays its Holiday Inn Express affiliation. It has heaps of character, starting from the tile-filled lobby with a fountain. Upgraded rooms have air-con, flat-screen TVs and CD players. Parking $10.

Hotel State Street
HOTEL **$**
(☏805-966-6586; www.hotelstatestreet.net; 121 State St; r without bathroom from $70; @🛜) You can't escape a certain institutional feel at this bare-bones downtown hotel, despite its attempts at whimsical decor. Pros: friendly staff, clean rooms, and the beach is two blocks away. Cons: noise from Amtrak trains (bring earplugs), no air-con, and shared bathrooms. Of course, bathroom sharing here isn't like a hostel or college dorm – you have privacy, European-style; just shut the door and lock it.

Santa Barbara Tourist Hostel   HOSTEL $
(📞805-963-0154; www.sbhostel.com; 134 Chapala St; dm $32-40; reception 🕙8:30am-12:30pm & 2:30pm-11:15pm; 📄@🛜) Traveling strangers, evening trains and a rowdy brewhouse only steps from your door – it's either the perfect country song or this low-slung bungalow right next to the train station (bring earplugs). Cramped and raucous, this hostel ain't the cleanest or safest, but the price is right for dorm beds – forget about private rooms. Bike and surfboard rentals available.

Motel 6 Santa Barbara   MOTEL $$
(📞805-564-1392, 800-466-8356; www.motel6.com; 443 Corona del Mar; r $120-175; 📄🛜🏊) The very first Motel 6 to 'leave the light on for you' has been remodeled with IKEA-esque contemporary design and flat-screen TVs. It fills nightly; book ahead. Pet fee $10.

Blue Sands Motel   MOTEL $$
(📞805-965-1624; www.thebluesands.com; 421 S Milpas St; r $160-240; 📄🛜🏊) This tiny two-story motel may be a bit kitschy, but who cares when you're just steps from East Beach? Ask the affable owners for an upgraded room. Pet fee $10.

El Prado Inn   MOTEL $$
(📞805-966-0807, 800-669-8979; www.elprado.com; 1601 State St; r incl breakfast $125-175; 📄@🛜🏊) North of downtown, the family-run El Prado has a 1960s mod exterior, spacious, above-average motel rooms and an outdoor heated pool. Continental breakfast included.

✖ Eating

Restaurants abound along downtown's State St and by the waterfront, where you'll find a few gems among the touristy clap-trap. Wander away from the beaten path to find interesting, affordably priced cafes, gourmet take-out and Mexicali taco shops.

TOP CHOICE Santa Barbara Shellfish Company   SEAFOOD $$
(230 Stearns Wharf; mains $10-20; 🕙11am-9pm; 📄🍴) 'From sea to skillet to plate' sums up this end-of-the-wharf seafood shack that's more of a buzzing counter joint than a sit-down restaurant. Chase away the seagulls as you chow down at wooden picnic tables outside. Awesome lobster bisque, ocean views and the same location for over 25 years.

Bouchon   FRENCH $$$
(📞805-730-1160; www.bouchonsantabarbara.com; 9 W Victoria St; mains $24-38; 🕙dinner) The perfect, unhurried, follow-up to a day in the wine country is the bright, flavorful French cooking at convivial Bouchon (meaning 'wine cork'). The California influence on the seasonal menu is obvious: locally grown farm produce and ranched meats that marry beautifully with the more than 30 local wines available by the glass. Lovebirds, book a table on the candlelit patio.

◻ Square One   CALIFORNIAN $$
(📞805-965-4565; www.squareonesb.com; 14 E Cota St; mains $14-25; 🕙5:30-9pm Tue-Sun) Make your way to this polished downtown gem for a hushed tête-à-tête. The organic, seasonally inspired Californian menu will pique jaded palates with the likes of seafood ceviche with grapefruit gelée or housemade duck-egg pasta topped by pecorino-dusted short ribs. Be prepared for slow-paced service. A svelte wine bar pours outstanding, eclectic California vintages.

Brophy Bros   SEAFOOD $$
(📞805-966-4418; www.brophybros.com; 119 Harbor Way; mains $10-20; 🕙11am-10pm Sun-Thu, to 11pm Fri & Sat) A longtime favorite for its fresh-off-the-dock fish and seafood, rowdy atmosphere and salty harborside setting. The slightly less claustrophobic tables on the upstairs deck are worth the long wait – they're quieter and have the best ocean views. Or skip the lines and start knocking back oyster shooters and Bloody Marys with convivial locals at the bar.

Tupelo Junction   SOUTHERN $$
(📞805-899-3100; www.tupelojunction.com; 1218 State St; mains breakfast & lunch $13-18, dinner $13-33; 🕙8am-2pm daily, 5-9pm Tue-Sat) Downtown, this sunlight-splashed cafe stirs up a gourmet Southern-inspired menu that's a masterpiece. From the cinnamon-apple beignets dipped in crème anglaise to shrimp and scallops with cheddar-jalapeño grits – it's enough to make a foodie lose their mind. Expect a wait for brunch; around dinnertime it's often deserted.

Metropulos   DELI $
(www.metrofinefoods.com; 216 E Yanonali St; dishes $6-10; 🕙8:30am-6pm Mon-Fri, 10am-4pm Sat) Before a hike or a day at the beach, pick up some gourmet salads and sandwiches at this 'fine foods merchant,' east of the railroad tracks in the Funk Zone. Artisan breads, over 100 cheeses and 50 cured

DIY DINING

Stock up on fresh produce, nuts and honey at the **farmers market** (www.sbfarmersmarket.org), held late afternoon Tuesday on the 500 and 600 blocks of State St between E Haley and E Ortega Sts, and from Saturday morning until early afternoon at the corner of Santa Barbara and Cota Sts. Make it a picnic with artisan loaves from **Our Daily Bread** (831 Santa Barbara St; ⊙6am-5:30pm Mon-Fri, 7am-4pm Sat), down the street from **C'est Cheese** (825 Santa Barbara St; ⊙10am-6pm Mon-Fri, 8am-6pm Sat). The best place for healthy, organic groceries is **Lazy Acres** (302 Meigs Rd; ⊙7am-10pm; P), south of Hwy 101 via W Carrillo St. North of downtown, **McConnell's Ice Cream** (201 W Mission St; ⊙10:30am-10:30pm Sun-Thu, to 11:30pm Fri & Sat; P) scoops up premium frozen treats. For more sweet endings, pop chocolate-sea salt truffles from **Chocolate Maya** (15 W Gutierrez St; ⊙11am-6pm Mon-Fri, 10am-4pm Sat).

meats, and California olives and wines will be bursting out of your picnic basket. It's a great refueling stop on the Urban Wine Trail (p384) too.

El Buen Gusto TAQUERÍA $
(836 N Milpas St; dishes $3-7; ⊙8am-9pm; P) At this low-slung, red-brick strip-mall joint, step right up to the counter and take your choice of authentic south-of-the-border tacos, tortas, quesadillas and burritos from the board overhead. Then kick back at plasticky booths with an *agua fresca* (sugary fruit drink) or cold bottles of Pacifico beer while Mexican music videos and soccer games blare from TVs. *Menudo* (tripe soup) and *birria* (spicy stew) are weekend specials.

D'Angelo Pastry & Bread BAKERY, CAFE $
(25 W Gutierrez St; dishes $2-8; ⊙7am-2pm) Tucked off lower State St, this retrolicious bakery with shiny-silver bistro sidewalk tables is a calming breakfast spot, whether you're sipping a frothy cappuccino and buttering up a croissant or forking into Iron Chef Cat Cora's favorite dish, Eggs Rose (poached eggs with artichoke paste on kal-

amata olive bread). The flakiest, oven-fresh pastries go quick, so get here early.

Olio e Limone ITALIAN $$$
(☎805-899-2699; www.olioelimone.com; 11 W Victoria St; mains lunch $12-18, dinner $24-34; ⊙lunch Mon-Sat, dinner daily) *Wine Spectator* gives the nod to the extensive cellar of Old and New World varietals at this Italian ristorante. Dishes hail from all over the boot, with special love reserved for the island of Sicily. Don't want to spend a fortune? Duck next door to the casual pizzeria and enoteca, where service is less snobby.

Palace Grill SOUTHERN $$
(☎805-963-5000; www.palacegrill.com; 8 E Cota St; mains lunch $8-13, dinner $16-26; ⊙11:30am-3pm daily, 5:30-10pm Sun-Thu, 5:30-11pm Fri & Sat) With all the exuberance of Mardi Gras, this N'awlins-style grill makes totally addictive baskets of housemade muffins and breads, and ginormous (if so-so) plates of jambalaya, gumbo ya-ya, blackened catfish and pecan chicken. Stiff cocktails and indulgent desserts make the grade. Act unsurprised when the staff lead the crowd in a rousing sing-along.

Sojourner Café HEALTHY $$
(www..sojournercafe.com; 134 E Cañon Perdido; mains $6-13; ⊙11am-11pm Mon-Sat, to 10pm Sun; ℗) Vegetarians rejoice – the menu is extensive at this cozy, mostly veggie 1970s-era cafe. While supporting local farms, cooks get creative with vegetables, tofu, tempeh, fish, seeds and other healthy ingredients. The tempeh taco salad is delish, as are tempting daily desserts, including vegan and wheat-free treats. Fair-trade coffees, local beers and wines.

Lilly's Taquería MEXICAN $
(310 Chapala St; dishes from $1.50; ⊙11am-9pm Mon & Wed-Thu, to 10pm Fri & Sat, to 9:30pm Sun) There's almost always a line roping around this taco shack at lunch. But it goes fast, so you'd best be snappy with your order – the *adobada* (marinated pork) is killer.

Natural Café HEALTHY $
(www.thenaturalcafe.com; 508 State St; mains $7-10; ⊙11am-9:30pm Sun-Thu, to 10pm Fri & Sat; ℗) This healthy, beachy hangout fills vegetarian bellies with 'spiritual spinach' salads, 'good karma' tempeh burgers and Buddha burritos. Grilled chicken pitas and turkey burgers will satisfy carnivores. Kids' menu available.

Backyard Bowls
HEALTHY $

(www.backyardbowls.com; 331 Motor Way; dishes $6-10; ⊙7am-6pm) This eco-minded little shop serves up real-food smoothies and heaping bowls of acaí berries, granola, coconut milk, honey and energy-boosting supplement for health nuts, including yogis from the nearby studio.

Roy
CALIFORNIAN $

(☏805-966-5636; www.restaurantroy.com; 7 W Carrillo St; mains $20-30; ⊙6pm-midnight) The classic Californian cooking has fallen off lately, but Roy's still serves later than almost any place in town. Food arrives more quickly at the bar, convenient if you're flying solo.

🍷 Drinking

Santa Barbara's after-dark scene revolves around lower State St, where most watering holes have happy hours, tiny dance floors and college nights, when the booze is cheap and the atmosphere rowdy. Just south of Hwy 101 and east of State St is the Funk Zone, an eclectic mix of bars and wine-tasting rooms that's a counter-cultural poke in the eye to downtown's conformity.

TOP CHOICE Brewhouse
BREWPUB

(www.brewhousesb.com; 229 W Montecito St; ⊙11am-11pm Sun-Thu, to midnight Fri & Sat) Perfect for a rowdy reunion down in the Funk Zone, the ever-popular Brewhouse crafts its own unique small-batch beer (Saint Barb's Belgian-style rules!), serves wines by the glass and awesome fries, and has cool art and rockin' live music Wednesday to Saturday nights.

French Press
COFFEEHOUSE

(1101 State St; ⊙6am-7pm Mon-Fri, 7am-7pm Sat, 8am-5pm Sun; 🛜) This State St coffee shop shames the chains with beans roasted in Santa Cruz, shiny silver espresso machines from Italy and baristas that really know how to pull their shots and mix spicy chais, too. Blueberry buckle, anyone?

Press Room
PUB

(15 E Ortega St; ⊙11am-midnight) This tiny pub can barely contain the rowdy locals, university students and European travelers who cram the place to its seams. No better place to catch soccer games, stuff the jukebox with quarters or be jovially abused by the British bartender.

Blenders in the Grass
JUICE, SMOOTHIES

(www.drinkblenders.com; 720 State St; items $3-6; ⊙7am-9pm Mon-Thu, 7am-10pm Fri, 8am-10pm Sat, 8am-9pm Sun) For a quick, healthy burst of energy, pop by this youthful, locally owned juice bar and down a wheatgrass shot, blueberry-licious 'Purple Banana' smoothie or date milkshake.

Endless Summer
BAR

(http://chuckswaterfrontgrill.com; 113 Harbor Way; ⊙11:30am-9:30pm) Upstairs from Chuck's Waterfront Grill, the scene here at the harbor is Jack Johnson–casual, with fish-and-chips, burgers, billiards and beer. Or clink mai-tai glasses outside overlooking the sailboats. Back inside, vintage surfboards hang on the walls and surfing videos loop well, endlessly.

James Joyce
PUB

(www.sbjamesjoyce.com; 513 State St; ⊙11am-2am) In the thick of the barflies' lower State St drag, this institution's most endearing quality is the inch-thick carpet of peanut shells. Live bands play almost nightly, with jazz most Saturdays. Darts, yes; dancing, no. Don't bother asking the bartenders if they've read *Ulysses*.

Santa Barbara Roasting Company
COFFEEHOUSE

(www.sbcoffee.com; 321 Motor Way; ⊙5:30am-9pm Mon-Fri, 6am-9pm Sat, 6:30am-9am Sun; 🛜) Intense-looking alternatypes fill the tables in this exposed-brick, industrial factory space. Poets? Hackers? Sociopaths? Who knows, who cares. Come for the potent java – this place roasts its own drip coffee.

Muddy Waters
COFFEEHOUSE

(☏805-966-9328; 508 E Haley St; ⊙6am-6pm Mon-Sat, later if there's a show; @🛜) A yard sale's mix of furniture? Check. Pool table? Check. Punk drinking microbrews at the bar? Check. A kick-ass backyard patio? Check. Live local bands and open-mic nights? Yup. It's got everything required for the quintessential indie coffeehouse, including baristas with attitude.

Hollister Brewing Company
BREWPUB

(www.hollisterbrewco.com; 6980 Marketplace Dr, Goleta; ⊙11am-9:30pm; 🅿) Home to over a dozen microbrews including a couple of seasonal specialties, this place draws the serious beer geeks out to Goleta, near the UCSB campus, off Hwy 101. IPAs are the permanent attractions, along with nitrogenated draft stout. Skip the food, though.

URBAN WINE TRAIL

No wheels to head up to Santa Barbara's wine country? No problem. Ramble between almost a dozen wine-tasting rooms (and a microbrewery, too) near the beach, just east of downtown. Pick up the **Urban Wine Trail** (www.urbanwinetrailsb.com) anywhere along its route. Most tasting rooms are open Thursday to Sunday afternoons and evenings, when crowds of 20- and 30-somethings rub shoulders as they sip outstanding glasses of pinot noir and viognier, listen to live music and play games. For a hip social scene, hit **Kunin Wines** (☑805-963-9696; www.kuninwines.com; 29 Anacapa St), nearby two other wine-tasting rooms and a surfboard shop. Then head up to Yaonali St, turning left to find another trio of tippling spots, one inside an old tire shop and another crafting Australian-style vintages. Don't miss a detour to refined **Carr Winery** (☑805-965-7985; www.carrwinery.com; 414 N Salsipuedes St), next door to **Telegraph Brewing Company** (☑805-963-5018; www.telegraphbrewing.com; 416 N Salsipuedes St), which makes robust ales and a 'rhinocerous' rye wine. Call ahead to double-check opening hours at all of these places.

Some of downtown's sexiest places for cocktails are inside restaurants, safely far away from lower State St's heaving meat-market masses:

Hob Nob   COCKTAIL BAR
(21 W Victoria St) Inventive cocktails, California wines and microbrews, and a chic crowd. The eclectic food menu ain't great.

Blue Agave   TEQUILA BAR
(20 E Cota St) Modern Mexican restaurant with a tequila bar, snuggly booths and a sexy fireplace. Lemongrass mojitos and cucumber martinis liven up the cocktails list.

Milk & Honey   TAPAS BAR
(30 W Anapamu St) Flickering candles and low tables fill this Spanish-Mediterranean tapas bar with the triple threat of margaritas, mojitos and martinis. Cool ambience, so-so food (vegetarians OK).

☆ Entertainment

Santa Barbara's appreciation of the arts is evidenced not only by the wide variety of performances available on any given night but also its gorgeous, often historic, venues. For a current list of live music and events, pick up the free weekly *Santa Barbara Independent* or Friday's 'Scene' guide in the *Santa Barbara News-Press*.

TOP CHOICE **Soho**   MUSIC
(☑805-962-7776; www.sohosb.com; 1221 State St, 2nd level) One unpretentious brick room plus live music almost nightly equals Soho, upstairs inside a downtown office complex behind McDonald's. Lineups range from indie rock, jazz, folk, funk and world

beats to weekend DJs and jazz every Monday. If there's a cover, it's around $10. Some all-ages shows.

Santa Barbara Bowl   MUSIC
(☑805-962-7411; www.sbbowl.org; 1122 N Milpas St; P) Built by Works Progress Administration (WPA) artisans during the Great Depression in the 1930s, this naturally beautiful outdoor stone amphitheater has ocean views from the highest cheap seats. Kick back in the sunshine or under the stars for live rock, jazz and folk concerts in summer. Big-name acts like Jack Johnson, Norah Jones and Primus take the stage here.

Arlington Theatre   MUSIC, CINEMA
(☑805-963-4408; www.thearlingtontheatre.com; 1317 State St) Harking back to 1931, this Mission Revival–style movie palace has a Spanish courtyard, and the gorgeous ceiling is spangled with stars. It's a drop-dead gorgeous place to see a show by anyone from Wynton Marsalis and Pink Martini to Ziggy Marley or Sonic Youth.

Velvet Jones   MUSIC, COMEDY
(☑805-965-8676; www.velvet-jones.com; 423 State St) Long-running downtown punk and indie dive for rock, hip-hop, comedy and 18-plus DJ nights for the city's college crowd. Many bands stop here between gigs in LA and San Francisco.

Zodo's Bowling & Beyond   BOWLING, BILLIARDS
(☑805-967-0128; www.zodos.com; 5925 Calle Real, Goleta; P ⛄) With over 40 beers on tap, pool tables and a video arcade (Skee-Ball!), this bowling alley near UCSB is good ol'

family fun. Call for schedules of open-play lanes and 'Rock 'n' Bowl' movie nights. From Hwy 101 west of downtown, exit Fairview Ave north.

Lobero Theatre · THEATER
(📞805-963-0761; www.lobero.com; 33 E Cañon Perdido St) One of California's oldest theaters presents modern dance, chamber music and jazz and world-music touring acts.

Granada Center for the Performing Arts · THEATER
(📞805-899-2222; www.granadasb.org; 1216 State St) This beautifully restored 1930s Spanish Moorish–style theater is home to the city's symphony, ballet and opera.

🛍 Shopping

Downtown's State St is packed with shops, from vintage and unique clothing boutiques to gung-ho outdoors stores. Even chain stores conform to downtown's red-roofed architectural style. Cheapskates should stick to lower State St, while trust-fund babies should head uptown (ie north). For more indie local shops, dive into the Funk Zone, east of State St and south of Hwy 101.

Blue Bee · CLOTHING, SHOES
(http://bluebee.com; 925 State St) At one of the city's best-loved indie boutiques you'll find style-savvy clothes, jewelry and shoes for women by under-the-radar designers. Wander downtown and you'll start seeing Blue Bee specialty shops everywhere you look, in fact. Its ever-expanding local empire includes a men's shop and another for its line of hip jeans.

TOP CHOICE | Channel Islands Surfboards · OUTDOORS
(www.cisurfboards.com; 36 Anacapa St; 🅿) Are you dying to take home a handcrafted, Southern California–born surfboard? In the Funk Zone, this sleek surf shack is the place for innovative pro-worthy board designs, as well as surfer threads and beanie hats.

Closet · SECONDHAND
(www.theclosetsb.net; 920 State St) This contemporary, cool resale clothing shop is a style maven's dream. No cluttered racks of vintage duds here – just lightly worn, stylish outfits from fashionistas like yourself. It's superpicky about what brands it accepts. (Jimmy Choo? Yes. Ann Taylor? Nuh-uh.)

Surf-n-Wear's Beach House · OUTDOORS
(www.surfnwear.com; 10 State St) Surfboards dangle from the ceiling at this beach-minded emporium where bikinis, shades, beachbags and flip-flops jostle for your attention. The shop's been around since before 1967's Summer of Love.

Diani · CLOTHING, SHOES
(www.dianiboutique.com; 1324 State St, Arlington Plaza) Carries high-fashion, Euro-inspired designs, with a touch of funky California soul thrown in for good measure. Think Diane von Furstenburg dresses, Rag & Bone skinny jeans and Chloé shoes.

CRSVR · CLOTHING, SHOES
(www.crsvr.com; 632 State St) Men, check out this sneaker boutique run by DJs, not just for limited-editions Nikes and other athletic-shoe brands, but also hip and trendy T-shirts, jackets, hats and more urban styles.

Mountain Air Sports · OUTDOORS
(www.mountainairsports.com; 14 State St) If you left your Camelbak pack or rock-climbing carabiners at home, this indie shop by the beach is the place to load up on outdoor gear, technical clothing and shoes for getting back to nature.

Downtown's most popular shopping malls and arcades:

Paseo Nuevo · MALL
(www.paseonuevoshopping.com; State St, btwn Cañon Perdido & Ortega Sts) This busy open-air mall is anchored by Macy's and Nordstrom department stores and clothing chains from Lululemon Athletica to Juicy Couture, plus eco-green goddess' bath, body and beauty shop Lush.

La Arcada · ARCADE
(www.laarcadasantabarbara.com; 1114 State St) Filled with jewelry and clothing

FIRST THURSDAYS

Prime time for downtown gallery hopping is **First Thursday** evenings, from 5pm to 8pm on the first Thursday of every month, when art galleries throw open their doors for new exhibitions, artists' receptions, wine tastings and live music, all free. For sneak peeks and schedules, visit www.santabarbaradowntown.com.

GO GREEN IN SANTA BARBARA

Are you a disengaged, greenwashing cynic? Keep reading – turns out that tree huggers are having the most fun.

One of the city's best-promoted initiatives is **Santa Barbara Car Free**. Visit www.santabarbaracarfree.org for tips on seeing the city without your car, plus discounts on accommodations and more. From LA, you can hop aboard the *Pacific Surfliner* for a three-hour coastal chug to the Amtrak station, a few blocks from the beach and downtown. Then hoof it or catch the electric shuttle that zips along State St or east–west along the coast. Take MTD line 22 (see to reach the mission and botanic gardens. For a self-guided cycling tour, drop by **Wheel Fun Rentals** (p374), just south of the train station.

Even Santa Barbara's wine country is getting into the eco swing of things. Vineyards are implementing biodynamic farming techniques and following organic guidelines. Many vintners and oenophiles are starting to think that the more natural the growing process, the better the wine, too. **Sustainable Vine Wine Tours** (p395) uses biodiesel vans to whisk you around ecofriendly vineyards, or minimize your carbon footprint even further by walking Santa Barbara's local **Urban Wine Trail** (p371).

Available free at many local markets, restaurants and wineries, **Edible Santa Barbara** (www.ediblecommunities.com/santabarbara) magazine publishes great articles about vineyards and restaurants that are going green. For our green-grazing faves, look for the 🖉 icon with reviews and see the 'DIY Dining' boxed text on p382.

Hiking, cycling, kayaking and surfing remain environmentally friendly outdoor activities, too (see p374). Just pay attention to posted guidelines and follow **Leave No Trace** (www.lnt.org) principles. If you're going whale-watching (p374), ask around to see if there are any alternative-fueled tour boats with trained onboard naturalists.

boutiques, restaurants and whimsical art galleries, this historic red-tile-roofed passageway was designed by Myron Hunt (builder of Pasadena's Rose Bowl) in the 1920s.

El Paseo ARCADE
(www.elpaseo.com; cnr State & De La Guerra Sts) Locally owned shops and restaurants overflow in this tiny, flower-festooned courtyard opposite Paseo Nuevo, as seen in *It's Complicated* when Meryl Streep's character bribes her psychotherapist with coffee cake.

❶ Information

Emergency
Santa Barbara Cottage Hospital (☎805-682-7111; cnr Pueblo & Bath Sts; ⏰24hr; Ⓟ) Emergency room open 24/7.

Internet Access
Central Public Library (www.sbplibrary.org; 40 E Anapamu St; ⏰10am-8pm Tue-Thu, 10am-5:30pm Fri & Sat, 1-5pm Sun; @🛜) Free walk-in internet terminals and wi-fi.

FedEx Office (www.fedexoffice.com; 1030 State St; per min 20-30¢; ⏰7am-11pm Mon-Thu, 7am-8pm Fri, 9am-5pm Sat & Sun) Self-service internet computer workstations.

Media
Santa Barbara Independent (www.independent.com) Published on Thursday, this free alternative weekly tabloid offers local eating and entertainment listings and reviews, plus an events calendar.

Santa Barbara News-Press (www.newspress.com) This daily newspaper has an events calendar and publishes Friday's arts-and-entertainment supplement 'Scene.'

Post
Main post office (www.usps.com; 836 Anacapa St; ⏰9:30am-6pm Mon-Fri, 10am-2pm Sat)

Tourist Information
Outdoors Santa Barbara Visitors Center (☎805-884-1475; www.outdoorsb.noaa.gov; 4th fl, 113 Harbor Way, Waterfront Center Bldg; ⏰11am-5pm) Helpful info on the Channel Islands and Los Padres National Forest. Great harbor-view deck.

Santa Barbara Visitors Center (☎805-965-3021; www.santabarbaraca.com; 1 Garden St; ⏰9am-5pm) Pick up maps and brochures while consulting with the helpful, but busy, staff. The website offers free downloadable DIY touring maps, from famous movie locations to wine trails and u-pick farms. Self-pay metered parking lot nearby.

ℹ Getting There & Away

The small **Santa Barbara Airport** (code SBA; ☎805-967-7111; www.flysba.com; 500 Fowler Rd, Goleta), about 10 miles west of downtown via Hwy 101, has scheduled flights to/from LA, Las Vegas, San Francisco, Sacramento and other western US cities. A taxi to downtown or the waterfront costs about $30 to $35 plus tip. The following agencies have car-rental desks at the airport:

Budget (☎805-964-6792, 800-527-0700; www.budget.com)

Enterprise (☎805-683-3012, 800-261-7331; www.enterprise.com)

Hertz (☎805-967-0411, 800-654-3131; www.hertz.com)

National (☎805-967-1202, 877-222-9058; www.nationalcar.com)

Santa Barbara Airbus (☎805-964-7759, 800-423-1618; www.santabarbaraairbus.com) shuttles between LA International Airport (LAX) and Santa Barbara ($48/90 one way/round-trip, 2¼ hours, nine departures daily). The more people in your party, the cheaper the fare. For discounts, prepay online.

Greyhound (☎805-965-7551, 800-231-2222; www.greyhound.com; 34 W Carrillo St) operates four buses daily to LA ($14 to $21, three hours) and up to six to San Francisco ($39 to $55, nine hours). **Vista** (☎800-438-1112; www.goventura.org) runs several daily 'Coastal Express' buses to Ventura ($2.50, 50 minutes).

Amtrak (☎800-872-7245; www.amtrak.com; 209 State St) has direct train services to LA ($16 to $26, three hours, six daily) and San Diego ($34 to $56, 5¾ hours to 6½ hours) via the *Pacific Surfliner* and *Coast Starlight,* which also stop in Carpinteria and Ventura.

Santa Barbara is bisected by Hwy 101. For downtown, take the Garden St or Carrillo St exits. Downtown street parking or in any of a dozen municipal lots is free for the first 75 minutes; each additional hour costs $1.50.

ℹ SANTA BARBARA CAR FREE

If you don't drive to Santa Barbara, you're eligible for 20% off Amtrak trains, plus discounts on some accommodations, restaurants, attractions, tours and outdoor activities, all courtesy of Santa Barbara Car Free (www.santabarbaracarfree.com). For more green travel tips, see the boxed text, opposite.

ℹ Getting Around

Local buses operated by the **Metropolitan Transit District** (MTD; ☎805-963-3366; www.sbmtd.gov) cost $1.75 per ride (exact change, cash only). Equipped with front-loading bike racks, these buses travel all over town and to adjacent communities; ask for a free transfer upon boarding. **MTD Transit Center** (1020 Chapala St) has details about routes and schedules.

BUS	DESTINATION	FREQUENCY
5	Arroyo Burro Beach	Hourly
11	State St, UCSB campus	Every 30 minutes
20	Montecito, Summerland, Carpinteria	Hourly
22	Mission, Museum of Natural History and (weekends only) Botanic Garden	Six to nine buses daily

MTD's electric **Downtown Shuttle** buses run along State St down to Stearns Wharf every 10 to 15 minutes from 10am to 6pm daily. A second **Waterfront Shuttle** route travels from Stearns Wharf west to the harbor and east to the zoo at 15- to 30-minute intervals from 10am to 6pm daily. In summer both routes also run every 15 minutes from 6pm to 10pm on Fridays and Saturdays. The fare is 25¢ per ride; transfers between routes are free.

The biodiesel **Santa Barbara Trolley** (☎805-965-0353; www.sbtrolley.com; adult/3-12yr $18/9) makes a hop-on, hop-off 90-minute narrated one-way loop starting from Stearns Wharf; stops include the harborfront, maritime museum, zoo, natural-history museum, mission and county courthouse on State St. One-way tickets are valid all day from approximately 10am to 4pm and include a free harbor cruise and discount coupons for various attractions. Pay the driver directly, or buy discounted tickets online in advance.

Lil' Toot water taxi (☎805-896-6900; adult/2-12yr $4/1; ⊗noon-6pm, till sunset in winter; ♿) provides an ecofriendly biodiesel-fueled ride between Stearns Wharf and the harbor. Look for ticket booths on the waterfront; trips run every half-hour.

Taxis are metered around $2 at flagfall, with an additional $2.80 to $3.25 for each mile. Try calling **Yellow Cab** (☎805-965-5111, 800-549-8294).

For bicycle rentals, see p374.

What to See

Rising from the coast, you'll leave oh-so civilized Santa Barbara behind and enter the Santa Ynez Mountains. You'll notice places where the hillsides have been scarred by wildfires, but don't be alarmed: wildfires are part of the natural process of birth and regrowth in SoCal forests.

CHUMASH PAINTED CAVE STATE HISTORIC PARK

This tiny, off-the-beaten path **historic site** (www.parks.ca.gov; admission free; ☉dawn-dusk) shelters pictographs painted by the indigenous Chumash tribes over 400 years ago. The sandstone cave is now protected from graffiti and vandalism by a metal screen, so bring a flashlight to get a good look. The turnoff to Painted Cave Rd is off Hwy 154 below San Marcos Summit, about 6 miles from Hwy 101. The two-mile twisting side road to the park is extremely narrow, rough and steep, and not accessible by RVs. Look for a small signposted pull-off on your left.

COLD SPRING TAVERN

A vintage slice of Americana, **Cold Spring Tavern** (☎805-967-0066; www.coldspring tavern.com; 5995 Stagecoach Rd; ☉breakfast, lunch & dinner) is an 1860s stagecoach stop that's still a popular watering hole. A rough-hewn plank floor connects a warren of dimly lit rooms decorated with an odd assortment of Western memorabilia. As for the food, call ahead to check when the BBQ grill is open, then order the Santa Maria-style tri-tip barbecue sandwich. The tavern's signposted turnoff from Hwy 154 is about a mile downhill from the mountain summit, around 9 miles from Hwy 101. Follow the signs for another 1.5 miles to the tavern; continue on and you'll hook back up to Hwy 154.

LOS PADRES NATIONAL FOREST

The **Los Padres National Forest** (www.r5.fs.fed.us/lospadres) stretches over 200 miles from the Carmel Valley to the western edge of Los Angeles County. It's great for hiking, camping, horseback riding and mountain biking.

SANTA BARBARA WINE COUNTRY

Oak-dotted hillsides, winding country lanes, rows of sweetly heavy grapevines stretching as far as the eye can see – it's hard not to gush when describing Santa Barbara's wine country, a primo spot for road tripping. From fancy convertibles and Harleys to eco-friendly touring vans and road bikes, you'll find an eclectic, friendly mix of travelers sharing these bucolic back roads.

Citizens here are typically friendly too, from longtime landowners and farmers displaying small-town graciousness to vineyard owners who've fled big cities to follow their passion. Ever more wine-makers are showing their passion for the vine in earth-conscious ways, implementing organic practices and biodynamic farming techniques. Many happily share their knowledge and fascinating histories, as well as their love of the land, in more intimate vineyard tasting rooms.

You may be inspired to visit by the Oscar-winning film *Sideways,* an ode to the joys and hazards of wine-country living, as seen through the misadventures of middle-aged buddies Miles and Jack. The movie is like real life in at least one respect: this wine country is ideal for do-it-yourself-exploring with friends.

With more than 100 wineries spread out across the landscape, it can seem daunting at first. But the Santa Ynez Valley's five small towns – Buellton, Solvang, Santa Ynez, Ballard and Los Olivos – are all clustered within 10 miles of one another, so it's easy to stop, shop and eat whenever and wherever you feel like it. Don't worry about sticking to a regimented plan or following overly detailed wine guides either. Just soak up the scenery and pull over where the sign looks welcoming.

There are several good US Forest Service (USFS) trails off Paradise Rd, which crosses Hwy 154 north of San Marcos Pass, just over 10 miles from Hwy 101. Try the 2-mile round-trip **Red Rock Trail**, where the Santa Ynez River deeply pools among rocks and waterfalls, creating a great swimming and sunning spot. The trailhead lies beyond the river crossing at the end of Paradise Rd.

En route, visit the **ranger station** (☎805-967-3481; 3505 Paradise Rd; ⊙8:30am-4:30pm Mon-Fri) for posted trail maps and information and a National Forest Adventure Pass ($5 per day), which is required for parking. Developed **campgrounds** (reservations ☎877-444-6777; www.recreation.gov; campsites $19-35) with first-come, first-served and reservable sites include Fremont, Paradise and Los Prietos before the ranger station and Upper Oso at the end of Paradise Rd.

CACHUMA LAKE RECREATION AREA

This county-run **park** (admission per vehicle $6) is a haven for anglers and boaters, with wildlife-watching **cruises** (☎805-686-5050/5055; adult/4-12yr $15/7) year-round. There's also a child-friendly **nature center** (⊙daily Jun-Aug, weekends only Sep-May) and a large **campground** (☎805-686-5055, recorded info 805-686-5054; www.cachuma.com; tent/RV sites $25/35, yurts $75-85) with hot showers. First-come, first-served sites fill quickly, especially on weekends. Book ahead for ecofriendly yurts.

The Route

From Hwy 101 west of downtown Santa Barbara, Hwy 154 (San Marcos Pass Rd) heads northwest, winding up through Los Padres National Forest and past Cachuma Lake. Past Santa Ynez and the Hwy 246 turnoff west toward Solvang, Hwy 154 bisects the wine-growing Santa Ynez Valley before rejoining Hwy 101, north of Los Olivos.

Time & Mileage

It's 35 miles from downtown Santa Barbara to Los Olivos, taking 45 minutes to drive with no stops (longer during weekday commute hours and busy weekend wine-country traffic). Returning to Santa Barbara, it's just under an hour's trip via Hwy 101 southbound.

🏃 Wineries

The three appellations for Santa Barbara's wine country are the **Santa Ynez Valley**, **Santa Maria Valley** and **Santa Rita Hills**. Wine-tasting rooms abound in Los Olivos (see p395) and also Solvang, handy for anyone with limited time.

The Santa Ynez Valley, where you'll find most of the wineries, lies south of the Santa Maria Valley. Hwy 246 runs east–west, via Solvang, across the bottom of the Santa Ynez Valley, connecting Hwy 101 and Hwy 154. North–south secondary roads where you'll find good wineries include Alamo Pintado Rd from Hwy 246 to Los Olivos, and Refugio Rd into neighboring Ballard.

For a half-day trip, expect to spend no less than four hours, which will allow you to see one winery or tasting room, have lunch and return to Santa Barbara. Otherwise make it a full day and plan to have lunch and possibly dinner before returning to the city.

SANTA YNEZ VALLEY

Popular wineries cluster between Los Olivos and Solvang along Alamo Pintado Rd and Refugio Rd, south of Roblar Ave and west of Hwy 154. Noisy tour groups, harried staff and stingy pours too often disappoint, but thankfully that's not usually the case at the following wine-tasting rooms.

Beckmen Vineyards   WINERY
(www.beckmenvineyards.com; 2670 Ontiveros Rd, Solvang; tastings $10-15; ⊙11am-5pm) Bring a picnic to the pondside gazebo at this tranquil winery, where estate-grown Rhône varieties flourish on the unique terroir of Purisima Mountain. Using biodynamic farming principles, natural (not chemical), means are used to prevent pests. To sample superb syrahs and a rare cuvée blend with grenache, mourvèdre and counoise, follow Roblar Ave west of Hwy 154 to Ontiveros Rd.

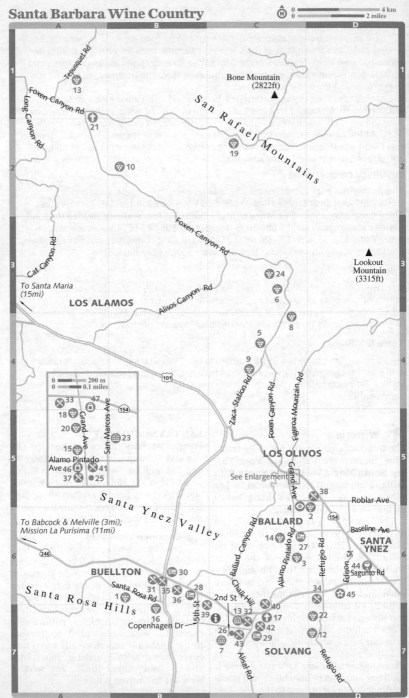

Lincourt Vineyard WINERY
(www.lincourtwines.com; 1711 Alamo Pintado Rd, Solvang; tastings $10; ☺10am-5pm) Respected winemaker Bill Foley, who runs Firestone Vineyard on the Foxen Canyon Wine Trail, founded this vineyard first in the late 1990s on a former dairy farm. Today you can still see the original 1926 farmhouse built from a Sears catalog kit. Inside the yellow cottage's tasting room, sip finely crafted syrahs and pinot noirs and a dry French-style rosé, all made from grapes grown in the Santa Maria Valley and Santa Rita Hills.

Kalyra Winery WINERY
(www.kalyrawinery.com; 343 Refugio Rd, Santa Ynez; tastings $7; ☺11am-5pm Mon-Fri, 10am-5pm

Sat & Sun) Australian Mike Brown has traveled halfway around the world to combine his two loves: surfing and winemaking. Try his unique shiraz–cabernet sauvignon blend, a true Australian shiraz made from imported Barossa Valley grapes, and an Eden Valley reisling, all in bottles with Aboriginal art–inspired labels. Kalyra also pours a variety of Santa Ynez Valley–grown white and red varietals here and along Santa Barbara's Urban Wine Trail (see p384).

Sunstone Vineyards & Winery WINERY
(www.sunstonewinery.com; 125 Refugio Rd, Santa Ynez; tastings $10; ☺10am-4pm) After a short jaunt on a dirt road, you'll discover what looks like an 18th-century stone

WINE COUNTRY CELEBRATIONS

The **Santa Barbara Vintners' Association** (☎805-668-0881; www.sbcountywines.com) publishes a free touring map of area wineries, which you can pick up at just about any winery or visitors center. Special events worth planning your trip around include the **Spring Vintners' Festival** held in early April and mid-October's **Celebration of Harvest** weekend.

farmhouse from Provence. Wander inside past the main tasting area into dimly lit hillside caves housing the barrel room and a library of vintages. Sunstone crafts Bordeaux-style wines and blends made from 100% organically grown grapes. Bring a picnic to eat in the courtyard beneath gnarled oaks.

Buttonwood Farm Winery WINERY
(www.buttonwoodwinery.com; 1500 Alamo Pintado Rd, Solvang; tastings $10; ⏰11am-5pm) Bordeaux and Rhône varieties do well in the sun-dappled limestone soil at this friendly winery best for wine-tasting neophytes. Founder Betty Williams is another earth-conscious wine grower; her family has implemented sustainable and environmentally sound growing practices. The trellised back patio, bordering the orchard, is a nice spot to relax with a bottle of Buttonwood's zingy sauvignon blanc.

FOXEN CANYON WINE TRAIL
The scenic Foxen Canyon Wine Trail runs north from Hwy 154, just west of Los Olivos, deep into the heart of the Santa Maria Valley, a more rural area with fewer visitors. It's a must-see for oenophiles or anyone wanting to get off the beaten path. For the most part, the wine trail follows Foxen Canyon Rd, with the following wineries listed in geographical order, south to north.

Firestone Vineyard WINERY
(www.firestonewine.com; 5000 Zaca Station Rd; tastings $15, incl tour $20; ⏰10am-5pm) Founded in 1972, Firestone is Santa Barbara's oldest estate winery. Sweeping views of the vineyard from the sleek, wood-paneled tasting room are as impressive as the chardonnay, syrah, pinot noir, merlot and Bordeaux-style wines. Arrive in time for a winery tour, offered at 11:15am, 1:15pm and 3:15pm daily.

Curtis Winery WINERY
(☎805-686-8999; www.curtiswinery.com; 5249 Foxen Canyon Rd; tastings $10; ⏰10:30am-5:30pm Apr-Sep, 10am-5pm Oct-Mar) Owned by the family of former *Bachelor* Andrew Firestone, this artisan winemaker specializes in Rhône-style wines, including outstanding syrahs, grenache, mourvèdre, viognier and roussanne.

Fess Parker Winery & Vineyard WINERY
(www.fessparker.com; 6200 Foxen Canyon Rd; tastings $10; ⏰10am-5pm) Pinot-noir sales jumped after the winery's appearance as Frass Canyon in the film *Sideways*. The winery's other claim to fame is its late founder Fess Parker, best known for playing Davy Crockett on TV. Even though Fess has now gone to those happy hunting grounds in the sky, his winery still gives away coonskin-cap-etched souvenir glasses.

Demetria Estate WINERY
(☎805-686-2345; www.demetriaestate.com; 6701 Foxen Canyon Rd; tastings $10; ⏰by appt only) Just north of tour-bus-filled Fess Parker, this retreat has the curving arches and thick wooden doors of your hospitable Greek uncle's country house. Tastings are by appointment only, but worth it to sample biodynamically farmed and gravity flowed pinot noir, syrah, chardonnay and pinot blanc, plus rave-worthy red and white cuvée blends.

Zaca Mesa Winery WINERY
(www.zacamesa.com; 6905 Foxen Canyon Rd; tastings $10; ⏰10am-4pm) Stop by smaller,

TOP FIVE WINERIES FOR PICNICS

You won't have any problem finding picnic fare in Santa Barbara's wine country. The region is chock-full of groceries, delis and bakeries serving up portable sandwiches and salads. When picnicking at a winery, remember it's polite to buy a bottle of wine before spreading out your blanket on the lawn.

» **Rancho Sisquoc**
» **Beckmen Vineyards** (p389)
» **Sunstone Vineyards & Winery** (p391)
» **Zaca Mesa Winery**
» **Lincourt Vineyard** (p391)

Though large-scale winemaking has only been happening here since the 1980s, the climate of Santa Barbara's wine country has always been perfect for growing grapes. Two parallel, east–west-trending mountain ranges (the Santa Ynez and San Rafael) cradle the region and funnel coastal fog eastward off the Pacific into the valleys between. The farther inland you go, the warmer it gets.

To the west, fog and low clouds may hover all day, keeping the weather chilly even in summer, while only a few miles inland, temperatures approach 100°F in July. These delicately balanced microclimates support two major varieties of grape. Near the coast in the Santa Maria Valley, pinot noir – a particularly fragile grape – and other Burgundy-style varieties like chardonnay thrive. Inland in the Santa Ynez Valley, Rhône-style grapes do best, including syrah and viognier.

As you wander around wine country, you'll see vineyards and wineries. They're not the same thing. The term 'vineyard' refers only to the place where grapes are grown, while a winery is the place where grapes are fermented into wine. If a winery uses grapes from its own vineyards, it's called an estate, as in 'estate grown' or 'estate bottled' wines. But estates ferment grapes from other vineyards too. 'Vineyard-designated' wines refer to when a winery buys grapes from a particular vineyard known for its superior quality.

barn-style Zaca Mesa for a rustic, sipping-on-the-farm ambience. The vibe is low-key but convivial, and the friendly tasting-room hosts are happy to share their knowledge. Santa Barbara's highest-elevation winery, it's known not only for its estate-grown Rhône varietals and signature Z Cuvée red blend, but also a life-sized outdoor chessboard, tree-shaded picnic area and a short, scenic trail overlooking the vineyards.

TOP CHOICE **Foxen** WINERY
(☑805-937-4251; www.foxenvineyard.com; 7200 & 7600 Foxen Canyon Rd, Santa Maria; tastings $10; ⊙11am-4pm) On what was once a working cattle ranch, Foxen excels at crafting many different varietals – warm cabernets, steel-cut chardonnays, full-fruited pinot noirs and great Rhône-style wines – sourced from standout vineyards. The new tasting room is solar powered, while the old 'shack' – a dressed-down space with a concrete floor, corrugated-metal roof and funky-cool decor – pours Bordeaux-style and Cal-Ital varietals under the 'Foxen 7200' label. Only those in the know make the journey to this special place.

Rancho Sisquoc WINERY
(www.ranchosisquoc.com; 6600 Foxen Canyon Rd, Santa Maria; ⊙10am-4pm Mon-Thu, to 5pm Fri-Sun) This tranquil gem is worth the extra mileage, not necessarily for its hit-and-miss wines (try the inky malbec) but for the charmingly rustic tasting room sur-

rounded by pastoral views. Turn off Foxen Canyon Rd when you spot **San Ramon Chapel**, a little white church built in 1875; it's on the east side of the road and worth a visit for those curious about local history and architecture. Incidentally, *sisquoc* is the Chumash term for 'gathering place.'

Kenneth Volk Vineyards WINERY
(☑805-938-7896; www.volkwines.com; 5230 Tepusquet Rd, Santa Maria; tastings $5; ⊙10:30am-4:30pm) Only an established cult winemaker could convince oenophiles to drive out of their way to taste rare heritage varietals like floral-scented malvasia and standard-bearing pinot noir, cabernet sauvignon, merlot and chardonnay.

SANTA RITA HILLS WINE TRAIL
Santa Rita Hills may be the new kid on the block, but when it comes to country-road scenery, eco-conscious farming practices and top-notch pinots, it holds its own. Almost a dozen tasting rooms line this scenic loop west of Hwy 101 via Santa Rosa Rd and Hwy 246. Be prepared to share the roads with cyclists and an occasional John Deere tractor.

Alma Rosa Winery & Vineyards WINERY
(www.almarosawinery.com; 7250 Santa Rosa Rd, Buellton; tastings $10; ⊙11am-4:30pm) Richard Sanford, founder of nearby Sanford Wineries, left the powerhouse bearing his name to start this new winery with his wife, Thekla, using sustainable,

CHRIS BURROUGHS: TASTING ROOM MANAGER

Alma Rosa Winery's tasting-room manager is already familiar to moviegoers for his appearance in the 2004 indie hit *Sideways* as – what else? – a cowboy-hat-wearing tasting-room manager. He shared a few smart wine-tasting tips with us.

Novices Never Fear

Don't let a lack of wine savvy keep you away. Winemakers enjoy sharing their passion and knowledge, and beginners are often their favorite guests.

Travel Light

Most tasting rooms aren't equipped for large crowds. Traveling in small groups means you'll have more time to chat with the staff.

Less is More

Don't keep a scorecard on the number of wineries visited. Spend time at only a handful of tasting rooms on any given day. Wine drinking is a social vehicle (not a mobile party crawl).

Stay Open-Minded

At most tasting rooms you'll sample six wines: three whites and three reds. Don't tell the staff you never drink chardonnay – who knows, the wine you try that day may change your mind.

Nice Guys Finish First

Smoking and heavy perfume? Not so considerate of others, and smoking dulls your wine-tasting senses besides. Be friendly, too. I'd rather drink a mediocre bottle of wine with a cool person than special wine with a jerk.

California-certified organic farming techniques. Cacti and cobblestones welcome you to the ranch, reached via a long, winding gravel driveway. In the tasting room, knockout vineyard-designated pinot noirs and a fine pinot blanc are poured.

Babcock WINERY
(www.babcockwinery.com; 5175 E Hwy 146, Lompoc; tastings $10; ☺10:30am-4pm) Family-owned vineyards overflowing with different varietals – chardonnay, sauvignon blanc, pinot gris, pinot noir, syrah, cabernet sauvignon, merlot and more – let innovative small-lot winemaker Bryan Babcock be the star. The Fathom red blend is pilgrimage-worthy.

Melville WINERY
(www.melvillewinery.com; 5185 E Hwy 146, Lompoc; tastings $10; ☺11am-4pm) Next door to Babcock, this Mediterranean hillside villa calls to oenophiles seeking tastes of estate-grown, small-lot bottled pinot noirs and chardonnays made by folks who believe in talking about pounds per plant, not tons per acre. Don't think there isn't variety

here, though, with over a dozen different clones of pinot noir alone grown.

Ampelos Cellars TASTING ROOM
(☎805-736-9957; www.ampeloscellars. com; 1633 W Central Ave, Lompoc; tastings $10; ☺11am-4pm Sat & by appt) Danish grower Peter Work and wife Rebecca display their passion for the vine through rigorous adherence to biodynamic farming techniques and encyclopedic knowledge of their lots. Their innovative pinot noirs and syrahs shine – too bad the tasting room is in an industrial area of Lompoc, far from the vineyards.

Hitching Post II WINE BAR
(www.hitchingpost2.com; 406 E Hwy 246; tastings $8; ☺4-6pm) Along Hwy 146 in Buellton, this steakhouse offers tastings ($8) of its own well-regarded pinots and syrahs at the bar nightly. Arrive early for a seat.

Mosby Winery WINERY
(☎805-688-2415; www.mosbywines.com; 9496 Santa Rosa Rd, Buellton; tastings $10; ☺10am-4pm Mon-Thu, to 5pm Fri-Sun)

Just west of Hwy 101, this casual red carriage house proffers unusual Cal-Italian varietals, including a lip-puckering, fruit-forward dolcetto and a crisp, citrusy estate-grown cortese.

Tours

Full-day wine-tasting tours average $100 to $175 per person; most leave from Santa Barbara, and some require a minimum number of participants.

 Sustainable Vine Wine Tours
WINE TASTINGS
(☎805-698-3911; www.sustainablevine.com) Biodiesel-van tours of wineries implementing organic and sustainable agricultural practices include lunch from an organic-minded deli.

Wine Edventures WINE TASTINGS
(☎805-965-9463; www.welovewines.com) Serves up a fun-lovin' side dish of local history and wine education on its shuttle-driven wine-tasting tours.

Santa Barbara Wine Country Cycling Tours WINE TASTINGS
(☎888-557-8687; www.winecountrycycling. com; 3630 Sagunto St; ◎8:30am-5pm Mon-Sat, Sun by appt) Guided and DIY cycling tours leave from Santa Ynez. Also rents road and hybrid mountain bikes (from $35/45 per half-/full day).

Los Olivos

POP 1300

The posh ranching town of Los Olivos is many visitors' first stop when exploring Santa Barbara's wine country. A four-block-long main street is lined with rustic tasting rooms, art galleries, restaurants, cafes and surprisingly fashionable shops seemingly airlifted straight out of Napa.

◉ Sights & Activities

Inside a rickety 19th-century general store, the **Los Olivos Tasting Room** (2905 Grand Ave; tastings $10; ◎11am-5:30pm) stocks rare vintages you won't find anywhere else. California's oldest independent tasting room, it specializes in high-end pinot noirs and other small lot batches from the region's top vineyards, some of which don't have their own tasting rooms. Well-oiled servers are by turns loquacious and gruff, but refreshingly blunt in their opinions about local wines, and pours are generous.

Run by one of the county's most experienced vintners, **Richard Longoria Wines** (www.longoriawine.com; 2935 Grand Ave; tastings $10; ◎11am-4:30pm) specializes in pinot noir, syrah, pinot grigio and a few Spanish varietals like albariño and tempranillo. As you sip, inspect the antique wine press or relax on the shady garden patio. Nearby **Qupé Wines** (www.qupe.com; 2963 Grand Ave; tastings $10; ◎11am-5pm) is of the most respected syrah and chardonnay producers on California's Central Coast. It also bottles other small-lot Rhône varietals.

Need a break from boozin'? The petite **Wildling Art Museum** (☎805-688-1802; www.wildlingmuseum.org; 2928 San Marcos Ave; adult/under 12yr $3/free; ◎11am-5pm Wed-Sun) has special exhibitions of wilderness-themed paintings and photography that will inspire you to go hiking in the mountains (for trails, see the boxed text, p389). More natural beauty awaits just outside town at family-owned **Clairmont Farms** (☎805-688-7505; www.clarimontfarms.com; 2480 Roblar Ave; ◎usually 10am-6pm), where purple lavender fields bloom like a Monet masterpiece, usually peaking from mid-June to late July. Snap photos, then peruse the lavender honey, lavender sea salt and aromatherapy, bath and body products.

WORTH A TRIP

MISSION LA PURÍSIMA

Perhaps the most evocative of all Southern California's missions, **La Purísima Mission State Historic Park** (☎805-733-3713; www.lapurisimamission.org, www.parks.ca.gov; 2295 Purísima Rd; admission per vehicle $5; ◎9am-5pm) was completely restored in the 1930s by the Civilian Conservation Corps (CCC). Today its buildings are furnished just as they were during Spanish colonial times. The fields still support livestock, and outdoor gardens are planted with medicinal plants and trees once used by Chumash tribespeople. Surrounding the mission are miles of peaceful hiking trails too. Free guided tours begin at 1pm daily. The mission is 15 miles west of Hwy 101 via Hwy 146.

For more postwine pampering, **Champagne Spa & Boutique** (☑805-686-9202; www.fessparker.com; Fess Parker Wine Country Inn & Spa, 2860 Grand Ave) is a downtown haven of relaxation. A 50-minute 'Vino Therapy' treatment – grapeseed-oil moisturizer and therapeutic massage – costs around $100, plus tip. Linger longer with a zinfandel-chocolate or viognier-apricot scrub and soothing body-butter massage (from $155).

🛏 Sleeping & Eating

Ballard Inn & Restaurant
B&B **$$$**

(☑805-688-7770, 800-638-2466; www.ballard inn.com; 2436 Baseline Ave, Ballard; r $245-315; 🖀) For honeymooners and romantics, this contemporary-built inn awaits in the 19th-century stagecoach town of Ballard, just over 2 miles south of Los Olivos heading toward Solvang. Wood-burning fireplaces make the private en-suite rooms feel even more cozy. Rates include a full hot breakfast and wine tastings. Reservations are essential for the rooms and also dinner at the inn's chef-driven Eurasian restaurant.

Los Olivos Café & Wine Merchant
CAL-MEDITERRANEAN **$$**

(☑805-688-7265; www.losolivoscafe.com; 2879 Grand Ave; mains $12-30; ⏲11:30am-8:30pm) *Sideways* promoted Los Olivos Café, and now Los Olivos Café promotes *Sideways* – buy a copy of the book here. With white canopies, a concrete floor and a wisteria-covered trellis, this happenin' wine bistro swirls up a casual-chic ambience that adds a nice finish to a long day of touring. It conveniently stays open between lunch and dinner for antipasto platters, hearty salads and crispy pizzas and wine flights at the bar.

Brothers' Restaurant at Mattei's Tavern
STEAKHOUSE **$$$**

(☑805-688-4820; www.matteistavern.com; 2350 Railway Ave; mains $20-45; ⏲dinner) Relaxing on an overstuffed sofa in the fireplace lounge, you half expect a stagecoach to come thundering up in time for dinner – which would've been the norm over a century ago at this one-time stagecoach stop and tavern dating from 1886. Today you can dine at checkered-tablecloth tables on bold American country flavors, such as hickory-smoked salmon and oven-roasted rack of lamb. Get gussied up, pardner.

Los Olivos Grocery
MARKET, DELI **$**

(http://losolivosgrocery.com; 2621 W Hwy 154, Santa Ynez; ⏲7am-9pm) This locavarian market heaps up BBQ tri-tip sandwiches and farm-fresh salads, artisan breads, specialty cheeses and everything you'll need for a vineyard picnic, or just grab a table on the screened-in front porch.

Panino
DELI **$**

(http://paninorestaurants.com; 2900 Grand Ave; sandwiches $8-10; ⏲10am-4pm) Take-out deli serves up a healthy selection of gourmet sandwiches such as curried chicken salad or roast turkey with brie, plus robust vegetarian options. Order at the counter, then eat outside at an umbrella-covered table.

🔒 Shopping

Boutiques and specialty shops cluster along Grand Ave.

Tin Roof Boutique
CLOTHING, JEWELRY

(www.tinroofboutique.com; 2982 Grand Ave) The roof's not rusted at this bright-red boutique where Valley fashionistas snap up stylin' tees, flouncy dresses, designer shoes and jewelry.

Jedlicka's Western Wear
CLOTHING, SHOES

(www.jedlickas.com; 2883 Grand Ave) Wranglers and prairie babes should mosey over to Jedlicka's for name-brand boots – Lucchese, Justin – as well as hats, jeans and jackets.

Wine Country Home
GIFTS

(2900 Grand Ave) Decorate your cottage with vineyard-inspired style accents, cookware and gourmet gifts.

Solvang

POP 5450

My God, captain, we've hit a windmill. Which can only mean one thing in wine country: Solvang, a Danish village founded in 1911 on what was once a 19th-century Spanish colonial mission and later a Mexican *rancho* land grant. This Santa Ynez Valley town holds tight to its Danish heritage – or at least its stereotypical images. With its knickknack stores and cutesy motels, the town is almost as sticky-sweet as the Scandinavian pastries foisted upon the wandering hordes looking for a point to it all. And what precisely is the point? Solvang's kitschy charms make it worth visiting – well, at least once – if only to gawk.

◎ Sights

Old Mission Santa Inés HISTORIC SITE
(www.missionsantaines.org; 1760 Mission Dr;
adult/under 12yr $4/free; ⊙9am-4:30pm) Along
Hwy 246 east of Alisal Rd, this was the
stage for a Chumash tribespeople's revolt
against Spanish colonial cruelty in 1824. It's
still an active parish today. Ask for a free
(albeit historically biased) audio guide tour.

Hans Christian Andersen Museum MUSEUM
(2nd fl, 1680 Mission Dr; ⊙10am-5pm) If you
remember childhood fairy tales with
fondness, stop by this tiny museum where
original letters and 1st-edition copies
of the Danish storyteller's books are on
display.

Elverhøj Museum of History & Art MUSEUM
(☑805-686-1211; www.elverhoj.org; 1624
Elverhoj Way; adult/under 13yr $3/free; ⊙1-
4pm Wed & Thu, noon-4pm Fri-Sun) South of
downtown on residential side streets, the
delightful little museum has modest, but
thoughtful exhibits on Danes in America
and Solvang's Danish history.

✦ Activities

Beyond its kitschy shops and buttery pastries, Solvang is a good jumping-off point
for wine-country explorations. Solvang is
well known in bicycling circles for **Solvang
Century** (www.bikescor.com/solvang) races
through the surrounding countryside in
March. Or just take it easy and unwind
with a one-hour Swedish massage and re-
flexology treatment (from $100 plus tip) at
De-stress Café (☑805-693-8776; 435 Second
St), a day spa. **Haven Spa** at the Hadsten
House Inn (see below) is more deluxe.

🛏 Sleeping

Sleeping in Solvang isn't cheap, not even in
old motels with faux-Danish exteriors (save
us, Holger Danske!). On weekends, rates
skyrocket and rooms fill fast, so book ahead
or make it a day trip from Santa Barbara
instead.

Hadsten House Inn BOUTIQUE HOTEL $$
(☑805-688-3210, 800-457-5373; www.hadsten
house.com; 1450 Mission Dr; r incl breakfast $120-
305; 🎈🐾) Why does my luxury inn look like
a dumpy two-story motel? Don't worry: this
revamped motel property has updated just
about everything, except for its uninspiring
exterior. Inside your room, it's surprisingly
plush, with flat-screen TVs, triple sheets,
comfy duvets and L'Occitane bath products.

There's an indoor heated pool too. Rates in-
clude a hot breakfast and afternoon wine-
and-cheese tasting.

Hotel Corque HOTEL $$
(☑805-688-8000, 800-624-5572; www.hotel
corque.com; 400 Alisal Rd; r $140-330; @🎈🐾)
Downtown, this clean-lined hotel is a relief
from all things Danish. Rooms may look
anonymous, but they're spacious. You've
also got access to the next-door fitness
center, where you can work off all those
Danish butter rings or dinner at the hotel's acclaimed restaurant, Root 246. More
Vegas-style hotel rooms await a few miles
away at the tribe's Chumash Casino Resort.

🍴 Eating

Tubs of Danish butter cookies and rich al-
mond kringles are popular takeaways from
the **Solvang Bakery** (www.solvangbakery.com;
460 Alisal Rd; ⊙7am-6pm), or gobble a cus-
tardy butter ring from **Mortensen's Bakery** (1588 Mission Dr; ⊙7:30am-7pm). For pancakes, Scandinavian or otherwise, take a
detour to Ellen's Pancake House in Buellton
(see p398).

Root 246 MODERN AMERICAN $$$
(☑805-686-8681; www.root-246.com; 420
Alisal Rd; mains lunch $14-20, dinner $19-35;
⊙lunch Sat & Sun, dinner daily) Next to the Ho-
tel Corque, star chef Bradley Ogden brings
creative farm-to-table cuisine to life with
an artful touch in cool, chic surrounds.
It's hard to beat the 'shake-and-bake' fried
chicken. Make reservations and dress to the
nines. Otherwise the no-reservations bar,
which serves haute appetizers and a luxu-
riously long list of California wines by the
glass, opens at 4pm.

El Rancho Market MARKET, DELI $
(2886 Mission Dr; sandwiches around $8; ⊙6am-
10pm) It's the best place to stop if you want
to fill a picnic basket, not to mention re-
integrate into society after a day of wind-
mills, clogs and abelskiver (small dough-
nut). An easy pull-off east of downtown
Solvang, this grocery store is known for
its fab deli case, smokin' barbecue takeout,
bargain wine room and espresso bar.

Solvang Restaurant BAKERY, CAFE $
(www.solvangrestaurant.com; 1672 Copenhagen
Dr; mains $6-12; ⊙6am-3pm Mon-Fri, to 5pm Sat
& Sun) Film buffs may recognize the Danish-
inscribed beams and decorative borders
from *Sideways*. The other reason to visit is
for abelskivers – round pancake balls with

sliced apples baked inside and covered in raspberry-jam sauce and powdered sugar. They're so popular, there's even a special take-out window.

New Frontiers Natural Marketplace

GROCERY STORE

(1984 Old Mission Dr; ☺8am-8pm Mon-Sat, to 7pm Sun; ✍) If you're trying to keep things organic, stop here for a tasty variety of deli sandwiches, salads and take-out dishes for picnicking.

Bit o' Denmark DANISH

(473 Alisal Rd; buffet $16; ☺11:30am-9:30pm Mon-Fri, 9am-9:30pm Sat & Sun) Tipple imported Danish liquors and beers at the bar, or try the all-you-can-eat smorgasbord, if you dare.

🍷 Drinking & Entertainment

Anywhere but here. Sorry, but true. After dinner this town is deader than an ancient Viking.

Maverick Saloon BAR, MUSIC

(☎805-686-4785; www.mavericksaloon.org; 3687 Sagunto St, off Hwy 246; ☺noon-2am) En route to the Chumash Casino, you'll pass by the one-horse town of Santa Ynez, home to this Harley-friendly honky-tonk with live country-and-western and rock bands, latenight DJs and dancing.

Chumash Casino Resort GAMBLING, MUSIC

(☎800-248-6274; www.chumashcasino.com; 3400 E Hwy 246; ☺24hr) If you're just one abelskiver from sugar-and-kitsch-induced insanity, drive east 3 miles on Hwy 246 to Solvang's vice-minded doppelganger, where the slots are plenty, the cocktails watereddown and the cigarette smoke so thick you could cut it with a Danish butter knife. Last-minute tickets for concerts by yesterday's pop and rock superstars are usually available.

🛍 Shopping

Downtown Solvang's notoriously kitschy shops cover about three square blocks south of Mission Dr (Hwy 246) between Atterdag Rd and Alisal Rd. If colorful quilts, miniclog magnets, and decorative Danish plates top your shopping list, you'll be crossing off items like mad. **Gaveasken** (433 Alisal Rd), aka 'The Gift Box,' displays a primo mix of Scandinavian wares: from ornamental silver trays and candelabras to paper-cut Christmas ornaments, it's all here. For Danish cookbooks, handcrafted quilts and pil-

lows and other homespun items, visit the **Elverhøj Museum** (see p397). For truly fine wooden furnishings, clocks, decorative art and jewelry from around Europe and America, step inside the museum-like **Solvang Antique Center** (http://solvang antiques.com; 486 First St).

Buellton

POP 3830

Somewhat misleadingly described as the gateway to Santa Barbara's wine country, tiny Buellton is best known for the awful landmark towering over the intersection of Hwys 101 and 246: Anderson's Pea Soup Restaurant, where you can indeed get heaping bowls of the green stuff (we would advise against it).

Ever since the release of *Sideways* in 2004, the **Hitching Post II** (☎805-688-0676; www.hitchingpost2.com; 406 E Hwy 246; mains $20-48; ☺dinner) has been giving Andersen's some competition as the town's most recognizable landmark. Seen in the movie as the restaurant where Miles meets waitress Maya, this legendary, dark-paneled chophouse offers oak-grilled Midwestern corn-fed steaks as well as baby back ribs and California quail. Every meal comes with a veggie tray, garlic bread, shrimp cocktail or soup, salad and a starch. The Hitching Post II makes its own pinot noir, and it's pretty darn good (see also p394); the bar opens at 4pm.

Buellton has slightly cheaper chain midrange motels and hotels than Solvang, about 3 miles east. **Pea Soup Andersen's Inn** (☎805-688-3216, 800-732-7687; www.pea soupandersens.com; 51 E Hwy 246; r $90-150; ❖🎮🕹🅿) has a central courtyard where kids go nuts for the minigolf course and pool. First-floor rooms with patio doors are fun for families; upstairs rooms are quieter. All rooms have air-con, but are otherwise outdated and worn-looking.

West of Hwy 101, old-fashioned and always busy **Ellen's Pancake House** (☎805-688-5312; 272 Ave of the Flags; mains $6-12; ☺6am-8pm Mon-Sat, to 4pm Sun) is where locals congregate for what they know are the wine country's best Danish pancakes, Danish sausages and not-so-Danish Belgian waffles. Hidden upstairs in an industrial space nearby, **Avant Tapas & Wine** (☎805-686-9400; www.avantwines.com; 35 Industrial Way; dishes $5-8; ☺11am-8pm Thu-

Sun) is another under-the-radar find for the hot and cold Cal-Spanish tapas, wood-oven pizzas and a DIY enomatic dispensing system pouring tastes of over 30 boutique wines fermented in the warehouse, where you can walk out onto the catwalk to take a look.

❶ Information

Solvang is the hub for wine-country visitors. Pick up free tourist brochures and winery maps at the **Solvang Conference & Visitors Bureau** (☎805-688-6144, 800-468-6765; www.solvang usa.com; 1639 Copenhagen Dr; ◷9am-5pm) in the town center, near the municipal parking lot and public bathrooms. For local guidebooks and trail maps, stop by Solvang's **Book Loft** (1680 Mission Dr; ◷9am-8pm Tue-Thu, to 9pm Fri & Sat, to 6pm Sun & Mon), a well-stocked indie bookstore. Enjoy wi-fi with your java next door at the **Bulldog Café** (◷6am-9pm Sun-Thu, to 11pm Fri & Sat; ☎).

❶ Getting There & Around

From Santa Barbara, you can drive to the wine country in under an hour. Via Hwy 101, it's 45 miles from Santa Barbara to Buellton. Hwy 246 runs east–west from Buellton to Solvang, then across the bottom of the Santa Ynez Valley to Hwy 154. From Santa Barbara, Hwy 154 is a more scenic route (see boxed text, p389). It's about 10 miles shorter than taking Hwy 101, but the road is often only two lanes wide with some slow-moving traffic. North of Hwy 246, Hwy 154 leads to Los Olivos.

Central Coast Shuttle (☎805-928-1977, 800-470-8818; www.cclax.com) will carry you from LAX to Buellton for $71/130 one way/round-trip, slightly less if you prepay 24 hours in advance. **Amtrak** (☎800-872-7245; www.amtrak.com) provides daily connecting Thruway buses to and from Solvang, but only if you're catching a train (or arriving on one) in Santa Barbara.

On weekdays Santa Barbara's **MTD** (☎805-963-3366; www.sbmtd.gov) runs late-afternoon 'Valley Express' commuter buses to Buellton and Solvang, returning to Santa Barbara in the early morning. The trip takes just over an hour; the one-way fare is $5 (cash only, exact change). **Santa Ynez Valley Transit** (☎805-688-5452; www.syvt.com) runs local buses equipped with bike racks on a loop around Buellton, Solvang, Santa Ynez, Ballard and Los Olivos from 7am to 7pm Monday through Saturday, costing $1.50 per ride (exact change only).

Many tour companies offer wine-tasting trips around the valley; see the Wine Country Tours section on p395 for recommended tours and also bicycle rentals.

Can't quit your day job to follow your bliss? Don't despair, a long weekend in the mountains, valleys and beaches between Santa Barbara and LA will keep you inspired until you can. In this land of daydreams, perfect waves beckon off Ventura's coast, shady trails wind skyward in the Los Padres mountains and spiritual Zen awaits you in Ojai Valley. Surf, stroll, seek – if outdoor rejuvenation is your goal, this is the place.

And then there's Channel Islands National Park, a biodiverse chain of islands shimmering just off the coast where you can kayak into majestic sea caves, scuba dive near wavy kelp forests, wander fields of wildflower blooms or simply disappear from SoCal's 'cultural apparatus' at a remote, soul-enriching campsite.

Montecito

POP 10,060

The well-heeled community of Montecito hovers just east of Santa Barbara like a hitherto-unknown cousin who has just inherited the family fortune. This leafy village in the Santa Ynez foothills is not just home to the rich and famous but to the obscenely rich and the uberfamous: it's the type of guarded enclave that would incite revolutions in eras past. But really, part-time residents like Oprah Winfrey, Ellen DeGeneres and Rob Lowe can't be all bad, right?

Though many homes hide behind manicured hedges, a taste of the Montecito lifestyle can be savored on the boutique-filled main drag, **Coast Village Rd** (exit Hwy 101 at Olive Mill Rd). **Dressed & Ready** (☎805-565-1253; www.dressedonline.com; 1253 Coast Village Rd) are twin couture shops that cater to a star-quality crowd with flirty fashions by hand-picked designers for women – everything from satin sheaths to crystal cuffs.

For brunch, nab a table on the outdoor patio at **Jeannine's Bakery Café** (☎805-969-7878; http://jeannines.com; 1253 Coast Village Rd; mains $9-13; ◷6:30am-4pm Mon-Thu, 6:30am-4:30pm Fri, 7am-4:30pm Sat & Sun) and watch the ritzy stroll past. The organic-ish menu of from-scratch goodness includes dishes such as challah French toast with

LOTUSLAND

The eccentric Madame Ganna Walka bought the 37 acres that make up **Lotusland** (☎805-969-3767, reservations 805-969-9990; www.lotusland.org; 695 Ashley Rd, Montecito; adult/5-18yr $35/10; ⊙tours by appt 10am & 1:30pm Wed-Sat mid-Feb–mid-Nov) in 1941, with money from the fortunes she inherited after marrying – and then divorcing – a string of wealthy men. She spent the next four decades tending and expanding this incredible collection of rare and exotic plants from around the world – there are over 120 varieties of aloe alone. Come in summer when lotuses bloom, typically from late June onward. Reservations are required for tours; the phone is only attended from 9am to 5pm weekdays, 9am to 1pm Saturday.

caramelized bananas in Kahlua sauce. To nibble on Anglo-Mexican seafood enchiladas, grilled fajitas or rock-shrimp soft tacos, hit the sometimes-too-hip-for-its-own-good **Cava** (☎805-969-8500; www.cavarestaurant. com; 1212 Coast Village Rd; mains lunch $12-20, dinner $15-25; ⊙11am-10pm).

From Santa Barbara, MTD bus 20 runs to and from Montecito ($1.75, 20 minutes) every hour or so.

Summerland

POP 1550

This drowsy seaside community is locally famous for its supernatural-minded origins. The town was founded in 1885 by HL Williams, a real-estate speculator. Williams was also a Spiritualist, a religion in vogue at the time, whose followers believed in the power of mediums to connect the living with the dead. Rumor had it that the spiritualists kept hidden rooms in their homes for seances to welcome the dearly departed – a practice earning the town the indelicate nickname of 'Spookville.'

Today, those wanting to connect to the past wander the town's antique shops, where you won't find any bargains, but you can ooh and ahh over beautiful furniture from decades or even centuries gone by. From Hwy 101 southbound, take exit 91 and turn north. Park on Lillie Ave and amble around town – you'll never be far from the hum of the freeway or the racket of the trains. To find the beach, turn south off exit 91 and cross the railroad tracks to **Lookout Park**, with a playground, picnic tables, BBQ grills and access to a wide, relatively quiet stretch of sand (leashed dogs OK).

Grab brunch at the Victorian seaside-style **Summerland Beach Café** (☎805-969-

1019; 2294 Lillie Ave; mains $7-10; ⊙7am-3pm Mon-Fri, to 4pm Sat & Sun), known for fluffy omelets and Crabby Bill's eggs Benedict, and enjoy the sea breezes on the outdoor patio. Or walk over to cheapskate **Stacky's** (2315 Lillie Ave; mains $4-8; ⊙6:30am-7:30pm Mon-Fri, 7am-7:30pm Sat & Sun), a pine-paneled, eat-out-of-a-basket greasy-spoon diner that delivers ginormous breakfast burritos. Then tip back a draft or two under the watchful eye of a mounted jackalope at the **Nugget** (2318 Lillie Ave; ⊙11am-9pm), a scruffy, wood-darkened locals' lair that grills pretty darn-good burgers.

From Santa Barbara, MTD bus 20 runs to Summerland ($1.75, 25 minutes, approximately hourly) via Montecito, continuing to Carpinteria.

Carpinteria

POP 14,400

Lying farther east of Santa Barbara, the time-warped beach of Carpinteria – so named because Chumash tribespeople once built seafaring canoes here – is a laid-back place. You could easily spend an hour or two wandering in and out of the beachy boutiques and vintage, antique and toy shops along **Linden Ave**, downtown's main drag. To gawk at the world's largest vat of guacamole, show up in early October for the **California Avocado Festival** (www. avofest.com).

Carpinteria State Beach (www.parks. ca.gov) is an idyllic, mile-long strand where kids splash around in the calm waters and go tide-pooling along the shoreline. Parking costs $10. In winter, you may spot seals and sea lions hauled out on the sand. Often crowded, **Carpinteria State Beach Camp- ground** (☎reservations 800-444-7275; www.reserveamerica.com; hike-&-bike

tent sites $10; campsites $35-50) offers cushy amenities like flush toilets, hot showers, picnic tables and BBQ grills.

Surf Happens (☎805-451-7568; www.surfhappens.com; 2hr lesson per 1/2 people $160/260) runs eco-conscious, family-friendly board classes led by expert staff that incorporate the Zen of surfing. In summer begin your spiritual journey atop the waves off Hwy 101 (exit Santa Claus Lane – yes, that's right). If you're already an expert, **Rincon Point** has long, glassy, right point-break waves; it's about 3 miles southeast of downtown, off Hwy 101 (exit Bates Rd).

Carpinteria's cookie-cutter chain motels and hotels are unexciting, but usually less expensive than those just up the road in Santa Barbara. Off Hwy 101 (exit Casitas Pass Rd), **Motel 6 Carpinteria South** (☎805-684-8602, 800-466-8356; www.motel6.com; 5550 Carpinteria Ave; r $56-116; 🖥🐾) has basic, pet-friendly motel rooms with mod upgrades like flat-screen TVs and IKEA-like interior design. For more spacious rooms, bed down at **Best Western Carpinteria** (☎805-684-0473, www.bestwestern.com; 5550 Carpinteria Ave; r $89-149; 🖥🐾). Air-con rooms are standard at both motels.

For breakfast, the fairy-tale-cute **Worker Bee Cafe** (973 Linden Ave; mains $5-11; ⊙6:30am-3pm) slaps big plates of diner delights like biscuits and gravy and egg scrambles down on your Formica table. Right by the beach, the **Spot** (389 Linden Ave; dishes $3-8; ⊙7:30am-7pm) is an authentically retro (since 1914) take-out counter for grilled burgers, fries and shakes. For classic steaks, seafood and cocktails, old-school chophouse **Sly's Restaurant** (☎805-684-6666; www.slysonline.com; 686 Linden Ave; mains lunch $12-28, dinner $20-50; ⊙dinner) is the kind of place that Don Draper would love, so shake that sand outta your shoes. Almost as posh, contemporary **Corktree Cellars** (☎805-684-1400; http://corktreecellars.com; 910 Linden Ave; small plates $5-15; ⊙11:30am-9pm, to 9:30pm Fri & Sat, closed Mon) is downtown's hip wine bar and bistro, proffering tasty tapas, charcuterie and cheese plates, and a dizzying number of wine flights. If you'd rather hang loose with beach bums, **Island Brewing Co** (www.islandbrewingcompany.com; 5049 6th St; ⊙2-9pm Mon-Fri, 11am-9pm Sat & Sun) is a locals-only, industrial space hidden next to the railroad tracks.

Carpinteria is 12 miles east of Santa Barbara via Hwy 101 (southbound exit Linden Ave, northbound Casitas Pass Rd). From Santa Barbara, take MTD bus 20 ($1.75, 40 minutes, approximately hourly), which stops at Montecito and Summerland. **Amtrak** (☎800-872-7245; www.amtrak.com; 465 Linden Ave) has an unstaffed platform downtown; buy tickets online or by phone, before catching one of five daily trains south to Ventura ($11, 25 minutes) and Los Angeles ($28, 2½ to three hours).

Ojai

POP 7775 / ELEVATION 746FT

Hollywood director Frank Capra chose the petite Ojai Valley to represent a mythical Shangri-la in his 1937 movie *Lost Horizon*. Today Ojai ('*oh-*hi', meaning 'moon' to the Chumash) attracts artists, organic farmers, spiritual seekers and anyone ready to indulge in spa-style pampering. Bring shorts and tank tops: Shangri-la gets hot in summer.

⊙ Sights & Activities

Inside downtown's historic firehouse, **Ojai Vineyard** (☎805-649-1674; www.ojaivineyard; 109 S Montgomery St; tastings $12; ⊙1-5pm Thu & Sun, to 7pm Fri & Sat) pours tastes of its primo small-batch reisling, chardonnay, pinot noir, grenache and syrah.

For the ultimate in relaxation, book a day at top-tier **Spa Ojai** (☎888-772-6524; www.ojairesort.com; Ojai Valley Inn & Spa, 905 Country Club Rd), where a 50-minute four-handed Ayurvedic massage costs $280. Without reservations, you can pay $20 to access the two pools, workout equipment and mind/body fitness classes. Day-trippers can also unwind in a hobbitlike cottage at **Day Spa of Ojai** (☎805-640-1100; www.thedayspa.com; 1434 E Ojai Ave), a mile east of downtown. One-hour armoatherapy massages cost from $85 plus tip, with optional add-ons like hot rocks ($20) and organic tea service ($15).

Though uncomfortably close to the highway, **Ojai Valley Trail**, converted from old railway tracks, is popular with walkers, joggers, cyclists and equestrians. Pick it up downtown two blocks south of Ojai Ave, then pedal west through the valley. Rent bikes downtown at **Bicycles of Ojai** (☎805-646-7736; 108 Canada St; per hr/day from $6/26; ⊙9:30am-5:30pm Mon-Fri, to 5pm Sat).

PINK MOMENTS

Ojai is famous for the rosy glow that emanates from its mountains at sunset, the so-called 'Pink Moment.' The ideal vantage point for catching the show is the peaceful lookout atop **Meditation Mount** (www.meditation.com; admission free), which closes after sunset. Head east of downtown on Ojai Ave (Hwy 150) for 2.5 miles, take a left at Boccali's farm-stand restaurant and drive another 2.5 miles on Reeves Rd until it dead-ends.

Gather camping tips and trail maps for hiking to hot springs, waterfalls and mountaintop viewpoints in the **Los Padres National Forest** (☎805-646-4348; www.fs.fed.us/r5/lospadres) at the **Ojai Ranger Station** (☎805-646-4348; 1190 E Ojai Ave; ⊙8am-4:30pm Mon-Fri). On weekends stop by **Wheeler Gorge Visitors Center** (17017 Matilija Hwy), 8 miles north of town via Hwy 33.

🛏 Sleeping & Eating

Blue Iguana Inn BOUTIQUE INN **$$**
(☎805-646-5277; www.blueiguanainn.com; 11794 N Ventura Ave; r incl breakfast $119-169, ste $159-299; 🐾🛜🌊) Artsy iguanas lurk everywhere at this funky Southwestern inn – on adobe walls, around Mediterranean-tiled fountains and anywhere else that amphibian style could bring out a smile. The staff is helpful, the bungalow and cottage suites unique, and the pool a social scene for LA hipsters. Rates include continental breakfast; advance pet approval required. For more romantic atmosphere, try the sister property Emerald Iguana Inn, just north of downtown.

Ojai Retreat B&B **$$**
(☎805-646-2536; www.ojairetreat.com; 160 Besant Rd; r & ste incl breakfast $89-249; @🛜) On a hilltop on the outskirts of town, this peaceful nonprofit inn has a back-to-nature collection of remodeled, country arts-and-crafts-style guest rooms and cottages, all perfect for unplugging. Find a quiet nook for reading or writing, ramble through the trees or join a yoga class. All air-con rooms. Rates include a healthy breakfast buffet.

Su Nido Inn BOUTIQUE HOTEL **$$**
(☎805-646-7080, 866-646-7080; sunidoinn.com; 301 N Montgomery St; r & ste $179-509; @🛜) A short walk from downtown shops and restaurants, this Mission Revival–style property's name means 'your nest' in Spanish.

With feather beds, mosaic-tiled tubs, gas-burning fireplaces, and a goodie basket of snacks and gourmet coffee, you and your lover may never want to leave.

Boccali's ITALIAN **$$**
(☎805-646-6116; www.boccalis.com; 3277 Ojai Ave; mains $10-18; ⊙4-9pm Mon & Tue, 11:45am-9pm Wed-Sun) This roadside farm stand, replete with red-and-white-checkered plastic tablecloths, does simple Italian and does it well. Much of the produce is grown in the gardens right behind the restaurant, and the fresh tomato salad is often still warm from the garden, but the real draw is the wood oven–baked pizzas, which take time to make. No credit cards. It's about 2.5 miles east of downtown.

Vesta CAFE **$**
(☎805-646-2339; 242 E Ojai Ave; mains $7-13; ⊙11am-9pm Tue-Sun) Forget about the indoor dining room – join the gossipy local crowds on the courtyard patio out back for lunchtime burgers, paninis and wraps, crunchy salads, sweet-potato fries and delish seven-layer carrot cake. Breakfast served all day. Vegetarians welcome.

Ojai Valley Inn & Spa RESORT
(☎805-646-1111, 888-697-8780; www.ojairesort.com; 905 Country Club Rd; @🛜🌊🐾) Pampering luxury resort at the west end of town has landscaped gardens, golf courses and a fabulous spa. Air-con standard. Complimentary spa entry for guests. Bicycle rental available. Online discounts.

Me Gusta Gourmet Tamales MEXICAN
(☎805-646-7715; 423 E Ojai Ave; dishes $3-5; ⊙8am-6pm) Fresh homemade tortillas, hot salsas and pillowy sweet-corn tamales filled with *pollo* (chicken), *carne asada* (beef) and more. It's a locals' hideout.

🛍 Shopping

Shoppers amble through **Arcade Plaza**, a maze of Mission Revival–style buildings on Ojai Ave (downtown's main drag), filled with gifty boutiques. **Human Arts Gallery** (246 E Ojai Ave) sells unique handmade jewelry, sculpture, wood carvings, glassworks, folk art and more. **Ojai Terrain** (318 E Ojai Ave) vends unique earth-friendly goods, like reclaimed T-shirts, BPA-free water bottles and woodblock-printed stationery. **Chameleon** (326 E Ojai Ave) is a divine post-spa stop for chic women's clothing, anything from cashmere wraps to strappy sandals. **Cowboy Babies** (423 E Ojai Ave) carries pint-sized Western wear and camouflage booties for tots ready to crawl the open range.

Uniquely indoor/outdoor **Bart's Books** (www.bartsbooksojai.com; 302 W Matilija St; ☺9:30am-sunset), one block north of Ojai Ave, sells new and well-loved tomes. It demands at least a half-hour's browse – just don't step on the lurking but nimble gray cat. **Soul Centered** (http://soulcentered.weebly.com; 311 N Montgomery St), a 'metaphysical shoppe,' shares Ojai's authentically hippie-dippie vibe with crystals, aura photography and magical books. Or mingle with residents at the rain-or-shine **farmers market** (300 E Matilija St; ☺9am-1pm Sun), where you'll find eggs, oils, jams, nuts and candles, along with locally grown fruit and vegetables.

ℹ Information

For tourist information, visit the **Ojai Chamber of Commerce** (☎805-646-8126; www.ojai-chamber.org; 201 S Signal St; ☺8:30am-4pm Mon-Fri). The **public library** (111 E Ojai Ave; ☺10am-8pm Mon-Thu, noon-5pm Fri-Sun; @) offers free internet access.

ℹ Getting There & Away

Ojai is 33 miles east of Santa Barbara via scenic Hwy 150, or 15 miles inland (north) from Ventura off Hwy 33. From downtown Ventura, catch **Gold Coast Transit** (☎805-487-4222; www.gold coasttransit.org) bus 16 at Main and Ventura Sts, connecting to downtown Ojai ($1.35, 50 minutes, every 75 minutes).

Ventura

POP 104,100

Primarily a pushing-off point for Channel Island trips, the beach town of San Buenaventura is not the most enchanting coastal city, but it has its ungentrified charms, especially in its historic downtown along Main St, north of Hwy 101 via California St.

◉ Sights & Activities

Ventura's Spanish-colonial roots go back to the 1782 **Mission San Buenaventura** (☎805-643-4318; www.sanbuenaventuramission.org; 211 E Main St; adult/under 17yr $2/50¢; ☺10am-5pm Mon-Fri, 9am-5pm Sat, 10am-4pm Sun), the ninth and final mission founded in California by Junípero Serra. A stroll around this mellow parish church leads you through a garden courtyard and a small museum, past statues of saints, centuries-old religious paintings and unusual wooden bells.

Albinger Archaeological Museum (☎805-648-5823; www.albingermuseum.org; 113 E Main St; ☺call for hr), just west of the mission, is for archaeology fans and history buffs. Artifacts include Chumash, Spanish and Mexican relics. Outside, you can see the mission's original foundations.

Across the street, the **Ventura County Museum of History & Art** (☎805-653-0323; www.vcmha.org; 100 E Main St; adult/6-17yr/senior $4/1/3; ☺10am-5pm Tue-Sun) has a mishmash of exhibits including Chumash baskets, 1920s-era wooden surfboards, and a massive stuffed California condor with wings outspread – a chihuahua wouldn't stand a chance, you know.

On the waterfront off Hwy 101, **San Buenaventura State Beach** (www.parks.ca.gov; ☺dawn-dusk; ♿) is perfect for swimming, surfing or just lazing on the sand. Parking costs $10. Recreational cycling paths connect to even more beaches. Ventura Harbor (southwest of Hwy 101 via Harbor Blvd) is the departure point for boats to the Channel Islands (p405).

🛏 Sleeping & Eating

Midrange motels and high-rise beachfront hotels cluster off Hwy 101 in Ventura. If you can't find any good deals, keep driving south on Hwy 101 for around 15 miles to Camarillo, where cheaper roadside chains abound.

Back downtown in Ventura, Main St downtown is chock a block with taco shops, healthy SoCal-style cafes and a rainbow of ethnic flavors.

Brooks MODERN AMERICAN $$$
(☎805-652-7070; www.restaurantbrooks.com; 545 E Thompson Blvd; mains $20-35; ☺dinner Tue-Sun) Chef Andy Brooks, who once worked alongside Bradley Ogden, executes top-notch creative cuisine such as cornmeal-fried oysters, roasted Niman Ranch

SANTA PAULA

Now calling itself 'the citrus capital of the world,' the small town of Santa Paula once found its treasure in black gold. If you've seen the movie *There Will Be Blood*, loosely based on the Upton Sinclair novel *Oil!*, then you already know that SoCal's early oil boom was a bloodthirsty business. Today the **California Oil Museum** (☏805-933-0076; www.oilmuseum. net; 1001 E Main St; adult/6-17yr/senior $4/1/3; ⊗10am-4pm Wed-Sun) tells the story of Santa Paula's 'black bonanza' with modest historical exhibits that include an authentic 1890s drilling rig and a collection of vintage gas pumps. Afterward take a walk around downtown Santa Paula's historic district with its interesting outdoor murals; pick up a free self-guided walking-tour map inside the museum. Santa Paula is around a 15-mile drive east of Ventura or Ojai, at the intersection of Hwys 126 and 150.

pork chops, Maytag blue cheesecake and cinnamon-roll bread pudding at this distinguished dining room just off Hwy 101. Small plates, Pacific Rim martinis and maverick Californian wines also served at the bar.

Mary's Secret Garden ECLECTIC **$$**
(☏805-641-3663; www.maryssecretgarden. com; 100 S Fir St; mains $10-16; ⊗4-9:30pm Tue-Thu, 11am-9:30pm Fri & Sat; ☏) On the corner of a park just south of Main St, this internationally spiced vegetarian and raw-food haven for hot soups, sandwiches and salads also makes fresh juices, creative smoothies (pistachio mint, anyone?) and out-of-this-world vegan cakes and dairy-free ice creams. Check Twitter (@MarysSecret Gard) for daily specials. Reservations recommended.

Drinking & Entertainment

You'll find plenty of rowdy dives down by the harbor.

Zoey's Café COFFEEHOUSE, MUSIC
(☏805-652-1137; www.zoeyscafe.com; 451 E Main St; ⊗11:30am-3:30pm Mon, Wed & Thu, to 10pm Fri & Sat, to 4pm Sun) Tucked at the end of a brick-lined passageway, this cozy coffeehouse showcases lives acts almost nightly – folk, soul, acoustic rock, bluegrass and comedy to name just a few. During the day it's a low-key cafe for convivial noshing.

Wine Rack BAR, SHOP
(☏805-653-9463; www.weaverwines.com; 14 S California St; ⊗4-9pm Mon & Tue, 2-9pm Wed & Thu, noon-10pm Fri & Sat, 2-8pm Sun) At this upbeat wine shop, novices can sidle up to the unpretentious bar for a $10 tasting, loiter over a tasty cheese plate and listen to live music some weekend nights. Show up before 7pm for happy hour.

Anacapa Brewing Co BREWPUB
(www.anacapabrewing.com; 472 E Main St; ⊗11:30am-midnight Tue-Sun, 5pm-midnight Sun) Beachy downtown brewpub crafts its own microbrews and makes a mean pulled-pork sandwich.

Rocket Fizz SHOP
(www.rocketfizz.com; 105 S Oak St; ⊗11am-7pm Mon-Wed, to 9pm Thu-Sun) Retro-styled soda pop and old-fashioned candy store for stocking your cooler before a day at the beach.

Shopping

There are kick-ass thrift shops and antique mini-malls in downtown Ventura. Most secondhand and vintage shops cluster on Main St west of California St. At the unbeatable **ARC Foundation Thrift Store** (265 E Main St), the hordes flipping through the racks can be daunting. For more upscale beach-living accessories, **B on Main** (337 E Main St) carries nifty reproductions of vintage surf posters and SoCal landscape art. Run by a third-generation Peruvian jewelry craftsman, **Ormachea** (451 E Main St) hammers out one-of-a-kind, handmade rings, pendants and bangles in a storefront studio. For steeply discounted designer duds, drive 20 minutes on Hwy 101 southbound to **Camarillo Premium Outlets** (www.premiumoutlets.com; 740 E Ventura Blvd, Camarillo; ⊗10am-9pm Mon-Sat, to 8pm Sun) shopping mall.

ⓘ Information

The **Ventura Visitors & Convention Bureau** (☏805-648-2075, 800-483-6214; www.ventura-usa.com; 101 S California St; ⊗8:30am-5pm Mon-Fri, 9am-5pm Sat, 10am-4pm Sun) hands out free maps and tourist brochures.

ⓘ Getting There & Away

Ventura is 30 miles southeast of Santa Barbara via Hwy 101. **Amtrak** (☑800-872-7245; www. amtrak.com) operates five daily trains north to Santa Barbara ($13, 40 minutes) via Carpinteria and south to LA ($22, two hours). Amtrak's platform **station** (cnr Harbor Blvd & Figueroa St) is unstaffed; reserve seats online or by phone. **Vista** (☑800-438-1112; www.goventura. org) runs several daily 'Coastal Express' buses between downtown Ventura and Santa Barbara ($2.50, 50 minutes).

Channel Islands National Park

Don't let this off-the-beaten-path national park loiter for too long on your lifetime to-do list. It's easier to access than you might think, and the payoff is immense. Imagine hiking, kayaking, scuba diving, camping and whale-watching, and doing it all amid a raw, end-of-the-world landscape. Rich with unique species of flora and fauna, tide pools and kelp forests, the islands are home to 145 plant and animal species found nowhere else in the world, earning them the nickname 'California's Galapagos.'

Geographically, the Channel Islands are an eight-island chain off the Southern California coast, stretching from Santa Barbara to San Diego. Five of them – San Miguel, Santa Rosa, Santa Cruz, Anacapa and tiny Santa Barbara – comprise Channel Islands National Park. Originally inhabited by the Chumash and Gabrieleño tribespeople (who were forced to move to mainland missions in the early 1800s), the islands were subsequently taken over by ranchers in the 19th century and the US military in the 20th, until conservation efforts began in the 1970s.

◉ Sights & Activities

Anacapa and Santa Cruz, the park's most popular islands, are within an hour's boat ride of Ventura. Anacapa is a doable day trip, while Santa Cruz is better suited for campers.

Most visitors arrive during summer, when island conditions are hot, dusty and bone-dry. Better times to visit are during the spring wildflower bloom or in early fall, when the fog clears. Winter can be stormy, but it's also great for wildlife-watching, especially whales.

Before you shove off from the mainland, stop by Ventura Harbor's **NPS Visitors Center** (p407) for educational natural-history exhibits, a free short nature film and family-friendly ranger-led activity programs on weekends.

ANACAPA ISLAND

Anacapa, which is actually three separate islets, gives a memorable introduction to the islands' ecology and is the best option for those short on time. Boats dock year-round on the East Island and after a short climb you'll find 2 miles of trails offering fantastic views of island flora, a historic lighthouse, and rocky Middle and West Islands. Kayaking, diving, tide-pooling and seal-watching are popular activities here. After checking out the small museum at the island's visitors center, ask about ranger-led programs. In summer scuba divers with video cameras occasionally broadcast images to a TV monitor you can watch.

PARADISE (ALMOST) REGAINED

Human beings have left a heavy footprint on the Channel Islands. Livestock overgrazed, causing erosion, and rabbits fed on native plants. The US military even used San Miguel as a practice bombing range. In 1969 an offshore oil spill engulfed the northern islands in an 800-sq-mile slick, killing off uncountable seabirds and mammals. Meanwhile, deep-sea fishing has caused the destruction of three-quarters of the islands' kelp forests, which are key to the marine ecosystem.

Despite past abuses, the future isn't all bleak. Brown pelicans – decimated by the effects of DDT and reduced to one surviving chick on Anacapa Island in 1970 – have rebounded. On San Miguel Island, native vegetation has returned – albeit 50 years later – after overgrazing sheep were removed. On Santa Cruz Island, the National Park Service (NPS) and Nature Conservancy have implemented multiyear plans to eliminate invasive plants and feral pigs, and hopefully their recovery efforts will meet with success.

ISLAND OF THE BLUE DOLPHINS

If you've got kids, for bedtime reading aloud around the campfire, pick up Scott O'Dell's Newberry Award–winning *Island of the Blue Dolphins*. This children's novel was inspired by the true life story of a Native American girl left behind on San Nicolas Island during the early 19th century, when indigenous peoples were forced off the Channel Islands. Incredibly the girl survived mostly alone on the island for 18 years, living in a whalebone hut and sourcing water from a spring, before being rescued in 1853. However, fate was still not on her side: she died just seven weeks after being brought to the mainland. Today her body lies buried in the graveyard at Mission Santa Barbara, where a commemorative plaque is inscribed with her Christian baptismal name, Juana María.

SANTA CRUZ ISLAND

Santa Cruz, the largest island at 96 sq miles, has two mountain ranges with peaks soaring to 2450ft (Mt Diablo). The western three-quarters of Santa Cruz is owned and managed by the **Nature Conservancy** (www.nature.org) and it can only be accessed with a permit (apply online at www.nature.org/cruzpermit). However, the remaining eastern quarter, managed by the National Park Service (NPS), packs a wallop – ideal for those wanting an action-packed day trip or a more laid-back overnight trip. You can swim, snorkel, scuba dive and kayak. Rangers meet incoming boats at Scorpion Anchorage, a short walk from historic **Scorpion Ranch**.

There are rugged hikes too, which are best not attempted at midday – there's little shade. It's a 1-mile climb to captivating **Cavern Point**; views don't get much better than from this windy spot. For a longer jaunt, continue 2 miles west – mostly along scenic bluffs – to **Potato Harbor**. From Scorpion Anchorage, the 4.5-mile **Scorpion Canyon Loop** heads uphill to an old oil well for fantastic views, then drops through Scorpion Canyon to the campground. Alternatively, follow Smugglers Rd all the way to the cobblestone beach at **Smugglers Cove**, a strenuous 7-mile round-trip from Scorpion Anchorage.

OTHER ISLANDS

The Chumash called **Santa Rosa** 'Wima' (driftwood) because of the logs that often came ashore here. They built plank canoes called *tomols* from the redwood logs. This island has rare Torrey pines, sandy beaches and hundreds of plant and bird species. There's beach and canyon hiking but high winds can make swimming, diving and kayaking tough for any but the most experienced.

San Miguel is the most remote of the four northern islands. While it can guarantee solitude and a wilderness experience, it's often windy and shrouded in fog. Some sections are off-limits to prevent disruption of the fragile ecosystem, which includes a caliche forest (containing hardened calcium-carbonate castings of trees and vegetation) and seasonal colonies of seals and sea lions.

Santa Barbara, only 1 sq mile in size and the smallest of the islands, is a jewel-box for nature lovers. Big, blooming coreopsis, cream cups and chicory are just a few of the island's memorable plant species. You'll also find the humongous northern elephant seal here as well as Xantus' murrelets, a bird that nests in cliff crevices. Get more information from the island's visitors center.

Tours

Most trips require a minimum number of participants, and may be canceled due to surf and weather conditions.

> ### ℹ CHANNEL CROSSINGS
>
> The open seas on the boat ride out to the islands may feel choppy to landlubbers. To avoid seasickness, sit outside on the second level – not too close to the diesel fumes in back. The outbound trip is typically against the wind and a bit bumpier than the return. Staring at the horizon may help. Boats usually brake for dolphin- and whale-spotting – always a nice distraction from any nausea. Over-the-counter motion-sickness pills (eg Dramamine) are effective but will make you drowsy.

CAMPGROUND NAME	NUMBER OF SITES	ACCESS FROM BOAT LANDING	DESCRIPTION
Anacapa	7	0.5-mile walk with 154 stairs	High, rocky, sun-exposed and isolated
Santa Cruz (Scorpion Ranch)	40	Flat 0.6 mile walk	Popular with groups, often crowded and partly shady
Santa Barbara	10	Steep 0.5-mile walk uphill	Large, grassy and surrounded by trails
San Miguel	9	Steep 1-mile walk uphill	Windy, often foggy with volatile weather
Santa Rosa	15	Flat 1.5-mile walk	Eucalyptus grove in a windy canyon

Island Packers WHALE-WATCHING
(☎805-642-1393; www.islandpackers.com;
1691 Spinnaker Dr, Ventura Harbor; 3hr tour
adult/child from $32/23, full-day trip from
$63/47) Offers whale-watching excursions
from late December to early April (gray
whales) and in summer (blue and humpback whales).

Truth Aquatics TOURS
(☎805-962-1127; www.truthaquatics.com;
301 W Cabrillo Blvd, Santa Barbara) Santa
Barbara–based concessionaire leads
diving, kayaking and hiking day trips
and multiday excursions, with excellent
interpretation.

Raptor Dive Charters TOURS
(☎805-650-7700; www.raptordive.com; 1559
Spinnaker Dr, Ventura) Runs scuba-diving
trips to Anacapa and Santa Cruz starting
at $110; equipment rentals available.

Paddle Sports of Santa Barbara TOURS
(☎805-899-4925, 888-254-2094; www.kayak
sb.com; 117b Harbor Way, Santa Barbara)
Organizes kayaking trips to Anacapa,
Santa Cruz and Santa Barbara (from
$175). Kayaks, paddles, wetsuits and life
vests are included; some trips are kid-
friendly.

For more kayaking tours, try **Aquasports**
(☎805-968-7231, 800-773-2309; www.island
kayaking.com; 111 Verona Ave, Goleta) or
Channel Islands Kayak Center (☎805-
984-5995; www.cikayak.com; 3600 S Harbor
Blvd, Oxnard), open at Ventura Harbor by
appointment.

🛏 Sleeping

All of the islands have primitive year-round
campgrounds (☎reservations 877-444-6777;
www.recreation.gov; tent sites $15) with pit toi-
lets and picnic tables. Water is only available
on Santa Rosa and Santa Cruz Islands. You
must pack everything in and out, including
trash. Due to fire danger, campfires aren't
allowed, but enclosed, gas campstoves are
OK. Limited backcountry camping is available on Santa Cruz and Santa Rosa Islands.
Advance reservations are required for all
island campsites.

ℹ Information

All of the trip-planning information, books
and maps you'll need are available at the **NPS
Visitors Center** (☎805-658-5730; www.nps.
gov/chis; 1901 Spinnaker Dr, off Harbor Blvd,
Ventura; ⊗8:30am-5pm) at Ventura Harbor on
the mainland.

ℹ Getting There & Away

You can access the national park by taking a boat
from Ventura or Oxnard or catching a plane from
Camarillo.

Near the NPS visitors center situated at Ventura Harbor, **Island Packers** (☎805-642-1393;
www.islandpackers.com; 1691 Spinnaker Dr, Ventura) offers boat rides to all the islands. Day trips
to East Anacapa start from $45 for adults (each
child $28); going to the other islands is more
expensive, and campers pay additional costs. If
you camp overnight and the seas are rough the
following day, beware you could get stuck for a
night or more. In short, a landing (or pick-up) is
never guaranteed. Reservations are essential,
especially on weekends and in summer.

If you're prone to seasickness, consider taking an alternative route – you can take a 25-minute scenic flight to Santa Rosa Island with **Channel Islands Aviation** ([☑]805-987-1301; www.flycia.com; 305 Durley Ave, Camarillo; day trips adult/child from $160/135, campers round-trip from $300).

To get to the NPS Visitors Center and the boat docks in Ventura from Hwy 101 northbound, exit at Victoria Ave, turn left on Victoria and right on Olivas Park Dr, then continue on to Spinnaker Dr. From Hwy 101 southbound, exit at Seaward Ave onto Harbor Blvd, then turn right on Spinnaker Dr.

Understand Southern California

population per sq mile

USA   California   Los Angeles

↑ ≈ 80 people

Southern California Today

New Natives

Today's Southern California, or 'SoCal,' is the culmination of the efforts of generations of big dreamers. Bear in mind that we're talking about one half of a single American state that has an economy roughly the equal of Spain. Its universities are plentiful and renowned. From Los Angeles the imagery spun by Hollywood dominates the digital transmissions and cultural trends of the entire planet. Surf, sand and sex will endure as long as there is a SoCal coast.

But SoCal is not a finished work. It remains one of the most dynamic places on earth in which to live and play. Just consider space probes, Disneyland, the internet, automotive and fashion design, and the movie industry and its media slaves – all are headquartered in or managed from here. The nightmares of the 1990s – including the race riots and the Northridge earthquake – seem already to belong to a different age.

» Size: 45,065 sq miles

» Population: 22 million

» GDP: $792 billion

» Average per capita income: $20,683

» Median single-family home price: $360,000

Growing Pains

The biggest problem now is growth itself. Perhaps because of its very adaptability, SoCal has found that the human wave of domestic migration and international immigration continues to crest. Every New Year's Day the largest commercial for living here – Pasadena's Rose Parade – snares the imaginations of folks freezing in Wisconsin or struggling to make ends meet in the Rust Belt. Many who heed the mid-19th-century advice to 'Go West, young man!' wind up on SoCal's sunny shores.

With this burgeoning humanity comes horrific traffic and the skyrocketing costs of living and real estate. Public transport is woefully inadequate, so everyone hits the tortured freeway systems, which move ever more slowly. Sheer human impaction is a palpable force and begs the question that Rodney King so famously asked: 'Can't we all get along?'

Top Books

» **The Tortilla Curtain** (TC Boyle) Engrossing tale about the clash of Mexican and American cultures and the elusive Californian dream.

» **My California: Journeys by Great Writers** (Angel City Press) Insightful stories by such talented chroniclers as Pico Iyer and Michael Chabon. Some proceeds benefit the California Arts Council.

» **Where I Was From** (Joan Didion) California-born essayist shatters palm-fringed fantasies while skewering the stinking rich and exposing the violence and shallowness of this warped shore.

» **Hollywood Babylon** (Kenneth Anger) Pulp 'tell-all' book about the tawdry and scandalous lives and times of Hollywood's Golden Era stars.

belief systems
(% of population)

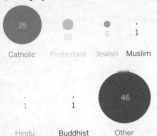

35 Catholic
10 Protestant
6 Jewish
1 Muslim

1 Hindu
1 Buddhist
46 Other

if Los Angeles were 100 people

45 would be White
33 would be Latino
11 would be African American
10 would be Asian
1 would be Native American

Multicultural Mosaic

The current mayor of Los Angeles – Antonio Villaraigosa, himself of Mexican descent – is a fellow with bold ideas about social initiatives and it's extremely difficult to envision LA ever returning to the infamous 'Zoot Suit Riots' of the '40s or the uproar that followed the 1992 'all-white jury' verdict in the beating case of Rodney King, an African American, by LA police. In fact, you may be surprised to see the happy ethnic and racial mix of colleagues and friends walking along boulevards and beaches or gathering for meals together in SoCal's plethora of globally inspired restaurants.

Work Smart, Play Hard

Some of the myths surrounding SoCal have come true. You really *can* surf in the morning, spend the afternoon skiing down alpine slopes and end the day with cocktails in the desert. Who wouldn't want to live here, even with the horrifying commute times? More to the point, who wouldn't want to visit, or even become part of, such a successful social experiment?

Time and again, SoCal has proven itself to be resourceful, resilient and innovative. After tourism, major drivers of the economy include international trade (LA and Long Beach form the nation's largest port), technology, finance, film and TV production, health services and design. With global warming threatening, you can bet the bank that Caltech, UCLA and other universities are using their big brains to solve the issues that challenge not just SoCal, but also the rest of the country and the world.

» Unemployment: 12.4%

» Residents who don't speak English at home: 40%+

» Annual passengers passing through LAX: 46 million

» Percentage of all North American adult films made in SoCal: 85%

Top Films

» **Sunset Boulevard** (1950)
» **Chinatown** (1974)
» **Boyz n the Hood** (1991)
» **LA Story** (1991)
» **The Player** (1992)
» **LA Confidential** (1997)
» **Sideways** (2004)

Top Downloads

» 'California Dreaming' (The Mamas and the Papas)
» 'LA Woman' (The Doors)
» 'Straight Outta Compton' (NWA)
» 'Los Angeles' (X)
» 'California Sun' (The Ramones)

» 'California Love' (2Pac)
» 'California' (Phantom Planet)
» 'All I Wanna Do' (Sheryl Crow)
» 'California Soul' (Fifth Dimension)
» 'Come On, Let's Go' (Ritchie Valens)
» 'Surfin' USA' (Beach Boys)

History

When European explorers arrived in the 16th century, over 100,000 Native Americans called this land home, speaking diverse languages and living in small villages along the coast, seasonal mountain camps or nomadically in the desert.

Spanish conquistadors combed through what they called 'Alta California' (Upper California, as opposed to Baja, or Lower, California) in search of a fabled 'city of gold' but left the territory virtually alone after failing to find it. Not until the Mission Period (1769–1810) did Spain make a serious attempt to settle the land, establishing 21 Catholic missions – many founded by peripatetic Franciscan priest Junípero Serra – for conversion purposes, and presidios (military forts) to keep out British and Russians.

After winning independence from Spain in 1821, Mexico briefly ruled California but then got trounced by the fledgling United States in the 1846–48 Mexican-American War. The discovery of gold soon sent the territory's population soaring from 14,000 to 92,000 by 1850, when California became the 31st US state.

Thousands of imported Chinese laborers helped complete the transcontinental railroad in 1869, which opened up markets on both coasts and further spurred migration to the Golden State. Mexican immigrants arrived during the 1910–21 Mexican Revolution and again during WWII to fill labor shortages.

During WWII, important military-driven industries developed, while anti-Asian sentiments led to the internment of many Japanese Americans, especially those living in LA. Reacting against the banal complacency of post-WWII suburbia, 1960s hippies flocked to California spreading poetry, free love and, later, gay pride.

The internet revolution, spurred by Silicon Valley up north near San Francisco, rewired the economy and led to a 1990s boom in overspeculated stocks. When the bubble burst in 2000, plunging the state's econ-

Top History Books

» *California: A History* (Kevin Starr)

» *A World Transformed: Firsthand Accounts of California Before the Gold Rush* (Joshua Paddison)

» *Cadillac Desert: The American West and Its Disappearing Water* (Marc Reisner)

TIMELINE

Around 20,000 BC

First people start crossing from Asia into North America via the Bering Strait land bridge. The bones of a human found on California's Santa Rosa Island date back 11,000 years.

1542

Portuguese navigator Juan Rodríguez Cabrillo and his Spanish crew become the first Europeans to sight the mainland of New Spain's west coast, anchoring in today's San Diego Bay.

1602

Sebastián Vizcaíno first sets foot on California soil on the feast day of San Diego de Alcalá. In honor of the saint, he names the spot San Diego.

omy into chaos, Californians blamed Governor Gray Davis (Democrat), especially when deregulation of the electricity market led to rolling blackouts and sky-high power bills.

In a controversial recall election, Californians voted in 2003 to give Arnold Schwarzenegger (Republican) a shot at fixing things. But five years later, the meltdown on Wall Street and lingering US recession caused another staggering financial crisis that state lawmakers have yet to resolve.

Ballistic population growth, pollution and traffic are among the problems that continue to cloud SoCal's sunny skies after the first decade of the new millennium. The need for public education and prison reform builds, while the conundrum of immigration from Mexico, which fills a critical cheap-labor shortage, is yet unsolved.

Native Californians

Immigration is hardly a new phenomenon here, since people have been migrating to Southern California for millennia. Many archaeological sites have yielded evidence – from large middens of seashells along the beaches to campfire sites on the Channel Islands – of humans living here as early as 11,000 years ago.

Traditional Ways of Life

The majority of Native Californians lived in small communities and a few migrated with the seasons. Their diet was largely dependent on acorn meal, supplemented by small game such as rabbits and deer, and fish and shellfish. By all accounts they were a crafty people, making earthenware pots, fish nets, bows, arrows and spears with chipped stone points. Many tribes developed a knack for weaving baskets made from local grasses and plant fibers and decorated with geometric designs. Some baskets were so tightly woven they would even hold water.

Coastal and inland peoples traded but generally didn't interact much, partly because they spoke different languages. Kumeyaay and Chumash villages dotted the coast, where tribespeople fished and paddled hand-hewn canoes, including to the Channel Islands. Inland, nomadic hunter-gatherer bands of Cahuilla and Mojave peoples found oases in the deserts, while Serrano tribes camped seasonally in the San Bernardino Mountains.

Although there was no concept of private land ownership among Native Californians, the most common cause of conflict between indigenous peoples (that is, until Europeans arrived) was trespassing on another tribe's traditional territory. Natural resources were scarce, especially in the harsh desert, where tribes frequently skirmished.

Native American History

» Chumash Painted Cave State Historic Park

» Indian Canyons & Tahquitz Canyon

» Museum of the American West

» Museum of Man

» Southwest Museum of the American Indian

1769	1781	1821–46	1848
Spanish captain Gaspar de Portolá leads the first European land expedition north, establishing colonial forts and missions, with the help of Padre Junípero Serra, in Alta California.	Mexican governor Felipe de Neve sets out from the Mission San Gabriel with a tiny band of settlers, trekking west just 9 miles to establish the future Los Angeles.	During Mexico's rule over California, Spanish missions are secularized (except Santa Barbara) and their land carved up into ranchos. Governor Pio Pico's brother-in-law snaps up San Juan Capistrano for $710.	Signing the Treaty of Guadalupe Hidalgo on February 2, Mexico turns over one third of its territory, including California, to the US in exchange for $15 million.

From Conquest to Tribal Revival

Starting in the late 18th century, Spanish colonizers virtually enslaved Native Americans. Despite pockets of armed resistance and violent revolts, tribespeople were made to construct the missions and presidios. Spanish soldiers, whose job was ostensibly to protect the missions and deter foreign intruders, became infamous for raping and pillaging. Meanwhile, European diseases such as smallpox and syphilis further decimated indigenous populations.

Native Californians were further dispossessed of their tribal lands during the Mexican colonial and early American periods. It wasn't until during the 20th century when the federal government began to recognize tribes as sovereign nations, including granting Native Americans citizenship and the right to vote in 1924, that indigenous populations once driven almost to the point of extinction started to rebound.

Political activism, including the 'Red Power' protests of the American Indian Movement (AIM) starting in the late 1960s, led not only to a cultural renaissance, but also secured some tribes economic assistance from state and federal agencies, including California's Native American Heritage Commission established in 1978.

Deprived of their traditional land base and means of livelihood centuries ago, many contemporary California tribes have now turned to casino gaming to relieve unemployment and poverty on their reservations. Today, tribal casinos support tens of thousands of jobs in Southern California.

A New World for Europeans

Following the conquest of Mexico in the early 16th century, the Spanish turned their attention toward exploring the edges of their new empire, fueled by curiosity, lust for power and, above all, greed. Tales of a golden island to the west circulated widely, and in 1542 the Spanish crown sent Juan Rodríguez Cabrillo, a Portuguese explorer and retired conquistador, to find it.

The fabled land, of course, proved elusive, but Cabrillo and his crew still made it into the history books as the first Europeans to see mainland California – today's San Diego. He claimed the land for Spain while sitting out a storm in the harbor before sailing northward. Stopping to check out the Channel Islands, Cabrillo broke a leg, fell ill, died and was buried on what is now San Miguel Island.

The Spanish left California alone for the next half century or so, until they decided they needed to secure some ports on the Pacific coast, and sent Sebastián Vizcaíno to find them. Vizcaíno's first expedition

---

HISTORY A NEW WORLD FOR EUROPEANS

A literally and symbolically colorful website, A People's Guide to Los Angeles (www.pgtla.org) documents milestones and places of racial and class struggle in LA County. Take a self-guided virtual tour.

If you're wondering about the traditions and lifestyles of SoCal's Native American tribes, find answers in the readable natural history guide *California Indians and Their Environment*, by Kent Lightfoot and Otis Parrish.

1849

Following the discovery of gold at Sutter's Creek in the Sierra Nevada foothills in 1848, the California gold rush sees the largest migration in US history.

1850

On September 9, California becomes the 31st state of the US, entering the Union as a free (non-slaveholding) state. Its first constitution is written in Spanish and English.

1869

Gold is discovered in Julian, near San Diego, sparking a frenetic local mining boom. Once the gold runs out, Julian goes back to being a sleepy little town.

» Gold-mining tour

was a disaster that didn't get past Baja California, but in his second attempt, in 1602, he rediscovered the harbor at San Diego and became the first European to set foot in what Spaniards called 'Alta' (Upper) California.

Mission Improbable

Everyone wanted a toehold on the west coast of the New World in the 18th century. Around the 1760s, as Russian ships sailed to California's coast in search of sea-otter pelts, and British trappers and explorers were spreading throughout the west, King Carlos III finally grew worried that Spain's claim to the territory might be challenged.

Conveniently, the Catholic Church was anxious to start missionary work among Native Californians, so the Church and Spanish crown combined forces and established missions protected by presidios. Native American converts were expected to live in the missions, learn trade and agricultural skills and ultimately establish pueblos, which would be like little Spanish towns. Or so the plan went.

On July 1, 1769, a sorry lot of about 100 missionaries and soldiers, led by the Franciscan priest Junípero Serra and the military commander Gaspar de Portolá, limped ashore at San Diego Bay. They had just spent several weeks at sea sailing from Baja California; about half of their cohort had died en route and many of the survivors were sick or near death. It was an inauspicious beginning for the Mission San Diego de Alcalá, the first of the chain of 21 California missions.

The missions did achieve modest success at farming, managing to just barely become self-sufficient, an essential achievement during the 1810–21 Mexican war for independence from Spain, when supplies from Mexico were cut off completely. As a way of colonizing California and converting the natives to Christianity, however, the mission period was an abject failure. The Spanish population remained small, the missions achieved little better than survival, foreign intruders were not greatly deterred and ultimately, more Native Americans died than were converted.

The Path to Statehood

Upon Mexican independence from Spain in 1821, many in that new nation looked to California to satisfy their thirst for private land. By the mid-1830s, almost all of the missions had been secularized and divvied up into land grants by Mexican governors. This gave birth to a system of ranchos, largely given over to livestock to supply the hide and tallow trade. The new landowners, called rancheros or Californios, prospered quickly and became the social, cultural and political fulcrums of Alta California.

The distance between each of California's missions equaled a day's journey by horseback. Learn more about the Spanish missions, both their cultural influence and their historical significance, on the comprehensive website www.california missions.com.

1874	1892	1902	1913
US Department of Agriculture ships three seedless navel orange trees to botanists in Riverside. By 1889 citrus orchards cover more than 13,000 acres, sending the local economy through the roof.	Oil is discovered by Edward Doheny in downtown LA, near where Dodger Stadium stands today, sparking a major oil boom. Within five years, 500 wells are operational.	The first Rose Bowl football game takes place in Pasadena, with the University of Michigan trouncing Stanford 49-0. The next game isn't held for another 14 years.	The Los Angeles Aqueduct, built under the direction of city engineer William Mulholland, starts supplying water from the Owens Valley, in the eastern Sierra Nevada.

Meanwhile, American explorers, trappers, traders, whalers, settlers and opportunists increasingly showed interest in California. Some Americans who started businesses here converted to Catholicism, married local women and assimilated into Californio society. Impressed by California's untapped riches and imbued with Manifest Destiny (an imperialist political doctrine of extending the USA's borders from coast to coast), President Andrew Jackson sent an emissary to offer the financially strapped Mexican government $500,000 for California in 1835.

But Mexicans were not interested in selling and soon a political storm was brewing. In 1836 Texas seceded from Mexico and declared itself an independent republic. When the US annexed Texas in 1845, Mexico broke off diplomatic relations and ordered all foreigners without proper papers to be deported from California. In turn, the US declared war on Mexico and began an invasion. Soon US naval units occupied every port on the California coast, but militarily California was a sideshow as the war was mostly fought in Mexico.

The capture of Mexico City by US troops in September 1847 put an end to the fighting and led to the signing of the Treaty of Guadalupe Hidalgo on February 2, 1848, in which the Mexican government ceded much of its northern territory to the US, including California, just in time for the gold rush era to begin.

Riches of Railroads & Real Estate

Many Mexican rancheros lost their land when the American government questioned their title under the 1851 Land Act. During this period of loose government, LA was a Wild West town, filled with saloons, brothels and gambling dens. Added to the mix were thousands of Chinese immigrants who'd arrived for the gold rush and railroad work. These foreigners were viewed by many with suspicion – the state even enacted a special 'foreign miner's tax' in 1852.

The perception of LA and the rest of the region as a lawless backwater began to change with the arrival of the railroad. The transcontinental railroad had been completed in 1869 and shortened the trip from New York to San Francisco from two months to less than four days, elevating the latter to California's metropolitan center. But SoCal's parched climate, its distance from fresh water and mining resources, and its relatively small population made it unattractive to railroad moguls. Wheeling and dealing resulted in a spur line to LA in the mid-1870s.

During the same period, agriculture diversified, with new crops – especially oranges – being grown in Southern California for markets on the East Coast and abroad. Unlike many fruits, oranges easily survive long-distance rail shipping. As oranges found their way onto New York grocery shelves, a hard-sell California advertising campaign began, as

The precise etymology of 'California' has never been convincingly established, though many think it derives from a 16th-century Spanish romance novel about a legendary island, fabulously rich in gold and inhabited only by black women warriors ruled by Queen Califia.

1915

German-born Carl Laemmle builds Universal Studios, selling lunch to curious guests coming to watch the magic of moviemaking.

1923

LA's famous landmark, the 45ft-tall Hollywood Sign, is built in the Santa Monica Mountains to promote the Hollywoodland subdivision. The 'land' drops off in 1949 but the sign survives.

» LA's advertising gimmick turned famous landmark

folks back East heeded the self-interested advice of crusading magazine and newspaper editor Horace Greeley to 'Go West, young man.'

But much of the land granted to the railroads in Southern California was sold in big lots to speculators who also acquired, with the help of corrupt politicians and administrators, much of the farmland that was released for new settlement. A major share of agricultural land thus became consolidated into large holdings in the hands of a few city-based landlords, establishing the still-existing pattern of industrial scale 'agribusiness,' rather than small family farms.

Never mind that SoCal's supply of fresh water was inadequate and that cheap farm agricultural labor often had to be imported. Sharp, conniving minds and determined spirits would eventually overcome these obstacles. Right?

Water, Water Nowhere

The growth of semiarid Los Angeles into a megalopolis would not have been possible without water. When the city's population surged in the early 20th century, it became clear that groundwater levels would soon

IMMIGRATION: TAKE IT, THEN LEAVE IT

Southern California has always had a love-hate relationship with its immigrants, but owes much of its success to its cultural diversity. Newcomers are typically welcomed in periods of rapid growth, only to be rejected when times get tough.

Chinese railroad workers, for instance, were in great demand in the 1860s, but ended up being discriminated against and even violently attacked in Los Angeles during the next decade. California's Alien Land Law of 1913 even prevented some Asian minorities from owning land.

During WWII 120,000 people of Japanese heritage – many of them American citizens – were forcibly placed in internment camps. African Americans came to SoCal in large numbers to take jobs in the postwar boom, but suddenly found themselves unemployed when the economy slowed down.

It is estimated that more than three million undocumented immigrants currently work in California, despite continuing efforts to seal the notoriously porous border (see boxed text, p424). Mexican and Latin American workers still do most of SoCal's farm labor and domestic work.

In 1994, in the face of increasing unemployment and state government deficits, Californians voted in favor of Proposition 187, which denied illegal immigrants access to state government services, including schools and hospitals. Illegal immigration remains a volatile political topic in California, especially among conservatives who often employ migrants as nannies and gardeners while simultaneously calling for their expulsion.

1925	1927	1929	1942
At 6:44am on June 29, a 6.3-scale earthquake levels most of downtown Santa Barbara, killing 13 people. The city rebuilds in Spanish colonial style.	*The Jazz Singer* premieres at downtown LA's Million Dollar Theater as the world's first 'talkie' movie, signaling the decline of the silent-film era. Hollywood booms.	The first Academy Awards ceremony takes place at the Hollywood Roosevelt Hotel, lasting only 15 minutes. Fewer than 300 people fork over $5 each to be part of the crowd.	US Executive Order 9066 banishes 120,000 Japanese Americans to internment camps. The federal government doesn't make monetary reparations until the 1990s.

STREETCARS

be inadequate to meet its needs, let alone sustain further growth. Water had to be imported and Fred Eaton, a former LA mayor, and William Mulholland, the powerful head of the LA Department of Water & Power (LADWP), knew just how and where to get it: by aqueduct from the Owens Valley, which receives enormous runoff from the Sierra Nevada Mountains.

The fact that the Owens Valley was settled by farmers who needed the water for irrigation purposes bothered neither the two men nor the federal government, which actively supported the city's less-than-ethical maneuvering in acquiring land and securing water rights in the area. Voters gave Mulholland the more than $25 million needed to build the aqueduct. An amazing feat of engineering – crossing barren desert floor as well as rugged mountain terrain for 233 miles – it opened to great fanfare on November 5, 1913.

The Owens Valley, however, would never be the same. With most of its inflows diverted, Owens Lake quickly shriveled up. A bitter feud between LA and Owens Valley farmers and ranchers grew violent when some opponents to the scheme tried to sabotage the aqueduct by blowing up a section of it. All to no avail. By 1928 LA owned 90% of the water in Owens Valley and agriculture was effectively dead. These early water wars formed the basis for the 1974 noir film *Chinatown*.

These days LA still gets about half of its water supply from this aqueduct, which was extended another 105 miles to Mono Basin in 1940. The remainder of the city's water is siphoned from the Sacramento and San Joaquin Rivers via the California Aqueduct and also from the Colorado River; only about 15% comes from groundwater.

Los Angeles once had a wonderfully efficient system of streetcars, until General Motors allegedly conspired to destroy it (search Google for 'GM streetcar conspiracy' and make up your own mind).

Military Might

Along with motion pictures (see p428), aviation was another major industry to have a significant impact on Southern California beginning in the early 20th century. During and after WWI, the Lockheed brothers and Donald Douglas established aircraft manufacturing plants in LA, while Glenn H Curtiss set up shop in San Diego and San Diego–based Ryan Airlines built the *Spirit of St Louis* for Lindbergh's celebrated transatlantic flight in 1927.

In the 1930s, the aviation industry – pumped up by billions of federal dollars for military contracts – helped lift SoCal out of the Great Depression. WWII had a huge impact on the region too. After the 1941 bombing of Pearl Harbor, San Diego became home to the headquarters of the US Pacific Fleet, changing the city forever. Further north, Camp Pendleton, a huge Marine Corps Base, was established in 1942. Throughout the war, aircraft manufacturing plants turned out planes by the thousands.

1943	1955	1965	1968
Tension between Americans and Mexicans reaches boiling point during the Zoot Suit Riots, which pit US military servicemen against zoot-suit-clad Mexican teens while LA police look on.	Disneyland opens in Anaheim on July 18 after a quick one-year construction period. Temperatures hit 101°F, ladies' high-heeled shoes sink into the soft asphalt and drinking fountains don't work.	It takes 20,000 National Guards to quell the six-day Watts Riots in LA, which cause death, devastation and $200 million in property damage. That same year, Rodney King is born.	Robert Kennedy is assassinated at the Ambassador Hotel in LA by Palestinian immigrant and anti-Zionist Sirhan Sirhan, who remains in jail today in Coalinga, California.

After WWII, many service people settled in SoCal. The area's military-industrial complex continued to prosper during the Cold War, providing jobs in everything from avionics and missile manufacturing to helicopter and nuclear submarine maintenance. The Marine Corps still trains recruits and the navy holds advanced training for fighter pilots here. There are submarine bases, aircraft testing facilities, air force bases and sprawling gunnery ranges.

Military spending peaked in the 1980s under ex-California governor and then US president Ronald Reagan, but the end of the Cold War spelled economic disaster. Budget cutbacks closed numerous military bases, forcing defense contractors to move on or diversify. Workers who had grown accustomed to regular paychecks from McDonnell Douglas

RACE RIOTS

LA's long history of racial strife reached an explosive peak in the 1960s. The city was booming but not everyone was invited to the party. Entire neighborhoods, predominantly black South Central foremost among them, had for decades been suffering from institutional neglect and lack of opportunity.

On a hot August day in 1965, frustration levels reached a boiling point when an African American motorist being pulled over on suspicion of drink-driving was beaten by police. Six violent days later, when the Watts Riots were over, 34 people were dead and more than 2000 were injured.

As the city licked its wounds, Governor Pat Brown appointed a commission to study the causes of the riots. They identified the problems – an unemployment rate double the LA average, overcrowded and underfunded classrooms, discriminatory housing laws etc – but lacked the vision, money and perhaps motivation to fix them. A generation later there would be a high price to pay for such indifference.

April 29, 1992: 'Not guilty.' The words cut through the stifling air of a hushed Simi Valley courtroom. More than a year earlier – in an eerie déjà vu of 1965 – four LAPD officers had stopped Rodney King, an African American, on suspicion of driving under the influence. When King initially resisted arrest, the cops allegedly started to kick, beat and shout at the man as he crouched on the sidewalk. Infamously, the whole incident was caught on videotape.

The cops' acquittal unleashed a replay of the Watts Riots on an even bigger scale, as rioting and looting spread through several neighborhoods. National Guards patrolled the streets with machine guns, businesses and schools were ordered to close and a dusk curfew was imposed. LA felt like a war zone. The shocking toll: 54 dead, over 2300 injured, 12,000 arrested and nearly $1 billion in property damage.

Still today, charges of police brutality and corruption splash news headlines. Given an abyss of distrust between police and some poor communities, it's anybody's guess what the future holds.

1969

UCLA professor Len Kleinrock sends data from a computer in Los Angeles to another at Stanford University, typing just two characters before the system crashes. The internet is born.

1984

Los Angeles hosts the Olympic summer games for the second time (the first was in 1932). The USSR doesn't show up, leaving US athletes to win 83 gold medals.

1992

After a 25-year hiatus California resumes executions at San Quentin by killing Robert Alton Harris in the gas chamber for killing two teenagers in San Diego in 1978.

1994

The 6.7-magnitude Northridge earthquake strikes at 4:31am on January 17, killing 72 and causing $20 billion in property damage. It's among the costliest natural disasters in US history.

Military
Museums &
Events
» USS Midway
Museum
» San Diego Air &
Space Museum
» Fleet Week &
Miramar Air Show
» Palm Springs
Air Museum

In 1997 the
Heaven's Gate
cult brought
unwanted public-
ity to the upscale
San Diego suburb
of Rancho Santa
Fe, when leader
Marshall Apple-
white convinced
38 followers to
commit ritual
suicide.

and other aerospace companies suddenly got laid off. The USA's current 'war on terror' has once again boosted military manufacturing in the region, however.

Social Movers & Shakers

Unconstrained by the burden of traditions, bankrolled by elite affluence and promoted by film and TV, California has always been a leader in new attitudes and social movements.

In the affluent 1950s, the emerging middle class moved to the sub-urbs, and no place in America better defined suburban life than Orange County. The Irvine Company, owner of almost 100,000 acres of pri-vate land (a legacy of 19th-century Mexican land grants), built the first 'Master Plan' communities. Strict rules governed their design – hence the county's uniform beige-box architecture. Everybody lived on quiet streets where children could safely play, while shopping centers and strip malls were concentrated along multilane boulevards that made owning a car necessary.

When the postwar Baby Boomers hit their late teens, many rejected their parents' values and heeded Timothy Leary's counsel to 'turn on, tune in, drop out.' Though the hippie counterculture was an interna-tional phenomenon, SoCal was at the leading edge of its music, psyche-delic art and new libertarianism. Sex, drugs and rock 'n' roll ruled the day. LA's Venice Beach was a major hub and hangout of Jim Morrison, Janis Joplin and other luminaries of that era.

In the late 1960s and early '70s, New Left politics, the anti–Vietnam War movement and Black Liberation forced their way into the political limelight, and flower power and give-peace-a-chance politics seemed naive. The 1968 assassination of Robert Kennedy in LA, the sometimes violent repression of demonstrations, and the death of a spectator at a Rolling Stones concert at the hands of security guards (Hells Angels the Stones had hired for the occasion) stripped the era of its innocence.

What a difference a few decades make. Since the 1980s, Southern California's new obsession has become the healthy lifestyle, with a mood-altering array of yoga and fitness classes and self-actualization workshops on offer. Leisure activities such as in-line skating, skate-boarding, snowboarding and mountain biking all originated in Califor-nia. Be careful what you laugh at: from pet rocks to soy burgers, SoCal's flavor of the month is often next year's global trend.

2003	2005	2007	2010
Arnold Schwarzenegger announces his Republican candidacy for governor on *The Tonight Show with Jay Leno.* In October's recall election, he gets 4.2 million votes.	Antonio Villaraigosa elected mayor of LA, the first Latino since 1872. Born poor in East LA, he said in his victory speech, 'I will never forget where I came from.'	Wildfires sweep across drought-stricken Southern California. One million people evacuate their homes from Santa Barbara to San Diego.	Proposition 8, a state constitutional ban on same-sex marriage, narrowly approved by voters in 2008, is challenged in federal court. A judge's decision is pending.

Life in SoCal

Regional Identity

Southern California is America at its extremes, with all the good and bad that this entails. Its people are among the nation's richest and poorest, most established and newest arrivals, most refined and roughest, most beautiful and most plain, most erudite and most airheaded. Success here can be spectacular, failure equally so.

What binds the residents of this region is that they are seekers. Nearly everyone – or their forebears – arrived by choice. Whether from across the country, across the border or across the globe, they were drawn by a dream, be it fame on the silver screen; sand, surf and sun; making a splash in business or research; or cash to send home to the family. It's as if America's dreamers rushed west and stopped where the continent ran out of land.

They found plenty of company.

The Stereotypes

Valley girls snap chewing gum in shopping malls, surfer boys shout 'Dude!' across San Diego beaches, new immigrants gather around street corners in search of day jobs, surgically enhanced babes sip margaritas poolside, rail-thin Orange County soccer moms in urban assault vehicles flip out in rush-hour traffic, and everyone works in 'the Industry.'

The Reality

As with everything in SoCal, if you're looking for the stereotype, that's what you'll tend to focus on. But keep your eyes open and you'll find that the reality is a lot more complex, and interesting. Here are some ways:

While in the northeastern parts of the US people might start a conversation by asking you where you went to college, or in the South where you go to church, in LA the first question you'll often hear from locals is 'What do you do for a living?' This is how people place each other and, unlike elsewhere in America, nobody here is very surprised if the answer takes more a minute; there's nothing unusual about waiting tables, for example, while working toward your dream job as a performer or screenwriter. The second question you might hear is 'Where are you from?' since most people seem to have come from elsewhere.

Hollywood happy talk trickles down to daily interaction, sometimes to the point that people from other places can have trouble understanding what locals mean. Saying someone has 'issues' is a polite way of implying that the person has problems. 'Let's get together' is often not to be taken literally; it can mean 'It was great talking with you, and now I have to go.'

> SoCal inventions include the space shuttle, Mickey Mouse, whitening toothpaste, the hula hoop (or at least its trademark), Barbie, skateboard and surfboard technology, the Cobb salad and the fortune cookie.

INVENTIONS

Just who lives in LA? If you believe the stereotypes, they're a flaky bunch. Liberal. Self-absorbed. Greedy. Botoxed and blow-dried. Though these adjectives may have a hint of truth for certain subgroups, with four million people crammed into the city's 465 sq miles and 10 million jostling for space in sprawling LA County, no one label fits all.

How is LA's ethnic diversity playing out in the early 21st century? Simmering issues of distrust linger between various communities but day-to-day life isn't quite as bleak as portrayed in Paul Haggis' 2005 Oscar-winning *Crash*. The main problem? People are quick to demand respect but slow to give it out. The town also runs high on false friendliness and let's-do-lunch superficiality; there's a bit more 'I' and 'me' than 'we' and 'us.'

But Angelenos aren't all bad. Optimism, open-mindedness and outside-the-box thinking are the norm (studios execs excluded), and people tend to work hard. From illegal immigrants on the corner ready for a long day's work and downtown office workers earning overtime for ballooning mortgage payments to Hollywood assistants holding dreary day jobs while cramming free hours with indie projects, everybody's hustling. Griffith Park might be in flames, the Hollywood Hills crumbling and the ground shaking under our feet, but if it's not blocking traffic, get out of the way. Yes, our reach may sometimes exceed our grasp, but isn't that what LA's for?

Then there's the car you drive. There's an underlying truth to the stereotype that the right car in California is what the right shoes are to Italians. Fancy imports, convertibles and muscle cars still turn heads, but the status symbol *du jour* is ecofriendly. Angeleno hipsters, even those with means, are increasingly forgoing cars entirely and moving to neighborhoods like Downtown and Hollywood that can be accessed by subway, bus and bike, and there's a growing urban scene in the glass skyscrapers of downtown San Diego.

Mike Davis' *City of Quartz* (1990) is an excoriating history of LA and a glimpse into its possible future; in *Ecology of Fear* he examines the decay of the natural environment in the LA Basin. Davis and collaborators also examined San Diego's underbelly in *Under the Perfect Sun: the San Diego Tourists Never See* (2003).

Beach Life

Beach culture colors Southern California in ways both subtle and in-your-face, but which beach determines which culture.

LA's Venice used to be the definitive hippie beach. Despite hippie-unfriendly real estate prices, some of that aesthetic remains on its boardwalk, a mile-and-a-half-long party of street performers, merchants and graffiti artists. Neighboring Santa Monica, meanwhile, is great for kids, including the amusement park on its pier.

For views, visit the wealthy beaches of Malibu, La Jolla or Santa Barbara County. For surf culture, try Orange County's Huntington Beach or San Diego's Oceanside, Encinitas, Mission or Pacific Beaches.

Beachwear is appropriate for the coastal strip but not in the rest of LA: 'No shoes, no shirt, no service' signs appear in establishments throughout town.

LA vs SoCal

Or rather, SoCal vs LA. Generally LA goes about its business and the rest of the region either depends on or resents it.

You can see this in politics, for starters. LA leans to the left – often there is no Republican candidate for mayor – and its politicians carry significant weight in Washington (eg Democratic Congressman Henry Waxman of West LA).

However, much of the rest of SoCal tends to behave more like a 'red state.' Generally, the further from the coast, the more conservative: the city of Santa Barbara votes blue, but inland Santa Barbara county votes red. A big exception is Orange County, a largely conservative stronghold with firebrand congressional representatives like Dana Rohrabacher. In Orange County we've heard progressive views met with 'Well, that's LA talking.' However, things are changing even here, as Democrats like Loretta Sanchez have taken over long-held Republican seats in congress.

Conservative politics extend to San Diego and the desert areas, largely because of the high numbers of military personnel and wealthy retirees who live there.

And then there's the rest of California. Angelenos visiting San Francisco are often greeted with 'Ugh!', 'How can you live there?!?', 'That place is a hellhole!' and worse, and much of the interior of the state reviles LA for having 'stolen' its water. We wouldn't call any of this a rivalry, though, as it seems to be one way. Angelenos generally seem to like the rest of the state, or are too busy to notice.

Majorities & Minorities

There were different races even among the first settlers to LA in 1781, and today it is one of only two major metro areas in the nation without a majority ethnic group (the other is Honolulu). Across the region, immigrants from over 140 countries have put down roots, creating the largest populations of Mexicans, Koreans, Armenians, Filipinos, Salvadorans, Guatemalans and Vietnamese outside their home countries, plus America's largest ethnic Cambodian, Japanese and Persian communities.

All this makes LA one of the most tolerant, cosmopolitan and open-minded societies anywhere. Although there are ethnic enclaves, it's not uncommon to interact with people of 10 ethnicities or more in a single day in any corner of the city. You might drop off your shirts with a Korean dry cleaner, have your nails done by a recent Vietnamese immigrant, pick up groceries from a Mexican grocer and a treat from the Cambodian-run doughnut shop. Dinner might just as easily be sushi, falafel, enchiladas or steak-frites, or maybe pad Thai while a Thai Elvis impersonator entertains. Interracial families barely raise an eyebrow.

Certainly, explosive race-related incidents have received high-profile exposure, as with the riots in 1965 in Watts and in 1992 in Los Angeles (p419), yet day-to-day civility between races is the norm. Animosity is hard to maintain when you encounter different races on a daily basis.

A dozen SoCal colleges and universities are ranked in the top 50 nationally.

Latino SoCal

Forty-eight percent of LA County's residents are Hispanic, according to the 2009 US census (the latest for which figures were available as we went to press), and Hispanics are soon projected to become the outright majority; the largest contingent is from Mexico, followed by Central

DAMN THAT TRAFFIC JAM!

Traffic is LA's great leveler. Outsiders often marvel that it's a city without a center; that's less true than it used to be thanks to Downtown LA development, but it's also more true in that business districts have dispersed in the last 10 years. So while you could once count on traffic into Downtown in the morning and out of Downtown in the evening, now it could happen any time of day. The same could happen anywhere in SoCal. Or you might just as easily find the roads mysteriously clear.

Subway and light rail lines have been extended of late, and long-range regional plans call for even more; as we went to press, LA was abuzz with a '30/10' plan to fast-track an estimated 30 years' worth of transit updates for completion in the next 10 years. For now, our advice is to double the time you think it will take to get anywhere (triple at rush hour), take your cell phone (with headset – it's the law), and should you get stuck in traffic, be Zen about it. Those waiting for you will understand.

Estimates put the number of undocumented/illegal immigrants in the US at around 11 million people (per US census and Department of Homeland Security estimates for 2009). About one-quarter of these immigrants live in California, and the majority in SoCal, performing low-paying work such as farm labor, construction, domestic and food service.

The equation is simple: for over a generation, the search for economic opportunity has driven Mexican laborers north, to earn money for relatives back home; remittances from these workers were about $21.1 billion in 2009, accounting for some 2.4 percent of Mexican GDP. North of the border, increasingly vocal opposition in the US is putting pressure on lawmakers to do something about those who have entered illegally, leading to hundreds of miles of border fence patrolled by National Guard troops.

Although immigration is under federal control, states have increasingly taken immigration issues into their own hands, with controversial laws preventing undocumented immigrants from obtaining driver's licenses, educational funding and social services. Some of these laws, such as a landmark 2010 bill in California's neighboring state of Arizona requiring police to ask for proof of citizenship from anyone suspected of being there illegally, continue to be the subject of roiling court battles.

The great recession and laws like these have slowed but hardly stopped immigration, but perhaps the only lasting solution will be for the Mexican economy to reach something like economic parity with the US economy. One visit to Tijuana will tell you there's still a way to go.

America. Their collective influence is huge. Spanish is the *lingua franca* of many SoCal restaurant kitchens, and there's a host of Latino products on grocery-store shelves. Even non-Latino Angelenos can expound on mole and corn versus flour tortillas. From radio and TV stations to Spanish-language billboards, you'll see and hear Latino culture across the Southland.

Despite their numbers, Latinos had little say in leadership until fairly recently. Now LA's mayor, county sheriff, members of the city council and the powerful county board of supervisors are Latino, as well as many representatives in the California State Assembly and US Congress from across SoCal. The hot-button issue is immigration and May Day in Downtown Los Angeles has become a de facto Mexican pride rally.

In his column 'iAsk a Mexican!', *OC Weekly* columnist Gustavo Arellano tackles such questions as why Mexicans swim with their clothes on, alongside weighty social issues involving immigrants' rights. See it at www.ocweekly.com.

Perhaps somewhat surprisingly, San Diego is more homogeneous (read: Caucasian) than LA despite its border location. That said, the 2010 census showed the percentage of non-White county residents reaching 50 percent for the first time.

Other Ethnic Groups

LA's – and SoCal's – vast space has allowed ethnic enclaves to thrive as in few other places. Neighborhoods throughout the region burst with ethnic cuisine, clothing and souvenir shops, and houses of worship. Add in community newspapers and social services in the native language, and it's possible to live day to day entirely in a language other than English.

LA's Koreatown is the largest, a vast swath between Hollywood and Downtown LA. The city boasts not one but three Japanese neighborhoods, America's first Thai Town, and enclaves from HiFi (Historic Filipinotown) to Little Ethiopia. LA's Chinatown offers Chinese dim sum and Vietnamese *pho* (soup), though the real center of modern Chinese immigration to SoCal is east of LA, in the suburban San Gabriel

Valley towns of Alhambra, Monterey Park and San Gabriel; Chinese signage is almost as prevalent as English. Venice Blvd in West LA bops with Brazilian cuisine and music, the mayor of Beverly Hills is Iranian-American, West Hollywood has a large Russian immigrant contingent, and it's not uncommon to see black-hatted Orthodox Jews walking to synagogue in the Fairfax and Pico-Robertson districts. Armenians form the largest ethnic group in Glendale, Signal Hill near Long Beach is home to a Cambodian community, Cerritos and Artesia (near the border of LA and Orange Counties) are the center of Indian activity, and Croatian seafarers made their home in the southern LA port enclave of San Pedro.

San Diego honors the heritage of Portuguese fisherfolk in the Point Loma neighborhood, and it has SoCal's only Little Italy, bursting with cafés and restaurants.

Little Saigon, in the Orange County towns of Garden Grove and Westminster, has the largest population of ethnic Vietnamese outside Vietnam; many residents emigrated around the end of the Vietnam war, and the population here tends to be vocally opposed to the current Vietnamese regime. Little Arabia in Anaheim offers restaurants, bookstores and clothing stores, and even some non-Muslim restaurants serve halal meat.

> In some of LA's more diverse neighborhoods, it's not uncommon to see mini-mall signage in multiple languages. Signage in Koreatown, for example, might be in Korean, Spanish, Thai and Armenian as well as English.

Gay & Lesbian SoCal

From shiny Palm Springs to San Diego's bohemian Hillcrest neighborhood, arty Laguna Beach and the booming LA enclaves of Silver Lake and West Hollywood, members of SoCal's gay and lesbian community are out and proud. High-profile gay men and lesbians can be found at all levels of society, from government to business and the arts. The *Advocate* magazine, PFLAG (Parents and Friends of Lesbians and Gays) and America's first gay church and synagogue all started in Los Angeles.

In spring 2008 the California Supreme Court ruled that gay and lesbian couples had the same right to marry as heterosexual couples, and over the next several months some 18,000 same-sex couples were married in the state. That ruling was overturned in the election of November 2008 when, in a statewide ballot measure known as Proposition 8, the state constitution was amended to specify that marriage had to be between one man and one woman. The California Supreme Court upheld Proposition 8 but also ruled that the same-sex marriages performed earlier that year remained valid. As we went to press, Proposition 8 continued to be the subject of court challenges, whose outcomes, like so much that originates in SoCal, are expected to have national implications.

See boxes in the regional chapters (p115, p289 and p347) and Directory A–Z (p455) for gay and lesbian listings and further info.

> SoCal's contributions to the political blogosphere run the gamut from progressive (www.huffingtonpost.com, operated by Arianna Huffington) to the conservative websites of Andrew Breitbart (http://biggovernment.com, http://bighollywood.com and more).

SCIENTOLOGY

The LA-based Church of Scientology follows beliefs articulated by L Ron Hubbard in his book *Dianetics* (1950). Scientology's celebrity followers include Tom Cruise and Katie Holmes, John Travolta, Beck, TV journalist Greta van Susteren and the late Isaac Hayes.

According to the church's website, following the methods of Dianetics 'increases sanity, intelligence, confidence and well-being' and removes 'unwanted sensations, unpleasant emotions and psychosomatic ills that block one's life and happiness.' Church members famously oppose drug abuse and psychiatry.

LA's sports teams have long and often winning histories, but they're also known as much for their celebrity quotient on and off the court or field as for any athletic prowess.

The Los Angeles Lakers basketball team plays at Staples Center, where you can watch the game alongside famous fans including Jack Nicholson, Tobey Maguire and Snoop Dogg. On the court, the Lakers' roster of fabled players includes household name Kareem Abdul-Jabbar, Magic Johnson, Shaquille O'Neal and current star Kobe Bryant, plus coach Phil Jackson (aka the Zen Master).

The Brooklyn Dodgers baseball team became the Los Angeles Dodgers in 1958, and New Yorkers have never quite forgiven LA. Ringed by hills, Dodger Stadium is one of the most beautiful in baseball, even if the team's current news is the ugly, tabloid-fodder divorce between its owners. San Diego's Petco Park is the gorgeous new home to the San Diego Padres, and in between are the successful if awkwardly named Los Angeles Angels of Anaheim.

The region's only professional football team is the San Diego Chargers. In LA, the ticket is college sports, particularly crosstown rivals the UCLA Bruins and the recently scandal-plagued USC Trojans.

LA's long-neglected Major League Soccer (MLS) team, the Galaxy, got a boost with the 2007 arrival of icon David Beckham and his $250 million price tag, but his career here has been less than stellar due to injury and the suspicion that Becks is generally past his prime.

Del Mar Racetrack in northern San Diego County is the ritziest of SoCal's horse-racing tracks, alongside Hollywood Park and Santa Anita Racetrack in LA County. The Grand Prix (p67), a Formula 1 race, takes over the streets of Long Beach every April.

Other professional teams include the following:

» Los Angeles Clippers – National Basketball Association. Home court: Staples Center.

» Los Angeles Sparks – WNBA (Women's National Basketball Association). Home court: Staples Center.

» Anaheim Mighty Ducks – National Hockey League. Home ice: the Pond of Anaheim.

» Los Angeles Kings – National Hockey League. Home ice: Staples Center.

Religion – Old & New

Despite, or perhaps because of, its freewheeling reputation, Southern California is one of the world's most religiously diverse regions, and religious tolerance is (mostly) the rule. LA is home to the nation's largest Roman Catholic archdiocese, one of the world's largest Jewish populations, and Bahais, Buddhists, Hare Krishnas, Hindus, Muslims, Sikhs and members of every imaginable Christian denomination are well represented. The world's second-largest Mormon temple is in the LA neighborhood of Westwood, while another spectacular Mormon temple towers over the I-5 near La Jolla, in San Diego County. All of these denominations are quite powerful, some controversially as with the sex abuse scandal in the Roman Catholic Church and Mormon support for Proposition 8 (p425).

Orange County is famously one of the USA's bastions of conservative Christianity, alongside well-known televangelists Pastor Rick Warren of Saddleback Church and the Schuller family of the 'Hour of Power' show from the Crystal Cathedral.

Other offshoots of mainstream religions include the yogic Self-Realization Fellowship, with large centers in Pacific Palisades and the

San Diego suburb Encinitas. West LA's Kabbalah Center has seen many celebrity practitioners of this Jewish mystical art, most notably Madonna, Demi Moore and Ashton Kutcher.

Religious cults have also thrived. Most famously, Heaven's Gate was based in a mansion in Rancho Santa Fe in northern San Diego County, where 38 members committed mass suicide in 1997.

Let's Get Physical

Southern California's outdoor lifestyle has made it a mecca for fitness buffs since early days. Starting with Muscle Beach in Venice, SoCal residents visit the gym with almost religious fervor. Marathons in LA (p67) and San Diego (p286) are major civic events, and no matter where you are in SoCal, you're never more than about 30 minutes from mountains for hiking, biking, climbing or horseback riding.

Fans of the Los Angeles Dodgers are (in)famous for leaving during the 8th inning in order to beat traffic exiting Dodger Stadium.

Surfing, Skating & Extreme Sports

Surfing first hit the US mainland in 1929, when Hawaiian surf legend Duke Kahanamoku gave a demonstration in Huntington Beach (Orange County). It's been Surf City ever since, with numerous competitions every year including the US Open of Surfing each July. Other surf competitions take place in Carlsbad and Oceanside (northern San Diego County) and at Trestles (San Clemente) and San Onofre State Beach in southern Orange County.

Extreme sports in SoCal go back to the 1970s when the Santa Monica–Venice border neighborhood was nicknamed 'Dogtown' for the proliferation of skateboarders who honed their craft by breaking into dry swimming pools in the backyards of mansions (the 2005 film *Lords of Dogtown* chronicles the rise of this group known as the Z-Boys). Things have developed rapidly since. Extreme sports deities Tony Hawk and Shawn White are from the San Diego area, and the X Games, which also include BMX and Moto X competitions, takes place each summer in Downtown LA.

As Seen on TV (& Film)

Try to imagine living in a world without Orson Welles whispering 'Rosebud,' Judy Garland clicking her heels three times, John Travolta dancing in his white suit or the Terminator informing us that he'll 'be back.' LA is where these iconic images are hatched, nurtured and set to fly.

But it's more than the movies. It seems like every other car commercial is shot in Downtown LA, fashion photographers are common on Santa Monica beach, and locations throughout LA County stand as a backdrops for your favorite TV series. The upshot: few people come to LA without seeing something – or someone – they recognize.

> Easily the most famous piece of footage shot in Orange County was the opening credits of the *Gilligan's Island* TV series, in Newport Harbor.

The 'Industry'

From the moment film – and later TV – became the dominant entertainment medium, LA took center stage in the world of popular culture and has been there ever since. It's also been the best (and sometimes the worst) ambassador of LA, and by extension California and the rest of America, to the world. You might know it as entertainment, but to Angelenos it's simply the 'Industry.'

It began when entrepreneurial moviemakers – most of them European immigrants – established studios here in the first decade of the 20th century. German-born Carl Laemmle built Universal Studios in 1915, selling lunch to curious guests coming to watch the magic of moviemaking; Polish immigrant Samuel Goldwyn joined with Cecil B DeMille to form Paramount Studios; and Jack Warner and his brothers arrived a few years later from Poland via Philadelphia. Perpetually sunny weather meant that most outdoor locations could be easily shot, and moviemaking flourished. Fans loved early film stars like Charlie Chaplin and Harold Lloyd, and the first big Hollywood wedding occurred in 1920 when Douglas Fairbanks wed Mary Pickford. What's more, the

RUNAWAY PRODUCTION

Entertainment is big business in LA County, bringing in around $35 billion in revenue and ranking third in employment behind tourism and international trade. There's a critical mass of studios and talent, and locations around LA often stand in for other cities: Downtown for Midtown Manhattan, Pasadena for the Midwest etc.

Other localities have caught on, though, and the high cost of filming in LA has sent location scouts looking elsewhere. States such as New Mexico, North Carolina, Louisiana and Connecticut have offered production credits, tax incentives, state-of-the-art facilities (particularly in New Mexico) and, in some cases, nonunionized workforces. And in Canada, film production is welcomed with open arms (and pocketbooks).

proximity of the Mexican border enabled filmmakers to rush their equipment to safety when challenged by the collection agents of patent holders such as Thomas Edison.

Although Hollywood became the cultural and financial hub of the movie industry, it's a myth that most production ever took place there; of the major studios, only Paramount Pictures is in Hollywood proper, albeit surrounded by block after block of production-related businesses like lighting and post-production. Studios were built in Culver City (MGM, now Sony Pictures), Studio City (Universal Studios Hollywood) and Burbank (Disney and Warner Bros), but historically moviemaking wasn't even limited to LA. American Film Company, founded in Santa Barbara in 1910, did box office for years and Balboa Studios in Long Beach was another major silent-era dream factory. And the first big movie palaces were not on Hollywood Blvd but on Broadway in Downtown LA.

Although LA sometimes feels like a company town, like Washington, DC for government or – at one time – Detroit for automobiles, the Los Angeles Economic Development Council reports that in 2009 only some 154,000 people in LA County were employed directly in film, TV and radio production. That doesn't tell the whole story, though, because the Industry churns more jobs, from high-powered attorneys to cater-waiters. Still, the region's economic reach is much more than making pretty pictures.

All that aside, for stargazers or movie buffs, LA is the equivalent of the Holy Grail. Experiences are infinite: you can tour major movie studios (p184), be part of a sitcom audience (p90), shop at boutiques favored by today's hottest stars (p97), see where celebs live (p66), eat, drink and party, buy their old clothes (p162) or attend a film festival (p430).

SoCal on Screen

Critics and cineastes have written volumes about Hollywood cinema, and at any time of the day you can turn on the TV for the latest entertainment news and gossip, so we're not going to attempt to cover that here. Instead, to put you in an LA mood, here's a catalog of Hollywood movies that feature the City of Angels – in some cases almost as a character in itself.

Classics

Perhaps the greatest LA film is Roman Polanski's *Chinatown* (1974), which is about early-20th-century water wars. Vincente Minelli's *The Bad and the Beautiful* (1952) takes a hard look at the film biz, with Lana Turner recalling the exploits of an aggressive, egotistic film producer played by Kirk Douglas. In David O Selznick's *A Star Is Born* (1937), Janet Gaynor plays a woman rising to stardom as her movie-star husband (Fredric March) declines in popularity. A 1954 remake starred Judy Garland; a 1976 remake starred Barbra Streisand.

AS SEEN ON TV (& FILM) SOCAL ON SCREEN

1893
Thomas Edison debuts the first motion picture projection device, the Kinetoscope, at the World's Fair in Chicago. Viewers sat in a small booth to watch short video clips.

1913
The first Hollywood movie, *Squaw Man,* is shot by Cecil B de Mille.

1915
Universal Film Manufacturing Company (now Universal Studios Hollywood) opens, charging visitors 25 cents including lunch to watch movies being made.

1918
Warner Bros studio opens.

1927
The first talkie, *The Jazz Singer,* ends the silent film era.

1927
Sid Grauman opens his Chinese Theater. Stars have been leaving their hand- and footprints ever since.

1928
The first Academy Awards ceremony takes place.

1928
Walt Disney releases *Steamboat Willie,* the first fully synchronized animated short starring a mouse named Mickey.

1939
The Wizard of Oz is the first wide-release movie to be shown in full color.

TOP FIVE FILM FESTIVALS *ADAM SKOLNICK*

In SoCal it's not love or money but movies that make the world go round. Besides churning out blockbuster productions, the region hosts dozens of film festivals, including such highly specialized ones as the Festival of Science Fiction, Fantasy & Horror and the Pan African Film & Art Festival. We've picked through the pile for our faves. Check the websites for lineups and ticket information.

AFI Fest (www.afi.com/afifest) One of the most influential festivals in the country presents top-notch films by newbies and masters from around the world. *Monster, The Cider House Rules* and other Academy Award winners premiered here.

Los Angeles Film Festival (www.lafilmfest.com) This June festival corrals the best in indie movies from around the world – from shorts and music videos to documentaries and features.

Outfest (www.outfest.org) The largest continuous film fest in SoCal, this GLBT celebration has been held every July in Los Angeles for over a quarter-century. It features more than 200 shorts, films and videos by and about the community. In 2010 it screened the Alan Ginsberg docudrama *Howl*, starring James Franco.

Palm Springs International Film Festival (www.psfilmfest.org) Founded in 1990 by Sonny Bono, this balmy January festival is getting more glam every year. It's an intimate yet star-studded affair with more than 200 films from dozens of countries.

Newport Beach Film Festival (www.newportbeachfilmfest.com) The buzz surrounding this April competition has been increasing steadily since Oscar-winner *Crash* premiered here in 2005.

The most memorable of James Dean's scenes in *Rebel Without a Cause* (1955) takes place above Los Angeles in Griffith Park. In *The Graduate* (1967), Dustin Hoffman and Anne Bancroft play a game of nihilism, floundering and sexual awakening in 1960s Pasadena. And although it was released in 1997, Curtis Hanson's *LA Confidential* deftly portrays the violent world of deals, sexual betrayal and double-crossing that drove both good and bad cops in the LA of the crime-ridden '50s.

Contemporary LA

Robert Altman's *Short Cuts* (1993) weaves together several stories by Raymond Carver, showing a sadly depraved Los Angeles. Another dispiriting, multistory tale is told in Paul Haggis' Oscar-winning ensemble drama *Crash* (2005). In Joel Schumacher's *Falling Down* (1993), Michael Douglas plays an unemployed defense engineer for whom a traffic jam triggers a war with the world. Quentin Tarantino, in Chandleresque fashion, creates a surreal Los Angeles from the bottom up in *Pulp Fiction* (1994).

Gritty city tales include *Stand and Deliver* (directed by Ramón Menéndez in 1988), based on a true story, starring Edward James Olmos as a take-no-prisoners LA high school teacher who whips a bunch of Latino gang members into shape by successfully teaching them college-level calculus. John Singleton's tragic *Boyz n the Hood* (1991) stars Cuba Gooding Jr and offers a major reality check on coming-of-age as a black teenager in the inner city. The 2007 film *Freedom Writers* (directed by Richard LaGravenese) stars Hilary Swank as a Long Beach high school teacher whose students work out their feelings about race and their personal hardships through writing.

In David Lynch's surrealist *Mulholland Drive* (2001), an amnesiac woman (played by Naomi Watts) tries to put her life back together through encounters with weird and terrifying people on various edges of dark LA mindscapes. *Laurel Canyon* (2002) shows another strange view of life in LA: a young med-school intern and his fiancée return

GETAWAY

Palm Springs became a favorite getaway of Hollywood stars in the mid-20th century partly because its distance from LA (just under 100 miles) was as far as they could travel under their studio contracts.

to live with his pot-smoking mother (Frances McDormand), who's producing her latest boy toy's rock-and-roll record (see p434).

Three of Paul Thomas Anderson's films have come to be called the 'Valley Trilogy' for their San Fernando Valley locations: *Boogie Nights* (1997) starred Mark Wahlberg as the prodigiously endowed porn star Dirk Diggler; *Magnolia* (1999) brought together luminaries including Tom Cruise, Jason Robards and Philip Seymour Hoffman in a tale of interwoven family dramas; and the darkly romantic *Punch Drunk Love* (2002) saw Adam Sandler's character overcome serious anger management issues to win a woman's (Emily Watson) affections.

LA Comedies

Tony Richardson's outrageously sardonic commentary *The Loved One* (1965), based on an Evelyn Waugh novel about the funeral industry, features Sir John Gielgud and Liberace (as a huckstering mortician). Amy Heckerling and Cameron Crowe collaborated on *Fast Times at Ridgemont High* (1982), which launched the careers of Sean Penn, Jennifer Jason Leigh, Nicolas Cage and Forest Whitaker among others, as students at a fictional San Fernando Valley high school (emphasis on the 'high' in the case of Penn's Jeff Spicoli). *Bill & Ted's Excellent Adventure* (1989) featured Keanu Reeves and Alex Winter as time-traveling San Gabriel Valley teen slackers, and Julia Roberts became a screen queen for playing the definitive hooker with a heart of gold in Garry Marshall's *Pretty Woman* (1990). Steve Martin's *LA Story* (1991) hilariously parodies LA life from lattes to colonics. He followed up with the wistful *Shopgirl* (2005), in which a lonely clerk (Claire Danes) selling gloves at Neiman-Marcus finds herself in a love triangle with a sophisticate (Martin) and a goofball (Jason Schwartzman).

The '90s offered some classic LA youth comedies. Heckerling returned to direct *Clueless* (1995), starring Alicia Silverstone as spoiled Beverly Hills teenager Cher Horowitz in an update of Jane Austen's *Emma*. *Swingers* (1996) was Vince Vaughn's breakout film as a Hollywood hipster, coining the word 'money' as the ultimate compliment, and bringing 'Vegas, baby, Vegas!' to the lexicon. And *Go* (1999), an ensemble piece about club kids and a drug deal gone bad, has a cast that reads like a *Fast Times* for the new generation: Katie Holmes, Taye Diggs, Timothy Olyphant and Jay Mohr.

More recently, LA has been the backdrop for the merry band of comedic actors headed by director Judd Apatow, in movies including *the 40-Year-Old Virgin* (2005) and *Knocked Up* (2007). *(500) Days of Summer* (2009, directed by Marc Webb), starring Joseph Gordon-Levitt and Zooey Deschanel, is not a love story but a lovely story about love – and architecture – in Downtown LA.

AS SEEN ON TV (& FILM) SOCAL ON SCREEN

1950
Sunset Boulevard debuts. Stars have been ready for their close-up ever since.

1958
The USA's first school of film and TV is established at the University of Southern California.

1960
The Hollywood Walk of Fame debuts.

1970s
The San Fernando Valley becomes home base to America's adult film industry.

1975
The age of the modern blockbuster begins with *Jaws*, by a young filmmaker named Steven Spielberg.

1982
Outfest becomes the first gay and lesbian film festival in the nation.

1989
Sony purchases Columbia Tri-Star Pictures.

1990s
Blockbuster production costs soar over $100 million. Runaway production takes off.

1999
Independent film *The Blair Witch Project* inaugurates the era of internet marketing.

2001
The Kodak Theater becomes the permanent home to the Academy Awards ceremony.

2009
Avatar becomes the highest grossing movie of all time, encroaching on $3 billion as we went to press.

Hollywood likes nothing better than to make movies about itself. Self-indulgent? Maybe, but often very entertaining.

» *Sunset Boulevard* (1950) – the ultimate Hollywood story. Gloria Swanson plays Norma Desmond, a washed-up silent film star pining for her return, and William Holden plays the screenwriter she hires to make that happen.

» *Singin' in the Rain* (1976) – exuberant musical fairytale about love in the time of talkies, starring Gene Kelly, Debbie Reynolds and Donald O'Connor.

» *Silent Movie* (1976) – screwball comedy from Mel Brooks about a director trying to revive a movie studio by producing the first silent film in decades.

» *Postcards from the Edge* (1990) – Mike Nichols directs Shirley MacLaine and Meryl Streep as a mother-daughter pair dealing with stardom's seamy underbelly.

» *Barton Fink* (1991) – John Turturro and John Goodman engage in a battle of wits over how to write a screenplay in this dark comedy by the Coen Brothers.

» *The Player* (1992) – one of the most accessible films by legendary director Robert Altman. Tim Robbins plays a studio executive who takes his power too far.

» *Ed Wood* (1994) – Tim Burton directs Johnny Depp as perhaps the worst director in Hollywood history, famous for wearing pink angora sweaters.

» *Get Shorty* (1995) – in Barry Sonnenfeld's comedy based on the Elmore Leonard novel, John Travolta plays a mafioso who gets entangled in Hollywood and wonders which industry has fewer scruples.

Beyond LA

In Jake Kasdan's *Orange County* (2002), a surfer tries to get into Stanford University and escape his oddball family; in the meantime you get a humorous snapshot of culture in OC. Nancy Meyers' comedy *It's Complicated* (2009) showed Meryl Streep, Alec Baldwin and Steve Martin putting on the dog around the ritzy Santa Barbara suburb of Montecito. Ask any oenophile about *Sideways* (2004), and you'll get an earful about Santa Barbara's wine country, pinot noir and Paul Giamatti.

The most famous film shot in San Diego was *Some Like it Hot,* starring Marilyn Monroe, Jack Lemmon and Tony Curtis, a classic even if the iconic Hotel del Coronado served as a stand-in for Florida. In addition to modern classics like *Top Gun* (1986, directed by Tony Scott), 21st-century box-office hits filmed here include *Almost Famous* (2000), *Anchorman* (2004), *Babel* (2006), *Bring it On* (2000), *Bruce Almighty* (2003) and *Traffic* (2000).

LA has the greatest number of small (under 100 seat) stage theaters in the US.

Television

Through the decades, iconic images of LA have been beamed into living rooms across America in shows such as *Dragnet* (1950s), *The Beverly Hillbillies* (1960s), *The Brady Bunch* (1970s) and *LA Law* (1980s), through to teen dramedies *Beverly Hills 90210* (1990s), which made zip codes into a status symbol, and *The OC* (2000s) set in Newport Beach. Among more recent shows, *Curb Your Enthusiasm* offers insights – if you can call them that – into Hollywood's smarmier side, while *Entourage* offers the highs, the lows and the intrigues of the Industry through the eyes of a rising star and his posse, and *Californication* shows us with no holds barred what happens when a successful New York novelist goes Hollywood. And even if you're not a fan of reality TV, you'll see SoCal in shows from *Top Chef* to *The Hills* and *Real Housewives of Orange County*.

See p90 for details of how you can attend your favorite show as an audience member.

Animation

A young cartoonist named Walt Disney arrived in LA in 1923, and five years later he had his first breakout hit, *Steamboat Willie,* starring a mouse named Mickey. That film spawned the entire Disney empire, and dozens of other animation studios have followed with films, TV programs and effects. Among the best known: Warner Bros (Bugs Bunny et al), Hanna Barbera (*The Flintstones, The Jetsons,* Yogi Bear and Scooby-Doo), Dreamworks (*Shrek, Madagascar*), Film Roman (*The Simpsons, King of the Hill*), Klasky Csupo (*Rugrats*), Nelvana (Babar, *Fairly Odd-parents*). Even if much of the hands-on work takes place overseas (eg South Korea), concept and supervision is done in LA.

Music & the Arts

Go ahead: mock. Bad-mouth, belittle, bemoan, besmirch, debase, decry, demean, disparage. Get it all out. Put down, reduce, ridicule, slam, sling mud, thrash, trash.

Now open wide and prepare to eat your words, because anyone who thinks that Southern California is all pop culture hasn't been paying attention. For most of the last century, LA in particular has been one of America's most prolific generators of music, art and literature of all stripes.

The cover image of the Eagles' album *Hotel California* is of the Beverly Hills Hotel, but the group remains unspecific as to which hotel inspired the title.

Music

The history of music in LA might as well be the history of American music, at least for the last 75 years. Much of the recording industry is based here, and the film and TV industries have proven powerful talent incubators. Today's pop princess troublemakers and airbrushed boy bands are here thanks to the work of thousands who came before.

Post WWII

LA's music biz and its attendant club scene arose out of the film industry and the massive post-WWII influx of classically trained European refugees and American jazz, R&B and country-music hopefuls.

Especially in the postwar boom days, LA was a churning, exploding mecca for live jazz, R&B, soul, gospel and rock-and-roll groups. Beat music clubs dotted the Sunset Strip in Hollywood, along La Brea Ave toward the Leimert Park/Crenshaw district and all the way down into 'the community' of Watts, Inglewood, Compton and all over South Central LA.

California Dreamin'

It's hard to say which Los Angeles band is the most emblematic of the 1960s: The Doors, The Beach Boys, The Mamas and The Papas, Joni Mitchell, The Byrds and Crosby, Stills & Nash are all essential LA music acts. The epicenter of this movement was the Laurel Canyon neighborhood, just uphill from the Sunset Strip and the legendary Whisky a Go-Go, ground zero for the psychedelic rock scene.

The country-influenced pop of The Eagles, Jackson Browne and Linda Ronstadt became America's soundtrack for the early 1970s, joined by the Mexican-fusion sounds of Santana and iconic funk bands War and Sly and the Family Stone, the latter two from South LA.

The 1980s brought such punk bands as X, Black Flag, Bad Religion and Suicidal Tendencies, while the more mainstream girl bands The Bangles and The Go-Gos, new wave band Oingo Boingo and rockers Jane's Addiction and Red Hot Chili Peppers took the world by storm. Guns N' Roses was the '80s hard rock band of record. On avant-garde rocker Frank Zappa's 1982 single *Valley Girl*, his 14-year-old daughter Moon Unit taught the rest of America to say 'Omigo-o-od!' like an LA teenager.

HOTEL CALIFORNIA

By the 1990s alternative rock acts like Beck and Weezer had gained national presence. Los Lobos was king of the Latino bands, an honor that has since passed to Ozomatli. Another key '90s band was the ska-punk-alt-rock No Doubt, of Orange County (which launched the solo career of lead singer Gwen Stefani).

Yo, West Coast!

The '90s West Coast gangsta rap acts included Ice T, Cypress Hill and NWA, whose *Straight Outta Compton* was a watermark for the genre. NWA's Dr Dre and Ice Cube went off to have their own solo careers, and Dr Dre fostered the careers of Snoop Dogg and Warren G, among others. Later, Korn, Limp Bizkit and Linkin Park combined hip-hop with metal and popularized nu metal.

The 21st Century

SoCal rock stars of the new millennium include the approachable hip-hop of the Black Eyed Peas, San Diego–based alt-rockers Stone Temple Pilots and pop-punksters Blink 182, Orange County's The Offspring, indie-rockers Rilo Kiley and, for better or for worse, whoever wins on *American Idol,* the finals of which are held at Downtown LA's Nokia Theater.

Film & TV Scores

Music born of the film and TV industries is some of the most recognizable in American culture. John Williams, a frequent collaborator with Steven Spielberg, is perhaps the best known of legions of film composers, having created music for *Jaws, Star Wars, ET, Raiders of the Lost Ark* and *Schindler's List,* to name just a few. The 1950s through 1980s were a golden age for film scoring, including works by Elmer Bernstein (*The Magnificent Seven, Airplane, Stripes, Ghostbusters* etc), Bernard Herrmann (*Psycho, The Day the Earth Stood Still,* the *Twilight Zone* TV series) and Ennio Morricone (*The Good, the Bad & the Ugly, A Fistful of Dollars*).

Present-day composers include Williams, Randy Newman (*The Natural, Toy Story, Monsters Inc., Cars*), Danny Elfman (*Pee-wee's Big Adventure, Edward Scissorhands, Men in Black, The Simpsons* theme), Marco Beltrami (*3:10 to Yuma, The Hurt Locker*) and Lalo Schifrin (*Mission: Impossible*) for starters.

A great place to hear film music is at the Hollywood Bowl, where clips from the films are screened while the live orchestra plays.

The lyrics for the definitive LA party song, Sheryl Crow's 'All I Wanna Do' (1994), are from the poem *Fun* by Wyn Cooper, although it contains no reference to Santa Monica Blvd.

MUSIC & THE ARTS MUSIC

MUSIC FESTIVALS

All over the Southland, annual festivals host a mix of big-name and local acts. Buy tickets early for station-sponsored shows. Some highlights:

» Coachella Valley Music & Arts Festival (p342) – sweat it in the desert in Indio, with indie bands, up-and-comers and the occasional blockbuster star (some woman named Madonna?) in mid-April.

» KROQ Almost Acoustic Christmas (www.kroq.com) – a winter punk and modern rock event at the Gibson Amphitheater at Universal City, December. Recent headliners include The Offspring and AFI.

» KROQ Weenie Roast (www.kroq.com) – alt-rock musicians like Kings of Leon, Jimmy Eat World and Hole perform in Irvine, Orange County, in May or June.

» Stagecoach Festival (p342) – all things country and western, from Willie Nelson and Emmylou Harris to BBQ, the weekend after Coachella and same location.

» Sunset Junction Street Fair (p68) – late-August festival where Sunset and Hollywood Blvds meet. It's part street fair, part multiband concert on multiple stages. Acts run from local bands to Conor Oberst and Arrested Development.

'THE DUDE' ABIDES

In 2009 Gustavo Dudamel, not yet 30 years old, took over as conductor of the Los Angeles Philharmonic from the iconic conductor-composer Esa-Pekka Salonen, and the city has taken to him *con gusto*. The Venezuelan Dudamel came up musically through El Sistema, that nation's program for creating youth orchestras, culminating with his conducting the Simón Bolívar Youth Orchestra. With his shock of wild, black curls, prodigious energy on the podium and youthful enthusiasm, 'the Dude' has energized LA in a way few thought possible. Just as importantly, he's brought techniques of El Sistema to this city where youth could no doubt use the outlet as much as – if not more than – those in his native land.

Classical Music

First stop for fans of 'serious music' should be Downtown LA's Walt Disney Concert Hall, home of one of the world's greatest symphony orchestras, the LA Philharmonic, under the baton of the young Venezuelan phenom Gustavo Dudamel. The LA Phil's summer home is the Hollywood Bowl, a favorite venue for classical, jazz and pop performances and even films accompanied by a live orchestra.

Not to be outdone, Orange County boasts the Orange County Performing Arts Center in Costa Mesa, with two state-of-the-art concert halls also recognized among America's finest. The San Diego Symphony (p297) performs at Copley Symphony Hall and at Marina Park South in summer. In Palm Springs, check the calendar at the Annenberg Theater at the Palm Springs Art Museum.

The Los Angeles Opera, under the artistic direction of Placido Domingo, plays at Music Center in the Dorothy Chandler Pavilion. San Diego also has an active opera company (p297).

Visual Arts

A 2006 exhibition at Paris' Pompidou Center called Los Angeles an 'Artistic Capital,' a designation that may have surprised folks who haven't spent time here. New York may be the nation's largest art market, but much of that art is made in LA. Large artist colonies have sprung up around Downtown LA, and there are burgeoning gallery scenes Downtown and in LA's Chinatown, as well as in Santa Monica and Culver City.

California Institute of Arts (Cal Arts), in the northern LA county suburb of Valencia, is one of the art world's premier schools. Heavy hitters including Laurie Anderson, John Baldessari, Jonathan Borofsky, Judy Chicago and Roy Lichtenstein have taught there.

For museum-goers, SoCal offers a wealth of opportunities. In Los Angeles alone, the Getty Center, the Los Angeles County Museum of Art (LACMA) and the Museum of Contemporary Art are world-class venues that keep evolving. The Broad Contemporary Art Museum in opened at LACMA in 2008, housing the renowned collection of local real estate magnate and philanthropist Eli Broad. As we went to press, he was busy at work on a new museum for his collection on Grand Ave in Downtown LA, scheduled for completion in 2012. Other unique venues include the Museum of Latin American Art in Long Beach and the Hammer Museum in West LA.

San Diego, too, has many fine museums, many within easy walking distance of each other inside Balboa Park, and its Little Italy neighborhood also boasts a growing number of galleries. In Orange County there's the Orange County Museum of Art in Costa Mesa; a growing art

Essential LA Music Radio Stations

» KCRW (89.9FM) – eclectic music mix.

» KROQ (106.7FM) – the latest contemporary rock.

» KRTH (101.1FM) – all-oldies soundtrack to an All-American stay.

» KOST (103.5FM) – soft rock and nightly lovesong requests.

» KTWV (94.7FM) – new age and smooth jazz.

scene in Santa Ana, home of the Bowers Museum; and the longstanding artist colony of Laguna Beach alongside its three-quarter-century-old Festival of Arts (p257), capped by the amazing Pageant of the Masters in which townspeople recreate paintings on stage.

Literature

Early 20th Century

Los Angeles sheltered many illustrious 20th-century writers, among them William Faulkner, F Scott Fitzgerald and Aldous Huxley. During WWII German writers Bertolt Brecht and Thomas Mann resided in LA, exiled from their war-torn homeland.

While much of the local writing talent always seems to be harnessed to the film industry – even Faulkner and Fitzgerald were in LA primarily to make a living by writing screenplays – LA provides an immense wealth of irresistible material to writers. Bookworms will find that novels about the city make for fascinating reading.

Los Angeles has been a favorite subject of novelists since the 1920s. Many have regarded LA in political terms, often viewing it unfavorably as the ultimate metaphor for capitalism. Classics in this vein include Upton Sinclair's *Oil!* (1927), a muckraking work of historical fiction with socialist overtones. Aldous Huxley's *After Many A Summer Dies the Swan* (1939) is a fine ironic work based on the life of publisher William Randolph Hearst (also an inspiration for Orson Welles' film *Citizen Kane*). F Scott Fitzgerald's final work, *The Last Tycoon* (1940), makes scathing observations about the early years of Hollywood by following the life of a 1930s movie producer who is slowly working himself to death.

LA literature is, rightly or wrongly, also associated with pulp fiction. Raymond Chandler is the genre's undisputed king. Start with *The Big Sleep* (1939) and after following Philip Marlowe, private eye, for one book, you may wind up reading all the others, too.

Late 20th Century

Because of the great proliferation of SoCal-based authors, this section will highlight titles that feature the region.

In 1964 English immigrant to LA Christopher Isherwood penned *A Single Man,* a landmark of LA (and gay) literature, made into a 2009 movie by Tom Ford. LA fiction's banner year was in 1970. Terry Southern's *Blue Movie* concerned the decadent side of Hollywood. Joan Didion's *Play It as It Lays* looked at Angelenos with a dry, not-too-kind wit. *Post Office,* by poet-novelist Charles Bukowski, captured the down-and-out side of Downtown. (Bukowski himself worked at Downtown's Terminal Annex.) *Chicano,* by Richard Vasquez, took a dramatic look at the Latino barrio of East LA.

The mid-1980s brought the startling revelations of Bret Easton Ellis' *Less Than Zero,* about the cocaine-addled lives of wealthy Beverly Hills teenagers. For a more comedic insight into LA during the go-go '80s, pick up Richard Rayner's *Los Angeles Without a Map* (1988), which

Nobody could break down into simpler terms the psychology of SoCal's culture of fads better than Dr Seuss (Theodor Geisel) in his story The Sneeches (1961). A collection of his works and drawings is in the library named for him at the University of California, San Diego.

Although Susan Sontag, the 'Dark Lady of American Letters,' lived much of her life in New York City, she spent her formative years in LA, and her much-sought-after papers are at UCLA.

MUSIC & THE ARTS LITERATURE

UCI

The writers program at the University of California Irvine, in central Orange County, is consistently rated as one of the top in the nation, producing dozens of leading American novelists including Michael Chabon *(The Amazing Adventures of Kavalier & Klay),* Richard Ford *(Independence Day),* Whitney Otto *(How to Make an American Quilt)* and Alice Sebold *(The Lovely Bones).*

follows a British man who gets lost in his Hollywood fantasies while chasing a Playboy bunny. Kate Braverman's *Palm Latitudes* (1988) traces the intersecting lives of a flamboyant prostitute, a murderous housewife and a worn-out matriarch who maintain their strength and dignity against the backdrop of the violence and machismo of LA's Mexican barrio.

Literary pulp fiction made a comeback in the 1990s. Walter Mosley's famed *Devil in a Blue Dress* (1990), set in Watts, places its hero in impossible situations that test his desire to remain an honest man. Elmore Leonard's *Get Shorty* follows a Florida loan shark who moves to SoCal and gets mixed up in the film industry. Both stories – like many of the genre – translated brilliantly into film.

Contemporary LA novelists to look for include for Aimee Bender whose acclaimed 2010 novel *The Particular Sadness of Lemon Cake* tells of a Westside teenager who tastes the emotions of the chefs who make food she eats. USC English professor T Coraghessan Boyle has written prolifically about the region in novels and short stories, including *The Tortilla Curtain* (1995). Michael Connelly is one heir to the region's crime novel tradition with the Hieronymus (Harry) Bosch series. Peter Lefcourt chronicles insider Hollywood in novels such as 2001's *The Deal,* while journalist Sam Quinones writes eloquently about the migrants and corruption in LA County's Mexican-American communities, in such works as *Antonio's Gun and Delfino's Dream* (2007). Last but not least are mother-and-daughter novelists Carolyn See (*There Will Never Be Another You,* 2006) and Lisa See. Lisa See's *Shanghai Girls* (2009) is set in LA's Chinatown in the 1950s, when anti-communist sentiment was prominent in American politics.

Outside LA

San Diego novelist Joseph Wambaugh draws on his own experience as a detective to craft crime-fiction novels such as *Floaters* (1996), which centers on the 1995 America's Cup race. Abigail Padgett, also from San Diego, writes engaging mysteries that weave together themes of Native American culture, mental illness and the SoCal desert. Sue Grafton, author of the Kinsey Millhone mystery series and the alphabet mystery series (*A is for Alibi* etc) sets her novels in Santa Barbara, though in the books it's called Santa Theresa.

To learn more about LA's literary scene, listen to the weekly 'Bookworm' program on Santa Monica-based radio station KCRW (88.9FM) or download it as a free podcast from www.kcrw. com.

Few writers nail SoCal's culture as well as Joan Didion. In *Where I Was From* (2003), she contrasts California's mythology and reality.

Notable Buildings & Architecture

SoCal may have a reputation for the urban sprawl by which all other sprawl is measured, but look closer and you'll discover – particularly in LA – one of the most architecturally dynamic regions in the world.

Spanish Mission & Victorian Styles

The first Spanish missions were built around courtyards, using materials the native Californians and padres found on hand: adobe, limestone and grass. The missions crumbled into disrepair as the church's influence waned, but the style remained practical for the climate. It was later adapted as the rancho adobe style, as seen at El Pueblo de Los Angeles, the Presidio in Santa Barbara, and in San Diego's Old Town.

During the late 19th century the upper class built grand mansions to keep up with East Coast fashion, which reflected popular design worldwide during the reign of the UK's Queen Victoria. One of the finest examples of Victorian whimsy is San Diego's Hotel del Coronado. San Diego's Gaslamp Quarter is also filled with smaller-scale Victorian buildings, as is the mountain hamlet of Julian.

With its more simple, classical lines, Spanish Colonial architecture – or mission revival, as it's also called – rejected the frilly Victorian style and hearkened back to the California missions with arched doors and windows, long covered porches, fountains, courtyards, solid walls and red-tile roofs. Spanish Colonial's heyday lasted from 1890 to 1915 and is the signature style of downtown Santa Barbara, while William Templeton Johnson and the young Irving Gill fortified this trend in San Diego. The train depots in LA (Union Station), San Juan Capistrano and San Diego (now part of the Museum of Contemporary Art) were built in this style. San Diego's Balboa Park also showcases some outstanding examples.

Craftsman & Art Deco

Charles and Henry Greene and Julia Morgan ushered in the Arts and Crafts (aka Craftsman) Movement of the early 20th century. Simplicity and harmony were key design principles in this movement, blending Asian, European and American influences in warm wooden interiors, typically in single-story bungalows. Overhanging eaves, terraces and

TIKI

Fans of tiki style will want to head to the Point Loma district of San Diego. Visiting hotels and restaurants on Shelter Island is like a trip to palmy Polynesia.

CHICKEN WIRE MUSEUMS?

Many of the buildings that now serve as stately Spanish-Colonial museums in San Diego's Balboa Park were originally built to last for the duration of big international exhibitions a century ago, using materials including stucco and chicken wire. Don't worry, though; these popular buildings were later rebuilt in more durable materials.

sleeping porches are transitions between, and extensions of, the house into its natural environment. Pasadena's Gamble House is one of the largest and most beautiful examples of this style. The Lodge at Torrey Pines in La Jolla is a massive, contemporary re-creation of this style.

By the early 1920s it became fashionable to copy earlier architectural periods. No style was off-limits: neoclassical, baroque, Moorish, Mayan, Aztec or Egyptian. Downtown LA's Richard J Riordan Central Library and the ziggurat-style roof of LA's City Hall are prime examples.

The Irvine Company, a private real estate firm, controls much of southern Orange County's architectural design. The predominant style is Tuscan.

Art deco also took off during the 1920s and '30s, with vertical lines and symmetry creating a soaring effect, often culminating in a stepped pattern toward the top. Heavy ornamentation, especially above doors and windows, featured floral motifs, sunbursts and zigzags. You can see it in the Eastern Columbia building (849 S Broadway, Los Angeles) in Downtown LA and the Sunset Tower Hotel in West Hollywood.

Streamline Moderne, a derivative of art deco, sought to incorporate the machine aesthetic, in particular the aerodynamic look of airplanes and ocean liners. Great examples of this style include the Coca-Cola Bottling Plant in Downtown LA, the Crossroads of the World building in Hollywood and the Shangri-La Hotel in Santa Monica.

Modernism

Also called 'International Style,' modernism was initiated in Europe by Bauhaus architects Walter Gropius, Ludwig Mies van der Rohe and Le Corbusier. Its characteristics include boxlike building shapes, open floor

---

DOWNTOWN LA'S GLAMOUR BUILDINGS

Don't leave Downtown without checking out some of these gems, mostly from the early 20th century.

Richard J Riordan Central Library (1922; 630 W 5th St) Bertram Goodhue, inspired by the discovery of King Tut's tomb, incorporated numerous Egyptian motifs in this library named for a former LA mayor. The Tom Bradley Wing is an eight-story glass atrium (four stories above ground, four below) added in 1993 and named for another former mayor.

US Bank Tower (633 W 5th St) The tallest building west of Chicago has 73 floors and juts 1017ft into the air. Designed by Henry Cobb, an architect from the New York firm of IM Pei, the US Bank Tower was attacked by an alien spaceship in the 1996 movie *Independence Day*. It's gone through many name changes, and some locals still call it the Library Tower.

One Bunker Hill (1931; 601 W 5th St) The reliefs above the entrance to this 12-story art deco Moderne office tower recall the building's former occupant, the Southern California Edison company, depicting energy, light and power. In the 40ft-high lobby are 17 types of marble, gold-leaf ceilings and a mural by Hugo Ballin, a set designer for Cecil B DeMille.

Millennium Biltmore Hotel (1923; 515 S Olive St) Dominating the Olive St side of Pershing Sq is one of LA's grandest and oldest hotels, designed by the team that also created New York's Waldorf-Astoria. It has hosted presidents, political conventions and eight Academy Awards ceremonies. The hotel's sumptuous interior boasts carved and gilded ceilings, marble floors, grand staircases and palatial ballrooms in styles ranging from Renaissance to Baroque to Neoclassical.

Oviatt Building (1928; 617 S Olive St) The 1928 Oviatt is an art deco gem conceived by the mildly eccentric James Oviatt, owner of the men's clothing store previously on the premises (now Cicada restaurant). Oviatt fell in love with art deco on a visit to Paris and had carpets, draperies and fixtures shipped over from France, including the purportedly largest shipment of etched decorative glass by René Lalique ever to cross the Atlantic.

Fine Arts Building (1927; 811 W 7th St) This 12-story Walker & Eisen structure is a visual feast inside and out. The facade is awash in floral and animal ornamentation; sculptures peer down from arcaded upstairs windows. The cathedral-like lobby is especially striking. Built in Spanish Renaissance style, it has a galleried mezzanine from which large sculptures representing the arts gaze down.

Among the most noteworthy buildings in LA in the last few years are several new educational institutions.

Robert F Kennedy Community Schools (2010; 3400 Wilshire Blvd) Civil rights leader and US Attorney General Robert F Kennedy was assassinated on this site in 1968, when it was the Ambassador Hotel. With the Kennedy family's approval, the hotel was mostly torn down to be made into a school. The exterior keeps the lines of the Ambassador and houses over 4200 students in seven separate schools (K–12) on 23 acres. The new building also has the distinction of being the city's most expensive school (some $578 million).

High School for the Visual and Performing Arts (2008; High School No 9; cnr N Grand Ave & W Cesar Chavez Blvd) The metal cladding on the exterior – by Austrian architecture firm Coop Himmelb(l)au – echoes the Walt Disney Concert Hall a few blocks away as if to inspire the students. Look for an (also inspirational) spiral ramp growing out of the main building and up toward the sky.

Southern California Institute of Architecture (2008; 960 E 3rd St) Gary Paige transformed the Santa Fe freight depot, in an unloved corner of Downtown LA, into the home base for SCI-Arc, one of the world's most avant-garde architecture schools. The building is as long as the Empire State Building is tall (around ¼ mile!), no doubt to inspire the next generation of school-builders.

plans, plain facades, abundant glass and, for residences, easy access between indoor and outdoor spaces. Austrian-born Rudolph Schindler and Richard Neutra brought early modernism to LA and Palm Springs, where Swiss-born Albert Frey also worked. Both Neutra and Schindler were influenced by Frank Lloyd Wright, who designed LA's Hollyhock House in a style he fancifully called 'California Romanza.' His son Lloyd Wright later followed in his footsteps, building the Wayfarer's Chapel atop the cliffs overlooking the Pacific in Palos Verdes.

Modernism has become the signature style of Palm Springs (see p338), but not so in the rest of the Coachella Valley, which feels more Spanish Colonial in style although it was mostly built later. But it's not just in Palm Springs that SoCal has begun to appreciate modernism: in 2010 the Los Angeles Conservancy launched a '60s turn 50' campaign, aimed at preserving the city's midcentury modern structures.

Postmodernism & Contemporary Architecture

Postmodernism was partly a response to the starkness of the International Style, and sought to re-emphasize the structural form of the building and the space around it. Richard Meier perfected and transcended the postmodernist vision at West LA's Getty Center (1997). The Cathedral of Our Lady of the Angels (2002), by José Rafael Moneo, echoes the plazas in front of churches in Mexico and Europe, albeit in poured-in-place concrete. LA-based Frank Gehry is known for his deconstructivist buildings with sculptural forms and distinctive facade materials like stainless steel. The sweeping curved exterior of his Walt Disney Concert Hall (2003) has become the emblem of the re-emergence of Downtown LA. Thom Mayne of LA's Morphosis firm has also made his mark with such avant-garde buildings as the Caltrans District 7 Headquarters. Both Gehry and Mayne are winners of the Pritzker Prize, the Oscars of architecture.

Long-term plans for Downtown LA call for a park and civic gathering space along Grand Ave, connecting the Music Center and City Hall with a master plan designed by Gehry.

When Walt Disney Concert Hall was first built, some of its stainless steel exterior panels reflected so brightly that neighbors' nearby apartments heated up, and the offending panels had to be sanded to dull the finish.

Flavors of SoCal

While Los Angeles is known for chichi, high-end restaurants run by celeb chefs, you don't have to drop a Benjamin just to eat well, especially with Little Tokyo and Thai Town just around the edible corner, for starters. Southern California's culinary scene is one of America's most diverse and cutting-edge. Many foodie trends have started in SoCal's coastal kitchens, from fusion sushi to Nuevo Latino fare. Best of all, the region's cuisine keeps redefining and refining itself – and the way the rest of America eats.

Trendy Menu Ingredients

» **Meyer lemon** Sweet local citrus

» **Heirloom tomatoes** In a rainbow of colors

» **Huitlacoche** Corn fungus, a traditional Mexican delicacy

» **Gem lettuces** Similar to butter lettuce

California Cookin'

The cardinal rule of California cuisine is that the ingredients should be extremely fresh, minimally processed and prepared so that the flavors speak for themselves. Locally grown and organic foods are increasingly used. Chefs generally rely on flavor-packed reduction sauces rather than fatty gravies. Apart from that, there are few rules, and influences may come from Europe, Asia and/or Latin America.

Californians adore culinary trends. Some crazes are silly and doomed to failure (eg chocolate pasta), others are good but overused (eg foams), while still others get integrated from foreign countries and become a popular part of the California repertoire. Perhaps no one has done as much to popularize California's healthy-minded, fusion-style cuisine nationwide as much as peripatetic Austrian-born chef Wolfgang Puck, who began his career as a celebrity restaurateur in Beverly Hills.

Apart from LA's mobile food truck revolution and hipster underground supper clubs, one of the hottest and most accessible trends these days is 'small plate' dining. That is, a group will order several appetizer-sized dishes of food, letting everyone at the table share. It's not unlike Spanish tapas, but in SoCal you're just as likely to find small-plate menus in French, Middle Eastern, Japanese and Chinese restaurants.

Starring Meryl Streep, the drama *Julie & Julia* (2009) in part dramatizes the real-life adventures of TV chef and French cookbook author extraordinaire Julia Child, who was born in Pasadena, an LA suburb.

It's All Fruits & Nuts, Honey

Make all the jokes you want about this being the land of fruits, nuts and flakes. It's true, and locals couldn't be prouder. You name it, Southern California grows it. Avocado, citrus, dates, berries and all manner of vegetables are just a sampling of the crops that flourish between Santa Barbara County and the Mexican border.

In salads, forget iceberg lettuce (although that too is grown here): a SoCal salad is likely to include endive, radicchio, arugula and other greens that won't pass your smartphone's spell-checker. Other classics: the Cobb salad (invented in Hollywood), the Caesar salad (invented in Tijuana, Mexico) and the Chinese chicken salad (popularized in LA during the health-conscious 1970s) – sliced Napa cabbage with slivered carrot, green onion, grilled chicken, toasted sesame seeds and a tangy soy-based dressing.

An Ominvore's Feast

You may associate SoCal with vegetarianism, but locals ardently love red meat too. Trendy new steakhouses are opening all the time, many proudly printing on the menu the names of local farms that supply grass-fed, free-range and hormone-free beef, pork, lamb, chicken, duck and even American heritage-breed turkeys. When it comes to comfort-food classics, downtown LA's Phillipe the Original claims to have invented the French-dip roast beef sandwich way back in 1908.

With hundreds of miles of coastline, fishing is not only a huge industry in SoCal, but also a popular sport. As you travel between Santa Barbara and San Diego, you'll often see halibut, rockfish, sablefish (black cod) and sand dabs on restaurant menus, much of it locally caught. (The most sustainable salmon is wild Alaskan, however.) A rare and pricey treat is farm-raised abalone, which has a delicate flavor and texture similar to squid.

Small World, Big Tastes

No less than Ruth Reichl, peripatetic Californian chef, food writer and former restaurant critic for the *Los Angeles Times,* has said that LA's real culinary treasure is its ethnic restaurants. With 140 nationalities in LA County alone, we can only scratch the surface, but the destination chapters will definitely get you started sniffing out the next great Korean BBQ truck, Japanese ramen shop or Persian ice-cream parlor.

You'll find Mexican restaurants on virtually any block, as well as Japanese places, though the latter are most concentrated in LA neighborhoods like downtown's Little Tokyo and Torrance, inland from the South Bay. LA's Chinatown and communities to its east in the San Gabriel Valley are the epicenter of Chinese cooking. LA's Koreatown and Orange County's Little Saigon are each the largest respective expat communities outside their home countries, while Anaheim's Little Arabia is tops for Muslim and Middle Eastern fare. San Diego has a thriving Little Italy too.

If you want to taste all of SoCal in just one place, downtown LA's Grand Central Market is stuffed with energetic vendors dishing up street food from around the globe, from two-bite Latin American *pupusas* (filled corn tortillas) and fresh-squeezed fruit *jugos* (juices) and *licuados* (smoothies) to Californicized fish tacos or Hawaiian BBQ.

SPANGLISH

FLAVORS OF SOCAL SMALL WORLD, BIG TASTES

In *Spanglish* (2004), Adam Sandler plays a chef in a top LA restaurant, who learns a thing or two about life from Flor, the family maid, played by Paz Vega. Top chef Thomas Keller, of Napa Valley's celebrated French Laundry restaurant, consulted on the food scenes.

GET SCHOOLED

Bring a taste of SoCal back to your table at home by checking out these cooking classes.

» **Balboa Food & Wine School** (☎619-557-9441; www.balboawinefood.com) Fun, fast cooking demonstrations and hands-on classes with San Diego chefs, plus wine and cheese tastings.

» **California Sushi Academy** (☎310-231-4499; www.sushi-academy.com) Apprentice in the art of finessing raw fish or sake tasting in LA.

» **Laguna Culinary Arts** (☎949-494-0745; www.lagunaculinaryarts.com) Gourmet home-chef classes and wine and cheese appreciation in Laguna Beach.

» **Montecito Country Kitchen** (☎805-965-5112; www.mckcuisine.com) Seasonal gourmet menus with global spices and epicurean wine country influences.

» **New School of Cooking** (☎310-842-9702; www.newschoolofcooking.com) Globally inspired classes built around a theme, technique, ingredient and/or country (eg Mexican tacos, Thai street food, Chinese wok cooking).

» **Roblar Winery Cooking School** (☎805-686-2603; www.roblarwinery.com) Cooking demos and wine-and-food-pairing classes in Santa Barbara's wine country.

FISH TACOS, SOCAL STYLE

San Diego may not have an official food, but the whole city obsesses over where to get the best fish tacos. The fish used can vary, but a firm variety like mahimahi works well. It's cut bite-sized, then seasoned and grilled, or – for 'Baja-style' tacos – battered and deep-fried. The cooked fish is placed inside a tortilla (purists say it must be made of corn) and drizzled in a creamy white sauce seasoned with jalapeño peppers, capers, cayenne pepper and other spices. On top of that goes shredded cabbage and fresh *pico de gallo* (chopped tomato, onion and chili) salsa. Squeeze a little lime, take a bite. It's addictive.

Andrew Bender & Sara Benson

Mexican

Mexican food is iconic here, and not exclusively among people of Latino heritage. Until you've sampled *carnitas* (braised pork), *al pastor* (marinated and grilled pork) or San Diego–style fish tacos washed down with a cold beer or a margarita, you haven't experienced SoCal culture.

Virtually any Cal-Mex lunch or dinner starts with tortillas (flatbread made of wheat or corn flour). Small ones are wrapped around grilled or roasted meat, cheeses and vegetables and called tacos; larger, rolled versions are enchiladas (traditionally pan-fried and covered in sauce then baked), while burritos are huge tortillas, stuffed with the same, well, stuff, plus rice and beans. Rather than slushy bottled brands, local salsa is a finely diced mix of fresh tomatoes, onions, cilantro and jalapeño peppers.

The original chopped Cobb salad – romaine lettuce, tomatoes, avocado, chicken breast, blue cheese, watercress, chives, a hard-boiled egg and old-fashioned French dressing – was invented in 1937 by Bob Cobb, owner of the Brown Derby restaurant in Hollywood.

Japanese

Angelenos were enthusiastically chowing down sushi and sashimi when most of America still considered it foreign fare not to be trusted. The quickest way to start a hot debate in LA? Ask locals who they think the city's best sushi-bar chef is.

SoCal's Japanese food scene goes far beyond raw piscine treats. Many a good meal starts with *edamame* (boiled soybeans in the pod) and continues with *yakitori* (grilled skewers of chicken or vegetables), tempura (lightly battered and fried vegetables or fish) and an endless variety of artful hot and cold appetizers, most often shared by groups of friends at an *izakaya* (gastropub).

Other Japanese restaurants might specialize in just one dish, such as ramen (noodle soup), cook-it-yourself *sukiyaki* and *shabu-shabu* hot pots, or *okonomiyaki* – vegetable, seafood and pork-filled pancakes topped with a savory, barbecue-like sauce, Japanese mayonnaise and crispy seaweed flakes.

Jonathan Gold, restaurant critic for the *LA Weekly*, won the Pulitzer Prize for criticism in 2007, the first time a restaurant critic won this award. To find out where Gold is eating these days, pick up the free alternative tabloid anywhere around town, or visit www.laweekly.com.

Chinese

Sure, you'll find familiar favorites like *kung pao* this and American-born General Tso's that. But if you can, gobble up Cantonese dim sum. A small army of servers stroll around cavernous rooms for hundreds of diners filled with circular tables, pushing carts loaded with dumplings like *har gao* (shrimp) and *shu mai* (pork). Regional cuisines, such as Hunan and Szechuan, abound, especially around LA.

Korean

The signature dish is beef ribs *(kalbi)*, marinated in soy, sesame oil, rice wine and garlic, then grilled at your table – vents above each table whisk away the smoke. *Bibimbap* is a large bowl of mixed Korean vegetables, sliced meat (usually beef) and a fried egg topped with hot chili sauce over a mini mountain of rice. All of these are served with a variety of healthy side dishes including *kimchi* (spicy pickled cabbage).

Vietnamese

Vietnam's national dish is *pho* (pronounced 'fuh'): white rice noodles in clear beef broth, topped with sliced meat (usually beef) and served with a plate of bean sprouts and Asian basil, which you add into the soup along with chili, bean or hoisin sauce and maybe some fresh-squeezed lime juice.

Thirsty for More?

Hanging on the Grapevine

Californians love wine. In fact, each year California bottles more than 563 million gallons of wine. That's enough to fill over 850 Olympic-sized swimming pools!

Excellent wines are produced up and down the length of the Golden State, but the largest SoCal growing regions are Santa Barbara County (known for pinot noirs and Rhône-style wines like syrah, mourvedre and viognier) and upstart Temecula, a wild West frontier town on the edge of the desert outside San Diego.

Many of the newest winemakers are implementing their passion for the vine in earth-conscious ways, using organic practices and biodynamic farming techniques while enthusiastically sharing their knowledge in intimate tasting rooms.

Cool Cocktails & Masterful Microbrews

The margarita (traditionally made with tequila, triple sec and lemon or lime juice, either frozen and blended or served straight-up 'on the rocks' with ice) is the drink of choice with Mexican cuisine. Go ahead, splurge on higher-grade tequilas – they say it will help avoid hangovers!

Many species of seafood are being overfished, some to the point of extinction. This is doubly true for what's being dished up at many sushi bars. To find out what's good to eat (and what's not), check the Monterey Bay Aquarium's **Seafood Watch List** (www.mbayaq.org/cr/seafoodwatch.aspx), available as a free iPhone app or printable pocket guides.

TOP 10 FOOD & WINE EVENTS

» **American Wine & Food Festival** (www.awff.org) LA's glam foodie fundraiser on the beach and Universal Studios' backlot in July and September.

» **California Avocado Festival** (www.avofest.com) Curious to see the world's largest vat of guacamole? Come to Carpinteria in October.

» **California Strawberry Festival** (www.strawberry-fest.org) Oxnard's family-fun festival features recipe cook-offs and chefs' demos in May.

» **dineLA Restaurant Week** (http://dinela.com) Take advantage of bargain-priced multicourse menus from some of LA's hottest chefs in October.

» **LA Street Food Festival** (http://lastreetfoodfest.com) Let the food trucks come to you at Pasadena's Rose Bowl in July.

» **Little Italy Festa** (www.littleitalysd.com) Over 100,000 hungry folks turn out for San Diego's Italian cultural celebration in October.

» **National Date Festival** (www.datefest.org) Save the date (get it?) for Indio's February celebration of its prime local product – with camel races!

» **San Diego Bay Wine & Food Festival** (www.worldofwineevents.com) Winemakers' tastings and dinners and top chefs' classes and competitions in November.

» **Santa Barbara Vintners' & Harvest Festival Weekends** (www.sbcountywines.com) SoCal's premier wine country hosts weekend bashes in April and October.

» **Taste of Newport** (www.tasteofnewport.com) This flashy food-and-wine fest shows off Orange County's best chefs, winemakers and brewmasters in September.

FLAVORS OF SOCAL GREEN GRAZING

LEGEND OF TWO-BUCK CHUCK

When Southern Californians say 'TJ,' they're talking about Tijuana, Mexico. But when they say 'TJ's,' they mean beloved **Trader Joe's** (☎800-746-7857; http://traderjoes. com). Many locals count this bargain-priced, global-cuisine market as one of life's essentials, alongside sunshine and the beach. TJ's, which started life in Pasadena in 1967, offers an amazing, budget-priced selection of great California wines, too. For informal gatherings, college students and penny-pinching artists swear by 'Two-buck Chuck', the nickname for Charles Shaw private-brand wines sold at Trader Joe's supermarkets. Chuck's varietal wines cost an unbelievably cheap $1.99 per bottle, but they've won numerous awards in wine competitions. Believe it, dude – the check-out staff in Hawaiian shirts wouldn't lie to you, would they?

SIDEWAYS

The outlandish film *Sideways* (2004) captures the folly and passion of California's wine snobbery. Pinot noir, a highly sensitive grape, becomes a metaphor for the beleaguered, middle-aged main character, Miles, brilliantly played by Paul Giamatti.

The last decade or so saw a big comeback of 1950s-style martini bars. Using vodka instead of the traditional gin allowed for such wacky deviations as lemon- and chocolate-flavored martinis that would make the Rat Pack wince. Retro-licious Palm Springs in particular adores martini culture.

Beer drinkers should seek out SoCal's burgeoning microbreweries, especially in coastal beach towns. Brewpubs usually serve good grub too.

But Wait, There's More!

No alcohol? No problem. Try the following refreshers instead.

» A treat that originated in Asian neighborhoods but can now be found in almost every SoCal strip mall is boba tea, sweetened milk tea with tapioca 'pearls' at the bottom, sipped through a super-thick straw.

» Cool fruit smoothies are another SoCal staple: fresh fruit blended with ice, frozen yogurt, sorbet, vitamins or 'energy boosters' and other (mostly) healthful goodies.

» For strong coffee and espresso drinks, locals swear by LA-based chain Coffee Bean & Tea Leaf, which opened in 1963. It also invented the frozen ice coffee blended drink, now SoCal's summertime standard for re-javanation.

Green Grazing

California cuisine is all about being local, organic and seasonal, so eating green like a slow-food-loving 'locavore' isn't a tall order. Certified farmers markets abound, as do natural and organic food stores. Many top chefs make a point of using organic produce whenever possible and only order fish, seafood or meat that's from local, sustainable sources. Bottled water shipped over from Fiji or France? No thank you, filtered tap will be fine (and cheaper). SoCal is also so vegetarian friendly that it's almost a cliché. While strictly vegetarian, vegan or raw-food restaurants are rare outside bigger cities, almost every restaurant offers at least a few vegetarian choices.

Farmers Markets

Cities throughout the Southland have farmers markets on select days of the week, where farmers and small artisanal producers of foods such as honey and cheese come to sell their best, often trucking it in themselves from the growing fields. Prices are higher than at supermarkets, but quality is excellent and much of what's on offer is organic. Most vendors offer free samples too. Keep an eye out for specialty items that are available only seasonally. Some farmers markets also kick off with live entertainment and appearances by star local chefs.

Wild Things

Much of Southern California's coast has a Mediterranean climate, meaning warm, dry summers and mild, wet winters. That makes it a haven for diverse plants and animals, from hillsides covered in golden poppies to majestic migratory gray whales and monarch butterflies. Keep your peepers open and you'll be surprised just how many critters call Southern California home, even as built up and congested as much of it is.

Animals

Marine Superstars

When it comes to superstar wildlife in SoCal, think big. School-bus big. Although they don't exactly have a permanent LA address, giant gray whales make cameo appearances every year between December and April. That's when they migrate along the Pacific coast, traveling from their summertime feeding grounds in the arctic Bering Sea, across to the southern breeding grounds off Baja California – and then all the way back again. Pregnant gray whales give birth to calves weighing up to 1500lb; if lucky, those newborn whales will live up to 60 years, some growing up to 50ft long and weighing as much as 40 tons.

You can occasionally see migrating whales spout and breach from SoCal's shoreline viewing spots, such as San Diego's Point Loma or Point Vicente on LA's Palos Verdes Peninsula. Better yet, head out to meet the cetaceans on their own by going on a whale-watching tour; see p44.

Year-round, you may spy pods of bottlenose dolphins and porpoises swimming and doing acrobatics in the ocean. Playful sea otters and harbor seals typically stick closer to shore, especially around public piers and protected bays. To see pinnipeds, such as barking sea lions and elephant seals, in the wild rather than at SeaWorld, take time to visit Channel Islands National Park.

Feathered Friends

Out on a boat, or just standing on the beach, you'll spot plenty of winged creatures, including hefty pelicans darting for lunch like top-gun pilots, and skinny sandpipers foraging for invertebrates in the wet sand.

SoCal is an essential stop on the migratory Pacific Flyway between Alaska and Mexico. Almost half the bird species in North America use coastal and inland refuges for rest and refueling, peaking during the wetter winter season. Grab a pair of binoculars and scan the skies for avocets, green-winged teals, northern pintails and more.

Some beaches may be closed between March and September to protect endangered western snowy plovers, who lay their eggs in exposed

---

SoCal for the Birds

» Ballona Wetlands

» Bolsa Chica State Ecological Reserve

» Malibu Lagoon State Beach

» Sonny Bono Salton Sea National Wildlife Refuge

» San Elijo Lagoon

» Upper Newport Bay Nature Preserve

The California condor is the largest flying bird in North America. In 1987 there were only two dozen or so birds left in the wild. Today, thanks to captive breeding and release programs, there are about 275.

SEX ON THE BEACH

It's raw, primal, juicy and has thousands of participants. Drawn by the sensuality of the full or new moon, countless writhing bodies hit the beaches of Southern California every summer, drawing gaping crowds of voyeurs. But lest you think this annual beachside orgy involves the gyrations of nubile teens, let it be known that we're talking about a phenomenon known as the 'running of the grunions.' These flagrant sexual champions are in fact...fish.

Grunions are somehow drawn to the warmth of Southern California, and for the very best of reasons. It's along these local beaches that 'scouts' from the endless offshore schools swim up to check out the conditions. If these are favorable, they send the 'all clear' signal whereupon the grunion minions begin to thrash upon the water's edge. The females half bury themselves tail-first in the sand and within moments have deposited their eggs. Then come multiple worthy male suitors to fertilize them to assure the next dynasty of grunion-hood.

The website http://grunion.org has more information, updates and locations where the grunions are expected to show up, mostly between March and August. First-timers can join the hugely popular grunion watches organized by LA's Cabrillo Marine Aquarium in San Pedro. And no, the grunions don't mind if you watch. All you need is a flashlight, bare feet and a sense of demure decency. Even fish deserve their 'private moments.'

ground scrapes in the sand. Give these easily frightened birds plenty of space, as the presence of humans – and especially dogs – can cause them to fatally abandon their young.

Also keep an eye out for the regal bald eagle, which soared off the endangered species list in 2007. These birds of prey have regained a foothold on the Channel Islands, and some spend their winters at Big Bear Lake.

The Audubon Society's California chapter website (http://ca.audubon.org) has birding checklists and a newsy blog.

Kings of the Mountains

Mountain lions – also called cougars or pumas – inhabit forests and mountains throughout SoCal, especially in areas teeming with deer. Reaching up to 8ft in length and weighing as much as 175lb, this solitary animal is a formidable predator. Only a few attacks on humans have occurred, mostly where encroachment has pushed hungry lions to their limits – for example, at the borders of wild lands and rapidly developing suburbs.

Although an estimated 25,000 to 30,000 black bears roam around California, the possibilities of close encounters with bears in the southern part of the state are extremely unlikely, and limited to the San Gabriel Mountains and the San Bernardino Mountains east of LA. The only place you'll possibly see a grizzly bear these days is on the state flag, as this species was extirpated from California during the early 1900s.

Wildlife-Watching Hot Spots

» Channel Islands National Park
» Death Valley National Park
» Los Padres National Forest
» Mt San Jacinto Wilderness State Park
» Santa Monica Mountains

Desert Critters

The desert is far from deserted, but most critters are too smart to hang out in the daytime heat, coming out only at night like bats do. Roadrunners, those black-and-white mottled ground cuckoos with long tails and punk-style mohawks, can often be spotted on the side of the road. Other desert inhabitants include burrowing kit foxes, tree-climbing grey foxes, hoppity-hopping jackrabbits and kangaroo rats, slow-moving desert tortoises and a variety of snakes, lizards and spiders. Desert bighorn sheep and myriad birds flock to watering holes to SoCal's native fan-palm oases.

Plants

Going Native

You've seen them on film, you've seen them on TV. Those swaying palm trees with trunks as slender as a giraffe's neck that are so evocative of Southern California. Well, those guys are like most locals: they're not really from here. In fact, the only native species is the fan palm, found naturally in southern desert oases.

Oak trees are a different story. California has 20 native species of oak. Live, or evergreen, oaks with hollylike leaves and scaly acorns, especially thrive. You'll traipse past them while exploring the Santa Monica Mountains and other coastal ranges. Other common plants include the aromatic California bay laurel, whose long slender leaves turn purple, and manzanita shrubs with intensely red bark and small berries.

Rarer Beauties

The Torrey pine is a gnarly tree that has adapted to sparse rainfall and sandy, stony soils. It only grows at Torrey Pines State Reserve near San Diego and on Santa Rosa Island, part of Channel Islands National Park, which is home to dozens more endemic plant species. The same is true of Catalina Island, where you'll find the Catalina ironwood, Catalina mahogany, Catalina bedstraw and Catalina live-forever (a succulent), all displayed at the Wrigley Memorial & Botanical Gardens.

Except for the deserts and alpine mountain ranges, the hills of Southern California turn green in winter, not summer. As soon as winter rains arrive, dried-out brown grasses spring to life. As early as February, wildflowers pop up, notably the bright-orange California poppy, the state flower, which blooms through May. Resist the temptation to pick one – it's illegal ($500 fine) and besides, they wilt almost instantly when plucked from the ground. In the mountains, purple wild irises flower until June.

AN AUDIENCE WITH A MONARCH

Monarch butterflies are delicate-looking orange creatures that follow remarkable migration patterns and – like many MidWesterners and Canadians – prefer to spend their winters in California and Mexico. Although many hang out on the Monterey and San Luis Obispo County coasts further north, the more intrepid make it all the way to Southern California and beyond. Walt Sakai, biology professor at Santa Monica College and a recognized authority on monarch butterflies, shares with us his favorite local viewing spots:

» SoCal's premier site is **Ellwood Main** in Gaviota, west of Santa Barbara. From Hwy 101, take the Storke exit south, turn right on Hollister Ave and left on Coronado. At the end of the road, walk into the gully and turn right towards a clearing. After Thanksgiving, in late November and early December, is the best time to see the butterflies.

» In Ventura, a good spot is **Camino Real Park** in December and January. Look for monarchs in the eucalyptus grove above the creek near the tennis courts, upstream and north of Telegraph Rd. Access is via the church parking lot and up the drainage. From Hwy 101, go north on Victoria Ave, left on Telegraph Rd, left on S Bryn Mawr St and right on Aurora Dr.

» In the Santa Monica Mountains, **Big Sycamore Canyon** in Point Mugu State Park also plays host to the butterflies, especially in sycamore trees by the hike-and-bike camping area. October is the best month to see them – they're often gone by mid-November.

Cacti & Their Cousins

Nothing says desert more than a cactus. Cacti and other desert plants have adapted to SoCal's arid climate with thin, spiny leaves that resist moisture loss (and deter grazing animals), and seed and flowering mechanisms that kick into gear during brief rains. Wildflowers bloom spectacularly in spring (roughly, from February through April), carpeting valleys and drawing thousands of onlookers and shutterbugs.

The sheer variety of cacti found here is astonishing. Among the most common and easy to identify is cholla, which appears so furry that it's nicknamed 'teddy-bear cactus.' But beware, it's far from cuddly and instead will bury extremely sharp, barbed spines in your skin at the slightest touch. In spring, it boasts bright, yellowish flowers. Also watch out for catclaw acacia, nicknamed 'wait-a-minute bush' because its small, sharp, hooked thorny spikes can snatch your clothing or skin as you brush past.

Almost as widespread is prickly pear, a flat, fleshy-padded cacti that produces showy flowers in shades of red, yellow and purple, and whose juice is traditionally used as medicine by Native Americans. Then there's the cactuslike creosote (actually a small evergreen bush with a distinctive smell) and the spiky ocotillo, which grows up to 20ft tall and has canelike branches that produce blood-red flowers.

Like figments from a Dr Seuss book, whimsical Joshua trees are the largest type of yucca and are related to agave plants. Their heavy, creamy greenish-white flowers erupt in spring. They were named by migrant Mormons, who thought the crooked branches resembled the outstretched arms of a biblical prophet. These iconic trees grow throughout the Mojave Desert, although their habitat and long-term survival is seriously threatened by global warming.

A colorful photographic survey of over 2250 of Southern California's varied wildflowers, from desert cactus species to alpine blooms, can be found at www.calflora.net/bloomingplants/.

Survival Guide

Directory A-Z

Accommodations

Amenities

» Our budget-conscious recommendations include campgrounds, hostels and motels, but because mid-range properties generally offer better value for money, most of our accommodations fall into this category.

» At midrange motels and hotels, expect clean, comfortable and decent-sized double rooms with at least a private bathroom and standard amenities such as cable TV, direct-dial telephone, a coffeemaker, perhaps a microwave and mini fridge.

» Top-end lodgings offer top-notch amenities and perhaps a scenic location, edgy decor or historical ambience. Pools, fitness rooms, business centers, full-service restaurants and bars and other convenient facilities are all standard.

» Where an indoor or outdoor pool is available, the swimming icon ☒ appears with the review.

» Air-conditioning is a standard amenity except at some beachfront properties, where only fans may be provided.

» Accommodations offering online computer terminals for guests are designated with the internet icon (@). A fee may apply (eg at full-service business centers inside hotels).

» When wireless internet access is offered, the wi-fi icon (🛜) appears. There may be a fee, especially for daily in-room access. Look for free wi-fi hot spots in hotel public areas (eg lobby, poolside).

Seasons & Reservations

» Rates listed in this book are for high season: June to August everywhere, except the deserts and mountain ski areas, where December to March are the busiest months.

» Demand and prices also spike around major holidays (p459) and festivals (p26), when some properties may impose multiday minimum stays.

» Reservations are recommended for weekend and holiday travel year-round, and any day of the week in high season.

» If you walk up without reservations, request to see a room before paying for it, especially at motels.

» By law, all modern motels and hotels must have at least one ADA-compliant room (see p460); always specify your needs when making reservations.

Rates & Discounts

» This book lists accommodations in order of author recommendation. Rates are categorized as $ (under $120), $$ ($120 to $250) or $$$ (over $250). Unless noted, rates do not include taxes.

» Rates quoted in this book do not – and in fact cannot – take into account seasonal variations or promotional deals. Always ask about discounts.

» Generally, midweek rates are lower except in city hotels geared to business travelers, which lure leisure travelers with weekend deals.

» Discount cards (p455) may get you 10% or more off standard rates at participating properties.

» Bargaining may be possible for walk-in guests without reservations, especially during off-peak times.

Smoking

» Smoking rooms are increasingly rare in health-conscious SoCal.

BOOK YOUR STAY ONLINE

For more accommodation reviews by Lonely Planet authors, check out hotels.lonelyplanet.com/california. You'll find independent reviews, as well as recommendations on the best places to stay. Best of all, you can book online.

PRACTICALITIES

» **Electricity** 110/120V AC, 50/60Hz

» **Newspapers** Major dailies: center-left *Los Angeles Times* (www.latimes.com), conservative *San Diego Union-Tribune* (www.signonsandiego.com), right-leaning *Orange County Register* (www.ocregister.com); alternative tabloids: *LA Weekly* (www.laweekly.com), *San Diego Reader* (www.sandiegoreader.com), *OC Weekly* (www.ocweekly.com)

» **Radio** National Public Radio (NPR), lower end of FM dial

» **TV** PBS (public broadcasting); cable: CNN (news), ESPN (sports), HBO (movies), Weather Channel

» **Video** NTSC standard (incompatible with PAL or SECAM); DVDs coded region 1 (USA & Canada only)

» **Weights & Measures** Imperial

» Where smoking rooms exist, they're often in less desirable locations or are the last to be renovated.

» Be careful: some motels and hotels levy a hefty 'cleaning fee' if you light up in a nonsmoking room.

» Some hotels are entirely smokefree, meaning you're not allowed to smoke anywhere on the property, or even outside within a certain distance of entryways.

B&Bs

Bed-and-breakfast lodgings are usually high-end accommodations in converted private homes, typically lovely old Victorians or other heritage buildings. Travelers in need of a fair amount of privacy may find B&Bs too intimate.

Rates often include a home-cooked breakfast. Amenities vary widely, but rooms with TV and telephone are the exception; the cheapest units share bathroom facilities. Standards are high at places certified by the **California Association of Bed & Breakfast Inns** (www.cabbi.com).

Most B&Bs require advance reservations, though some will accommodate the occasional drop-in guest. Smoking is generally prohibited and minimum stays are common in high season and on weekends.

Camping

Camping in Southern California is a lot more than just a cheap way to spend the night. The best campsites have you waking up to ocean views, awesome rock formations or a canopy of pines. Many campgrounds are open year-round, and the most popular ones (eg near the beach) fill up in peak season, so make reservations or arrive early.

Basic campsites with fire pits, picnic benches and access to drinking water and pit toilets are common in national forests and on Bureau of Land Management (BLM) land. Campgrounds in state and national parks usually have flush toilets, sometimes hot showers and RV (recreational vehicle) hookups. Private campgrounds are often located close to towns and cater more to the RV crowd.

Many public campgrounds accept reservations for all or some of their sites through one or both of the following agencies:

National Recreation Reservation Service (NRSS; ☎877-444-6777, outside the US 518-885-3639; www.recreation.gov; campsites $10-25) Camping reservations in national parks, national forests (USFS) and other federal recreation lands (eg BLM).

Reserve America (☎800-444-7275, outside the US 916-638-5883; www.reserveamerica.com; campsites $10-70, cabins $40-100) For those California state park campgrounds and cabins that accept reservations.

Hostels

SoCal has five hostels affiliated with **Hostelling International USA** (HI-USA; ☎301-495-1240; www.hiusa.org). There are two each in San Diego and LA, and one in Fullerton near Disneyland. Dorms in HI hostels are typically gender-segregated and alcohol and smoking are prohibited. HI-USA membership cards ($28 per year for over-18s) entitle you to $3 off per night.

Indie hostels are most common in Hollywood, Venice and San Diego. They're generally more convivial with guest parties and other events. Some include a light breakfast in their rates, arrange local tours or pick up guests at transportation hubs. No two hostels are alike but typical facilities include communal kitchens, lockers, internet access, laundry and TV lounges.

Besides dorms (usually mixed) of varying sizes, many indie hostels have pricier private rooms, although bathrooms are usually shared. Some hostels say they accept only international

GOING GREEN

Many hotels in Southern California have not yet jumped on the environmental bandwagon. Apart from offering you the option of reusing your towels and sheets, even such simple eco-initiatives as switching to bulk soap dispensers or replacing plastic and Styrofoam cups and dropping prepackaged items from the breakfast buffet are still pretty rare.

More committed hotels recycle food and other waste, and some put green-colored recycling baskets in guestrooms. A few hotels loan guests bicycles for free or a small fee. You can help raise awareness among hotel staff by thanking them for any eco-friendly programs they offer; if they don't have any, encourage the manager to do so and offer a few constructive hints.

The **California Green Lodging Program** (www.calrecycle.ca.gov/epp/greenlodging/) is a voluntary state-run certification program; look for properties that have achieved the 'Leadership Level,' denoted by two palm trees.

Business Hours

Unless otherwise noted with reviews, standard opening hours for listings in this guide are as follows:

Banks 9am-5pm Mon-Fri, some 9am-1:30pm Sat

Bars 5am-2am daily

Business hours (general) 9am-5pm Mon-Fri

Post offices 8:30am-4:30pm Mon-Fri, some 9am-noon Sat

Restaurants 7:30am-10:30am, 11:30am-2:30pm & 5:30-10pm daily

Shops 10am-6pm Mon-Sat, noon-5pm Sun (malls open later)

Supermarkets 8am-9pm daily

Courses

For wine and cooking classes, see p443.

Silverlake Conservatory of Music (☎323-665-3363; www.silverlakeconservatory. com; 3920 Sunset Blvd, Los Angeles) Flea's music school offers affordable, professional private lessons for every instrument imaginable, and tremendous two-week summer sessions for kids.

New York Film Academy (☎818-733-2600; www.nyfa. com; 3801 Barham Blvd, Los Angeles) NYFA's West Coast branch is located on the Universal Studios lot. Learn about acting, filmmaking, screenwriting, and music videos in full programs or workshops lasting from one to 12 weeks. Courses start at $1375.

Robert McKee's Story Seminar (☎888-676-2533; www.mckeestory.com) Even seasoned writers come to pick up tips and inspiration from McKee's three-day seminar featured in the movie *Adaptation*. Former students include the screenwriters of *A Beautiful Mind*

visitors (basically to keep out homeless locals), but Americans who look like travelers (eg you're in possession of an international plane ticket) may be admitted, especially during slow periods.

Dorm-bed rates range from $14 to $40, including tax. Most hostels take bookings online or over the phone. Many indie hostels belong to reservation services like www.hostels.com, www.hostelz.com and www.hostelworld.com, which sometimes offer lower rates than the hostels directly.

Hotels & Motels

Hotel and motel rooms are often priced by the size and number of beds in a room, rather than the number of occupants. A room with one double or queen-size bed usually costs the same for one or two people, while a room with a king-size bed or two double beds costs more. 'Suites' may simply be oversized rooms, not necessarily two separate rooms; ask when booking.

Rooms with two double beds can accommodate up to four people, making them a cost-saving choice for families and small groups. A small surcharge often applies to the third and fourth person, but children under a certain age limit may stay free. Cribs or rollaway beds usually incur an extra charge.

The room location may also affect the price. Recently renovated or larger rooms, or those with a view, are likely to cost more. Beware that descriptors like 'oceanfront' and 'oceanview' are liberally used, and may require a periscope to spot the surf.

Rates may include breakfast, which could be just a stale donut and wimpy coffee, an all-you-can-eat buffet with hot and cold comfort-food favorites, or anything in between.

You can make reservations at chains by calling their central reservation lines, but to learn about specific amenities and local promotions, call the property directly. Every review in this book includes local direct numbers.

and *Lord of the Rings*. Offered in LA several times a year for $745.

Upright Citizens Brigade (☎323-908-8702; http://losangeles.ucbtheatre.com; 5919 Franklin Ave, Los Angeles) Learn the improv basics, the famed Harold structure, or delve into sketch writing during eight three-hour classes at Amy Pohler's improv theater founded in NYC. Alumni have gone on to write for the *Daily Show,* Conan O'Brien and *The Office* (US version). Tuition from $350.

Customs Regulations

Currently, non-US citizens and permanent residents may import:

» 1L of alcohol (if you're over 21 years old)
» 200 cigarettes (one carton) or 50 (non-Cuban) cigars (if you're over 18)
» $100 worth of gifts.

Amounts higher than $10,000 in cash, traveler's checks, money orders and other cash equivalents must be declared. Don't even think about bringing in illegal drugs.
    For more complete, up-to-date information, check with **US Customs and Border Protection** (www.cbp.gov).

Discount Cards

For discounts for children, see p53.

American Association of Retired Persons (☎800-566-0242; www.aarp.org; $13) Advocacy group for Americans 50 years and older offers member discounts (usually 10%) on hotels, car rentals and more.

American Automobile Association (AAA; ☎877-428-2277; www.aaa.com; annual membership from $47) Members of AAA and its foreign affiliates (eg CAA) qualify for small discounts (usually

10%) on Amtrak trains, car rentals, motels and hotels, chain restaurants, shopping, tours and theme parks.

Go Los Angeles Card (one-day pass adult/child $60/50) and **Go San Diego Card** ($69/58) Both include admission to major SoCal theme parks (but not Disney); for the best deals, buy them online in advance at www.smartdestinations.com.

International Student Identity Card (ISIC; www.isic.org; $22) Offers savings on airline fares, travel insurance and local attractions for full-time students.

International Youth Travel Card (IYTC; $22) For non-students under 26 years of age, this card grants similar benefits to the ISIC. Both cards are issued by student unions, hostelling organizations and youth-oriented travel agencies.

Senior Discounts People over the age of 65 (sometimes 55, 60 or 62) often qualify for the same discounts as students; any ID showing your birthdate should suffice as proof.

Southern California CityPass (www.citypass.com) If you're visiting SoCal theme parks, the CityPass costs from $269 (child aged three to nine $229). It covers three-day admission to Disneyland and Disney's California Adventure and one-day admission each to Universal Studios and SeaWorld, with another day at either the San Diego Zoo or the San Diego Zoo Safari Park. Passes are valid for 14 days from the day of the first use and may be purchased online or at any of the attractions.

Student Advantage Card (☎877-256-4672; www.studentadvantage.com; $23) For international and US students, it offers 15% savings on Amtrak and Greyhound, plus discounts of 10% to 20% on some airlines, chain shops, hotels and motels.

Electricity

120V/60Hz

120V/60Hz

Gay & Lesbian Travelers

SoCal is a magnet for LGBT travelers, with the hot spots West Hollywood (WeHo), Silver Lake and Long Beach around Los Angeles, the

Hillcrest quarter of San Diego and the desert resort of Palm Springs. The scene can be predominantly male-oriented, although lesbians won't feel left out. See p115 for an overview of gay and lesbian LA, p289 for San Diego and p347 for Palm Springs.

California offers gays and lesbians extensive domestic rights but currently stops short of the legalization of gay marriage and civil unions. Southern Californians tend to be tolerant, but bigotry has not been completely rooted out and there have been bashings even in metro areas.

Helpful Resources

Damron (www.damron.com) Classic, advertiser-driven international gay travel guides, including *Men's Travel Guide, Women's Traveller* and *Accommodations;* digital editions and a US-based 'Gay Scout' iPhone app available.

Gay.com (http://daily.gay .com/travel/) City guides, blog-style travel news and Pride events coverage.

Gay & Lesbian National Hotline (☎888-843-4564; www.glnh.org; ☉1-9pm Mon-Fri, 9am-2pm Sat) For counseling and referrals of any kind.

Gay & Lesbian Yellow Pages (www.glyp.com) Includes ads for restaurants, bars and clubs.

Gay Travelocity (www .travelocity.com/gaytravel) LGBT travel articles and hotel, guided tour and activity bookings.

Out Traveler (www.outtravel er.com) Free online magazine, trip planner, destination guides and e-newsletter.

Purple Roofs (www .purpleroofs.com) Online directory of LGBT accommodations.

Southern California Pride Guide (www.southern californiaprideguide.com) Free downloadable travel information.

Health

Healthcare & Insurance

» Many health-care professionals demand payment at the time of service, especially from out-of-towners. Except for medical emergencies (in which case call ☎911 or go to the nearest 24-hour hospital emergency room, or ER), phone around to find a doctor who will accept your insurance.

» Keep all receipts and documentation. Some insurance policies require you to get pre-authorization for medical treatment before seeking help. Overseas visitors with travel health-insurance policies may need to contact a call center for an over-the-phone assessment before getting medical treatment.

Dehydration, Heat Exhaustion & Heatstroke

» Take it easy as you acclimatize to SoCal's high temperatures. Always drink plenty of water. One gallon per person per day minimum is recommended when you're active outdoors.

» Dehydration (lack of water) or salt deficiency can cause heat exhaustion, often characterized by heavy sweating, fatigue, lethargy, headaches, nausea, vomiting, dizziness and muscle cramps.

» Long, continuous exposure to high temperatures can lead to possibly fatal heatstroke, when body temperature rises to dangerous levels. Warning signs include altered mental status, hyperventilation and flushed, hot and dry skin (ie sweating stops). Hospitalization is essential. Meanwhile, get out of the sun, remove clothing that retains heat (cotton is OK), douse the body with water and fan continuously; ice packs can be applied to the neck, armpits and groin.

Hypothermia

» Skiers and hikers will find that temperatures in the mountains and desert can quickly drop below freezing, especially during winter. Even a sudden spring shower or high winds can lower your body temperature rapidly.

» Instead of cotton, wear synthetic or woolen clothing that retains warmth even when wet. Carry waterproof layers (eg Gore-Tex jacket, plastic poncho, rain pants) and high-energy, easily digestible snacks like chocolate, nuts and dried fruit.

» Symptoms of hypothermia include exhaustion, numbness, shivering, stumbling, slurred speech, dizzy spells, muscle cramps and irrational or even violent behavior.

» To treat hypothermia, get out of bad weather and change into dry, warm clothing. Drink hot liquids (no caffeine or alcohol) and snack on high-calorie food. In advanced stages, carefully put hypothermia sufferers in a warm sleeping bag cocooned inside a wind- and water-proof outer wrapping. Do not rub victims, who must be handled gently.

» For more hiking safety tips, see p40.

Insurance

See p456 for health insurance and p466 for car insurance.

Travel Insurance

Getting travel insurance to cover theft, loss and medical problems is highly recommended. Some policies do not cover 'risky' activities such as scuba diving, motorcycling and skiing, so read the fine print. Make sure the policy at least covers hospital stays and an emergency flight home.

Paying for your airline ticket or rental car with a credit card may provide limited travel accident insurance. If you already have private health insurance or a homeowners or renters policy, find out what those policies cover and only get supplemental insurance. If you have prepaid a large portion of your vacation, trip cancellation insurance may be a worthwhile expense.

Worldwide travel insurance is available at www .lonelyplanet.com/travel_ser vices. You can buy, extend and claim online anytime, even if you're already on the road.

Internet Access

» Internet cafes listed throughout this guide typically charge $3 to $12 per hour for online access.

» With branches in most So-Cal cities and towns, **FedEx Office** (☏800-254-6567; www.fedex.com) offers internet access at self-service computer workstations (20¢ to 30¢ per minute) and sometimes free wi-fi, plus digital-photo printing and CD-burning stations.

» Accommodations, cafes, restaurants, bars etc that provide guest computer terminals for going online are identified by the internet icon @; the wi-fi icon 🛜 indicates that wireless access is available. There may be a fee for either service.

» Free or fee-based wi-fi hot spots can be found at major airports; many hotels, motels and cafes; and some tourist information centers, museums, bars and restaurants.

» Free public wi-fi is proliferating and even some state parks are now wi-fi–enabled (for a list, click to www.parks .ca.gov/wifi).

» To find more public wi-fi hot spots, search www .wififreespot.com/ca.html or www.jiwire.com.

» Public libraries have internet terminals (on-line time may be limited, advance sign-up required and a nominal fee charged for out-of-network visitors) and increasingly, free wi-fi access.

Legal Matters

MINIMUM LEGAL AGE TO...

Drink alcohol	21
Drive a car	16
Fly a plane	17
Have sex	18
Own a gun	18
Smoke tobacco	18
Vote in an election	18

Drugs & Alcohol

» Possession of under 1oz of marijuana is a misdemeanor in California. Possession of any other drug or more than an ounce of weed is a felony punishable by lengthy jail time. For foreigners, conviction of any drug-related offense is grounds for deportation.

» Police can give roadside sobriety checks to assess if you've been drinking or using drugs. If you fail, they'll require you to take a breath, urine or blood test to determine if your blood-alcohol is over the legal limit (0.08%). Refusing to be tested is treated the same as if you had taken and failed the test.

» Penalties for driving under the influence (DUI) of drugs or alcohol range from license suspension and fines to jail time.

» It's illegal to carry open containers of alcohol inside a vehicle, even if they're empty; store 'em in the trunk instead.

» Consuming alcohol anywhere other than at a private residence or licensed premises is a no-no, which puts parks and beaches off-limits.

Police

» If you are stopped by the police, be courteous. Don't get out of the car unless asked.

» There is no system of paying fines on the spot. Attempting to pay the fine to the officer may lead to a charge of attempted bribery.

» If you are arrested, you have the right to remain silent and are presumed innocent until proven guilty. Everyone has the right to make one phone call. If you don't have a lawyer, one will be appointed to you free of charge.

» Due to security concerns about terrorism, never leave your bags unattended, especially at airports or bus and train stations.

» Littering along California's highways is punishable by a $1000 fine. Like Woody says, 'Give a hoot, don't pollute.'

Smoking

» Smoking is generally prohibited inside all public buildings, including airports, shopping malls and train and bus stations.

» There is no smoking allowed inside restaurants, although lighting up may be tolerated at patio or sidewalk tables.

» At hotels, you must specifically request a smoking room; note some properties are entirely nonsmoking by law.

» In some cities and towns, smoking outdoors within a certain distance of any public business is now *verboten*.

Maps

Visitors centers distribute free (but often very basic) maps. If you're doing a lot of driving, you'll need a more detailed road map or map atlas. Members of the **American Automobile Association** (AAA; ☏800-874-7532; www.aaa.com) or its international affiliates (eg CAA) can get free driving

INTERNATIONAL VISITORS

Entering the USA

See Customs (p455), Passports (p462) and Visas (p460). Under the US Department of Homeland Security (DHS) registration program, **US-VISIT** (www.dhs.gov/us-visit), almost all visitors (excluding, for now, most Canadian and many Mexican citizens) will be digitally photographed and have their electronic (inkless) fingerprints scanned upon arrival; the process typically takes less than a minute.

Embassies & Consulates

Most foreign embassies are in Washington, DC, but some countries have consular offices in LA, including the following:

Australia (☏310-229-2300; 2029 Century Park E, 31st fl) Near Beverly Hills.
Canada (☏213-346-2700; 550 S Hope St, 9th fl) Downtown.
France (☏310-235-3200; 10390 Santa Monica Blvd, Suites 115 & 410) Westwood.
Germany (☏323-930-2703; 6222 Wilshire Blvd, Suite 500) Mid-City.
Japan (☏213-617-6700; 350 S Grand Ave, Suite 1700) Downtown.
New Zealand (☏310-566-6555; 2425 Olympic Blvd, Suite 600E) Santa Monica.
UK (☏310-481-0031; 11766 Wilshire Blvd, Suite 1200) Near Westwood.

For countries not listed here, visit www.sos.ca.gov/business/ibrp/consulates.htm.

Money

See p459. For US-dollar exchange rates and setting your trip budget, see p18.

Post

The **US Postal Service** (USPS; ☏800-275-8777; www.usps.com) is inexpensive and reliable. Postcards and standard letters up to 1oz (about 28g) cost 46¢ within the US, 80¢ to Canada, 85¢ to Mexico and $1.06 to all other countries. Postal rates increase by a few pennies every couple of years.

Telephone

CELL (MOBILE) PHONES

You'll need a multiband GSM phone in order to make calls in the US. Popping in a US prepaid rechargeable SIM card is usually cheaper than using your own network. They're available at any major telecommunications or electronics store. If your phone doesn't work in the USA, these stores also sell inexpensive prepaid phones, including some airtime.

For short stays, you could rent a cell phone, eg from **TripTel** (☏310-645-3500; www.triptel.com) at Los Angeles International Airport (outside the customs gate in the Tom Bradley International Terminal). Rentals cost from $3 per day ($15 per week) plus at least 95¢ per minute for incoming/outgoing calls within the US ($2.50 per minute for international calls).

DIALING CODES

» US phone numbers consist of a three-letter area code followed by a seven-digit local number.
» When dialing a number within the same area code, use the seven-digit number.
» Long-distance calls must be preceded by ☏1.
» Toll-free numbers begin with ☏800, ☏866, ☏877 or ☏888 and must be preceded by ☏1.
» For local or long-distance directory assistance, dial ☏800-466-4411 (no charge).
» For direct international calls, dial ☏011 plus the country code plus the area code plus the local phone number.
» If you're calling from abroad, the country code for the US is ☏1.

maps from any local AAA office. Benchmark Maps' comprehensive *California Road & Recreation Atlas* ($25) shows campgrounds, recreational areas and topographical land features, although it's less useful for navigating congested urban areas. **Google Maps** (www.maps.google.com) offers free downloadable maps and driving directions.

Money

ATMs

ATMs are available 24/7 at most banks, shopping malls, airports and grocery and convenience stores. Expect to be hit with a minimum surcharge of $2 per transaction, in addition to any fees charged by your bank back home. Most ATMs are connected to international networks and offer decent exchange rates.

Credit Cards

Credit cards are almost universally accepted. You'll find it hard or impossible to rent a car, book a hotel room or order tickets over the phone without one. Visa, MasterCard and American Express are most common.

Moneychangers

You can exchange money at major airports, some banks and all currency-exchange offices such as American Express or Travelex; always enquire about rates and fees. Outside big cities, exchanging money may be a problem, so make sure you have plenty of cash or a credit card.

Traveler's Checks

Traveler's checks have pretty much fallen out of use. Big city restaurants, hotels and larger stores often will accept traveler's checks in US dollars only, but smaller businesses, markets and fast-food chains may refuse them.

Public Holidays

On the following national holidays, banks, schools and government offices (including post offices) all close, and transportation, museums and other services operate on a Sunday schedule. Holidays falling on a weekend are usually observed the following Monday.

New Year's Day January 1
Martin Luther King Jr Day Third Monday in January
Presidents' Day Third Monday in February
Memorial Day Last Monday in May
Independence Day July 4 (aka Fourth of July)
Labor Day First Monday in September
Columbus Day Second Monday in October
Veterans' Day November 11
Thanksgiving Day Fourth Thursday in November
Christmas Day December 25

School Holidays

Colleges take a one- or two-week 'spring break' around Easter, sometime in March or April. Some hotels and resorts, especially along the coast and in the deserts, may raise their rates during this time. School summer vacations make July and August the busiest travel months.

Safe Travel

Earthquakes

Earthquakes happen all the time but most are so tiny they are detectable only by sensitive seismological instruments. If you're caught in a serious shaker:

» If indoors, get under a desk or table or stand in a doorway.

» Protect your head and stay clear of windows, mirrors or anything that might fall.

» Don't head for elevators or go running into the street.

» If you're in a shopping mall or large public building, expect the alarm and/or sprinkler systems to come on.

» If outdoors, get away from buildings, trees and power lines.

» If you're driving, pull over to the side of the road away from bridges, overpasses and power lines. Stay inside the car until the shaking stops.

» If you're on a sidewalk near buildings, duck into a doorway to protect yourself from falling bricks, glass and debris.

» Prepare for aftershocks.

» Turn on the radio and listen for bulletins.

» Use the telephone only if absolutely necessary.

Riptides

The biggest hazard lurking in the ocean is the dangerous ocean current called a riptide. If you find yourself being carried offshore by a rip, the important thing is to just keep afloat. Don't panic or try to swim against the current, as this will quickly exhaust you and you may drown. Instead, try to swim parallel to the shoreline and once the current stops pulling you out, swim back to shore.

Tipping

Tipping is *not* optional. Only withhold tips in cases of outrageously bad service.

» **Airport skycaps and hotel bellhops** $2 per bag, minimum per cart $5

» **Bartenders** 10% to 15% per round, minimum $1 per drink

» **Concierges** No tips required for simple information, up to $20 for securing last-minute restaurant reservations, sold-out show tickets etc

» **Housekeeping staff** $2 to $4 daily, left under the card provided; more if you're messy

» **Parking valets** At least $2 when handed back your car keys

» **Restaurant servers and room service** 15% to 20%, unless a gratuity is already charged

» **Taxi drivers** 10% to 15% of metered fare, rounded up to the next dollar

Tourist Information

For pretrip planning, peruse the information-packed website of the **California Travel & Tourism Commission** (www.visitcalifornia .com). This state-run agency also operates several **California Welcome Centers** (www.visitcwc.com), where staff dispense maps and brochures and may help find accommodations. More local tourist information offices and visitor centers are listed in the destination chapters.

Travelers With Disabilities

Southern California is reasonably well-equipped for travelers with disabilities. Disneyland is a shining example when it comes to catering to visitors with special needs (see p37).

» Telephone companies provide relay operators (dial ☎711) for the hearing impaired.

» Many banks provide ATM instructions in Braille.

» Most intersections have dropped curbs; some have audible crossing signals.

» The Americans with Disabilities Act (ADA) requires public buildings, including restrooms, to be wheelchair-accessible.

» For nonpublic buildings, such as historic hotels,

restaurants, museums and theaters, there are no accessibility guarantees.

» When making lodging reservations, state your specific needs; at other venues, call ahead to find out what to expect.

» Most national and many state parks and other outdoor recreation areas have paved or boardwalk-style nature trails.

Transportation

» All major airlines, Greyhound buses and Amtrak trains can accommodate people with disabilities, usually with 24 to 48 hours of advance notice required.

» Major car-rental agencies offer hand-controlled vehicles and vans with wheelchair lifts at no extra charge, but you must reserve these well in advance.

» For renting wheelchair-accessible vans, also try **Mobility Works** (☎877-275-4915; www.mobilityworks.com) in northern LA County.

» Local buses, trains and subway lines usually have wheelchair lifts.

» Seeing-eye dogs are permitted to accompany passengers traveling on public transportation.

» Taxi companies have at least one wheelchair-accessible van, but you'll usually need to call first.

Helpful Resources

A Wheelchair Rider's Guide: Los Angeles and Orange County Coast (http://scc.ca.gov/publica tions/) Free downloadable PDF covers wheelchair access at beaches, parks and more.

Access Guide: In San Diego (www.accessandiego .org) Downloadable city guide booklet ($3).

Discover Los Angeles (http://discoverlosangeles .com/guides/la-living/) Tips for accessible sightseeing and entertainment.

MossRehab Resource Net (www.mossresourcenet.org/ travel.htm) Useful links and general info enabling accessible travel.

Theme-Park Access Guide (www.mouseplanet .com/tag/dlintro.htm) An insider's view of Disneyland and other parks 'on wheels.'

Visas

» Depending on your country of origin, the rules for entering the USA keep changing. Double-check current visa and passport requirements *before* coming to the USA.

» Currently, under the US Visa Waiver Program (VWP), visas are not required for citizens of 36 countries for stays up to 90 days (no extensions) as long as you have a machine-readable passport (MRP; see p462). If you don't have an MRP, you will need a visa to enter the USA.

» Citizens of VWP countries must also register with the Electronic System for Travel Authorization (ESTA) online (https://esta.cbp.dhs.gov/) at least 72 hours before travel. Once approved, the registration is valid for up to two years.

» Citizens from all other countries need to apply for a visa in their home country. The process costs a nonrefundable $131, involves a personal interview and can take several weeks, so apply as early as possible.

» For up-to-date information about entry requirements and eligibility, check the visa section of the **US Department of State website** (http://travel.state.gov) and the travel section of the **US Customs & Border Protection website** (www.cbp.gov). If you're still in doubt, contact the nearest US embassy or consulate in your home country (for a complete list, see www.usembassy.gov).

Volunteering

Casual drop-in volunteer opportunities are most common in SoCal cities, where you can socialize with locals while helping out nonprofit organizations. Browse upcoming projects and sign up online with local organizations such as **LA Works** (www.laworks .com), **Volunteer San Diego** (www.volunteersandiego. org) or **Volunteer Center Orange County** (www.vol unteercenter.org). For more opportunities, check local alternative weekly newspapers and **Craigslist** (www .craiglist.org).

Helpful Resources

826LA (http://826la.org) Nonprofit creative writing and tutoring center for young students offers long-term volunteering positions in LA,

California Volunteers (www.californiavolunteers.org) Official state volunteer directory and matching service, with links to national service days and long-term AmeriCorps programs.

Habitat for Humanity (www.habitat.org) Nonprofit organization helps build homes for impoverished families, including weekend and week-long projects.

Idealist.org (www.idealist .org) Free searchable database covers both short- and long-term volunteer opportunities.

Sierra Club (www.sierra club.org) Day or weekend projects and longer volunteer vacations (including for families), mostly focused on conservation; annual membership $25.

TreePeople (www.treepeople .org) Organizes half- and full-day group tree-planting projects around LA, from urban parks to wildfire-damaged forests.

Worldwide Opportunities on Organic Farms (www .wwoofusa.org) Long-term volunteering opportunities on local organic farms; online membership fee $30.

Transportation

GETTING THERE & AWAY

Flights, tours and rail tickets can be booked online at lonelyplanet.com/bookings.

Entering the Region

California is an important agricultural state. To prevent the spread of pests and diseases, certain food items (including meats, fresh fruit and vegetables) may not be brought into the state. Bakery items, chocolates and hard-cured cheeses are admissible. If you drive into California across the border from Mexico or from the neighboring states of Oregon, Nevada and Arizona, you may have to stop for a quick inspection and questioning by officials of the California Department of Food and Agriculture.

For Mexico land border crossings, see p463. For visa requirements, see p460.

Passports

» Under the Western Hemisphere Travel Initiative (WHTI), all travelers must have a valid machine-readable (MRP) passport when entering the US by air, land or sea.

» The only exceptions are for some Canadian and Mexican citizens who can present other WHTI-compliant documents (eg pre-approved 'trusted traveler' cards).

» MRP passports issued or renewed after October 26, 2006 must be e-passports (ie have a digital photo and integrated chip with biometric data).

» MRP passports issued or renewed between October 26, 2005 and October 25, 2006 must have a digital photo or integrated chip on the data page.

» If your passport was issued before October 26, 2005 it will be accepted only if it's an MRP (ie the data page has two lines of letters, numbers and <<< at the bottom).

» For more information, consult www.cpb.gov/travel.

Air

Airports & Airlines

Southern California's primary international airport:

Los Angeles International Airport (www.lawa.org/lax) Most international flights arrive here at California's largest and busiest airport, 20 miles southwest of Downtown LA, near the coast.

Regional hubs more often served by low-cost domestic carriers:

Bob Hope Airport (www.burbankairport.com) Also known as Burbank Airport, in northern LA County, close to Universal Studios Hollywood.

John Wayne Airport (www.ocair.com) In Santa Ana, Orange County, convenient for Disneyland.

LA/Ontario International Airport (www.lawa.org/ont) In Riverside County, east of LA, closer to some desert destinations.

Long Beach Airport (www.longbeach.gov/airport) Easy access to LA and Orange County.

Palm Springs International Airport (code PSP; 760-318-3800; www.palmspringsairport.com) Easy in, easy out; no international flights to speak of.

San Diego International Airport (www.san.org) Also known as Lindbergh Field, just west of downtown. Handles mostly domestic flights, but also a few international routes to Canada and Mexico.

Santa Barbara Airport (www.flysba.com) Tiny and hassle-free, west of downtown near UCSB campus.

Domestic airlines:

Alaska/Horizon (800-252-7522; www.alaskaair.com)
Allegiant (702-505-8888; www.allegiantair.com)
American (800-433-7300; www.aa.com)
Continental (800-523-3273; www.continental.com)
Delta (800-221-1212; www.delta.com)
Frontier (800-432-1359; www.frontierairlines.com)

CLIMATE CHANGE & TRAVEL

Every form of transport that relies on carbon-based fuel generates CO_2, the main cause of human-induced climate change. Modern travel is dependent on aeroplanes, which might use less fuel per kilometer per person than most cars but travel much greater distances. The altitude at which aircraft emit gases (including CO_2) and particles also contributes to their climate change impact. Many websites offer 'carbon calculators' that allow people to estimate the carbon emissions generated by their journey and, for those who wish to do so, to offset the impact of the greenhouse gases emitted with contributions to portfolios of climate-friendly initiatives throughout the world. Lonely Planet offsets the carbon footprint of all staff and author travel.

Hawaiian (☎800-367-5320; www.hawaiianair.com)

Horizon (☎800-547-9308; www.alaskaair.com)

Jet Blue (☎800-538-2583; www.jetblue.com)

Northwest (☎800-225-2525; www.nwa.com)

Southwest (☎800-435-9792; www.southwest.com)

Spirit (☎800-772-7117; www.spiritair.com)

United (☎800-864-8331; www.united.com)

US Airways (☎800-428-4322; www.usairways.com)

Virgin America (☎877-359-8474; www.virginamerica.com)

International airlines:

Aeroméxico (www.aeromexico.com)

Air Canada (www.aircanada.com)

Air France (www.airfrance.us)

Air New Zealand (www.airnewzealand.com)

Alitalia (www.alitalia.com)

British Airways (www.britishairways.com)

Cathay Pacific (www.cathaypacific.com)

Iberia (www.iberia.com)

Japan Airlines (www.jal.com)

KLM (www.klm.com)

Lufthansa (www.lufthansa.com)

Mexicana (www.mexicana.com)

Qantas (www.qantas.com)

Singapore (www.singaporeair.com)

V Australia (www.vaustralia.com)

Virgin Atlantic (www.virgin-atlantic.com)

WestJet (www.westjet.com)

Land

Border Crossings

On the US–Mexico border between San Diego and Tijuana, San Ysidro is the world's busiest border crossing. Traveling into Mexico is usually not a problem but coming back into the US almost always entails a long wait, especially if you're driving. The website http://apps.cbp.gov/bwt shows current border wait times.

US citizens and residents do not require a visa for stays of 72 hours or less when within the border zone (ie as far south as Ensenada). To get back into the USA:

» US citizens will need to present a valid US passport or another WHTI–compliant document (see www.getyouhome.gov). A regular US driver's license is no longer sufficient as proof.

» Non-US citizens may be subject to a full immigration inspection upon returning to the US, so bring your passport (p462) and US visa if required (see p460).

For more on traveling between San Diego and Tijuana, see p285.

Bus

Greyhound (☎800-231-2222; www.greyhound.com) is king of the road, ploughing a nationwide route system serving dozens of destinations in Southern California. Some US routes connect with **Greyhound Canada** (☎800-661-8747; www.greyhound.ca) and **Greyhound México** (☎800-010-0600; www.greyhound.com.mx). Greyhound's **Discovery Pass** (www.discoverypass.com) is good for unlimited travel throughout the US and Canada for seven ($239), 15 ($339), 30 ($439) or 60 ($539) consecutive days. If you're starting your trip in the US, passes may be bought at Greyhound terminals or online (to be picked

WARNING

In late 2010, the **US State Department** (http://travel.state.gov) issued a travel alert about increasing Mexican drug-cartel violence and crime along the US–Mexico border. Travelers should exercise extreme caution in Tijuana (see p285), avoid large-scale gatherings and demonstrations, and not venture out after dark, especially in cars with US license plates.

GO GREEN

Southern California is practically synonymous with car culture but, with time and patience, you can get around using public transportation. The trick is to focus your itinerary and do in-depth explorations of smaller areas rather than a sweeping loop. Even if you have a car, consider ditching it for at least part of the time. If you're renting a car, choose a fuel-efficient model, preferably a hybrid, and decline those 'free' upgrades – how big a car do you really need?

Amtrak's *Pacific Surfliner* links all the coastal cities from San Diego to Santa Barbara, while some inland destinations are served by Greyhound buses. Many cities and towns have local bus, trolley and shuttle systems too. Even in LA you'll be OK as long as you limit your ambition to seeing only one or two neighborhoods a day. Santa Barbara, Palm Springs and Orange County beach towns are compact enough to explore by bicycle. If you take an organized tour, ask about sustainable itineraries and alternative-fuel vehicles.

up later at the terminal) up to two hours before starting your trip.

See p465 for more information on bus tickets, reservations and fares.

Car & Motorcycle

Tips for driving to/from the USA:

» If you're driving to the USA from Canada or Mexico, bring your vehicle's registration papers, liability insurance and driver's license.

» Unless you're planning an extended stay in Mexico, taking a car from the US across the border to Tijuana is more hassle than it's worth (see p285 for other transportation options).

» If you're interested in driving someone else's car to California to save money, **Auto Driveaway** (☎800-346-2277; www.autodriveaway.com) has dozens of offices nationwide, or browse www.movecars.com.

For more information about driving in Southern California, including road rules, car rentals and road distance charts, see p466.

Train

Amtrak (☎800-872-7245; www.amtrak.com) operates a fairly extensive rail system throughout the US. Trains are comfortable, if slow, and are equipped with dining and lounge cars for long-distance travel.

Major long-distance routes:

Coast Starlight Travels the West Coast daily from Seattle to LA (from $102, 35 hours) via Portland, Sacramento and Oakland.

Southwest Chief Daily departures between Chicago and LA (from $146, 43 hours) via Kansas City, Albuquerque and Flagstaff.

Sunset Limited Thrice-weekly service between New Orleans and LA (from $136, 37 hours) via San Antonio and Tucson.

See p468 for intra-California routes.

Amtrak's USA Rail Pass is valid for coach-class travel for 15 ($389), 30 ($579) or 45 ($749) days; children aged two to 15 pay half-price. Actual travel is limited

to eight, 12 or 18 one-way 'segments,' respectively. A segment is *not* the same as a one-way trip. That means if reaching your destination requires riding more than one train, you'll use up multiple pass segments. You'll also need to make reservations for each segment. Purchase passes online or through international travel-agency representatives.

For Amtrak's California Rail Pass, see p469.

GETTING AROUND

Air

Although it is possible to fly from, say, LA to San Diego or Palm Springs, the time and cost involved don't make airplanes a sensible way to get around Southern California.

Bicycle

Cycling around Southern California is a great, nonpolluting way to travel. But it's really only a feasible option if you're in good shape and able to cope with high temperatures, especially midsummer.

Helpful organizations:

Adventure Cycling Association (www.adventure-cycling.org) Excellent online resource for purchasing bicycle-friendly maps, long-distance cycling route guides and gadgets.

Better World Club (☎866-238-1137; www.betterworldclub.com) Annual membership costs $40 (plus $12 enrollment fee), including two free 24-hour emergency roadside pickups with transportation to the nearest bike-repair shop within a certain distance.

Road Rules

» Cycling is allowed on all roads and highways – even along freeways if there's no suitable alternative, such as a smaller parallel road; all mandatory exits are marked.

» Some cities have designated bicycle lanes, but make sure you have your wits about you when venturing out into heavy traffic.

» Cyclists must follow the same rules of the road as vehicles, but don't expect drivers to always respect your right of way.

» Wearing a helmet is mandatory for bicycle riders under 18 years old.

Rental & Purchase

» Most towns have at least one bike-rental shop; many are listed throughout this book. Rates range from about $10 to $20 per hour or $30 to $45 per day (more for high-tech mountain bikes); multiday and weekly discounts may be available.

» You can buy new models from specialty bike shops, sporting-goods stores and discount-warehouse stores, or used from notice boards at hostels, cafes and universities. Also check online bulletin boards such as **Craigslist** (www.craigslist.org).

Theft

» Bicycle theft is fairly common, so protect yours with a heavy-duty bicycle lock and park in well-lit, busy areas.

» Some parking garages have special bicycle parking areas.

» If possible, bring your bicycle inside your hotel room at night.

Transporting Bicycles

» Some local transportation companies operate buses equipped with bike racks.

» Greyhound transports bicycles as luggage (surcharge varies, usually around $15 to $25), provided the bicycle is disassembled and placed in a box (available at terminals for $10).

» Most of Amtrak's *Pacific Surfliner* trains (p468) feature special racks where you can secure your bike unboxed, but be sure to reserve a spot when making your ticket reservation (fee $5 to $10, depending on the destination). On Amtrak trains without racks, bikes must be put in a box and checked as luggage (fee $5, box $15).

Bus

Southern California cities served by **Greyhound** (☎800-231-2222; www.greyhound.com) include LA, Long Beach, Santa Barbara, San Diego, Anaheim, Oceanside and Temecula. Frequency of service varies, but main routes operate every hour or so, sometimes round the clock.

Greyhound buses are usually clean, comfortable and reliable modes of transport. The best seats are typically toward the front and away from the bathroom. Limited onboard amenities include icy air-conditioning (bring a sweater) and slightly reclining seats. Smoking on board is strictly prohibited. Bus stations are dreary places and often in sketchy areas; this is especially true of LA and Palm Springs.

Greyhound can accommodate travelers with disabilities if you call ☎800-752-4841 at least 48 hours before traveling.

Costs

It's easy to buy tickets online with a credit card, then pick them up (bring photo ID) at the terminal. You can also buy tickets over the phone or in person from an Amtrak ticket agent.

You may save a few dollars by purchasing round-trips and traveling between Monday and Thursday. Other promotions, including companion fares (50% off), are often available, though they may have restrictions or blackout periods. Check the Greyhound website for a rundown of the current fare specials.

Discounts are regularly available – on unrestricted fares only – for seniors over 62 (5% discount), AAA (see p466) members (10%) students (20%) with a Student Advantage Card (p455) and children aged 2 to 11 (25%). Children under 2 years of age ride free.

For bus passes, see p463.

Reservations

» Most boarding is done on a first-come, first-served basis.

» Even buying tickets in advance does not guarantee you a seat on any particular bus unless you also purchase priority boarding (add $5).

» Arrive at least one hour prior to the scheduled departure time to secure a seat; allow extra time on weekends and around holidays.

SAMPLE GREYHOUND FARES

ROUTE	ADULT FARE	DURATION	FREQUENCY
LA–Anaheim (Disneyland)	$8-15	¾-1½hr	7 per day
LA–Las Vegas	$42-63	5-8hr	13 per day
LA–San Diego	$14-22	2¼-3¼hr	20 per day
LA–Santa Barbara	$14-21	3hr	5 per day

Car & Motorcycle

Automobile Associations

For 24-hour emergency roadside assistance, free maps and discounts on lodging, attractions, car rentals and more:

American Automobile Association (AAA; ✆800-564-6222; www.aaa.com) Walk-in offices throughout Southern California, plus reciprocal agreements with some international auto clubs (eg CAA in Canada) – bring your membership card from home.

Better World Club (✆866-238-1137; www.betterworldclub.com) This eco-friendly alternative supports environmental causes and also offers cyclists' emergency roadside assistance (see p464).

Driver's License

» Visitors may legally drive a car in California for up to 12 months with their home driver's license.

» If you're from overseas, an International Driving Permit (IDP) will have more credibility with traffic police and also simplify the car-rental process, especially if your license doesn't have a photo or isn't written in English.

» To drive a motorcycle, you'll need a valid US state motorcycle license or a specially endorsed IDP.

Fuel

» Gas stations in California, nearly all of which are self-service, are ubiquitous, except in national parks and some sparsely populated desert and mountain areas.

» Gas is sold in gallons (one US gallon equals 3.78L). At press time, the cost for mid-grade fuel ranged from $3 to $3.50.

Insurance

California law requires liability insurance for all vehicles. When renting a car, check your auto-insurance policy from home to see if you're already covered. If you're not, expect to pay about $15 per day. Foreign visitors should check their travel insurance policies (p456) to see if rental cars are covered.

Insurance against damage to the car itself, called Collision Damage Waiver (CDW) or Loss Damage Waiver (LDW), costs about $15 per day; the deductible may require you to pay the first $100 to $500 for any repairs. Some credit cards will cover this, provided you charge the entire cost of the car rental to the card; check with your card issuer to determine the extent of coverage.

Rental

CARS

To rent your own wheels, you'll typically need to be at least 25 years old, hold a valid driver's license and have a major credit card (not a check or debit card). A few companies may rent to drivers under 25 but over 21 for a surcharge (around $25 per day). If you don't have a credit card, you may occasionally be able to make a large cash deposit instead.

With advance reservations, you can often get an economy-size vehicle from about $30 per day, plus insurance, taxes and fees. Rates usually include unlimited mileage. Expect surcharges for rentals originating at airports and train stations, for additional drivers and for one-way rentals. Child or infant safety seats are compulsory (see p467); reserve them (for around $10/50 per day/week) when booking your car.

Major international car-rental companies:

Alamo (✆877-222-9075; www.alamo.com)

Avis (✆800-331-1212; www.avis.com)

Budget (✆800-527-0700; www.budget.com)

Dollar (✆800-800-3665; www.dollar.com)

Enterprise (✆800-261-7331; www.enterprise.com)

Hertz (✆800-654-3131; www.hertz.com)

National (✆877-222-9058; www.nationalcar.com)

Thrifty (✆800-847-4389; www.thrifty.com)

Overseas travelers should look into prepaid deals or fly-drive packages arranged in their home country, which

ROAD DISTANCES (KM)

	Big Bear Lake	Death Valley	Las Vegas	Los Angeles	Newport Beach	Palm Springs	San Diego	San Francisco	Santa Barbara
Big Bear Lake	84								
Death Valley	283	236							
Las Vegas	263	216	141						
Los Angeles	26	96	289	270					
Newport Beach	19	96	297	276	44				
Palm Springs	91	83	300	280	110	104			
San Diego	96	144	350	331	120	90	140		
San Francisco	405	474	528	568	379	426	486	498	
Santa Barbara	123	189	377	357	95	138	200	220	334
Tijuana	110	157	363	345	135	104	155	17	831	229

often work out cheaper than on-the-spot rentals. Search the rental and airline companies' websites as well as online travel agencies for deals.

If you'd like to minimize your contribution to So-Cal's polluted air, a few major car-rental companies (including Avis, Budget and Hertz) offer 'green' fleets of hybrid rental cars. Expect to pay more for these models. Other options:

Simply Hybrid (323-653-0011, 888-359-0055; www.simplyhybrid.com) With rental rates from $60/330 per day/week, these cars are more expensive, but you'll get a break at the pump. Free delivery and pickup from select LA locations (three-day minimum rental required).

Fox Rent-a-Car (310-641-3838, 800-225-4369, ext 1; www.foxrentacar.com) Rents hybrids from $65/245 per day/week, with offices at LAX, Burbank, Ontario, John Wayne (Orange County) and San Diego airports.

Zipcar (866-494-7227; www.zipcar.com) Currently in LA, San Diego, Santa Barbara, Pasadena and Long Beach, this car-sharing club charges usage fees (from $8/66 per hour/day) including free gas, insurance and limited mileage. Apply online (foreign drivers OK); annual membership $50, application fee $25.

To find and compare independent agencies, try **Car Rental Express** (www.carrentalexpress.com), which is especially useful for searching out cheaper long-term rentals. Some companies that may rent to drivers under 25:

Rent-a-Wreck (www.rentawreck.com) Minimum rental age and surcharges vary by location. SoCal branches include LA, Burbank, Pasadena and North Hollywood.

Super Cheap Cars (www.supercheapcar.com) LA (310-645-3993; 10212 La Cienega Blvd, Inglewood); Orange County, it costs $100 (949-752-6499; Suite P, 18017 Sky Park Circle, Irvine) No surcharges for under-25s with full-coverage CDW/LDW insurance. Free pickups from select locations.

MOTORCYCLES

Motorcycle rentals and insurance are not cheap, especially if you've got your eye on a Harley. Depending on the model, it costs $100 to $250 per day plus taxes, including helmets, unlimited miles and liability insurance; collision insurance (CDW) costs extra.

Eagle Rider (310-536-6777, 888-900-9901; www.eaglerider.com) Rental outlets include LA, San Diego, Palm Springs and Las Vegas. You can rent in one city and return in another (surcharge from $150).

Route 66 (310-578-0112, 888-434-4473; www.route66riders.com; 4161 Lincoln Blvd, Marina del Rey) Harley-Davidson rentals in LA's South Bay from $195 per day, including taxes, fees and mileage.

RECREATIONAL VEHICLES

RVs are a popular way to travel. It's easy to find coastal campgrounds with electricity and water hookups, but in big cities RVs are a nuisance, since there are few places to park or plug them in. RVs are also cumbersome to navigate and burn fuel at an alarming rate, but they do solve transportation, accommodation and cooking needs in one fell swoop.

Rental RV costs vary by size, model and mileage; expect to pay at least $100 per day. Some rental agencies:

Cruise America (480-464-7300, 800-671-8042; www.cruiseamerica.com)

El Monte (562-483-4956, 888-337-2214; www.elmonterv.com)

Happy Travel Campers (310-928-3980, 800-370-1262; www.camperusa.com) LA-based.

Road Bear (818-865-2925, 866-491-9853; www.roadbearrv.com) LA-based.

Road Rules

» Drive on the right-hand side of the road.

» Talking on a cell phone while driving is illegal.

» The use of seat belts is required for drivers, front-seat passengers and children under age 16.

» Infant and child safety seats are required for children under 6 years old or weighing less than 60lbs.

» All motorcyclists must wear a helmet. Scooters are not allowed on California freeways.

» High-occupancy (HOV) lanes marked with a diamond symbol are reserved for cars with multiple occupants, sometimes only during morning and afternoon rush hours.

» Unless otherwise posted, the speed limit is 65mph on freeways, 55mph on two-lane undivided highways, 35mph on major city streets and 25mph in business and residential districts and near schools.

» It's forbidden to pass a school bus when its rear red lights are flashing.

» Except where indicated, turning right at red lights after coming to a full stop is permitted, although intersecting traffic still has the right of way.

» At four-way stop signs, cars proceed in the order in which they arrived. If two cars arrive simultaneously, the one on the right has the right of way. When in doubt, politely wave the other driver ahead.

» When emergency vehicles (ie police, fire or ambulance) approach from either direction, carefully pull over to the side of the road.

» When parking, read all posted regulations and pay close attention to any colored curbs and parking meters, or you may be ticketed or towed.

» California has strict anti-littering laws; throwing trash from a vehicle may incur a $1000 fine.

» Driving under the influence of alcohol or drugs is illegal (see p457).

For other questions, consult the *California Driver Handbook* and *California Motorcycle Handbook* (available as free downloads from www.dmv.ca.gov).

Tours

Adventure Bus (☎909-633-7225, 888-737-5263; www.adventurebus.com) Offers springtime hiking tours of Death Valley and Joshua Tree National Parks, departing from Las Vegas. Similar to Green Tortoise (ie you'll sleep aboard a bus), but for all ages.

California Motorcycle Tours (☎858-677-9892; www.ca-motorcycletours.com) This San Diego–based outfit offers guided trips on Harley Davidsons, including beaches, mountains, deserts and Mexico's Baja Peninsula.

Exploritas (☎800-454-5768; www.exploritas.org) Formerly known as Elderhostel, this nonprofit organization offers learning trips (including bus and walking tours and outdoor-sports adventures) for active people aged over 50.

Green Tortoise (☎415-956-7500, 800-867-8647; www.greentortoise.com) Backpacker-budget trips that utilize converted sleeping-bunk buses; the four-day 'Mojave Desert Loop' route visits Joshua Tree National Park and Las Vegas, departing from LA.

Train

Amtrak

Amtrak (☎800-872-7245; www.amtrak.com) operates train services throughout California. At some stations, trains are met by Thruway buses for onward connections to smaller destinations. Smoking is prohibited on board both buses and trains.

The *Pacific Surfliner* is Amtrak's main rail service within Southern California. Sleek, double-decker trains have on-board bicycle and surfboard racks and a cafe car. Business-class seats feature slightly more legroom, electrical outlets and sometimes wi-fi internet access.

Up to 12 trains daily ply the *Surfliner*'s LA–San Diego route, making stops in Oceanside (for Legoland), San Juan Capistrano and Anaheim (for Disneyland), among others. Some trains continue north to Santa Barbara via Burbank, Oxnard, Ventura and Carpinteria. The trip itself, which hugs the coastline for much of the route, is a visual treat.

Of Amtrak's long-distance trains (see p464), the *Coast Starlight* stops in Santa Barbara and LA, while the *Sunset Limited* travels to LA and northern Palm Springs.

COSTS

Purchase tickets at train stations, by phone or online. Fares depend on the day of travel, the route, the type of seating etc. Fares may be slightly higher during peak travel times (eg summer). Round-trip tickets cost the same as two one-way tickets.

Usually seniors over 62 and students with an ISIC or Student Advantage Card (see p455) receive a 15% discount, while up to two children, aged two to 15 and accompanied by an adult, get 50% off. Children under two years of age ride free. AAA members (p466) save 10%. Special promotions can become available anytime, so check the website or ask about them when making reservations.

RESERVATIONS

Amtrak reservations can be made up to 11 months prior to departure. In summer and around holidays, trains sell out quickly, so book tickets as early as possible. The cheapest coach fares are usually for unreserved seats; business-class fares typically come with reserved seats.

SAMPLE AMTRAK FARES

ROUTE	COACH	BUSINESS CLASS	DURATION
LA–Anaheim	$11	$21	¾hr
LA–Santa Barbara	$16-24	$37	3hr
LA–San Diego	$30	$44	2¾hr
San Diego–San Juan Capistrano	$18	$30	1½hr
San Diego–Oceanside	$14	$24	1hr
San Diego–Santa Barbara	$33	$50	5½hr

TRAIN PASSES

Amtrak's California Rail Pass costs $159 ($80 for children aged two to 15) and is valid on all trains (except certain long-distance routes) and most connecting Thruway buses for seven days of travel within a 21-day period.

Metrolink

Southern California's major population centers are linked to LA by a commuter-train network called **Metrolink** (☎800-371-5465; www.metro linktrains.com). Seven lines connect Downtown LA's Union Station with the surrounding counties – Orange, Riverside, San Bernardino and Ventura – as well as northern San Diego County.

The most useful line for visitors is the Orange County Line, stopping in Anaheim, Orange, Santa Ana, San Juan Capistrano, San Clemente and Oceanside. The Ventura County Line stops at Bob Hope Airport in Burbank.

Most trains depart between 5am and 9am and 3pm and 7pm Monday to Friday, with only one or two services operating during the day. Some lines offer limited weekend services. Tickets are available from station vending machines; fares are zone-based.

behind the scenes

SEND US YOUR FEEDBACK

We love to hear from travelers – your comments keep us on our toes and help make our books better. Our well-traveled team reads every word on what you loved or loathed about this book. Although we cannot reply individually to postal submissions, we always guarantee that your feedback goes straight to the appropriate authors, in time for the next edition. Each person who sends us information is thanked in the next edition – and the most useful submissions are rewarded with a free book.

Visit **lonelyplanet.com/contact** to submit your updates and suggestions or to ask for help. Our award-winning website also features inspirational travel stories, news and discussions.

Note: We may edit, reproduce and incorporate your comments in Lonely Planet products such as guidebooks, websites and digital products, so let us know if you don't want your comments reproduced or your name acknowledged. For a copy of our privacy policy visit lonelyplanet.com/privacy.

OUR READERS

Many thanks to the travelers who used the last edition and wrote to us with helpful hints, useful advice and interesting anecdotes:

Paul Beckwith, Lalimarie Bhagwani, Michael Brae, Greg Butterfield, Richard Edwards, Gentry Fischer, Marg Gibson, Kathy Lewis, Ralph Meyer, Dennis Mogerman, Heather Monell, Jennifer Nash, Michelle Nguyen, Jerry Patel, Mona Reed, Raphael Richards, Stephen Rogowski, Howard Rutenberg, Elizabeth Saenger, Lisa Scalia, Joe Silins, Alex Wong

THIS BOOK

The 3rd edition of *Los Angeles, San Diego & Southern California* was researched and written by Sara Benson (coordinating author), Andrew Bender and Adam Skolnick. The previous edition was written by Andrea Schulte-Peevers, Amy C Balfour and Andrew Bender. This guidebook was commissioned in Lonely Planet's Oakland office, and produced by the following:

Commissioning Editors Suki Gear, Kathleen Munnelly

Coordinating Editors Andrea Dobbin, Chris Girdler

Coordinating Cartographer Valeska Canas

Coordinating Layout Designer Frank Deim

Managing Editors Helen Christinis, Bruce Evans

Managing Cartographers Shahara Ahmed, Alison Lyall

Managing Layout Designer Celia Wood

Assisting Editors Monique Choy, Peter Cruttenden, Laura Gibb, Kim Hutchins, Amy Karafin, Charlotte Orr

Assisting Cartographers Mark Griffiths, Brendan Streager

Cover Research Naomi Parker

Internal Image Research Sabrina Dalbesio

Thanks to Lisa Knights, Mark Adams, Imogen Bannister, David Connolly, Stefanie Di Trocchio, Janine Eberle, Joshua Geoghegan, Mark Germanchis, Michelle Glynn, Indra Kilfoyle, Lauren Hunt, Laura Jane, David Kemp, Nic Lehman, John Mazzocchi, Wayne Murphy, Adrian Persoglia, Piers Pickard, Lachlan Ross, Michael Ruff, Julie Sheridan, Laura Stansfeld, John Taufa, Sam Trafford, Juan Winata, Emily Wolman, Nick Wood

AUTHOR THANKS

Sara Benson

Thanks to Suki Gear, Kathleen Munnelly and everyone at Lonely Planet for making this book happen. Without such talented SoCal co-authors, I could never have put together this guide – thank you, Andrew Bender and Adam Skolnick. I'm grateful to everyone on the road who shared their local expertise and tips, including my nomadic friends and family, especially the Boyles, Starbins, Connollys Sr and Evan Baxter. PS to Mike Jr: Hey, look: no wildfires this time!

Andrew Bender

Andy Sklar and Dan Young, Joe Timko, Kate Buska, Mark Graves, Hilary Angel and, in house, Suki Gear, Sam Benson and Laura Stansfield for the opportunity and their good cheer and advice, as well as editors Andrea Dobbin and Helen Christinis, Bruce Evans and cartographer Valeska Canas.

Adam Skolnick

Thanks to Dan Cohn – the man knows where to eat, Jon Regardie at Downtown News,

Eddie Lin, Trisha Cole, Guru Singh, Burton Breznick, Paul Feinstein, Chris Sorensen and Adria Heath, Patricia Chen, Emilce Martinez, Robyn Frazer – night music connoisseur, the always fashionable Onelia Estudillo, Stephanie and Niki Shadrow, Sarah at Voyeur, Josh at Warp Records, Kate and Andy Lipkis, Jason Bentley and Rachel Reynolds at KCRW, Sam, Andrew, Suki and the entire Lonely Planet squad, and to the sweet and gorgeous, Georgiana Johnson.

471

BEHIND THE SCENES

ACKNOWLEDGMENTS

Climate map data adapted from Peel MC, Finlayson BL & McMahon TA (2007) 'Updated World Map of the Köppen-Geiger Climate Classification', *Hydrology and Earth System Sciences*, 11, 163344.

Cover photograph: Houses in Santa Monica, Micha Wright, LPI

Many of the images in this guide are available for licensing from Lonely Planet Images: www.lonelyplanetimages.com.

index

Map Pages **p000**
Photo Pages **p000**

Map Pages **p000**
Photo Pages **p000**

Map Pages **p000**
Photo Pages **p000**

how to use this book

These symbols will help you find the listings you want:

- ☉ Sights
- 🎋 Festivals & Events
- ☆ Entertainment
- 🏃 Activities
- 🛏 Sleeping
- 🛍 Shopping
- 🍴 Courses
- ✕ Eating
- ℹ Information/Transport
- 👉 Tours
- 🍷 Drinking

Look out for these icons:

- **TOP CHOICE** Our author's recommendation
- **FREE** No payment required
- 🌿 A green or sustainable option

Our authors have nominated these places as demonstrating a strong commitment to sustainability – for example by supporting local communities and producers, operating in an environmentally friendly way, or supporting conservation projects.

These symbols give you the vital information for each listing:

- ☑ Telephone Numbers
- ☎ Wi-Fi Access
- 🚌 Bus
- ☉ Opening Hours
- 🏊 Swimming Pool
- ⛴ Ferry
- Ⓟ Parking
- 🥗 Vegetarian Selection
- Ⓜ Metro
- ⊖ Nonsmoking
- 📖 English-Language Menu
- Ⓢ Subway
- ❄ Air-Conditioning
- 👪 Family-Friendly
- ⊖ London Tube
- @ Internet Access
- 🐾 Pet-Friendly
- 🚊 Tram
- 🚆 Train

Reviews are organised by author preference.

Map Legend

Sights
- Beach
- Buddhist
- Castle
- Christian
- Hindu
- Islamic
- Jewish
- Monument
- Museum/Gallery
- Ruin
- Winery/Vineyard
- Zoo
- Other Sight

Activities, Courses & Tours
- Diving/Snorkelling
- Canoeing/Kayaking
- Skiing
- Surfing
- Swimming/Pool
- Walking
- Windsurfing
- Other Activity/Course/Tour

Sleeping
- Sleeping
- Camping

Eating
- Eating

Drinking
- Drinking
- Cafe

Entertainment
- Entertainment

Shopping
- Shopping

Information
- Post Office
- Tourist Information

Transport
- Airport
- Border Crossing
- Bus
- Cable Car/Funicular
- Cycling
- Ferry
- Metro
- Monorail
- Parking
- S-Bahn
- Taxi
- Train/Railway
- Tram
- Tube Station
- U-Bahn
- Other Transport

Routes
- Tollway
- Freeway
- Primary
- Secondary
- Tertiary
- Lane
- Unsealed Road
- Plaza/Mall
- Steps
- Tunnel
- Pedestrian Overpass
- Walking Tour
- Walking Tour Detour
- Path

Boundaries
- International
- State/Province
- Disputed
- Regional/Suburb
- Marine Park
- Cliff
- Wall

Population
- Capital (National)
- Capital (State/Province)
- City/Large Town
- Town/Village

Geographic
- Hut/Shelter
- Lighthouse
- Lookout
- Mountain/Volcano
- Oasis
- Park
- Pass
- Picnic Area
- Waterfall

Hydrography
- River/Creek
- Intermittent River
- Swamp/Mangrove
- Reef
- Canal
- Water
- Dry/Salt/Intermittent Lake
- Glacier

Areas
- Beach/Desert
- Cemetery (Christian)
- Cemetery (Other)
- Park/Forest
- Sportsground
- Sight (Building)
- Top Sight (Building)

OUR STORY

A beat-up old car, a few dollars in the pocket and a sense of adventure. In 1972 that's all Tony and Maureen Wheeler needed for the trip of a lifetime – across Europe and Asia overland to Australia. It took several months, and at the end – broke but inspired – they sat at their kitchen table writing and stapling together their first travel guide, *Across Asia on the Cheap*. Within a week they'd sold 1500 copies. Lonely Planet was born.

Today, Lonely Planet has offices in Melbourne, London and Oakland, with more than 600 staff and writers. We share Tony's belief that 'a great guidebook should do three things: inform, educate and amuse'.

OUR WRITERS

Sara Benson

Coordinating Author, Disneyland & Orange County, Santa Barbara After graduating from college in Chicago, Sara jumped on a plane to California with just one suitcase and $100 in her pocket. She has bounced around the Golden State ever since, in between stints living, working and backpacking abroad, including in Asia. Her travel writing features on popular websites and in magazines and newspapers including the *Los Angeles Times*. Already the author of dozens of travel and nonfiction books, Sara has contributed to Lonely Planet's *California, Coastal California, California Trips, Las Vegas Encounter, Route 66, USA* and *USA's Best Trips* guides. Her biggest surprise on this research trip? Finding authentic Japanese ramen in Orange County. Follow more of her adventures around the country and the world online at www.indietraveler.net, www.indietraveler.blogspot.com and @indie_traveler on Twitter.

Read more about Sara at:
lonelyplanet.com/members/lostasia

Andrew Bender

San Diego, Palm Springs & The Deserts Andy is a true Angeleno, not because he was born in LA but because he's made it his own. Two decades ago this native New Englander packed up the car and drove cross-country to work in film production, and eventually realized that the joy was in the journey (and writing about it). His work has since appeared in the *Los Angeles Times, Forbes*, over two dozen Lonely Planet titles and on his blog, www.wheres-andy-now.com. Current obsessions: San Diego–style fish tacos, Palm Springs' midcentury architecture, the next great ethnic enclave and winter sunsets over the bike path in Santa Monica.

Adam Skolnick

Los Angeles Adam is a third-generation Los Angeleno whose family moved from the old country to Boyle Heights, the Fairfax district and finally to Santa Monica. A freelance journalist, he writes about travel, culture, health, sports and the environment for Lonely Planet, *Men's Health, Outside, Travel & Leisure* and *Spa*. He has authored and coauthored nine previous Lonely Planet guidebooks, and a few unsold screenplays. He lives in Santa Monica and Bali, but has an increasing fondness for Downtown and Echo Park. You can read more of his work at www.adamskolnick.com. His new web series, *Aspiring*, is online at www.youtube.com/user/The-Holdingpattern.

Published by Lonely Planet Publications Pty Ltd
ABN 36 005 607 983
3rd edition – March 2011
ISBN 978 1 74179 315 4
© Lonely Planet 2011   Photographs © as indicated 2011
10 9 8 7 6 5 4 3 2 1
Printed in China